From Coexistence to Conquest

'This is an elegant and forceful narrative by a young Palestinian scholar.'
Boutros Boutros Ghali, Former UN Secretary-General

'By placing international law within its proper political and historical context, Victor Kattan offers a fresh analysis of a conflict with far-reaching implications for the region and beyond, and which should have ended long ago. If the Middle East is to develop an intra-independency of sovereign states, then issues of legitimacy, authority and jurisdiction must not only be addressed, but defined. *From Coexistence to Conquest* as a piece of scholarship is a welcome addition to the search for a peace in the Middle East with human dignity for all its peoples at its centre.'
His Royal Highness Prince El Hassan bin Talal of Jordan

'Kattan's book constitutes an exceptionally important contribution to the literature on the history of the Arab–Israeli conflict. Most importantly, it highlights the centrality of international law in the search for a durable solution to the conflict. As Kattan amply demonstrates, a solution that is not "rights-based" will have little chance of finding public acceptance and therefore of being sustainable in the long term.'
Lex Takkenberg, General Counsel, United Nations Relief and Works Agency for Palestinian Refugees in the Near East (UNRWA), and author of *The Status of Palestinian Refugees in International Law*.

'Differing historical narratives and competing legal claims have characterized the Palestinian issue for over a hundred years. Victor Kattan gives them new meaning in his excellent study, which contains much new historical material and many new legal insights. His portrayal of issues such as the Balfour Declaration, the establishment and operation of the Mandate, the Partition proposal, the expulsion of Palestinians from their homes in 1948–49 and the consequent refugee crisis serves to remind us of how international law has failed the Palestinians. At the same time it is a warning that a settlement of the Palestinian issue not premised on international law is doomed to fail.'
John Dugard, Professor of Public International Law Emeritus, Leiden University and UN Special Rapporteur to the Occupied Palestinian Territories 2000–08

'No conflict in modern history has presented so many legal issues, which presumably could have been solved applying international law. This book highlights a number of these issues as they relate to the establishment of the State of Israel. The author's style is crisp and direct, making it easy for the reader to follow complex legal issues.'
M. Cherif Bassiouni, Distinguished Research Professor of Law at DePaul University College of Law and President Emeritus of the International Human Rights Law Institute

'Readers, whatever their view of the Arab–Israeli conflict, will appreciate this lucid and scholarly work. Kattan explains how Jews and Palestinians were tragically caught up in the net of Great Power politics. His critique of Zionism, while robust, fully acknowledges the oppression that the Jews of Europe suffered through antisemitism, a subject that he treats with sensitivity and insight. This is one reason why, beyond explaining the origins of the conflict, this book could contribute to its resolution.'
Brian Klug, Senior Research Fellow & Tutor, St. Benet's Hall, University of Oxford

'This is a trenchant analysis of the critical early decisions that led to the failure of the international community to resolve the conflict over Palestine.'
John B. Quigley, President's Club Professor of Law, Ohio State University

'This is a well researched and extremely informative and well argued book. As to the material, it is one of the best, if not the best, on the subject.'
Dr. Anis al-Qasem, Barrister-at-Law, Lincoln's Inn, and formerly Chairman of the Legal Committee of the Palestinian National Council

FROM COEXISTENCE TO CONQUEST

International Law and the Origins of the Arab–Israeli Conflict, 1891–1949

Victor Kattan

Foreword by Richard Falk

PlutoPress
www.plutobooks.com

First published 2009 by Pluto Press
345 Archway Road, London N6 5AA and
175 Fifth Avenue, New York, NY 10010

www.plutobooks.com

Distributed in the United States of America exclusively by
Palgrave Macmillan, a division of St. Martin's Press LLC,
175 Fifth Avenue, New York, NY 10010

British Library Cataloguing in Publication Data
A catalogue record for this book is available from the British Library

ISBN 978 0 7453 2579 8 Hardback
ISBN 978 0 7453 2578 1 Paperback

Library of Congress Cataloging in Publication Data applied for

10 9 8 7 6 5 4 3 2

Designed and produced for Pluto Press by
Chase Publishing Services Ltd, Sidmouth, England
Typeset from disk by Stanford DTP Services, Northampton, England
Printed and bound in the European Union by
CPI Antony Rowe, Chippenham and Eastbourne

This book is dedicated to the memory of my grandmother:

Marguerite Kattan

1915–2008

And to the grandfather I never knew:

Victor Giries Kattan

1910–1980

Contents

Foreword

Richard A. Falk

The prevailing discourse relating to the unresolved Israel/Palestine conflict is dismissive of any recourse to history, contending that it is irrelevant to present realities. In essence, the Israeli contention, backed by Washington, is that how we reached the present impasse is of no practical use in mapping a beneficial future. All that counts, according to this view, is the present relation of forces, 'the facts on the ground' that the Israelis have been unilaterally shaping to their advantage for many decades, and continue to do so in the Palestinian territories occupied since 1967. Of course this Israeli position is extremely self-serving, and confronts the Palestinians with an unpalatable choice between swallowing non-sustainable, unjust peace offerings and continuing their struggle under the highly adverse conditions of a prolonged occupation of their territories carried out in manner violative of international humanitarian law.

Victor Kattan, with the discipline and knowledge of a serious scholar, proceeds from a premise that historical understanding matters fundamentally, indispensably helping us realize why the long evolution of the conflict remains both unresolved and the source of so much suffering since its point of origin in the late 19th century. We can be here likewise instructed by the poetic wisdom of T.S. Eliot's 'Burnt Norton':

> Time present and time past
> Are both present in time future,
> And time future contained in time past.

In keeping with this spirit, we can never and should never escape our history if we are to construct a worthwhile future. We cannot grasp the meaning of the present without attentiveness to history, and we cannot hope for a benevolent future without relying on historical knowledge that is interpreted with as much objectivity as first-class scholarship enables. Kattan's scholarly achievement is to provide us with this historical understanding.

What Kattan's scrupulous presentation of the historical narrative tells us above all is that the Zionist Project from its inception in the latter decades of the 19th century was colonialist in its essence, initially threatening and displacing, and later dispossessing an indigenous and deeply rooted people from their homes and their land. It is important to recognize that the Arab inhabitants of Palestine opposed this systematic Jewish settlement from its earliest beginnings, understanding that it was aimed at transforming their homeland from without. They were deeply and justifiably suspicious of and hostile to the Zionist vision, fully realizing that if it were ever achieved, it would be almost totally at their expense.

The possibility of this exploitative interaction between Zionist settlers and the indigenous population was greatly facilitated by the two-faced, cynical British diplomacy practiced during World War I that promised one thing to Arab leaders in the Middle East and another in London to the Jewish leaders of the Zionist movement. Perhaps, this double message, with its resulting ambiguities, would have amounted to nothing very significant with respect to Palestine absent the huge push given to Zionist goals by Nazi Germany in the 1930s and 1940s, stimulating massive Jewish migration from Europe in search of sanctuary. The impact of this horrifying Nazi phenomenon was abetted by the Western liberal democracies, especially Britain and the United States, which refused to open their doors to Jewish refugees, thereby making refuge in Palestine a matter of virtual necessity for many Jews.

Kattan carefully and reliably shows that all along the Zionist side was able to take far more effective tactical advantage of these ambiguities than did their Arab counterparts in Palestine and in the region. Step by step the Zionist Project moved from being a vague and romantic dream with no prospect of realization to becoming a plausible political undertaking, especially by overcoming the original demographic imbalance arising from the Jewish minority being less than 10% of the whole through waves of settlement and by land purchases, although these never amounted to more than 7–8% of the whole of Palestine.

Again we might still be tempted to react by saying 'this is all very sad and lamentable, but why should we be now concerned with remembering these largely forgotten parts of the story?' There is no single persuasive answer to such a question, but there are some relevant observations. This narrative has intrinsic importance to the extent that it illuminates how the present tragic standoff evolved out of a one-sided pattern of unequal and manipulative power relations that embodied the colonialist ethos. More pointedly, the British obtained Jewish financial and diplomatic support in their struggle with Germany at the expense of Arab interests in the Middle East. It is this kind of manipulation, combined with Zionist ingenuity and passion, that has led to so much bloodshed over many years. Although colonialism has collapsed as a global phenomenon, some of its remnants have been sustained by the practice of geopolitics as administered by the US Government, and none more abusively than the denial to the Palestinian people of their right of national self-determination.

The second main tenet of Kattan's illuminating book is that Palestinian rights under international law were consistently violated or ignored, and with great consequences. Britain as the occupying power of Palestine after World War I had a fundamental legal obligation to uphold the rights and well-being of the indigenous population, and not to interfere with the existing laws in Palestine whilst it was under belligerent occupation. Recalling that Palestine had been freed from Ottoman rule in an international context in which self-determination had been promised to the previously subjugated peoples, the

European powers engineered a compromise by way of the mandates system in which a colonial power would administer a given territory as 'a sacred trust of civilization' and guide the population toward political independence and the exercise of its right of self-determination, relinquishing control at the appropriate moment. Britain was designated as the mandatory power for Palestine, and presided over a course of political development that eventuated in the emergence of Israel, and the marginalization of the Palestinian people in what was supposed to have been their own country. This supposition was undermined at its core because the mandate also incorporated the legally dubious Balfour Declaration with its promise to the Zionist movement of support for its efforts to establish a Jewish national home in Palestine. All this was done in violation of the most basic responsibility to protect the native population that had been written into the Covenant of the League of Nations as binding the behavior of the mandatory power in its role as representative of the organized international community. As Kattan makes clear, and it remains important for the legal and political debate, the Palestinians enjoyed a right of self-determination *prior* to and *independent* of its incorporation into contemporary international law after World War II. Their status as a people subject to a Class A Mandate meant that Britain as the mandatory power had a solemn legal and moral obligation to lead the Palestinian people toward full independence, including their right to shape their own future as a sovereign state. It is this mandatory right that became generalized international law through the anti-colonial movement, and assumed fundamental importance and respect as the core rule of the law of international human rights, comprising common Article 1 of the 1966 International Covenant of Civil and Political Rights and the International Covenant of Social, Economic and Cultural Rights.

It requires only minimal knowledge of recent 'peace diplomacy' (Oslo, Camp David II, Annapolis) to appreciate that Israel has induced the Quartet (US, Russia, the EU, and the UN) to ignore Palestinian rights under international law in their search for a solution. It is obvious why: international law essentially supports all of the basic Palestinian grievances – obligation to withdraw to the 1967 borders, to dismantle the Israeli settlements and the wall/barrier, to share control over the city of Jerusalem, and to grant Palestinian refugees a right of return. Israel has consistently avoided accountability under international law in its diplomacy, insisting instead on negotiating a bargain that reflects the relative strength of the two sides, an approach that implicitly ratifies past illegalities. In practice, this has meant giving the Palestinians a take it or leave it proposition to build their future on a small fraction of the original Palestine (considerably less than 22%) as a political entity with such curtailed rights that would at most constitute a *nominal* sovereign state. It should come as no surprise that such offers have been unacceptable to the Palestinian people and their political representatives. And all the while, the bodies keep piling up!

The great merit of Victor Kattan's elegantly presented historical study is that it makes clear that it was this persistent refusal to respect international law and Palestinian rights that brought us step by step to the present impasse.

The book's conclusion is edifying for all of us: namely, that current efforts to resolve the conflict are 'doomed to fail' unless based on 'equity, justice and the principles of international law'. Such a conclusion is not put forward as a matter of rigid legalism. Kattan is fully sensitive to the importance of compromise and political accommodation as integral to the search for peace, yet recognizing that a viable peace process cannot achieve its goals unless it acknowledges the relevance of international law in fixing the parameters of mutually responsible negotiations. Hitherto, the exclusion of international law from Israel/Palestine negotiations has falsely supposed the conflict could be resolved by a bargaining process heavily weighted to favor the stronger Israeli side, which has been further bolstered in its domineering posture by having the supposed intermediary, the United States, in its corner at all crucial diplomatic moments.

Until a solution that fulfills the general assessment set forth by Kattan is accepted and acted upon by all sides to the conflict there will be no ending of this tragedy that has befallen both peoples, but unequally. This calls for either a territorial partition of historic Palestine that achieves viable self-determination and full sovereign status for both peoples, shared or internationalized sovereignty over Jerusalem, dismantling most settlements, a negotiated compromise on the right of return of Palestinian refugees, agreed allocation of ground water, or a single unified state based on constitutional democracy and equal rights for all residents. Above all, the past and present, as well as considerations of fundamental fairness, converge on the realization that without a genuine realization of the right of self-determination for the Palestinian people, there will neither be peace nor justice. The insecurities confronting Israel are genuine and likely to persist, but these provide no excuse for the acute daily suffering visited upon the Palestinian people as a whole for decades, aggravated in recent years beyond the 'normalcy' of an oppressive occupation for the 1.5 million Palestinians living in Gaza, nor for the Israeli refusal to respect the authority of the United Nations, and withdraw from occupied Palestine. Reading Kattan helps us appreciate how this set of circumstances emerged historically, as well as prefiguring and depicting a tenable escape from the current morass should an authentic peace process (unlike any so proclaimed to date) be established in the future.

RICHARD A. FALK
Albert G. Milbank Professor Emeritus of
International Law, Princeton University,
and Visiting Professor, Global Studies,
University of California, Santa Barbara

Acknowledgements

Writing a book is a rewarding, exhausting and time consuming endeavour. It is also a process of learning. It took four years of my life to write this book. Initially, I had intended to write a basic introduction to the Arab–Israeli conflict examining its legal aspects for journalists. However, my publisher Roger van Zwanenberg talked me out of this approach and instead encouraged me to write a broader and more analytical book that would appeal to a wider audience. He also encouraged me to tackle the conflict's controversial and dark history with which I was not initially familiar. I am grateful to him for his suggestions and patience and to Sharif Hikmat Nashashibi for introducing us.

There are many people I would like to thank for making this book possible, some who wish to be acknowledged and others, for their own personal reasons, who do not. I would like to begin by thanking Ray Addicott and Oliver Howard at Chase Publishing Services and Robert Webb at Pluto for preparing the manuscript and the maps so that they could be published as a book. On questions of law I extend my thanks to Rosalie Balkin and Don Grieg for looking over an earlier draft as well as to John Dugard who also commented on it. Catriona Drew, Lady Hazel Fox, Robert McCorquodale, John McHugo, Anis Qasem, John B. Quigley, and two other international lawyers who wish to remain anonymous, were kind enough to read through later drafts, which they commented on and offered suggestions for improving. In addition, I must thank Malgosia Fitzmaurice and Matthew Craven for reading through Chapter 4 and Ilan Pappé for taking the time to comment on my first draft of Chapter 7. I am most grateful to Richard Falk, currently UN Special Rapporteur for Human Rights in the Occupied Palestinian Territories, for agreeing to write the foreword. I should add that Chapters 1 and 2, the epilogue and parts of the introduction were substantially re-written after Richard had already completed the foreword. Indeed, this book was delayed by several months due to the changes which I subsequently introduced into the text. The reason for the changes was my discovery of the 'Jewish Question' which to my shame, I was wholly ignorant of, before I came across several books about it in the rare reading room at the Cambridge University Library. Once I familiarised myself with the question and the history of anti-Semitism I was able to make the connections between British colonialism at the turn of the twentieth century and the Royal Commission on Alien Immigration (1903), the Aliens Act (1905), and the Balfour Declaration (1917). I wholeheartedly thank Brian Klug for being so gracious as to read over and offer comments on my sections on the Jewish Question and anti-Semitism at short notice. Of course, it goes without saying that I am solely responsible for the views expressed in this book which are mine alone and should not be associated with anyone who kindly commented on what I have written.

The late David Walters, my history teacher at St Edmund's College in Ware, Hertfordshire, who sadly passed away whilst I was half way through my A-levels in 1997, instilled in me a deep interest in all things historical. I will always remember writing an essay as part of my GCSE course in history when we were asked to empathise with the victims of the *Shoah* for which he gave me the highest mark possible. I do not know what he would make of this book if he were still alive to read it, but I hope that he would have found it of some interest. I often thought of him when writing this book.

The librarians at Birzeit University, Cambridge University, the Foreign and Commonwealth Office, the Hebrew University of Jerusalem, the Institute of Advanced Legal Studies, the Institute of Commonwealth Studies, the London School of Economics and Political Science, the School of Oriental and African Studies, Senate House, the Squire Law Library at Cambridge University, the Weiner Institute of Contemporary History, the British Library, the British Newspaper Library, the Peace Palace in The Hague, and finally, the National Archives in Kew, Surrey, were always courteous and helpful. I thank them all for their assistance. A special thanks to Hugh Alexander at the National Archives for giving me permission to reproduce the colourful maps of the Middle East from the Foreign and Colonial Office files in Kew.

I would like to thank all of my colleagues at the British Institute of International and Comparative Law in Russell Square who provided an academic, congenial, collegial and friendly atmosphere, which was of enormous support both when it came to researching and writing this book. There are too many people I could list here, but a debt of gratitude must go to Ruth Eldon and Gillian Triggs for welcoming me to the Institute, initially as a Visiting Fellow, and to Robert McCorquodale who was so kind as to allow me to complete my book in my final year there. I have very fond memories of sharing an office at the Institute in Charles Clore House, at first with Aphrodite Smagadi and Nisrine Abiad for two years on the Iran human-rights project, in whose company much of this book was written, and in my final months with Sergey Ripinsky and Justine Stefanelli.

Finally, I would like to express my profound gratitude to my father William, who always made himself available to read through the innumerable drafts of this manuscript, even when he was very busy at work or travelling to legal conferences in faraway lands. My mother Josephine and my sister Leyla have also provided me with a constant source of encouragement and advice in numerous ways over many years, as has more recently, my girlfriend, Vibeke Jensen – who is especially associated with this book.

Preface

International lawyers are often discouraged from writing about themselves lest it affect the neutrality of their scholarship. Whilst this approach might be acceptable when writing about the specificities of technical aspects of the law, I am not persuaded that this should be a rule of thumb in all situations, especially when one is writing on such a highly controversial subject. I would imagine that most readers will want to know more about an author, particularly if the subject one is writing on is politically contentious. Moreover, as students, scholars, authors, and practitioners, we are all affected by our backgrounds, our experiences and family circumstances, as well as where we were educated, what we uncovered in our research, and the places we have worked in. So I will digress from the usual practice and briefly explain why I have spent several years working on this book, which marks a culmination of my research interests on the Palestine question.

In 2003–04, I spent several months living and working in the Occupied Palestinian Territories during the *intifada* (uprising) as a UN Development Programme TOKTEN (transfer of knowledge through expatriate nationals) consultant to the BADIL Resource Centre for Palestinian Residency and Refugee Rights, which is a Palestinian NGO based in Bethlehem. What I witnessed whilst working there – the checkpoints, the relentless settlement construction, the creation of new by-pass roads, the wall/fence/barrier, the behaviour of the Israeli Army at checkpoints, the impact of Israel's closure policy and permit system on Palestinian residents of the West Bank and East Jerusalem, the daily harassment, the restrictions on internal Palestinian movement, Palestinian refugee children walking around barefoot in Jalazone, being tear gassed in Qalqilya, having a gun trained on me every time I crossed into Bethlehem from Jerusalem, inadvertently traversing across a shootout between Israeli soldiers and Palestinian gunmen by the Bethlehem checkpoint, and on one occasion arriving at the scene of a morning ambush which left three Israeli soldiers dead on the settler bypass road between Bethlehem and Hebron – left an indelible impression on me. So did the overwhelming fact that notwithstanding the start of the so-called 'peace process' at Madrid in 1991, the human rights of the Palestinian people continue to be infringed to the extent that one must seriously question why the process negotiated in Oslo has failed to improve their lot.

That much of the legal scholarship I had come across on the conflict was anachronistic, in some cases not even factually accurate, and in most instances paid scant regard to history, further confirmed my image of professors of international law living in their ivory towers. I sought to remedy this void in the literature through my own scholarship. Sadly, there are very few Palestinians who have published articles about the conflict in international law journals, which is perhaps a reflection of the reality that for most Palestinians, particularly those from the refugee camps in the West Bank and in the Gaza Strip, a good university education outside of the occupied territories remains a dream. A recent example of the difficulty Palestinians face in obtaining access to higher education was a decision by the US State Department reported by the *Guardian* and *Ha'aretz* in May 2008 to withdraw several Fulbright scholarships awarded to Palestinian students from Gaza to study at universities in the US because they could not obtain permission from Israel to leave that small strip of land – and this was not even an isolated incident. It seems clear to me that Palestinians in the Diaspora, who are not affected by Israel's closure policy, have a responsibility to speak out for those who cannot.

No doubt my family background has played a major role in nurturing my interest in the conflict. This book is dedicated to the memory of my grandparents, Victor and Marguerite Kattan, who grew up in Bethlehem where they met and married in the Roman Catholic Church of St Catherine, aside the Church of the Nativity, before moving to the Sudan, then another British colony, in 1936. My interest in the Middle East and in British colonial history more generally, has no doubt been affected by the stories my grandmother used to tell me about her youth in Palestine, the photographs she used to show me of her life there, and in the Sudan. One particular story my grandmother was fond of recalling was of a visit that King Abdullah made to the Seil ('the valley') which was my great-grandfather's house in Beit Jala, near Bethlehem. Little did I know that a few years later I would write a book that would touch upon a controversial correspondence between King Abdullah's father, Hussein Ibn Ali, the Sherif of Mecca, and Henry McMahon, the British High Commissioner in Egypt. The source of this controversy was whether Palestine was, or was not, pledged to be 'Arab and independent' by McMahon, a subject which I explore in some depth in this book.

However, unlike some Palestinians in the Diaspora, I did not have much knowledge of or any experience of what it was like to live in the Middle East, until I visited the Holy Land when I was 16. Of course, I knew that my father's family was from the region. That was clear from hearing my father conversing with his mother and his siblings in Arabic and of course, when he or my grandmother prepared a meal. It was not my mother's Yorkshire puddings I looked forward to, but some *warak-enab*, *hummus*, *tabbouleh*, and *shish kebab*. The fact that I never knew either of my grandfathers may have contributed to my curiosity in all things historical. Ian, my maternal grandfather, an Anglo-Scot, died in 1967, partly as a result of the injuries he received during the Second World War fighting against Rommel's *Deutsches Afrikakorps* as a Bombardier with the Royal Horse Artillery, which was then attached to the 8th Army. He saw active service in North Africa in Benghazi, Tripoli, Derna, Bardia, Tobruk and El Alamein, where he was injured in 1943, before local Bedouin rescued him. Victor, my paternal grandfather, was from a completely different part of the world. He was born in Bethlehem to a prominent Christian Palestinian family. I was named after him, and he passed away, not in Palestine, his country of birth where his family had lived for hundreds of years, and to which he had always wanted to return before his death, but in Khartoum, Sudan, where he had gone as a young man to seek his fortunes in the family business in Omdurman.

It seems to me that the pre-eminent question that one needs to ask oneself before coming to terms with the Arab–Israeli conflict is how the conflict started. It seems obvious, but this question is often overlooked in the legal literature on the subject, which is surprising since the same problems keep reappearing: violent Palestinian resistance to occupation and to political Zionism, the conduct of hostilities between Arabs and Jews, territorial questions concerning title, sovereignty, and their relationship to the right of all peoples to self-determination, as well as the legacy from the expulsion and exodus of almost an entire people from their homeland. We can only engage with these complex and difficult issues if we have a thorough grasp of the conflict's history.

In this connection I have endeavoured to place the international legal issues in their broader political and historical contexts rather than approach the subject strictly from the black letter of the law. This enables one to have a better understanding of why, for instance, Britain issued its Balfour Declaration in 1917. Only once this is fully understood can one have a real appreciation for the way in which people thought at the time and what they intended to achieve from the decisions they made. Words and phrases can mean different things depending on the way they are interpreted and understood by the reader. We cannot take colonial documents at face value. They are a product of time, place, and circumstance, and reflect the prejudices of their authors. We must not forget that the world we inhabit today is a very different place from the worlds inhabited by Balfour, Curzon, and Montagu, a century ago, when anti-Semitism and racism were rampant, and when colonialism was at its zenith. One only has to read through some of the classical nineteenth-century authors of international law such as John Westlake at Cambridge University and James Lorimer at Edinburgh University to see how they described the non-Anglo-Saxon world for a flavour of the nature of British imperialism.

An advantage in writing a legal history of the Arab–Israeli conflict today is the availability of declassified government documents. Often we do not really know what governments have been saying behind closed doors. We have to rely on what they tell the press and of course they are often economical with the truth, only revealing what suits their interests. But with the passage of time, many government documents are declassified and made available to scholars. Sometimes these are republished in bulky volumes, such as *Documents on British Foreign Policy*, *Foreign Relations of the United States* or *Documents on the Foreign Policy of Israel*. More recently, scholars have even scanned archival documents and made them available on electronic databases. However, the vast majority of the most interesting material is not always republished or available electronically either on special databases or on the Internet, and therefore one will have to undertake research in the National Archives, as I did with this book. Of course, the 'truth' is not an objective criterion. However, if a particular historical event is mentioned in the British archives, the Israeli archives and the US archives, and they all correspond, one is probably as close to the 'truth' as one is ever likely to be. Furthermore, the situation is made slightly easier for international lawyers, who are accustomed to undertaking textual analysis of official documents. We can all offer our own views of what we think a sentence or a phrase in a treaty might mean. But it is all the more fascinating when the government lawyer, adviser, or politician, who drafted a particular document, gives his own view of what his government intended.

In the following pages, I bring much new material to light that has not been published in any other international law book on the Palestine question, such as Foreign Office legal advice on the 1947–48 conflict and the creation of Israel. This material, I am sure, will be of interest not only to the general reader but also, perhaps, to the specialist as well. In fact those who may think they are already familiar with the history of the conflict, may be surprised to come across new material and facts which they are unlikely to have been exposed to before unless they have undertaken in-depth archival research in this particular area. In this regard it would probably be fair to say that what is different about this book is its use of sources: declassified legal opinions, minutes, telegrams, reports and memoranda, in addition to the usual sources such as treaties, UN documents, cases and the secondary literature in books and law journals. I have also occasionally cited contemporary newspaper reports to spice things up. Although the subtitle of the book mentions the year 1891, I do not cover Ottoman Palestine in any great detail. I have only chosen to stress this date, as this was when the first protest against Jewish immigration into Palestine was recorded. I also do not deal with the legal status of Jerusalem in any great detail, although I briefly mention the League of Nations commission which visited Jerusalem in 1929, because I think it deserves a special study singularly devoted to it. Rather, the focus of this book is on the international law and politics of the period when Britain ruled over Palestine as the mandatory power.

Law has always been intricately involved in the Arab–Israeli conflict ever since those curious words 'public law' appeared in the first resolution adopted by the first Zionist Congress in Basel in 1897. ('The aim of Zionism is to create for the Jewish people a home in Palestine secured by public law.') It is therefore hardly surprising that many of the questions addressed in this book have necessitated recourse to legal norms, whether it is regarding questions relating to the laws of war which are addressed in Chapters 3 and 7, to the interpretation of treaties and to what, in fact, constitutes a treaty, which is explored in Chapters 2 and 4. I have devoted a whole chapter to the Hussein–McMahon correspondence which I have placed half-way through this book because it was only in 1939, when the British Government finally agreed to publish the correspondence, that this issue came to the fore. I have chosen to highlight the correspondence because it is often overlooked by international lawyers who mention it only in passing before moving on to the Balfour Declaration. As a matter of law, I think the correspondence raises serious questions for international lawyers, questions which have never been examined before such as the fact that states entered into treaty relations with non-state actors on a relatively regular basis throughout the colonial period. The Arabs certainly took the correspondence seriously and they even attempted to refer it to the International Court of Justice for an advisory opinion in 1947. Territorial questions are also considered in this book concerning sovereignty, self-determination and statehood, which are examined in Chapters 2, 5 and 9. Then there is the issue of British colonial law and the dispositary powers of the League of Nations and the United Nations to affect territorial change, which are analysed in Chapters 2, 5, 6 and 9. Evidently, any attempt to conclude a peace treaty, which is a legal document, is likely to make reference to international law, a point I make in my conclusion.

This book makes the case that the claims of the Palestinian people to independence and statehood finds ample justification in international law, leaving elementary considerations of justice aside, even according to the positive tradition of international law associated with British imperialism and colonialism. The Palestinian people's strong legal entitlement to self-determination which is inherently intertwined with the fate of the Jewish people can be traced back to the Paris Peace Conference in 1919, the drafting of the British Mandate of Palestine, and British colonial policy and practice in Palestine between 1922 and 1948. Whereas the Zionists' claim to self-determination found expression through an instrument of British colonial policy, namely the Balfour Declaration as it was incorporated into the Mandate, national self-determination for the Palestinian people as a whole was based on effective occupation. Moreover, those indigenous Christians, Jews and Muslims who had continuously inhabited Palestine for centuries before the emergence of Zionism in the late nineteenth century, had a right not to be exploited, expelled or harmed in any way. In essence, this was what 'the sacred trust' enshrined in the Covenant of the League of Nations was all about. The fact that the Palestinians have still not been given an opportunity of creating a state of their own – despite the numerous pledges, promises and unilateral declarations made over so many years – makes their case stand out from other contemporary self-determination claims and justifies the number of UN resolutions and heightened interest in resolving this dispute by that organisation.

There is a common misperception that the Arab–Israeli conflict was inevitable. I have sought to challenge this view with my choice of words 'from *coexistence* to conquest' in the title. Christians, Jews, Muslims, and others, have lived together in relative harmony in North Africa and the Middle East for thousands of years. Even in biblical times, Jews did not only inhabit the Holy Land. There was always a significant Jewish population in Egypt and Iraq, a situation which did not change substantially until the calamities of the twentieth century. It was European anti-Semitism and British colonialism which caused the conflict in Palestine, attributes of which continue to linger in the region until this very day. Indeed it may be fair to say that colonialism has never really ended in Palestine since the end of the British Mandate in 1948. Jordan annexed the West Bank in 1950, a measure which is commonly associated by international lawyers with colonialism. And since 1967, Israel has 'administered' the West Bank and Gaza as an occupying power, a regime which also has many features associated with colonialism; primarily, the ability through a prolonged military occupation of denying the people of that territory from being in a position to exercise their right of self-determination. The fact that the Palestine Liberation Organisation agreed in 1994 to create the Palestinian National Authority as Israel's surrogate in administering the occupied territories has done little to change things. Those territories still remain occupied and subject to the laws of belligerent occupation. It may therefore be fair to conclude that the Palestinians are one of the longest colonised peoples in history.

VICTOR KATTAN
The British Institute of International and Comparative Law,
Charles Clore House, Russell Square, London
October 2008

Chronology

1517	Palestine is conquered by Turkey and becomes an integral part of the Ottoman Empire.
1799	Napoleon invades Palestine and Syria but is defeated by the Turks.
1830	British consulate opens in Jerusalem.
1831–40	Ibrahim Pasha, the son of Muhammad Ali, occupies Palestine.
1834	Revolt in Palestine against Egyptian rule.
1840	Turkey recaptures Palestine from Egypt.
1853–56	The Crimean War.
1860	Massacre of Christians in Lebanon provokes France to send troops there to quell it.
1869	Suez Canal opens.
1874–75	The governments of Egypt and Turkey both go bankrupt. The British Government under the leadership of Benjamin Disraeli subsequently purchases 44 per cent of the shares of the Suez Canal Company to the tune of £4,000,000 loaned to it from the British branch of the Rothschild family.
1882	Russia enacts the May Laws.
1882–1903	First wave of Jewish immigration (*aliyah*) into Palestine. However, for most immigrants, the US is their Promised Land, not Palestine. Between 1.5 and 2 million Eastern European Jews immigrate to the United States, their destination of choice, and a further 350,000 go to Western Europe.
1884–85	General Act of the Conference of Berlin is convened to regulate European colonisation and trade in Africa. In the following years Africa would be partitioned and colonised by the Great Powers.

1891	First Arab protest against Jewish immigration into Palestine is made.
1897	First Zionist Congress is held in Basel.
1898	Jewish Colonial Trust is established at the Second Zionist Congress.
1900	The Fourth Zionist Congress is held in London. Theodor Herzl drafts a Charter for a Jewish-Ottoman Land Company.
1902	Theodor Herzl and Adolf Böhm, prominent leaders of the Zionist Organisation, are invited to give oral evidence to the Royal Commission on Alien Immigration. Herzl meets Joseph Chamberlain in his efforts to establish a Jewish homeland in the Sinai Peninsula. A technical commission is sent by Lord Cromer to the Sinai. The commission rules out Jewish colonisation there due to a lack of available water. Chamberlain suggests to Herzl that he consider instead a Jewish homeland in East Africa.
1903	The report of the Royal Commission on Alien Immigration is published by His Majesty's Government. Lloyd George drafts a Jewish Colonisation Scheme for East Africa in collaboration with the Zionist Organisation.
1905	The report of a commission sent to East Africa by the Zionist Organisation to examine its suitability for Jewish settlement is published. Parliament passes the Alien Act 1905 in order to restrict Jewish immigration into Britain.
1908	The Jewish National Fund and the Palestine Land Development Company begin their work purchasing land in Palestine for Jewish settlement.
1914–18	The First World War.
1915–16	Turkey at the Battle of Gallipoli defeats Britain and the Allies. The Hussein–McMahon correspondence is exchanged.
1916	Britain and France conclude the Sykes–Picot agreement. Lloyd George replaces Herbert Asquith to become British Prime Minister. The Hejaz joins the Allies and declares war against Turkey. In November, the Sherif of Mecca declares himself the King of Hejaz, which, in December, is recognised by Britain and France.

1917 In November (October on the Julian calendar), the Bolsheviks seize power and Russia makes preparations to withdraw from the war. That same month, Britain issues the Balfour Declaration. In December, the British Army led by General Allenby marches victoriously into Jerusalem. Palestine is placed under British military occupation (1917–20). It then had a population of 688,957 Arabs (including Christians, Muslims and other non-Jewish minorities) and a population of 58,728 Jews.

1918 In January, President Woodrow Wilson sets out his Fourteen Points to both Houses of Congress. In the same month, Commander Hogarth and the Sherif of Mecca reach an understanding regarding Jewish settlement in Palestine on the condition that 'no people shall be subject to another' and that Jewish settlement in Palestine would be government policy 'in so far as is compatible with the freedom of the existing population both economic and political'. In November, the Anglo-French Declaration is published calling for 'the complete and definite emancipation of the peoples so long oppressed by the Turks and the establishment of national governments and administrations deriving their authority from the initiative and free choice of the indigenous populations'.

1919 Feisal and Weizmann conclude an agreement on Jewish settlement in Palestine, although the former inscribed a reservation to the document. The Peace Conference takes place in Paris. The Hejaz was invited as one of the Allied and Associated Powers and signed the Versailles Treaty with Germany. The Great Powers agree to establish the League of Nations and a Covenant is drafted, which provides for the creation of the Mandates in Article 22. Palestine is deemed an A-class mandate. The Great Powers agree to send a commission of inquiry to the Middle East to determine the wishes of the inhabitants. In Damascus, the commission was told that the Arabs opposed the Zionist project to establish a Jewish national home in Palestine.

1919–22 The mandates for Palestine and the Levant are drafted at the Foreign Office in London and the Quai d'Orsay in Paris in close collaboration with members from the Zionist Organisation.

1920 At San Remo, the Great Powers determine the allocation of the A-class mandates. Britain is appointed the mandatory power over Palestine and Iraq. France is given a mandate over the rest of the Levant (Lebanon and Syria). Rioting breaks out between Arabs and Jews in Jerusalem and a military commission of inquiry is asked to look into the causes of the disturbances. It concludes that the Zionists are largely responsible for the violence 'by their impatience, indiscretion and attempts to force the hands of the Administration' in providing for Jewish settlement in Palestine. In July, Britain terminates its occupation of Palestine and Herbert Samuel is appointed the first High Commissioner of Palestine. His first task was to establish a civilian administration to replace the British Army.

1921 The US restricts immigration. In Jaffa, there are large-scale riots between Arabs and Jews. The Haycraft Commission of Inquiry is appointed by the British Government to examine the causes of the riot. It concludes 'had there been no Jewish question, the Government would have had no political difficulty of any importance to deal with so far as domestic affairs are concerned'. It adds: 'Any anti-British feeling on the part of the Arabs that may have arisen in the country originates in their association of the Government with the furtherance of the policy of Zionism.'

1922 The Council of the League of Nations agrees to the text of the British Mandate of Palestine. The Palestine Order-in-Council of 1 September separates Palestine from the Emirate of Transjordan, which is established to the east of the River Jordan. The Colonial Secretary, Winston Churchill, in a statement on British policy rejects the claim that Palestine was to become 'as Jewish as England is English'. He declares: 'His Majesty's Government regard any such expectation as impracticable and have no such aim in view.' He adds that: 'the status of all citizens of Palestine in the eye of the law shall be Palestinian, and it has never been intended that they, or any section of them, should possess any other juridical status'. In an exchange of correspondence with the Palestine Arab delegation, Churchill recognises 'the people of Palestine', specifically referring to Palestine's Arab community.

1923 The Treaty of Lausanne between the Allies, the Associated Powers and Turkey is concluded on 24 July. The Mandate enters into force on 29 September, after signature, but before ratification of the Lausanne Treaty. Britain proposes to create an Arab Agency in Palestine to have the same powers as the Jewish Agency for the purposes of advising and cooperating with the British authorities in Palestine concerning matters of interest specifically affecting the Arab population. However, Palestine's Arab leaders reject it on the grounds that 'the Arabs, having never recognised the status of the Jewish Agency, have no desire for the establishment of an Arab Agency on the same basis'.

1928–29 Riots break out between Arabs and Jews at the site of the Western Wall in Jerusalem. This quickly spreads to Hebron and other parts of Palestine. The Shaw Commission of Inquiry concludes that racial animosity on the part of the Arabs, consequent upon the disappointment of their political and national aspirations and fear for their economic future, is the fundamental cause of the outbreak of violence.

1930 The League of Nations agrees to a British proposal to send an ad hoc commission to Palestine to examine the rights and claims of Jews and Muslims to the Holy Places. The Commission rules in favour of Muslim proprietary rights but concludes that Jews should have free access to the Western Wall for the purposes of devotions at all times. The British Government subsequently appoints Sir John Hope-Simpson to undertake a study on land cultivation and settlement possibilities in Palestine. He concludes that there is no room for a single additional Jewish settler if the standard of life of the Arab villager is to remain at existing levels. The British Government then publishes a White Paper endorsing his findings, which provokes a storm of protest from the Zionists. In response, Prime Minister Ramsay MacDonald 'clarifies' his government's policy towards the Jewish national home as set out in the White Paper. He reaffirms Britain's intention to stand by the Mandate, to uphold the policy of the Jewish national home by further land settlement and immigration, and to condone the Zionist insistence on Jewish labour for work on Jewish enterprises. The Palestine Arabs who interpret this as a complete volte-face refer to this letter as the 'Black Letter'.

1931 Haj Amin al-Husseini – head of the Supreme Muslim Council – organises a large international gathering in Jerusalem attended by Muslims from all over the world to defend Al-Aqsa and the Islamic Holy Places.

1932–33 Overt Nazi persecution of German Jews begins. Jewish immigration into Palestine increases three-fold.

1935 Annual Jewish immigration into Palestine peaks at 61,854 persons. This meant that more Jews entered Palestine in that year alone than had inhabited Palestine in 1917 when the Balfour Declaration was published.

1936 The Mufti and the Arab Executive Committee call for a general strike. Six weeks of rioting follow directed at the British Government. The Murison Commission of Inquiry concludes that the immediate cause of the riot was 'to protest against the policy of the Government, the ground for which was prepared by a general feeling of apprehension amongst the Arabs engendered by the purchase of land by the Jews and by Jewish immigration'. Britain's High-Commissioner proposes to amend the Legislative Council so as to reflect the fact that Arabs were numerically preponderant – but these proposals are rejected by Westminster.

1936–39 The Great Arab Revolt takes place. Military Courts are established under the Defence (Military Courts) Regulations Laws. The British Army sends in an extra 20,000 troops to Palestine to crush the rebellion. At the end of the conflict approximately 5,000 Palestinian Arabs have been killed, 10,000 wounded and 5,670 detained. This means that over 10 per cent of the adult male Arab population was killed, wounded, imprisoned, or exiled.

1936–37 The Peel Commission of Inquiry concludes that the underlying causes of the initial disturbances were the desire of the Arabs for national independence and their hatred and fear of the establishment of the Jewish national home. It recommends that Britain terminate its mandate over Palestine and partition it between an Arab and a Jewish state with the exception of Jerusalem, Bethlehem, Nazareth and the Sea of Galilee, which would remain under British control in the form of a mandate so as to ensure free access to the Holy Places. The plan envisages population transfers between the Arab and the Jewish states, which are to have special treaty relations with Britain. Both the Arabs and the Zionists reject the plan.

1938 Sir John Woodhead concludes in a Government report that the partition of Palestine is impracticable.

1939 The British Government publishes a White Paper in which it declares that 'it is proper that the people of the country [that is, the Palestinians] should as early as possible enjoy the rights of self-government which are exercised by the people of neighbouring countries'. Accordingly, the British Government desires 'to see established ultimately an independent Palestinian State. It should be a state in which the two peoples in Palestine, Arabs and Jews, share authority in government in such a way that the essential interests of each are shared.' At a conference held in St James's Palace in London, the British Government formerly acknowledges that during the First World War it had conducted a series of secret exchanges with the Sherif of Mecca via its High Commissioner in Egypt. It agrees to publish the Hussein–McMahon correspondence for the first time. Sir Michael

McDonnell, who served as Chief Justice in the Supreme Court of Palestine from 1927 to 1937, argues that in his opinion, it was sufficiently clear from reading the Hussein–McMahon correspondence that Palestine was to be included in the Arab state. However, the British Government disagrees with him, although it is telling that its arguments were considered so thin that it did not even convince its own civil servants in the Foreign and Colonial Office of its case.

1939–45 The Second World War. Britain restricts, but does not halt, Jewish immigration into Palestine.

1941 President Theodor Roosevelt and Prime Minister Winston Churchill agree to the Atlantic Charter aboard the HMS *Prince of Wales*.

1942 On 20 January, a plan for the annihilation of Europe's Jews was finalised by the German Government at Wannsee, just outside Berlin. Over the next three years, some 6 million Jews were systematically and ruthlessly killed in extermination camps throughout Europe. On 11 May, an extraordinary conference of American Zionists at the Biltmore Hotel in New York City passes a resolution calling for the whole of Palestine to be established as a Jewish commonwealth.

1945 The United Nations Conference on International Organisation is convened at San Francisco. There, delegates review and rewrite the Dumbarton Oaks proposal which results in the creation of the UN Charter, a treaty which is opened for signature on 26 June. The British Government examines secret proposals to partition Palestine.

1946 The Anglo-American Committee of Enquiry tours the concentration and extermination camps of Europe, after which it recommends that whilst some refugees (approx. 100,000) should be allowed into Palestine, its territorial integrity should nevertheless be kept intact. It recommends that Palestine 'shall be neither a Jewish state nor an Arab state'.

1947 The United Nations Special Committee for Palestine (UNSCOP) visits Palestine as well as the concentration camps of Europe. It recommends the partition of Palestine between an Arab and a Jewish state. The UN then asks an ad hoc committee to examine the matter. It produces two reports. The majority favoured partition and the minority a single unitary state with strong protections for minorities. The UN General Assembly accepts the findings of majority report and recommends the partition of Palestine with economic union. It proposes that Jerusalem and Bethlehem be established as a separate body under some form of UN territorial administration. It envisages voluntary population transfers between the two states, which were to draft constitutions enshrining democratic governance and protecting human rights. The Zionists tacitly accept the UN Partition Plan and the Arabs oppose it because they consider it unfair, unworkable and inequitable – as does Britain. Egypt and Syria attempt to refer the legality of the UN Partition Plan to the International Court of Justice in The Hague for an advisory opinion but they are defeated by one vote in the UN General Assembly and so the question is never rendered to the Court. Fighting breaks out between Arabs and Jews in December, with the former protesting against partition and calling for immediate independence.

1948 Civil war breaks out on a wider scale in Palestine. In March, the US concludes that partition is unworkable and reverses its policy. It declares itself in favour of a UN Trusteeship for Palestine in a single unitary state. A UN Trusteeship Agreement is subsequently drafted. The Jewish Agency condemns it, goes on the offensive and avows to proclaim a Hebrew Republic on 16 May. In April, the Haganah implements Plan Dalet. Thirteen military operations follow, eight of which are beyond the boundaries set out for the Arab state in the UN Partition Plan. On 9 April, a massacre is perpetrated by the Irgun with the support of the Haganah in the Palestinian Arab village of Deir Yassin, near Jerusalem. By May, the Zionists have conquered Jaffa (which was supposed to be part of the Arab state as envisaged in the UN Partition Plan) and Haifa, causing their Arab populations to flee to secure ground. At midnight on 14/15 May the last British High Commissioner in Palestine terminates the Mandate and departs Haifa. The *Yishuv* concomitantly proclaims the establishment of the state of Israel. By this time, over 350,000 Palestinian Arabs have been evicted from their homes. The Arab Legion, commanded by British officers, enters Palestine on the pretext that it is defending the population of Palestine from further attacks by the Haganah and the Irgun. It is supported by troops from Lebanon, Syria, Egypt and Iraq. The fighting escalates. In July, the Haganah captures Lydda, Ramle and Nazareth expelling its Arab populations. By the time hostilities come to an end some 750,000 Palestinian Arabs and 17,000 Jews are displaced by the fighting. In December, the UN General Assembly passes a resolution providing that: 'the refugees wishing to return to their homes and live at peace with their neighbours should be permitted to do so at the earliest practicable date, and that compensation should be paid for the property of those choosing not to return and for loss of or damage to property which, under principles of international law or in equity, should be made good by the Governments or authorities responsible'.

1949 Israel formally concludes armistice agreements with Egypt, Lebanon, Syria and Transjordan. The fighting officially comes to an end, although expulsions of Palestinian Arabs (like that at Wadi Fukin) and the Bedouin continues. The Government of Israel refuses to allow the vast majority of Arabs to return to their homes in Palestine but allows Jews to do so. In an exchange of notes, the US Government declares that Israel's opposition to repatriation is not in conformity with UN General Assembly resolution 194 (III). They also threaten to review their relationship with Israel and to undertake countermeasures. Under pressure, Israel does agree to allow, in principle, a return of 100,000 refugees. However, talks break down and nothing comes of this. The vast majority of Palestinians displaced in 1948 continue to languish in refugee camps in the Middle East to this day.

About the Author

Victor Kattan was born in Khartoum, Sudan in 1979 to a Palestinian father and British mother. He graduated with an LL. B (Hons) from Brunel University in 2001, an LL. M from Leiden University in 2002, and is currently pursuing his Doctorate at the School of Oriental and African Studies (SOAS), University of London, for which he was awarded a scholarship from the Arts and Humanities Research Council. His previous publications include *The Palestine Question in International Law* (editor), and his scholarly articles have been published in international law journals in Europe and the United States.

In 2003–04, he worked as a consultant with the United Nations Development Programme in Jerusalem on secondment to the Badil Resource Centre for Palestinian Residency and Refugee Rights in Bethlehem. In 2004–06, he worked as a journalist with Arab Media Watch and was one of its Directors. In December 2006, he tendered his resignation to become a Research Fellow at the British Institute of International and Comparative Law to work on their project on Human Rights in International Law and Iran, as well as to research and write this book. He is currently a teaching fellow in International Law at the Centre for International Studies and Diplomacy at SOAS.

About the Authors

Map 1 'Russia in Europe, Map showing Pale of Jewish Settlement', from *The Persecution of the Jews in Russia* (London: Wertheimer, Lea & Co., 1890). Reprinted with permission. © British Library Board. All rights reserved 4033.c.57.

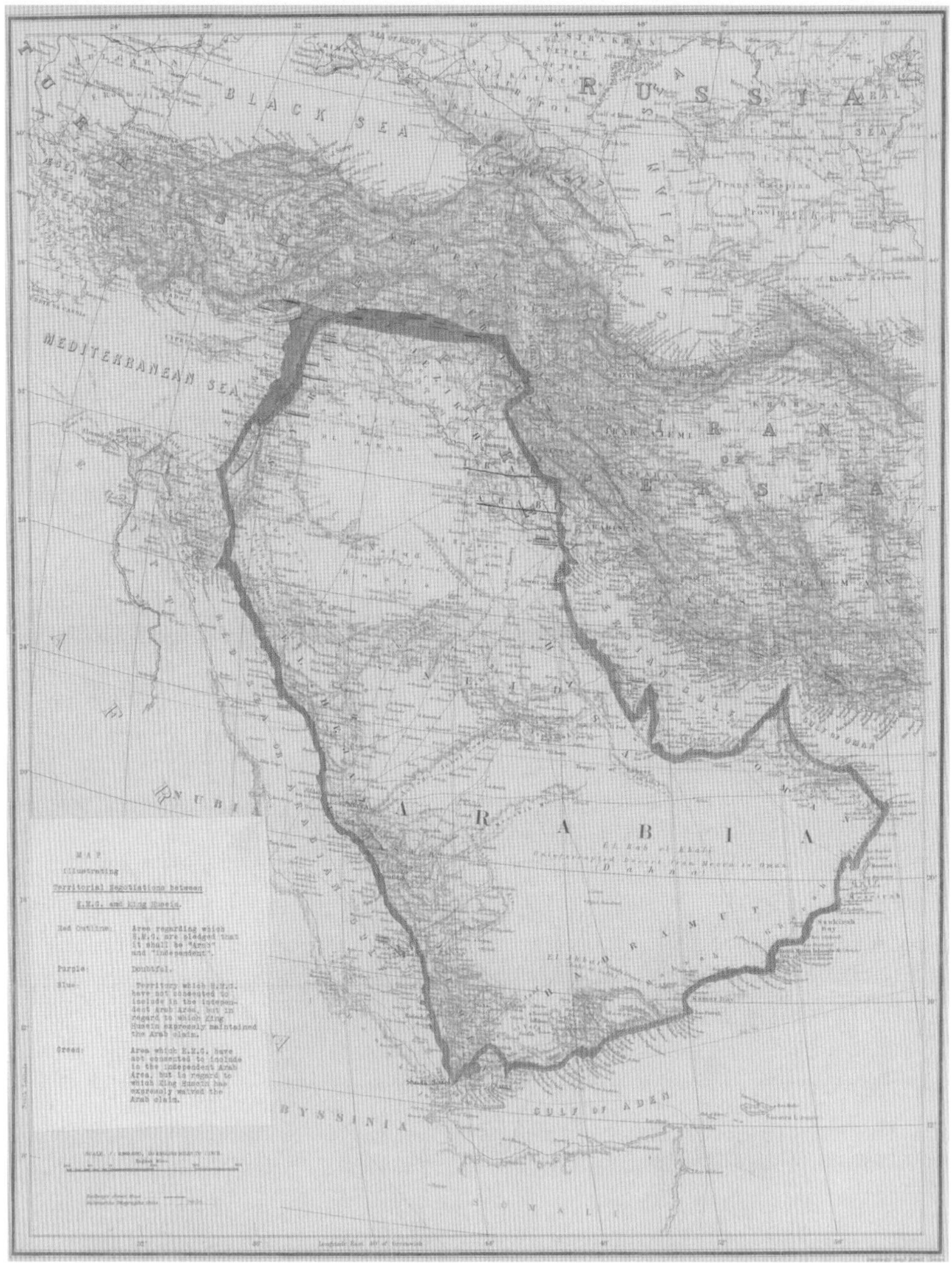

Map 2 'Map illustrating territorial negotiations between H.M.G. and King Hussein. Red Outline: Area regarding which H.M.G. are pledged that it shall be "Arab" and "independent".' Courtesy of The National Archives UK, MFQ 1/357.

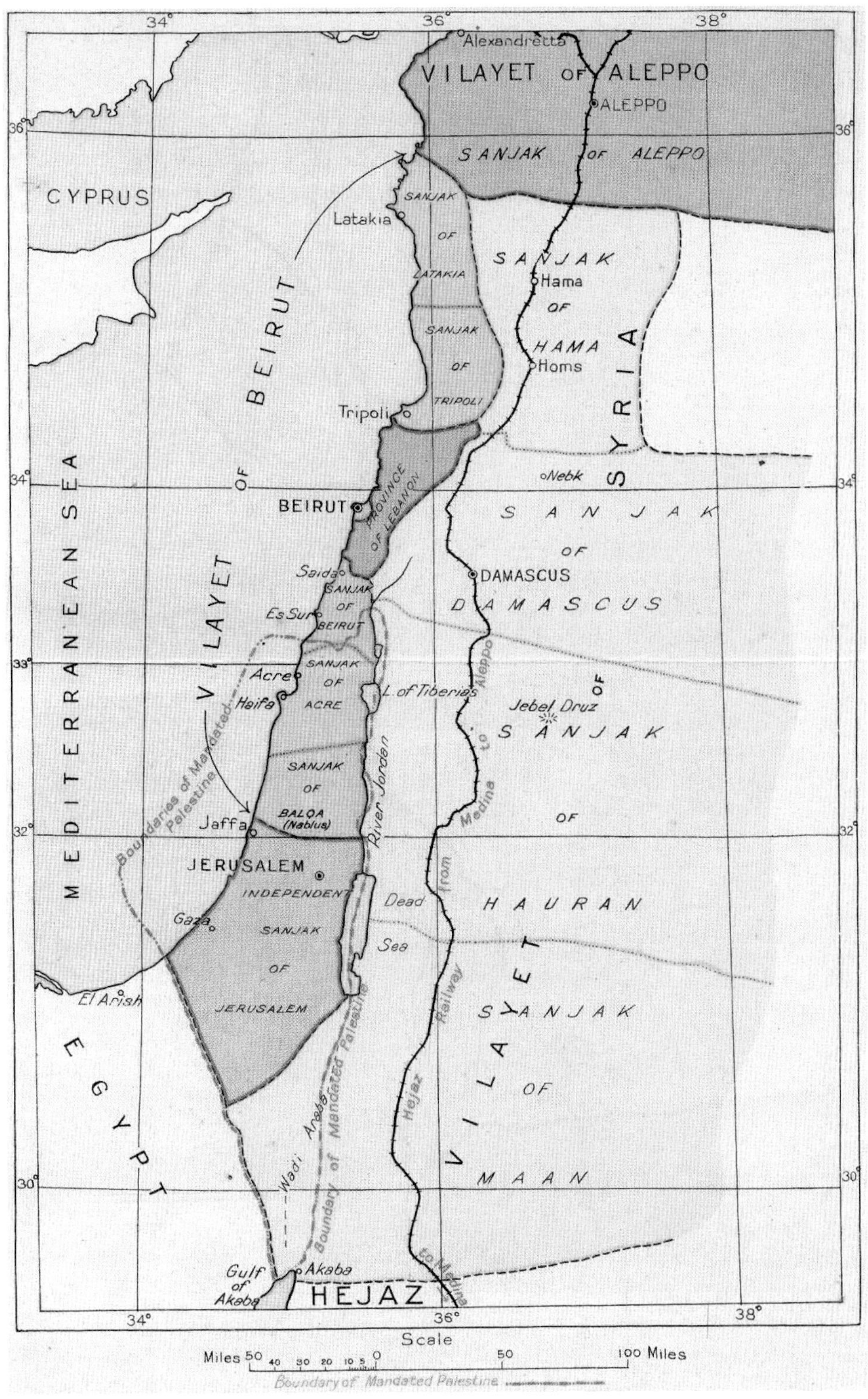

Map 3 'Pre-war Turkish Administrative Districts comprised in Syria and Palestine showing the boundaries of mandated Palestine and the Hejaz railway.' Courtesy of The National Archives UK, MFQ 1/388.

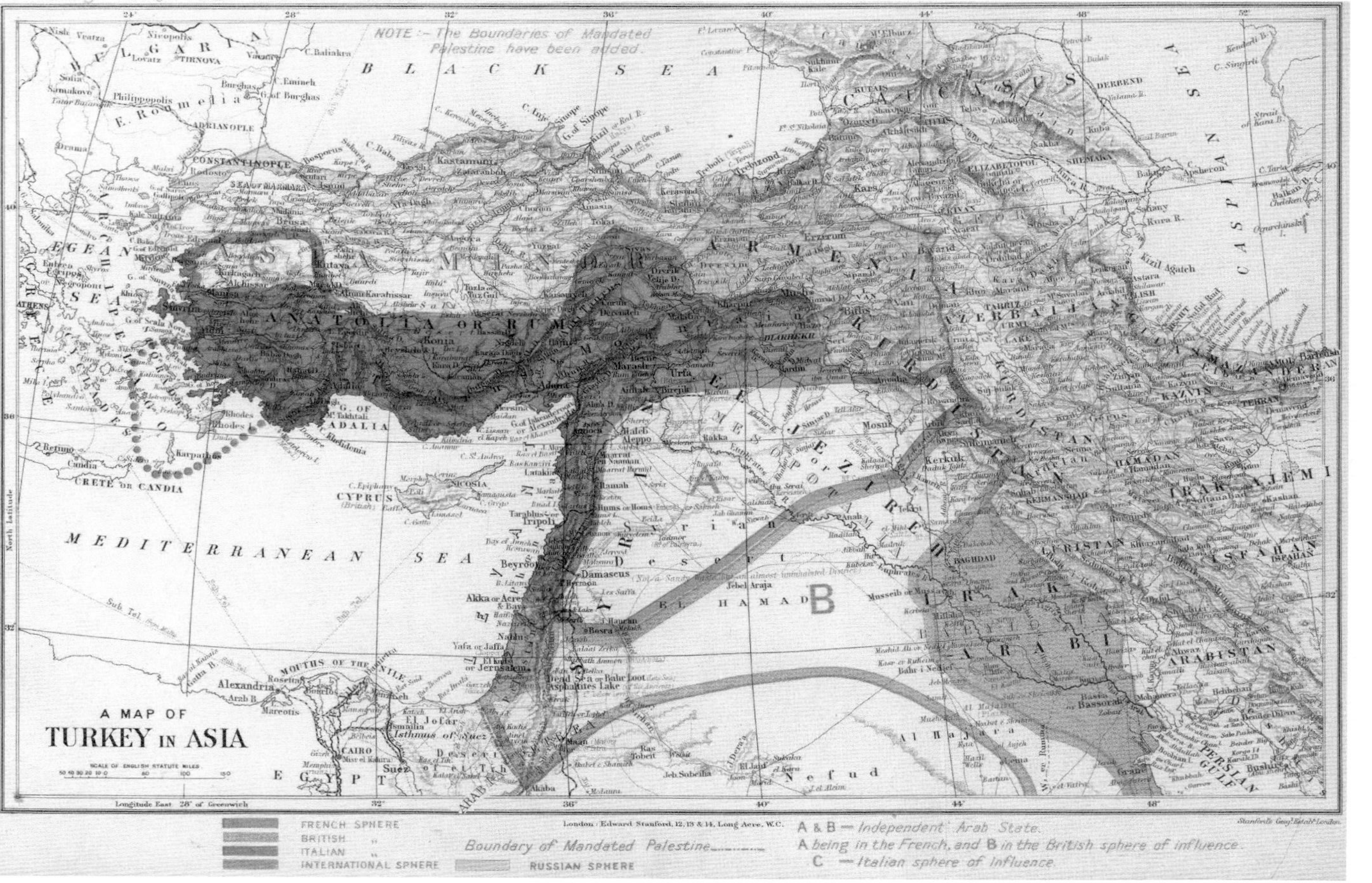

Map 4 'The Sykes–Picot Arrangement of 1916 in regard to Syria and Palestine. Map to illustrate the Agreement of 1916 in regard to Asia Minor, Mesopotamia, &c.' Courtesy of The National Archives UK, MFQ 1/388.

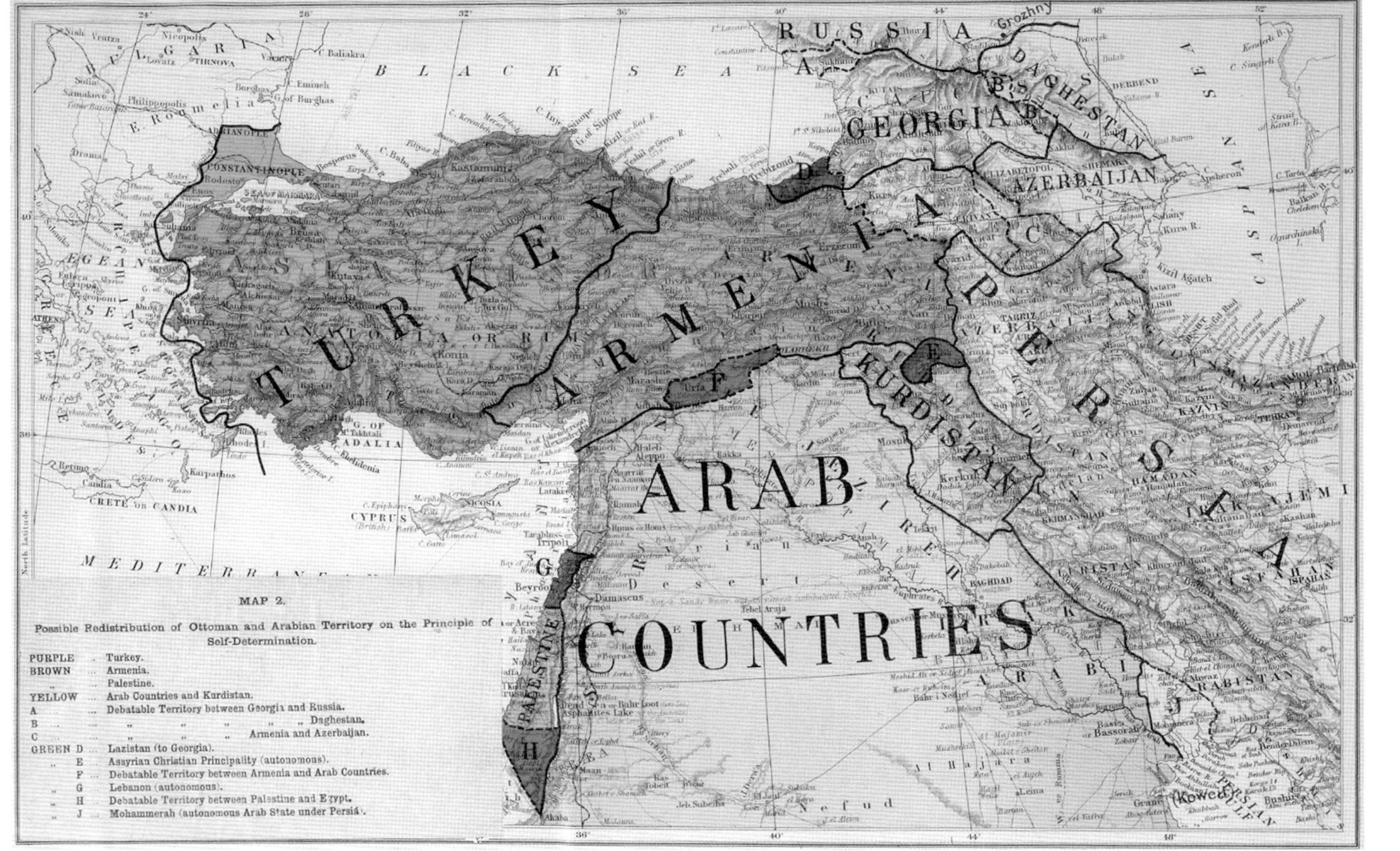

Map 5 'Map illustrating possible redistribution of Ottoman and Arab territory on the Principle of Self-Determination.' Courtesy of The National Archives UK, FO 925/41231.

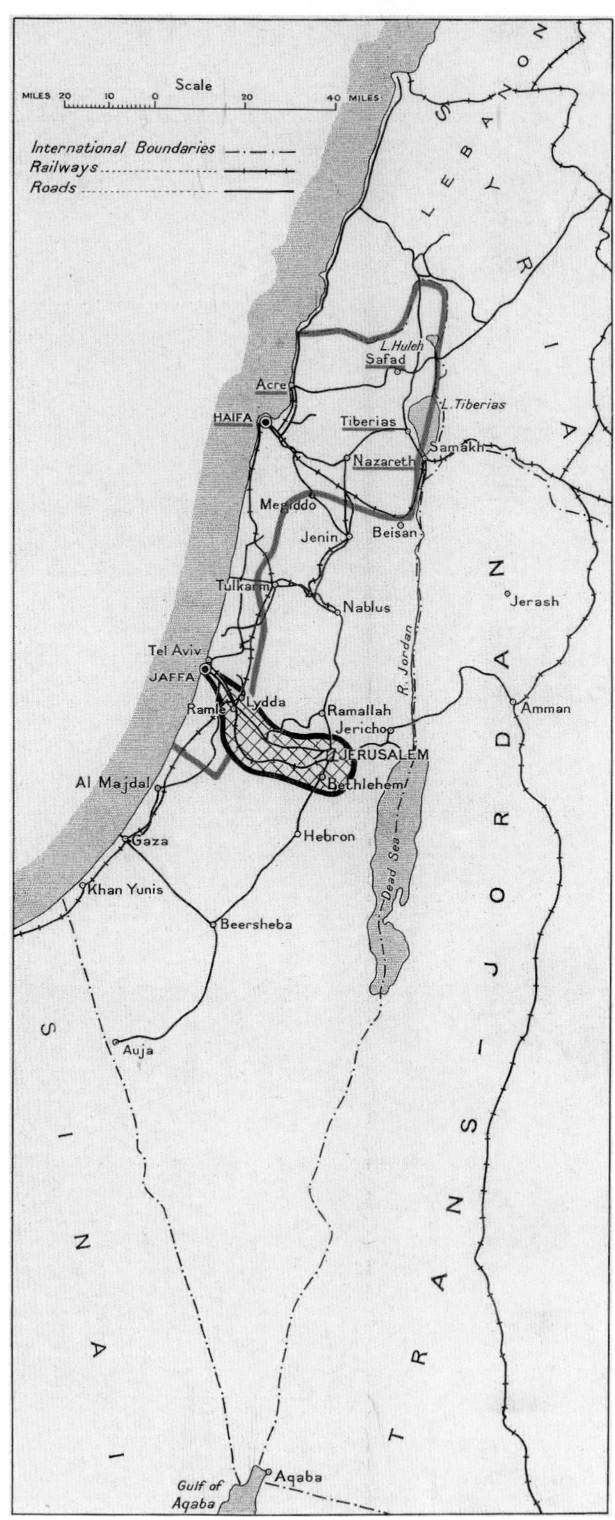

Map 6 'Map of the Royal Commission's Partition Plan (Peel Commission) 1937.' Courtesy of The National Archives UK, MFQ 1/465.

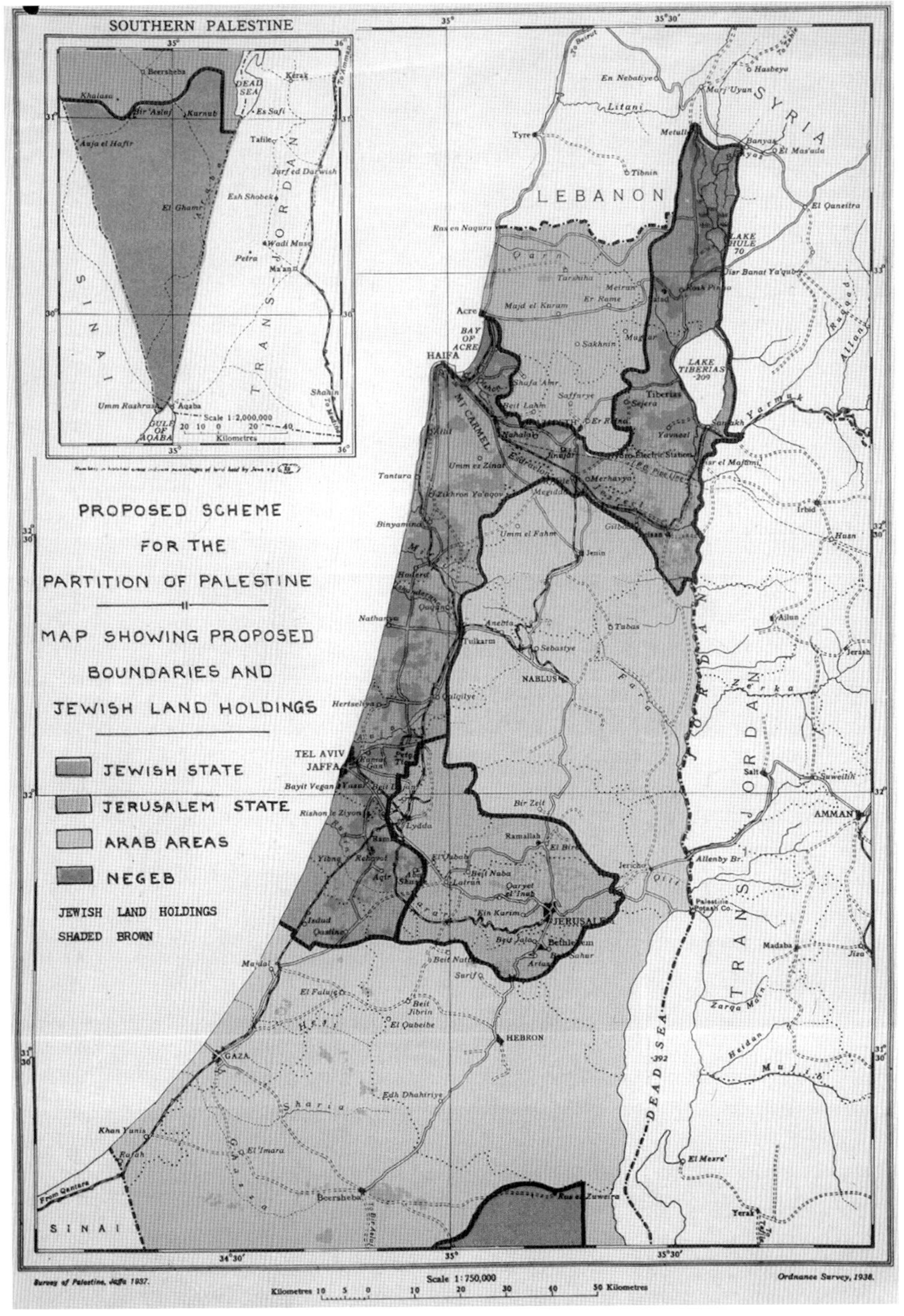

Map 7 'Proposed Scheme for the Partition of Palestine: Map Showing Proposed Boundaries and Jewish Land Holdings, April 1945.' Courtesy of The National Archives UK, PREM 4/52/1.

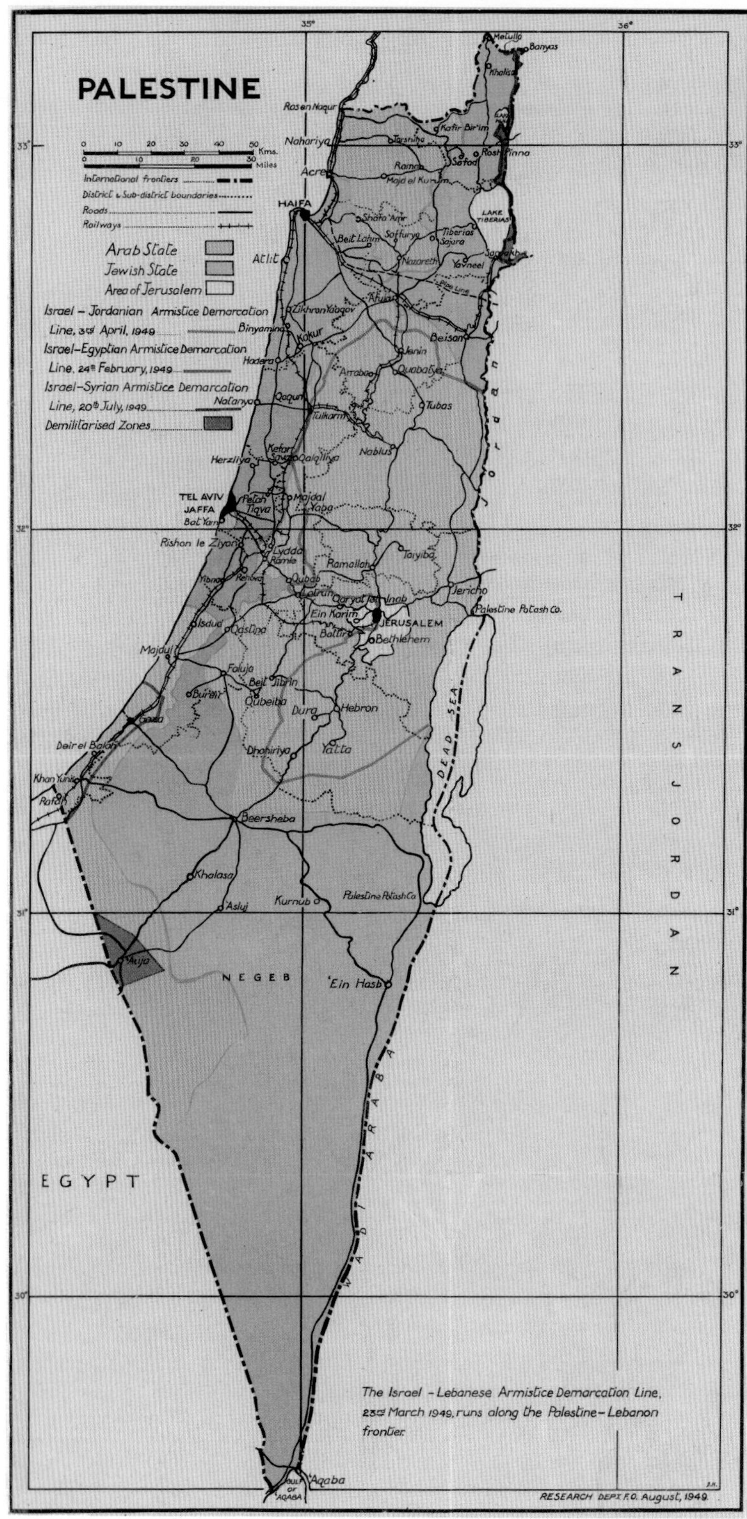

Map 8 'Palestine: Map of 1949 Armistice Lines & Boundaries in Partition Plan.' Courtesy of The National Archives UK, MFQ 1/1396/1.

Introduction

It is usually said that the Arab–Israeli conflict is intractable because it consists of two competing nationalisms vying for control over the same territory.[1] Whilst there is intrinsic merit in the supposition that Arab and Jewish nationalisms are violently at odds, it is, nevertheless, inherently flawed in that it does not explain how these two sets of nationalisms emerged in Palestine to begin with.[2] Jewish nationalism never existed in Palestine historically amongst the small number of oriental Jews who lived in peace with the Arabs, both Christians and Muslims, for over a thousand years. Rather, it emanated from Central and Eastern Europe where anti-Semitism was endemic and where Zionism was born amongst the *Ashkenazim* who were being oppressed. In order to understand how Jewish nationalism emerged in Palestine and did not remain in Europe, one must trace the roots of the conflict to the colonial era when the British Empire ruled over a quarter of the globe. This is because without colonialism there would have been no Balfour Declaration, no British Mandate of Palestine, no mass immigration of Jews into Palestine, and no Jewish national home. In fact, without colonialism the state of Israel would most likely not exist today and these two sets of nationalisms could never have clashed. Religion, poverty, political violence and race are only contemporary attributes of the conflict. They do not explain why the conflict commenced or why it continues.

The Arab–Israeli conflict is not old. It has not been going on for centuries or since 'time immemorial'. It is not as long-lived as the conflict was in Ireland for example.[3] It has nothing to do with the Bible or with the Qur'an, although Palestine being the centre for the three monotheistic religions – Christianity, Islam and Judaism – has undoubtedly complicated matters. Yet despite the importance of religion in the region the conflict remains inherently nationalistic, with the Zionists and the Palestinian Arabs as the principal protagonists. The former are predominately, but not exclusively, Jewish immigrants who settled in Palestine mostly from Central and Eastern Europe since the late nineteenth century fleeing European anti-Semitism and persecution.[4] In contrast, the Palestinians are an indigenous people descended from those who lived in the land between the Mediterranean Sea and the Jordan River in antiquity.[5] Their demographics have changed over the ages by migration, settlement, war, famine and a whole variety of other factors which usually explain the demographic composition of other peoples throughout history. It is said that the ancestors of today's Palestinians included the Canaanites, Hittites, Philistines, Phoenicians, Egyptians, Hebrews, Samaritans, Persians, Greeks, Assyrians, Armenians, Romans, Arabs, Crusaders and Turks.[6] Over the past millennia, Jews, Christians, Muslims, and peoples of other faiths, and those of no faith, have inhabited that land. In the course of time its inhabitants were Judaised, Christianised and Islamised, their language being transformed into Hebrew, then to Aramaic, and then to Arabic.[7] However, without question, Palestine has been a predominantly Arab country for the greater part of its modern history, and Sunni Islam has been the religion of the overwhelming majority of its inhabitants, prior to the Zionist conquest. The word 'Palestine' was first used by Heredotus, the ancient Greek historian, and adopted after him by early Christian historians.[8] The word derives from the Philistines, a migrating twelfth-century people from the Aegean civilisation (3000–1100 BC).[9]

It is futile to dwell on trying to ascertain who Palestine's first inhabitants were because there is simply no way of proving it. But even if that could be established, it would make little difference to resolving today's conflict which is a modern political phenomenon that began in the late nineteenth century, during the heyday of European colonial expansion. It perhaps suffices to say, in this regard, that some Zionists trace their roots back to the ancient Israelite tribes to seek to prove that they have a better title to the land than the Palestinian Arabs.[10] The problem with this argument, however, apart from the general problem associated with advancing claims based on ancient title, is that some Palestinians claim they are descended from the Canaanites, an indigenous people who inhabited the land of Palestine prior to the creation of ancient Israel.[11] Of course, this is contested too, which provides yet another good reason obviating the need to revert to the ancient scriptures to come to terms with a conflict which is not as complicated as it might appear on initial inspection.[12] This is because it is not necessary to trace the origins of the conflict back to the dawn of history to understand it. For the purposes of international law, the question of who inhabited the land first is not strictly speaking relevant. Otherwise, the Muslims could advance territorial claims to Spain, Sicily, Greece and most of the Balkans; the Greeks to Turkey, Iraq, Iran and Palestine; and the Italians to England, France and Spain. It would be a recipe for chaos. Rather, international lawyers are interested in finding out who has sovereignty over the territory at the critical date, which is usually based on effective occupation and longevity of control over it. In its most basic and simplistic conception the question of sovereignty is concerned with the question of who had a better title to the territory at the date conflict ensued.

It is not disputed by either the Palestinians or the Zionists that Turkey had sovereignty over Palestine until it ratified the Lausanne Treaty in 1923, although it had lost *de facto* control over Palestine in December 1917. After this, things get problematic, and the remainder of this book is devoted to the question of what happened in the years when Palestine was placed under a League of Nations Mandate that was entrusted by the Great Powers to Great Britain to the time when war broke out between the Zionists and the Palestinian Arabs in the years 1947–49. Although it is arguable that many of the problems associated with the present predicament trace their roots to the first Arab–Israeli conflict in 1947–49, which saw the expulsion of two-thirds of Palestine's pre-war Arab population, this does not explain why there was a conflict to begin with.[13] Nor is tracing the violence to the June 1967 war in which Israel captured East Jerusalem, the West Bank, the Gaza Strip, the Golan Heights and the Sinai Peninsula in a mere six days sufficient to explain it.[14] This presupposes that everything would be peaceful if Israel remained within its 1949 ceasefire boundaries, when Jerusalem was divided, when Egypt occupied the Gaza Strip and when Jordan was in possession of the West Bank.[15]

The Arab–Israeli conflict, like many conflicts in Africa and Asia, traces its roots to the colonial confrontation when vast swathes of the planet were placed under the control of a number of European powers. There were two phases to this process of European expansion. The first took place in Berlin in 1884–85, when the colonial powers gathered to regulate their conquest of Africa, the 'dark continent', which in due course would be partitioned into fragmented territories, called colonies, by the Great Powers as if the continent was a white space on a map.[16] The second phase occurred in Paris in 1919 when the Great Powers assembled to reshape the world after the First World War.[17] It was there that the area we now refer to as the 'Near East' or the 'Middle East' was to be remodelled in the shape of European mini states.

When Palestine was carved out of the Ottoman Empire, it had in 1918 a population of 688,957 Arabs (including Christians, Muslims and other minorities) and 58,728 Jews.[18] At that time there were more Christian Arabs living in Palestine than Jews.[19] Moreover the majority of Jews were indigenous, that is, they had been living in Palestine for more than several generations. However, this was about to change significantly. Zionism, which is sometimes referred to as the 'national liberation movement of the Jewish people', was to mimic the European practice of colonialism so successfully, that within a matter of five decades they would gain control over most of Palestine. And of course the Zionists were not indigenous; most of them had never set foot in the country before, let alone the Middle East.

The colonisation of Palestine was accomplished through a process of immigration, settlement, land purchase and ultimately conquest. And it was during the 1922–48 mandate, when Britain facilitated the Zionists in their colonial enterprise, through which international law was instrumental, that the seeds of conflict were first sown. Indeed, Britain's 31 years of administering Palestine, three years as an occupying power, and 28 years as the mandatory power, was marred by a litany of violent incidents, which were marked by riots, protests and petitions against the Zionist project, which was referred to by colonial civil servants at the time as 'the national home policy'. That is, the policy of establishing a Jewish national home in a country that was in 1918, overwhelmingly populated by Arabs.

So what can international lawyers learn from the turbulent legal history of the British Mandate of Palestine? First, that international law gave the Zionists the legitimacy they craved, as manifested in the Balfour Declaration, the British Mandate of Palestine and the UN Partition Plan.[20] Once the Great Powers sanctioned these agreements it became very difficult for those Palestinians who opposed Zionism in the 1920s, 1930s and 1940s to be granted political legitimacy. The same goes for those organisations, like Hamas, who oppose the state of Israel today, and who are under pressure to adhere to another series of international agreements, collectively known as the 'Oslo Accords'.[21] As long as they refuse to sign up to these agreements and recognise Israel it is likely that they will continue to be ostracised by the international community, even though they were elected through a democratic process. And yet, excluding the Palestinians from being in a position to pursue a truly independent political strategy that challenges the *status quo* is not an entirely new phenomenon. After all, the proposals[22] submitted by the High Commissioner in Palestine in 1936 for a Legislative Council which would have reflected the fact that the indigenous Arab Christians and Muslims were numerically preponderant in Palestine were vetoed by the House of Commons because they feared that this could have enabled the Palestinian Arabs to scupper the Zionist project.[23]

In this regard it could be argued that international law has had a malign effect on the welfare of the Palestinian people, which has been used and abused by the Great Powers to advance their respective agendas. As a consequence, many see international law as it is applied in the Middle East as an illegitimate, and immoral tool that is intimately associated with Western power, culture and imperialism.[24] As a result, international law's agents, as reflected through the work of international organisations like the United Nations, the European Union and even the International Committee of the Red Cross, have increasingly become an object of armed attack in the Arab world.[25]

Alternatively, one could point to the 'civilising nature' of the aforesaid agreements as an example of international law's concern for humanity, development and progress. After all, the whole raison d'être behind the concept of the mandate, its sacred trust, and international humanitarian law are 'the duty of civilisation'. In this regard, it will be recalled that the Balfour Declaration contained a safeguard clause stipulating that nothing should be done 'which may prejudice the civil and religious rights of existing non-Jewish communities in Palestine', and Article 22 of the Covenant of the League of Nations provided that the well-being and development of peoples placed under the mandatory system of administration 'form a sacred trust of civilisation'. Moreover, the UN Partition Plan and the draft for a UN Trusteeship Agreement had elaborate provisions for minorities and human rights. From this perspective, one could advance the argument that the problem is not international law *per se* but its lack of enforcement; that in the Middle East international law is closer to power than to justice.[26]

Secondly, it would seem that even if one analyses the origins of the Arab–Israeli conflict from a strictly positivist perspective, that is without taking into account other factors such as culture, fairness and justice, it is apparent that in nurturing the development of a Jewish national home in Palestine the colonial powers departed from the very rules they freely consented to and helped to develop. That is, at a time when principles such as the self-determination of peoples, the norm of territorial integrity, the prohibition of armed conflict and the protection and promotion of human rights were gaining currency, the

Great Powers were supporting an experiment that had all the hallmarks of a nineteenth-century colonial project. In other words, the creation of a Jewish state in Palestine in 1948–49 was arguably as much of an anachronism then, as it would be if it were created today. The Jewish state was, after all, created after the establishment of the United Nations in 1945 and after many of the violent tactics employed during the Arab–Israeli conflict in 1947–49 had been condemned as contrary to the law of nations by the International Military Tribunals in Nuremberg, Tokyo and elsewhere.[27]

In this regard, it is rather paradoxical that today the reverse of what was promised to Lord Rothschild in 1917 has transpired: instead of there being a Jewish national home in Palestine, as envisaged by the Balfour Declaration and the Mandate, we essentially have a situation where a 'Palestinian national home' may be established within a Jewish state. In other words it is not entirely unfeasible that the Palestinian state the 'international community' is contemplating will be anything but independent or viable, at least if they are seriously considering establishing one in the fragmented territory of the West Bank and Gaza. In such a situation it is more than likely that the Palestinian entity created will either be a puppet state, a client state or even an apartheid state where a minority of Israeli settlers rule over the majority of Palestinians living in the West Bank.[28] This was certainly not what was envisaged by even the most ardent supporters of Zionism within the British political establishment in 1917, although of course many of the founding fathers of the Zionist movement harboured intentions to establish a state with a majority Jewish population from the very beginning.[29] In other words, what most British statesmen meant by the term 'a Jewish national home', differed significantly from how it was interpreted by the Zionists, although the more politically erudite amongst them were aware that it could cause difficulties. Even Lord Balfour, with his strong sympathies for Zionist aspirations, said that he never wanted the indigenous Palestinian Arab population to be dispossessed or oppressed.

Moreover, if anything can be learned from the various arguments employed for and against the partition of Palestine in 1947, it is that a Palestinian state in East Jerusalem, the West Bank and Gaza will be an unviable entity that will be dependent on handouts from the international community. As Britain's Foreign Secretary, Ernest Bevin, said in a 1947 House of Commons debate on Palestine: 'I have never yet been able to see how a little country like that, with railways, telegraph and the rest, can be economically run and can be viable if divided.'[30] If the Arab state as envisaged in the 1947 UN Partition Plan, which was more than twice the size of what the Palestinian leadership is demanding today, was economically unviable, how can a 'state' in a mere 22 per cent of mandatory Palestine be considered independent and viable today when the West Bank has effectively been dissected into several parts and surrounded by walls, fences, trenches and armed watchtowers? Moreover, it is more than likely that the envisaged 'state' will be completely dependent on Israel economically and for transport and communications. If partition is ever to be a viable prospect in this day and age, then it will surely necessitate territorial concessions from Israel, a dismantling of the settlements and unhindered access for Palestinians to the Holy Places.

Thirdly, the passage of the UN Partition Plan accompanied by the acrimonious debates in the UN General Assembly as well as the debates concerning a UN Trusteeship Agreement in the days preceding Israel's unilateral declaration of independence at midnight on 14/15 May 1948, are a testimony to the limits of international law when domestic politics affects the actions of the Great Powers. In this respect, Zionist interference in American foreign policy is not something new, but was very much prevalent during the UN debates from November 1947 to May 1948. As Philip C. Jessup, the US judge appointed to the International Court of Justice in 1961 recalled in his memoirs of his time at the UN when the Provisional Government of Israel issued a Declaration of Independence:

> Neither I nor my advisers at the United Nations in New York had ever been told that it was the President's policy to recognize the state of Israel the moment it was proclaimed. Our official information in the delegation had been to the contrary. Secretary Marshall himself did not know it until May 14. And President Truman evidently was not aware that all of the friendly delegations who were working with us to bring about a peaceful solution of the Palestine crisis were taken completely by surprise. Diplomacy by surprise is a dangerous practice. It may be useful from the point of view of domestic politics, but it can be ruinous to our relations with other countries.[31]

In this regard it would seem that not much has changed since 1949. The Arab world is still implacably hostile to a Jewish state in control of the Holy Places, that is seemingly allowed to violate the human rights of the Palestinian people with impunity, and that continues to construct settlements in the territories it occupied in the June 1967 war.[32]

Finally, just as the British narrowly interpreted the recommendations of their own White Papers, policy statements and the numerous Commissions of Inquiry sent to Palestine as well as a Military Commission of Inquiry, which suggested that Britain should seriously reconsider the national home policy, or abandon it entirely as the King–Crane Commission had suggested, Britain strove on relentlessly. There are many reasons, which may explain why Britain was so persistent in a policy that many considered doomed from the beginning and a recipe for future disaster. These ranged from strategic considerations associated with Empire to a revolutionary solution for a European minority problem.[33] Of course the problems associated with European anti-Semitism had nothing to do with the peoples of the Arab world when Theodor Herzl first published *Der Judenstaat* in 1896.[34] And just like most political activists of his era, he showed scant regard for the indigenous peoples of the territories he suggested colonising. Rather, at the turn of the twentieth century, Zionism was seen by both Zionists and anti-Semites as a solution to the 'Jewish Question', because it encouraged Jewish immigration out of Europe. This is one of the primary reasons why Balfour supported the Zionists, because they provided him with an opportunity to divert Jewish immigration away from Britain and into Palestine which was to become 'the national home for the Jewish people'.

In 1919, Lord Curzon, warned Lord Balfour, rather prophetically, about the perils of the contradictory policy their government was pursuing in Palestine, creating a Jewish national home in a land that was almost entirely Arab:

> 'Personally, I am so convinced that Palestine will be a rankling thorn in the flesh of whoever is charged with its Mandate, that I would withdraw from this responsibility while we yet can.'[35]

However, the British did not withdraw from this responsibility. Instead they ignored Curzon's advice and that of Edwin Montagu, who were some of Britain's most experienced politicians of the time, particularly when it came to the administration of colonial territories, to implement a policy that promised two peoples self-determination in the same country without seriously considering how this could be accommodated in a single geographic entity. It can safely be said that had there been no British Mandate of Palestine, with its promise to establish a Jewish national home without prejudicing the civil and religious rights of its indigenous Arab population or the political rights of Jews in other countries, there would have been no conflict to write of. As it happened, history tells us another story, and as will become evident in the following pages, the conflict, and many of the problems associated with it, can be traced back to the Mandate.

1
Anti-semitism, Colonialism and Zionism

'Dr. Herzl was indifferent at first whether he led them to Argentina or to Palestine, he quickly perceived the commercial value of keeping the name of the old firm on his prospectus ... And the promoters knew their public. Poor Jews, who would have preferred the fleshpots of Egypt to the unknown terrors of South America, jumped at the sound of Jerusalem.'

Aspects of the Jewish Question by a Quarterly Reviewer with a Map
(London: John Murray, 1902), p. 20

'The Congo State has land enough which we can use for our settlement. We can take over part of the responsibilities, that is, pay an annual tax, which may be fixed later, to the Congo State, in return for which we naturally lay claim to self-government ... If King Leopold turns a willing ear to the matter, I shall go to see him at once.'

Theodor Herzl, 12 July, 1903 in Raphael Patai (ed.),
The Complete Diaries of Theodor Herzl, Vol. IV
(New York: Herzl Press, 1960), pp. 1511–12

'There is only one cure for this world-evil, and that is for all the Christian white races to combine and to repatriate to Palestine and the neighbouring territories every Jew, male and female, and to take the most drastic steps to see that, once they have founded their Zionist state in their own Promised Land, they permanently remain there.'

The Jews' Who's Who: Israelite Finance. Its Sinister Influence,
Popular Edition (London: The Judaic Publishing Co.,
H.H. Beamish, Proprietor, 1921), p. 43

'What the French could do in Tunisia, I said, the Jews could do in Palestine, with Jewish will, Jewish money, Jewish power and Jewish enthusiasm.'

Dr Chaim Weizmann, *Trial and Error*
(New York: Shocken Books, 1966), p. 244

If there were three words which could explain the success which lay behind the creation of Israel and the conquest of Palestine in 1948 they would be anti-Semitism, colonialism and Zionism. Not only do these words end with the same suffix, but they all contributed directly to the decision by Britain to support Jewish colonisation in Palestine. And law, being the end product of politics, was there every step of the way providing legitimacy and a legal framework through which Jewish immigration into Britain would be controlled and restricted in 1905, before being redirected into Palestine after the Balfour Declaration of 1917, and regulated thereafter through the implementation of a League of Nations Mandate from September 1923 until May 1948. It therefore becomes necessary to take a closer look at the history behind these three inter-related phenomena, as well as the colonisation of Palestine that had already begun in the nineteenth century, before analysing the big international legal issues, with which the rest of this book is devoted.

ANTI-SEMITISM

Anti-Semitism, that is, hostility towards Jews as Jews,[1] is a phenomenon, which manifested itself in its most extreme form in Nazi Germany in the 1930s where the Jews were stripped of all civil and political rights before being subjected to the extermination camps and the gas chambers during the Final Solution (1942–45).[2] This form of racism and religious and ethnic persecution was not, however, new. It had been around for over a millennium, particularly in Christian Europe where Jews were expelled from England[3] in the thirteenth century, and from Spain and Portugal[4] in the fifteenth century. Indeed, many of the Jews expelled from the Iberian Peninsula, the *Sephardim*, would find refuge in North Africa and the Middle East. Then, it was the Muslims who welcomed them and the Roman Catholics who drove them from their homes. But the maltreatment of Jews did not end in the fifteenth century. In the nineteenth century, Jews were not only expelled from their places of origin, but they were killed in organised pogroms in Russia and Romania which led to a Jewish exodus westwards, primarily into Britain, France, Germany, and the United States, as well as into Palestine where a very small number of Russian Jews established colonies.[5] Yet, even after all the appalling atrocities the Jews had been subjected to in those countries they were not always welcomed, even in the 'enlightened' states of Western Europe.[6] Indeed, today it is common to blame the Germans, and almost they alone, for the scourge of anti-Semitism – and for good reason. After all, German intellectuals from the nineteenth and twentieth centuries, like Johann Gottlieb Fichte, Eugen Dühring, Heinrich von Treikschke, Heinrich Class, Ludwig Woltmann, Wilhelm Marr, Konstantin Frantz, Johannes Scherr, Adolf Stoecker, Wilhelm Stapel, Hans Blüher, Richard Wagner, Max Wundt, and Johannes Pfeffrkorn, among many others,[7] were all self-professed anti-Semites who argued that there was no place for the Jews in modern Germany.[8] They considered anti-Semitism as a natural reaction of the German *Volksgefühl* (popular consciousness) against a 'foreign element' that they claimed never intended to assimilate.[9] They had a particular dislike for the *Ostjuden*, those Jews who had been arriving in Germany and other places from the ghettos of Eastern Europe and Russia in an area called the Pale of Jewish Settlement created by Catherine the Great in 1791 (see Map 1).[10] Ultimately these German intellectuals provided the political and philosophical foundations that would give succour to the crazed conspiracy theories of Alfred Rosenberg who incorporated it into Nazi dogma, and which ultimately influenced the policies of Adolf Hitler.[11]

Yet we forget just how widespread anti-Semitism was. Germany was not the only country to produce intellectuals and politicians who viewed these Eastern European Jews with suspicion. For instance, the 'Jewish Question', coined by Bruno Bauer,[12] which, among other things, concerned the question as to whether members of the Jewish faith could be 'true patriots', if they refused to assimilate with non-Jews, was also something debated quite openly in Britain especially amongst the educated elite.[13] Indeed, there was a certain commonality between the anti-Semites and the Zionists. For those same German intellectuals, mentioned earlier, who considered the Jews alien to Germany, were, in fact, the most ardent Zionists, because Zionism supported their philosophy of encouraging the Jews to remove themselves from Germany and into Palestine.[14] In the words of the eighteenth-century German idealist philosopher Johann Fichte: 'I see no other way to protect ourselves from the Jews, except if we conquer their promised land for them and send all of them there.'[15] The Zionist concept of the Jews as a distinct national or racial community, deserving its own homeland or state, coincided with the anti-Semitic view of the Jews as a 'foreign body'. Its appeal to them lay in the Zionists' ultimate acceptance of the exclusion of the Jewish people from the German *Volksgemeinschaft* (racial community) and the necessity of a Jewish homeland in Palestine or elsewhere overseas, capable of drawing Jews away from Europe.[16] Theodor Herzl, the Austro-Hungarian journalist and founding father of political Zionism, was well aware of this paradox and realised that his movement could expect considerable support from the anti-Semites.[17] 'The anti-Semites will have carried the day', Herzl confided in his diary in 1895.[18] 'Let them have this satisfaction', he wrote, 'for we too shall be happy. They will have turned out to be right because they *are* right.'[19] Herzl's alliance with the anti-Semites did not, however, pass without comment. He was attacked quite vociferously in liberal Jewish quarters:

> Dr. Herzl and those who think with him are traitors to the history of the Jews, which they misread and misinterpret. They are themselves part authors of the anti-Semitism they profess to slay. For how can the European countries which the Jews propose to 'abandon' justify their retention of the Jews, if the Jews themselves are to be the first to 'evacuate' their position, and to claim the bare courtesy of 'foreign visitors'?[20]

Zionism's 'dark side' is that it was the twin of anti-Semitism.[21] As Herzl told the First Zionist Congress in his opening address in Basel on 29 August 1897, 'Anti-Semitism ... is the up-to-date designation of the [Zionist] movement.'[22] Instead of struggling for equal civil and political rights with Europe's Christian majority, and by accepting the premise that the Jews were, in fact, a separate 'race' in need of their own state, Herzl and his Zionists were giving succour to the anti-Semites who were essentially making the same argument.[23] It also affirmed the prejudices of Adolf Hitler, who in *Mein Kampf*, made the following observation about Jews and Zionism whilst wandering the streets of Vienna:

> Yet I could no longer very well doubt that the objects of my study were not Germans of a special religion, but a people in themselves; for since I had

begun to concern myself with this question and to take cognisance of the Jews, Vienna appeared to me in a different light than before. Wherever I went, I began to see Jews, and the more I saw, the more sharply they become distinguished in my eyes from the rest of humanity. Particularly the Inner City and the districts north of the Danube Canal swarmed with a people which even outwardly had lost all resemblance to Germans.

And whatever doubts I may still have nourished were finally dispelled by the attitude of a portion of the Jews themselves.

Among them there was a great movement, quite extensive in Vienna, which came out sharply in confirmation of the national character of the Jews: this was the *Zionists*.[24]

In Hitler's eyes Zionism reconfirmed his pre-existing bigoted and racially narrow-minded views about the Jews not being 'true' Germans and being responsible for all that was wrong with his vision of what Germany should be. Therefore, like Fichte and the other German anti-Semites, Hitler supported the emigration of the Jews to Palestine as one way of solving Germany's Jewish Question. Indeed, today, it is all too often overlooked that Hitler, who greatly admired the British Empire throughout most of his adult life, and lamented the loss of Germany's colonies in Africa and the Pacific at the end of the First World War, supported the policy of encouraging the Jews to immigrate to Palestine for almost a decade prior to the Final Solution. Indeed, once in power, he probably did more than anyone else to encourage Zionism and the largest influx of Jewish immigrants into Palestine (1932–36) occurred when he was the Fuehrer of the Third Reich (see Table 1).

Table 1 Annual Immigration into Palestine, by Race, 1931–36

Year (September–October)	*Recorded Immigration*	
	Jews	*Non-Jews*
1931	4,075	1,458
1932	9,553	1,736
1933	30,327	1,650
1934	42,359	1,784
1935	61,854	2,293*
1936	29,727	1,944†

* Of these 903 were Arabs.
† Of these 675 were Arabs.

Source: Palestine Royal Commission Report, July 1937, Cmd 5479, p. 279.

As the commission which compiled these statistics noted, by 1936 immigration from Russia had almost entirely ceased, its place being taken over by Germany which supplied the largest proportion of immigrants overall after Poland and Russia.[25] These statistics did not include illegal Jewish immigration into Palestine, however, and so the true figures were higher.[26] That immigration peaked in 1935 was no coincidence. In that year on 15 September, Germany passed the Nuremberg Law for the Protection of German Blood and Honour, which, among other things, prohibited marriages between Germans and Jews as well as extramarital intercourse and the flying of the Reich flag by Jews.[27] With regard to Zionism, the introduction accompanying that law included the following statement:

> If the Jews had a state of their own in which the bulk of their people were at home, the Jewish question could already be considered solved today, even for the Jews themselves. The ardent Zionists of all people have objected least of all to the basic ideas of the Nuremberg Laws, because they know that these laws are the only correct solution for the Jewish people.[28]

In 1937, the Palestine Royal Commission Report was published, which for the first time envisaged establishing a Jewish state in Palestine. The report provoked intense debate within the German Foreign Ministry where the pros and cons of encouraging Jewish emigration from Germany into Palestine were debated.[29] Finally, the ministers involved decided to ask Hitler for a final ruling, and he, in turn, asked Rosenberg for a special report. After studying the document he received from his racial expert, Hitler's decision was communicated by the Foreign Affairs Office of the Nazi Party to all the Ministries concerned. They were told that the Fuehrer had decided again that: 'Jewish emigration from Germany shall continue to be promoted by all available means. Any question which might have existed up to now as to whether in the Fuehrer's opinion such emigration is to be directed primarily to Palestine has thereby been answered in the affirmative.'[30] Although Jewish immigration into Palestine fell significantly after 1937, the number of German immigrants as a proportion of the total number of immigrants entering Palestine was still high and increased appreciably in 1939.[31] According to *A Survey of Palestine* prepared in 1945–46 for the information of the Anglo-American Committee of Inquiry, emigration from Germany overtook that of Poland in 1938 and surged in 1939.[32] However, by that time Britain had decided to restrict Jewish immigration into Palestine.

Table 2 Annual Immigration into Palestine, by Race, 1937–42
(Total number of persons registered as immigrants)

Year	*Total*	*Jews*	*Arabs*	*Others*
1937	12,475	10,536	743	1,196
1938	15,263	12,868	473	1,922
1939	18,433	16,405	376	1,652
1940	5,611	4,547	390	674
1941	4,270	3,647	280	343
1942	3,052	2,194	423	435

Source: *A Survey of Palestine*, December 1945–January 1946, p. 185.

In 1961, Adolf Eichmann was indicted before the District Court of Jerusalem on 15 charges, which included crimes against humanity, crimes against the Jewish people, and being a member of an outlawed organisation.[33] At the trial he attempted to defend his horrendous actions when he was working for the Department of Jewish Emigration, which was responsible for deporting hundreds of thousands of Jews to their deaths, which led, after 1942, to the mass murder of millions, by claiming that the initial *emigration* policy of the National Socialist Party was consistent with Zionism. He told the District Court that Theodor Herzl's *Der Judenstaat* ('The Jewish State') and Adolf Böhm's *Die Zionistische Bewegung* ('The History of Zionism') were required reading by the employees of that Department.[34] Eichmann also told the Court that he protested the desecration of Herzl's grave in Vienna in 1939 and that he even commemorated the 35th anniversary of his death.[35] During the cross-examination he told the presiding judge, to the bemusement of those sitting in the gallery, that in Vienna he regarded the Jews as opponents with respect to whom a 'mutually fair solution' had to be found:

> That solution I envisaged as putting firm soil under their feet so that [the Jews] could have a place of their own, soil of their own. And I was working in the direction of that solution joyfully. I cooperated in reaching such a solution, gladly and joyfully, because it was also the kind of solution that was approved by movements among the Jewish people themselves [that is, the Zionists], and I regarded this as the most appropriate solution to this matter.[36]

Eichmann was essentially echoing what Hitler wrote in *Mein Kampf*; that Zionism was compatible with the emigration policy of the National Socialist Party in Germany, although obviously not with the extermination of European Jewry that became part of official Nazi policy at the House of Wannsee Conference in 1942.[37] In its judgment, the District Court of Jerusalem referred to Eichmann's testimony, just quoted, which formed a part of the Madagascar Plan.[38] In short, this plan entailed the total deportation of the Jews from German-ruled territory, which at that time numbered four million, to Madagascar where they could create their own 'homeland'. However, it was not to be as 'joyful' as Eichmann had rather disingenuously suggested to the Court. According to the judgment:

> ... even deportation to Madagascar would have been preferable to the physical extermination which later befell European Jewry. But ... the Madagascar Plan must be viewed in terms of the pre-extermination period. It is sufficient to glance at the details of the written plan in order to discover its true significance: the expulsion of four million Jews – the whole of European Jewry at that time under the rule of the Hitler regime – within four years into exile, and their complete isolation from the outside world. It was stated explicitly that the organization of the Jews as an independent State was out of the question and that this would be a 'police state' supervised

> by RSHA [the Reich Main Security Office] men ... the economic living conditions of millions of Jews in their new abode did not particularly worry the authors of the plan. They had in mind employing them for many years on public works such as draining swamps and building roads, that is to say, on forced labour under the supervision of the German masters of the island ... as for finance, this in part would come from the property of the Jews themselves, which would be confiscated on their leaving their places of residence and transferred to 'a central settlement fund', while the rest would be raised by imposing a tax on Jews of the Western Powers, payment to be guaranteed by the peace treaty. Western Jewry would also pay for the transport of the deportees to Madagascar, as 'reparations for damage caused to the German nation by the Jews economically and otherwise as a result of the Versailles Treaty'.[39]

Eichmann and others devised the Madagascar Plan in the Nazi bureaucracy after Hitler's blitzkrieg against France in May 1940. Madagascar was a French colony. The Nazis envisaged a 'peace treaty' with France whereby the latter would cede its colony to Germany so that they could carry out their 'Master Plan'. As the District Court noted in its judgment, the Madagascar Plan was occasionally referred to in government circles in Germany as the 'Final Solution of the Jewish problem'.[40] The plan according to Eichmann was compatible with Zionism, a view which was condemned in the most stringent terms by the District Court.[41] In 1939, Britain had restricted Jewish immigration into Palestine and German citizens as well as those persons in German-occupied territory were considered 'enemy nationals'. The Nazis therefore had to find another outlet to solve its 'Jewish problem' and this is where the Madagascar Plan came in. Had Germany not lost it colonies at the end of the First World War, when they were confiscated by the Entente and turned into B- and C-class League of Nations mandates, it is not entirely implausible that the Nazis might have encouraged Jewish emigration from Germany to one of its former colonies, such as South-West Africa, the Cameroons or Tanganyika, and claimed that this was consistent with political Zionism. The problem was that Zionism, like other political ideologies of that era such as capitalism, communism, fascism and socialism, was capable of being interpreted *differently* by different actors. After all, in *Der Judenstaat*, Herzl specifically listed Argentina, and not only Palestine, as an ideal location for establishing his Jewish state – and the Jewish Territorial Organisation led by Israel Zangwill was advocating creating a state elsewhere other than Palestine.[42] In other words, Zionism, as a political creed, could be appropriated by others and used for their own selfish ends. Indeed, Britain, Germany, and the Soviet Union, produced their own versions of Zionism; in Britain, it was, initially, the 'Uganda Plan', in Germany it was the 'Madagascar Plan' and in the USSR it was 'Birobidzhan' in the Soviet Far East, which still exists today as the Jewish Autonomous Region.[43]

But how was it that two very different visions of Zionism, the British theory, advocated by A.J. Balfour, more of which is described below, and the German one, advocated by Hitler and his acolytes, have originated from the same source, that is, Theodor Herzl's *Der Judenstaat*? The fundamental flaw was a central tenet of Herzl's thesis. It was his suggestion that anti-Semitism was inevitable wherever there were Jews in significant numbers, that if the Jews were to be 'honest' with themselves they could not be Frenchmen, Englishmen or Germans, and that there was no other way to combat anti-Semitism other than to agree with the anti-Semites that the Jews were a 'foreign body' who needed to sever their links with their countries of origin in favour of a territorial solution based upon nineteenth-century notions of nationality and race.[44] In the eyes of a sociopath like Hitler, saying this was tantamount to treason. As many Jewish anti-Zionists in the early twentieth century tried to stress time and time again this was an inherently flawed and extremely dangerous thesis that would be used and abused by the anti-Semites. This is why Edwin Montagu, Lucien Wolf, Laurie Magnus, Claude Montefiore, and many other Western-educated Jews who were content with their status as Englishmen vigorously opposed Zionism. As they noted, the anti-Semites were always very sympathetic to Zionism. This would explain why, for instance, many statesmen who supported Zionism in its early days, such as Sir Mark Sykes[45] and Colonel Richard Meinertzhagen[46] were anti-Semitic, even in Britain, which was widely seen as a bastion of liberal democracy. This is also why, in addition to a safeguard clause protecting Arab rights there was a safeguard clause specifically protecting the rights and political status of *Jews* inserted into the Balfour Declaration in 1917, which is examined in detail in the next chapter.

Although this book is principally concerned with the Arab–Israeli conflict, it is important to stress that Jews, and not only Arabs, were victims of European colonialism, imperialism and nationalism as well as anti-Semitism. One cannot understand Edwin Montagu's vehement opposition to Zionism, as explained in more depth in the next chapter, without comprehending the political and social situation of the Jews in Europe at the dawn of the twentieth century. Likewise, one cannot determine whether the establishment of a Jewish state in 1948 breached the safeguard clauses inserted into the Balfour Declaration as it was incorporated into the Mandate without taking into account the fate of German Jews and those who lived in Nazi-occupied Europe during the Second World War. As it happened, at the turn of the twentieth century, a very small number of Jews, mostly from Eastern Europe and Russia, who called themselves the 'Zionists', and who at the time represented less than 1 per cent of Jewish opinion in the world, were quite prepared to allow themselves to be manipulated by the Great Powers in their quest to colonise the Holy Land.[47] As a result, they were pitted into a conflict with that country's indigenous inhabitants, a conflict that shows no signs of abating. Of course, anti-Semitism did not only exist in Germany. It was also widespread in Britain. However, British anti-Semitism was peculiarly connected to xenophobia and the question of alien immigration.[48] It was not based on warped Germanic racial theories.

BRITISH ANTI-SEMITISM AND ALIEN IMMIGRATION

In Britain, at the dawn of the twentieth century, an acrimonious debate raged over the question of alien immigration into the country and whether restrictions should be placed upon it. Those who argued in favour of restrictions justified their position quite openly and had no qualms about using intemperate language. Two extracts from a book entitled *Alien Immigration: Should Restrictions be Imposed?*[49] published a year before the British Government, under the leadership of A.J. Balfour, who successfully passed the Aliens Act 1905 through Parliament, left little to the imagination of the reader:

> The 'two nations' of Disraeli were never more separate than to-day in London, and the weaker nation – England's poor – are face to face with a third nation whose rivalry threatens to deprive them of the result of fifty years of struggle for human conditions of labour ... Alone among the nations of the world we allow the scum of the earth to enter our land, and, naturally, taking the line of least resistance, they come to us in ever increasing numbers, since the rest of the world is closed to them.[50]

Such sentiments were perhaps common to much racist literature, and the extract just quoted could have referred to any immigrant community. Its author was alluding to Prime Minister Benjamin Disraeli's novel *Tancred: Or, the New Crusade* whose hero is an English Lord who strongly reacts to the social conditions of the 'Two Nations', in Britain, the rich and the poor, after returning from a visit to the Middle East.[51] Yet, if there were any doubts regarding the target for the author's racial outburst in the passage quoted above, it becomes clear from a second extract from the same book which particular community its author sought to vent his ire:

> It is an unfortunate fact that the alien immigrant is generally a Jew, for anything savouring of religious intolerance is sure of condemnation to-day. And yet we are experiencing in England on a small scale what Russia has endured for centuries on a large scale – the evils due to the presence in a State of a body of men alien in thought, sympathies, and beliefs to the mass of their fellow citizens.[52]

Racial stereotypes of Jews were rife in Britain in the early twentieth century, and common amongst men and women from all walks of life.[53] A book published in 1900, called, *The Jew in London: A Study of Racial Character and Present-Day Conditions being Two Essays Prepared for the Toynbee Trustees*,[54] to which a Member of Parliament[55] and a clergyman[56] were quite happy to have their names associated, spoke of the Jews as being 'self-assertive and loud' and going 'after money as if it were his god'.[57] However, it was not the assimilated Jew that concerned the clergyman and the many who thought like him, but the *Ostjuden* who so infuriated German anti-Semites:

> The Jew, who is by nature spiritual, tends to become material or sensuous, and in East London is sometimes notable for his coarseness and vulgarity. Altogether he has not popular qualities. His virtues raise him above his neighbours, his ability enable him to pass them in the race for wealth, and his manners give him the appearance of superiority. The immigrant Jew has, moreover, habits of living acquired in other countries which offend the prejudiced Englishman, who is apt to call 'dirty' whatever is foreign.[58]

As Herzl noted in his diary, it was the emancipation of the Jews in the nineteenth century that was causing anti-Semitism.[59] He made this prescient observation in 1895 when he was walking in the 'green meadows' philosophising with his friend Speidel. Whilst pontificating, Herzl provided the following explanation for what he thought caused the anti-Semitism that he was experiencing as a journalist with the *Neue Freie Presse*:

> We Jews have maintained ourselves, even if through no fault of our own, as a foreign body among the various nations. In the ghetto we have taken on a number of anti-social qualities. Our character has been corrupted by oppression, and it must be restored through some other kind of pressure. Actually, anti-Semitism is a consequence of the emancipation of the Jews. However, the peoples who lack historical understanding – that is, all of them – do not see us as an historical product, as the victims of earlier, crueller, and still more narrow-minded times. They do not realize that we are what we are because they have made us that way amidst tortures, because the Church made usury dishonourable for Christians, and because the rulers forced us to deal in money.[60]

Unfortunately, most anti-Semites did not understand this, or care to comprehend it. To them the Jews were considered a foreign and unwanted element in their societies, whether they were in France, scandalised by the Dreyfus affair, Germany, or even the United States, which experienced the Saratoga incident, and Britain where the Marconi scandal took place, in which Herbert Samuel, Sir Rufus Isaacs, and other prominent British Jews were accused of insider trading, which fuelled allegations of anti-Semitism.[61]

At the turn of the last century, most of the Jews inhabiting the East End of London had emigrated there from Eastern Europe and it was in this context that an attempt was made to curb Jewish immigration into Britain, which quintupled between 1880 and 1920 from an original 60,000.[62] In 1903, amidst complaints regarding the effects of immigration on the working conditions and loss of employment in Britain's largest cities, the Report of the Royal Commission on Alien Immigration was published.[63] Its Terms of Reference had been to inquire into – (1) The character and extent of the evils which are attributed to the unrestricted immigration of Aliens, especially in the Metropolis; and (2) The measures which have been adopted for the restriction and control of Alien Immigration in Foreign Countries, and in British Colonies. The Commission cited the May Laws enacted in Russia in

1882 and the oppressive measures taken in Romania as the main reasons causing the Jewish exodus.[64] Regarding the nature of the Aliens, several allegations were submitted, including:

> (1) That on their arrival they are (a) in an impoverished and destitute condition, (b) deficient in cleanliness, and practicing unsanitary habits, (c) and being subject to no medical examination on embarkation or arrival, are liable to introduce infectious diseases.
> (2) That amongst them are criminals, anarchists, prostitutes, and persons of bad character, in number beyond the ordinary percentage of the native population.
> (3) ...
> (4) That on their arrival in this country they congregate as dwellers in certain districts, principally in the East End of London, and especially in the Borough of Stepney, and that when they so settle they become a compact, non-assimilating community.[65]

Point nine singled out one group of persons in particular:

> (9) In addition to these allegations it was complained in respect to immigrants of the Jewish faith (a) that they do not assimilate and intermarry with the native race, and so remain a solid and distinct colony; and (b) that their existence in large numbers in certain areas gravely interferes with the observance of the Christian Sunday.[66]

It was Balfour, who, as Prime Minister, steered the passage of the Aliens Act through Parliament in 1905 that restricted this westward movement of Jewish immigration into Britain which was used by many as a point of embarkation for the United States which in turn restricted immigration from Europe in 1921.[67] Between 1.5 and 2 million Eastern European Jews made the United States, not Palestine, their destination of choice, and a further 350,000 chose to go to Western Europe.[68] During the debates, Balfour told the Commons that the oppression of Jews tarnished the fair fame of Christendom and said that it was their duty to do anything that could diminish its effects.[69] This is why he thought the British Government's decision to offer land for Jews to settle in British East Africa in 1903 would make a 'good asylum'. This is what is recorded in Hansard:

> Mr. A. J. BALFOUR said that he did not intervene in order to reply to some of the very singular attacks which had been made upon him in the course of the last two hours, although he might well have asked permission to do so. One hon. Gentleman seemed to think that he was justly open to the charge of inhumanity, and that he was indifferent to the sufferings of the Jewish race in Russia and other Eastern countries because he did not think that their rights, or indeed any serious respect their interests, would be interfered with by the Bill ... So far as he knew, alone among the nations of the world, and

> certainly alone among the Governments of this country, they had offered to the Jewish race a great tract of fertile land in one of our possessions in order that they might, if they desired it – [ironical OPPOSITION laughter] – find an asylum from their persecutors at home. He did not know whether that offer was regarded as contemptuous or derisory, he could only say that such an offer had never yet been made by any country to the people on whose behalf the hon. Gentleman spoke.[70]

Balfour's 'humanitarian gesture' was, however, very contradictory and some might say rather disingenuous which would explain the ironical opposition laughter and the singular attacks made upon him by his colleagues.[71] On the one hand he was calling on Parliament to do all it could to help the Jews, and at the same time he was persuading them to restrict Jewish immigration into the country. On the other hand the solution he envisaged for these poor Jews fleeing Russian persecution was not the chance to make a new start in Britain but to send them to mosquito-ridden East Africa. It did not occur to him that these Jewish immigrants wanted to actually reside in Britain and that their integration and assimilation into British society would take time. In the debate on the Second Reading of the Aliens Bill, which was passed by a 211 majority vote, with only 59 MPs opposing it (including Herbert Samuel and L.W. Rothschild), Balfour told the House of Commons that although serious national danger from these foreigners was still remote, in the future

> … a state of things could easily be imagined in which it would not be to the advantage of the civilisation of the country that there should be an immense body of persons who, however patriotic, able, and industrious, however much they threw themselves into the national life, still, by their own action, remained a people apart, and not merely held a religion differing from the vast majority of their fellow-countrymen, but only intermarried among themselves.[72]

In other words, even if the Jews were indeed patriotic, which many anti-Semites in Britain and Germany questioned, Balfour still did not want them in England because they refused to assimilate with his fellow Anglo-Saxons, for example, through intermarriage. This did not suit his conception of what an Englishman was. As one historian aptly put it, in early twentieth-century Britain, '[t]he patriotism of a Gentile Englishman formed a congruent hierarchy – loyalty to England, to Britain, to the British Empire, to the Anglo Saxon race, to Western civilisation, to humanity. How did Jewish race patriotism fit into this?'[73] It is therefore not surprising that contemporary historians have called Balfour an anti-Semite.[74] Indeed when Balfour was Foreign Minister in 1917, he refused to intercede with Russia to ameliorate conditions in the Pale of Jewish Settlement because he did not want to interfere in the domestic affairs of an ally. This is what he is alleged to have said:

> ... it was also to be remembered that the persecutors had a case of their own. They were afraid of the Jews, who were an exceedingly clever people ... wherever one went in Eastern Europe, one found that, by some way or other, the Jew got on, and when to do this was added the fact that he belonged to a distinct race, and that he professed a religion which to the people about him was an object of inherited hatred, and that, moreover, he was ... numbered in millions, one could perhaps understand the desire to keep him down ...[75]

It is in this context that the declaration which bears Balfour's name, and which is examined in some detail in the next chapter, should be properly understood. It was not merely a propaganda document, or born of strategic necessity, but a potential solution, in Balfour's eyes, to stem the flow of European Jewish immigration into Britain. It must be remembered that in the years 1905–14 there was an intensification of hostility towards Jewish immigrants, particularly those from Eastern Europe and Germany who were seen to be sympathetic to the Kaiser, and that during the First World War the British Government deported 20,000 'aliens' and interned a further 32,000, which included many Jews.[76]

Ultimately, Zionism provided a pretext for people like Balfour to justify the removal of these unwanted people from England's shores by arguing that they were not being anti-Semitic because the Jews themselves supported it. This was one of the reasons, in addition to considerations of *realpolitik*, and his religious upbringing, why Balfour found Zionism so appealing.[77] However, the vast majority of British Jews were either ambivalent about Zionism or indifferent.[78] Some, however, such as Edwin Montagu, and others, were outright hostile to it, and opposed Zionism and the 'Balfour Declaration' when it was issued in November 1917.[79] To them, Judaism was a religion and not a nationality. They argued that they were not a separate race, as Balfour saw them, and this was one of the primary reasons Montagu would draft the first of three memoranda which he submitted to the British cabinet in 1917, when Balfour was Foreign Minister, provocatively entitled 'The Anti-Semitism of the Present Government.'[80] It is quite telling that the only Jew in the British Government responsible for the affairs of India, which was then Britain's largest colony, and whom his colleagues specifically consulted about the declaration, thought that the government he served was initiating a policy, the effect of which would be anti-Semitic. As Montagu recognised, Zionism actually provided Balfour and those who thought like him with the perfect pretext to reduce Jewish immigration into Britain whilst portraying themselves, falsely, as 'humanitarians' concerned about their welfare. This is what Balfour wrote in the conclusion to his introduction to Nahum Sokolow's epic book, the *History of Zionism, 1600–1918* (1919):

> If [Zionism] succeeds, it will do a great spiritual and material work for the Jews, but not for them alone. For as I read its meaning it is, among other things, a serious endeavour to mitigate the age-long miseries created

> for western civilisation by the presence in its midst of a Body which it too long regarded as alien and even hostile, but which it was equally unable to expel or absorb. Surely, for this if for no other reason, it should receive our support.[81]

That Balfour had the gall to write this in a book on Zionism was foreboding. One can only imagine what he wrote about the Jews in private or in correspondence that was destroyed or lost. But there is little reason to doubt that his views, even then, would have been regarded as anti-Semitic. At least this is how Herzl would have described it. For Herzl anti-Semitism was not to be associated with 'the old religious prejudice'.[82] Rather, '[f]or the most part it is a movement among civilized nations whereby they try to exorcize a ghost from out of their past'.[83] If this was how anti-Semitism, as opposed to Philo-Semitism, was understood to be at the dawn of the twentieth century, then those who described Balfour as an anti-Semite, then and now, must surely be right.[84]

Zionism, however, had another aspect to it. Not only was it intricately linked to anti-Semitism but it appealed to a certain type of Briton, Balfour included, because it was an essentially imperialist project that provoked excitement in those who were sent to 'redeem' and 'rebuild' the Holy Land which they had read about in the Bible.[85] Indeed, already during the nineteenth century, antiquarianism, the passion for authenticating the Bible, and Evangelical hopes for the conversion of the Jews, had all inspired British visitors and missionaries to Palestine.[86] Moreover, many nineteenth-century philanthropists who donated money to colonise Palestine were from England, France and Germany, the very countries where anti-Semitism was at its most virulent.

COLONIALISM AND ZIONISM

In early twentieth-century Britain, not only was anti-Semitism acceptable, but so was colonialism, which was seen by many as an admirable venture associated with the British Empire and imperialism.[87] In fact, colonialism was looked at favourably amongst most classes of British society, and it did not have the pejorative connotation with alien subjugation, domination and exploitation, which it has been associated with since decolonisation in the 1960s.[88] It is in the context of European anti-Semitism, and the escape that colonialism offered the Zionists, that the project to create a homeland for the Jewish people as outlined by the first Zionist Congress in Basel in August 1897 should be viewed and understood.[89] And public international law, which is the law that applies between states and international organisations, as opposed to individuals, was the very vehicle through which the Zionist project was to be brought to fruition.[90] As the first declaration adopted by the Zionists in Basel in 1897 made clear: 'The aim of Zionism is to create for the Jewish people a home in Palestine secured by public law.'[91] A home secured by public law, '*eine oeffentlich-rechtlich gesicherte Heimstaette*', implied that the colonisation of Palestine by the Zionists would be accomplished through legal means.

And yet, the Zionist project was, from its inception, mired in controversy. Herzl originally wanted to hold his first Zionist congress in Munich, but the rabbis there told him that they did not like his political Zionism and they forced him to relocate his congress to Basel instead.[92] 'Judaism obliges its followers', they wrote, 'to serve the country to which they belong with the utmost devotion, and to further its interest with their whole heart and all their strength.'[93] They also thought that Herzelian Zionism was 'antagonistic to the messianic promises of Judaism as contained in the Holy Writ and in later religious sources'.[94] But this did not stop Herzl. According to the 'Basel Program' adopted by the first Zionist congress in 1897:

> The aim of Zionism is to create for the Jewish people a home in Palestine secured by *public law*.
>
> The Congress contemplates the following means to the attainment of this end:
>
> 1. The promotion, on suitable lines, of the *colonization* of Palestine by Jewish agricultural and industrial workers.
> 2. The organization and binding together of the whole Jewry by means of appropriate institutions, local and international *in accordance with the laws of each country*.
> 3. The strengthening and fostering of Jewish national sentiment and consciousness.
> 4. Preparatory steps towards obtaining government consent, where necessary to the attainment of the aim of Zionism.[95]

International law was pivotal to the development of the Jewish national home. Without it, Israel would not exist today. Nor should there be any doubt about the colonial origins of the Zionist project as the Zionists themselves frequently referred to it in this light in their founding document and in their literature.[96] In fact, from its very inception, the institutions and character of Jewish settlement in Palestine were an imitation of other colonial models.[97] For instance, in the late nineteenth century, Baron Edmond de Rothschild, who financed settlements for the first wave of Jewish immigrants into Palestine, recruited French colonial agronomists from North Africa to reorganise the failing settlements of the first *aliyah* by copying the model of colonial agriculture in Algeria, Egypt and Tunisia.[98] In Argentina, Baron Maurice de Hirsch and his Jewish Colonisation Association spent 50 million francs towards the mass resettlement of Jews there because of its cheap arable land, plentiful rainfall, and relatively well developed transportation system.[99] Hirsch's colonisation of Argentina was similar to Palestine where private capital was also used to settle the colonists and indeed his Jewish Colonisation Association provided financial aid to those Jewish colonies in Palestine that were not receiving aid from Rothschild.[100] However, neither of the Barons were Zionists in the political sense, at least not initially. They did not set out to create a Jewish state in Palestine as advocated by Herzl and indeed their relationship with the Austrian journalist was often tense and at times acrimonious.[101] Although Baron Edmond de Rothschild met Herzl and his associates several times, he told his colleague Max Nordau that his brand of Zionism was dangerous because he was 'rendering the patriotism of the Jews suspect'.[102] In Germany, by contrast, many of the founders of the Jewish National Fund, the body tasked with providing capital to purchase land in Palestine on behalf of the Zionist movement for Jewish settlement, were directly influenced by Herzlian Zionism. Most of them were involved in the German colonisation of Posen, which was then in German-occupied Poland.[103] The leaders of the Zionist Organisation, such as Adolf Böhm, Franz Oppenheimer, Arthur Ruppin, and Otto Warburg, were familiar with the national conflicts within the Habsburg Empire, where large peasant populations of various nationalities threatened the dominance of the German-speaking elite.[104] The German Zionists, in contrast to the Barons, were state builders. Their colonisation efforts were not philanthropic but nationalistic and they sought to lay the foundations for ultimately establishing a Jewish state in Palestine. They found the Barons tiresome and irksome (as did the Barons find the Zionists) and questioned the wisdom of relying on private capital alone to colonise Palestine.[105] This is why they decided to establish the Jewish National Fund to purchase land in Palestine and hold it in trust for the Jewish people.

Although Rothschild sought to emulate the French colonial model in North Africa he was not necessarily concerned with their *mission civilisatrice*, and only hired Arab peasants to work in the fields of the Jewish settlements due to the colonists' lack of farming experience and familiarity with local conditions.[106] The German Zionists also sought to avoid the use of Arab labour through the strategy of 'conquest of labour', which aimed to create a homogeneous labour market in which Arab workers would be excluded from working with Jews.[107] Although the German Zionists saw this strategy as a doctrine that was essential for national revival, it was resented by the Arabs, and caused friction between the two communities in Palestine. When some Jewish-owned companies actually decided to ignore the ban and employ Arab labour, because it was less expensive and more productive, the Arabs being accustomed to local conditions, they often met with opposition from the Jewish workers they employed who refused to till the fields with the Arabs.[108]

By the turn of the twentieth century, the colonisation of Palestine gathered pace. At the Second Zionist Congress in Basel in 1898, the Jewish Colonial Trust, the parent company of the Anglo-Palestine Bank, was established, which became the 'Bank Leumi Le-Israel' following the establishment of the state of Israel.[109] Herzl saw the establishment of the Jewish Colonial Trust as a financial tool for the realisation of the idea of the Jewish state, which would serve the political and economic activity of the Zionist Organisation.[110] By raising capital in this way, he wanted to implement a programme of large-scale immigration, retraining, and rapid economic development in Palestine that would entail large investments in infrastructure, agriculture, and industry.[111] Herzl sought to emulate the great European colonial companies and investment banks of his day through the Anglo-Palestine Bank.[112] Then in 1900, due to a lack of return on his investments, Rothschild decided to turn over his vast property portfolio, holdings, and financial assets in Palestine and hand it over to the Jewish Colonisation Association that was being run be Hirsch.[113] In his later years, it was said that Baron Edmond de Rothschild started to sympathise with the political Zionists, although his memories of Herzl remained unpleasant, but he nevertheless preferred to create a Jewish homeland in Palestine by quiet immigration and settlement.[114] In short, the colonisation of Palestine was progressively being institutionalised and nationalised.

But Herzl remained restless. He still wanted his charter to legalise his colonisation efforts. In 1900, in furtherance of his aims, Herzl drafted a Charter for a Jewish-Ottoman Land Company, which he intended to present to the Grand Vizier, who was the representative of the Ottoman Sultan in Istanbul, in the hope of persuading him to support the creation of a Jewish homeland in Palestine.[115] According to Adolf Böhm, a confidant and a member of the Zionist hierarchy, Herzl wanted to emulate the successes of the British and Dutch East India Companies in colonising the Holy Land.[116] This is why he was intent on drafting a charter that would legalise the whole expedition. In this regard, some of the principal clauses of his draft, translated from German from the Herzl Archive in Vienna, are of interest, and included the following principal provisions:

AGREEMENT[117]

> concerning the privileges, rights, liabilities, and duties of the Jewish-Ottoman Land Company (JOLC) for the settlement of Palestine and Syria.
>
> His Majesty the Sultan grants and guarantees the JOLC the following special rights and privileges for the purpose of settling Palestine and Syria with Jews who assume Ottoman citizenship [in order to enable them] to open up the natural food and occupation resources of these countries under the following conditions, and in return for assuming the obligations listed below.
>
> I. A special right to purchase large estates and small farms, and to use them for agriculture, horticulture, forestry, and mining … On these areas [the JOLC] may build all installations, roads, bridges, buildings and houses, industrial and other facilities, which it considers appropriate, without being restricted in the choice of means to be used, and without having to apply for special permits. [The JOLC is entitled] to drain and utilize swamps (if there are any) by planting or any other way, to establish small and large settlements, and to settle Jews in them.
>
> II. The limited proprietorship of all estates and landed properties belonging to His Majesty the Sultan in the above mentioned 'Privileged Territories.' [The JOLC shall express its] eternal recognition of his supreme proprietorship through a permanent annual payment of 3 Turkish Piasters per dunum.[118] This refers to the areas which

[the company] has the right to utilize according to article I of this agreement. Likewise, a special right to occupy all those areas for which nobody can prove legal title or the right of ownership ...

III. ...

IV. ...

V. The JOLC will take over taxation in the 'Privileged Territory,' stipulating that it [the company] is entitled to reform taxation and make it more efficient ... if it imposes customs duties, it has to respect the international treaties of the Ottoman government, adhering to the customary procedures and amounts ...

VI. Within its 'Privileged Territory,' and under the protection of His Majesty the Sultan, the JOLC has complete autonomy, guaranteed by the Ottoman Empire. But it is obliged to ensure on its territory the maintenance of law and order, as well as the personal security and the property of both of the inhabitants and of peaceful visitors and groups of pilgrims from foreign countries ...

VII. A. All Jews whom the JOLC has settled in the 'Privileged Territory' become subjects of His Majesty the Sultan by virtue of their acceptance as colonists or their employment as functionaries; they enjoy full Ottoman citizenship. By joining the JOLC as colonists or as its functionaries they ipso facto abandon their former citizenship. The same applies for Jews who are already settled in Palestine and Syria, who consider themselves protégés of the JOLC, and who sign a certificate of admission of the Company.

B. Every protégé of the JOLC is subject to military service in the Imperial Ottoman Syrian-Palestinian Land [IOSPL] or Navy [SPN] division: Upon reaching the age of 19 he is subject to a year-long service in the standing army and a 1/2-year long cadre service [*Cadredienst*]; until he reaches 26 he serves in the militia [*Lanwehr*], including three weeks of maneuvre per year; finally, between the age of 27 and 35 he is part of the general levy [*Landsturm*]. The two divisions mentioned above are to be entirely composed of Jewish soldiers, and foreign nationals can only be accepted temporarily as instructors and trainers ...

Although Herzl decided against showing this draft to the Grand Vizier, it gives an indication of his intentions in colonising Palestine for the Zionist movement.[119] When Herzl mentioned orally to the Vizier's officials his desire to set up a company to facilitate Jewish immigration to the Ottoman Empire, he was told in reply that the Grand Vizier was happy for them to settle wherever they liked in his empire, with the sole exception of Palestine, as long as they became Turkish subjects. Herzl, however, rejected this.[120]

As regards the text of Herzl's draft agreement, it is apparent that he was not only interested in Palestine, but Syria too, which then included what we know today as Lebanon and Jordan. Indeed, in his diaries, Herzl described the area of the Jewish state he envisioned as stretching 'from the Brook of

Egypt to the Euphrates'.[121] Herzl evidently did not give much consideration to the indigenous inhabitants of the land he desired to colonise. He does not mention them at all, although he certainly knew they were there. Herzl probably realised that his request for substantial autonomy in his 'Privileged Territory', would attract controversy in the Porte, particularly as he wanted to go about setting up an army and a navy to protect it. Interestingly, in view of subsequent events (see the section on nationality in Chapter 8), all Jews who became citizens of this territory or signed a certificate of admission to the Jewish-Ottoman Land Company were to acquire their new citizenship *ipso facto*, and lose their former one. Indeed, in view of the substantial powers Herzl was proposing to ask the Ottoman Government to bestow upon his Company, it seems that what he was really asking for was a permit to lay the legal foundations for ultimately creating a Jewish state.

THE BRITISH CONNECTION

It was only when Herzl's venture with the Ottoman Vizier failed that he turned to Britain, the greatest imperial power at the time, for support.[122] There, the Zionists would have more success and again anti-Semitism enters the picture with British statesmen associating the Jews with money. For instance, in 1840, Lord Palmerston, the Foreign Secretary, wrote to his Ambassador in Istanbul about the financial benefits that would accrue by encouraging the Jews to go to Palestine: 'It is well known that the Jews of Europe possess great wealth; and it is manifest that any country in which a considerable number of them might choose to settle, would derive great benefit from the riches which they would bring into it ...'[123] Many Western clergymen, statesmen and diplomats, supported the establishment of a Jewish homeland in Palestine, with Lord Shaftesbury, Lord Palmerston, Napoleon Bonaparte, Edward Mitford, George Gauler and Charles Henry Churchill being some of the outstanding gentiles who favoured returning the Jews to Palestine.[124] However, their support was rarely altruistic. They saw commercial and strategic advantages in encouraging Jewish immigration into Palestine.[125]

In the years 1874–75, an opportunity presented itself for greater British involvement in the Near East, when the governments of Egypt and Turkey both went bankrupt. The Khedive of Egypt, Ismail Pasha, had little choice but to sell his shares in the Suez Canal Company.[126] The British Government under the leadership of Benjamin Disraeli subsequently purchased 44 per cent of the shares to the tune of £4,000,000[127] (equivalent to 8.3 per cent of the entire British budget net of debt charges) loaned to it from the British branch of the Rothschild family.[128] Although Britain did not own an outright majority of the shares, it gave it an additional interest in the Suez Canal Zone, which gave it further leverage to expand its sphere of influence in the Middle East.[129] The Rothschilds too, benefited enormously from the deal, financially and politically, coming to the assistance of a Government which needed a large sum of money at very short notice and which could not be acquired from other sources such as the Bank of England without attracting unwarranted attention from rival French and German banks (and their governments).[130] In a letter to the Prince of Wales, Disraeli wrote the following:

> Our friends, the Rothschilds, distinguished themselves. They alone cd. have accomplished what we wanted, & they had only 4 & 20 hours to make up their minds, whether they wd, or could, incur an immediate liability of 4 millions. One of their difficulties was, that they cd. not appeal to their strongest ally, their own family in Paris, for Alphonse is si francese that he wd. have betrayed the whole scheme instantly.[131]

This convergence of interests between the Rothschilds and the British Government was, however, not restricted to the Middle East. The Rothschilds also financed the activities of Cecil Rhodes in southern Africa and sponsored his wars against the Matebele in what would become known as Rhodesia (named after Cecil Rhodes), the southern part of which is today known as Zimbabwe.[132] As one of Britain's leading historians has noted: '... like that other very different visionary of the period, Theodor Herzl – Rhodes saw the legendary Lord Rothschild as the one man with resources capable of making his dreams a reality'.[133] It is therefore, perhaps, not in the least surprising that the Balfour Declaration promising the Jews a national home in Palestine would be addressed to a member of the Rothschild family. In fact, by the First World War, Lord L.W. Rothschild (although he was a minority within his family) viewed British imperialism and Zionism as complementary.[134] But the connection between British imperialism and Zionism went deeper than mere finances, which was an unfortunate fact in and of itself because it was used by the anti-Semites who saw in it grand plans for a Jewish conspiracy to take over the world as had been predicted in that scandalous forgery *The Protocols of the Elders of Zion*.[135] It was lamentable that some Zionists such as Herzl sought to play on the connection between Jews and money because they thought it would impress upon the British Government their scheme to colonise the Holy Land. It was to prove disastrous.

In an entry dated 23 October 1902, Herzl writes in his diary of his first meeting with Joseph Chamberlain.[136] Herzl had requested the meeting so that he could introduce the Colonial Secretary to Zionism, the movement he led. Herzl told Chamberlain that he wanted England to give him Cyprus, El Arish, and the Sinai Peninsula for Jewish colonisation.[137] Chamberlain replied by saying said that as Colonial Secretary, he could only speak about Cyprus, which fell under his mandate, whereas Egypt was under the responsibility of the Foreign Office.[138] He then told Herzl that Greeks and Muslims lived in Cyprus and that 'he could not crowd them out for the sake of new immigrants'.[139] Rather, it was his duty to stand by them.[140] He then told Herzl that if he could show him a spot in the English possessions where there were no white people, he would be happy to talk to him about utilising it for Jewish colonisation.[141] But Herzl pressed Chamberlain:

> Once we establish the Jewish Eastern Company, with 5 million pounds capital, for settling Sinai and El Arish, the Cypriots will begin to want that golden rain on their island, too. The Moslems will move away, the Greeks will gladly sell their lands at a good price and migrate to Athens or Crete.[142]

Herzl writes that Chamberlain 'seemed to take the idea'.[143] But he remained non-committal and told him to go and speak to Lord Cromer, then Consul-General of Egypt. In anticipation of his meeting with Cromer, Herzl drafted a memorandum, which made the following connection between British imperialism and the Jewish Question:

> Milord:
>
> In accordance with your kind oral request I have the honor to submit herewith a brief sketch of my plan.
>
> It is a matter of solving the Jewish Question of Eastern Europe in a way that redounds to England's honour, but also to her advantage.
>
> *The stimulus for the British government to occupy itself with this question is supplied by the immigration to the East End of London.*
>
> It is true, this is still no calamity worth mentioning, and I hope it will never become one to the extent that England would have to break with the glorious principle of free asylum. But the fact that a Royal Commission was appointed for the matter will make it sufficiently plausible in the eyes of the world if the British government considers itself *impelled to open up a special territory for the Jews who are oppressed everywhere and thus gravitate to England ...*
>
> To the southeast of the Mediterranean England has a possession which at present is worthless and almost uninhabited. It is the coastal area of El Arish and the Sinai Peninsula.
>
> This area could be made the place of refuge, the home, of the Jews hard-pressed all over the world, if England permits the establishment of a Jewish colony there.[144]

Prior to meeting Chamberlain, Herzl had appeared as an expert before the Royal Commission on Alien Immigration in 1902, which he alluded to in his memorandum to Cromer.[145] The Commission, of whom Lord Rothschild was a member, allowed Herzl to read out a pre-prepared speech. Herzl did not hesitate to tell the Commission what he thought was the real motive underlying the convening of a commission on alien immigration:

> ... I cannot regard the question before the Commission as a small one in comparison – a question, for instance, of local housing or local overcrowding. As to these I know little so far as they affect the districts of the East End of London. The most I know is what I have read of the evidence placed before the Commission; and that evidence tells me quite plainly that questions of

> overcrowding and of housing are at most incidental, that the forces at work are the identical forces at work against our people elsewhere – the forces which I have denominated 'Forces of common trade jealousy, of inherited prejudice and of pretended self-defence.' These forces are at work here, and, mask it in any way you choose, the cry for restricting alien immigration arrives from the presence here of a perceptible number of Jews, and the desire that that number shall not be perceptibly increased.[146]

In so many words, Herzl was essentially telling the Commission that behind their façade was the curse of anti-Semitism. All the other factors, such as overcrowding, loss of jobs, 'interfering' with the Christian worship on Sundays, were just a masquerade. Herzl then presented the Commission with his 'solution' to the Jewish Question:

> ... the solution of the Jewish difficulty is the recognition of Jews as a people, and the finding by them of a legally recognised home, to which Jews in those parts of the world in which they are oppressed would naturally migrate, for they would arrive there as citizens just because they are Jews, and not as aliens. *This would mean the diverting of the stream of emigration from this country and from America*, where so soon as they form a perceptible number they become a trouble and a burden to a land where the true interest would be served by accommodating as many as possible.[147]

In essence, Herzl was trying to sell Zionism to the British Government as a form of immigration control. Anti-Semitism according to Herzl was a 'natural phenomenon' that occurred wherever there were Jews in large numbers. The only way to solve this 'problem', was to establish a legally recognised home for these people:

> ... I felt very strongly that nothing will meet the problem the Commission is called upon to investigate and advise upon except a diverting of the stream of migration that is bound to go on with increasing force from Eastern Europe. The Jews of Eastern Europe cannot stay where they are – where are they to go? If you find they are not wanted here, then some place must be found to which they can migrate without by that migration raising the problems that confront them here. These problems will not arise if a home be found them which will be legally recognized as Jewish.[148]

When Herzl met with Cromer in Cairo he tried to stress his ties to the Rothschild dynasty in an attempt, most probably, to play on the connection between Jews and money, by showing him a letter and a telegram from Lord Rothschild supporting his scheme.[149] But Cromer reacted coolly to the proposal and interjected when Herzl started to talk about building a railroad unaware that at the time there was a serious confrontation between Britain and Turkey over the Sinai Peninsula, the Suez Canal and the Hejaz railway.[150] But he assented to Herzl's proposal to send a commission there to examine its suitability for Jewish colonisation. Cromer, however, warned Herzl not to speak to the Turkish commissar about it and told him instead to go and speak to the Egyptian Prime Minister Boutros Ghali, which he did.[151] But Ghali, in Herzl's words, 'flatly refused' to accede to a Charter providing for El Arish and the Sinai to be colonised by Jewish immigrants from Eastern Europe, although he did not oppose the scheme in principle so long as they became Ottoman subjects.[152] The technical commission then returned from the Sinai. Its conclusions were summarised in a letter that Herzl wrote to Lord Rothschild:

> My whole Sinai plan has broken down. Everything was ready. It now depended simply and solely on Sir William Garstin's verdict as to whether we could get the Nile water that we needed. However, after his return from Uganda Sir William questioned the calculations of our engineer, Stephens. He declared that we would need five times as much Nile water as Stephens had calculated, and Egypt could not spare this much. With this the whole project collapsed.[153]

But Herzl's hopes were not completely dashed. On 24 April 1903, he met Chamberlain for the second time. On this occasion Herzl described meeting the Colonial Secretary 'like an old acquaintance'.[154] Chamberlain referred to the Sinai commission report calling its conclusions 'not favourable' for Jewish colonisation due to the scarcity of water there.[155] He then said: 'I have seen a land for you on my travels, and that's Uganda.'[156] He told Herzl that although it was hot on the coast (he was actually referring to what we now know as Kenya), further inland the climate became excellent, 'even for Europeans'.[157] He said that one could raise sugar and cotton there. However, he knew that Herzl really desired Palestine, then under Turkish sovereignty. The conversation then became political. This is how Herzl recalled it:

> 'In Asia Minor,' Chamberlain said, 'we have fewer and fewer interests. Some day there will be a showdown over that region between France, Germany and Russia – whereas we are increasingly drawn to more distant points. I am wondering, in such a case, what would be the fate of your Jewish colony in Palestine, supposing you have succeeded in establishing it in the meantime?'
>
> I said: 'I believe that then our chances would be even better. For we shall be used as a small *buffer-state. We shall get it not from the goodwill, but from the jealousy of the powers!* And once we are at El-Arish under the *Union Jack*, then Palestine too will fall into the *British sphere of influence.*'
>
> That seemed to make quite a bit of sense to him.[158]

However, for the time being, Palestine was out of bounds because it was not a British possession or yet within its sphere of influence. Accordingly, Herzl decided to take Chamberlain up on his offer of establishing a Jewish colony in East Africa. The task for drawing up a Jewish colonisation scheme there was given to David Lloyd George, who was then a solicitor with the law firm of Lloyd George, Roberts & Company as well as being a Member of Parliament.[159] The British Government's legal expert C.J.B. Hurst subsequently examined the document drafted by Lloyd George.[160] The memorandum Lloyd George prepared was far more elaborate than Herzl's original draft for a Jewish-Ottoman Land Company, which was akin to a treaty with an elaborate preamble, articles and clauses. It also provided for arbitration in case of any disagreement between the concessionaires and the Government.[161] Article 1 provided:

> 1. That the Jewish Colonial Trust (Juedische Colonialbank) (hereinafter called 'the Concessionaires') may and are hereby authorised to enter into and upon the lands comprised in His Majesty's dominions in British East Africa for the purpose of inspecting and examining the same and of ascertaining the condition thereof and the suitability of the same or any part thereof for the establishment of Jewish Settlement or Colony ... with full power to use for any of the purposes aforesaid any road or ways constructed therein and to plot out and survey the same to the intent that a portion thereof ... if and when found suitable may be identified and with the boundaries and abuttals thereof duly determined by the Concessionaires may be submitted to His Majesty's Secretary of State for the approval of His Majesty's Government.[162]

More controversially, Article 5 included the following provisions:

> 5. THAT at any time subsequent to the approval of the said lands and before the said 31st December 1909 the Concessionaires may submit to His Majesty's Government for approval by the said Government the terms of a Constitution for the regulations administration and good government of the Settlement whereby provision shall be made *inter alia* for the following matters and things:--
>
> (a) FOR the introduction and establishment of a form of popular government in the territory which shall be Jewish in character and with a Jewish Governor to be appointed by His Majesty in Council.
> (b) FOR the granting to the settlement all necessary and proper powers to make ordinances and regulations for the internal administration and all matters necessary for the welfare and good government of the Jewish community and other persons in the said settlement.
> (c) FOR the levying in and upon the said territory all such tax or taxes and assessments as the settlement may decide for the said purposes of administration and good government ...
> (d) FOR defining the relationship and status of the settlement and all persons therein with any other part or parts of His Majesty's

dominions beyond the seas and with any Foreign State and with the Chief of independent tribes in British East Africa ...

(e) ...

(f) ...

(g) ...

(h) FOR granting to the settlement power to exclude from the said territory any person or persons proposing to enter or settle in the same who shall or may be deemed to be opposed to the interests of the settlement or the governments thereof or the dignity of His Majesty the King and the power ... to expel from the territory without being liable for compensation or otherwise any person not fully and completely abiding by the ordinance rules and regulations for the time being in force in the territory or committing or conniving at a breach of the Constitution of the settlement.

(i) ...

(j) ...

(k) FOR the preservation of the customs and laws of the native people of the territory with respect to the holding possession transfer and disposition of interests in lands and goods and the succession thereto ...

(l) FOR the non-interference by the Settlement (except insofar as may be necessary in the interests of humanity and for the preservation of peace) with the religion of any class or tribe of the native peoples of the territory and all forms of religious worship and ordinances as heretofore exercised and practised in the territory.

(m) ...

(n) FOR calling of the said settlement by the name of 'New Palestine' ...[163]

As will become evident in later passages of this book, there is continuity between Herzl's initial draft for a JOLC, Lloyd George's draft for a Jewish colonisation scheme in East Africa, and the mandate for Palestine that would eventually be drafted by the Zionists in collusion with the British Foreign and Colonial Office. And each time, the draft drawn up by the Zionists was 'watered down' by officials at the Foreign and Colonial Office, but their essential objective remained the same throughout: they wanted ultimately to create a Jewish state in Palestine where they would encourage Jews from all over the world to settle so as to solve the Jewish Question and alleviate Britain's 'immigration problem'. In short, Britain was using the Zionists. There is no other way they could have had such intimate and close access to British officials high up in the Foreign and Colonial Office unless the British Government saw some benefit to be gained from it.

According to Lloyd George's draft the main colonisation vehicle was the Jewish Colonial Trust, which then had a capital of £2,000,000. Its principal object was 'the settling of Jews under conditions favourable to their retention and encouragement of the Jewish national idea'. The preamble stipulated that Great Britain's dominions in East Africa 'would be greatly enhanced in value by the foundation there of a Jewish settlement and the creation and direction of public works and the promotion therein of commercial enterprises and the establishment of commercial relationships with neighbouring districts'. It was envisaged that the Jewish Colonial Trust would be the vehicle through which an investigation of East Africa would be financed to inspect the land to ascertain whether it was adequate for Jewish colonisation.[164]

In commenting on the preamble, the Foreign Secretary, Lord Lansdowne noted in the margin that it was 'superfluous, and it contains some objectionable passages'. The Government lawyer C.J.B. Hurst did not comment on the preamble but he objected to the proposal to create a constitution for the Jewish settlement that would give it the right to define its relationship and status with other parts of the British Empire, with any other foreign state or with the chiefs of independent tribes in British East Africa. 'Any such provision quite impossible', he noted in the margin. He added, 'foreign relations must remain entirely in the hands of the Crown and without any fetters imposed by previous definition'.[165] It is noteworthy that one of the conditions for statehood in modern international law is the capacity to enter into relations with other states.[166] Evidently, the British Government did not agree to allow the Zionists to create a state in East Africa; they were to remain subject to the laws and regulations of the British Crown at all times.

Hurst also objected to a clause in the charter, which would have allowed the Jewish settlement the right to exclude and expel any persons entering the settlement who were opposed to the interests of the settlement. He noted that the settlement would have this power if it owned all the land as it could let it out on terms as it pleased. He wrote: 'Even the Commissioner [for East Africa] has no power conferred on him to arbitrarily exclude or expel, and it would not do to confer larger powers on a municipality.'[167] He further objected to a clause in the charter 'for the preservation of the customs and laws of the people of the territory', because 'the colonists would not be concerned with the natives and would not exercise jurisdiction over them'.[168] However, Lord Lansdowne noted that 'there might be natives within the assigned area, and it would be necessary to provide for their protection'. Undoubtedly, what was meant by Hurst's comment was that it was unnecessary to provide for such a provision since the Act of the Conference of Berlin 1884–85 already provided protection for the natives.[169] He was not suggesting that the natives were not to be protected; quite the contrary.

This is an important point to make, as the idea of transfer was not alien to the Zionist movement even at the turn of the twentieth century. On 12 June 1895 in an entry reflecting on his ideas of creating a Jewish state, Herzl confided in his diary[170] that:

> ... We must expropriate gently the private property on the estates assigned to us.

> We shall try to spirit the penniless population across the border by procuring employment for it in the transit countries, while denying it any employment in our own country.
>
> ... Both the process of expropriation and the removal of the poor must be carried out discreetly and circumspectly.[171]

It would seem that the British were opposed to any interference by the Zionists with the welfare of the indigenous population of East Africa. So too, presumably, were the Africans of what would become known as Kenya where the settlement was to be located on a tract of land some 200 miles in length, between Nairobi and the Mau escarpment, on the Uganda railway. The missionaries were certainly opposed to the Jewish settlement as were prominent British Jews such as Lucien Wolf who thought the proposal was 'unnecessary' and 'mischievous' and said so in a letter to the editor of *The Times* (of London).[172] Upon hearing of the Jewish colonisation scheme for East Africa one Christian missionary based in Nairobi wrote to the High Commissioner Sir Charles Elliot complaining that the scheme would interfere with the white man's mission to advance Christian civilisation among the black African native heathens.[173]

The Zionists tried to appeal to the British Government by arguing that their cause was advantageous for the British Empire. In a letter written by Leopold J. Greenberg, Herzl's representative in London, to Joseph Chamberlain, then Secretary of State for the Colonies, which enclosed the draft prepared by Lloyd George on the Jewish colonisation scheme, Greenberg reiterated his hope 'that it may prove in every way most desirable for the British Empire'.[174] The Zionists sought to use the Jewish Colonial Trust, an English registered company, which would operate under the protection of the British Empire (or any Empire which would agree to support them), to colonise a location they deemed suitable. Their preference was always for Palestine, although the Zionists seriously considered other locations such as Argentina, as well as the Sinai and Cyprus among other places. Herzl wanted to use Cyprus as a base to obtain Palestine, either through force, or by bartering for it.[175] Other locations Herzl considered included the Congo, Mozambique and Libya.[176] In a letter to a Mr Philippson, who was a member of the Jewish Colonisation Association in Brussels, he asked:

> Do you have personal connections with the King? Can you sound him out? The Congo State has land enough which we can use for our settlement. We can take over part of the responsibilities, that is, pay an annual tax, which may be fixed later, to the Congo State, in return for which we naturally lay claim to self-government and a not too oppressive vassalage to the Congo State.
>
> These are the great outlines, the principle. If King Leopold turns a willing ear to the matter, I shall go to see him at once.[177]

When Herzl met with King Victor Emmanuel of Italy in December 1903, he raised the idea of channelling 'surplus' Jewish immigration into Tripoli, the capital of today's Libya, which was then within Italy's sphere of influence.[178] In response, Victor Emmanuel politely reminded Herzl that it was 'someone else's house'.[179]

As regards Chamberlain's idea to establish a Jewish state in East Africa, which Herzl assented to and which was the most serious proposal the latter considered and which was a real possibility, the British Foreign Office official, Sir Clement Hill, who was the superintendent in charge of the African protectorates and President of the African Society, made the following note after reading the charter drafted by Lloyd George:

> I have looked at the scheme, which appears to me to contemplate the creation of an *imperium in imperio* [an Empire within an Empire] which would be anomalous and, to say the least, inconvenient. If the promoters wish to obtain a large land grant in East Africa where Jews alone should be allowed to reside, it is possible that such a grant might be made tho' [*sic*] I doubt whether it would be compatible with the free ideas of the Berlin Act.[180]

In another note written by Hurst, reflecting on the memorandum, he wrote:

> There would, I suppose, be no objection to a Jewish colony, if it was subject to the ordinary laws of the Protectorate ...
>
> If the promoters are looking for more than this and want a petty State of their own, something more than townships and municipalities, the scheme would, I think, be open to great objection ...
>
> The scheme they have sent in seems to me to go further than is reasonable, and I should have thought, further than was necessary for their purposes.[181]

As things transpired nothing would come of the Zionist scheme to colonise part of East Africa, as a commission that they financed to go there to inspect the land, was, on the whole, negative about prospects for Jewish colonisation.[182] The only Jewish member of the three-man commission, N. Wilbusch, was dead set against the idea from the beginning.[183] In contrast to his British counterpart, Major A. St Hill Gibbons, who viewed the colonisation of East Africa in a more favourable light, Wilbusch thought that the land 'was well-adapted for cattle breeding, but by natives only'.[184] He also thought that industry and agriculture were out of the question and that only a few families could settle there. With this conclusion, the Zionist colonial project in Africa came to an end and the Uganda Plan was rejected by the Seventh Zionist Congress in 1905.

LAYING THE FOUNDATIONS FOR COLONISING PALESTINE

Despite Herzl's attempts to seek locations other than Palestine to colonise, it was always the Holy Land the Zionists really desired. In 1908, Zionist settlement activity in Palestine took formal root when the Jewish National

Fund and the Palestine Land Development Company were put into operation for the first time to purchase land in Palestine for Jewish settlement.[185] The Zionist Organisation held voting shares in the Jewish Colonial Trust and appointed members to the General Assembly of the Jewish National Fund, which in turn put up half the shares in the formation of the Palestine Land Development Company, which purchased land in Palestine on their behalf.[186] The Anglo-Palestine Bank, which was entitled to British consular protection because it was registered in London, facilitated the flow of capital from Europe to Palestine so that it could grant loans to Jews to buy land there.[187] Through this arrangement private capital was used to acquire land in Palestine although the Zionists never succeeded in purchasing more than 5–6 per cent of the total area of Palestine by the time Arab–Jewish hostilities escalated in the late 1930s.[188] A resolution adopted by the International Zionist Congress in July 1920 stipulated that the Jewish National Fund was to use voluntary contributions and private capital received from Jewish individuals and organisations to make the land of Palestine 'the common property of the Jewish people'.[189] This meant that land purchased by the Fund was taken off the market and nationalised with the result that it could only be leased on a hereditary basis (that is, to Jews).[190] In other words, land purchased by the Jewish National Fund from Palestinian Arabs and other landowners became the perpetual and collective property of the Jewish people with the result that it could only sublet, and then only to Jews.[191] This is why private land ownership is so rare in Israel, even to this day.

International law was integral to the Zionist movement, which was inherently linked to European colonialism, British imperialism and Western capitalism as well as European notions of nationalism, self-determination and anti-Semitism. The charters drafted by Lloyd George and by Theodor Herzl were essentially legal documents that could only be put into operation with the consent of the British and Ottoman governments. The Jewish Colonial Trust, the Jewish National Fund and the Palestine Land Development Company, were legal instruments through which private capital could be utilised effectively towards the colonisation of Palestine. In this regard it is important to note that although international law facilitated these enterprises it also placed constraints upon them. Notably, Britain did not consent to the establishment of a Jewish state in one of her colonies or to conferring powers on the Zionists that would allow them to expel indigenous Africans, because of the provisions of the Berlin Act. These factors are important to bear in mind due to subsequent events.

Ultimately, international law would give the Zionist movement legitimacy once they had succeeded in persuading the British to support them 14 years later. Although Herzl would pass away in 1904, his movement lived on. By the outbreak of the First World War they were in a much stronger position to enter into negotiations with the British Government. The Zionists were also fortunate that the very man who had drafted the Jewish Colonisation Scheme for East Africa in 1903, David Lloyd George, would become British Prime Minister in 1916, and Arthur James Balfour who was British Prime

Minister when the Zionists were negotiating with the British Foreign Office in 1903, and who along with Herzl saw in Zionism a solution to the 'Jewish Question', would be appointed Foreign Secretary in Lloyd George's cabinet in 1916. Moreover, Chaim Weizmann, who was the leader of the Zionist movement in Britain, was appointed a Professor of Chemistry at Manchester University in 1904, and the MP of his constituency happened to be none other than Arthur Balfour who he met when the latter was campaigning there in the 1906 General Election.[192] It was through Weizmann that Balfour was given a 'proper introduction' to the aims and ambitions of the Zionists and Zionism although he was aware of the movement long before then. And indeed Zionism proved useful to British imperialism and vice versa: The Zionists wanted to use it to create a Jewish colony in Palestine for the millions of Jewish immigrants they envisaged emigrating there from Eastern Europe and the British realised that such a colony could help it solve its 'immigration problem', as well as serve its imperial interests in the race for hegemony over the Middle East amongst the other Great Powers, most notably France.[193] Moreover, Weizmann played on the anti-Semitic canard of global Jewish power by successfully creating amongst British leaders an identity between the Zionist movement and 'world Jewry'.[194] However, it was all a farce. The movement that was supposed to be a centre for world influence only occupied four small, dark rooms in Piccadilly Circus in London; its entire archives were kept in a single box in a small hotel room, under the bed of Nahum Sokolow, who was then the leader of the Zionist Organisation.[195]

2
Palestine and the Scramble for the Middle East

'With regard to Palestine, His Majesty's Government are committed by Sir H. McMahon's letter to the Sherif on the 24 October, 1915, to its inclusion in the boundaries of Arab independence.'

Memorandum with regard to British Commitments to King Hussein,
Foreign Office, Political Intelligence Department, FO 608/92,
Peace Conference, British Delegation 1919

'The Covenant of the League of Nations acknowledges 'that the communities formerly belonging to the Turkish Empire have reached a stage of development when their existence as independent nations' should be recognised. The Muslim view is that this 'independence' should not be curtailed by placing those Communities under the control of any alien nation however advanced the latter might be.'

Yakub Nasan, Minister of the Madras Legislative Council,
Delegate of the All-India Muslim League and Representative of the
Khilafat Committee of Bombay. Telegram to Rt. Hon. A.J. Balfour, 1919,
FO 608/98 Peace Conference, British Delegation 1919

'The Zionists are after a Jewish State with the Arabs as hewers of wood and drawers of water. So are many British sympathisers with the Zionists. Whether you use the word Commonwealth or State that is what it will be taken to mean. This is not my view. I want the Arabs to have a chance and I don't want a Hebrew State.'

George Curzon, British Foreign Secretary, 1920 quoted in Doreen Ingrams,
Palestine Papers 1817–1922: Seeds of Conflict (London: John Murray, 1972), p. 96

'Palestine belongs to the Arabs in the same sense that England belongs to the English or France to the French. What is going on in Palestine today cannot be justified by any moral code of conduct. The mandates have no sanction but that of the last war. Surely it would be a crime against humanity to reduce the proud Arabs so that Palestine can be restored to the Jews partly or wholly as their national home.'

Mahatma K. Gandhi, 'The Jews in Palestine', *Harijan*, 26 November 1938

The Middle East has been an area of strategic importance to the Great Powers for over a century. In 1919, when Great Britain entered into negotiations with the Allies at the Paris Peace Conference it had a vested interest in maintaining control of the various land and sea routes to India, the Crown Jewel of the British Empire, via the Suez Canal and the Gulf.[1] Britain needed a buffer to prevent Russian expansion southwards towards the Indian Ocean, to protect its commercial interests in the region, and to extract petroleum, which had recently been discovered in Iraq and Persia.[2] The French also had commercial and political interests in the region dating back centuries, as did the Italians. The US, by contrast, was at that time mainly interested in maintaining its various missionary activities in the Middle East.[3] As Chamberlain had predicted in his meeting with Theodor Herzl in 1903, and which was briefly described in the previous chapter, there was going to be a scramble for the Middle East between the Great Powers just as there had been over Africa.[4] Palestine, in particular, was considered strategically important by British military planners because in British hands it could be used as a bulwark to prevent any Turkish and German attempts to encroach towards the Suez Canal via the Negev and the Sinai Peninsula which they had been attempting to do via the construction of a branch of the Hejaz railway from Aqaba to the banks of the Suez Canal.[5] It was in the context of French and Turkish intrigues over Suez that Britain was to send its Army to capture Palestine from Turkey in 1917.[6] And it was during the discussions at the Paris Peace Conference in 1919 that the region was to undergo a radical transformation from being mere provinces of a crumbling Ottoman Empire to being carved up into separate territories by the Great Powers and remodelled according to European economic and geopolitical interests with little regard being given to the interests of its inhabitants. Logistical, military, and strategic considerations are what dictated the modern map of the Middle East. A prime example of this was a Ministry of Defence plan to construct an oil pipeline between Mosul and Haifa along with a railroad and an air corridor.[7] The borders that still exist between the modern states of Iraq, Jordan and Syria were drawn up to satisfy British military planners to ensure that the pipeline that traversed those territories would not fall solely under the French sphere of influence in Syria.[8]

THE HUSSEIN–McMAHON CORRESPONDENCE

During the First World War, Great Britain needed the support of the Arabs in its struggle against the Central Powers, Bulgaria, Germany, Austria-Hungary and Turkey.[9] In 1915, the war was going badly for Britain and its Allies in the Middle East, and consequently Arab support to defeat the Turks was given a high priority by the Foreign Office and by its advisers in Cairo and Khartoum.[10] The attack on Gallipoli had failed, Egypt was under threat, and the Turks in the north of Yemen had invaded Aden, then a small British protectorate strategically situated on the southwestern tip of the Arabian Peninsula. Britain needed the Arabs to be quiescent in the struggle with Turkey, which was then aligned to Germany, for mastery over the Middle East so as to avoid antagonising the rulers of the Holy Places lest they issue a declaration of *jihad* against the Empire which then included territories inhabited by millions of Muslims. After the Turkish surrender, which Britain was confident would happen, the Foreign Office envisaged replacing the Ottoman Caliphate, which had been based in Istanbul, and had seen itself as a federal system of political leadership for Sunni Muslims, with an Arab Caliphate based in the Hejaz, and in the Sherif of Mecca they found someone who would suit this role.[11]

It was in this context that Britain made its first promise in an exchange of letters (July 1915–March 1916) between Sir Henry McMahon, the British High Commissioner in Cairo, and the Sherif of Mecca who was the main spokesman for the pan-Arab cause.[12] From the terms of the correspondence (examined in greater detail in Chapter 4) the Sherif was under the impression that, with the exception of Lebanon, which had a significant Christian population, Britain had agreed to grant him independence in those territories which today comprise Israel/Palestine, Iraq, Jordan, Saudi Arabia and Syria, although Britain stipulated that it wanted to have 'special administrative arrangements' with the Arabs over Baghdad and Basra (which are situated in modern-day Iraq). In the letter, Sir Henry McMahon wrote that Britain was 'prepared to recognise and support the independence of the Arabs in all the regions within limits demanded by the Sherif of Mecca' with the exception of the two districts of Mersina and Alexandretta (situated in modern-day Turkey) and portions of the Levant lying to the west of the districts of Damascus, Homs, Hama and Aleppo (situated in modern-day Syria).

Even from a cursory glance at a map it seemed evident that the 'portions of Syria lying to the west of the districts of Damascus, Homs, Hama and Aleppo' included Lebanon but not Palestine, which the Arabs desired. Consequently, if Palestine was excluded from McMahon's letter, it would form part of the independent Arab state, or states, whereas Lebanon would not. This was the conclusion reached by the Political Intelligence Department at the Foreign Office: 'The whole of Palestine, within the limits set out in the main body of the memorandum, lies within the limits which H.M.G. have pledged themselves to Sherif Hussain that they will recognise and uphold the independence of.'[13] The Foreign Office cartographers even produced a map to this effect in which Palestine was included in the area (outlined in red) that had been pledged by the British Government to the Sherif of Mecca (see Map 2). That Palestine had first been pledged to the Sherif was also acknowledged by the House of Lords in a debate in 1922 in which they condemned the Balfour Declaration and the Mandate.[14] In 1947 several Arab states attempted to refer the correspondence to the International Court of Justice in the form of a question in which they asked for an advisory opinion (see Chapter 6).

THE 'SYKES–PICOT' AGREEMENT

However, after the exchange of correspondence with the Sherif, Britain concluded another secret agreement on 16 May 1916 with the French Government in which they agreed to carve up Turkey's former possessions in the Middle East between them with the exception of Arabia, which is now known as Saudi Arabia, whose independence they would recognise, in the event of an Allied victory.[15] What became known as the Sykes–Picot agreement, named after Sir Mark Sykes, a distinguished British orientalist and MP, and M. Charles François Georges-Picot, formerly French Consul in Beirut, envisaged giving the French control of parts of southern Turkey, Kurdistan, Syria, Lebanon and a part of what was then referred to as Mesopotamia (that is, Iraq); giving the British control of the remainder of Iraq, including Basra and Baghdad; the Italians, control of southern Turkey; and the Russians, control of the Caucasus and Armenia. Substantial parts of what is known today as Syria, Jordan and the remainder of Iraq were to become an 'independent Arab state' or a 'confederation of states', under the suzerainty of an Arab chief whereby Britain and France would supply 'advisers or foreign functionaries' with a view to administering the territory. An international administration was to be established in Palestine, the form of which was to be decided upon after consultation with Russia, the other allies, such as the Italians, and the representatives of the Sherif of Mecca. The relevant provisions of the agreement were contained in a letter from the British Foreign Minister to his French counterpart:

> It is accordingly understood between the French and British Governments –
> 1. That France and Great Britain are prepared to recognise and protect an independent Arab State or a Confederation of Arab States in the areas (A) and (B) marked on the annexed map, [see Map 4] under the suzerainty of an Arab chief. That in area (A) France, and in area (B) Great Britain, shall have priority of right of enterprise and local loans. That in area (A) France, and in area (B) Great Britain, shall alone supply advisers or foreign functionaries at the request of the Arab State or Confederation of Arab States.
> 2. That in the blue area France, and in the red area Great Britain, shall be allowed to establish such direct or indirect administration or control as they desire and as they may think fit to arrange with the Arab State or confederation of Arab States.
> 3. That in the brown area [that is, Palestine] there shall be established an international administration, the form of which is to be decided upon after consultation with Russia, and subsequently in consultation with the other Allies, *and the representatives of the Shereef of Mecca.*[16]

The Russian connection was considered important due to the presence of the Russian Orthodox Church in Jerusalem as was the Greek Orthodox Church and the Roman Catholic Church for the same reasons. At that time no one envisaged a Zionist presence in Palestine even though the holiest sites in Judaism are located in Jerusalem. According to the text of the Sykes–Picot agreement the only other representatives, apart from the Russians and the other allies that were to be consulted about the 'brown area', that is, Palestine, were 'the representatives of the Shereef of Mecca'. This would seem to be consistent with the view that Palestine was not, in fact, excluded from the area pledged to the Sherif of Mecca by McMahon in their correspondence. If Palestine had been specifically excluded, then why would the British and French governments consult the Sherif of Mecca about establishing an international administration there? It is therefore arguable that the Sykes–Picot agreement was not incompatible with the Hussein–McMahon correspondence. In fact, as will become apparent in Chapter 4, the Sykes–Picot agreement was actually based upon the Hussein–McMahon correspondence as Lloyd George acknowledged during the negotiations with France at the Paris Peace Conference.[17] What came next, however, was a completely different story.

THE BALFOUR DECLARATION

Following the Sykes–Picot agreement, the British Government published a declaration which, on the face of things, seemed to directly contravene what the Sherif had been pledged in the Hussein–McMahon correspondence. In his correspondence with McMahon, the Sherif was promised independence so long as it did not affect French interests in its traditional sphere of influence in Syria and subject to the rendering of British advice, assistance, and guidance. No mention was made in the Hussein–McMahon correspondence or the Sykes–Picot agreement of anything relating to Zionist aspirations for establishing a Jewish homeland in Palestine.[18] Yet on 2 November 1917, Britain's Foreign Secretary A.J. Balfour published a declaration promising precisely this in *The Times*[19] addressed to Lord Rothschild,[20] a wealthy British banker and zoologist, who, as described in Chapter 1, had been a part of the Royal Commission on Alien Immigration in 1903. In the declaration the British Government viewed with favour the establishment in Palestine of a national home for the Jewish people on the condition that it was clearly understood that nothing was to be done which might prejudice the civil and religious rights of existing non-Jewish communities in Palestine or the political rights of Jews in other countries.

Foreign Office,
November 2nd, 1917

Dear Lord Rothschild,

I have much pleasure in conveying to you, on behalf of His Majesty's Government, the following declaration of sympathy *with Jewish Zionist aspirations* which has been submitted to, and approved by, the Cabinet.

'His Majesty's Government view with favour the establishment in Palestine of a national home for the Jewish people, and will use their best endeavours to facilitate the achievement of this object, *it being clearly understood* that nothing shall be done which may prejudice the civil and religious rights of existing non-Jewish communities in Palestine, or the rights and political status enjoyed by Jews in any other country.'

I should be grateful if you would bring this declaration to the knowledge of the Zionist Federation.

Yours sincerely,
Arthur James Balfour[21]

As one would expect, the Balfour Declaration was met with great fanfare by the Zionists, with the exception of some ultra Orthodox Jews who were initially hesitant and many of whom still oppose its very existence today.[22] It is also noteworthy that this was a 'declaration of sympathy with *Jewish* Zionist aspirations'. This was an admission, perhaps, by the British Government, that

Zionist aspirations were not necessarily or exclusively Jewish. The Balfour Declaration was not, however, universally welcomed even across the Atlantic – at least not initially. In the United States, Robert Lansing, the Secretary of State, and a prominent international lawyer, who would lead the US delegation to the Paris Peace Conference in 1919, objected to the Balfour Declaration on political grounds, writing the following letter to President Woodrow Wilson:

> Washington, December 13, 1917.
>
> MY DEAR MR PRESIDENT: There is being brought considerable pressure for the issuance of a declaration in regard to this Government's attitude as to the disposition to be made of Palestine. This emanates naturally from the Zionist element of the Jews.
>
> My judgment is that we should go very slowly in announcing a policy for three reasons. First, we are not at war with Turkey and therefore should avoid any appearance of favouring taking territory from that Empire by force. Second, the Jews are by no means a unit in the desire to reestablish their race as an independent people; to favor one of the other faction would seem to be unwise. Third, many Christian sects and individuals would undoubtedly resent turning the Holy Land over to the absolute control of the race credited with the death of Christ.
>
> For practical purposes I do not think that we need go further than the first reason given since that is ample ground for declining to announce a policy in regard to the final disposition of Palestine.
>
> Faithfully yours,
> ROBERT LANSING.[23]

The Balfour Declaration was also opposed by a substantial number of British Jews such as Edwin Montagu and Lucien Wolf. Predictably, Arabs of Syrian-Palestinian origin reacted with fury to the news and wrote petitions of complaint to the British Government from as far away as Santiago de Chile and New York.[24] Their essential concern was that as they were indigenous to Palestine, their country should not be given to anyone else.[25] In Jerusalem, a conference was hastily convened by Christian and Muslim Palestinian Arabs to express their opposition to the Declaration, preferring a union with Syria which they considered themselves connected to 'by national, religious, linguistic, natural, economical and geographical bonds'.[26] A British intelligence officer present at the conference wrote a report to London in which he said that the Arabs were dumbfounded that the Allies could talk about the rights of small nations, protection of the minority, self-determination etc. and then 'proceed to hand over Palestine to an alien people, now in a minority, who would eventually dispossess them of their lands and undoubtedly tyrannise over them'.[27] The officer from the Secret Service Bureau then warned:

> I have personally heard many Arabs, both Christians and Moslems, declare that they will forcibly resist any attempt to set up in this land a Jewish State or anything resembling it. The pan-Arab young bloods, very bold in speech, say so openly on every hand. Others, not so bold and perhaps more candid, declare that they will sell out and leave the country. I do not think the threat of the young Arabs is to be taken lightly, as they might cause much trouble by appealing to the fanaticism of the villagers and as they would certainly be supported by Arabsoutside [*sic*] of Palestine.[28]

It is somewhat perplexing that Britain did not take these warnings seriously, as the Arabs would repeatedly reiterate their opposition to Zionism on many occasions; but then, perhaps, she was blinded by the 'Zionist experiment', which was how the colonisation of Palestine was referred to by British politicians and civil servants at the time, and by imperial grandeur. Indeed, it is a curious aspect of the Balfour Declaration that neither Britain nor the Zionists had sovereignty over, nor any effective connection to, that territory other than the fact that the British Army had overrun it in December 1917 after which it was intended that Turkey's colonies would be carved up and distributed to the victors (principally, Britain, France and Russia).[29] In fact, Britain was not even in effective control of Palestine when it issued its declaration in sympathy of 'Jewish Zionist aspirations'. This is because the Balfour Declaration was published in November 1917; and Allenby's forces did not capture Palestine until the following month. So the Balfour Declaration was essentially a statement of intention. In the period *preceding* the First World War, conquest[30] was considered a legitimate mode of acquiring territory, although it was subject to the laws of belligerent occupation.

However, as will be seen later, the League of Nations mandates system was a very different arrangement to conquest.[31] When, on 9 November 1917, the Balfour Declaration was published in the *Manchester Guardian*, alongside a report of the Bolshevik revolution in Petrograd, international law was still heavily influenced by the policies and practices of the colonial powers.[32] Partly as a response to the Balfour Declaration[33] the Bolsheviks exposed[34] Britain's duplicity by publishing the Sykes–Picot agreement, which until then had been kept secret, as evidence of what they saw as Western and Tsarist imperialism.[35] In essence, the Balfour letter acknowledged that a people already inhabited Palestine, of who over 90 per cent were non-Jewish despite its declared intention to establish a Jewish homeland there.[36] How Great Britain would assist with establishing a national home for the 'Jewish people' without prejudicing the civil and religious rights of the indigenous non-Jewish population or the rights and political status enjoyed by Jews elsewhere was never seriously addressed.

CONFLICTING PLEDGES

The problem was that at the same time as the British Government came out in support of Zionism, Arab nationalism was on the rise. To the Arabs, the Zionists were seen as settler-colonialists whose aims and ambitions in the region they diametrically opposed.[37] They viewed the encroachment of Zionism and the mass influx of Jewish immigrants that would accompany it as a threat to their own claims to independence. However, Zionism was arguably more than a colonialist movement because it also had the attributes of a nationalist movement. This is because the Zionists did not merely want to settle in Palestine in search of opportunities and a better way of life, but to recreate a Jewish state in the land of their ancestors. They hoped that in time the land of Palestine would serve as a national rallying point to arrest the assimilation of Jews throughout the world.[38] The Zionists saw in Zionism a solution to the Jewish Question and a cure for centuries of anti-Semitism. But the Arabs did not see it like this and swore that they would sacrifice body and soul to fight the Zionist menace. And in exchange for their support, the British Government made a series of conflicting pledges to both Arabs and Zionists over the allocation of land and resources in the Middle East that were inherently at odds. As a result Britain sowed the seeds of future strife, when it promised to recognise the independence of an Arab state in the Middle East, without explicitly excluding Palestine from its boundaries, whilst also promising the Zionists self-government in Palestine.

In a debate in the House of Lords over the pledges given by Britain to the Arabs, Viscount Grey of Fallodon, who, as Sir Edward Grey, was one of the longest serving British Foreign Ministers of all time, said that he could not see how the Government could establish a Zionist home in Palestine where 93 per cent of the population was Arab without prejudicing their civil rights.[39] He therefore suggested that the Government release the papers, which could give clarification to the commitments his Government made to the Arabs when he was Foreign Minister.[40] He said that:

> It would be very desirable, from the point of view of honour, that all these various pledges should be set out side by side, and then, I think, the most honourable thing would be to look at them fairly, see what inconsistencies there are between them, and, having regard to the nature of each pledge and the date at which it was given, with all the facts before us, consider what is the fair thing to be done.[41]

Although the instructions given to McMahon were not published during Grey's lifetime – he died in 1933 – they have since been declassified.[42] In his telegram, Grey instructed McMahon 'to give an assurance of Arab independence saying that we will proceed at once to discuss boundaries if they will send representatives for that purpose, but if something more precise than this is required *you can give it*'.[43] In other words, Grey left the question of boundaries to McMahon's absolute discretion. It is therefore apparent that when he drafted his letter to the Sherif, McMahon was acting with full governmental authority. In his reply to Grey, drafted after he had written to the Sherif, McMahon wrote the following telegram explaining what had been promised:

> 4. I have been definite in stating that Great Britain will recognise the principle of Arab independence in purely Arab territory, this being the main point of which agreement depends, but have been equally definite in excluding Mersina, Alexandretta and those districts *on the northern coast of Syria*, which cannot be said to be purely Arab, and where I understand that French interests have been recognised.[44]

Location is a question of fact. At no point in the twentieth century, or even prior to it, was Palestine considered to be situated 'on the northern coast of Syria'. Even in biblical times, Palestine was always understood to refer to the coastal plains of southern Syria, which British politicians brought up on the Bible would have recognised.[45] One must therefore conclude that McMahon did not intend to exclude Palestine from his pledge. It is abundantly clear from both the actual text of the Hussein–McMahon correspondence, and from the correspondence between Grey and McMahon, that Palestine was not excluded from the territory promised to Hussein in which he was to create his 'Arab Caliphate of Islam'. Indeed, this probably accounts for the inconsistencies between the pledges Britain made to the Arabs both *before* the publication of the Balfour Declaration, such as the pledges made in the Hussein–McMahon correspondence, and *afterwards*.

In fact, only eleven months after General Allenby captured Jerusalem on 9 December 1917, he issued the following Proclamation:

> The object of the war in the East on the part of Great Britain was the complete and final *liberation of all peoples* formerly oppressed by the Turks and the establishment of national governments and administrations in those countries deriving authority from the initiative and *free will of the people* themselves.[46]

Allenby's Proclamation was closely modelled on the Anglo-French Declaration of 7 November 1918, in which it was said:

> The object aimed at by France and Great Britain in prosecuting in the East the War let loose by the ambition of Germany is the complete and definite *emancipation* of the peoples so long oppressed by the Turks and the establishment of national governments and administrations deriving their authority from the initiative and *free choice* of the *indigenous* populations.[47]

Not only did the Balfour Declaration conflict with the Hussein–McMahon correspondence, but it also seemed to conflict with General Allenby's Proclamation at Jerusalem as well as the Anglo-French Declaration: how could the Zionist Organisation with its headquarters in London[48] (and prior to that in Berlin) claim to be 'formerly oppressed by the Turks'? Surely, a national government in Palestine could only derive its authority from the free will of the indigenous and predominantly Arab population of Palestine?

Yet here it was being promised by a third party, the British, to another third party, the Zionists, without any consideration being given to the interests and free choice of the indigenous populations – despite the numerous pledges and lofty declarations on self-determination, independence and statehood made to them by the Allies.

It would seem that the only possible explanation for this anomaly was that either these principles were not supposed to apply to the people of Palestine or if they did, then they were to apply also to the Jewish people who had not yet made their home there. Some support for this latter proposition is provided for in a message that Commander Hogarth, then the Director of the Arab Bureau in Cairo, was instructed to deliver to the Sherif of Mecca in January 1918. The relevant passages of this message provided:

> (2) So far as Palestine is concerned we are determined that no people shall be subject to another ...
>
> (3) Since the Jewish opinion of the world is in favour of a return of Jews to Palestine and inasmuch as this opinion must remain a constant factor, and further as His Majesty's Government view with favour the realisation of this aspiration, His Majesty's Government are determined that *in so far as is compatible* with *the freedom of the existing population* both economic and *political*, no obstacle should be put in the way of the realisation of this ideal.[49]

It therefore seemed that Britain genuinely believed that it could reconcile the conflicting interests of both Arabs and Zionists in relation to Palestine even though the vast majority of the latter were not resident in the country.

Perhaps then, this was a sign of the times, when the colonial powers could more or less do as they pleased. After all, the Balfour Declaration was negotiated only 32 years after the General Act of the Conference of Berlin in 1885, which effectively 'legalised' the scramble for Africa during an age of unbridled colonialism where the 'dark continent' was partitioned into spheres of influence between the Great Powers.[50] In this respect, it should be stressed that Africa was not considered *terra nullius*, that is, vacant land which was declared abandoned, in order to justify its colonisation, for African peoples and tribes had inhabited the continent since time immemorial.[51] Instead, the powers of the day entered into treaties of cession with local tribal leaders which allowed them to exploit African land.[52] In fact, Africa had seen the rise and development of flourishing states and empires, and this may partly explain why at Berlin, the powers of the day, which included Muslim Turkey and the United States of America, agreed to '... *bind themselves* to watch over the *preservation* of the native tribes, and to care for the improvement of the conditions of *their moral and material well-being* and to help in suppressing slavery ...'.[53] This suggests that even in classical cases of colonialism, the preservation, moral and material well-being of indigenous peoples was considered, at least on paper, to be binding upon the colonial powers – although the lands they inhabited could be exploited.[54] After all, as mentioned in Chapter 1, the Foreign Office Legal Adviser C.J.B. Hurst noted that several provisions of the draft charter for a Jewish colonisation scheme for East Africa would be contrary to the Berlin Act.[55] As international law at that time drew a distinction between different forms of 'civilisation', with Palestinian Christians, Jews and Muslims being higher up 'the evolutionary chain' because they formed a part of the Ottoman Empire, they were not exploited to the extent that indigenous Africans were.[56] At an absolute minimum, it would therefore seem that Palestine's indigenous inhabitants had a right to self-preservation; they could not be dispossessed or oppressed, as this would not be in the interests of 'their moral and material well-being'. As will be seen later, the principle of the 'sacred trust' which was subsequently enshrined in the League of Nations Covenant had its origins in the Conference of Berlin and was intimately connected with 'the duty of civilisation'.[57] The colonial powers party to that Covenant were consequently bound to pay due regard to the preservation, moral and material well-being of all of Palestine's indigenous inhabitants.

THE FOURTEEN POINTS

Unfortunately for indigenous peoples, the Great Powers were able to partition the region into separate territories with little regard for the interests of the inhabitants because international law had not outlawed colonialism in the days of the First World War. Rather, the victorious powers sought to 'civilise' the peoples of the colonial territories they acquired from Germany and Turkey through a system of mandates, although no attempt was made to apply the mandate idea to any territory that had been within Austria-Hungary as that country had been dissolved before the Peace Conference at Versailles.[58] The word 'mandate' originated from the reign of the Roman Emperor Justinian whose jurists advised him that he who discharges a mandate may not exceed its limitations.[59] Essentially, the mandate was a tool through which the Great Powers could undertake their 'civilising mission'. It was in this context, and in the aftermath of the 'war to end all wars', that President Woodrow Wilson wanted to create a world, which would be made 'fit and safe to live in'.[60] In order to achieve this, 'every peace-loving nation' would be 'assured of justice and fair dealing by the other peoples of the world as against force and selfish aggression'.[61] Wilson wanted to create a new world order avowedly based on peace and justice. Before he delivered his famous Fourteen Points to both houses of Congress on 8 January 1918 he said: 'All the peoples of the world are in effect partners in this interest, and for our own part we see very clearly that unless justice be done to others it will not be done to us.'[62] The twelfth of Wilson's fourteen points, which was relevant to the situation then prevailing in the Middle East, provided that the other nationalities which were then under Turkish rule should be assured an 'undoubted security of life' and an 'absolutely unmolested opportunity of autonomous development'.[63] The mandates system was promoted by Wilson as a device designed to avoid the traditional European practice of dividing the spoils among the victors in a war.

Following Wilson's address to Congress, and after negotiations with Premiers Lloyd George and Georges Clemenceau at the Paris Peace Conference over the disposition of Ottoman territory, Wilson promptly dispatched a fact-finding committee to the Middle East. It was comprised of Charles R. Crane, a wealthy American philanthropist, and Henry Churchill King, an American theologian, who were sent to Syria of which Palestine, at that time, was an integral part, to determine, among other things, which of the victorious allied nations in the First World War should act as the mandatory power for Palestine. As it happened, the Palestinian Arabs wanted the United States to be the mandatory power and were opposed to Britain and France, the traditional colonial powers.[64] On 2 July 1919, the King–Crane Commission was presented with a memorandum by the General Syrian Congress in Damascus. The Congress claimed to represent the indigenous Arab peoples of the Southern, Eastern and Western Zones of Syria (that is, the *Sham*), which included Christians, Jews, Muslims and other minorities.[65] The Congress was authorised to represent the inhabitants of each of these districts. Its representatives agreed on the following point unanimously:

> 7. We oppose the pretensions of the Zionists to create a Jewish commonwealth in the southern part of Syria, known as Palestine, and oppose Zionist migration to any part of our country; for we do not acknowledge their title but consider them a grave peril to our people from the national, economic, and political points of view.[66]

The King–Crane Commission completed their report on 28 August, 1919, although it was not published for three years due to British and French opposition. They recommended 'serious modification of the extreme Zionist program for Palestine of unlimited immigration of Jews, looking finally to make Palestine distinctly a Jewish state'.[67] They noted that 'a national home for the Jewish people' is not equivalent to making Palestine into a Jewish state.[68] They considered that the creation of such a state could not be accomplished 'without the gravest trespass' upon the 'civil and religious rights of existing non-Jewish communities in Palestine'.[69] They said this fact came out repeatedly in their meetings with Jewish representatives, who 'looked forward to a practically complete dispossession of the present non-Jewish inhabitants of Palestine, by various forms of purchase'.[70] The Commissioners, who 'began their study of Zionism with minds predisposed in its favour', then issued this stark warning:

> The [Paris] Peace Conference should not shut its eyes to the fact that the anti-Zionist feeling in Palestine and Syria is intense and not lightly to be flouted. No British officer, consulted by the Commissioners, believed that the Zionist program could be carried out except by force of arms. The officers generally thought that a force of not less than fifty thousand soldiers

> would be required even to initiate the program. That of itself is evidence of a strong sense of the injustice of the Zionist program, on the part of the non-Jewish populations of Palestine and Syria. Decisions, requiring armies to carry them out, are sometimes necessary, but they are surely not gratuitously to be taken in the interests of a serious injustice.[71]

King and Crane noted that the Zionists' claim that they have a 'right' to Palestine, based on an occupation of two thousand years ago, 'can hardly be seriously considered'. Indeed, international law recognises no such right.

TITLE TO TERRITORY AND EFFECTIVE OCCUPATION

In 1906, a dispute arose between the Netherlands and the United States of America over who had sovereignty over the Islands of Palmas (or Miangas), which are situated between Indonesia, then a Dutch colony, and the Philippines, then a US colony.[72] In a special agreement concluded between the two countries, the famous Swiss jurist Max Huber was appointed arbitrator at the Permanent Court of Arbitration.[73] In his Award he held that 'the actual continuous and peaceful display of State functions is in case of dispute the sound and natural criterium of territorial sovereignty'.[74] In other words what is essential is 'the continuous and peaceful display of *actual power* in the contested region' which reflected customary international law.[75] This is because the continuous and peaceful display of territorial sovereignty is as good as title and is one of the most important considerations in establishing boundaries between states.[76] However, the Zionists, as opposed to a small number of persons of the Jewish faith who inhabited Palestine and others who in the late nineteenth and early twentieth centuries had immigrated there in small numbers for purposes of devotion, had not displayed any continuous and actual power in Palestine since biblical times. They were essentially a group of immigrants, drawn mainly from Eastern and Central Europe, who were promised a home in a territory that was inhabited by another people by a third party. For the previous two millennia European Jewry had not inhabited Palestine and had shown little interest in colonising it until the late nineteenth century. As Huber concluded in his arbitral award in the *Palmas* case:

> International law, like law in general, has the object of assuring the coexistence of different interests which are worthy of legal protection. If, as in the present instance, only one of two conflicting interests is to prevail, because sovereignty can be attributed to but one of the Parties, the interest which involves the maintenance of a state of things having offered at the critical time to the *inhabitants of the disputed territory* and to other States a certain guarantee for the respect of their rights ought, in doubt, to *prevail* over an interest which – supposing it to be recognized in international law – has not yet received any concrete form of development.[77]

Even if it could be argued that the Zionists had a 'right' to advance claims to sovereignty in Palestine at the time of the Paris Peace Conference in 1919, this could not prevail over the rights of the inhabitants of the territory that was to be placed under the mandate. This is because it is the continuous and peaceful display of territorial sovereignty in the territory concerned that conveys title. In other words, the continuous and peaceful display of the functions of a state within a given region is a constituent element of territorial sovereignty.[78] Yet in 1919, the Zionists were not the territorial sovereign of Palestine and moreover their claim to it would have been contested by the former sovereign, Turkey, as well as by its indigenous inhabitants. In fact, Turkey had been suspicious of the small trickle of Russian Jewish immigration into Palestine that began in the 1880s because of the system of capitulations that were in force there which allowed them to seek protection from the Russian consul, in case of a conflict of laws, with the result that Ottoman law did not apply to them causing a rift with the Turkish authorities which saw them as potential outlaws.[79] Aside from this, the continuous and peaceful display of territorial sovereignty was something the Zionists were not, in any event, capable of ever accomplishing after 1919 in the face of persistent opposition from the Palestinian Arabs.

As regards claims to sovereignty based on ancient or historic title, a dispute before the International Court of Justice between France and Britain over who had sovereignty over a group of islands off the Isles of Jersey dating back to the times of William the Conqueror and the Norman conquest of Britain in 1066, is elucidating.[80] There, the Court concluded that attributing legal effects to a situation after an interval of several centuries 'seems to lead far beyond any reasonable application of legal considerations'.[81] The Court considered that what was of decisive importance was not indirect presumptions deduced from events in the Middle Ages, but the evidence which related directly to the possession of the islands in question.[82] In other words, in the context of the Arab–Israeli dispute, what mattered is that for centuries prior to creation of the Zionist movement in the late nineteenth century, the Turks had been exercising state functions in Palestine. They accordingly had sovereignty over it. Any claims advanced by the Zionists based on biblical texts or archaeological digs dating back well over a millennium were irrelevant.[83] Moreover, in his Declaration, Judge Alvarez complained that the parties had attributed 'excessive importance to historical titles'.[84] He chastised them for not sufficiently taking into account the state of international law as it existed at the time:

> The task of the Court is to resolve international disputes by applying, not the traditional or classical international law, but that which exists at the present day and which is in conformity with the new conditions of international life, and to develop this law in a progressive spirit.[85]

In another legal dispute concerning sovereignty over Western Sahara, a situation not too dissimilar to the problems facing the Palestinian people today, who like the indigenous Sahrawis people are unable to exercise sovereignty over their homeland, the International Court of Justice concluded in an advisory opinion that what matters in determining title to territory 'is not indirect inferences drawn from events in past history but evidence directly relating to effective display of authority'.[86] When the Balfour Declaration was issued in November 1917, the Zionists did not and could not display any effective authority over Palestine. This was because neither they nor Britain were in effective control of Palestine at that time, as Allenby's forces had not yet penetrated that part of the Middle East. Rather, Palestine was still part of the Ottoman Empire where it had been governed for centuries as a distinct autonomous province. The Turks maintained their control over Palestine until the Allied Powers defeated them on 9 December 1917, although Turkey did not explicitly agree to transfer sovereignty to the Allied Powers in either the Treaties of Sèvres or Lausanne (Turkey merely renounced its rights over its former provinces).[87]

In this regard, it is noteworthy that in a case between France and Greece over who had sovereignty over the islands of Crete and Samos before 1913, for the purposes of solving a conflict concerning concessionary rights over lighthouses in those territories, the Permanent Court of International Justice, which was the predecessor to the International Court of Justice, concluded that even though the Sultan had been obliged to accept important restrictions on the exercise of his rights of sovereignty in Crete, that sovereignty had not ceased to belong to him, however qualified it might be from a juridical point of view.[88] This situation persisted until the time when Crete was separated from the Ottoman Empire by treaties of cession.[89] One may therefore conclude that sovereignty over Palestine remained vested at least *hypothetically*, although not in practice, in the Ottoman Empire until it agreed to renounce its rights in the Treaty of Lausanne on 24 July 1923.

CATEGORIES OF COLONISATION

Palestine was not colonised in the same manner as Africa due to the degree of political status the Palestine Arabs enjoyed under Turkish rule where they attained high executive, legislative and administrative posts in the Ottoman Empire.[90] Instead Palestine, as a former province of that Empire, was subject to a mandate even though the Syrian General Congress protested to the King–Crane Commission that the 'Arabs inhabiting the Syrian area are not naturally less gifted than other more advanced races and that they are by no means less developed than the Bulgarians, Serbians, Greeks and Roumanians at the beginning of their independence.'[91] In this regard, it should be stressed that a mandate was not analogous to a colony, as Palestine was not a British possession.[92] Britain was merely an administrator.

In his treatise on *The Acquisition and Government of Backward Territory in International Law*, Sir Mark Frank Lindley noted that the mandates relating to territories, which had previously belonged to Turkey, were 'more advanced' than those covered by other mandates.[93] This is because according to Article 22 of the Covenant of the League of Nations each mandate differed according to the stage of development of the people of the territory, its geographical situation and its economic conditions.[94] As Lindley noted, Palestine, as a former Turkish colony, was considered an 'A-class' mandate (as opposed to a 'B- or C-class' mandate), which signified that it had reached a stage of development where its existence as an independent nation was provisionally recognised.[95] In 1924, Mr Ormsby-Gore, who was then the Under-Secretary of State for the Colonies, told a meeting of the Permanent Mandates Commission that:

> Consideration of the reports on Palestine showed that the problem was entirely different from that of B and C mandates, where African and Polynesian inhabitants were under consideration. Palestine occupied a unique position in international politics, since it was the Holy Land for Jews, Christians and Mohammedans. The object of the British Government was to treat all Palestinians on a basis of complete equality.[96]

Palestine was explicitly mentioned in an earlier draft of Article 22 that was presented to the Paris Peace Conference, which concerned the A-class mandates, as was Kurdistan.[97] America never joined the League of Nations due to domestic opposition and the premature death of Wilson in October 1919, which was why Britain was given the mandate over Palestine, and France over the rest of the Levant (Lebanon and Syria).[98]

TRANSJORDAN

On 1 September 1922, Britain effectively partitioned Palestine into two nations either side of the river Jordan: Palestine was situated on the West Bank, and the Emirate of Transjordan, a new mandate created by the British to give to Abdullah, the eldest son of the Sherif of Mecca, was established, where the terms of the Balfour Declaration and those articles in the Mandate regarding the national home policy would not apply.[99] In this connection, the argument has been advanced in certain circles, that by dividing Palestine in 1922, Britain was fulfilling its pledge to both the Zionists and the Arabs by giving Palestine to the Jews and Transjordan to the Arabs.[100] However, despite the beguiling simplicity of this argument, there is one fundamental flaw: Palestine was subject to the Balfour Declaration, which was conditional upon safeguarding the civil and religious rights of the Arab population. That Declaration did not give the Zionists any right to create a Jewish state over the whole of Palestine. Nor did it give them a right to remove Palestine's Arab population. Rather, a Jewish national home was to be established within the Palestine mandate.[101] Palestine and Transjordan were separate legal entities. In the words of the Supreme Court of Palestine:

> ... Trans-Jordan has a government entirely independent of Palestine – the laws of Palestine are not applicable in Trans-Jordan nor are their laws applicable here. Moreover, although the High Commissioner of Palestine is also High Commissioner for Trans-Jordan, Trans-Jordan has an entirely independent government under the rule of an Amir and apart from certain reserved matters the High Commissioner cannot interfere with the government of Trans-Jordan – at the most he can advise from time to time. His Britannic Majesty has entered into agreements with His Highness the Amir of Trans-Jordan in which the existence of an independent government in Trans-Jordan under the rule of the Amir has been specifically recognised ... It is clear therefrom that Trans-Jordan exercises its powers of legislation and administration through its own constitutional government which is entirely separate and independent from that of Palestine.[102]

ARTICLE 22 AND THE LEAGUE OF NATIONS COVENANT

It has been said that a booklet entitled *The League of Nations: A Practical Suggestion*, which was written by General Jan Smuts and published in 1918, influenced the drafting of Article 22.[103] Apparently, Smuts had been impressed by the cry for self-determination in Central and Eastern Europe, and in German and Russian socialist circles in 1917, although he did not envisage it applying to the C-class mandates, such as South-West Africa, which had been a German colony before the war.[104] He did, however, envisage the principle applying to Syria, which he considered to be close to what he called 'complete statehood'.[105] With regard to Palestine, Smuts recognised that administrative cooperation between the Jewish minority and the Arab majority 'would not be forthcoming' and autonomy 'in any real sense' would be out of the question.[106] This is why he thought they would need 'the assistance and control of an external authority', such as Great Britain. In this respect Article 22 of the Covenant of the League of Nations provided:

> To those colonies and territories which as a consequence of the late war have ceased to be under the sovereignty of the States which formerly governed them and which are inhabited by peoples not *yet* able to stand by themselves under the strenuous conditions of the modern world, there should be applied the principle *that the well-being and development of such peoples form a sacred trust of civilisation* and that securities for the performance of this trust should be embodied in this Covenant.
>
> The best method of giving practical effect to this principle is that the tutelage of such peoples should be entrusted to advanced nations who by reason of their resources, their experience or their geographical position can best undertake this responsibility, and who are willing to accept it, and that this tutelage should be exercised by them as Mandatories *on behalf of the League*.

> The character of the mandate must differ according to the stage of development of the people, the geographical situation of the territory, its economic conditions and other similar circumstances.
>
> Certain communities formerly belonging to the Turkish Empire have reached a stage of development *where their existence as independent nations can be provisionally recognised* subject to the rendering of administrative advice and assistance by a Mandatory until such time as they are able to stand alone. The wishes of these communities must be a principal consideration in the selection of the mandatory.[107]

Article 22 explicitly provided that those communities formerly belonging to the Ottoman Empire had reached a stage of development where their existence as independent nations was provisionally recognised. The only proviso was that Britain and France had the right to render administrative advice and assistance until the time when they were able to stand alone (that is, attain independence). The use of the word 'yet' in the phrase 'not yet able to stand by themselves' at the beginning of Article 22 suggested an expectation that capacity for self-determination and eventual independence would arise at some point in the future, which will be examined in more detail in Chapter 5.[108] In other words, it was never envisaged that these territories would remain mandates *ad infinitum*. Rather, the 'advanced nations' concerned were to help these peoples who were 'not yet able to stand by themselves under the strenuous conditions of the modern world' until they could do so. The eventual goal, particularly for those communities formerly belonging to the Turkish Empire, was self-determination and independence.[109]

Paragraph four of Article 22 of the Covenant provided that: 'The wishes of *these communities* must be a principal consideration in the selection of the Mandatory.' In context, 'these communities' could only refer to Palestine's indigenous inhabitants who included established communities of Christians, Jews, Muslims and others. In this regard it could therefore be argued that it was inconsistent with the recognition of a community as independent to provide that its territory or part of its territory was to be the national home of a foreign people who were to immigrate there from all over the world until they formed the majority of the population; so that when self-government was granted the governing majority were not the people who were there in 1923 (when the Mandate entered into force) and whose independence had been provisionally recognised but another people altogether.[110] It would therefore not be an understatement to say that the incorporation of the Balfour Declaration into the British Mandate of Palestine providing preference for a national home for the 'Jewish people' clashed with the political aspirations of the indigenous population who, given half a chance, would have undoubtedly opted for independence.[111] It also clearly contradicted the whole raison d'être of the mandates system which viewed the well-being and development of indigenous peoples a 'sacred trust of civilization'. The Allied Powers therefore clearly acquiesced[112] in this colonialist adventure, even though the Balfour

Declaration was inconsistent with the terms of Article 22 and Article 23 of the Covenant. The latter article required the Members of the League to 'undertake to secure just treatment of the *native* inhabitants of territories under their control'.[113] It would be difficult to describe Jewish émigrés from Europe and Russia in the early twentieth century as 'native' to Palestine.

THE MANDATES, SOVEREIGNTY AND THE SACRED TRUST

The question of who had sovereignty over the mandates was a cause of controversy amongst international lawyers in the inter-war years.[114] Some scholars such as Hersch Lauterpacht thought sovereignty vested in the League; others, such as Quincy Wright thought that communities of an A-class mandate 'doubtless approach very close to sovereignty'; and yet others like Arnold McNair thought that sovereignty was in abeyance because it had no application to the mandates system.[115] Another view expressed by both Arab and Jewish scholars was that sovereignty was actually vested potentially in the peoples of an A-class mandate.[116] It is not necessary to dwell at length on these points, however, as it is generally recognised that upon the relinquishment of the mandate, sovereignty would automatically vest in the people of the territories concerned regardless of where it was located prior to the territory's independence.[117]

In contrast, there was no such controversy over the term a 'sacred trust of civilization' which was a device borrowed from Anglo-Saxon common law.[118] Great Britain, as the mandatory power, had undertaken to act 'on behalf of the League' in a capacity akin to a fiduciary.[119] In other words, Britain was arguably vested with fiduciary duties in relation to the beneficiaries of this trust who were the indigenous peoples of Palestine. Inherent in the notion of a 'sacred trust' is the principle that the fiduciary must not profit from its position and must not allow personal interest to prevail over the duty owed to the principal (in this case, the League).[120] A fiduciary must also act in good faith and not place itself in a position where its duty and its interest may conflict.[121] Although not entirely analogous to the concept of trusts in English equity, the British and American lawyers who drafted the Covenant were greatly influenced by the trust concept in their own legal systems.[122] And although the trust was not a tool common to civil law countries, there was nothing original in the concept of a mandate, which traced its origins to Roman law.[123] As Sir Arnold McNair, the British judge on the International Court of Justice wrote in his Separate Opinion on the *International Status of South-West Africa*:

> Nearly every legal system possesses some institution whereby the property (and sometimes the persons) of those who are not *sui juris* ... can be entrusted to some responsible person as a trustee or *tuteur* or *curateur*. The Anglo-American trust serves this purpose, and another purpose even more closely akin to the Mandates system, namely, the vesting of property in trustees, and its management by them in order that the public or some class

> of the public may derive benefit or that some public service may be served. The trust has frequently been used to protect the weak and the dependent, in cases where there is 'great might on the one side and unmight on the other', and the English courts have for many centuries pursued a vigorous policy in the administration and enforcement of trusts.[124]

An early proponent of a system similar to that of the mandates was Francisco de Vitoria, a professor of theology at the University of Salamanca, who is widely regarded as one of the founding fathers of modern international law. Writing 40 years after the discovery of the Americas by Christopher Columbus, Vitoria noted in his classic *De Indis et De Jure Belli* that the sovereigns of sixteenth-century Spain could, in their own interests, undertake the administration of Indian territories by providing them with prefects, governors and lords for their towns 'so long as this was clearly for their benefit [that is, for the benefit of the Indians]'.[125] He cautioned that 'any such interposition' in the lives of the natives should be for their welfare and interests 'and not merely for the profit of the Spaniards'.[126] In this respect, the Dutch jurist Hugo Grotius, who is also credited as one of the founding fathers of modern international law, agreed with Vitoria. 'Surely it is a heresy', he wrote,

> to believe that infidels are not masters of their own property; consequently to take from their possessions on account of their religious belief is no less theft and robbery than it would be in the case of Christians. Vitoria then is right in arguing that the Spaniards have no more *legal right* over the East Indians because of their religion than the Indians would have over the Spaniards if they happened to be the first foreigners to come to Spain.[127]

In other words there was no principle of international law, provided in the mandates or in custom, which allowed a nation to expropriate the properties of another people on account of their colour, race or religion – for this would be tantamount to theft. Ultimately, the mandate was a compromise between progress towards a decolonisation process and the manifestation of imperial rule over peoples not yet able to govern themselves.[128] As Lord McNair wrote in his preface to the English translation of Norman Bentwich's 1929 Hague Academy of International Law lecture[129] on mandates:

> It is unthinkable that a large part of the population of the world should remain in permanent subjection to a section of the other part, merely because their colour is different or their political experience is at present inferior. The Mandate system points the road to their ultimate emancipation, and so rapidly is the development of some races that have habitually been regarded as 'backward' that this goal may in many cases be reached sooner than some of us think.[130]

Although decolonisation was not explicitly referred to in the Covenant, the overall concept behind Article 22 could be regarded as the first manifestation of the ultimate goal to abrogate the colonial systems that were still being pursued by many European states at the time.[131] After all it is arguable that the mandate system – just as the UN Charter system – did not explicitly promote continued or new colonial power. And it was the idea underlying the concept of the mandate and its 'sacred trust' that would eventually work its way into the Trusteeship System of the United Nations.

THE BALFOUR DECLARATION AND THE MANDATE

It will be recalled that the Balfour Declaration was incorporated in a letter addressed to Lord Rothschild concerning a national home for the Jewish people, which merely conveyed a promise from the British Government to a private British subject as to the course of future British policy in Palestine.[132] Although under international law, declarations made by way of unilateral acts can produce legal obligations, this is only so if it is the intention of the state making the declaration that it should become bound according to its terms.[133] Usually, this intention is specific and expressed clearly and precisely.[134] In this respect, it may be questioned whether Britain gave an undertaking to be bound by the Balfour Declaration in November 1917, especially since His Majesty's Government only viewed 'with favour the establishment in Palestine of a national home for the Jewish people', and only agreed to use its 'best endeavours' to achieve this objective. In contrast when it came to the civil and religious rights of the 'existing non-Jewish communities in Palestine', the British Government wanted it to be 'clearly understood that nothing shall be done' which may prejudice their rights. In other words, the promise to establish a Jewish national home was made *conditional* upon safeguarding the civil and religious rights of the indigenous population of Palestine.

Although the Balfour Declaration would subsequently be incorporated into the second preambular paragraph of the Mandate of Palestine and referred to in Article 2, it was not cast in imperative terms, only requiring that Great Britain as the mandatory 'should be responsible for putting into effect the [Balfour] declaration'.

> ... Whereas the Principal Allied Powers have also agreed that the Mandatory *should* be responsible for putting into effect the declaration originally made on November 2nd, 1917, by the Government of His Britannic Majesty, and adopted by the said Powers, in favour of the establishment in Palestine of a national home for the Jewish people, *it being clearly understood* that nothing should be done which might prejudice the civil and religious rights of *existing non-Jewish communities in Palestine*, or the rights and political status enjoyed by Jews in any other country; and
>
> Whereas recognition has thereby been given to the historical connection of the Jewish people with Palestine and to the grounds for reconstituting their national home in that country;
>
> ...

> *Article 2*
>
> The Mandatory shall be responsible for placing the country under such political, administrative and economic conditions as will secure the establishment of the Jewish national home, as laid down in the preamble, and the development of self-governing institutions, and also for safeguarding the civil and religious rights of *all the inhabitants of Palestine*, irrespective of race and religion.[135]

It is noteworthy that the safeguard clauses protecting Palestine's indigenous population are mentioned in both the preamble as well as in Article 2 and they were also mentioned in the original Balfour Declaration. Moreover, whereas the preamble speaks of 'existing non-Jewish communities' in Palestine, Article 2 widens this to safeguard the rights of 'all the inhabitants of Palestine, irrespective of race and religion'. What did these additional words mean? Under a Privy Council ruling in a case on appeal from the Supreme Court of Palestine, it was held that these additional words meant that 'the Mandatory shall not discriminate in favour of persons of any one religion or race'.[136] In other words, the full powers of legislation granted to the mandatory in Article 1 of the Mandate could not be used to pass legislation that would discriminate between Palestine's Jewish and non-Jewish inhabitants.

THE JEWISH NATIONAL HOME

The term 'a Jewish national home', as employed in the preamble and in Article 2 of the Mandate did not imply that Britain intended to establish a Jewish state in Palestine.[137] If the British Government had intended to create a Jewish state, then presumably they would have used terminology that would not cause confusion. This is because it is a canon of statutory interpretation that in legal drafting, the legislature or in this case, the state concerned which was Britain, uses English words in their ordinary senses and that if a particular word has been used it cannot be disregarded or be given a totally different meaning.[138] As Ernst Frankenstein, a professor at the Hague Academy of International Law, writing in 1948, noted in an article he published in the first and only volume of *The Jewish Yearbook of International Law*: 'Logically ... a national home appears to be an equivalent for State. But the very fact that it was found necessary to create the new term indicates that a national home is not a State but something less than a State.'[139] Moreover, it is a well-established rule of customary international law that a treaty is to be interpreted in good faith in accordance with the ordinary meaning to be given to the terms of the treaty in its context and in the light of its object and purpose.[140] This is a rule of international law regarding the interpretation of treaties, which dates back to at least the nineteenth century.[141] In its ordinary meaning a 'home' cannot possibly be synonymous with a state, even if it is called a 'national home'. For since when was a 'home' a 'state' for the purposes of international law? According to the minutes of a meeting of the

War Cabinet when they were discussing the terms of the Balfour Declaration it meant an international protectorate where 'full facilities would be given to the Jews to work out their own salvation and to build up, by means of education, agriculture, and industry, a real centre of national culture and a focus of national life'.[142] This did not necessarily involve the establishment of a Jewish state although it was envisaged that such a state could be created at some point in the future.[143]

Even if the 'Jewish national home' really meant a 'Jewish state', as the Zionists sought to interpret it, the declaration provided that it would be established in Palestine, not instead of Palestine.[144] This meant that even if the Zionists were entitled to create a state at some point in the future, that state could only be created in a part of Palestine. It could not be created in place of Palestine or involve the subordination of its Arab population. Therefore, if the envisaged 'home' were to become a state at some point in the future, it would have to be either a bi-national state or a state in only a part of Palestine, whilst being subject to the safeguard clauses mentioned above.[145] In other words, the envisaged Jewish state could not discriminate between Jews and non-Jews or harm the latter's civil and religious rights. This is important to emphasise because the safeguard clauses were specifically added by the British War Cabinet to the text which had initially been drafted by the Zionist Organisation when they were considering various drafts of a declaration in October 1917.[146] The original draft of what would become the Balfour Declaration, was written by the Political Committee of the Zionist Organisation and handed over to Balfour on 18 July 1917:

> His Majesty's Government, after considering the aims of the Zionist Organization, accept the principle of recognizing Palestine as the National Home of the Jewish people and the right of the Jewish people to build up its national life in Palestine under a protection to be established at the conclusion of peace, following upon the successful issue of the war.
>
> His Majesty's Government regard as essential for the realization of this principle the grant of internal autonomy to the Jewish nationality in Palestine, freedom of immigration for Jews, and the establishment of a Jewish National Colonizing Corporation for the re-establishment and economic development of the country.
>
> The conditions and forms of the internal autonomy and a Charter for the Jewish National Colonizing Corporation should, in the view of His Majesty's Government, be elaborated in detail and determined with the representatives of the Zionist Organization.[147]

The idea of a colonising corporation was not a novel phenomenon.[148] They had existed in Africa, the East Indies, India, and North America and had the power to acquire, retain and govern territory.[149] However, the Zionists were not going to get their Jewish National Colonising Corporation. In fact, Weizmann was very disappointed with the final draft of the Balfour

Declaration because it was a far cry from what the Zionists were asking for. It made no mention of a Jewish National Colonising Corporation. Nor did it provide for the *right* of the Jewish people to establish Palestine as *the* National Home. Moreover, it included the two safeguard clauses protecting indigenous rights and the rights of Jews in other countries. In his memoirs, Weizmann described this as a 'painful recession'.[150] He was particularly perturbed by the inclusion of the clause safeguarding the civil and religious rights of existing non-Jewish communities in Palestine because he thought it would 'imute [*sic*] possible oppressive intentions to the Jews' and could be 'interpreted to mean such limitations on our work as completely to cripple it'.[151]

The first safeguard clause regarding indigenous rights was inserted due to a memorandum submitted by Curzon to the cabinet at the eleventh hour in which he expressed his opinion that Palestine was already inhabited by a half a million Arabs who 'will not be content either to be expropriated for Jewish immigrants or to act merely as hewers of wood or drawers of water for the latter'.[152] He added that the most that could be done would be 'to secure to the Jews (but not to the Jews alone) equal civil and religious rights with the other elements of the population'.[153] In other words, by inserting the safeguard clause at Curzon's suggestion, it was never agreed that the Palestine's indigenous Arab population did not have political rights on a par with the Jews. It was quite to the contrary. Jewish immigration into Palestine was to be encouraged but not at the Arabs' expense. Rather, it was thought that the latter would actually benefit from the national home policy. The second clause safeguarding Jewish rights was inserted because Montagu argued that his home was Britain rather than Palestine, that most English-born Jews were opposed to Zionism, and that the declaration was anti-Semitic.[154]

The only other precedent for the 'national home' terminology was in the case of the debates at the Lausanne Peace Conference in 1922 over the Armenian question.[155] There the British Government was presented with letters and memoranda from 'La Ligue Internationale Philarménienne', the British Armenia Committee and the Armenia American Society asking for action to be taken at the Lausanne Peace Conference to create a national home for the Armenian people, and to protect minorities in Turkey.[156] However, at the conference, Turkey was not persuaded and the Treaty of Lausanne made no provision for the Armenian National Home.[157] Similarly, negotiations for establishing autonomy for the Assyrian Christians within Turkey also failed to get anywhere at Lausanne.[158] However, there was one noticeable exception to this. In 1928, the Soviet Union set aside an area called Birobidzhan in the Soviet Far East for a Jewish homeland as an alternative to Palestine where Russian Jews were encouraged to settle.[159] In 1934, it was officially set aside as the Jewish Autonomous Region, which still exists today.[160]

Reading through the *travaux préparatoires* of what would become the British Mandate for Palestine that was drafted in the years 1919–22, it seems evident that the word 'state' was deliberately avoided by the Zionists, as they must have been aware that they had no chance of getting that word included in the draft.[161] This would explain why in early drafts of the Mandate the Zionists wanted to include the phrase: 'The *reconstitution* of Palestine as *the* national home.'[162] And during the negotiations over the terms of the Mandate, they hoped the High Contracting Parties would 'recognise the historic *title* of the Jewish people to Palestine'.[163] However they were unsuccessful with these endeavours, as the final draft of the Mandate only mentioned the words 'establishment' and 'a national home' when recalling the Balfour Declaration in the preamble, and merely recognised 'the historical connexion [note, not title] of the Jewish people with Palestine and to the grounds for reconstituting their national home *in* that country'.[164] Curzon, who was Britain's Foreign Minister when the Mandate was being drafted, said that he 'objected to the phrase [the reconstitution of Palestine as the national home] in toto'. He minuted one of his colleagues in the Foreign Office, saying: 'I do not myself recognise that the connection of the Jews with Palestine, which terminated 1200 [*sic*] years ago, gives them any claim whatsoever. On this principle we have a stronger claim to parts of France. I would omit the phrase.'[165] It would be difficult to describe the phrase that eventually found its way into the Mandate – '[w]hereas recognition has thereby been given to the historical connexion of the Jewish people with Palestine and to the grounds for reconstituting their national home in that country' – as a declaration of statehood or a promise to provide the Zionists with a basis to establish a state immediately. If such a state were to be created, it had to be accomplished progressively, and subject to the safeguard clauses protecting the civil and religious rights of the Palestine Arabs. As Professor Ernst Frankenstein of the Hague Academy noted: '... the Jews were given their National Home instead of a State precisely because there were others in the country. It was felt that the non-Jewish inhabitants of Palestine had to be protected against the possible consequences of a wide construction of the term "National Home".'[166] In correspondence with Field-Marshall Viscount Allenby, Curzon wrote that although the Balfour Declaration had been endorsed by the Allied and Associated Powers at the Paris Peace Conference, it did not contemplate 'the flooding of Palestine with Jewish immigrants', nor 'spoliation or eviction of the present landowners in Palestine'.[167] Furthermore, rather than Palestine being reconstituted as the national home, as the Zionists desired, the national home was to be reconstituted *in* Palestine. As is clear from the *travaux*, Curzon was adamantly opposed to the creation of a Jewish state in Palestine and was of the opinion that what was promised at San Remo, where the Balfour Declaration was incorporated into the Treaty of Sèvres, which was never ratified, 'was far from constituting anything in the nature of a legal claim'.[168]

It would therefore seem from its plain and ordinary meaning that the declaration envisaged granting the 'Jewish people' the right to participate in the affairs of the country specifically affecting the interests of the Jewish population subject to laws and regulations of Palestine. Hence in early drafts of the Mandate, the Zionists desired 'the creation of an autonomous commonwealth'.[169] But even this was restricted by Article 3 of the Mandate, which provided that, 'The Mandatory shall, *so far as circumstances permit*, encourage local autonomy.' In his White Paper of 1922, Winston Churchill, then Secretary of State for the Colonies provided an authoritative interpretation of what was meant by the phrase 'the development of the Jewish National Home in Palestine'. According to the Paper, this was

> not the imposition of a Jewish nationality upon the inhabitants of Palestine as a whole, but the further development of the existing Jewish community, with the assistance of Jews in other parts of the world, in order that it may become a centre in which the Jewish people as a whole may take, on grounds of religion and race, an interest and a pride.[170]

Churchill made it clear that the British Government 'never contemplated, at any time, the disappearance or the subordination of the Arabic population, language or culture in Palestine'.[171] After all, as he pointed out, the Balfour Declaration did not contemplate that 'Palestine as a whole should be converted into a Jewish National Home, but that such a Home should be founded in Palestine.'[172]

Britain had also proposed to establish an Arab agency in Palestine which was to occupy a position exactly analogous to that accorded to the Jewish agency under Article 4 of the Mandate. That is, to be recognised as a public body for the purpose of advising and cooperating with the administration of Palestine in such economic, social and other matters as may affect the interests of the non-Jewish population, and, subject to the control of the administration, of assisting and taking part in the development of the country.[173] However, this offer was unanimously declined by the Arab leaders of the day on the grounds that 'the Arabs, having never recognised the status of the Jewish Agency, have no desire for the establishment of an Arab Agency on the same basis'.[174] Britain also attempted to create a semi-elected Legislative Council composed of the High Commissioner as President, and of 22 members, ten of whom were British officials, and twelve elected members which would include two Jews.[175] However, the Arabs rejected this offer because they contended that it would not be representative of the Palestinian people because it included nominated British officials.[176] They argued that to participate in any council, no matter what its form, would indicate on their part an acceptance of the Mandate and the Constitution, which they declined to accept.[177] Under the proposed Legislative Council the elected members would have no powers and so it could at any time be outvoted by the Government and by Jewish votes.

ANTI-SEMITISM AND BRITISH SUPPORT FOR ZIONISM

In early 1915, Herbert Samuel MP submitted the first of two memoranda to the Cabinet entitled 'The Future of Palestine'. With Britain's declaration of war against Turkey on 5 November 1914, Samuel realised that in the aftermath of a British victory, the Zionists had an opportune moment to put their plans into place. They just needed to persuade the British Government to support them. In the first memorandum Samuel suggested that the British

Empire annex Palestine with a view to encouraging it to be colonised by the Zionists so that in time they could be granted self-government there. 'Jewish immigration, carefully regulated, would be given preference so that in the course of time the Jewish people, grown into a majority and settled in the land, may be conceded such a degree of self-government as the conditions of that day may justify.'[178] He appealed to the strategic advantages of annexing Palestine, its proximity to Egypt and the Suez Canal, as well as its importance to the traditional Protestant sympathies being home to the Christian Holy Places. He then conceded that whilst Palestine alone could not solve the Jewish Question in Europe, it could, in time, hold 3–4 million Jews so that some relief could be given 'to the pressure in Russia and elsewhere'.[179] By 'elsewhere', Samuel was most probably alluding to America and Britain. He concluded:

> Let a Jewish centre be established in Palestine; let it achieve, as I believe it would achieve, a spiritual and intellectual greatness; and insensibly, but inevitably, the character of the individual Jew, wherever he might be, would be ennobled. The sordid associations attached to the Jewish name would be sloughed off, and the value of the Jews as an element in civilisation of the European peoples would be enhanced.[180]

In March, Samuel circulated a revised version of his memorandum which gave greater consideration to the strategic and *realpolitik* considerations in favour of a British protectorate over Palestine.[181] It still, however, made the connection between the Jewish Question and Palestine: 'A country the size of Wales, much of it barren mountain and part of it waterless, cannot hold 9,000,000 people. But it could probably hold in time 3,000,000 and some relief would be given to the pressure in Russia and elsewhere.'[182] However, initial reactions to Samuel's suggestions were cool. In a letter to Venetia Stanley, of whom Prime Minister Herbert Asquith was very fond, he confided:

> I think I told you that H Samuel had written an almost dithyrambic memorandum urging that in the carving up of the Turks Asiatic dominions, we should take Palestine, into which the scattered Jews cd. in time swarm back from all quarters of the globe, and in due course obtain Home Rule. (What an attractive community!) Curiously enough, the only other partisan of this proposal is Lloyd George, who, I need not say, does not care a damn about the Jews or their past or their future, but who thinks it would be an outrage to let the Christian Holy Places ... pass into the possession or under the protection of 'Agnostic Atheistic France'! Isn't it singular that the same conclusion shd. be capable of being come to by such different roads?[183]

When Herbert Samuel was the Home Secretary in 1916, he was faced with a serious controversy with Britain's Russian Jewish immigrant community who refused to enlist in the British Army to fight alongside Russia, the country they fled, against Germany.[184] Out of a total of 70,000 Russian Jews who were eligible for military service, only 700 volunteered.[185] Samuel was in an untenable position and had little choice but to threaten them with the prospect of enforced conscription for which he received praise from the *East London Observer*.[186] The newspaper congratulated Samuel for his firmness towards the Russian Jews whom it called 'parasites' and 'uninvited "guests" who have long outstayed their welcome'.[187] The paper then warned of the danger of disturbances: 'The misbehaviour of any offensive foreign bounder, or the impertinence of a Whitechapel Jew boy, may light the smouldering fires of native feeling.'[188] On 3 November 1916, the Cabinet approved of Samuel's proposals to pass legislation to bring the recalcitrant Jewish immigrants who refused military service 'within the sphere of the Military Services Acts'.[189] If anti-Semitism was this widespread amongst the general public in Britain during the First World War, then it is perhaps not so surprising that their elected representatives in Parliament, including Prime Minister Asquith, Balfour and Lloyd George, with the exception of its Jewish members, must have also thought like them. It must have been a harrowing experience for Samuel and entrenched his Zionism.[190]

So perhaps it was no surprise that when he was appointed to the position of High Commissioner in Palestine in July 1920, Samuel accepted it with joy and went about avidly laying the foundations that would ultimately lead to the establishment of a Jewish state in Palestine.[191] The British Government appointed Norman Bentwich, who was related to Samuel, and who was also a Zionist, to the position of Attorney General.[192] In an article published in the *American Jewish Chronicle*, Bentwich was described as 'the son of the well-known English Zionist leader, Herbert Bentwich, the father-in-law of Dr. Israel Friedlander'.[193] The article said that he had been 'affiliated with the Zionist movement since its inception'.[194] Bentwich was not, however, devoid of controversy. He had already been singled out for specific criticism by Edwin Montagu because of a statement he made to a journalist in 1909 in which he said that a British Jew cannot be as entirely English 'as the man who is born of English parents and descended from ancestors who have mingled their blood with other Englishmen for generations'.[195] In view of the fact that the British Government was appointing well-known Zionists to positions of prominence in Palestine, which would give them a substantial say in the operation of the government and the judiciary, it was somewhat unsurprising that most of these measures and political appointments were opposed by the indigenous inhabitants, the Palestine Arabs, who, fearful of Zionist aspirations, resisted intellectually, economically and often violently.[196] A typical example of a British appointee and Zionist sympathiser was Colonel Richard Meinertzhagen, the Chief Political Officer in Palestine, who was working for the Egyptian Expeditionary Force. In September 1919, he wrote a letter to Lord Allenby, in which he expressed some extreme opinions:

General Headquarters,
Egyptian Expeditionary Force,
Cairo.
26.9.1919

My Lord,

I have the honour to submit some observations on the state of Zionism as I find it at present in Palestine.

As the value of any opinion on controversial matter is enhanced by a knowledge of the personal leanings of the informent, I wish to make my own position vis-à-vis Zionism perfectly clear.

My inclination towards Jews in general is governed by an anti-Semitic instinct which is invariably modified by personal contact. My views on Zionism are those of an ardent Zionist. The reasons which induced in me a fascination for Zionism are many and complex, but in the main were governed by the unsatisfactory state of the Jews of the world, the great sentimental attraction of re-establishing a race after banishment of 2,000 years, which is not without its scientific interest, and the conviction that Jewish brains and money could, when backed by such a potent idea as Zionism, give to Palestine that impetus in industrial development which it so sorely needs after lying fallow since the beginning of the world...

My first introduction to Zionism was in 1917 when I met the Aaronshon family and visited the Zionist colonies of south Palestine. My close relation with Zionism since that date and an established friendship with many of the Zionist leaders in Paris and London have only increased my respect for Zionism and all that it means.

I do not therefore approach Zionism in Palestine with an open mind, but as one highly prejudiced in its favour ...

It has been well known in Paris and London for some months past that there is strong local opposition to Zionism in Syria and Palestine, which is frequently being voiced by nearly all communities and classes. Neither is such opposition entirely confined to non-official elements. The reasons underlying such opposition are varied and spring from many sources, but they are mainly traceable to a deliberate misunderstanding of the Jew and everything Jewish – this in its turn is based on contact with the local Jew, the least representative of Jewry or Zionism ...

All non-Zionist feeling in Palestine also views with alarm the question of immigration, which is regarded as the unlimited dumping of undesirable Jews from Eastern Europe.

The acknowledged superiority of Jewish brains and money forces landowners and businessmen to realize their impotence to withstand eventual eviction, and they look on Zionism as synonymous with complete Jewish control and possession of land and industrial development in Palestine. The Jew is regarded as a parasite among Nations, indigestible to his host, and therefore scarcely able to assimilate himself to Nationhood.

The Moslem element in Palestine is also inclined to direct its antagonism to Zionism along fanatical channels – cries out against the minority ruling the majority and strongly resents a policy being imposed on Palestine against the wishes of the majority.

It is not therefore difficult to understand that in Palestine every man's hand is against Zionism ...

I have the honour to be, etc.

(sgd) R. Meinertzhagen
Colonel.[197]

In this regard it is intriguing that Meinertzhagen viewed Zionism and anti-Semitism as synonymous, just as Herzl predicted. The Zionists with whom Meinertzhagen was personally acquainted must have realised this as well. It is noteworthy that the Jews who were already living in Palestine were not considered 'good Zionists'. In Meinertzhagen's words, the local Jew was 'the least representative of Jewry or Zionism'. Of course, Meinertzhagen's views may not have reflected the sentiment of his colleagues. But then, A.J. Balfour, Lloyd George, and Mark Sykes, the latter a strict Roman Catholic, who, like Robert Lansing, would have believed in deicide, and who had told a friend of his that he had his writings suppressed by the censorship in Palestine,[198] all had very strange views of the Jews generally. They also all considered themselves to be Zionists.

It was Mark Sykes who sought out the Zionists and who started the negotiations that would lead to the Balfour Declaration, which has been described as one of the greatest mistakes in British imperial history.[199] Nahum Sokolow, the leader of the Zionist Organisation, recalled that Sykes was instrumental in nurturing the Zionist cause. 'For more than two whole years we were in daily intercourse with him', he wrote.[200] When Sokolow went to Rome in April 1917, Sykes, he noted, had been there before him:

> ... [Sykes] could not wait my arrival. He had gone to the East. I put up at the hotel. Sykes had ordered rooms for me. I went to the British Embassy. Letters and instructions from Sykes were waiting for me. Then I went to the Italian Government offices. Sykes had been there too. Then to the Vatican, where Sykes had again prepared my way. It seemed to me as if his presence was wherever I went, but all the time he was far away in Arabia, whence I received telegraphic messages.[201]

This is a rather poetic way of saying that the British Government had adopted Zionism and not vice versa.[202] In Sokolow's own words: 'Until November [Sykes] was arranging the preliminaries to the Balfour Declaration ... everything had to pass through Sykes's hands.'[203] And yet Sykes, brought up a strict Roman Catholic, was suspicious of the Jews, as was his mother, who blamed Jewish financiers for being behind the Boer War.[204] In a letter to C.P. Scott of the *Manchester Guardian*, Edward Granville Browne, Britain's foremost academic authority on the Middle East, who was Adams Professor of Arabic at Cambridge University, wrote that Sykes, one of his former students, had learned nothing from him and 'sees Jews in everything'.[205] During the war, Sykes even made a propaganda film called *The Hidden Hand*, a term associated with international conspiracy theories for world Jewish domination.[206] So what did Sykes, the anti-Semite see in Zionism? In a memorandum addressed to the cabinet written in 1917, Sykes drew a distinction between the assimilated Jew who, in his view, was Westernised and who cared more for Karl Marx and socialism and the Zionists who Sykes looked upon more favourably because they wanted to recreate their homeland in the land of their ancestors through colonisation under British tutelage 'with privileges equal to the various religious and racial nationalities in the country'.[207] With regards to Sykes's views towards Zionism and Palestine, a most peculiar passage appears in a book entitled *Mark Sykes: His Life and Letters* published posthumously after Sykes succumbed to the Spanish flu epidemic in Paris in 1919, and in which Winston Churchill MP wrote the introduction:

> In his last months and in his death he became closely associated with Zionism. Before the war he had disliked it as 'bad cosmopolitanism and finance' ... It was his Catholicism which assisted Mark to understand the Jewish tragedy. He was interested in the ethos of the real Hebrew, not in the Anglicized Jew ...
>
> The Sephardim of Salonica, driven out of Spain, instinctively supported Turkey against Russia. Russia fell, and *Mark felt that the problems of Palestine and the Jewish question could be solved together if Zionism tended to draw the Salonica Jews out of the Ottoman rut*. He decided that there was room for a Jewish as well as an Arab nationality.[208]

As described in Chapter 1, it was Theodor Herzl who had first suggested to Lord L.W. Rothschild and the British Government before the Royal Commission on Alien Immigration in 1902 that sending the Jews to Palestine was one way of solving Britain's 'immigration problem', something he repeated to Joseph Chamberlain and Lord Cromer in conversation as recorded in his personal diaries for creating a Jewish homeland in the Sinai.[209] In 1906, Nahum Sokolow received a letter from Lord Robert Cecil (who, as the Parliamentary Under-Secretary of State for Foreign Affairs, would later be involved in the negotiations over the Balfour Declaration) in which he wrote: 'The central idea underlying the Zionist movement seems to me worthy of all our support. Apart from all other considerations, it appears to me that the restoration of the Jewish nation offers a satisfactory solution, if it can be accomplished, *of those problems raised by Jewish emigration*, which are otherwise very difficult of adjustment.'[210] The link between Zionism, alien immigration, the Jewish Question, and the British Empire was also suggested by Herbert Samuel in the two memoranda he had drafted in 1915 and presented to the cabinet which had been dismissed by Asquith in his letter to Venetia Stanley. In 1916, Asquith's Government fell and Lloyd George became Prime Minister. It was

Lloyd George who drafted the Jewish colonisation scheme for East Africa in 1903, A.J. Balfour, appointed Foreign Minister by Lloyd George, whose government passed the Aliens Act in 1905 restricting Jewish immigration into Britain, and it was Herbert Samuel who introduced Mark Sykes to Zionism.[211] Then there was Gerald Fitzmaurice (not to be confused with the international lawyer of the same name), who as the First Dragoman and adviser on oriental affairs at the British Embassy in Istanbul, and who attended the same Jesuit public school (Beaumont College) as Sykes, thought that the Committee of Union and Progress, or the Young Turkey Party, was part of a Jewish Freemason network that sought to take control of the Ottoman Empire.[212] 'The Oriental Jew is an adept at manipulating occult forces', Sir Gerard Lowther, the British Ambassador in Istanbul, wrote to the Foreign Office heeding Fitzmaurice's advice.[213] If Sykes also shared the same prejudices as his friend Fitzmaurice and viewed the Salonica Jews as subversive, because of their alleged role in the 1908–09 Turkish revolution, then sending them to Palestine where they would be taught to be 'good Hebrews' under British tutelage would most probably have been viewed in a favourable light.

Further support for the view that creating a Jewish home in Palestine was seen as a form of Anglo-Saxon 'immigration control', a potential solution to the Jewish Question, and preserving Empire from revolutionary movements, is provided by the extracts from a conversation between A.J. Balfour and Justice Louis Brandeis of the US Supreme Court at the Paris Peace Conference in 1919, the notes of which were taken down by Felix Frankfurter, who was then a young Professor at Harvard Law School:

> Mr. Balfour expressed great satisfaction that Justice Brandeis came to Europe. He said the Jewish problem (of which the Palestinian question is only a fragment but an essential part) is to his mind as perplexing a question as any that confronts the statesmanship of Europe. He is exceedingly distressed by it and harassed by its difficulties. Mr. Balfour rehearsed summarily the pressure on Jews in Eastern Europe and said that the problem was, of course, complicated by the extra-ordinary phenomenon that Jews now are not only participating in revolutionary movements but are actually, to a large degree, leaders in such movements. He stated that a well informed person told him only the other day that Lenin also on his mother's side was a Jew.
>
> Justice Brandeis stated that he had every reason to believe that this is not so and that Lenin on both sides is an upper class Russian. He continued to say that after all this is a minor matter, that all that Mr. Balfour said was quite so. He believes every Jew is potentially an intellectual and an idealist and the problem is one of direction of those qualities. He narrated his own approach to Zionism, that he came to it wholly as an American, for his whole life had been free from Jewish contacts or traditions. *As an American he was confronted with the disposition of the vast number of Jews, particularly Russian Jews, that were pouring into the United States year by year.* It was then that by chance a pamphlet on Zionism came his

> way and led him to the study of the Jewish problem and to the conviction that Zionism was the answer.[214]

This extract seems to confirm both Balfour's anti-Semitism, the Jews being responsible for the Russian Revolution because Lenin and others allegedly had Jewish roots, and that in Zionism both he and Brandeis saw in it a solution to the Jewish Question and a way of stemming the flow of Jewish immigration into their own countries.

It was in the context of British prejudices and widespread anti-Semitism that the British Government was to be deluded into thinking that a declaration favouring Zionism would, in addition to providing a solution to the Jewish Question, 'secure for the Entente the aid of Jewish financial interests' and 'greatly influence American opinion in favour of the Allies'.[215] Apparently, it was said that after the fall of Romania the Allies were so concerned about the attitude of Jews in neutral countries who were anti-Russian, that they issued the Balfour Declaration 'to prevent the incalculable and universal influence of Jewry being exerted on the side of the Central Powers'.[216] According to this view, Britain wanted 'to transfer this highly important influence to the cause of the Entente'.[217] Many academics writing in the inter-war years took at face value the claims that a mythical body, represented by 'international Jewry', had the power to assist the war effort by bringing the United States into the war on Britain's side, and by preventing Russia from leaving that war.[218] Other reasons adduced for Britain's alliance with the Zionists include the effects of the Russian revolution in November 1917[219] which had weakened the struggle against Germany in the East, and that the Germans were about to transfer divisions from the Russian to the Western front before American troops could reach France.[220] Apparently, Britain also feared that if it did not issue a declaration of support for a Jewish national home in Palestine, Germany would, although in view of the Kaiser's alliance with the Ottoman Empire, in retrospect, this seems highly questionable.[221] It was also thought that a reliable Jewish presence in Palestine would be of use to the British Empire because of its strategic importance as the military gate to Egypt and the Suez Canal.[222] It has even been suggested that the religious persuasion of the British War Cabinet was a factor in motivating British sympathy for the Zionist aspirations.[223] But one of the most convincing explanations, in the short term, was that the British Government sincerely believed in the power of 'international Jewry' to foment revolutionary political change in Russia and Turkey, so much so, that having them 'on side' was considered necessary to win the war. Seen in this light, it has been argued that the Balfour Declaration was issued primarily to enable a global Zionist propaganda campaign to capture the support of world Jewry for the British war effort particularly in the United States.[224] And the British Zionists, led by Chaim Weizmann, were keenly aware of this and used it to their advantage. Indeed, when Weizmann met with William Yale, a Special Agent with the US State Department in the Near East, in 1919, he had by then caught on to the fact that fears of a Jewish conspiracy could work in the Zionists' favour. He told Yale that if

Britain did not support a national home for the Jews in Palestine, the Zionists would 'smash the British Empire as we smashed the Russian Empire'.[225] Of course, this was a fantastic claim. But Weizmann knew he had an audience to play to and that many statesmen believed in the myth that the Bolshevik revolution and the Turkish revolution were Jewish conspiracies to take over the world.[226] In addition to this, Zionism offered the prospect of diverting the steady stream of Russian Jewish immigration away from America and Britain towards Palestine which could provide a potential 'solution' to the Jewish Question as some British statesmen like Balfour hoped it would. Finally, a pliant Jewish community in Palestine grateful to Britain could aid that country with its 'civilising mission' in the Middle East and also act as a 'wedge' to counter French claims to the Holy Land at the Paris Peace Conference.

JEWISH OPPOSITION TO POLITICAL ZIONISM

However, not all was rosy. Herbert Samuel faced fervent opposition to his advocacy of uprooting millions of Jews from Europe and settling them in Palestine from his cousin Edwin Montagu, the Secretary of State for India (1917–22). Montagu was opposed to the Balfour Declaration because he thought that the effect of a Zionist policy would be anti-Semitic, and that Zionism was itself 'a mischievous political creed'.[227] In contrast to Samuel, Montagu did not agree that anti-Semitism was inevitable wherever Jews settled in large numbers. Nor did he believe that Zionism was the answer to the Jewish Question. On the contrary, he thought that Zionism was extremely dangerous because it would encourage the anti-Semites to view the Jews as foreign elements in their societies. He also had the foresight to warn his colleagues of the conflict that would arise between the Jews who settled in Palestine and its indigenous inhabitants. So zealous was Montagu's opposition to Zionism that he drafted three memoranda on the subject which he presented to the cabinet in as many months. In his first memorandum entitled 'The Anti-Semitism of the Present Government', Montagu wrote in his opening paragraph:

> I have chosen the above title for this memorandum, not in any hostile sense, not by any means as quarrelling with an anti-Semitic view which may be held by my colleagues, not with a desire to deny that anti-Semitism can be held by rational men, not even with a view to suggesting that the Government is deliberately anti-Semitic; but I wish to place on the record my view that the policy of His Majesty's Government is anti-Semitic in result and will prove a rallying ground for Anti-Semites in every country in the world.[228]

Montagu said that he had been prompted to write the memorandum after he received correspondence between Lord Rothschild and A.J. Balfour on Palestine being a Jewish national home. He felt that as he was 'the one Jewish Minister in the Government' that he may be allowed to express his views on the subject which he held very strongly. He then referred to the easing of restrictions on Jews in Russia and then waxed lyrical:

> ... at the very time when these Jews have been acknowledged as Jewish Russians and given all liberties, it seems to be inconceivable that Zionism should be officially recognised by the British Government, and that Mr. Balfour should be authorised to say that Palestine was to be reconstituted as the 'national home of the Jewish people.' I do not know what this involves, but I assume that it means that Mohammedans and Christians are to make way for the Jews, and that the Jews should be put in all positions of preference and should be peculiarly associated with Palestine in the same way that England is with the English or France with the French, that Turks and other Mahommedans [*sic*] in Palestine will be regarded as foreigners, just in the same way as Jews will hereafter be treated as foreigners in every country but Palestine. Perhaps also citizenship must be granted only as a result of a religious test.[229]

Montagu wrote this memorandum in August 1917 without the benefit of hindsight. Over the next three decades Jews were encouraged to relocate from many places in Europe and move to Palestine, thereby effectively becoming 'strangers' in their former countries of origin. And after Israel was created in 1948, which is described in Chapter 9, its legislature enacted a Law of Return which grants citizenship only to Jews, on the basis of *Halakha* (Jewish religious law), precisely as Montagu had predicted.[230] But this was not the only prescient observation Montagu made. He went on to set out four principles in the memorandum, the second of which makes rather prophetic reading:

> 2. When the Jews are told that Palestine is their national home, every country will immediately desire to get rid of its Jewish citizens, and you will find a population in Palestine driving out its present inhabitants, taking all the best in the country, drawn from all quarters of the globe ...[231]

Indeed, Montagu's fears were not unfounded. Only two years after he wrote this memorandum, the anti-Semitic Britons, which continued to publish English translations of the *Protocols of the Elders of Zion* as late as the 1970s,[232] was founded by Henry Hamilton Beamish who advocated removing all Jews from Britain, encouraging their 'return' to Palestine, and nationalising their property.[233] Indeed by 1920, and even before then, the ideas contained in the *Protocols* were gaining popularity with *The Spectator* (of London) going so far as to describe them as 'brilliant in (their) moral perversity and intellectual depravity' and as 'one of the most remarkable productions of their kind'.[234] The *Protocols* would not be exposed as a forgery until the following year by *The Times* newspaper,[235] and even then many people continued to peddle its falsehoods and myths.[236] In fact, throughout the 1920s and 1930s sales of the *Protocols* were astronomical – it was said to be the most widely distributed book in the world after the Bible.[237] In the 1917 edition of the *Protocols*, its

Russian author Sergyei Nilus added the following tract making a direct link between Zionism and a Jewish conspiracy to control the world which he claimed had been hatched up at the Zionist Congress in 1897:

> ... only now have I learned authoritatively from Jewish sources that these Protocols are nothing else than a strategic plan for the conquest of the world, putting it under the yoke of Israel, the struggle against God, a plan worked out by the leaders of the Jewish people during the many centuries of dispersion, and finally presented to the Council of Elders by 'The Prince of the Exile,' Theodor Herzl, at the time of the first Zionist Congress, summoned by him at Basel in August, 1897.[238]

Now of course there was no truth to this. But was it a coincidence that in the year in which Nilus added this passage, the British Government had been debating for months over whether to issue the Balfour Declaration? From the point of view of someone wanting to create fears of a Jewish conspiracy to take over the world an organised Jewish movement which had received the British Government's sympathy to create a 'home' in Palestine made a good story. It also provided fodder for the anti-Semites. Montagu was therefore right to fear its consequences. In this connection the following extract which appears in a book published by Henry Beamish sheds some light on the thought processes of a vicious anti-Semite and explains why Montagu so derided Balfour for coming out in favour of Zionism in 1917 because it would give ammunition to the anti-Semites:

> It is of vital importance that the Jews do not leave [Palestine] once they are established there, and for this purpose the 'League of Nations,' which at present is simply a Jew-devised and Jew-controlled affair, should be transformed into a 'League of *Christian* Nations,' and be given the task of seeing (1) that no Jew leaves the Promised Land; (2) that no Christian enters the country. Similar tactics as to segregation are being adopted in South Africa with regard to the Natives there, and in dealing with the Jews, nothing short of complete segregation will avert the menace, destroy the all-polluting International Finance, and permit the Christian races to live at peace with each other.[239]

Montagu's well-founded fears can only be understood in the social and political context of the times in which the Balfour Declaration was announced and its impact on furthering the causes of the anti-Semites within Britain and elsewhere. Hence it was hardly surprising that he wrote: 'I would be almost tempted to proscribe the Zionist organization as illegal and against the [British] national interest.'[240] Nor was Montagu a lone voice amongst Anglo Jewry. This is what he wrote in his third memorandum on the subject:

> 4. I have obtained a list of a few prominent anti-Zionists. It will be noticed that it includes every Jew who is prominent in public life, with the exception of the present Lord Rothschild, Mr. Herbert Samuel, and a few others.
>
> Dr. Israel Abrahams, M.A., University of Cambridge
> Sir Lionel Abrahams, K.C.B.
> Professor S. Alexander, M.A., University of Manchester
> D.L. Alexander, Esq., K.C., J.P.
> Captain O.E. d'Avigdor-Goldsmid
> Leonard L. Cohen, Esq.
> Robert Waley Cohen, Esq.
> Dr. A. Eicholz.
> S.H. Emanuel, Esq., B.A., Recorder of Winchester.
> Ernest L. Franklin, Esq.
> Professor I. Gollancz, M.A., Secretary of the British Academy
> Michael A. Green, Esq.
> P.J. Hartog, Esq., M.A., Registrar, University of London.
> Captain Evelyn de Rothschild, New Court, E.C.
> Major Lionel de Rothschild, New Court, E.C.
> Captain I. Salmon, L.C.C.
> Sir Harry S. Samuel, Bart.
> Edmund Sebag-Montefiore, Esq.
> Oswald J. Simon, Esq.
> Dr. Charles Singer, M.A., Ec., 33 Upper Brook Street, W.
> H.S.Q. Henriques, Esq., M.A.
> Sir Charles S. Henry, Bart., M.P.
> J.D. Israel. Esq.
> Benjamin Kisch, Esq.
> Rev. Ephraim Levine, M.A.
> Joshua M. Levy, Esq., Chairman of the Council, Jews' College.
> Major Laurie Magnus.
> Sir Philip Magnus, Bart., M.P.
> Sir Alfred Mond, M.P.
> C.G. Montefiore, Esq., M.A.
> A.R. Moro, Esq.
> Sir Matthew Nathan, G.C.M.G.
> J. Prag, Esq. J.P.
> The Right Hon. Viscount Reading, G.C.B, K.C.V.O.
> Captain Anthony de Rothschild, New Court, St. Swithin's Lane, E.C.
> Sir Isidore Spielman, C.M.G.
> Marion H. Spielmann, Esq.
> Meyer A. Spielman, Esq.
> Sir Edward D. Stern.
> Lord Swaythling.
> Philip S. Waley, Esq.
> Professor A. Wolf, M.A., University College, London
> Lucien Wolf, Esq.
> Albert M. Woolf, Esq.
>
> These are all men who lead an English life as well as acknowledging and rendering their services to their fellow-religionists in this country and abroad. They contain among them ultra-orthodox as well as certain heterodox Jews'.[241]

That Montagu felt compelled in his third and final memorandum to go to the length of actually compiling a list of prominent British Jews who were opposed to Zionism and the Balfour Declaration, is perhaps a sign that he knew he was facing a losing battle. As far as Balfour was concerned these British Jews were only a minority. The 'real' Jews, in Balfour's eyes – that is, the *Ostjuden* – were Zionists; and that, as far as he was concerned, was all that mattered. Zionism was going to have the British Government's sympathy.

However, the fact was that even amongst the *Ostjuden* Zionism had a small following. Balfour had been hoodwinked by Weizmann into thinking that Zionism was a bigger and more powerful movement amongst 'international Jewry' than it ever really was.

Of course not all British politicians were anti-Semitic or blind to the rift that a national home for the Jews in Palestine, however one understood it, would cause with its indigenous inhabitants. On 21 June 1922, a motion was passed in the House of Lords by a majority of 60 to 29 rejecting a mandate for Palestine that incorporated the Balfour Declaration.[242] Since the great majority of Palestine's indigenous inhabitants opposed Zionism, Lord Islington (John Poynder Dickinson), who served as Under-Secretary of State for India and the Colonies, urged that ratification be postponed until amendments were made annulling the Balfour Declaration.[243] The Motion provided:

> That the Mandate for Palestine in its present form is unacceptable to this House, because it directly violates the pledges made by His Majesty's Government to the people of Palestine in the Declaration of October, 1915, and again in the Declaration of November, 1918, and is, as at present framed, opposed to the sentiments and wishes of the great majority of the people of Palestine; that, therefore, its acceptance by the Council of the League of Nations should be postponed until such modifications have therein been effected as will comply with the pledges given by His Majesty's Government.[244]

The House of Lords non-binding motion was, however, 'signally overruled' by the Government of the day and consequently the British Mandate of Palestine included Balfour's pledge for a Jewish national home there.[245] Nevertheless, this was not the end of the matter as there was also opposition to British policy in Palestine in the House of Commons. Sir William Johnson-Hicks MP, who would go on to become the Home Secretary during the premiership of Stanley Baldwin, enquired whether there was such a thing as self-determination.[246] He asked the House: 'Surely you must ask the inhabitants of the country to let the Jews in as friends and neighbours, but not to lead ultimately to the establishment of a Jewish nation ultimately forming a Jewish commonwealth.'[247] He continued: '... if the Zionists are able to import thousands and thousands until they get a majority over the Arabs, the Arabs are entitled, in the first place, to say, "We represent 90 per cent of the population. We are entitled to self-determination ..."'[248]

In response to these murmurs of discontent, Winston Churchill, who seemed to be labouring under the impression that the Zionists' claim to be able to control the politics of both the United States and Russia had some credence, which as it turns out was not the case, reminded his colleagues of the reasons underlying British policy in Palestine:

> Pledges and promises were made during the War, and they were made, not only on the merits, though I think the merits are considerable. They were

> made because it was considered they would be of value to us in our struggle to win the War. It was considered that the support which the Jews could give us all over the world, and particularly in the United States, and also in Russia, would be a definite palpable advantage.[249]

If Churchill sincerely believed what he was saying to the House of Commons then he had fallen for the canard which Montagu had sought to dispel, and which the Zionists had played on – the myth that 'the Jews control the world'. Just because a few Jews were prominent in American society in the judiciary, such as Felix Frankfurter and Justice Louis Brandeis, being friendly with Woodrow Wilson and that many of the leaders of the Bolshevik revolution, such as Leon Trotsky, were Jewish, did not mean that they controlled the corridors of power or were necessarily pro-Zionist.[250] However, at the time the forged *Protocols* were thought to be genuine by many British statesmen and Churchill even received a copy.[251] We can never know whether he read the *Protocols* but its ideas certainly seemed to have made quite an impression on him. In an article he published in the *Illustrated Sunday Herald* on 8 February 1920 entitled 'Zionism versus Bolshevism', Churchill categorised Jews into 'Good and Bad Jews', 'National Jews', 'International Jews', and 'Terrorist Jews'.[252] Under the heading 'International Jews', Churchill wrote:

> In violent opposition to all this sphere of Jewish effort rise the schemes of the International Jews. The adherents of this sinister confederacy are mostly men reared up among the unhappy populations of countries where Jews are persecuted on account of their race. Most, if not all, of them have forsaken the faith of their forefathers, and divorced from their minds all spiritual hopes of the next world. This movement among the Jews is not new. From the days of Spartacus-Weishaupt to those of Karl Marx, and down to Trotsky (Russia), Bela Kun (Hungary), Rosa Luxembourg (Germany), and Emma Goldman (United States), this worldwide conspiracy for the overthrow of civilisation and for the reconstitution of society on the basis of arrested development, of envious malevolence, and impossible equality, has been steadily growing.[253]

Churchill saw in Zionism the Jewish answer to international communism and called on Jews in every country to come forward and assume a prominent role in combating the Bolshevik conspiracy. 'In violent contrast to international communism', Churchill wrote, '[Zionism] presents to the Jew a national idea of a commanding character.'[254] This was one of the reasons why the British Government, according to Churchill, came out in support of Zionism. But Churchill's views of the Jews did not pass without controversy. Indeed they sounded eerily similar to the *Protocols*. Hence it was hardly surprising that the *Jewish Chronicle* took strong objection to his article and subsequently published an editorial in which it condemned Churchill.[255] But if a man of the stature of Churchill could think like this, then what of other British politicians and diplomats? Did they too draw the false conclusions about the supposed link between 'good and bad Jews', 'international Jews', 'terrorist Jews' and the Bolshevik revolution? After all, had this 'worldwide Jewish conspiracy' not all been predicted in the *Protocols*? And were they not called the Elders of *Zion* as opposed to the Elders of Israel or the Elders of Jewry?[256] In 1919, Churchill made a speech in which he referred to the Hungarian Communist leader as 'Bela Kun or Bela Cohen', trying to draw a connection to his Jewish roots.[257] And when Prime Minister Lloyd George asked Churchill for his opinion concerning changes to his cabinet and the return of Herbert Samuel, he replied: '... there is a point about the Jews which occurs to me – you must not have too many of them'.[258] At that time it did not occur to Churchill and his contemporaries that the *Protocols* were a malicious and anti-Semitic document which had no basis whatsoever and would bring untold misery to millions of Jews once it got into Hitler's hands whose Nazi propaganda machine propagated it the world over.[259] In 1934, Nahum Sokolow even had to defend himself in a South African court to the charge that he and his fellow Zionists had concocted the whole plan behind the scenes at the first Zionist Congress in 1897.[260]

More pertinently, as regards the Palestine question, Churchill was forgetting that pledges and promises were also given to the Arabs in exchange for their actual material and logistical support in that war, and these were given two years *before* the Balfour Declaration was issued. Evidently, British policy must have therefore changed at some point, which may explain why it had to backtrack on its wartime pledges to the Arabs. However, at no time was it envisaged that the whole of Palestine was to be converted into a Jewish State. As the Minister for the Co-ordination of Defence noted in a memorandum he was instructed to draft for the Ministry of Defence when Britain was contemplating partitioning Palestine in the 1930s as part of its policy of imperial defence: '... the Balfour Declaration was not originally intended to provide for the conversion of Palestine from an Arab into a Jewish State, or to establish a policy which – as is now recognized – can only end in the suppression or eviction of its native population'.[261] It was partly because the British Government eventually came to recognise that the aims of the Balfour Declaration were essentially irreconcilable with the rights of the Arab population in a single Palestinian state, which led them to come out in favour of partition throughout the 1930s and 1940s. The fact was that Zionism was to provoke a violent reaction from the Palestinian Arabs, who saw it as an attempt by a group of foreign immigrants to take their country away from them. This reaction is the subject of the next chapter.

3
ARAB OPPOSITION TO POLITICAL ZIONISM

'The Palestinians desire their country for themselves and will resist any general immigration of Jews, however gradual, by every means in their power, including active hostilities ... A British mandate for Palestine on the lines of the Zionist programme will mean the indefinite retention in the country of a military force considerably greater than that now in Palestine.'

General Clayton to Lord Curzon, 5 May 1919, in Woodward and Butler (eds), *Documents on British Foreign Policy 1919–1939*, p. 272

'... any anti-British feeling on the part of the Arabs that may have arisen in the country originates in their association of the Government with the furtherance of the policy of Zionism'.

Palestine: Disturbances in May, 1921, *Reports of the Commission of Inquiry with Correspondence Relating Thereto*, p. 44

'In less than ten years three serious attacks have been made by Arabs on Jews. For eighty years before the first of these attacks there is no recorded instance of any similar incidents. It is obvious then that the relations between the two races during the past decade must have differed in some material respect from those which previously obtained.'

Report of the Commission on the Palestine Disturbances of August, 1929, in *Parliamentary Papers of Interest to the Foreign Office* (1930), p. 150

Traditionally, international law has recognised only five modes of acquiring territorial sovereignty.[1] These were (1) by an act of conquest or subjugation; (2) through accretion, which occurs when territory increases through a new formation such as where an island rises within the maritime belt; (3) by cession, when one state cedes its sovereignty to another state by agreement, usually undertaken through a treaty; (4) through occupation, not to be confused with belligerent occupation, which takes place where the territory subject to occupation is not under the sovereignty of another state; and (5) through prescription, according to which undisturbed possession can under certain conditions produce a title for the possessor, if the possession has lasted for some length of time. However, prescription would not apply in the face of protest and opposition.[2] Consequently, with the exception of conquest/subjugation, none of these modes of acquiring territory would be of assistance to the Zionist movement in acquiring sovereignty over Palestine unless a representative of the Palestinian people agreed to cede it to them. Since the Palestine Arabs never agreed to a treaty of cession during the Mandatory years, the Zionists could not have acquired sovereignty there through this mode.[3] Nor was Palestine ever *terra nullius*. Consequently, the only option available to the Zionists to acquire territorial sovereignty over Palestine was to conquer it, as described in Chapters 7 and 9.

This chapter traces the roots of Palestinian opposition to Jewish immigration from 1891, that is six years prior to the decision by the first Zionist Congress in 1897 to establish a Jewish national home there, and their subsequent opposition to political Zionism until the outbreak of the Second World War in 1939. It will become apparent that the Palestinian Arabs never acquiesced to Zionist attempts to acquire sovereignty over Palestine. Instead, the Zionists faced opposition every step of the way.

THE ROOTS OF REBELLION

Opposition to Jewish immigration, and subsequently to political Zionism in Palestine, emerged decades before the Balfour Declaration was published in November 1917.[4] In fact, the conflict between Arabs and Jewish settlers began almost as soon as the latter began immigrating to Palestine in large numbers from Eastern Europe and Tsarist Russia in the 1870s and 1880s. Most of the initial disputes were over land and in particular over grazing rights and rights of access to farmland between the settlers and the *fellaheen* (that is, the Arab peasantry).[5] Misunderstandings caused by language barriers were very common as most of the Jewish immigrants did not speak Arabic and were ignorant of Arab customs and culture. Amongst Arab notables in the major towns and cities there was consternation that the Jewish immigrants (known as 'the lovers of Zion') did not respect the laws then prevailing in the country; the settlers would build houses without permits, and plant vineyards without asking the Government if they were permitted to do so.[6] However, it was only when Jewish immigration into Palestine took a formal footing with the establishment of the British Mandate that large-scale violence erupted.

The Arabs, both Muslims and Christians, were well informed about the Zionist movement from its inception.[7] On 24 June 1891, the first Arab protest against modern Jewish settlement in Palestine was made in the form of a telegram from Jerusalem, asking the Grand Vizier to prohibit Russian Jews from entering Palestine and acquiring land there.[8] Local merchants and craftsmen feared economic competition, which would almost certainly follow if Jewish immigration continued.[9] It was therefore apparent that almost three decades before the Balfour Declaration, the Arabs spelt out their demands which they never abandoned thereafter: a halt to Jewish immigration into Palestine, and an end to land purchase by them.[10] In 1914, Raghib al-Nashashibi, a candidate for the 1914 elections to the Ottoman Parliament, declared: 'If I am elected as a representative I shall devote all my strength day and night to doing away with the damage and threat of the Zionists and Zionism.'[11] He was elected by an overwhelming majority.[12] It would therefore be no exaggeration to say that the Balfour Declaration was not so much a starting point of the conflict, as a turning point, which greatly aggravated an existing trend.[13]

The roots of rebellion in modern Palestinian history can be traced back to 1834 when the Ottomans lost control of Palestine to Egypt, which occupied it until 1840.[14] When the Egyptian General Ibrahim Pasha, the son of Muhammad Ali, the founder of modern Egypt, demanded conscripts for his wars, which the Palestinians knew was little more than a death sentence, they revolted.[15] The revolt began in May 1834, in and around the cities of Nablus, Jerusalem and Hebron. The riots first broke out in the Hebron region when *fellaheen* from the village of Sair, supported by the Bedouin, killed 25 Egyptian soldiers.[16] In Hebron, the local population overcame the Egyptian garrison and arrested Ibrahim's governor before moving towards Jerusalem.[17] However, by 4 July 1834, Ibrahim Pasha responded by crushing the nascent rebellion, an event which is described in vivid detail by Israeli sociologists and historians Kimmerling and Migdal:

> The Egyptian soldiers reduced 16 villages to ash on their route, including those dominated by major rebel leaders. After a bloody battle, the Egyptians routed the fellaheen, publicly decapitating their leaders; they took Nablus on July 15. The final battle occurred in Hebron on August 4: The Egyptian victory there was complete and included leveling of the city, rape of the women, mass killing and conscription of the men, the furnishing of 120 adolescents to Egyptian officers to do with as they pleased.
>
> Throughout the country, the rebels were cruelly handled. About 10,000 fellaheen were recruited and shipped to Egypt. Sections of entire towns, including the Muslim quarter of Bethlehem, were destroyed, and their inhabitants expelled or killed.[18]

As is evident from the historical record, it was clear that Palestinian Arab opposition to political Zionism did not occur in a vacuum. Rather, the seeds of rebellion were sown in Palestine years before Zionism came onto the scene. Their opposition to Zionism had little to do with the fact that the Zionist movement was primarily comprised of persons of the Jewish faith. They opposed anyone, including their fellow Muslim Arab brothers, such as the Egyptians, from occupying their lands although they were not strong enough to oppose the Turks who recaptured Palestine from the Egyptians in 1840.

THE ORIGINS OF THE LAWS OF WAR

It is said that the first systematic code of war was that of the Saracens (Muslim Arab jurists) and was based on the Holy Qur'an.[19] The rules of war were also described in the writings of Hindus, Babylonians, Egyptians, ancient Hebrews, Sumerians, Hittites, Greek philosophers and by classical international lawyers like Francisco de Vitoria (1483–1546),[20] Alberico Gentili (1552–1608),[21] Balthazar Ayala (1548–1584),[22] Hugo Grotius (1583–1645)[23] and others.[24] However, the occupation of Palestine by Egyptian troops preceded the development of modern international humanitarian law, which provides the rules regarding the manner in which conflict may lawfully be fought.[25] This is because no laws regulating the conduct of modern armed conflict were codified in any form until the latter half of the nineteenth century, during the American Civil War (1861–65).[26] It was not until 1899 that the first fully-fledged international convention on the laws and usages of war on land was signed at the Hague Peace Conference convened on the initiative of the Czar of Russia, Nicholas II.[27] And even though, according to Muslim jurists[28] the *shari'a* (Islamic law) prohibits the killing of 'protected persons' (that is, those civilians who do not take part in hostilities), it was apparent from the way in which the Egyptians treated Arab detainees during their six-year occupation of Palestine, that its injunctions were not always adhered to in practice.[29]

Instead, customary international law regulated the conduct of warfare, with the common traditions and practices of states (mainly European at that time), military manuals of national armies and bilateral agreements concluded in wartime between belligerents, contributing to the formation of the laws of war.[30] It was only towards the end of the nineteenth century, that a growing conviction spread over the Western world that as civilisation was rapidly advancing it was imperative 'to restrain the destructive force of war'.[31] As with the case of mandated territories, the laws of war were concerned with the 'ever increasing requirements of civilization'.[32]

BRITISH MILITARY OCCUPATION OF PALESTINE 1917–20

Palestine was placed under British Military Occupation from the moment it was captured in December 1917 until July 1920, when a civilian administration was installed.[33] Palestine was then a part of what was known as Occupied Enemy Territory Administration (OETA), the area conquered by Lord Allenby's Army with the assistance of the Sherif of Mecca in 1917. Palestine comprised OETA South, with the Levant coast (West), inland Syria (North), and Transjordan (East) making up the rest of the occupied territory.[34] The applicable rules of humanitarian law were codified by conventions concluded at the 1899 and 1907 Hague Peace Conferences, which provided that the status quo in the occupied territory be maintained.[35] Turkey, which previously had sovereignty over Palestine, had ratified the Hague Convention with Respect to the Laws and Customs of War on Land and its Annex: Regulations Concerning the Laws and Customs of War on Land of 1899 (1899 Hague Regulations) on 12 June 1907, as had Britain on 4 September 1900.[36] That convention was therefore binding between the belligerents. According to Article 43 of the 1899 Hague Regulations:

> The authority of the legitimate power having actually passed into the hands of the occupant, the latter shall take all steps in his power to re-establish and insure, as far as possible, public order and safety, while respecting, unless absolutely prevented, the laws in force in the country.[37]

The phrase 'public order and safety' was a mistranslation of the French 'l'ordre et la vie publics' which, when correctly translated, refers to 'public order and life', implying a broader obligation not to interfere with a country's existing institutions.[38] The principles enunciated in Article 43 were subsequently mentioned in the 1914 edition of the *Manual of Military Law* published by the War Office for members of His Majesty's Armed Forces.[39] In his instructions to his troops, General Allenby gave the order that:

> The system of administration will be in accordance with the laws and usages of war as laid down in Chapter 14, Section 8, Manual of Military Law, and no departures from these principles will be permitted without the approval of C-in-C. As far as possible the Turkish system of government will be continued and the existing machinery utilized ...[40]

Paragraph 353 of the *Manual of Military Law* provided that: 'The occupation of enemy territory during war creates a condition entirely different from subjugation through annexation of the territory.'[41] In other words, Britain was not free to dispose of the territory as it wished. There were certain obligations it had to take into account. According to the chapter of the manual on the laws and usages of war on land which was written in part by Mr Lassa Oppenheim, a prominent German jurist of international law who made his home in England and was appointed to the Whewell Professorship of Public International Law at the University of Cambridge:

> ... During the occupation by the enemy the sovereignty of the legitimate owner of the territory is only temporarily latent, but it still exists and in no way passes to the occupant. The latter's rights are merely transitory, and he shall only exercise such power as is necessary for the purposes of the war, the maintenance of order and safety, and the proper administration of the country.
>
> 354. It is no longer considered permissible for him to work his will unhindered, altering the existing form of government (a), upsetting the constitution and the domestic laws, and ignoring *the rights* of the inhabitants.[42]

This meant that sovereignty, even though it was only temporarily latent, remained vested at least hypothetically in the 'legitimate owner', which at that time would have probably still been Turkey. As mentioned in Chapter 2, Turkey formally relinquished its sovereignty at the Treaty of Lausanne on 23 July 1923. However, there is a paradox here because Article 22 of the League of Nations Covenant provided that 'those colonies and territories which as a consequence of the late war have ceased to be under the sovereignty of the States which formerly governed them'. Consequently, it may be fair to conclude that between December 1917 and July 1923, Turkey's sovereignty over Palestine was 'temporarily latent' to the extent that it ceased to be directly applicable to its former possessions in the Middle East. Instead sovereignty was either in abeyance or, alternatively, the Mandatory Power was temporarily exercising attributes of it until the beneficiaries of its trust were in a position to exercise it independently.

It was clear, however, that Britain did not have sovereignty over Palestine as the Occupying Power. Whilst it might have been able to exercise attributes of sovereignty, it was subject to international humanitarian law throughout the duration of its occupation of Palestine as enshrined in the 1899 Hague Regulations and customary international law. Britain was consequently not supposed to interfere with the legislative framework that existed in Palestine. Rather it could only introduce legislation to the extent that it was necessary to preserve the public order and life of the population there. It would have been impossible for Britain to have remained in conformity with the law of belligerent occupation if it had changed the law wholesale.[43] An Occupying Power can only make minor legislative changes.[44] It was partly due to these legal restrictions that the Zionists came into increasing conflict with the British Army, which placed restrictions on their colonisation activities as described below. However, occasionally, the Zionists got their way, and the laws of belligerent occupation were set aside infringing Article 43.

THE JERUSALEM RIOTS OF 1920

By 1920, the conflict that had been brewing between the Arabs and the Zionists came to a head and Arab riots broke out in Jerusalem during the Nebi Musa pilgrimage protesting the policy of the Jewish national home.[45] On the weekend of 2–4 April 1920, the annual pilgrimage (which is a Muslim festival honouring Moses who is still believed by Muslims to be buried where a mosque was later erected off the highway between Jerusalem and the Dead Sea, which one can visit) coincided with Good Friday and the Jewish Sabbath. On the Sunday, fighting broke out between Jews and Arab pilgrims from Hebron who were parading through Jaffa Gate, which is one of the main entrances into the Old City of Jerusalem. A number of Arabs and Jews were arrested and then subsequently released upon which further fighting took place. During the fighting, nine people were killed, 22 were seriously wounded and 220 people (mostly Jews) were lightly wounded (of the dead, five were Jews and four were Arabs).[46] Before the outbreak of violence, there were demonstrations and political speeches made at the balcony of the Arab Club in Jerusalem in support of King Feisal who had just crowned himself King of Greater Syria.[47] Cries for independence were heard during the rally and Zionism was condemned.[48]

To examine the causes of the riot, the British military authorities in Port Said established a Court of Inquiry,[49] which was presided over by Major General P.C. Palin of the British Army in Egypt. The two other military members of the court were Brigadier General G.H. Wildblood and Lieutenant Colonel C. Vaughan Edwards. Mr A.L. Barnet, a British judge at the Courts of Appeal in Egypt, was appointed the legal adviser. The Court was tasked with recording 'the evidence as to the circumstances which gave rise to the disturbances which took place at and near Jerusalem on the occasion of the Nebi Musa

Pilgrimage on 4th April and following days'.[50] The inquiry was subsequently enlarged by the addition of the words 'and as to the extent and causes of racial feelings that at present exist in Palestine' by a cable received from General Headquarters on 22 April 1920.[51] The Court sat for a period of 50 days, exclusive of Sundays, and examined 152 witnesses. These examinations were conducted in open court, although due to the political sensitivity of the inquiry, portions of the evidence were heard in camera. After sentencing 23 people to prison for rioting, the Court came to the following conclusions in an 82-page report, the principal ones being:

1. That the causes of the alienation and exasperation of the feelings of the population of Palestine are: -
   (a) Disappointment at the non-fulfillment of promises made to them by British propaganda.
   (b) Inability to reconcile the Allies' declared policy of self-determination with the Balfour Declaration, giving rise to a sense of betrayal and intense anxiety for their future.
   (c) Misapprehension of the true meaning of the Balfour Declaration and forgetfulness of the guarantees determined therein, due to the loose rhetoric of politicians and exaggerated statements and writings of interested persons, chiefly Zionists.
   (d) Fear of Jewish competition and domination, justified by experience and the apparent control exercised by the Zionists over the administration.
   (e) Zionist indiscretion and aggression, since the Balfour Declaration aggravating such fears.
   (f) Anti-British and Anti-Zionist propaganda working on the population already inflamed by the sources of irritation aforesaid.
2. That the Zionist Commission and the official Zionists by their impatience, indiscretion and attempts to force the hands of the Administration, are largely responsible for the present crisis ...[52]

The Court was highly critical of the Zionists, because they had made numerous attempts to coerce the military administration in Palestine to bend the rules of international humanitarian law, in particular the principle enshrined in Article 43 of the 1899 Hague Regulations, referred to above, which provided that the Occupying Power should respect the laws of the previous sovereign and maintain the status quo. In a letter to Arthur Balfour, Dr Chaim Weizmann, the leader of the British Zionists, claimed that the policy of maintaining the status quo as decreed by international law was '... a formula which has been violated by every belligerent power during this war [referring to the First World War], and has lost all relation to reality'.[53] Weizmann said that he wanted the British authorities to allow the Zionists to establish a Jewish University in Palestine, to give the Western Wall (also known as the 'Wailing Wall' and Al Buraq to Palestinians, which is *Waqf* property and forms a part of the Haram-al-Sherif, the third most holiest site in Islam and the first *qibla* or direction to which

Muslims prayed before it was moved to Mecca) to the Zionists.[54] Weizmann also wanted the Zionists to be given permission to take over a large tract of land in southern Palestine, which, while formerly owned by a number of people, was largely unoccupied.[55] Balfour subsequently wrote to Major-General Gilbert Clayton who informed him that he would not assent to the land scheme or to the transfer of the Western Wall.[56] The High Commissioner in Egypt had also received reports of attempts by 'certain Zionists to buy up as much German owned land in Haifa as they can' in the name of the Anglo-Palestine Company.[57] The military authorities promptly informed the Palestine authorities that this procedure was 'in direct contravention of the proclamation issued in OETA South dated Nov 1st 1918'.[58]

The Court went on to lambast the military administration in Palestine for allowing people to deliver inflammatory speeches during the pilgrimage and for withdrawing troops from inside the Old City on Monday 5 April, when the further rioting took place.[59] They said the military was slow in obtaining full control of the city after martial law had been proclaimed.[60] Finally, they concluded their judgment by saying that 'the situation at present obtaining in Palestine is exceedingly dangerous and demands firm and patient handling if a serious catastrophe is to be avoided'.[61] This judgment was delivered on 1 July 1920, the day after the British military occupation of Palestine came to an end. When Herbert Samuel's civilian administration took over one of the first things he did, as Britain's first High Commissioner to Palestine, was to ensure that the findings of the inquiry never saw the light of day.[62] In a telegram to the Foreign Office he wrote that he strongly deprecated publication. He said that there was a new administration, amnesty had been declared, passions had subsided, and the atmosphere was excellent. He wrote: 'Publication must necessarily revive controversy. Eder, Zionist commissioner agrees.'[63] The Foreign Office and the Military Administration in Cairo agreed with their man on the spot, and the report was never seen again until it was declassified decades later.[64]

THE JAFFA RIOTS OF 1921

However, if Samuel sincerely believed that the atmosphere in Palestine was excellent, he was deluding himself as well as his colleagues in the British Government. Less than a year later, riots on a much larger scale than that of Nabi Musa broke out between Arabs and Jews in Jaffa.[65] In an Interim Report on the Civil Administration of Palestine presented to the League of Nations, Samuel described the riot as follows:

> On May 1st there was a riot at Jaffa. Disturbances continued during the following days. Attacks were made from Arab villages upon the Jewish colonies of Petah Tikvah and Chederah. Troops were employed and suppressed the disturbances, and the attacks on the colonies were dispersed with considerable loss to the attackers. Martial law was proclaimed over the area affected, but much excitement prevailed for several days in Jaffa

> and the neighbouring districts, and for some weeks there was considerable unrest. 88 persons were killed and 238 injured, most of them slightly, in these disturbances, and there was much looting and destruction of property. There were no casualties among the troops.[66]

Samuel established a three-man commission of inquiry chaired by Sir Thomas Haycraft to examine the causes of the disturbances (the Haycraft Commission of Inquiry).[67] Mr H.C. Luke, Assistant Governor of Jerusalem and Mr Stubbs of the Legal Department assisted Haycraft with the inquiry.[68] In their report the commissioners considered that 'had there been no Jewish question, the Government would have had no political difficulty of any importance to deal with so far as domestic affairs are concerned'.[69] They thought 'any anti-British feeling on the part of the Arabs that may have arisen in the country originates in their association of the Government with the furtherance of the policy of Zionism'.[70] Regarding the reasons underlying the riot, they found 'no evidence worth considering, to show that the outbreak was planned and organized'.[71] They found a 'general belief that the aims of the Zionists and Jewish immigration are a danger to the national and material interests of Arabs in Palestine is well nigh universal amongst the Arabs, and is not confined to any particular class ... the people participate with the leaders, because they feel that their political and material interests are identical'.[72] In their opinion they thought that the two issues, which above all caused Arab grievance towards the Zionists, were Jewish immigration and land transfer. The Arabs were under the impression that the Transfer of Land Ordinance, 1920, which forbade the transfer of land to persons other than those who were already resident in Palestine, had been introduced to keep down the price of land which would allow the Zionists to purchase it at a low price.[73] They also contended that a temporary provision which prohibited the export of cereals by Arab farmers was enacted 'to oppress the native landowners so as to compel them to sell their land, and at the same time to provide cheap food for Jewish immigrants'.[74] As regards immigration, the commissioners reported that it could be summed up 'in the fear that through extensive Jewish immigration Palestine will become a Jewish dominion'.[75] What they meant by this, the commissioners said, was that 'the Jews when they had sufficiently increased in numbers would become so highly organized and so well armed as to be able to overcome the Arabs, and rule over and oppress them'.[76] The commissioners were convinced that there was 'no animosity towards the Jews as such; that there is no inherent anti-Semitism in the country, racial or religious'.[77] They said educated Arabs credibly assured them that 'they would welcome the arrival of well-to-do and able Jews who could help develop the country to the advantage of all sections of the community'.[78]

THE 1928–29 RIOTS OVER THE WESTERN WALL

In the following years, relations between Arabs and Jews deteriorated further as had been predicted by the Military Court of Inquiry and by the Haycraft

Commission of Inquiry. Despite the rosy assurances of Herbert Samuel, by the time his successor arrived in Palestine it was virtually a tinderbox. By 1928–29, demonstrations occurred between Jews and Arabs over rights of worship at the Western Wall in the Old City of Jerusalem. The conflict began right after the Jewish Day of Atonement on 24 September 1928, when the police removed the dividing curtain from the pavement in front of the Western Wall during Jewish prayers, which provoked a sharp reaction from them. Demonstrations followed. The Muslims viewed Jewish encroachment on what was lawfully *Waqf* property as a potential threat to their own rights of worship and they also feared that this was just the first step in a Zionist plot to take control of the compound.[79] The problem was that the rights and claims to that part of the Old City had not been juridically determined in a manner that pleased all those concerned. In this connection, Article 14 of the British Mandate provided:

> A special Commission shall be appointed by the Mandatory to study, define and determine the rights and claims in connection with the Holy Places and the rights and claims relating to the different religious communities in Palestine. The method of nomination, the composition and the functions of this Commission shall be submitted to the Council of the League for its approval, and the Commission shall not be appointed or enter upon its functions without the approval of the Council.

Due to a disagreement between Great Britain and the League of Nations in 1922, the Commission was never appointed and the dispute concerning the Holy Places went unresolved.[80] The conflict concerned the pavement, courtyard and dwellings in front of the Western Wall, which though sacred to Jews, were part of the Abu Madian Waqf, a Muslim religious and charitable trust, which was founded at the time of Saladin for the benefit of a sect of Muslims of Moroccan origin known as the Mughrabis.[81] It was also where, according to tradition, the prophet Muhammed's horse, 'Burak', was stabled when he made his celestial journey from the Dome of the Rock. Surrounding the area were a number of small houses, which were inhabited by poor Moroccan families.[82] Before and after the First World War, a number of prominent Jews such as Nissim Bechar and Baron Edmond De Rothschild had made attempts to acquire the area adjacent to the Western Wall by various forms of purchase.[83] Statements had also been made to the press, that certain Zionists envisaged rebuilding the Third Temple, as the Romans had destroyed the Second Temple in 70 AD.[84] As the site of the Second Temple is reputedly situated beneath the Dome of the Rock this naturally aroused the suspicions of the Muslims and gave the Mufti of Jerusalem, Haj Amin al-Husseini, an excuse to politicise the issue, whip up support, and agitate the masses.[85]

These factors formed the background to the riots that would engulf Palestine in the ensuing months. This led to the deaths of 67 Jews in the City of Hebron, another place of religious significance where the Cave of the Patriarchs is located known to Muslims as the Mosque of Ibrahim, holy to all three of the monotheistic faiths, where Abraham is buried with his wife and children.[86] Only one British policeman was present in Hebron at the time and he was unable to control the violence, which caused an exodus of Jews from that city.[87] There was also rioting in the 'religious cities' of Jerusalem and Safed. In all, 133 Jews and 116 Arabs were killed in a week of violence, and 339 Jews and 232 Arabs were wounded, the latter mostly by British police.[88]

According to the Commission of Inquiry sent to Palestine to investigate the disturbances (the 'Shaw Commission of Inquiry') Arab grievances had their origin long before the Day of Atonement in 1928. These grievances concerned Jewish immigration, Jewish land purchase and Palestine's Constitutional provisions, which gave preference to the Zionists, even though the Arabs formed the majority of the community in Palestine at that time.[89] The Commission also concluded that the Arabs were angered by the Rutenberg concession for the provision of electricity and water to the City of Jerusalem because the profits would be for the benefit of foreign capitalists and not for the people of the country.[90] Both the denationalisation of persons of Palestinian Arab origin who had left Palestine before 1919 and the high level of taxation, which was disproportionate to the low standard of Arab living, also caused concern.[91] In other words, it was the policy of the Jewish national home, through which all these grievances were linked, that was causing the problem. The Commission noted that Palestinian society was highly politicised and well informed. In the Commission's own words:

> The contention that the fellah takes no personal interest in politics is not supported by our experience in Palestine ... villagers and peasants alike are taking a very real and personal interest both in the effect of the policy of establishing a national home and in the question of the development of self-governing institutions in Palestine. No less than fourteen Arabic newspapers are published in Palestine and in almost every village there is someone who reads from the papers to gatherings of those villagers who are illiterate ... it is not unusual for part of the address in the Mosques on Friday to be devoted to political affairs. The Arab fellaheen and villagers are therefore probably more politically minded than many of the people of Europe.[92]

The Commission concluded their report by stating that in their view there could be no doubt that racial animosity on the part of the Arabs, consequent upon the disappointment of their political and national aspirations and fear for their economic future, was the fundamental cause of the outbreak of violence.[93] They also noted that in less than ten years three serious attacks (Jerusalem in 1920, Jaffa in 1921, and Jerusalem, Hebron and Safed in 1929) had been made by Arabs on Jews. Yet for eighty years before the first of these attacks there had been no recorded instance of any similar incidents.[94] What had changed since then they pondered? Evidently, it was Britain's policy of creating a Jewish national home whilst trying to assuage Arab concerns that they would not be detrimentally affected. The Palestinian Arabs were not convinced.

THE LEAGUE OF NATIONS COMMISSION AND THE HOLY PLACES

After the disturbances, the British Government appointed an *ad hoc* International Commission to examine the rights and claims of Jews and Muslims to the Holy Places on 13 September 1929, although it was not to be identified with the functions of the Holy Places Commission as envisaged in Article 14 of the British Mandate, which was never appointed.[95] On 14 January 1930, the proposal to send a Commission to Palestine was approved of by the League of Nations after it had heard the views of the Permanent Mandates Commission. On 15 May 1930, the Council approved of the composition of the International Commission which was comprised of three persons, none of whom could be British subjects: Eliel Löfgren, formerly Sweden's Minister for Foreign Affairs, Charles Baroe, Vice-President of the Court of Justice at Geneva, and C.J. Van Kempen, Member of the States-General of the Netherlands and a former Governor of the East Coast of Sumatra (now known as Indonesia).[96]

The Commission arrived in Jerusalem on 19 June 1930 and stayed there for one month. They examined the Western Wall and its environs, the documents relating to the history of the dispute and heard the claims of Jews and Muslims. The Commission noted that from the latter part of the sixteenth century onwards, questions as to the possession of the Holy Places in Palestine had been at the forefront of international politics.[97] They recalled that controversies on points concerning the Holy Places was one of the causes of the Crimean War and that at the conclusion of peace in 1856,[98] the matters in dispute being still left undecided were submitted to the Signatory Powers, who undertook to guarantee in every respect the *status quo ante bellum*.[99] They also noted that at the conclusion of the Russo-Turkish War in 1878, the Peace Treaty[100] laid down the requirement that no alterations were to be made to the status quo without the consent of all the Signatory Powers (Austria-Hungary, France, Germany, Great Britain, Italy, Russia and Turkey).[101] The Commission then carefully considered the issues of controversy concerning ownership of the Western Wall and rights of Jewish access for the purposes of devotion, and came to the following principal conclusions:

A. To the Moslems belong the sole ownership of, and the sole proprietary right to, the Western Wall, seeing that it forms an integral part of the Haram-esh-Sherif area, which is a Waqf property.

   To the Moslems there also belongs the ownership of the Pavement in front of the Wall and of the adjacent so-called Moghrabi (Moroccan) Quarter opposite the Wall, inasmuch as the last-mentioned property was made Waqf under Muslim Sharia Law, it being dedicated to charitable purposes.

   Such appurtenances of worship and/or such other objects as the Jews may be entitled to place near the Wall either in conformity with the provisions of this present Verdict or by agreement come to between the Parties shall under no circumstances be considered as, or have the effect

> of, establishing for them any sort of proprietary right to the Wall or to the adjacent Pavement.
>
> On the other hand, the Moslems shall be under the obligation not to construct or build any edifice or to demolish or repair any building within the Waqf property (Haram area and Moghrabi Quarter) adjacent to the Wall, in such a manner that the said work would encroach on the Pavement or impair access of the Jews to the Wall or involve any disturbance to, or interference with, the Jews during the times of their devotional visits to the Wall, if it can in any way be avoided.
>
> B. The Jews shall have free access to the Western Wall for the purposes of devotions at all times – subject to the explicit stipulations hereinafter to be mentioned, viz.,[102]

The explicit stipulations mentioned by the Commission included restrictions on the following: blowing the Ram's horn (*shofar*) near the Wall and bringing to the Wall any tent or curtain. The Muslims were urged not to carry out a *Zikr* ceremony close to the pavement during the progress of Jewish devotions, though they had a right 'to go to and fro in an ordinary way' along the pavement by the Wall. It was prohibited for any person to make a political speech or a demonstration in front of the Wall.[103]

THE HOPE-SIMPSON REPORT

One of the other recommendations of the Shaw Commission of Inquiry was that a scientific study should examine land cultivation and settlement possibilities in Palestine. Consequently, the British Government appointed Sir John Hope-Simpson, formerly of the Indian Civil Service, to conduct such a study.[104] In his report he concluded that there was no room for a single additional Jewish settler if the standard of life of the Arab villager was to remain at existing levels.[105] He recommended 'an active policy of agricultural development, having as its object close settlement on the land and intensive cultivation by both Arabs and Jews', without which, he considered, the obligations of the mandate could not be fulfilled.[106] In the meantime, he was opposed to the admission of further Jewish immigrants as settlers on the land.[107]

Concurrently, with the Hope-Simpson report, the British Government issued its White Paper of 1930.[108] In that paper, the Government accepted most of the views expressed by Hope-Simpson in his report, which 'provoked a storm of protest from the Jews and their supporters'.[109] Dr Weizmann protested that the White Paper 'was inconsistent with the terms of the Mandate' and marked a 'reversal of policy'.[110] As a result, it seems, of pressure exerted upon the British Government, Ramsay MacDonald, the British Prime Minister, published a letter in which he 'clarified' his government's policy towards the Jewish national home as set out in the White Paper. He reaffirmed Britain's intention to stand by the Mandate, to uphold the policy of the Jewish national home by further land settlement and immigration, and to condone the Zionist insistence on Jewish labour for work on Jewish enterprises.[111] This letter was subsequently referred to as the 'Black Letter' by the Palestine Arabs who interpreted it as a complete *volte face*.[112] They regarded it 'as plain proof of the power which world Jewry could exercise in London' and lost their faith in the British Government.[113] As a result, the Arabs decided to cease cooperation with the Zionists in every field.[114]

In the meantime, Haj Amin al-Husseini, head of the Supreme Muslim Council, set up a campaign in defence of Al-Aqsa and the Islamic Holy Places in the late 1920s which would eventually lead in December 1931, to a large international gathering in Jerusalem attended by Muslims from all over the world.[115] From then on, Arab resistance to Zionism began to take on an overtly Islamic character. The struggle had moved from the educated classes and their lofty ideals of self-determination, majority rights and anti-imperialist slogans to the struggle for Al-Aqsa and Palestine's Holy Places. One Palestinian newspaper summed up the mood using the following words: 'The Muslims of Palestine are determined to sacrifice body and soul in order to safeguard their religious rights. It is not enough that their national rights have been stolen from them.'[116] The Dome of the Rock, Al-Aqsa and the Muslim Holy Places in Palestine became a symbol in the battle for control over Palestine. Al-Husseini had succeeded in bolstering support from the Islamic world, which continues until the present day.[117]

JEWISH IMMIGRATION INTO PALESTINE

Jewish immigration into Palestine rapidly increased from 9,553 persons in 1932 to 30,327 persons in 1933, a three-fold increase (which is equivalent to 1,800,000 immigrants arriving to the UK in one year alone at present day population levels or 9,000,000 persons arriving in the US).[118] In 1934, this figure increased to 42,359 before peaking at 61,854 persons for 1935 according to figures provided by the Palestine Government and the Jewish Agency.[119] This meant that more Jews entered Palestine in that year alone than had inhabited Palestine in 1917 when the Balfour Declaration was issued.[120] In 1936, the British Government predicted that if the annual rate of Jewish immigration was 30,000 persons per year, the year in which the Jewish population would equal the Arab population would be mid 1960.[121] If it was higher, at 60,000 persons per year, then this could happen as early as 1947, although Jewish immigration never reached this figure again.[122] If the figure was lower than 30,000 it could take until 1970 to reach parity.[123] These calculations did not, however, take into account a surge in the Arab growth rate or a further fall in the Jewish immigration rate which would have delayed Arab–Jewish population parity still further.[124]

The sharp increase in immigration to Palestine in the 1930s was caused by the policies of Adolf Hitler's Nationalist Socialist Party in Germany. German citizens of Jewish ancestry were progressively being stripped of their German citizenship and were prevented from undertaking employment in many professions.[125] Great Britain, the United States and many other countries refused to relax their immigration restrictions, effectively shutting their doors to these people desperately seeking safety and security.[126] And these restrictive measures were supported by public opinion. For instance, *The Daily Mail*, a British newspaper, campaigned aggressively against Jewish immigration into Britain even though they were fleeing persecution. An article published on 20 August 1938, reported Mr Herbert Metcalfe, the Old-street magistrate, saying: 'The way stateless Jews from Germany, are pouring in from every port of this country is becoming an outrage. I intend to enforce the law to the fullest.'[127] With these words, Mr Metcalfe sent three Jewish refugees to six months' hard labour, with a recommendation that they be deported.[128] This was not an isolated incident, however.[129] Sentences like these were a common occurrence, 'a problem' as *The Daily Mail* claimed, to which it 'has repeatedly pointed'.[130] Although Britain attempted to offer refuge in some of its isolated colonies, in many cases these Jewish refugees had no other choice but to seek refuge in Palestine. This is especially as Austria, Italy, Spain and many other European countries fell prey to Nazi ideology, and were hostile to the Jews who were fleeing in droves. The Nazis even had the audacity to complain over a British proposal to send the refugees to Tanganyika (formerly German East Africa), which the German press described as a device to perpetuate a 'robbery' of Germany's colonies.[131]

However, the Arabs who were already in conflict with the Zionists in Palestine viewed this massive influx of Jewish immigrants with alarm. In their eyes, these Jewish immigrants were perceived as being aligned to the Zionists who were intent on taking over the country. Most Palestinian Arabs did not fully appreciate the hideous nature of the Nazi regime or anticipate the catastrophe that was to come. The *fellaheen* probably did not even know where Germany was on a map let alone understand the politics of that country, what the Jewish Question was all about, or even what anti-Semitism was. Their sole concern was their own survival in a country which they viewed as their own.

THE PALESTINE RIOTS OF 1936

This massive demographic shift in the size of Palestine's Jewish population led the Mufti and the Arab Executive Committee to call for a general strike outside Government offices in Jerusalem in April 1936. This was followed by six weeks of rioting in Jaffa, Haifa and Nablus, which led to the deaths of 27 people.[132] This time the focus of Arab fury, as already alluded to, was the British Government. There was very little inter-communal violence between Arabs and Jews.[133] Following the unrest, another Commission of Inquiry was appointed, which Sir William Murison headed. His report concluded that the immediate cause of the riot was 'to protest against the policy of the Government, the ground for which was prepared by a general feeling of apprehension amongst the Arabs engendered by the purchase of land by the Jews and by Jewish immigration'.[134]

In the following years, relations between the British Government and the Palestine Arabs deteriorated still further. As well as political activity by the Supreme Muslim Council and the Arab Executive Committee, several independent Arab political parties were established, as well as a youth movement.[135] In 1935, the British discovered that there were armed underground Arab organisations operating in Palestine. In November of that year, British troops killed Sheikh Izzed Din al-Qassam.[136] They had previously discovered large quantities of arms being shipped from Belgium to Jews in Jaffa, which provoked the Arabs into calling for a one-day strike to protest.[137] This led to rumours that the Zionists were arming themselves and so the Arabs prepared themselves for battle. It was during this time of tension that al-Qassam was killed.

On 25 November 1935, the leaders of five Arab political parties presented a memorandum to the British High Commissioner demanding: The establishment of democratic government; the prohibition of the transfer of Arab lands to the Jews; and the immediate cessation of Jewish immigration, the formation of a competent committee to determine the absorptive capacity, legislation requiring the carrying of identity cards and an immediate investigation into illegal immigration.[138]

Upon receiving this memorandum, the High Commissioner sent a proposal to Arab and Jewish leaders for the establishment of a Legislative Council with a large unofficial majority, comprised of the following: five officials, two nominated representatives of commerce; eight elected and three nominated Muslims; three elected and four nominated Jews and one elected and two nominated Christians.[139] The President would be an impartial person unconnected to Palestine. However, there were three safeguards: (1) The validity of the Mandate was not to be questioned; (2) The High Commissioner would be empowered to legislate in certain circumstances; and (3) The High Commissioner would continue to determine the labour schedule of the immigration quota.[140]

Although the proposals were criticised in the Arab press, the Arab political parties did not reject them.[141] However, the Jewish leaders refused to accept the proposals and both Houses of Parliament in Britain rejected them.[142] It was only after these legislative changes were discarded by Westminster that the Arabs lost their faith in the political process since all their attempts at being given political parity with the Zionists were hindered (even though they formed the majority of the population).[143] It was the last straw. They had exhausted all diplomatic and peaceful avenues to vent their frustrations. In due course the Palestinian Arabs would embark on a serious guerilla war against the British authorities in Palestine, which would catch them by surprise and would last for three years until the outbreak of the Second World War.

THE GREAT ARAB REVOLT OF 1936–39

The Great Arab Revolt began with a call for a general strike, which was supported by all the major factions, Christians and Muslims alike.[144] It lasted for six months. On 8 May 1936, at a conference in Jerusalem, the Arabs resolved that they would no longer pay taxes, and in June the port at Jaffa was put out of action. This was followed by demonstrations and assaults on Jews, the destruction of Jewish property and sniping at Jewish settlements. There were also attacks on railway lines, which derailed two trains, roads were barricaded and telephone wires cut.[145] Armed bands, swelled by volunteers from Syria and Iraq, appeared in the hills.[146] However, the Zionists were not the main targets of Arab attacks – the British authorities in Palestine bore the brunt.[147]

At first, the British did not take the revolt seriously and thought that, like the previous riots in 1920, 1921, 1929 and 1933, it could be contained.[148] But as the revolt developed, the British authorities called for reinforcements from Egypt and Malta. They appointed another Commission of Inquiry, this time a Royal Commission, which was sent to Palestine to investigate the causes of the unrest although the commissioners were specifically instructed not to question the terms of the Mandate.[149]

THE PEEL COMMISSION OF INQUIRY

The Royal Commission of Inquiry to Palestine (known as the Peel Commission of Inquiry) concluded that the underlying causes of the disturbances were the desire of the Arabs for national independence and their hatred and fear of the establishment of the Jewish national home.[150] In the first six months of violence, 314 people were killed (195 Arabs and 80 Jews) and over 1,000 were wounded.[151] The Commission recommended that Britain terminate its mandate over Palestine and partition it between an Arab and a Jewish state with the exception of Jerusalem, Bethlehem, Nazareth and the Sea of Galilee which would remain under British control in the form of a mandate so as to ensure free access to the Holy Places that would accord with Christian sentiment in the world at large.[152] They also recommended that the Arab state envisaged by their plan would be united with Transjordan.[153] The policy of the Balfour Declaration was to be revoked.[154]

The Jewish state they envisaged was rather small comprising the Galilee, the Jezreel Valley and the coastal plain from Acre to Tel Aviv where the most fertile land was located.[155] The rest of the territory went to the Arab state although it was mostly desert and scrubland (see Map 6). Partly for this reason and the loss of taxable capacity of the Jewish Area, the Commission recommended that the Jewish state pay a subvention to the Arab state, which had happened when Sind had been separated from Bombay and Burma from the Indian Empire.[156] The plan also envisaged population transfers between the two states,[157] which were to have special treaty relations with Britain although they recognised that the transfer would be difficult to apply in Palestine because of the large number of Arabs inhabiting the area that was to be allocated to the Jewish state and the lack of cultivable land in the envisaged Arab state.[158]

In the end the plan got nowhere because the Arabs rejected the partition proposal and demanded the recognition of their right to complete independence in Palestine and the termination of the Mandate.[159] The partition proposal divided the Zionists but ultimately they too rejected it.[160] The Permanent

Mandates Commission declared itself in favour of the principle of partition but was opposed to the idea of the immediate creation of two new independent states. It considered that there should be a prolonged period of political apprenticeship before independence.[161]

THE BRITISH RESPONSE TO THE ARAB REVOLT

In September 1937, Arab irregulars murdered the Acting District Commissioner of the Galilee District, and his British police escort. The violence intensified. In response, the British mandatory authorities outlawed the Arab Higher Committee and deported six leading Arab politicians to the Seychelles.[162] Haj Amin al-Husseini was deprived of his position as President of the Supreme Muslim Council and of membership of the General Waqf Committee of which he was chairman. He fled to Lebanon.[163]

On 11 November 1937, Military Courts were established under the Defence (Military Courts) Regulations Laws[164] for the trial of offences connected with the discharge or carrying of firearms, which were punishable by death.[165] The regulations also gave the High Commissioner in Palestine the right to appropriate any immovable property of those persons engaged in violent offences and demolish it or dispose of it any manner in which he thought appropriate.[166] These regulations also provided for 'collective fines', whereby whole villages could be financially penalised if they failed to surrender the rebels or were suspected of aiding them.[167] The laws were amended in 1938 so that inquests could be dispensed with if the rebels were killed by British troops.[168] In 1938 alone, an inordinate number of laws was passed giving the Government wide powers to restore law and order, ranging from curfews, censorship, closing cinemas and roads, to banning plays, among other things.[169] Torture was also employed.[170] One author writing in the 1940s described British counter-insurgency operations in Palestine:

> Fines of up to £2000 were inflicted upon villages, and collected in kind and in cash. The houses of suspects were dynamited by administrative order and their families rendered homeless. In one case at least this form of vengeance was taken on the relatives of a man who had already expiated his crime by his death. In other cases the best houses in villages near which the crime had occurred were destroyed without regard to the character of the owners. Wholesale arrests of notables and commons were made by administrative order, and soon the concentration camps housed six or seven hundred untried prisoners.[171]

The Arab town of Jaffa was particularly hard hit: bulldozers flattened whole rows of houses.[172] Black and white photographs of the damage, which was very extensive, are available in the National Archives.[173] The British authorities, did, however, accept responsibility and make provision for the payment of compensation.[174]

By August 1938, the British Army had to be reinforced with an additional 20,000 soldiers, which included 18 infantry battalions.[175] Two Royal Air Force squadrons and 3,000 additional British police were also made available.[176] Air Commodore Arthur Harris was the RAF commander in Palestine at the time. He claimed, 'the only thing the Arab understands is the heavy hand'.[177] In his opinion, the key to counter-insurgency problems in Palestine could be solved by 'one 250lb or 500lb bomb in each village that speaks out of turn within a few minutes or hours of having so spoken'.[178]

In the summer of 1938, there were discussions at the Colonial Office regarding the rules relating to the aerial bombing of houses in Palestine.[179] These were set out as follows: (1) The authority to undertake such action could only be given to experienced pilots; (2) the pilots taking such action had to be certain as to the buildings from which fire was being directed against them; and (3) the bombing had to be directed solely against the building from which the fire was coming.[180] On 21 June 1938, Prime Minister Neville Chamberlain told the House of Commons that three principles of international law were applicable to warfare from the air, which were reiterated by the League of Nations in a unanimous resolution adopted on 30 September 1938:

> [The League of Nations] [r]ecognizes the following principles as a necessary basis for any subsequent regulations:
>
> (1) The intentional bombing of civilian populations is illegal;
> (2) Objectives aimed at from the air must be legitimate military objectives and must be identifiable;
> (3) Any attack on legitimate military objectives must be carried out in such a way that civilian populations in the neighbourhood are not bombed through negligence'.[181]

In an internal military inquiry, which was never officially published, the British Army came to the following conclusions about the causes of the revolt, which are worth quoting *in extenso*:

> The rebellion of 1936 was the fifth outbreak of violence since the British occupation of Palestine. It was the first to be directed deliberately against the Government and against British authority. The riots of 1920, 1921, 1929 and 1933 had been solely of an inter-racial character, being directly by the Arabs against the Jews as the latter developed with unprecedented rapidity from an unobtrusive minority into a community of great political, industrial and agricultural importance. The years 1934 and 1935 saw an enormous increase in Jewish immigration – over 100,000 being admitted legally during that period – which, together with extensive land purchases by Jews, profoundly disturbed the Arab population. At the same time they noted with deep interest the gaining of independence by Iraq and the example of a prolonged and successful strike in Syria against the French authorities. On top of this came the Mediterranean crisis in the autumn of

> 1935, which followed upon the Italian invasion of Abyssinia. Its immediate consequences in Palestine were the failure of the tourist season, with the very serious local losses which that involves, and a marked lowering of British prestige.[182]

In other words, the causes of the violence had not changed much since 1920. The Arabs were opposed to the establishment of a Jewish national home in Palestine and they were prepared to use force to stop it. At first they fought the Zionists and then they turned against the British. In every single instance they lost and ended up worse off. By the end of the three-year revolt in 1939, approximately 5,000 Palestinian Arabs had been killed, 10,000 were wounded and 5,670 were detained.[183] This effectively meant that over 10 per cent of the adult male population was killed, wounded, imprisoned, or exiled.

The fighting capability of the Arab forces was greatly affected by the British crackdown on the Arab revolt. By the time war broke out again in 1947, most of the Arab leadership of the revolt were dead, imprisoned or in exile. In contrast, the Zionists benefited from their association with the British police who used them to suppress the revolt. Special Night Squads were established which utilised Jewish irregulars who greatly benefited from the expertise provided by British soldiers such as Orde Wingate.[184] One of those was Moshe Dayan who would go on to command Israel's victories in the 1948, 1956 and 1967 Arab–Israeli conflicts.[185] Consequently, the Zionists were in a more advantageous position when the 1947–49 conflict broke out and were in a better situation to use armed force to create their state. They accomplished this by committing acts of terrorism against the British mandatory authorities to drive them out before expelling the Arabs. As a result, the international community was presented with a *fait accompli* with the creation of the Jewish state in May 1948, which is described in more detail in Chapters 7 and 9. And yet, Palestine had been promised to the Sherif of Mecca in 1915, something which the British Government almost admitted in public when it published the correspondence for the first time in 1939, the subject of the next chapter.

4
The Hussein–McMahon Correspondence

'A treaty is a treaty.'
Prime Minister Lloyd George,
Paris Peace Conference, 1919

Historians have argued for almost a century about a series of letters exchanged between Sir Henry McMahon, the British High Commissioner in Egypt, and King Hussein, the Sherif of Mecca, over whether or not Palestine was pledged to be Arab and independent.[1] While it is unlikely that this controversy will be resolved to everyone's satisfaction, some historians have, in addition to questioning whether Palestine was ever promised to the Arabs, advanced the argument that the pledges made in that correspondence have no legal validity because they did not amount to a treaty.[2] In this chapter, it will be argued that the doubts that have been placed on the legal validity of the Hussein–McMahon correspondence are not persuasive and that contrary to the assertions of some of these historians, a strong argument can be advanced that Palestine was not specifically excluded from McMahon's pledge. In the light of Britain's subsequent pledge to the Zionists in the Balfour Declaration of November 1917, it will become clear that there is some truth to the saying that Palestine was the 'twice promised land'.

A SECRET TREATY IS A TREATY

The Hussein–McMahon correspondence is best described as a secret treaty.[3] This is an agreement which is usually concluded between two states or a number of states but which is not published or acknowledged to exist. Secret treaties have been a part and parcel of diplomatic intercourse since time immemorial and are considered necessary to protect a state's national security interests. Usually, they are concluded between allies in times of war or in anticipation of war.[4] Paradoxically, many blamed the existence of secret treaties as a reason for the outbreak of the First World War. As described in Chapter 2, when the Bolsheviks seized control of Russia in 1917, they exposed the Sykes–Picot agreement, another secret treaty, which was concluded between France and Britain, and which violated the pledges made in the Hussein–McMahon correspondence. Yet despite the efforts by the Bolsheviks to abolish the practice of negotiating secret treaties, they would make use of them once they had consolidated power, most notoriously when they connived with Nazi Germany to partition Poland in the Molotov–Ribbentrop Pact in August 1939 at the onset of the Second World War.[5]

The Hussein–McMahon correspondence was a treaty born of war, hence its origins have been shrouded in secrecy, but this did not necessarily mean that it had no legal consequences. This is especially true since, and as will be explained later in this chapter, the British Government considered it to be a treaty when they were negotiating with the French Government over the disposition of Ottoman territory at the Paris Peace Conference in 1919. Although little has been written on secret treaties from the perspective of international law, one can deduce from logic, common sense, and from those secret treaties that have been exposed, by drawing an analogy from private contract law as well as from the principles of public international law that the signatories to a secret treaty would be bound by it. Otherwise, there would be little point in taking the trouble to negotiate them in the first place. Whether or not a secret treaty is subsequently exposed or published would not seem to make the slightest difference towards its obligatory force, as what counts is the intention of the states entering into the secret treaty at the time it was negotiated.[6]

In the Hussein–McMahon correspondence, His Majesty's Government conveyed its intention to recognise and support the independence of the Arabs on condition that they assisted it in fighting the Turks.[7] And the Arabs kept their side of the bargain by stirring up trouble for the Turks in Syria and in the Hejaz (which is situated in modern-day Saudi Arabia) and actual participation in the war against Turkey.[8] In exchange, Great Britain provided the Sherif with money, manpower and guns.[9] Clearly then, both Great Britain and the Sherif acted upon their reciprocal commitments, which is integral to the creation of a treaty in international law.[10] That there was an exchange of pledges was not only evident from the fact that the parties acted upon their commitments but also by the terminology employed by McMahon, which, as it will be recalled, he utilised only after having consulted the Foreign Minister in advance, who by virtue of his position can bind his state in international law:

> I have ... lost no time in informing the Government of Great Britain of the contents of your letter, and it is with great pleasure that I communicate to you on their behalf the following statement, which I am confident you will receive with satisfaction: –
>
> The two districts of Mersina and Alexandretta and portions of Syria lying to the west of the districts of Damascus, Homs, Hama and Aleppo cannot be said to be purely Arab, and should be excluded from the limits demanded.
>
> With the above modification, and without prejudice to our existing treaties with Arab chiefs, we accept those limits.
>
> As for those regions lying within those frontiers wherein Great Britain is free to act without detriment to the interests of her ally, France, I am empowered in the name of the Government of Great Britain to give the following *assurances* and make the following reply, to your letter: –

(1) Subject to the above modifications, Great Britain is prepared to recognise and support the independence of the Arabs in all the regions within the limits demanded by the Sherif of Mecca.
(2) Great Britain will guarantee the Holy Places against all external aggression and will recognise their inviolability.
(3) When the situation admits, Great Britain will give to the Arabs her advice and will assist them to establish what may appear to be the most suitable forms of government in those various territories.
(4) On the other hand, it is understood that the Arabs have decided to seek the advice and guidance of Great Britain only, and that such European advisers and officials as may be required for the formation of a sound form of administration will be British.
(5) With regard to the *vilayets* of Bagdad [*sic*] and Basra, the Arabs will recognise that the established position and interests of Great Britain necessitate special administrative arrangements in order to secure these territories from foreign aggression, to promote the welfare of the local populations and to safeguard our mutual economic interests.

I am convinced that this declaration will assure you beyond all possible doubt of the sympathy of Great Britain towards the aspirations of her friends the Arabs *and will result in a firm and lasting alliance*, the immediate results of which will be the expulsion of the Turks from the Arab countries and the freeing of the Arab peoples from Turkish yoke, which for so many years have pressed heavily upon them.[11]

In his first letter to McMahon, the Sherif had, among other things, demanded:

Firstly. – England to acknowledge the independence of the Arab countries, bounded on the north by Mersina and Adana up to the 37° of latitude, on which degree fall Birijik, Urfa, Mardin, Midiat, Jezirat (Ibn 'Umar), Amadia, up to the border of Persia; on the east by the borders of Persia up to the Gulf of Basra; on the south by the Indian Ocean, with the exception of the position of Aden to remain as it is; on the West by the Red Sea, *the Mediterranean Sea up to Mersina*. England to approve of the proclamation of an Arab Khalifate of Islam.

...

Thirdly. – For the security of this Arab independence and certainty of such preference of economic enterprises, both *high contracting parties* to offer mutual assistance, to the best ability of their military and naval forces, to face any foreign Power which may attack either party. Peace not to be decided without agreement of both parties.

Fourthly. – If one of the parties enters upon an aggressive conflict, the other party to assume a neutral attitude, and in case of such party wishing the other to join forces, both to meet and discuss the conditions.

...

Sixthly. – Articles 3 and 4 *of this treaty* to remain in vigour for fifteen years, and, if either wishes it to be renewed, one year's notice before lapse of *treaty* to be given.[12]

Clearly, the Sherif considered his correspondence with McMahon to amount to a treaty. Although McMahon was more careful with his language, he did set out in his letter five assurances responding to what the Sherif had demanded after having consulted his government. In contrast to the Balfour Declaration, which before its incorporation into the Mandate of Palestine was not legally binding, the declaration in the Hussein–McMahon correspondence arguably conveyed a sense of legal obligation. First, Britain agreed to the Sherif's demands regarding Arab independence with the exception of the 'two districts of Mersina and Alexandretta and portions of Syria lying to the west of the districts of Damascus, Homs, Hama and Aleppo'. Thus, although Britain had no sovereignty over these territories because it still belonged to Turkey, it clearly supported the Arabs in their claims to these areas, which Britain pledged that it would be prepared to recognise and support. And as a matter of fact, Britain subsequently did recognise and support Arab claims to sovereignty over the territories concerned. Secondly, Britain agreed to the Sherif's request for financial aid and military assistance in fighting the Turks and entered into an alliance with them. Plainly then, there was, in this instance, an intention to create a series of obligations in the shape of a *quid pro quo*: Britain transferred arms to the Arabs and they in turn assisted the war effort on the side of the Allies by declaring war against Turkey. Thirdly, Great Britain was to 'guarantee' the Holy Places against all external aggression and recognise their inviolability.[13] Arguably, this created an obligation on the part of Britain. Fourthly, in exchange for British support for Arab claims to sovereignty in the event of a successful insurrection against the Turks, the Arabs pledged themselves to recognise the position and interests of Britain to administer the *vilayets* of Baghdad and Basra. And all this was to result, in McMahon's own words, in a 'firm and lasting alliance'.

In addition to the pledges just quoted, McMahon wrote in later correspondence with the Sherif that he had been directed by the British Government to inform him that he 'may rest assured' that Great Britain had no intention of concluding any peace in terms of which the freedom of the Arab peoples from German and Turkish domination does not form 'an essential condition'.[14] He also alluded to the other treaties, which had been concluded by Great Britain with Arab chiefs, noting that his government could not repudiate 'engagements which already exist'.[15] Furthermore, in his letter of 25 January 1916, McMahon wrote in language that would appeal to Hussein in which he invoked 'God' who would 'grant that the result of our mutual efforts and co-operation will bind us in a lasting friendship to the mutual welfare and happiness of us all'.[16] The British must have been aware that the use of this language especially when translated into Arabic would have been interpreted by the Sherif as binding him into an alliance with the British in the war against Turkey, and this was also evident from their subsequent actions when Britain and the Sherif did indeed enter into such an alliance. Finally, in his last letter to the Sherif of 10 March 1916, McMahon agreed to requests for money and ammunition which the Arabs were to use to expel the Turks from Arabia as had been agreed upon: 'I am pleased to be able to inform you that His Majesty's Government have approved of meeting your requests, and that which you asked to be sent with all haste is being despatched with your messenger, who is also the bearer of this letter.'[17] That money was exchanged and that the parties acted upon what had been agreed to 'in all haste' all point to the conclusion that even if Britain considered their agreement to be no more than a political undertaking, they clearly felt some obligation to be bound by it.

It is important to bear in mind that the manner in which treaties were concluded at the turn of the twentieth century, was very different to the way in which states conclude agreements today.[18] At the turn of the twentieth century, secret treaties, like the Hussein–McMahon correspondence and the Sykes–Picot agreement, were a relatively common phenomenon partly due to the fact that before the creation of the League of Nations there was no obligation in custom or in general international law which required a state to publish a treaty.[19] Even today, it is not necessary for a state to publish a treaty. A treaty will still be considered binding as long as it creates rights and obligations for the parties to it in international law.[20] It is generally considered that an agreement concerning territorial questions is *a priori* a matter of international law.[21] Consequently, most agreements concerning territorial questions create rights and obligations for the parties concerned in international law. Moreover, the legal validity or efficacy of an international agreement has never been dependent on the form of the instrument used for its conclusion.[22] An exchange of letters, notes, or even agreed minutes, can create legal obligations if the parties consented to be bound by what had been agreed and if it created legal rights and obligations.[23] The Sykes–Picot agreement was, after all, an exchange of notes between Britain's Foreign Minister and the French Ambassador to London.[24] During the First World War, there was no particular form through which British Foreign Office diplomats were required to conclude international agreements.[25] Even the notes recorded during meetings between senior government officials have been held by the Permanent Court of International Justice to give rise to an international obligation where a promise was made with little regard for form.[26] This is because it is the common intention of the parties, not the form through which that intention is expressed, that is important.[27] As the Permanent Court of International Justice stated in its advisory opinion on the *Customs Régime between Austria and Germany* concerning the legal status of a Protocol concluded in 1922: 'From the standpoint of the obligatory character of international engagements, it is well known that such engagements may be taken in the form of treaties, conventions, declarations, agreements, protocols, or exchanges of notes.'[28] With regards to the Hussein–McMahon correspondence, it would seem that, at the very least, it amounted to a series of mutually agreed commitments by both parties towards an agreed and clearly identifiable goal: the expulsion of the Turks from Arabia. There was consequently an expectation by both parties that the commitments they had agreed to in order to achieve their end result would be fulfilled. Strictly speaking, it did not really matter whether the documents they used to come to this arrangement amounted to a treaty or not. Both the Sherif and McMahon considered themselves bound by it.

SHEIKHS, STATES AND TREATIES

Although it was generally thought during the nineteenth century and at the turn of the twentieth century, that treaties could only be concluded between states, there were exceptions to this rule.[29] For instance, treaties concluded between the British Government and Arab Sheikhs (as opposed to states) was a relatively common practice.[30] In the years 1820, 1835, 1853, 1861 and 1868, as well as in later years, the British Government concluded a number of treaties with the Sheikhs of Bahrain, Abu Dhabi, Qatar, Sharjah and Dubai over acts of piracy in the Gulf.[31] And in the same year as Britain was corresponding with the Sherif (1915–16), treaties were concluded with Ibn Saud who, a decade later, would force the Sherif out of the Arabian Peninsula, and with the Idrisi Sayyid of Sabya.[32] Not once did Britain claim that these agreements were not binding between them because the Sheikhs did not have the capacity to enter into binding obligations with Britain. The fact is that Britain did conclude treaties with non-state entities – before, during and after the First World War.[33] Consequently, the argument that Britain could only enter into treaty relations with other states seems to be rather tenuous as state practice in these cases is clearly to the contrary.

Although the Sherif of Mecca was appointed by the Ottoman Sultan, he had considerable authority over his subjects in the Hejaz and was effectively the sovereign there: He controlled Hejazi territory, fought off invaders, collected monies from the pilgrimage and received ambassadors and foreign dignitaries who had their consulates in Jeddah, near Mecca.[34] He was, moreover, able to act on his own initiative without referring to the Porte or seeking its approval.[35] He had his own administrative departments, his own prisons, his own budget and his own courts, which passed their sentences according to the *shari'a*.[36] He was the chief executive officer in Mecca and alone could call up any Hejazi for military service.[37] His temporal authority varied with the strength of the Ottoman Empire; if the latter was weak then he was the source of real power throughout north-western Arabia.[38] For example, an attempt to prevail upon the Hejazis, who were normally exempt from military service, to accept conscription in 1914 was successfully resisted by the Sherif.[39] By the time he began his negotiations with the British in 1915, the Ottomans were no longer in a position to exert their authority in his Emirate,[40] which was a distinct administrative unit within the Ottoman Empire with established borders delimiting it from the Governorate of Jerusalem and the Sinai Peninsula.[41] On 5 June 1916, the Sherif entered the war on the Allied side and by 9 July he forced the Ottomans out of the Arabian Peninsula with the exception of Medina, which the Turks held until the final armistice.[42] In November 1916, the Sherif proclaimed himself 'King of the Arab countries' and in December, he was recognised by Britain and France as 'King of the Hejaz'.[43] (Although the Sultan appointed Sherif Ali Haidar to replace Hussein as the Sherif of Mecca, he never made it there and took refuge in Lebanon.)[44] By July 1917, the Sherif's forces had captured Aqaba and advanced on Damascus in concert with Lord Allenby's operation from Egypt.[45] Vast territories formerly belonging to the Ottoman Empire fell to the Allies.

From these facts it was therefore apparent that Hussein had been recognised by both Britain and France as 'King of the Hejaz' whilst the terms of the Hussein–McMahon correspondence were being put into effect. In this regard, it is interesting to note that in all the discussions which took place in later years over the terms of the Hussein–McMahon correspondence, not once did the British Government advance the argument that it was not binding because Hussein did not have the capacity to enter into a legal relationship with them. It is even arguable that if Britain had wanted to contest the validity of the Hussein–McMahon correspondence, it would be estopped from doing so after the Sherif had relied upon it to enter into an alliance with Britain in the war against Turkey.[46] As regards the legal status of the Hejaz, the authoritative history by H.W.V. Temperley[47]of the Paris Peace Conference that led to the Versailles Treaty explicitly states that the Hejaz was already an independent sovereign state when Britain began its negotiations with the Sherif.[48] Whilst this may be stretching things a little, it was apparent that in the years 1915–16 when correspondence was exchanged between the Sherif and McMahon, Britain clearly recognised Hussein as the sovereign of Mecca with a legal personality that allowed him to conclude binding agreements under international law. In fact, it could be argued that by 1917 the Hejaz was a state,[49] which had effectively seceded from the Ottoman Empire, for unlike Bahrain, Kuwait, Qatar and the Trucial states of Oman (now the United Arab Emirates),[50] the Hejaz was not a protected state or a protectorate. This was made clear in a letter from the Foreign Office to the British Embassy in Rome concerning the delivery by the Italian Government of heavy weaponry to the Sherif. Mr Graham, then Secretary of State for Foreign Affairs, wrote in a memorandum to the British Chargé d'Affaires in Italy:

> The attitude of His Majesty's Government towards the new Arab Kingdom has from the first been to maintain the independence of King Hussein and the integrity of his dominions. They have always felt that it would be undesirable that the Arab Power in possession of the Holy Places should, as regards its internal affairs, be under the influence of any European Power.[51]

In the original draft of the letter, the following paragraph was removed:

> His Majesty's Government have, indeed, no desire to extend their sphere of political influence in Arabia, *still less to assume a Protectorate* over that country. Their desire is to diminish, not to increase, their responsibilities.[52]

It is therefore arguable that sometime in the latter half of 1917, the Hejaz was recognised as a sovereign and independent state for the purposes of international law by at least three of the Great Powers (Britain, France and Italy). If this is considered too premature, then surely by 1919 when it was welcomed as a fully-fledged member of the family of nations as an 'Associated Power' at the Paris Peace Conference, the Hejaz must have been recognised as a state.[53] And unlike India, which was a member of the League of Nations, Britain never claimed that it had sovereignty over Arabia or that it was a dominion of the British Empire, probably because it did not want to infuriate the Muslims by claiming to have sovereignty over Mecca and Medina. The King of the Hejaz (formerly the Sherif of Mecca) was represented at the Paris Peace Conference by Mr Rustem Haïdar and Mr Aouni Abdul Hadi, the latter a prominent Palestinian. There, they signed on his behalf the Treaty of Peace between the Allied and Associated Powers and Germany.[54] In that year they also signed several other treaties relating to arms traffic[55] and air navigation[56] as well as a peace treaty and protocol concluded between the Allied and Associated Powers and Bulgaria.[57] The Hejaz was also one of the Principal Allied Powers, which signed the Treaty of Sèvres with Turkey.[58] Article 98 provided for Turkish recognition of the Hejaz 'as a free and independent State', and renounced 'in favour of the Hedjaz [*sic*] all rights and titles over the territories of the former Turkish Empire situated outside the frontiers of Turkey'.[59] As Quincy Wright, a famous American political scientist and scholar of international law, wrote: 'Of the former Turkish territories, the Hedjaz was recognized as completely independent and included in the Annex to the Covenant, though it actually has not been admitted to the League of Nations.'[60]

In this regard, it is interesting to note that in the first case ever to come before the Permanent Court of International Justice over the rights of passage for shipping through the Kiel Canal of those nations at peace with Germany as expressly provided for in Article 380 of the Versailles Treaty, the court considered that 'the right of entering into an international engagement is an attribute of State sovereignty'.[61] Although Henry McMahon and Sherif Hussein corresponded whilst the Hejaz was effectively in *statu nascendi*, this did not affect the binding quality of that secret wartime correspondence. Britain regularly entered into agreements with non-state entities, as evinced by the number of agreements it concluded with the Sherif's neighbours in the Gulf.[62] Moreover, as previously mentioned, the Hejaz had a special status as a distinct province within the Ottoman Empire with the capacity to have international relations with other powers concerning the Holy Places, such as with the Moghuls and subsequently with India's Muslims who would make pilgrimages there.[63]

In this respect, the International Court of Justice in a decision *Concerning Right of Passage over Indian Territory*, considered that an agreement concluded in the last quarter of the eighteenth century between Portugal and the leader of the Marathas people in India was binding upon the parties.[64] This was the case even though the document had not been ratified simultaneously by the two contracting parties and even though there was disagreement as to which of the documents was the 'authentic' text.[65] It was sufficient that there was a common agreement creating mutual rights and obligations between two legal persons recognised as such in their international relationships.[66] The same could be said of the Hussein–McMahon correspondence where there were disagreements over the translations concerning the meaning of the term '*vilayet*' which in Arabic is translated as 'district'. Moreover, in the *Western Sahara* advisory opinion, evidence was produced during the oral pleadings to show that in the eighteenth and nineteenth centuries, treaties of peace, commerce and amity had been concluded between the Sultan of Morocco and tribal chiefs in Western Sahara, which implicitly recognised their sovereignty over the territory.[67] And in the actual text of the Hussein–McMahon correspondence, reference was made to Britain's 'existing treaties with Arab chiefs'.[68] Why would McMahon mention these treaties if he did not think that his government was entering into a legal relationship with the Sherif of Mecca? Moreover, in his letter of 14 July 1915, the Sherif was very specific and precise as regards the areas in which he wanted Britain to acknowledge the independence of the Arab countries ('bounded on the north by Medina and Adana up to the 37° latitude etc ...') and to approve of the proclamation of an Arab Caliphate of Islam.[69] The terminology employed by the Sherif in this instance was hardly vague or unclear. He knew exactly what he wanted and McMahon understood this perfectly well. In his letter of 24 October 1915 McMahon replied by saying 'Great Britain is prepared to recognise and support the independence of the Arabs in all the regions within the limits demanded by the Sherif of Mecca' with the exception of those areas in which it would have been detrimental to France. And it will be recalled (see Chapter 2) that Palestine was not excluded, as was clear from McMahon's telegram to Grey concerning what had actually been pledged:

> 4. I have been definite in stating that Great Britain will recognise the principle of Arab independence in purely Arab territory, this being the main point of which agreement depends, but have been equally definite in excluding Mersina, Alexandretta and those districts *on the northern coast of Syria*, which cannot be said to be purely Arab, and where I understand that French interests have been recognised.[70]

McMahon seemed to be quite clear in what he understood by what he was trying to convey to the Sherif in his telegram to Grey ('I have been definite in stating', 'have been equally definite in excluding' ...). Only those districts on the *northern* coast of Syria were excluded in his pledge. It would take some creative thinking and an exercise in geographic acrobatics to argue that Palestine was in 1915, situated on the northern coast of Syria (see Map 3). McMahon clearly did not intend to exclude Palestine from his pledge to the Sherif despite his later protestations.[71] In this regard it should be emphasised that it was what McMahon said and did in his official capacity in 1915 that counts and not what he 'recalled' years later, when he was old, forgetful and retired from the civil service. As the International Court of Justice stated in the *Qatar v. Bahrain* case:

> The Court does not find it necessary to consider what might have been the intentions of the Foreign Minister of Bahrain or, for that matter, those of the Foreign Minister of Qatar. The two Ministers signed a text recording commitments accepted by their Governments, some of which were to be given immediate application. Having signed such a text, the Foreign Minister of Bahrain is not in a position subsequently to say that he intended to subscribe only to a 'statement recording a political understanding', and not to an international agreement.[72]

DISCLOSURE AND THE TALKS AT ST JAMES'S PALACE

In 1939, the British Government published the Hussein–McMahon correspondence for the first time. A Committee was subsequently established to 'consider certain correspondence between Sir Henry McMahon and the Sherif of Mecca'.[73] The meetings were held at St James's Palace in the presence of a number of Arab notables (such as Nuri al-Sa'id, the Iraqi Prime Minister who attended two meetings and George Antonius, one of the first historians to write about the rise of Arab nationalism) with the Lord Chancellor, Lord Maugham and Sir Grattan Bushe, a Legal Adviser at the Colonial Office, amongst others. During one of the meetings, Sir Michael McDonnell, who served as Chief Justice in the Supreme Court of Palestine from 1927 to 1937, argued that in his opinion, it was sufficiently clear from reading the Hussein–McMahon correspondence that Palestine was to be included in the Arab state. He noted that in McMahon's second letter to the Sherif, he had written that the area to be excluded from the pledge to Hussein consisted of coastal regions populated by peoples who could not be said to be 'purely Arab'. McDonnell thought it was of the 'highest significance' that:

> the portions of Syria which may accurately be described as lying to the west of the districts of Damascus, Homs, Hama and Aleppo comprised exactly these areas of Latakia and of the Lebanon and Tripoli where the minorities in question are to be found. Further, an area of which it emphatically could not be said that the population was not purely Arab was Palestine, where notwithstanding the presence of a number of Christian European institutions, at that time at least 95 per cent of the population was Arab.[74]

In the exchange of correspondence with the Sherif, McMahon explicitly mentioned that Britain could not award territories to the Arabs that would be to the detriment and interests of her ally, France. McDonnell thought that it was natural to suppose that the British Government had in mind the 'large Christian Maronite community in the Lebanon which had for years looked upon France as its protector and which was the only Christian community living in a compactly defined sphere in the whole area in question'.[75] In this respect it is worth recalling that in 1860, Charles Louis Napoléon Bonaparte (that is, Napoleon III) sent a force of some 6,000 soldiers there to quell a massacre of Christian Maronites by Muslim Druze, which left 11,000 dead.[76] This early form of 'humanitarian intervention' in the Lebanon was authorised by an agreement concluded between the Ambassadors of the five great powers (Austria, Britain, France, Prussia and Russia) and Turkey on the condition that France withdrew its forces after a six-month period which was subsequently extended for a further three-month period at the request of the Russian Ambassador.[77] It was, perhaps, only natural that the Arabs concluded that Britain was referring to that area of Syria known as Lebanon and not to Palestine in its correspondence with McMahon as the French evidently seemed to consider Syria as falling within their sphere of influence.[78] And as things transpired, Britain agreed to cede Syria to France at the 1920 San Remo Conference in exchange for Palestine, which then included what would become known as Transjordan.[79] Although Britain maintained throughout the talks that it was not its intention to include Palestine in those territories that would form part of an independent Arab state, McDonnell stressed that this was irrelevant from a strictly legal point of view:

> ... I would point out that it is only when, from the imperfection of language it is impossible to know what the intention is without enquiring further, that then it is legitimate to see what the circumstances were with reference to which the words were used and what was the object appearing from those circumstances which the person using them had in view ...
>
> In my contention the grammatical and ordinary sense of the words used in the correspondence lead to no absurdity and no inconsistency, and for that reason it is not necessary, indeed it is not legitimate, to consider any surrounding circumstances in order to modify their meaning.[80]

McDonnell's opinion was significant because he considered the text to be a legal, and not purely a diplomatic, document. It should also be stressed that what matters when an international agreement is concluded is the common intention of the parties *at the time* the agreement was concluded and not what one of the parties thought of it years later.[81] The principle of *pacta sunt servanda* ('agreements must be kept'), is one of the oldest principles of international law, and provides that every treaty in force is binding upon the parties to it and must be performed in good faith.[82] Respect for the obligations arising from treaties is indispensable to predictability and stability in international relations, allowing states to expect that their mutual treaty commitments will be fulfilled in good faith. It would cause anarchy in international relations if the parties to an agreement could simply renege on it on the flimsy pretext that they did not intend to promise X or Y when they concluded an agreement – despite clear indications to the contrary. There is simply no doubt from the exchange of correspondence between Sir Edward Grey, the Foreign Secretary, and Sir Henry McMahon, that Palestine was not excluded from the territories he pledged to Hussein to create his 'Arab Caliphate of Islam'.[83]

In this regard, it is noteworthy that a special map[84] 'illustrating territorial negotiations between H.M.G. and King Hussein' produced by the Foreign

Office explicitly acknowledged that Palestine was included in King Hussein's original demands and that it had not been excluded in McMahon's letter to him of 24 October 1915 (see Map 2). Palestine, which was clearly marked by a red outline, was, according to the cartographer of this particular map, 'pledged that it shall be "Arab" and "independent"'. The fact that this map was produced by the British Foreign Office would seem to accord it greater evidentiary value than say, if it had been produced by the Sherif's *diwan*.[85] In other words, the Foreign Office had produced a map of its own accord, which seemed to clearly indicate what had been pledged. It had also been produced by the Foreign Office at the time of the controversy, rather than years later, when the original participants were dead and buried. This would seem to accord it more evidentiary weight, as the arbitrator in the *Beagle Channel* arbitration would conclude in relation to a series of maps concerning a dispute between Argentina and Chile over a group of islands in Patagonia.[86] Furthermore, a memorandum prepared by the Foreign Office's own Political Intelligence Department on 'British commitments to King Hussein', concluded that: 'With regard to Palestine, His Majesty's Government are committed by Sir H. McMahon's letter to the Sherif on the 24 October, 1915, to its inclusion in the boundaries of Arab independence.'[87]

Behind the scenes, the Foreign Office and the Colonial Office were so concerned with the ramifications of the recently exposed correspondence (which they only published in 1939 after it had been discovered by the Cambridge educated Lebanese scholar, George Antonius[88] who wrote about it in his classic book, *The Arab Awakening*) that they joined forces to draft a memorandum on the 'juridical basis of the Arab claim to Palestine', which was 'prepared as a basis for consideration of certain points to which it is desirable to have the answers ready when the Arab delegations reach this country in January'.[89] The legal document, which they prepared, was, however, very thin. It mainly focused on linguistics and on the differences between the English and Arabic translations of the correspondence. The author of the document also attempted to argue that Article 22 of the Covenant of the League of Nations was permissive only with regard to the question of independence. However, this persuaded no one, not even within the Foreign Office where one unnamed official wrote, '... after going into the whole question of the McMahon-Hussein correspondence again, our position in regard to this correspondence seems to me even weaker than it did before'.[90]

DISCUSSIONS AT THE PARIS PEACE CONFERENCE

The truth was that their position on the Hussein–McMahon correspondence was very weak, as the following account of the debates, which took place at the end of the First World War, will demonstrate. According to the notes of a meeting recorded by an American delegate at the British Prime Minister's flat on the Rue Nitot, in Paris, a dispute arose between France and Britain over the disposition of Ottoman territory during a meeting of the Council of Four (the British Empire, France, Italy and the USA).[91] France claimed a right to Syria as an undivided unit, which included Palestine.[92] The British protested and said that this would not be consistent with the terms of the Sykes–Picot agreement of 1916.[93] A discussion then took place between Prime Minister Lloyd George and the French Foreign Minister, Pichon. Lloyd George claimed that a proper understanding of the Sykes–Picot agreement was dependent on Britain's 'bargain' with the Sherif of Mecca.[94] He then asked whether France intended to occupy Damascus with French troops. If this was the case, he said, 'it would clearly be a violation of the *Treaty* with the Arabs'.[95] Monsieur Pichon then protested that France did not have a 'convention' with King Hussein and that the undertaking had been made by Britain alone.[96] Lloyd George responded by saying that although the agreement had been concluded by Britain alone, it was the British Army who had organised the whole Syrian campaign.[97] He said there would have been no question of capturing Syria from the Turks, but for the use of British troops in the war against Turkey, and that Arab help had been essential, a view which General Allenby, who was also present, endorsed, describing it as 'invaluable'.[98] What these discussions at Paris therefore show is that the British Prime Minister was clearly aware of the Hussein–McMahon correspondence, indeed he even quoted from it, and he described it as being a treaty. He also clearly considered Britain (and France as it happened) bound by it as a matter of law. In a later discussion, after Britain and France had come to an agreement over partitioning Syria between themselves (it transpired that the British wanted a corridor from Mosul to Haifa in Palestine so they could construct an oil pipeline, as well as a corridor between Baghdad and Haifa for a railway and an air route), they said, whilst referring to the Sykes–Picot agreement that: 'A treaty is a treaty and could not be departed from.'[99]

It has, however, been argued by one scholar of the correspondence that the Arabs did not fulfil their side of the bargain because they did not succeed in raising a large-scale revolt against the Turks.[100] However, despite Hussein's outlandish claims there was a revolt.[101] The fact that it would not have been such a success without British support and manpower is immaterial. This is because the Hussein–McMahon correspondence was not predicated upon the *performance* of the Sherif's soldiers. Rather it was based on the *success* of the revolt.[102] And the revolt was a success. As Lloyd George noted in a sternly worded letter he wrote to Georges Clemenceau in October 1919:

> You will observe that the acceptance of the agreement by Great Britain was made conditional upon the Arabs obtaining the four towns of Damascus, Homs, Hama and Aleppo. If that condition is not fulfilled, the whole agreement clearly falls to the ground. There was also the further condition that the Arabs should fulfil their part. In view of the fact that the Arabs remained in the war until the end and played an indispensable part in the overthrow of Turkey, there can be no question that this condition has been fulfilled.[103]

The agreement that Lloyd George was referring to in this instance was the Sykes–Picot agreement which was based upon the Hussein–McMahon correspondence as noted in Chapter 2. In the words of Lloyd George, the Arabs 'played an indispensable part in the overthrow of Turkey'. Whilst legitimate questions might be raised as to whether the Sherif was ever really considered an Arab leader, in the pan-Arab sense, and whilst his desert Bedouin soldiers were no match against the Turks alone, they did fight side by side with the British Army and were allied to the Entente. The Sherif took a huge risk in siding with Britain and he would have been viewed as a traitor by many of his compatriots. His alliance with Britain was no small matter. It was a serious and risky venture. Contrary therefore to the assertions of some historians, it is arguable that the Hussein–McMahon correspondence was considered as binding between the parties in the years 1915–16 and moreover that Palestine was included in that pledge.[104] Certainly, many members of the British Government who were privy to the exchange of correspondence were under the impression that it was binding upon Britain.[105] And even if this view is not accepted, there is little reason to doubt that today such an agreement would be considered as legally binding. In this respect it should be remembered that the correspondence was a secret wartime agreement, which explains why it was not published at the time, but the fact is that secret treaties are binding because it is the intention of the parties to the treaty to create binding legal obligations that counts.[106] The reason for secrecy was twofold: First, because the Turks would have considered it to be an act of treason; and second, because publication of this fact would have precipitated a storm of indignation in the Muslim world, particularly in British India (which back then included the northern territories of the Punjab as well as Kashmir, Sindh and Baluchistan, which would become Pakistan in 1947, as well as Bangladesh which would become an independent state in 1971). It ought to be reemphasised that for the purposes of international law, the form through which an international agreement is expressed is not important – for it is the substance that counts and the circumstances in which the agreement was concluded.[107]

THE FEISAL–WEIZMANN AGREEMENT

So how could the Hussein–McMahon correspondence be reconciled with the Balfour Declaration? In 1919, the Sherif of Mecca sent his third son Feisal to the Paris Peace Conference to present the case of the Arabs before the Great Powers where negotiations were taking place over the spoils of war. On his way to Paris, Feisal sojourned in London where the Foreign Office pressed him to enter into an agreement with Dr Weizmann, the leader of the British Zionists. In the light of the Balfour Declaration, the British Government wanted the young Feisal to give formal recognition to Zionist aspirations in Palestine, as did the Zionists, of course. The fact that Britain was so intent on this is perhaps further testimony to the fact that they were aware that his father had a legitimate claim to Palestine according to the Hussein–McMahon correspondence. This would explain why they were so keen for Feisal to reach an understanding with Weizmann as they would have been aware that there was a flagrant contradiction between their pledges to the Sherif concerning Palestine and the Balfour Declaration. An agreement between Feisal and Dr Weizmann could rectify this. The fact that the Zionists viewed their agreement with Feisal as being a matter of the utmost importance (even today, it is listed as a reference document on Israel's Foreign Ministry website in its peace process category) assumes that Emir Feisal, representing and acting on behalf of the Kingdom of Hejaz, had a say in the future disposition of Palestine, presumably based on the Hussein–McMahon correspondence (which is not listed on Israel's Foreign Ministry website).[108] By concluding this agreement with Feisal, the Zionists were clearly seeking Arab acquiescence over their claims to Palestine in order to legitimise Jewish immigration and settlement there.

Feisal, according to George Antonius, the only author to have been given exclusive access to his diaries, tried to obtain specific instructions from his father on how to negotiate with the Zionists over Palestine.[109] But the Sherif stuck to his guns, telling his son that he was to accept nothing less than the fulfilment of the pledges made by Britain in 1915. According to the account by Antonius, this frustrated Feisal, who did not speak English and who was not familiar with the methods of European diplomacy, as it did not give him much room for negotiations with the British and the Zionists. He was also aware that the French Government was hostile to him and that his only ally at that time was Britain.[110] After all, many of his friends, such as Colonel T.E. Lawrence (popularly known as 'Lawrence of Arabia'), had fought side by side with him against the Turks. He therefore heeded their advice, and agreed to meet with Dr Weizmann to try to reach an understanding with him. This resulted in the Feisal–Weizmann agreement, which provided, among other things, for Zionist immigration to Palestine 'so long as the Arab peasant and tenant farmers shall be protected in their rights'.[111] Though young and ignorant, Feisal was not, however, naïve. He attached a reservation, inscribed in Arabic, to his agreement with Weizmann, which is vividly described by Antonius:

> ... torn as he was between his reluctance to commit his father without previous consultation and his desire to placate the Foreign Office, he took the only course that in the circumstances he felt was open to him. He consented to sign the Agreement, but made his consent conditional upon the fulfilment by Great Britain of her pledges respecting Arab independence. The stipulation was inscribed by him on the text of the Agreement which he signed. It was couched in such sweeping and categorical terms as to leave the main issue untouched; and, since the condition which he attached was not fulfilled, the Agreement never acquired validity.[112]

It is an interesting question whether such an agreement could be characterised as a treaty, since the Zionists at that time, unlike the Hejaz, were not a sovereign entity or a state and had no legal status, as such, under international law.[113] On the other hand, agreements between states and non-state actors, such as those concluded between Britain and the Arab Sheikhdoms in the Gulf, had been described as treaties in the past. In any event, even if one were to conclude that the Feisal–Weizmann agreement amounted to a legally binding agreement, Feisal was acting in his capacity as his father's agent, who had given his son strict instructions not to depart from what the British had agreed to in the Hussein–McMahon correspondence. Although this might not absolve Feisal from incurring the international responsibility for the Kingdom of the Hejaz even if he had exceeded his father's authority and instructions, it is highly questionable whether there had been a common intention or a 'meeting of the minds' in concluding the agreement.[114] Moreover, as Antonius has already alluded to, the reservation attached by Feisal to his agreement with Weizmann was sweeping and categorical:

> Provided the Arabs obtain their independence as demanded in my memorandum dated 4th of January, 1919, to the Foreign Office of the Government of Great Britain, I shall concur in the above articles [referring to the Feisal–Weizmann Agreement]. But if the slightest modification or departure were to be made [*sc.* in relation to the demands in the memorandum] I shall not then be bound by a single word of the present Agreement which shall be deemed void and of no account or validity, and I shall not be answerable in any way whatsoever.[115]

Lawrence was with Feisal when he signed the agreement with Weizmann. He told Arnold Toynbee of the Foreign Office that in the original agreement Weizmann had used the phrases 'Jewish State' and 'Jewish Government'.[116] These were, however, altered by Feisal, who replaced them with 'Palestine', and 'Palestinian Government', to which Weizmann reluctantly agreed. This prompted Toynbee to comment in the memo accompanying the agreement in the Foreign Office files: 'Dr. Weizmann has accepted the principle that the State is not to be Jewish to the detriment of the Arabic-speaking inhabitants, but this will have to be looked after by the Mandatory Power.'[117]

In his original memorandum to the Foreign Office, which was stipulated in his reservation to his agreement with Weizmann, Feisal requested that the Great Powers allow his father to create one Arab state throughout the Middle East uniting the Arab races (see Map 2). He implored them not to partition the area into spheres of influence:

> We believe that our ideal of Arab unity in Asia is justified beyond need of argument. If argument is required, we would point to the general principles accepted by the Allies when the United States joined them, to our splendid past, to the tenacity with which our race has for 600 years resisted Turkish attempts to absorb us, and, in a lesser degree, to what we tried our best to do in this war as one of the Allies.
>
> My father has a privileged place among Arabs, as their successful leader, and as the head of their greatest family, and as Sherif of Mecca. He is convinced of the ultimate triumph of the ideal of unity, if no attempt is made now to force it, by imposing an artificial political unity on the

> whole, or to hinder it, by dividing the area as spoils of war among great Powers.
>
> ...
>
> In Palestine the enormous majority of the people are Arabs. The Jews are very close to the Arabs in blood, and there is no conflict of character between the two races. In principle we are absolutely at one. Nevertheless, the Arabs cannot risk assuming the responsibility of holding level the scales in the clash of races and religions that have, in this one province, so often involved the world in difficulties. They would wish for the effective super-position of a great trustee, so long as representative local administration commended itself by actively promoting the material prosperity of the country.
>
> ...
>
> ... if our independence be conceded and our local competence established, the natural influences of race, language, and interest will soon draw us together into one people; but for this the Great Powers will have to ensure us open internal frontiers, common railways and telegraphs, and uniform systems of education. To achieve this they must lay aside the thought of individual profits, and of their old jealousies. In a word, we ask you not to force your whole civilisation upon us, but to help us pick out what serves us from your experience. In return we can offer you little but gratitude.[118]

In a debate in the UN General Assembly in 1947, Weizmann claimed that with the independence of the Arab countries, Feisal's reservation had been adhered to.[119] However, his claim was disingenuous since the Great Powers decided, contrary to Feisal's memorandum, to partition the Middle East into separate entities.[120] No unified Arab state was created as demanded by Feisal and as stipulated in the Sherif of Mecca's original demands, which the British accepted in the Hussein–McMahon correspondence (see Map 2). Moreover, Feisal never accepted the principle of a Jewish state. In a very revealing interview with the *Jewish Chronicle* in October 1919, Feisal said that he had no objections to Palestine becoming a Jewish cultural centre, especially as he saw the Jews as Semites, as his 'cousins' and would willingly make them 'brothers'. He compared the Zionist claim to Palestine with that of the Arabs to Andalucía:

> Andalusia has very tender memories for Arabs. It was in quite modern times founded upon Arab culture, and for centuries belonged to the Arabs. Now, supposing we Arabs were to say to Spain: 'Your country had old memories for us, and we wish to return there.' We might even point to a few Arabs being resident there. What do you think the Spanish Government would say if we started an agitation for the purposes of making Spain as Arab as today she is Spanish? It is such hothead talk as this that is likely to create a very great deal of friction, which I am particularly anxious to avoid.[121]

On Palestine, Feisal was adamant. He told his interviewers that: '… we Arabs cannot yield Palestine as part of our Kingdom. Indeed, we would fight to the last ditch against Palestine being other than part of the Kingdom and for the supremacy of Arabs in the land.'[122] When Feisal spoke before the Great Powers at the Paris Peace Conference he did not agree to Palestine being converted into a Jewish state. Rather, he wanted Palestine to be included within the boundaries of the proposed Arab state as had been agreed to in the Hussein–McMahon correspondence. As the US delegate Robert Lansing noted:

> The Emir's desire seems to have been to include Palestine within the boundaries of the proposed state, a not unreasonable desire in view of the fact that nearly nine tenths of the population of that territory are today of Arab blood, though I think that he could not have been sanguine of achieving this wish in view of the Zionist Movement which had received the unqualified support of the British Government.[123]

Feisal was not, however, opposed to the idea of Palestine being used as a refuge for persecuted Jews, even if it was under the tutelage of one of the Great Powers, so long as this was not to the detriment of the Arabs, who at that time, formed the majority of the population. After all, Palestine, as the 'Terre Sainte' (Holy Land) with the 'Lieux Saints' (Holy Places), had been the cause of many wars between the Great Powers and was, and still is, coveted by the major religions of the world and their numerous sects. This was a responsibility, which the Sherif of Mecca, weak as he was, could not accept alone. Moreover, there was an economic advantage, which Feisal and his father recognised, to be gained from Jewish immigration and with having one of the Great Powers in control of Palestine. As Commander Hogarth reported to the Foreign Office after a meeting with the Sherif of Mecca in January 1918, where they discussed Palestine:

> The King would not accept an independent Jewish State in Palestine, nor was I instructed to warn him that such a State was contemplated by Great Britain. He probably knows nothing of the actual or possible economy of Palestine, and his ready assent to Jewish settlement there is not worth very much. But I think he appreciates the financial advantage of Arab co-operation with the Jews.[124]

GREAT POWER POLITICS

The Great Powers are called 'Great' for a reason. And so Feisal's speech before them at the Paris Peace Conference had little impact; Great Britain and France were intent on dismembering the Middle East to create new political entities under their control. Greater Syria was divided into four parts: Lebanon, Palestine, Transjordan and Syria. The French forced Feisal from Damascus in 1920, despite the fact that he had helped the Allies in prosecuting the war against Turkey. In fact, Lloyd George had written to Clemenceau, prior to the latter's visit to Paris in October 1919, imploring him to treat Feisal with the courtesy and respect owed to him as one of the Allies, but this was to no avail:

> The British Government knows that when the Emir Feisal does come to Paris, you will, notwithstanding the tone of your language, treat him with the courtesy and consideration which one of the Allies deserves. They would remind you that he initiated a revolt against Turkish rule at a time when Allied fortunes were at a very low ebb; that he was loyal to the alliance to the end; and that he and his followers played an indispensible part in overthrowing Turkey, which was the prelude to the collapse of the German combination. The Emir Feisal is the representative of a proud and historic race with whom it is essential that both the British and French should live in relations of cordial amity. He is further a member of the Peace Conference of which you are yourself the distinguished president. The British Government *is bound to him by solemn engagements*, and the area he controls lies opposite to both the French and British spheres.[125]

To compensate Feisal, Britain made him King of Mesopotamia. As regards the Hussein–McMahon correspondence, it seems to have been either set aside or forgotten for a number of years,[126] until interest in it was rekindled in 1939, by which time Palestine had already been placed under a British Mandate which provided that it was to become a 'Jewish national home', on the condition that nothing was done which might prejudice the civil and religious rights of Palestine's predominantly non-Jewish population.

At the heart of all these conflicting pledges, lay the question of self-determination and how the national aspirations of the Palestinian Arabs and the Zionists could be accommodated in a single Palestinian state. The problem that this created is examined in the next two chapters, on self-determination and partition.

5
The Question of Self-determination

'We shall never recognize as just the imposition of an alien will on any people.'

All-Russian Central Executive Committee, 1 January 1918

'Self-determination' is not a mere phrase. It is an imperative principle of action which statesmen will henceforth ignore at their peril.'

President Woodrow Wilson, Address to both Houses of Congress, 11 February 1918

'... once you appeal to the principle of self-determination, both Arabs and Zionists are prepared to make every use of it they can. No doubt we shall hear a good deal of that in the future, and indeed, in it we may find a solution of our difficulties'.

George Curzon, British Foreign Secretary, 1918 quoted in David Lloyd George, *The Truth About the Peace Treaties*, Vol. II (London: Victor Gollancz, 1938), p. 1144

'The immediate establishment of a complete and purely Jewish state would mean placing a majority under the rule of a minority; it would therefore run counter to the first principles of democracy; and would undoubtedly be disapproved by public opinion of the whole world ...'

Herbert Samuel, Britain's first High Commissioner to Palestine, in *Zionism: Its Ideals and Practical Hopes*, 1920, p. 2

'The Arab in Palestine has the *right* of self-determination.'

David Ben-Gurion, Secretary-General of *Histadrut*, Lecture in Berlin, 1931

'His Majesty's Government ... desire to see established ultimately an independent Palestine State. It should be a State in which the two peoples in Palestine, Arabs and Jews, share authority in government in such a way that the essential interests of each are shared.'

British White Paper, 1939

In many respects Zionism was at odds with twentieth-century notions of self-determination. This is because prior to the insertion of the Balfour Declaration into the British Mandate of Palestine, the Zionists had no territory to claim as their own. And prior to the Zionist conquest and the expulsion of the Palestinian Arabs, Jews never formed the majority of Palestine's population. Moreover, Zionism needed the support of a colonial power to nurture the development of a Jewish national home in Palestine. And yet, self-determination as it developed in the twentieth century was inherently anti-colonial and was intricately linked to decolonisation. But what happened in Palestine was precisely the reverse of decolonisation. If there were any word to accurately describe it, it would be 'recolonisation'. The paradox of the

Balfour Declaration did not pass without comment however. In the words of Balfour's Private Secretary, Lord Eustace Percy:

> In Palestine, a country peopled for the most part by an Arab race, whose independence they are equally pledged to recognise and guarantee, a 'national home' is to be created for a people whose only connection with that country for 1800 years was one of historic sentiment and religious tradition. This pledge [the Balfour Declaration] violates all current ideas of self-determination. It stands isolated and unique among the various phases of settlement.[1]

The Zionists' claim to self-determination in Palestine was indeed both 'isolated' and 'unique'. It was not based on effective occupation, the 'free will of the people', majority rule, or decolonisation. Rather, it was based on a colonial document. This was self-determination by treaty.

THE ANTECEDENTS OF SELF-DETERMINATION

Self-determination is one of the most widely disputed areas of public international law and is customarily invoked by all the sides to a conflict. Although its status as a norm of law is no longer disputed, its content and its application to specific situations remains hotly contested.[2] This is especially the case with long-standing territorial disputes between different ethnic groups which can become particularly acute in the cases of states with large minority populations. When making claims to self-determination, however, it is necessary to demonstrate a link between the people concerned and territory. This is because without a connection to territory a people cannot exercise their right of self-determination. Indeed, this was the fundamental dichotomy facing the Zionist movement at the dawn of the twentieth century. How could the Jewish people dispersed throughout all the corners of the globe claim to have a right of self-determination if they did not have a territory in which to exercise it? This is why Zionism needed to find a colonial power which could allocate them a territory.

Although today, the right of self-determination does not necessarily give a people a right to create a separate state, known to legal scholars as external self-determination, in the heady days of colonialism this is how it was understood by most people. For instance, Lenin, writing as early as 1914, was of the opinion that 'it would be wrong to interpret the right of self-determination as meaning anything but the right to existence as a separate state'.[3] In March 1917, Lenin declared publicly that when the Bolsheviks took power in Russia, their peace plan would include 'the liberation of all colonies; the liberation of all dependent, oppressed, and non-sovereign peoples'.[4] It was through the Bolsheviks' insistence during their negotiations with Germany and Austria-Hungary in the lead up to the conclusion of the treaty of Brest-Litovsk in March 1918, that self-determination became the dominant issue for international diplomacy at the end of the war.[5] The Marxists associated the principle of self-determination with secession, that is, the right to break away, which partly explains why the Soviet constitutions of 1918 and 1936 recognised the right of secession for its constituent republics.[6] Moreover, the Soviet principle of self-determination was not just a whimsical rhetorical device, for it was actually put into practice with immediate effect within the former Russian Empire following the Bolshevik Revolution.[7] Trotsky, the Russian Commissar for Foreign Affairs, challenged the western allies' (Britain, France, Italy and the US) commitment to the principle of self-determination in a speech he made on 29 December 1917:

> Are they asking, like we ourselves, that the right of the determination of their own destinies should be given to the peoples of Alsace-Lorraine, Galicia, Posen, Bohemia and South Slavonia? If they are doing so, are they willing also to recognise the right to the peoples of Ireland, Egypt, India, Madagascar, Indo-China, and other countries, just as under the Russian Revolution this right has been given to the peoples of Finland, Ukraine, White Russia and other districts?[8]

The Bolsheviks' pronouncement in support of self-determination acted as a spur to Woodrow Wilson's Fourteen Points speech to Congress, which was briefly mentioned in Chapters 2 and 4.[9] Wilson was anxious to persuade the Russians to stay in the war by publicly displaying his commitment to democratic and liberal principles, including national self-determination, as the framework for an Allied-constructed peace settlement.[10] Lloyd George too, reacted to Trotsky's speech by saying that self-determination would apply outside Europe, specifically listing Arabia, Armenia, Mesopotamia, Syria, and Palestine.[11] Lenin's concept of self-determination was, however, more radical than Wilsonian self-determination. In contrast to Wilson, Lenin envisaged the principle applying to all colonial territories, including those of the European colonial maritime powers.[12] However, this interpretation of self-determination was not widely accepted at the time, particularly by the Great Powers, such as Britain, France and Italy that were jealously guarding their colonies.[13] It was not until decolonisation in the 1960s, accompanied by its numerous conflicts (mostly Soviet sponsored), that self-determination became a rule of customary international law applicable to all colonised peoples, as opposed to a vague political principle. Even today, questions concerning the scope of self-determination, which peoples may invoke it, and whether a right of unilateral or remedial secession exists under international law remain controversial. In this regard it should be said that self-determination can be as much a cause of conflict as providing a solution to it. This is especially when there are more than one people entitled to it competing for effective control over the same territory. Palestine is a case in point.

SELF-DETERMINATION AND THE PARIS PEACE CONFERENCE

Although 'self-determination' was a relatively novel phenomenon in 1919 which traced its roots to the American and French revolutions, the Great

Powers were cognisant of what they were doing by referring to it at the Paris Peace Conference. The leaders of the day were well-informed of what the principle of self-determination entailed and they realised that it was such an elastic concept that it could be invoked by almost any group in support of their political claims to independence.[14] And neither did Wilson, one of its greatest champions, exclude non-European peoples from the right of self-determination as a matter of principle.[15] Rather, in contrast to Lenin, he envisaged them achieving it through an evolutionary process under the benevolent tutelage of a 'civilised' power that would prepare them for self-government.[16] This did not mean that the principle was not without controversy or that it raised expectations which Wilson could not guarantee. This is why Robert Lansing, the US Secretary of State, who was leading the American delegation to the Paris Peace Conference, was so concerned about what he referred to as 'the *right* of self-determination', that he jotted down the following note to himself:

> The more I think about the President's declaration as to the right of 'self-determination', the more convinced I am of the danger of putting such ideas into the minds of certain races ...
>
> What effect will it have on the Irish, the Indians, the Egyptians, and the nationalists among the Boers? Will it not breed discontent, disorder, and rebellion? Will not the Mohammedans of Syria and Palestine and possibly of Morocco and Tripoli rely on it? How can it be harmonized Zionism, to which the President is practically committed?
>
> The phrase is simply loaded with dynamite. It will raise hopes which can never be realized. It will, I fear, cost thousands of lives ...[17]

In December 1917, when the British Army occupied Palestine, the Arabs could not independently invoke a right of self-determination under general international law even though they had long been numerically preponderant in Palestine, owning most of the land, and even reaching high political office under the Turks. This is because at that time self-determination was, at best, a political principle. It did not exist as an independent legal right, which all peoples could invoke. However, the Arabs were represented at the Paris Peace Conference. Emir Feisal was given a right of audience by the Great Powers and in his speech before them he did assert a claim to Palestine.[18] Moreover, President Woodrow Wilson invoked the principle of self-determination in a speech he gave to a joint session of the two Houses of Congress five weeks after his Fourteen Points speech when he said that self-determination was not a mere phrase, but 'an imperative principle of action which statesmen will henceforth ignore at their peril'.[19] He added: '... peoples and provinces are not to be bartered about from sovereignty to sovereignty as if they were mere chattels and pawns in a game, even the great game, now forever discredited of the balance of power'.[20] Wilson's understanding of what the principle of self-determination entailed would find direct application in the League of Nations mandates system as provided for in the fourth paragraph of Article 22 of the Covenant, which partly explains why Lansing was so concerned about it. Wilson did not leave his ideas behind him in Washington DC. He brought them with him to Paris.[21] As will be explained in the following pages, those mandates established in the Middle East, which included Palestine, were classified as A-class, where the principle of self-determination was applicable to the communities living there (see Map 5). Whether self-determination was viewed as a principle as opposed to a right, and the terms were used interchangeably at the time, was, perhaps, beside the point, as the existence of the A-class mandates as 'independent nations' was 'provisionally recognised' by the Great Powers at the Paris Peace Conference in 1919.[22]

BRITISH POLICY TOWARDS PALESTINE

The policy of the British Government on the question of self-determination in Palestine can be summed up in an extract from a letter that the Foreign Secretary, Arthur J. Balfour, wrote to Prime Minister Lloyd George on 19 February 1919:

> The *weak* point of our position, of course, is that in the case of Palestine we deliberately and rightly decline to accept *the principle of self-determination.* If the present inhabitants were consulted they would unquestionably give an anti-Jewish verdict. Our justification for our policy is that we regard Palestine as being absolutely exceptional; that we consider the question of the Jews outside Palestine as one of world importance, and that we conceive the Jews to have historic claim to a *home* in their ancient land; provided that *home* can be given them *without either dispossessing or oppressing* the present inhabitants.[23]

Essentially, Balfour was making the argument that the principle of self-determination was not to apply to Palestine, as it did in the other A-class mandated territories. Rather, in his view, it was to be set aside in Palestine because the British Government wanted to create a Jewish home provided that it did not dispossess or oppress its present inhabitants. But was Balfour right when he said that his government declined to accept the principle of self-determination in Palestine? Or was he merely expressing his own private opinion?

In 1919, there was undoubtedly no obligation in customary international law to consult the inhabitants of a particular territory on their political development. The decision by the Great Powers at the Paris Peace Conference to send the King–Crane Commission of Inquiry to consult the inhabitants of the Middle East on their political aspirations was an exception to the general rule. But the A-class mandates were different. In spite of Balfour's reservations about the principle being applied to Palestine, self-determination was applicable as it was reflected in Article 22 of the Covenant of the League of Nations, a view which is also supported by state practice, as all those territories would become independent states after the Second World War.[24] The view that self-determination was applicable to the A-class mandates would also be subsequently endorsed by the International Court of Justice in its 1971 advisory opinion on the *Namibia* case, which is referred to below. And even during the mandatory years (1923–48) the British Government accepted that Palestine was an A-class mandate entitled to independence. As Britain's Colonial Secretary told the Permanent Mandates Commission in 1937: '... the Palestine mandate is an A mandate. The essence of that is that it marks a transitory period, with the aim and object of leading the mandated territory to become an independent self-governing State.'[25] Moreover, whatever Balfour's personal feelings may have been in 1919, the British Government evidently considered that all of Palestine's inhabitants were entitled to self-determination by 1939, when it published its White Paper. Then, the British Government categorically declared that:

> It is proper that the people of the country should as early as possible enjoy the rights of self-government which are exercised by the people of neighbouring countries. His Majesty's Government are unable at present to foresee the exact constitutional forms which government in Palestine will eventually take, but their objective is self government, and they desire to see established ultimately an independent Palestine State. It should be a State in which the two peoples in Palestine, Arabs and Jews, share authority in government in such a way that the essential interests of each are shared.[26]

The reason why Balfour wanted to sideline the principle of self-determination in Palestine in 1919 was because he was aware that were they to consult its predominantly Arab population on what they thought of Zionism, they would have unquestionably given, as he admitted, an 'anti-Jewish' verdict (that is, they would have opposed Zionism) and ended the experiment right there and then. And of course, his fears were well founded as the Palestinian Arabs, as explained in Chapter 2, resolutely opposed Zionism in their submissions to the King–Crane Commission in Damascus. Despite Balfour's opposition to Palestinian self-determination, he was, however, clear that he never envisaged nor wanted Palestine to be converted into a Jewish state nor for the Zionists to dispossess or oppress Palestine's indigenous Arab population. It seems that he sincerely believed that Arabs and Jews could coexist in Palestine when he said that Britain would provide the Jews with a home there on the condition that it could be given to them 'without either dispossessing or oppressing the present inhabitants'.

BALFOUR VS. CURZON

It is also important to note that Balfour conceded that the British Government's position was weak. In fact, after his resignation as Foreign Secretary, he wrote another memorandum on Palestine, this time to his successor Lord Curzon, in which he admitted that there was a flagrant contradiction between the

Government's Palestine policy, the letter of the Covenant, and the policy of the Allies.[27] In the memo he wrote:

> The contradiction between the letter of the Covenant and the policy of the Allies is even more flagrant in the case of the 'independent nation' of Palestine than in the 'independent nation' of Syria. For in Palestine we do not propose even to go through the form of consulting the wishes of the present inhabitants of the country, though the American Commission has been going through the form of asking what they are. The four Great Powers are committed to Zionism. And Zionism, be it right or wrong, good or bad, is rooted in age-long tradition, in present needs, in future hopes, of far profounder import than the desires and prejudices of the 700,000 Arabs who now inhabit that ancient land.
>
> In my opinion that is right. What I have never been able to understand is how it can be harmonized with the [Anglo-French] declaration, the [League of Nations] Covenant, or the instructions to the [King–Crane] Commission of Enquiry.[28]

Is this not an admission by a former senior member of the British Government and possibly one of the most pro-Zionist cabinet members of all time, that the Zionist project was inconsistent, if not contrary, to the League of Nations Covenant, the declared policy of the Allies in prosecuting the war, and the self-determination of peoples? If so, Balfour must have been aware that he could not unilaterally set aside the principle of self-determination in Palestine merely because it suited his own personal view of what he thought British foreign policy in the Middle East should be, which widely diverged from that of his successor Lord Curzon.[29] In fact, Curzon did his best to 'water down' the proposed mandate for Palestine that had been drafted by his predecessor. Replying to a minute written by Sir John Tilley on the draft Mandate in which Tilley objected to the Arabs being described as 'non-Jewish communities' because it 'sounds as if there were a few Arab villages in a country full of Jews', Curzon wrote:

> I have never been consulted as to this mandate at an earlier stage, nor do I know from what negotiations it springs or on what undertakings it is based ...
>
> But here I may say that I agree with Sir J. Tilley and that I think the entire conception is wrong.
>
> Here is a country with 585,000 Arabs and 30,000 or is it 60,000 Jews (by no means all Zionists). Acting upon the noble principles of self-determination and ending with a splendid appeal to the League of Nations, we then proceed to draw up a document which reeks of Judaism in every paragraph and is an avowed constitution for a Jewish State.
>
> Even the poor Arabs are only allowed to look through the keyhole as a non-Jewish community.

> It is quite clear that this mandate has been drawn up by someone reeling under the fumes of Zionism. If we are all to submit to that intoxicant, this draft is all right.
>
> Perhaps there is no alternative.
>
> But I confess I should like to see something worded differently.[30]

When Curzon alluded to the fact that the Mandate had been drawn up by 'someone reeling under the fumes of Zionism', he was primarily referring to Balfour.[31] Throughout the remainder of his time as British Foreign Minister, Curzon did his best to modify the terms of the British Mandate of Palestine, as described in Chapter 2, so that it could be reconciled with the League of Nations Covenant and the principle of self-determination.[32] He also wanted to ensure that the indigenous Arab population would be protected from an expansive interpretation of the phrase, 'a national home for the Jewish people'. For instance the Palestine Committee, which was set up by the Foreign Office to redraft the Mandate, considered that the proposed reference in the draft preamble to the 'claim' of the Jewish people to Palestine should be omitted. As recorded in the minutes: 'It was agreed that they had no *claim*, whatever might be done for them on sentimental grounds; further, that all that was necessary was to make room for Zionists in Palestine, not that they should turn "it", that is the whole country, into their home ...'[33] When the original draft of the Mandate was shown to the French Foreign Minister, M. Millerand, he apparently 'nearly jumped out of his skin'.[34] Moreover, in a memorandum drafted by Curzon on 30 November 1920 for the Cabinet, he wrote that the French and Italian governments were very critical of it because the interests and rights of the Arab majority were almost completely ignored.[35] There was strong objection to the notion that Palestine could be reconstituted as *the* National Home. This is what Curzon then wrote:

> It was pointed out (1) that, while the Powers had unquestionably recognized the historical connection of the Jews with Palestine by their formal acceptance of the Balfour Declaration and their textual incorporation of it in the Turkish Peace Treaty drafted at San Remo, *this was far from constituting anything in the nature of a legal claim*, and that the use of such words might be, and was, indeed, certain to be used as the basis of all sorts of political claims by the Zionists for the control of Palestinian administration in the future, and (2) that, while Mr Balfour's Declaration had provided for the establishment of a Jewish National Home in Palestine, this was not the same thing as the reconstitution of Palestine as a Jewish National Home – an extension of the phrase for which there was *no justification*, and which was certain to be employed in the future as a basis for claims to which I have referred.
>
> On the other hand, the Zionists pleaded for the insertion of some such phrase in the preamble, on the ground that it would make all the difference to the money that they aspired to raise in foreign countries for the development of Palestine.

> Mr Balfour, who interested himself keenly in their case, *admitted, however, the force of the above contentions*, and, on the eve of leaving for Geneva suggested an alternative form of words which I am prepared to recommend.
>
> Paragraph 3 of the Preamble would then conclude as follows 'whereas recognition has thereby (i.e. by the Treaty of Sèvres) been given to the historical connection of the Jewish people with Palestine, and to the grounds for reconstituting their National Home in that country' ...[36]

Even Balfour, the principal architect of the Zionist project, who had aligned himself so closely with their cause, ultimately conceded that the Zionists had no legal claim to Palestine. At the very most, they could create a National Home in Palestine, but not in place of it. The idea that the Zionists could not lay a claim to the whole of Palestine would be repeatedly reiterated throughout the years when Britain was the mandatory power, by British politicians from Churchill to MacDonald. It also indirectly contributed to the partition of Palestine, which is examined in the following chapter.

ENTITLEMENT TO SELF-DETERMINATION

The difficulty for the Zionists was that they lacked a legal nexus to territory. This is why they needed a charter to give their colonisation of Palestine a seal of approval where they could exercise their 'right' of self-determination. Essentially, the claim of Palestine's indigenous inhabitants to self-determination was based on effective occupation and continuous habitation whereas the Zionists' was aligned to British imperialism. Without British support there was simply no way in which the Zionists could create their national home in Palestine. But on what basis *in law* could the Zionists advance a claim to Palestine if they were not considered a people, which is a necessary precondition for self-determination? This paradox was noted by the eminent scholar Dr Frankenstein of the Hague Academy of International Law, who made the following illuminating observation:

> A normally situated people does not need a home. It is concentrated in a particular country and, by this very fact, is always in its home, even if it is not independent. But the Jewish people is not in a normal situation. It is not concentrated in a particular country but dispersed over the world. It thus lacks an essential characteristic of a people, i.e., the connection with a country.[37]

If the Jewish people were not a 'people' for the purposes of international law in 1917 when the Balfour Declaration was issued, then how could they assert a claim to self-determination in Palestine? In 1917, the 'Jewish people' was not a cohesive political group. Moreover, they lacked any collective connection to territory. The enforcement of the Mandate on 29 September 1923, however, remedied this situation by connecting the Jewish people to Palestine subject to clauses safeguarding the civil and religious rights of all the inhabitants of Palestine and the political status of Jews in other countries.

But if the principle of self-determination was applicable to the Jewish population of Palestine after 1923 then it must have also applied to the Arabs. This is especially as the principles enshrined in the Covenant of the League of Nations took precedence over the terms of the Mandate. If the principle of self-determination in Palestine applied to the Zionists when most of them were resident overseas and nationals of other states, then surely the indigenous Arab population who had physically resided in Palestine for centuries and were the overwhelming majority of the population, were entitled to invoke it as well? After all, General Allenby's Proclamation of November 1918 did invoke the 'free will of the people' in promising the Arabs liberation and an end to oppression:

> The object of the war in the East on the part of Great Britain was the complete and final liberation of all peoples formerly oppressed by the Turks and the establishment of national governments and administrations in those countries deriving authority from the initiative and free will of the people themselves.[38]

This British promise, as well as the Anglo-French Declaration which was drafted along the lines of Allenby's Proclamation as mentioned in Chapter 2, created a legitimate expectation on the part of the Arabs that these promises would be fulfilled.[39] And there is no doubt that this declaration applied to the *Palestinian* Arabs as it was announced by Allenby inside the walls of Jaffa Gate in the Old City of Jerusalem. Moreover, as mentioned in Chapters 2 and 4, unilateral declarations can create legal obligations for the purposes of international law.[40] As Balfour noted in the same memo cited earlier:

> In 1915 we promised the Arabs independence; and the promise was unqualified, except in respect of certain territorial reservations. In 1918 the promise was by implication repeated; for no other interpretation can, I think, be placed by any unbiased reader on the phrases in the declaration about a 'National Government', and 'an Administration deriving its authority from the initiative and free choice of the native population'.[41]

Therefore the only way in which the Balfour Declaration could be reconciled with the League of Nations Covenant as it was subsequently incorporated in the Mandate, would be to conclude that both Palestine's indigenous Jewish and Arab inhabitants had a claim to Palestine on the basis of the principle of self-determination.[42] But *how* this would actually be *realised* was another matter entirely, and indeed this is something which has never been resolved and which is still a source of controversy today.

However, it would seem that in the event of conflict between the interests of the two communities, international law would give first consideration to the interests of the original and indigenous inhabitants over those who had recently immigrated there from overseas. This was the opinion the Japanese representative, Mr Yanaghita, who, in a report he presented to the Permanent Mandates Commission in 1923, wrote:

> If ... it happens that the interests of the two classes of inhabitants – those previously living in the mandated areas and those arriving later prove irreconcilable, the Mandatory administration will naturally give first consideration to those of the original inhabitants.[43]

Moreover, in a British Colonial Office memorandum on the status of Indians in Kenya, which, as explained in Chapter 1, was seriously considered as a place for Jewish settlement in 1903, the policy of the British Government was explained in this manner:

> Primarily, Kenya is an African territory, and His Majesty's Government think it necessary definitely to record their considered opinion that the interests of the African natives must be paramount, and that if, and when, the immigrant races should conflict, the former should prevail.[44]

Yet in Palestine, Britain was committed to the Balfour Declaration. Consequently, the rights of the indigenous Palestinian Arab population were not considered paramount. However, this did not mean that they did not have any rights at all. Rather, their rights were to be accommodated in the light of Britain's pledges to the Zionists. In other words, they could not invoke the principle of self-determination to prevent Britain from implementing the terms of the Mandate as regards the Jewish National Home. But nor could the Zionists invoke the Balfour Declaration to lay a claim to the whole of Palestine. As explained in Chapter 2, a Jewish national home was to be established in Palestine, but not in place of it. In other words, the Balfour Declaration did not apply to the whole of Palestine. Rather, the national home was to be established *in* Palestine, within a territorial sphere, which had not yet been delimited.[45] Moreover, this pledge was conditional on the safeguard clauses respecting the civil and religious rights of the non-Jewish population and the political status of Jews in other countries.

SELF-DETERMINATION AND THE BRITISH MANDATE OF PALESTINE

The Mandate considered Palestine as a territorial unit, inhabited for the purposes of development by a single political community who were being nurtured by the British towards self-government and independence as a separate state. Although Britain was essentially creating a new political entity carved out of Syria, the idea of *Filastín* or Palestine was not new.[46] Even before the arrival of the British Army in 1917, Palestinian Arabs were regularly referring to *Filastín* as an area of its own, separate from Syria.[47] In this regard, Palestine always had a special significance, particularly for its Christian population, as the Holy Land, which marked it out from the rest of the Arab world. For instance, the jurisdiction of the Greek Orthodox Patriarch of Jerusalem, which had been in existence without a break since the Roman period, extended over western Palestine and Transjordan – as did the Latin Patriarchate of Jerusalem (re-established in 1847) and the Anglican Bishop of Jerusalem (appointed in 1841).[48] In 1910, a Court of Appeal was established in Jerusalem and cases were heard there, rather than in Damascus.[49] Moreover, by 1911, Palestinian newspapers were making extensive use of the term *Filastín* as a territorial location.[50] For instance, one Jaffa newspaper was actually called *Filastín*. As Yehoshua Porath – one of Israel's leading orientalist historians on Palestinian history and Professor Emeritus of Middle East History at the Hebrew University of Jerusalem – concluded in a study on the subject: '... at the end of the Ottoman period the concept of *Filastín* was already widespread among the educated Arab public, denoting either the whole of Palestine or the Jerusalem *sanjak* alone'.[51]

The Palestinian community was comprised of Christians, Jews, Muslims and others who inhabited that part of the *Bilad al-Sham* which would become Palestine and who were mostly Arabic speaking.[52] The mandate system therefore envisaged one people for the purposes of self-determination. Jewish self-determination was envisaged in the light of the Mandate but only within the context of the self-determination of Palestine as a whole.[53] It was not considered a principle that was given to the Jewish community independently of the Palestinian community.[54] Under the Mandate, Arabs and Jews were referred to as Palestinians, their religion and ethnicity being no longer relevant. As Churchill stipulated in his 1922 White Paper: '[T]he status of all citizens of Palestine in the eyes of the law shall be Palestinian, and it has never been intended that they, or any section of them, should possess any other juridical status.'[55] The Mandate was drafted in the belief that the Mandatory would find a common ground on which both Arabs and Jews could coexist. This was in line with the Balfour Declaration, the Hogarth Message, the Feisal–Weizmann agreement, and the Mandate itself. But it did not envisage that self-determination would apply exclusively to those Jews who immigrated to Palestine from overseas to the detriment of Palestine's indigenous inhabitants.

In this regard it will be recalled that although the Mandate included numerous provisions regarding the establishment of the Jewish national home in Palestine, this did not negate the rights of the Palestine Arabs. That they were not specifically mentioned in the Balfour Declaration other than as the 'existing non-Jewish' community did not affect this. In fact, the Mandate alluded to the presence of another people in Palestine in several of its principal provisions. For example, Article 2 safeguarded the civil and religious rights of *all the inhabitants of Palestine*; Article 6 ensured that the rights and position of *other sections of the population* would not be prejudiced; Article 9 provided that the judicial system in Palestine would assure to foreigners, *as well as to natives*, a complete guarantee of their rights; Article 11 provided that the Administration of Palestine would take all necessary measures to safeguard the interests of the *community* in connection with the development of the country;

and Article 18 provided that the Administration of Palestine could impose such taxes and custom duties as it considered necessary and to take such steps as it thought best to promote the development of the natural resources of the country and to safeguard the interests of the *population*.[56] These provisions referred to the indigenous population of Palestine, with Palestinian Muslim and Christian Arabs comprising the overwhelming majority in 1923, when the Mandate entered into force. After all, the Zionists, not being physically present in Palestine in large numbers, needed assistance with creating their national home there, whereas the Palestine Arabs did not, as they had already been living there for centuries. In this respect, their rights were not 'virtual' rights, a description which could only apply to a group of people, such as the Zionists, who were not physically rooted to the territory of Palestine because they resided abroad.[57]

In other words, the reason why the Mandate contained so many provisions for Jewish settlement was precisely because the vast majority of Jews in the early 1920s were not resident in Palestine. There was no need to insert provisions in the Mandate facilitating the immigration of Arabs to Palestine, as they were already there. Admittedly, the phrase 'non-Jewish communities' is not the most flattering description for the Palestinian Arabs, especially when they formed over 90 per cent of the population.[58] But the fact of the matter is that Britain would explicitly recognise their political rights, when it began administering Palestine as the mandatory power, as will be explained below. Finally, the League of Nations Covenant which was the principal juridical document which provided the legal basis for the mandates system, spoke of '[c]ertain communities formerly belonging to the Turkish Empire'. The only community inhabiting Palestine, who satisfied that description was its indigenous population. It would therefore seem that during the drafting of the Mandate, the Zionists and the British Government were attempting to modify the principle of self-determination in Palestine so that the Arab population would not be in a position to prevent the fulfilment of the Mandate in relation to the minority Jewish population. As noted in a Foreign Office memorandum written by Balfour on the drafting of the Mandate:

> The problem of Palestine cannot be *exclusively* solved on the principles of self-determination, because there is one element in the population – the Jews – which, for historical and religious reasons, is entitled to a greater influence than would be given to it if numbers were the sole test. It is necessary, therefore, to devise some scheme of Government which will at once protect Arab interests, and give effect to the national aspirations of the Jewish race.[59]

Although the problem of Palestine could not be solved exclusively on the principle of numerical self-determination as suggested in Balfour's memorandum, this did not mean that it did not apply at all. This is because the memorandum was predicated on the very premise that the self-determination framework was, in principle, applicable to Palestine. Otherwise, Balfour would not have mentioned self-determination at all. The problem was that in Palestine, other factors had to be taken into consideration, namely Britain's avowed promise to establish a Jewish national home there. Consequently, the principle of self-determination was being modified in Palestine so that it could apply to the immigrant Jewish population and not only to the indigenous Arab population. Effectively, Arab self-determination in Palestine was being temporarily *postponed* so as to give the Zionists an opportunity to create their home. As noted by the Attorney-General of Palestine, Norman Bentwich:

> The principle of self-determination had to be modified because of the two national selves existing in Palestine; and the majority Arab population could not be allowed to prevent the fulfillment of the Mandate in relation to the minority Jewish population ... Palestine is [therefore] designed to be a bi-national country: and could not be placed under a form of national government in which the people of one nationality would dominate people of the other. The trustee therefore, has, for a time to secure fair treatment and justice for the two communities, till the two have come to understand one another better.[60]

This view is also consistent with the position taken by the British Government at a meeting of the Permanent Mandates Commission in 1924, where Mr Ormsby-Gore said:

> The British Government was of the opinion that the Balfour Declaration involved that neither a Jewish State nor a purely Arab Government should be instituted. It regarded itself as a trustee and as required to see fair play between races and religions until free government and institutions should be given to Palestine.[61]

Further support for the view that the principle of self-determination applied to the Arabs of Palestine and not only to the Zionists, is evident from the fact that Britain wanted to create an Arab Agency which was to have occupied a position exactly analogous to the Jewish Agency under Article 4 of the Mandate which was described in Chapter 2.[62] This would have provided the Arabs with a public body to advise, cooperate and consult with the British authorities in Palestine regarding its administration as well as on the economic and social development of the Arab population.[63] The only reason why it was not eventually created was because the Arabs opposed it for political reasons. They were offended that the Zionists were being treated on a par with the Arabs, when they formed the overwhelming majority of the population.[64] The Arabs were also represented in the Legislative Council. However, British and Jewish officials collectively outnumbered them so that they could not disrupt the national home policy, which was another source of controversy contributing to Arab frustration and discontent. It is consequently arguable that the principle of self-determination had been modified in Palestine, so that the Arabs would not be able to prevent the fulfilment of the Mandate vis-à-vis Palestine's minority Jewish population by passing legislation restricting Jewish immigration or by rejecting the budget for political reasons.[65] However, the fact that Arabs were represented on the Legislative Council (numerically, there were more Arabs than Jews, although the former did not have a majority because of the presence of British officials who buttressed the Jewish vote) and that Britain wanted to create an Arab Agency is evidence that the Colonial Office tacitly recognised that the Palestinian Arabs had political rights. That the British High Commissioner in Palestine even proposed granting the Arabs greater political power in the Legislative Council in 1936 provides further support for the view that they were entitled to political rights and to further participate in the governance of the country.[66] It will be recalled (see Chapter 2) that the Hogarth Message of 1918 provided:

> (3) Since the Jewish opinion of the world is in favour of a return of Jews to Palestine and inasmuch as this opinion must remain a constant factor, and further as His Majesty's Government view with favour the realisation of this aspiration, His Majesty's Government are determined that in so far as is compatible with the freedom of the *existing* population both economic and *political*, no obstacle should be put in the way of the realisation of this ideal.[67]

At the San Remo Conference in 1920, the Great Powers agreed that the 'civil rights' of the non-Jewish population as stipulated in the Balfour Declaration as it was incorporated into the British Mandate of Palestine, included political rights.[68] In other words, it was not the case that the phrase 'it being clearly understood than nothing should be done which might prejudice the civil and religious rights of existing non-Jewish communities in Palestine' did not include political rights as had been argued.[69] In discussions on the drafting of the Mandate, Lord Curzon said that he did not understand the precise significance of 'political rights' in French law. He told his colleagues that in British law, all ordinary rights included 'civil rights'.[70] Curzon said that he was anxious to avoid introducing into the Mandate a word which might have a different meaning for the French and the British texts.[71] In reply, Monsieur Millerand said that the reason why the French delegation wished to insert the word 'political' was that they were anxious that non-Jewish communities should not be deprived of existing political rights, which he understood to include the right to vote and to take part in elections.[72] Signor Nitti of the Italian delegation then intervened to say that the difference of opinion between the French and British delegation was one of form and not of substance.[73] In others words, they all understood the term 'civil rights' as it was incorporated into the Mandate to include political rights. There was no distinction between the two terms. As Curzon noted, for the purposes of British law, civil rights were inclusive of political rights.

Moreover, throughout the years when Britain administered Palestine as the mandatory power, it was understood that the Arabs had political rights.

They were not mere pawns whose 'natural rights' could be ignored. The minutes of the Permanent Mandates Commission of June 1939 record the following statement:

> M. MacDonald reiterated that the Palestine mandate was different from all the others; but it was, nevertheless, a mandate and had to embody the spirit and principles of the mandate system. It was not so different that its provisions could contradict those principles. If the Arabs of Palestine, alone among all the populations of territories under mandate, were to be deprived of normal political rights, it would amount to saying that the Palestine mandate contradicted the spirit of the mandates system. The essential difference was that this mandate sought to establish in a country already inhabited by Arabs a National Home for the Jews. His Majesty's Government was proud of its association with that work but did not believe that it was ever intended to deprive the other sections of the population of their natural rights.[74]

Further support for the position that the Palestine Arabs had political rights in Palestine appears in a top-secret memorandum prepared by Foreign Office legal advisers in 1947.[75] In the memorandum, they conceded that the word 'position' in Article 6 of the Mandate, which provided for Jewish immigration to Palestine subject to the condition that the rights and *position* of other sections of the population were not prejudiced, referred to the 'political position' of the Palestine Arabs.[76] In fact, Britain controversially restricted Jewish immigration into Palestine in the 1940s during the *Shoah* on the basis of Article 6 of the Mandate contending that the sheer number of Jewish immigrants fleeing into Palestine from occupied Europe to escape Nazi persecution was causing political instability in the country. In this regard, a memorandum on British defence policy, which was drafted in the late 1930s, summed up the position on Jewish immigration as follows:

> The provision subsequently adopted in Article 6 of the Mandate, of which the Mandatory should 'facilitate Jewish immigration into Palestine', was specifically limited by the proviso in the same article that the position of the existing population was not thereby to be prejudiced, a proviso which again would be meaningless if Jewish immigration were to be allowed to extend to the creation of a Jewish majority. But, when the Mandate was drawn up, the Jewish population of Palestine was so small that there was ample room for a large immigration of Jews, without any serious interference with the rights and position of the native population of the country.[77]

This extract from the memorandum provides further evidence that whilst the Jews were allowed to immigrate to Palestine to create their national home, this could not be at the expense of its indigenous and predominantly Arab population, as this would interfere with the latter's political rights, which included eventual self-government and independence. This is one of the reasons why Britain would suggest partition throughout the 1930s and 1940s as a way out of the predicament it had got itself into, as a result of the conflicting obligations in the Balfour Declaration, and it is telling that the extract just quoted is from a document on partition. That Britain considered partitioning Palestine into an Arab state and a Jewish state on several occasions, as described in the next chapter, provides further evidence that the Palestine Arabs and not only the Jews were considered by the British as being entitled to self-determination as well as independence.

SOVEREIGNTY, SELF-DETERMINATION AND *TERRA NULLIUS*

In the first year of the League of Nations (1919–20) an influential committee of jurists – comprised of Professors Ferdinand Larnaude, Antonius Alexis H. Struycken, and Max Huber – were appointed to give an independent legal opinion on a dispute between Finland and Sweden over the sovereignty and political fate of the Aaland Islands.[78] At the time, the Permanent Court of International Justice had not yet been established. Consequently, a special committee of jurists was assembled to look into the legal aspects of the Finnish–Swedish dispute. Accordingly, the committee found that in situations of unresolved sovereignty the principle of self-determination applied.[79] The jurists said that a people in such a situation had a right to choose between forming an independent state and merging with an existing one:

> New aspirations of certain sections of a nation, which are sometimes based on old traditions or on a common language and civilization, may come to the surface and produce effects which must be taken into account in the interests of the internal and external peace of nations.
>
> The principle recognising the rights of peoples to determine their political fate may be applied in various ways; the most important of these are, on the one hand the formation of an independent State, and on the other hand the right of choice between two existing States. This principle, however, must be brought into line with that of the protection of minorities; both have a common object – to assure to some national Group the maintenance and free development of its social, ethnical and religious characteristics.[80]

In the dispute before it, the committee noted that: ‘By the application of a purely legal method of argument it might be said that a kind of acquired right exists in favour of the Aaland Islands which would be violated if Finland were allowed to suppress it retrospectively.’[81] A similar logic could be applied to the case of Palestine where the issue of sovereignty was unresolved, as briefly described in Chapter 2, with some jurists holding that it was vested in the League, others in its inhabitants and others in abeyance.[82] On the one hand, Turkey had not agreed to transfer sovereignty to the Allied Powers over any of its former territories in the Middle East in the treaties concluded between them in the aftermath of the First World War.[83] On the other hand, it was clear that Turkey did not have any sovereignty over its former possessions, particularly after it had concluded the Treaty of Lausanne, and it was also clear that the Principal Allied Powers did not have sovereignty there either.[84] In Palestine, Great Britain was merely the mandatory power. It claimed no sovereignty over Palestine. Moreover, its scope of authority there was curtailed by the terms of Article 22 of the Covenant.[85]

In any event, it was apparent that sovereignty in an inhabited territory, as opposed to *terra nullius*, that is vacant or abandoned territory, had to vest somewhere at some point in time. This is because sovereignty in an inhabited territory could not be suspended indefinitely, for self-determination prevents states from regarding as *terra nullius* territories inhabited by organised collectivities lacking the hallmarks of state authority in such cases where the territory was abandoned by the sovereign state previously wielding authority.[86] Even if this view is not accepted and it is alleged that the doctrine of *terra nullius* was still applicable at the turn of the twentieth century when colonialism was legitimate, it would not necessarily follow that this view should remain so today.[87] In the *Western Sahara* advisory opinion the International Court of Justice questioned whether the colonial powers actually colonised north-west Africa on the basis of the doctrine of *terra nullius*, since it concluded treaties with indigenous tribes. The ICJ noted:

> Whatever differences of opinion there may have been among jurists, the State practice of the relevant period indicates that territories inhabited by tribes or peoples having a social and political organization were not regarded as *terra nullius*. It shows that in the case of such territories the acquisition of sovereignty was not generally considered as effected unilaterally through 'occupation' of *terra nullius* by original title but through agreements concluded with local rulers.[88]

Britain never justified its administration of Palestine on the basis of *terra nullius*. Rather, it was given the right of administering Palestine temporarily by virtue of a League of Nations Mandate. Moreover, Palestine was to be administered by Britain as 'a sacred trust of civilisation', which implied that it had no sovereignty over the territory, as it was not to be annexed. As M. Viviani told the League of Nations Council in 1922:

> When the war came to an end, the Great Powers had not wished, as in the past, violently to annex territories and to oppress their inhabitants. The mandatory would take the inhabitants under its protection, it would administer the territories in the interests of all, and it would be responsible to the Council and the Assembly until these young peoples were able to conduct their affairs without further assistance.[89]

Furthermore, it would have been difficult for Britain to have argued that the land was empty and therefore open to colonisation as it had already conceded that it was inhabited by Arabs through the numerous promises it made to them during the course of the First World War, as described in Chapter 2. The Holy Land had been continuously inhabited for centuries before the arrival of the British Army in 1917 as a part of Syria, which was then a part of the Ottoman Empire.[90] The Great Powers were well aware of this through their commercial and missionary activities. They even had consulates in Jerusalem. Palestine could hardly be described as empty or as being possessed of a community which had no social and political organisation. As Herbert Samuel told the Permanent Mandates Commission in 1924, there had been in Palestine, under the Ottomans, a system of government where there were taxes, newspapers, schools, a system of land registration, political parties, a judicial system, hospitals and a railway.[91] Moreover, the Turkish Government enforced legislation in Palestine, such as the granting of concessionary rights to third parties, for example, in regard to public works in Jerusalem and at the Dead Sea, which was adjudicated in a case before the Permanent Court of International Justice.[92] All these factors point towards the conclusion that Palestine was under effective occupation when General Allenby's troops marched into Jerusalem in December 1917.[93] Prior to that date, the Turks had not abandoned it, and so it could not, by any stretch of the imagination, be described as *terra nullius* – as some Zionists sought to characterise it and which was epitomised in one of their favourite phrases, that Palestine was 'a land without a people, for a people without a land'.[94]

In effect, the aspirations of the Palestinian people to self-determination was being held for them in a 'sacred trust' by Britain, the mandatory, on behalf of the League until they had reached the stage where they could exercise that right independently. Ultimately, it did not really matter whether sovereignty was in suspense or whether it was vested in the people of the territory concerned: If it was in suspense, then it would have, in the words of Judge McNair, 'revived and vested' in the people under mandatory tutelage upon independence.[95] After all, upon independence, which was envisaged for all 'A-class' mandates, the peoples of these territories would be in a position to exercise their sovereign rights. In this respect, sovereignty and self-determination go hand in hand. This was, of course, what was envisaged for Palestine, which according to Article 22 of the League of Nations Covenant was provisionally recognised as an independent nation.

As regards the question of whether the Palestinian people was in fact a 'people' and recognised as such with a distinct identity, language and culture, it is instructive to note that the British Government recognised that they had such a status in 1922. In an exchange of correspondence between the Palestine Arab delegation and J.E. Shuckburgh who was instructed to write on behalf of Winston Churchill, then Secretary of State for the Colonies, the British Government referred to the Palestinians as 'a people' no less than six times and they were specifically referring to Palestine's Arab community.[96] For example, in the correspondence Britain said that '[t]here is no question of treating *the people of Palestine* as less advanced than their neighbours in Iraq or Syria' and that 'His Majesty's Government are ready and willing to grant to *the people of Palestine* the greatest measure of independence consistent with the pledges referred to.'[97] David Ben-Gurion, who would become Israel's first Prime Minister, even went so far as to recognise that Palestine's indigenous Arab inhabitants had the *right* of self-determination:

> The right to self-determination is a universal principle. We have always and everywhere been among the most fervent defenders of this principle. We are entirely for the right of self-determination of all peoples, of all individuals, of all groups, and it follows that the Arab in Palestine has the *right* of self-determination. This right is not limited, and cannot be qualified by our own interests ... It is possible that the realization of the aspirations [of the Palestinian Arabs] will create serious difficulties for us but this is not a reason to deny their *rights*.[98]

Although Palestine was not an independent or sovereign state for the purposes of international law during the mandatory years, it was accepted that communities under mandates were subjects of international law which possessed a national status, and could acquire rights or be held to their obligations.[99] Former Turkish nationals habitually resident in Palestine on 1 August 1925 did not become nationals of the mandatory power. They became Palestinian citizens with a distinct national status of their own (according to the Ottoman Nationality Law all persons living in the area from 1869 to 1925 were considered Turkish nationals).[100] This was in line with a resolution adopted by the League of Nations on 22 April 1923, which provided: 'The status of the native inhabitants of a mandated territory is *distinct* from that of the Mandatory Power ...' [101] This was also the opinion of Norman Bentwich, who it will be recalled was Britain's Attorney-General in Palestine in the 1920s.[102] Their distinct national status was further confirmed in the decisions of several tribunals in Britain, Egypt and Palestine.[103] Palestinian nationals were treated in Great Britain on the same footing as British Protected Persons, although they were not subject to the obligations of national service in the same way as British subjects.[104] So even though Palestine was not an independent and sovereign state during the mandatory period it paradoxically had all the attributes of a state. That is, it had a population, a territory, a government in effective control of the territory and the capacity through the mandatory to enter into international relations with other subjects of international law and was regarded as such in theory and in practice.[105] Despite complaints levelled by the Zionists against the British Mandatory Government for not employing more Jews, Arabs dominated the Civil Service in all the departments in Palestine, including the judiciary, the railways, the post office and the ports.[106] Whilst Britain was the ultimate authority in Palestine, the country was effectively being run by Arabs. Palestine at this time would probably be best described as an 'infant' or 'virtual' state without independence or sovereignty under the guardianship of the mandatory.[107] It was governed not by the authority of Parliament but by that of the Crown under the British Foreign Jurisdiction Act of 1890, an arrangement that emphasised its separateness from the home government.[108] Mr Orts, the Chairman of the 32nd session of the Permanent Mandates Commission, even expressed his view that:

> Palestine, as the mandate clearly showed, was a subject under international law. While she could not conclude international conventions, the Mandatory Power, until further notice, concluded them *on her behalf*, in virtue of Article 19 of the mandate. The mandate, in Article 7, obliged the Mandatory to enact a nationality law, which again showed that the Palestinians formed a nation, and that Palestine was a State, though provisionally under guardianship.[109]

In this regard, Article 30 of the Treaty of Lausanne, which provided for nationality in the territories detached from Turkey, notably referred to them as states:

> Turkish subjects habitually resident in territory which in accordance with the provisions of the present Treaty is detached from Turkey will become *ipso facto*, in the conditions laid down by the local law, nationals of the *State* to which such territory is transferred.[110]

Moreover, a judgment handed down by the Mixed Court of Mansura in Egypt[111] went so far as to conclude that Lebanon and Syria, being A-class mandates, were effectively independent. By analogy, the same reasoning could be applied to Palestine:

> Syria and the Lebanon, being countries placed under an 'A' Mandate, are, in accordance with the Covenant of the League of Nations, to be deemed to be independent States and persons of public international law, and the inhabitants have acquired the nationality of those States.[112]

Whilst it may be questioned whether the A-class mandates could ever be really independent when they were dependent on an external power for their independence, there was no doubt that they had many of the attributes of a state and were being prepared by the mandatory for independence. In the words of Mr Ormsby-Gore:

> His Majesty's Government conceived it as of the essence of such a mandate as the Palestine mandate, an A mandate, and of Article 22 of the Covenant, that Palestine should be developed, not as a British colony permanently under British rule, but as a self-governing State or States with the right of autonomous evolution.[113]

Therefore when the Palestine Mandate was terminated by Great Britain at midnight on 14/15 May 1948, sovereignty was vested in the Palestinian *people* (that is, Arabs and Jews with Palestinian nationality) to determine their political destiny.[114] This is because the mandates system was an exception to the general rule which prevailed during the colonial era that sovereignty could only be vested in the state.[115] This is especially as Article 22 of the League of Nations Covenant spoke of 'certain *communities*' who had reached a stage of development where their existence as independent nations was 'provisionally recognised'. Consequently, a community inhabiting an A-class mandate were entitled to exercise sovereignty when the mandatory power had relinquished control.[116] After all, their territory, Palestine, was being held in a 'sacred trust' for them until it could 'stand alone' as an independent state. There is nothing in the League of Nations Covenant which provided that sovereignty could be given to any other community, apart from 'certain communities formerly belonging to the Turkish Empire'.

THE LEAGUE OF NATIONS COVENANT AND SELF-DETERMINATION

Although there was in 1920 no general right of self-determination in international law, it did apply by way of exception to those territories and peoples provisionally recognised as independent nations by the mandatory system as provided for in Article 22 of the Covenant of the League of Nations.[117] In the *South-West Africa* (Namibia) cases, the ICJ held that the mandates system recognised that the peoples of the territories concerned had certain rights conferred on them by international law and that the mandatories were required to promote the well-being and development of the peoples concerned as a sacred trust of civilisation.[118] Article 22 of the League of Nations Covenant acknowledged the existence of the A-class mandates, communities formerly belonging to the Turkish Empire, and recognised them as 'independent nations', which included Palestine, who were to be advised and assisted by a mandatory, 'until such time as they are able to stand alone', which was a euphemism for the principle of self-determination – since the role of the mandatory power was to assist these peoples' economic, social and cultural development towards self-government and independence, rather than to perpetuate colonial domination through annexation.[119] That self-determination was principally of a political nature did not deprive it of having legal effect, as it was embodied in both the Covenant of the League of Nations and in the Mandate, the latter being equivalent to a treaty or convention, and was therefore comprised of a legal character.[120]

On the other hand it has been argued that Article 22 of the League of Nations Covenant did not provide for the principle of self-determination, and that in spite of the arguments presented here, the Arabs of Palestine could not invoke such a right in any event because they were not entitled to it.[121] Such an argument, however, flies in the face of the very wording of Article 22 which provided for the 'well-being and development' of the peoples concerned which formed 'a sacred trust of civilization'. Moreover, certain 'communities', i.e. peoples, formerly belonging to the Turkish Empire, had 'reached a stage of development where their existence as independent nations can be provisionally recognized'. Evidently, this terminology only applied to the Arabs of Palestine and not to the Zionists who at that time were primarily

Jews of European origin. Finally, the mandatory was to give 'administrative advice and assistance ... until such time as they are able to stand alone'. In other words, the mandatory was to assist the peoples concerned, that is, the Arabs of Palestine, by giving administrative advice and assistance until they had reached a stage of development when they could govern themselves without any outside assistance as independent nations. There is nothing in the wording of Article 22 which provided that the peoples of A-class mandates could be governed forever.[122] On the contrary, their existence as independent nations had already been recognised and the sole role of the mandatory was to provide administrative advice and assistance until the peoples concerned were 'able to stand alone'. This is why Article 28 of the British Mandate for Palestine made express provision for its termination.[123] It is irrelevant that Article 22 does not actually use the word 'self-determination', as this is implicitly provided for through the use of the phrases 'well-being and development', 'independent nations', and 'until such time as they are able to stand alone', which all point towards eventual self-government and independence. Moreover, Article 22 was drafted with the principle of self-determination specifically in mind. For instance, President Wilson's Third Draft presented to the Paris Peace Conference on 20 January 1919 explicitly invoked what was termed 'the *rule* of self-determination'. It provided:

> In respect of the peoples and territories which formerly belonged to Austria-Hungary, and to Turkey, and in respect of the colonies formerly under the dominion of the German Empire, the League of Nations shall be regarded as the residuary trustee with the right of oversight or administration in accordance with certain fundamental principles hereinafter set forth; and this reversion and control shall exclude all rights or privileges of annexation on the part of any Power.
>
> These principles are, that there shall in no case be any annexation of any of these territories by any State either within the League or outside of it, and that in the future government of these peoples and territories *the rule of self-determination*, or consent of the governed to their form of government, shall be fairly and reasonably applied, and all policies of administration or economic development be based primarily upon the well-considered interests of the people themselves.[124]

Although 'the rule of self-determination' was dropped from the fourth draft Wilson presented to the Paris Peace Conference a month later, in February 1919, it was still evident that it formed the whole philosophy upon which Article 22 would subsequently be drafted. According to Wilson's fourth draft:

> The object of all such tutelary oversight and administration on the part of the League of Nations shall be to build up *in as short a time as possible* out of the people or territory under its guardianship a *political unit* which can take charge of its own affairs, determine its own connections, and choose its

> own policies. The League may at any time release such people or territory from tutelage and consent to its being set up as an *independent* unit.[125]

This was self-determination in all but name. Instead of using the word 'self-determination', Wilson was essentially setting out what he thought that application of that principle entailed which would find expression in the final draft of Article 22 that would eventually find its way into the terms of the League of Nations Covenant.

Finally, even if, despite the clear wording of Article 22, it is still asserted that the Covenant of the League of Nations did not provide for the principle of self-determination, but rather was merely a political document whose sole purpose was to perpetuate colonial rule over dependent peoples, this would no longer have any legal resonance today. This is because Article 64 of the Vienna Convention on the Law of Treaties of 1969, states: 'If a new peremptory norm of general international law emerges, any existing treaty which is in conflict with that norm becomes void and terminates.'[126] It is indisputable today that the right of all peoples to self-determination is one of the essential principles of contemporary international law.[127] Moreover, the International Court of Justice has authoritatively ruled that it is also an obligation *erga omnes* – in other words, an obligation owed to all, a peremptory norm of international law.[128] Therefore, even if the argument is advanced that the Covenant of the League of Nations did not provide for the principle of self-determination in 1919, but rather, provided for the formal continuation of colonialism, this would have no legal effect today. In the words of the ICJ in its seminal 1971 advisory opinion on South-West Africa (Namibia):

> Mindful as it is of the primary necessity of interpreting an instrument in accordance with the intentions of the parties at the time of its conclusion, the Court is bound to take into account the fact that the concepts embodied in Article 22 of the Covenant – 'the strenuous conditions of the modern world' and 'the well-being and development' of the peoples concerned – were not static, but were by definition evolutionary, as also, therefore, was the concept of the 'sacred trust'. The parties to the Covenant must consequently be deemed to have accepted them as such. That is why, viewing the institutions of 1919, the Court must take into consideration the changes which have occurred in the supervening half-century, and its interpretation cannot remain unaffected by the subsequent development of international law, through the Charter of the United Nations and by way of customary law. Moreover, an international instrument has to be interpreted and applied within the framework of the entire legal system prevailing at the time of the interpretation. In the domain to which the present proceedings relate, the last fifty years, as indicated above, have brought important developments. These developments leave little doubt that the ultimate objective of the sacred trust was the self-determination and independence of the peoples concerned.[129]

SELF-DETERMINATION AND THE NATIONALITY LINK

In any event, it is argued that, for the reasons already mentioned, the principle of self-determination was applicable to A-class Mandates in 1919. However, in practice, Palestinian citizens could only exercise self-determination in Palestine. It would be difficult for nationals of other states to exercise it because then any group of peoples anywhere in the world could claim a right of self-determination which could potentially cause endless instability. Moreover, there is no basis in international law to support the claim of a group of refugees or temporary workers to create a state or lay a claim to self-government in the country where they happen to be residing even if they have a special emotional or historic attachment to it. In order to exercise a right of self-determination, there has to be some link or legal nexus between a people and a territory, which is provided by the law of nationality.[130] Yet in the dying years of the British Mandate, Jews constituted only a third of the total population of Palestine – 608,230 Jews out of a total population of 1,972,560 – with only one-tenth of these Jews being indigenous to Palestine and with only a third of them acquiring Palestinian citizenship.[131] It should be stressed that self-determination does not give a right to minorities *even if they are nationals of the state concerned* to secede or break away, let alone foreign immigrants. Moreover, there is nothing in the text of the British Mandate of Palestine that gave the Jewish people a right to break away and create a Jewish state. Rather, Article 6 of the Mandate provided that a Nationality Law would be enacted to facilitate the acquisition of Palestinian citizenship by Jews who took up their *permanent* residence in Palestine. Jews had to acquire Palestinian citizenship to establish their national home.

In a case between Liechtenstein and Guatemala concerning a dispute over the nationality (under international law, the terms 'nationality' and 'citizenship' are often used as synonyms) of a Mr Nottebohm, the International Court of Justice reached the conclusion after surveying the decisions of international arbitrators in the field, that:

> They have given their preference to the real and effective nationality, that which accorded with the facts, that based on stronger factual ties between the person concerned and one of the States whose nationalities is involved. Different factors are taken into consideration, and their importance will vary from one case to the next: the habitual residence of the individual concerned is an important factor, but there are other factors such as the centre of his interests, his family ties, his participation in public life, attachment shown by him for a given country and inculcated in his children ... Similarly, the courts of third States, when they have before them an individual whom two other States hold to be their national, seek to resolve the conflict by having recourse to international criteria and their prevailing tendency is to prefer the real and effective nationality.[132]

Although the case concerned a conflict over dual nationality, the principle involved, that of the real and effective nationality is significant. As the ICJ noted, nationality 'must correspond with a factual situation' which is based on a 'genuine connection' between the individual and the state.[133] The concept of the 'real and effective' nationality, endorsed by the ICJ in the *Nottebohm* case, has been approved of by other international tribunals and is said to reflect customary international law.[134] Even if this was not the case in the first half of the twentieth century, the Convention on Certain Questions Relating to Conflict of Nationality Laws and its Protocols of 1930 was ratified by Britain and extended to Palestine and was published in the *Palestine Gazette*, being directly applicable there.[135] Article 5 of the Convention included the 'effective link test' to determine the nationality of dual nationals.[136] In other words, and as elaborated in the *Nottebohm* case, the individual concerned claiming Palestinian nationality must have a strong factual tie to a state either through habitual residency, employment, family ties and place of birth or through the fact that the state concerned had deemed it necessary to grant a particular individual its nationality, perhaps because of special services to the state.[137]

In Palestine, the vast majority of Jewish immigrants would have had to apply for a certificate of naturalisation to obtain Palestinian citizenship, unless they had been born in Palestine to a Palestinian citizen or had been a Turkish subject habitually resident there on 1 August 1925.[138] According to the Palestine Citizenship Order, the High Commissioner of Palestine could grant such a certificate if the person making the application had satisfied him: (a) That he had resided in Palestine for a period of not less than two years out of the three years immediately preceding the date of his application; (b) That he was of good character and had an adequate knowledge of either the English, the Arabic or the Hebrew language; and (c) That he intended, if his application was granted, to reside in Palestine.[139] The applicant concerned then had to swear an oath of allegiance to the Government of Palestine and surrender his passport or laissez-passer.[140] Only when these requirements had been satisfied, and with the approval of the High Commissioner of Palestine who had an absolute discretion to withhold a certificate of naturalisation, could an individual be granted Palestinian citizenship.[141]

Since only one third of Palestine's total Jewish population had acquired Palestinian citizenship by 1947, the Jewish community then existing in Palestine was composed mainly of foreigners.[142] It is therefore difficult to see how they could exercise a 'right' of self-determination in Palestine *at the expense* of Palestine's indigenous inhabitants. By the terms of the Mandate, the Zionists had a right to determine their own future in Palestine by creating a Jewish national home, but this could only be established *within* a Palestinian state. The Mandate conferred no right on the 'Jewish people' to convert Palestine into a Jewish state to the detriment of the majority Palestinian Arab population. It is evident that the community then existing in Palestine during the mandatory years was predominantly Palestinian Arab, both by origin and nationality, and they, like all other mandated communities sought self-determination and independence.[143]

SELF-DETERMINATION AND THE UNITED NATIONS

Although the UN Charter only mentions self-determination in Articles 1 (2) and 55 leading some scholars to conclude that it did not provide all peoples with a right of self-determination,[144] Palestine, as has already been explained, was a legacy of the League of Nations. In other words, Palestinian self-determination is not based on any provision of the UN Charter but on Article 22 of the League of Nations Covenant. What is significant about the UN Charter in the context of Palestinian self-determination is Article 80 which preserves the *rights* of peoples subject to a mandate.[145] It has been pointed out in this regard that the carefully drafted and equally authentic French text of the Charter provides in Article 1, paragraph 2: 'du principe de l'égalité de droits des peuples et de leur droit à disposer d'eux-mêmes ...' In this regard it has been argued that by using the word 'droit' in connection with self-determination, the French text removes any possible ambiguity as to whether this is a right or simply a principle of international law.[146]

With respect, this is probably not the correct interpretation of the Charter.[147] However, it is not insignificant. Whilst it might not have provided a basis for all peoples to claim a right of self-determination it is arguable that it augmented a pre-existing right to self-determination especially when read in conjunction with Article 80. Bearing in mind that the UN Charter entered into force on 24 October 1945, the Palestine Mandate being terminated on 15 May 1948, the Palestinian people's aspirations to self-determination in those two and a half years was preserved and augmented by the principles and purposes of the UN Charter as enshrined in Article 1 (2) which is '[t]o develop friendly relations among nations based on respect for the principle of equal rights and self-determination of peoples, and to take other appropriate measures to strengthen universal peace'.[148] In this context the 1947 UN Partition Plan was an embodiment of this principle. Consequently it is arguable that any measures prohibiting the Palestinians from achieving their independence by resorting to armed force not only infringed Article 22 of the League of Nations Covenant but a fundamental purpose of the United Nations.

It would be wrong to argue that because self-determination was not a right in customary international law in 1948 that the Palestinian people were not allowed to rely on it. As already mentioned, Article 22 of the League of Nations Covenant provisionally recognised Palestine as an independent nation in 1919. Taking into account the legal and political developments that occurred in Palestine during the Mandate years, including the 1937 Peel Partition Plan, the promises of independence set out by the British Government in its 1939 White Paper, as well as the provisions regarding the establishment of an independent Arab state in the 1947 UN Partition Plan and in the 1948 UN draft Trusteeship Agreement, as well as the fact that all the other A-class mandates had become independent states, it is arguable that by 1948 the Palestinian Arabs were entitled to self-determination as a matter of *right*, and not on sufferance, just like their Jewish counterparts. It is difficult to understand why they would have to wait until the Declaration on the Granting of Independence to Colonial Countries and Peoples twelve years later in 1960 before they could assert such a right. Although the other Arab countries achieved independence during the time of the League, Transjordan became an independent state *after* the dissolution of the League of Nations in 1946. Clearly then, the right of the people of an A-class mandated territory to independence was not predicated on the existence of the League of Nations. This was further precedent, perhaps, that Palestine too should have become an independent state just as the other A-class mandated territories, either as a single geographic unit encompassing a Jewish national home within its borders, or as a separate Arab state, in economic union with a Jewish state.

In its advisory opinion on the *International Status of South-West Africa*, rendered only four years after the creation of the United Nations, the ICJ concluded that the well-being and development of peoples as envisaged in the 'sacred trust of civilisation' did not depend on the existence of the League of Nations.[149] In other words, the fulfilment of the trust could not be brought to an end merely because this supervisory organ ceased to exist. The Court observed that the rights of states and peoples as envisaged under the mandatory system did not automatically lapse with the League, for it 'was the intention to safeguard the rights of States and peoples under all circumstances and in all respects, until each territory should be placed under the Trusteeship system'.[150] The Court decided that the UN General Assembly was competent to exercise the supervisory functions formerly exercised by the Council of the League of Nations in supervising the administration of the Mandate, receiving reports and making recommendations to the other members of the UN on any matters within the scope of the Charter.[151] In other words, whilst the British Mandate of Palestine and its corresponding provisions supporting Jewish settlement there were terminated on 15 May 1948, the obligations to safeguard the rights of the Palestinian people as envisaged in the 'sacred trust' as mentioned in Article 22 of the League of Nations Covenant being preserved by Article 80 were not. Instead that 'sacred trust of civilisation' lives on, the responsibility of which has been transferred to the UN General Assembly as the successor to the Council of the League of Nations.[152] That body is consequently obliged under international law, to supervise and closely monitor the Palestinian people's well-being and development with a view to the implementation of their right of self-determination.[153] The fact that self-determination is today a peremptory norm of international law has converted the obligation of securing the Palestinian people's right of self-determination into an obligation *erga omnes*. In other words, all states are obliged to do what they can to secure Palestinian self-determination.

In this regard it is telling that the only two mandated territories which did not become independent states after the dissolution of the League of Nations on 18 April 1946 or were transferred to a UN Trusteeship, were Palestine and South-West Africa (Namibia).[154] In 1966 the UN General Assembly revoked South Africa's mandate over South-West Africa on the basis that it had 'failed to fulfil its obligations in respect of the administration of the Mandated Territory and to ensure the moral and material well-being and security of the indigenous inhabitants' of that country.[155] The right of revocation was regarded as an implied part of the mandates system, as the obligation of accountability by a Mandatory to the League for the administration of its 'sacred trust' included the sanction of revocation as the ultimate deterrent against abuse of the trust.[156] By the late 1930s, the British Government realised that it had created a dangerous situation where there were essentially two nationalities and two nationalisms in Palestine that were mutually antagonistic. To escape this conundrum so as to allow both communities to exercise their respective claims to self-determination peacefully in Palestine, partition, the subject of the next chapter, would be proposed, this time, by the United Nations.

6
The Partition of Palestine

'It would not be easy to persuade the Arab Governments that it is equitable or consonant with the mandate, or with the Atlantic Charter, or with our own war-time publicity, to include in the Jewish State all the best land, practically all the industries, the only good ports and about a third of the Arab inhabitants.'

Foreign Secretary Anthony Eden,
Top-Secret Memorandum to Winston Churchill, 1945

'We shall first cut the body of Palestine into three parts of a Jewish State and three parts of an Arab State. We shall then have the Jaffa enclave; and Palestine's heart, Jerusalem, shall forever be an international city. That is the beginning of the shape Palestine shall have.'

'Having cut Palestine up in that manner, we shall then put its bleeding body upon a cross forever. This is not going to be temporary; this is permanent. Palestine shall never belong to its people; it shall always be stretched upon the cross.

'What authority has the United Nations to do this? What legal authority, what juridical authority has it to do this, to make an independent State forever subject to United Nations administration?'

Sir Mohammed Zafrullah Khan, UN debates, 1947

'The General Assembly partitioned what it had no right to divide – an indivisible homeland. When we rejected that decision, our position corresponded to that of the natural mother who refused to permit King Solomon to cut her son in two when the unnatural mother claimed the child for herself and agreed to his dismemberment'.

Yasser Arafat, Chairman of the Executive Committee of the Palestine Liberation
Organisation, Address to the UN General Assembly, 13 November 1974

The partition of Palestine came in the wake of the division of the Indian subcontinent as the British Empire was on the wane and wanted a quick exit route.[1] The trend had begun in Ireland and would be suggested in later years to resolve the Cyprus debacle.[2] Korea was also a concern at the United Nations in 1948, having already been *de facto* partitioned between the Soviet Union and the United States in 1945 at the 38th parallel.[3] In 1945, Germany had unconditionally surrendered whereby Britain, France, the Soviet Union and the United States assumed 'supreme authority' over it in four zones of occupation.[4] There were also problems in Indochina that would be partitioned in 1954, as well as in Ethiopia, Eritrea, and in later years in Ruanda-Urundi and the Northern Cameroons.[5] Of course, partition had also been proposed within Palestine by Lord Peel in 1937 and was being considered by Winston Churchill during the course of the Second World War. It therefore did not come as a complete surprise that the UN proposed to partition Palestine in 1947. However, the proposals to partition Palestine contained in the UN Partition Plan, particularly the manner in which the line was delimited paid little heed to Palestine's population distribution, land ownership, and the economic viability of the envisaged Arab state, was certainly novel and even inconsistent with prior state practice. This is because the partition was being linked by its authors directly to the Jewish refugee problem in Central and Eastern Europe. Rather than encouraging countries throughout the world to open their doors to these Jewish refugees, the Great Powers were encouraging them to go to Palestine even though this was not the first choice of destination for many of these people.[6] This would explain why the 1947 UN Partition Plan was far more generous in granting the envisaged Jewish state territory than the 1937 Peel Partition Plan was, even though Jewish immigration into Palestine had been restricted by the British mandatory authorities and rigorously implemented since 1939.

THE UN SPECIAL COMMITTEE ON PALESTINE

On 15 May 1947, the UN General Assembly created a United Nations Special Committee on Palestine (UNSCOP) to prepare a report on 'such proposals as it may consider appropriate for the solution of the problem of Palestine'.[7] Four months later UNSCOP reported back to the General Assembly.[8] It observed:

> With regard to the principle of self-determination, although international recognition was extended to this principle at the end of the First World War and it was adhered to with regard to other Arab territories, at the time of the creation of the 'A' Mandates, it was not applied to Palestine, obviously because of the intention to make possible the creation of the Jewish National Home there. Actually, it may well be said that the Jewish National Home and the *sui generis* Mandate for Palestine run counter to that principle.[9]

As mentioned in Chapter 5, it is doubtful whether UNSCOP was correct with regard to its view of the application of the principle of self-determination to Palestine. The fact that the Arabs boycotted UNSCOP did not help things, as it was not presented with the Arab point of view, and was more likely to be swayed by the arguments advanced by the Zionists who had ready-made partition proposals to hand it.[10] Moreover, the members of UNSCOP seemed to be tying the fate of Palestine to the *Shoah*; they visited the concentration camps in the Allied-occupation zones, and witnessed the tragedy of the *Exodus*, a ship full of Holocaust survivors who were turned away by the British authorities in Palestine because they had no legal immigration certificates to enter the country.[11] But if self-determination did not apply to Palestine as UNSCOP suggested then on what basis did the Zionists have a right to create a state there? Surely, the only logical explanation is that it must have applied to Palestine as the Arabs were entitled to it on the basis of Article 22 of the League of Nations Covenant and Zionists on the basis of the Balfour Declaration after it was incorporated into the Mandate. Moreover, the various attempts to divide Palestine between an Arab and a Jewish state, which are examined in the following pages, provide further support for the view that the principle of self-determination was applicable to Palestine's Arab and Jewish inhabitants. Otherwise, on what basis did the Arabs have a right to a state according to the UNSCOP proposals and the UN Partition Plan which set out to create one? As many of the delegates speaking in favour of partition at the UN General Assembly debates in November 1947 recognised, partition via the creation of an Arab and a Jewish state in Palestine was tantamount to accepting that both communities were entitled to self-determination.[12]

Despite reaching the erroneous conclusion that self-determination did not apply to Palestine, UNSCOP paradoxically accepted that 'the Arab population is and will continue to be the numerically preponderant population in Palestine ...'[13] It also found that '[t]he Arab population in Palestine, despite the strenuous efforts of Jews to acquire land in Palestine, at present remains in possession of approximately 85 percent of the land'.[14] It was therefore quite odd that after acknowledging these incontestable facts, UNSCOP considered the establishment of a single unitary state with strong protections for minorities an 'extreme solution', even though this was the preferred outcome of the Arab Higher Committee (that is, the embryonic Government of Palestine).[15] UNSCOP then went on to dismiss the 'binational solution' advocated by the President of the Hebrew University of Jerusalem Dr Judah Leon Magnes as 'complicated', 'patently artificial' and of 'dubious practicality'.[16] The 'cantonal solution', UNSCOP found, 'might easily entail an excessive fragmentation of the governmental processes' and 'would be quite unworkable'.[17] It therefore proposed by a majority of seven members the partition of Palestine into a Jewish state and an Arab state qualified by economic union. Three members supported the federal-state plan.[18]

THE ATTEMPT TO PETITION THE ICJ FOR AN ADVISORY OPINION

After receiving the UNSCOP report, the UN General Assembly constituted an Ad Hoc Committee on the Palestine Question to frame the Palestine issue for plenary debate, comprised of all UN member states.[19] The Ad Hoc Committee set up two sub-committees. The first was to draw up a detailed plan for partition and the second was to draw up a plan for a single state. As Nabil Elaraby, a former ICJ judge, wrote:

> It seems anomalous that the procedure adopted for the consideration of the report was delegated to two subcommittees of the Ad Hoc Committee, one composed of pro-partition delegates and the other of Arab delegates plus Colombia and Pakistan, which were sympathetic to the Arab cause. It was obvious that those two sub-committees were so unbalanced as to be unable to achieve anything constructive. As was later evident, the task

of reconciling their conflicting recommendations was impossible. In such circumstances, it was not surprising that no serious attention was given to the legitimate aspirations of the Palestinians.[20]

To protest the legality of the measures under consideration by Sub-Committee 1, the representatives of several Arab states formally proposed to request an advisory opinion from the ICJ on the legality of partitioning Palestine before the Assembly proceeded to act on the UNSCOP majority recommendation.[21] Holding that partition violated both the UN Charter and a people's democratic right to self-determination, the representatives of Egypt, Iraq, Lebanon, Saudi Arabia, Syria and the Yemen declared themselves in favour of an independent unitary state embracing all of Palestine, in which the rights of the minority would be scrupulously safeguarded.[22] The representatives of Afghanistan, Argentina, Cuba, India, Iran, Pakistan and Yugoslavia supported them in their opposition to the Partition Plan.[23] During the general debate in the Ad Hoc Committee, Egypt, Iraq, and Syria proposed that the ICJ consider a number of 'legal questions' in its advisory capacity.[24] At its first meeting on 23 October 1947, Sub-Committee 2 elected Alberto Gonzalez Fernandez of Colombia as chairman and Sir Mohammed Zafrullah Khan of Pakistan as rapporteur.[25] After Fernandez resigned, Khan was elected chairman in his stead, while at the same time retaining his position as rapporteur of the sub-committee.[26] During the debate on partition in the UN General Assembly, Khan explained that Fernandez 'felt very uncomfortable' with the way in which the sub-committees had been constituted and that in order to make it more balanced, changes would have to be made.[27] In this regard, two of the Arab states let it be known that they were anxious to step down from Sub-Committee 2 so that it might be reconstituted on a fairer basis with countries both for and against partition working together.[28] But the chairman of the Ad Hoc Committee rejected the proposal. In the words of Khan: 'It was either partition or nothing.'[29] There was no middle way.[30] The Lebanese Ambassador to the UN, Camille Chamoun, who would become the President of that country in 1952, probably most eloquently expressed the Arab position on the Palestine problem in these words:

> Today, as before, we are ready to listen to, study and discuss any conciliatory formula likely to offer a reasonable and just solution of the Palestine problem. We shall do so not out of weakness, but with the greatest willingness, for we consider that our Organization's task is to recommend, not solutions which can be applied only by force or the threat of force, but solutions which by reason of their objective and equitable character command universal acceptance.[31]

The second sub-committee concentrated on three broad issues concerning the question of Palestine and resolutions were drafted on the following issues: (1) the legal questions connected with the Palestine problem; (2) the problem of Jewish refugees and displaced persons in Europe; and (3) the establishment of an independent and unitary Palestinian state.[32] Regarding the question of partition, the sub-committee drafted a resolution referring certain legal questions to the ICJ.[33] The preamble to the draft resolution recalled the legal controversies associated with 'the inherent right of the indigenous population of Palestine to their country and to determine its future'. These concerned the 'pledges and assurances given to the Arabs in the First World War regarding the independence of Arab countries including Palestine, the validity and scope of the Balfour Declaration and the Mandate, the effect on the Mandate of the dissolution of the League of Nations and of the declaration by the Mandatory Power of its intentions to withdraw from Palestine [*sic*]'.[34] The preamble also considered that the question of Palestine raised other legal issues 'connected with the competence of the United Nations to recommend any solution contrary to the Covenant of the League of Nations or the Charter of the United Nations, or to the wishes of the majority of the people of Palestine'.[35] The draft envisaged the UN General Assembly requesting 'the International Court of Justice to give an Advisory Opinion under Article 96 of the Charter and Chapter IV of the Statute of the Court'.[36] What followed were eight questions drafted by Egypt and Syria on a range of legal and political issues.[37] It may fairly be asked whether these questions would have satisfied the requirements set out in the UN Charter and the statute of the ICJ, which provides the UN General Assembly with the competence 'to give an Advisory Opinion on any legal question'.[38] In the debate on the reports of Sub-Committees 1 and 2 on 24 November 1947, the French Ambassador to the UN, Alexandre Parodi, felt that questions 1 to 7 in the draft resolution 'were so general in character as not to constitute legal matters, of which the Court could make a precise study'.[39] He therefore requested that questions 1 to 7 be voted separately from question 8, which asked:

> Whether the United Nations, or any of its Member States, is competent to enforce or recommend the enforcement of any proposal concerning the constitution and future Government of Palestine, in particular, any plan of partition which is contrary to the wishes, or adopted without the consent of, the inhabitants of Palestine.[40]

In the vote, questions 1 to 7 were defeated by 25 votes to 18 with 11 abstentions.[41] Question 8, however, was defeated by only one vote. France and India voted in favour of question 8 and Belgium, Czechoslovakia and Luxembourg decided to abstain rather than vote against it.[42] Included in those countries which abstained were the Netherlands and the United Kingdom. It was the policy of the Soviet Union and the states which were then allied to it (like Byelorussia and the Ukraine) to object to requests for advisory opinions from the ICJ, particularly on questions relating to the interpretation of the Charter.[43] Had the Soviet Union or just one of its satellite states voted in favour of question 8, it would have been submitted to the ICJ for an advisory opinion. One can only speculate what impact this would have had on subsequent events, but as the delegation of Colombia pointed out to the Ad Hoc Committee: 'The Mandatory Power was not going to have its force withdrawn in the next three months, and, while the Court studied the matter, an active, well directed attempt might be made toward conciliation.'[44] It was proposed that the advisory opinion of the Court and the results of conciliation under UN auspices could have been considered in a special session of the General Assembly.[45] An American jurist writing in 1948, was of the opinion that it was 'highly possible that the International Court of Justice would have rendered a liberal opinion on the matter' along the lines of its advisory opinion concerning the Nationality Decrees issued in the French zone of Tunis and Morocco[46] which affected British subjects living there.[47] He even thought that 'from a strictly logical or legalistic point of view the Arab position has much to be said for it'.[48] He added that: 'The Arabs deny the binding force of the Mandate, now or ever, as they deny the validity of the Balfour Declaration on which it is based, and again they are probably quite correct juridically.'[49] He expressed his opinion that 'it would be politically very difficult if not impossible for the United Nations to dictate a solution in Palestine not acceptable to both Arabs and Jews, and practically impossible to execute such a program in the absence of United Nations armed forces'.[50]

Paradoxically, ten days prior to the debate on the reports of the sub-committees, the General Assembly considered that 'in virtue of Article 1 of the Charter, international disputes should be settled in conformity with the principles of justice and international law'.[51] It declared:

> Considering that the International Court of Justice could settle or assist in settling many disputes in conformity with these principles if, by the full application of the provisions of the Charter and of the Statute of the Court, *more frequent use were made of its services*.[52]

THE UN GENERAL ASSEMBLY RESOLUTION TO PARTITION PALESTINE

On 29 November 1947, the UN General Assembly voted by a 33–13 majority with 10 abstentions to recommend the partition of Palestine with economic union.[53] The Plan proposed to create an Arab state and a Jewish state with Jerusalem and Bethlehem established as a *corpus separatum* (that is, a separate body), which was to be administered by the UN. Part B.I.B of the UN Partition Plan set out the procedural steps which were to be taken preparatory to the independence of the two states concerned, which required the progressive withdrawal of the mandatory power's armed forces from the territory, and the attendant assumption of administrative powers by a UN Commission, operating through Arab and Jewish Provisional Councils of Government. As regards the substantive parts of the Plan, Jaffa, a predominantly Arab city situated by the Mediterranean Sea to the south of Tel Aviv, was to be an enclave belonging to the Arab state within the Jewish state. According to figures provided by UNSCOP, in the proposed Arab state there would have been 10,000 Jews and almost 1 million Arabs. In the proposed Jewish state there would have been 498,000 Jews and 407,000 Arabs.[54] However, the figures used by UNSCOP did not include the Bedouin population. A more accurate British figure estimated the population figures at 509,780 Arabs and 499,020 Jews in the Jewish state, which meant the Arabs would have remained a majority.[55]

Although Jews only constituted 33 per cent of the population of Palestine in 1947 (a figure which included Jewish immigrants), they were awarded 57 per cent of Palestine's landmass.[56] And according to the document circulated by a British delegate at the UN Sub-Committee, 84 per cent of the agricultural land was to be allocated to the Jewish state, with only 16 per cent of it going to the Arab state.[57] This would have devastated the Arab citrus industry, which was the Palestinian Arabs' largest export.[58] In the Negev, where 15 per cent of the land was privately owned (14 per cent by the Arabs, and 1 per cent by the Jews) the Jewish state was awarded all of it, even though only 1,020 Jews inhabited the area as opposed to 103,820 Arabs.[59] It was therefore hardly surprising that the Arab Higher Committee rejected the Plan. In fact, they were not alone in thinking the UN Partition Plan unjust. Britain's Secretary of State for Foreign Affairs, Ernest Bevin, thought it was 'manifestly unfair to the Arabs',[60] as did General Sir Alan Cunningham, the last British High Commissioner of Palestine.[61] Although the Jewish Agency reluctantly agreed to accept the UN Partition Plan as it provided for the creation of a Jewish state albeit in only half of Palestine, they did so only as the 'indispensable minimum'.[62] Yet even then, many were unhappy with the Plan – as it was all of Palestine they desired.[63] As Menachem Begin, the leader of the Irgun who would eventually become Israel's Prime Minister, declared:

> The partition of the Homeland is illegal. It will never be recognized. The signature by institutions and individuals of the partition agreement is invalid. It will not bind the Jewish people. Jerusalem was and will for ever be our capital. Eretz Israel will be restored to the people of Israel. All of it. And for ever.[64]

Leaving aside Begin's sweeping objections, it is telling that those countries which voted against partition at the UN General Assembly included those with a direct interest in events in Palestine such as the neighbouring countries of Egypt, Lebanon and Syria (Jordan was not yet a member of the UN).[65] The non-Arab states of Cuba, Greece, India, Iran and Turkey also voted against the Plan. In fact, not one Muslim state voted in favour of it, which was problematic since the Jewish state was to be created in a region of the world where the vast majority of people were Muslims who clearly sympathised with the plight of the Palestinians. Moreover, the Jewish state, whether it liked it or not, was going to have predominately Muslim states as its neighbours for the foreseeable future. Even Britain, the mandatory power, abstained from the vote in favour of partition as did Argentina, Chile, El Salvador, Mexico and Yugoslavia. In an assessment undertaken by British diplomats in January 1947 on the voting intentions of the various member states of the UN General

Assembly it had been predicted that a resolution proposing partition would have received 17 adverse votes, whereas a proposal to establish a unitary independent state would have received only 16 adverse votes.[66] At the time, the UN was comprised of 55 member states, and therefore a proposal could be blocked by 19 adverse votes if every delegation cast a vote. Article 18 of the UN Charter provides that decisions of the General Assembly on important questions, which includes recommendations with respect to the maintenance of international peace and security, shall be made by a two-thirds majority of the members present and voting.

Belgium, France, Haiti, Liberia, Luxembourg, the Netherlands, New Zealand, Paraguay and the Philippines were allegedly subject to American threats to cut aid if they voted against partition. In his memoirs, Truman wrote that he had never experienced 'as much pressure and propaganda aimed at the White House' as he had in this instance.[67] It is ironic that before switching its vote, the Philippines delegate had said that his country could not support any proposal for the dismemberment of Palestine, since his country thought this would not be in accordance with the principles of the UN Charter.[68] In his memoirs, Sir Mohammed Zafrullah Khan recalled the following incident:

> The representative of Haiti met me in the lounge and with tears literally coursing down his cheeks, said, 'Mr Minister, what can I do? I have now received instructions that in spite of my speech, in accordance with the instructions of my Government and my declaring that we were opposed to the partition, I have to vote for it.'[69]

As was evident, had it not been for combined Zionist and US pressure, the partition proposal would have probably failed at the first hurdle, as it is likely that it would have been blocked by 19 adverse votes. According to the assessment undertaken by the British diplomats, the Philippines would have voted against partition, though they were not sure of France's intentions. They did, however, think that the attitude of the US would be 'of the greatest importance' as the Latin American states would be influenced by its vote.[70]

The legality of the UN's recommendation provoked quite a debate in the legal literature at the time, and still does to this day. It concerns two related issues: (a) whether the UN General Assembly has the competence to partition a mandated territory, and (b) whether the Plan was binding under international law or whether it was merely a recommendation.[71]

Some international lawyers have argued that the resolution recommending the adoption of the Partition Plan was *ultra vires* (that is, beyond its powers) because the UN General Assembly does not have the capacity to convey title as it cannot assume the role of a territorial sovereign.[72] Although it is true that the UN Charter does not explicitly give the UN General Assembly the power to partition mandated territories *per se*, and although the UN does not have the capacity to act as a territorial sovereign, there is nothing expressly prohibiting it from recommending to states that they consider partitioning a particular territory.[73] This is because according to the theory of 'implied powers', under which the UN is deemed to have those powers which, though not expressly provided in the Charter, are conferred upon it by necessary implication as being essential to the performance of its duties, the UN General Assembly may recommend such a course of action.[74] This is especially the case if the partition is being undertaken in the interests of international peace and security.[75] Article 10 of the Charter explicitly provides that the UN General Assembly may discuss any questions or any matters within the scope of the Charter or relating to the powers and functions of any of its organs, which would presumably include the powers, and functions of the General Assembly itself. In the cases of the peoples inhabiting territories placed under mandates and trusteeships, the UN has a special responsibility for their well-being. Therefore it is arguable that if the rationale underlying the Partition Plan was that it was in the interests of the well-being of the inhabitants of those territories, then it was lawful.

In this regard it will be recalled that in its 1950 advisory opinion on the *Status of South-West Africa* the ICJ unanimously concluded that the Union of South Africa acting with the consent of the UN had the competence to determine and modify the international status of a mandated territory.[76] And in the many submissions to the ICJ in that advisory opinion, not once did any of the lawyers advance the argument that the 1947 Partition Plan was *ultra vires* – even when they explicitly referred to it.[77] There is consequently no basis in the UN Charter or in international law to argue that the General Assembly does not have the power to *recommend* to states that they adopt a plan partitioning a particular territory over which it has a special responsibility. However, the case would perhaps be different if the Security Council upon a recommendation from the General Assembly tried to enforce a partition *by using force* against the express wishes of the peoples inhabiting the territory to be divided. The consent of the people is of the utmost importance.[78] In its *Status* opinion, the ICJ repeated that 'the normal way of modifying the international status of the Territory [referring in this particular instance to the Mandate of South-West Africa] would be to place it under the Trusteeship System by means of a Trusteeship Agreement in accordance with the provisions of Chapter XII of the Charter'.[79] In other words, the UN should have considered placing Palestine under a Trusteeship before going on to recommend partition as a course of action, although it is noteworthy that South-West Africa would become the independent state of Namibia in 1990 without it ever being placed under a UN Trusteeship.[80] It may therefore be concluded that the UN General Assembly, acting with the consent of the mandatory, can modify the status of a mandated territory and that, in so doing, it is competent to decide on claims of self-determination put forward by communities living in the territory.[81]

Regarding the question as to whether the UN General Assembly resolution was binding or not, it is instructive to note that UN Secretary-General Trygve Lie thought that the resolution was legally binding because it constituted a decision taken by the UN General Assembly, which as a successor to the

Council of the League of Nations had in his opinion the competence to partition a mandated territory.[82] The Government of Israel also argued that it was binding and based its claim to statehood on the strength of the UN Partition Plan.[83] The District Court at Haifa actually referred to the Partition Plan as 'a document having validity under international law'.[84]

However, despite the opinions of these authorities, the better view would seem to be that although the resolution was drafted with the intention that the Partition Plan would actually be implemented and expressly referred to possible enforcement action under Articles 39 and 41 of the UN Charter, the resolution was ultimately only a recommendation and not a legally binding decision.[85] This is because according to Articles 10–14 of the UN Charter, the General Assembly can only make recommendations.[86] This view is supported by the fact that both the Security Council[87] and the mandatory power[88] refused to enforce the UN Partition Plan. It is also apparent from the very terms of UN General Assembly resolution 181 which states that the General Assembly: '*Recommends* to the United Kingdom ... and to all other Members of the United Nations the adoption and implementation ... of the Plan of Partition.'[89] In the words of Philip C. Jessup, a former Professor of International Law at Columbia University, who represented the US at the UN in 1948, before becoming a judge at the ICJ: '... I do not believe that the most ardent advocates of the binding legal effect of such resolutions would attribute legislative force to the partition resolution. Like most General Assembly resolutions, it was merely a recommendation.'[90] Moreover, a working paper prepared by the UN Secretariat on the powers of the UN to enforce the UN Partition Plan concluded that whilst the UN Security Council was competent to enforce the recommendation of the UN General Assembly, if so requested, it was not bound by it because it was only a recommendation.[91] In the words of the Secretariat, UN General Assembly resolution 181 (III) had 'no obligatory character whatsoever'.[92] It will also be recalled that the initial question posed by Britain to the UN General Assembly concerning 'the future Government of Palestine' of 3 April 1947, explicitly stipulated that the General Assembly was acting under Article 10 of the UN Charter, which only provides that body with the power of making recommendations to other UN members.[93]

It is only the UN Security Council that can make legally binding decisions within the meaning of Article 25 of the UN Charter and enforce them by invoking its enforcement powers, which are provided for in Chapter VII (principally Articles 39, 41 and 42 of the Charter).[94] The UN General Assembly does not have the power to enforce its recommendations or to make law, as it is not a legislative body.[95] However, having said this, some UN General Assembly resolutions if they are adopted by a majority verging on unanimity, or virtually without opposition, may contribute to the formation of a customary rule of international law, or be evidence that it is already formed, although these rules would not be binding against a state that persistently objects to them.[96]

LEGAL OBJECTIONS TO THE UN PARTITION PLAN

It is, however, apparent that the plan to partition Palestine was not entirely without its faults. Even if one ignored for the moment, the question as to whether the UN Partition Plan was validly adopted, it faced several objections on legal, moral and political grounds. For instance, on 6 February 1948, Mr Isa Nakleh, the representative of the Arab Higher Committee, accused the US of placing undue influence, which he described as being 'nothing short of political blackmail', on states to vote in favour of partition.[97] Accordingly, the Arab Higher Committee refused to participate in the work of the Palestine Commission.[98] Yet despite the question of undue influence and whether the partition resolution was null and void, as the Palestinian Arabs claimed it was,[99] there were also substantive problems with the UN Partition Plan. To begin with it would seem that, on the face of it, the Plan was contrary to the principles of self-determination and majority rule as the Arab population of Palestine opposed partition. This was one of the arguments advanced by Loy W. Henderson, who was then serving as Director of the Office for Near Eastern and African Affairs at the US Department of State. In a top-secret memorandum to George Marshall, the Secretary of State, he wrote:

> These proposals [of the majority of UNSCOP proposing partition], for instance, ignore such principles as self-determination and majority rule. They recognize the principles of a theocratic racial state and even go so far in several instances as to discriminate on grounds of religion and race against persons outside of Palestine ... We are under no obligation to the Jews to set up a Jewish state. The Balfour Declaration and the Mandate provided not for a Jewish state, but for a Jewish national home. Neither the United States nor the British Government has ever interpreted the term 'Jewish national home' to be a 'Jewish national state'.[100]

Of course the contrary argument could be advanced that the Partition Plan was consistent with the self-determination of both peoples, although not with the concept of majority rule, as it provided for the creation of both a Jewish and an Arab state.[101] On the other hand, allowing a minority of the population to partition the country against the wishes of two-thirds of the population is a very odd way of giving effect to rights, which the Covenant of the League of Nations regarded as being vested in the population as a whole.[102] In this respect, it has been argued that the Covenant conferred rights on the inhabitants of Palestine which could not be revoked without their consent, in the same way that a treaty can sometimes confer an irrevocable right on a third state.[103]

Another criticism of the Partition Plan was that it was inequitable[104] in that the Jewish state was to have received the majority of the land, including quality farmland, even though the inhabitants of the putative Arab state owned most of it. According to British statistics on Arab land ownership in 1945, in every single sub-district of Palestine – Safad, Acre, Tiberias, Beisan, Nazareth, Haifa,

Jenin, Nablus, Tulkarem, Ramallah, Jerusalem, Hebron, Jaffa, Ramle, Gaza and Beersheba – the Arabs owned most of the land.[105] Even in Safad, which was awarded to the Jewish state by the UN Partition Plan, the Arabs owned 68 per cent of the land whereas Jews owned a mere 18 per cent; yet despite this, the latter got the lot.[106] Although land ownership is not commensurate with territorial sovereignty under international law, one would have thought that in marking the frontier between the Jewish state, the Arab state and the *corpus separatum* (Jerusalem and Bethlehem), the boundary commission would have taken into consideration those areas in which the land was predominantly Arab owned and partitioned it from those areas where it was predominantly Jewish owned or alternatively partitioned those areas in which Arabs formed a majority of the population from those parts where Jews were preponderant. Taking into account demographics and land ownership, and then marking out a frontier as the Peel Commission did in 1937, would certainly have been a more equitable, just, and practical partition.

Yet as things transpired the Arabs owned most of the land that was awarded to the Jewish state and it seems that a majority of the inhabitants in the Jewish state would have also been Arab. One possible explanation for this anomaly is that UNSCOP wanted to ensure that there would be enough space for those Jewish refugees from Europe who had survived the *Shoah* to immigrate to the envisaged Jewish state to settle there and develop the land.[107] However, it is noteworthy that this issue had already been looked into in some detail by the Anglo-American Committee of Enquiry of 1946[108] whose members toured the concentration camps of Europe, after which they recommended that whilst some refugees (approx. 100,000 persons) should be allowed into Palestine, its territorial integrity should nevertheless be kept intact.[109]

Tellingly, the US State Department and the American delegation in New York had actually proposed to amend UNSCOP's majority proposal so that the Negev that they had awarded to the Jewish state, and which was predominantly Arab, would be awarded to the Arab state instead.[110] However, they encountered resistance to this proposal from the Zionists. Weizmann called President Truman on the telephone, and managed to persuade him to leave the Plan unchanged.[111] In this regard it is significant that in a top-secret War Cabinet memorandum prepared especially for British Prime Minister Winston Churchill on post-war planning in Palestine in 1945, the Negev was to be awarded to neither state although it would have had continuity with the Arab state (see Map 7).[112] Moreover, even after the Partition Plan had been recommended by the UN in 1947, the UN mediator Count Folke Bernadotte had proposed that the Negev should be awarded to the Arab state in his last progress report to the UN General Assembly in 1948.[113] As the Syrian representative exclaimed to the UN General Assembly when they were debating the merits of partition in 1947 with particular reference to the Negev:

> The southern part of Palestine, inhabited exclusively by Arabs, has been given to the proposed Jewish State on the excuse that a desert region like the Negev is of no use to the Bedouins. This is a type of logic quite peculiar

> to the Zionists and their friends; they claim that a desert like the Negev or Sinai is useless to the Bedouins but can be of great use to the Jews of Warsaw and Riga. What logic![114]

In this regard it is intriguing that in the Armenia–Turkey boundary case of 1920, the arbitrator, who happened to be President Woodrow Wilson, concluded that where

> the requirements of a correct geographic boundary permitted, all mountain and valley districts along the border which were predominantly Kurdish or Turkish have been left to Turkey rather than assigned to Armenia, unless trade relations with definite market towns threw them necessarily into the Armenian State. Whenever information upon tribal relations and seasonal migrations was obtainable, the attempt was made to respect the integrity of tribal groupings and nomad pastoral movements.[115]

In addition, the arbitrator suggested to the boundary commission, in regard to one portion of the frontier, 'the desirability of consulting with the local inhabitants with a view to possible modification' of the boundary.[116]

During the partition of Ireland a boundary commission was asked to 'determine in accordance with the wishes of the inhabitants, so far as may be compatible with economic and geographic conditions, the boundaries between Northern Ireland and the rest of Ireland ...'[117] The three-man commission interpreted its terms of reference so that an inhabitant was someone who had a permanent connection to the area concerned and in order to assess the wishes of the inhabitants they made use of the census returns of 1911, showing the religious denominations to which the inhabitants belonged.[118] It was taken for granted that members of Protestant denominations wanted to be in Northern Ireland and that Roman Catholics preferred to be in the Irish Free State.[119]

In the *Jaworzina* case of 1923, which concerned a section of the frontier between Poland and Czechoslovakia, the Permanent Court of International Justice affirmed that the question of its delimitation had been settled by a decision of the Conference of Ambassadors (which was comprised of the USA, the British Empire, France, Italy, Japan and the Principal Allied and Associated Powers).[120] In that decision, the Conference of Ambassadors had established a Frontier Delimitation Commission which was empowered to propose 'any modifications which it may consider justified by reason of the interests of individuals or of communities in the neighbourhood of the frontier line and having regard to settled local circumstances'.[121]

When the Peel Commission first recommended partitioning Palestine it suggested that the 'natural principle' for the partition of Palestine would be to separate land and settlements from the areas in which the Jews have acquired land and settled from those which are wholly or mainly occupied by Arabs.[122]

Moreover, the boundary commission that was established by the British Government to partition the Punjab after the decision to partition British India had been announced was instructed to 'demarcate the Boundaries of the two parts of the Punjab on the basis of ascertaining the contiguous majority areas of Muslims and non-Muslims'.[123]

It therefore seemed that UNSCOP was departing from established practice in that it neither consulted the Arab population of Palestine, although this may have been because the Arab Higher Committee boycotted the commission, nor took into consideration those areas in which they formed a majority of the population or where they were the major landowners, in recommending partition.[124] Then there was also the question of economic viability, which the arbitrator in the Armenia–Turkey boundary case considered of the utmost importance.[125] In this respect it was highly questionable whether the Arab state – as opposed to the Jewish state – would be economically viable and this was one of the reasons why the Arab states opposed partition because they thought that the proposed Arab state would be dependent on handouts from the international community.[126]

It is noteworthy that when partition was being considered by the British War Cabinet in 1945, the Foreign Secretary, who was then Anthony Eden, wrote in a top-secret memorandum to Prime Minister Winston Churchill that he was opposed to partitioning Palestine, because in his view: 'It would not be easy to persuade the Arab Governments that it is equitable or consonant with the mandate, or with the Atlantic Charter, or with our own war-time publicity, to include in the Jewish State all the best land, practically all the industries, the only good ports and about a third of the Arab inhabitants.'[127] Eden's reference to the Atlantic Charter – the precursor to the UN Charter – was significant. This is because it provided, in its second principle, that the US and Great Britain 'desire to see no territorial changes that do not accord with the freely expressed wishes of the peoples concerned'.[128] And yet, the partition of Palestine seemed to expressly violate the principle concerned. Moreover, it would also seem that the method through which Palestine was to be partitioned according to the 1947 UN Partition Plan was contrary to the spirit of the UN Charter in that it would have had to be enforced by recourse to armed force,[129] which is in direct contradistinction to the preamble and a number of purposes and principles enumerated in Articles 1 and 2. And in fact this was the principal reason why the UN did not ultimately pursue partition, as the mandatory power opposed enforcing it against the wishes of both the Arabs and the Jews.[130] The Americans also decided not to place the Partition Plan before the UN Security Council when they realised that any UN force sent to Palestine would have included Soviet troops, as they did not want to give them a foothold in that part of the Middle East.[131] Moreover, every country in the region and some beyond were also opposed to the Partition Plan. Although the first purpose of the UN is to maintain international peace and security, the Partition Plan was so inequitable that it seemed self-evident that it would lead to conflict.

In this regard it is worth mentioning that in the Indo-Pakistan Western Boundary Case, which concerned a part of the boundary that was not delimited by the boundary commission headed by Sir Cyril Radcliffe during the 1947 partition of British India, Gunnar Lagergren, the Chairman of the three-man tribunal, took into account 'the paramount consideration of promoting peace and stability in the region' in determining the boundary between India and Pakistan in the Rann of Kutch (which is a salty marsh of some 10,000 square miles).[132] He also invoked considerations of equity, in awarding 10 per cent of the territory to Pakistan since not doing so in the particular circumstances of the case 'would be conducive to friction and conflict'.[133] There were good reasons why the Swedish Chairman invoked considerations of equity in promoting peace and stability between India and Pakistan: the two countries have gone to war several times since, most recently in the *Atlantique* incident in 1999.[134]

Moreover, in a dispute over the inter-entity boundary line in the Brčko area, which is a town located in a strategic location along the partitioned territories of Republika Srpska and the Federation of Bosnia and Herzegovina, the arbitral tribunal concluded that any 'simple solution' had to be rejected in favour of an approach 'that is consistent with law and equity and is designed gradually to relieve the underlying tensions and lead to a stable and harmonious solution'.[135]

The UNSCOP would perhaps have been wise to have taken into account considerations of equity, peace and stability when they recommended partitioning Palestine. In awarding so much territory to a minority community, many of whom had no legal connection to Palestine either through citizenship (as many were foreign immigrants) or through habitual residence, they provided the Arabs of Palestine with a cause to fight which has in turn contributed to civil strife and conflict. In this connection the citizenship provisions of the UN Partition Plan which granted citizenship on the basis of foreign *residence*, as opposed to domicile or habitual residence, have also been criticised as being contrary to state practice.[136] Had the Partition Plan been implemented it would have meant that a recent immigrant to the country would have been given the same rights to citizenship as someone who had been living in the country for several generations. According to the *Survey of Palestine*, in 1946, it was estimated that 91 per cent of the foreigners in Palestine were Jewish and only 6 per cent were Arab.[137]

During the debates in the UN General Assembly on the Partition Plan, the delegate from Cuba, Mr Ernesto Dihigo (and this was, it will be recalled, pre-Castro's Cuba) opposed partition on the grounds that 'the plan would mean deciding the fate of a nation without consulting it on the matter, and depriving it of half the national territory which it had held for many centuries'.[138] 'We consider the plan illegal,' he said, 'because it is inconsistent with the self-determination of peoples, an essential principle of the Covenant of the League of Nations.' He continued: 'We are not convinced by the argument which has been put forward to the effect that Palestine is not a State and therefore is not subject to international law, because these provisions [referring to Article 1 (2), and paragraph 6 of Article 76 of the UN Charter] speak of peoples not States and there can be no doubt that the inhabitants of Palestine are a people.'[139]

Mr Dihigo then went on to explain why Cuba, despite the pressure exerted upon it by the US, was opposed to the very principle of partitioning Palestine because it implied the establishment by the UN General Assembly of the principle that any racial or other minority may ask to secede from the political community of which it forms part. In this respect he recalled that not so many years ago,

> ... Cuba was in danger of losing part of its territory owing to immigration of United States citizens into Pinos Island.[140] Fortunately for us, and to the honour of the United States Government, which was magnanimous enough to recognize our rights, this attempt failed. Nevertheless, we cannot forget how much that danger meant to us; and, knowing what our feelings would have been if we had lost part of our territory in that way, we can easily imagine the feelings of the Palestine Arabs if the partition plan were approved. We cannot vote in favour of doing to them what we were not prepared to have done to us.[141]

Mr Dihigo added that it was useless to tell Cuba 'that a political solution must sometimes be accepted despite the fact that it is unjust; for international peace and friendship cannot be built upon injustice'.[142]

Similarly, the UN delegate of the Philippines, Mr Romulo, said that his government was opposed to the 'political disunion and the territorial dismemberment of Palestine', although ultimately his government was induced by the US to approve of the UN Partition Plan. Before switching his vote, Mr Romulo told the UN General Assembly:

> My country was, not so long ago, before we became independent, under grave threat of territorial dismemberment by a unilateral act of the metropolitan Power. The reasons given then were curiously similar to those that are being advanced now in the case before us. It was said that the part of my country which was to be segregated from the rest of the archipelago – Mindanao and Sulu – was inhabited by Mohammedans, as distinguished from the more numerous Christians who lived there and elsewhere. It was also claimed that the area was, so sparsely settled and so little developed that it was not to be left closed to foreign capital and enterprise.
>
> Our people fought this infamous proposal, which was presented to the United States Congress as the Bacon Bill, with all the force at their command. They denounced it as an act that was completely opposed to the spirit which, until then, had animated the policies of the United States towards the Philippines. They resisted it as a blow that was aimed by certain elements in the United States at the very heart of the nationalistic movement among the Filipino people.

> It is a tribute both to the character of the Filipinos and to the good sense of the people of the United States that we were able to overcome that menace. And so, today, we stand here to attest to the powerful spirit of union that now holds all the various elements of our population together – a spirit that, in its devotion to the ideals of religious tolerance, national co-operation and freedom, has survived with flying colours the two-fold devastation of conquest and liberation.[143]

When the Polish delegate came out in favour of the UN Partition Plan, the delegate from Syria reminded him that when his country was partitioned between its neighbours, Austria, Prussia and Russia, the only country that refused to recognise that partition was the Ottoman Empire, of which Palestine was part.[144] Then, for good measure, he expressed his opinion as to why he thought Poland was voting in favour of partition: 'The Polish delegation, which is usually so punctilious with regard to interpretations of the terms of the Charter, is silent when it is a question of violating that same Charter, because that violation is aimed at founding a Jewish State in Palestine which would allow Poland to get rid of its own Jews.'[145] Taken at face value this statement might seem a little extreme, but when one considers the social and political context in which the Balfour Declaration was issued in Britain in 1917, that the biggest rate of Jewish immigration into Palestine came from Germany, Poland and Russia, countries not known for treating their Jews well, one might understand what the Syrian delegate was suggesting. This is especially when one takes into account that the Soviet Union was actually forcing Jewish concentration camp survivors into the western zones of occupation from Poland so as to encourage their flight to Palestine.[146]

It is also arguable that the UN Partition Plan was inconsistent with the terms of the Mandate itself, which never envisaged partitioning Palestine into two separate states (rather, it provided for the creation of a Jewish national home in Palestine). If it had been the intention of the Principal Allied Powers to partition Palestine into a Jewish state and an Arab state, then presumably they would have stipulated this in the Mandate. After all, this was done in the Mandate for Syria and the Lebanon, which explicitly provided in Article 1 that the mandatory would 'enact measures to facilitate the progressive development of Syria and the Lebanon as independent States'.[147]

Furthermore, partitioning Palestine would arguably conflict with Article 5 of the Mandate, which provided that Britain was responsible 'for seeing that no Palestine territory shall be ceded or leased to, or in any way placed under the control of the Government of any foreign Power'. The Partition Plan granted a considerable share of Palestine to the Zionists, who were then represented on the international plane by the Jewish Agency, an arm of the Zionist Organisation, which, as the governing body of an international organisation, could by analogy be described as the government of a 'foreign power', as indeed, could the United Nations. And, as a matter of fact, the Partition Plan actually gave control over Jerusalem and economic policy to the UN via the establishment of a Joint Economic Board, which was to consist of three representatives of each of the two states and three foreign members appointed by the UN's Economic and Social Council, which was to realise the objectives of the economic union.[148] In fact, the whole plan hinged on the success of this economic union and this was one of the reasons why partition was opposed by the Arab states. They simply did not think it would work. They thought that it would be impossible to combine economic union with political division.[149]

Moreover, whilst it is true that Article 5 of the Mandate only applied to the mandatory power and to no one else, such as the member states of the UN, and that the functioning of the League of Nations with respect to the mandates had come to an end at the 21st and last session of the Assembly in 1946, the mandates themselves had *not* actually been terminated.[150] As Sir Arnold McNair stated in his Separate Opinion in the ICJ's *Status* advisory opinion:

> The dissolution of the League on April 19, 1946, did not automatically terminate the Mandates. Each Mandate has to be considered separately to ascertain the date and the mode of its termination. Take the case of Palestine. It is instructive to note that on November 29, 1947, the General Assembly of the United Nations adopted a resolution approving a plan of partition for Palestine, which was firmly based on the view that the Palestine Mandate still continued, as is evident from Articles 1 and 2 of Part A and Article 12 of Part B of the Plan ...[151]

Instead, those members of the League administering mandated territories were to continue administering them for the well-being and development of the peoples concerned in accordance with the obligations contained in their respective mandates, until other arrangements had been agreed to between the UN and the respective mandatory powers.[152] In this respect, it is questionable whether the UN General Assembly had the power to recommend a course of action, which directly conflicted, with the explicit terms of the Mandate. This is because the Mandate was still in force when Britain requested that the UN make a recommendation, under Article 10 of the Charter, concerning the future Government of Palestine.[153] As the UN never took control of Palestine, because the Partition Plan was never implemented, international legal responsibility remained vested with Britain, which was obliged to administer it according to the terms of the Mandate until its dissolution at midnight on 14/15 May 1948.[154] Therefore Article 5 remained in force throughout this period of time.

In this regard it is significant that the only provision of the UN Charter to mention the term 'Mandate' at all is Article 77, which deals with trusteeships.[155] It would seem that the expectation of those who drafted Article 77 was that territories placed under a Mandate would be placed under a UN Trusteeship if they were not yet considered ready for independence otherwise the territories concerned should have become independent.[156] In this connection, Article 80 of the UN Charter provides that nothing in Chapter XII (which deals with trusteeships) 'shall be construed in or of itself to *alter in any manner* the rights whatsoever *of any States or any peoples or the terms of existing international instruments* to which Members of the United Nations may respectively be parties'.[157] Article 80 was based on a proposal by the US delegate during the initial drafting of what would eventually become the UN Charter at Dumbarton Oaks in Washington DC. This was where a preliminary conference attended by Great Britain, China, the Soviet Union and the US on creating a world organisation in 1944 took place. The conference laid the foundations for the Conference on International Organisation in San Francisco, which created the United Nations Organisation in the following year. The original draft of Article 80 used the following language: '... nothing in the Charter should be construed in and of itself to alter in any manner the rights of any State or any peoples in any territory, *or the terms of any mandate*'.[158] This, perhaps, provides further evidence that the terms of the British Mandate of Palestine continued to apply, even after the creation of the UN, until the Mandate was dissolved by Britain at midnight on 14/15 May 1948.[159]

It is also important to point out that the UN Partition Plan was seriously flawed. As previously mentioned, the populations of the envisaged states were inaccurate. The fact is that there would have been more Arabs in the Jewish state than Jews, which is ironic given that it was supposed to be a 'Jewish state'. Even if one contests these figures, there would have been so many Arabs in the Jewish state according to UNSCOP, that it is unlikely that it could have survived for long without it becoming an 'Arab' state. In fact, according to a telegram sent from the British authorities in Palestine to the Foreign Office after the UNSCOP's recommendations were released, the Arab population of Palestine was reported to have responded to the Plan with incredulity:

> The immediately striking feature of the plan is that on the Committee's own figures (including 90,000 Bedouins), the Jewish State would contain actually more Arabs than Jews ... The Arab population is larger than in any plan yet seriously propounded. It is, in fact, so large that Arab opinion here still finds it difficult to regard the plan as a serious proposition at all. The absence of any immediate violent reaction by the Arabs can be attributed to this incredulity, and many Arabs regard it rather as a joke.[160]

What was also unique about the Partition Plan was that one of the communities, namely the Jewish community, was being awarded a state even though the vast majority of them were foreign immigrants (in other words, they were nationals of other countries) who were effectively being given the right to break up the territorial integrity of a territory to which they previously had no physical connection.[161] In other words, a minority people, united by religion and ideology, were being awarded a state in the territory of another people, where they would have remained a minority. It is therefore difficult to see how they could have formed a Jewish state according to the UN Partition Plan. This may also explain why the Zionists resorted to violence in order to carve out the territory in which they would proclaim their future state.

As previously mentioned, this was not the first time partition had been proposed as a solution to the problems in Palestine. Almost ten years earlier, a Royal Commission of Enquiry under Lord Peel had come to a similar conclusion, only for its recommendations to be rejected by the Arabs and by the Zionists,[162] as well as by Sir John Woodhead's Palestine Partition Commission who were specifically asked to study the feasibility of partition.[163] Several studies by His Majesty's Government on the ramifications of partitioning Palestine in 1939, 1944 and 1945 were also rejected.[164] In 1939, in a statement presented to Parliament by the Secretary of State for the Colonies, Malcolm MacDonald, the son of Ramsay MacDonald, declared:

> 4. His Majesty's Government, after careful study of the Partition Commission's report, have reached the conclusion that this further examination has shown that the political, administrative and financial difficulties involved in the proposal to create independent Arab and Jewish States inside Palestine are so great that this solution of the problem is impracticable.[165]

Six months after issuing this statement, Great Britain declared that since partition was not acceptable to either the Jews or the Arabs it was free to formulate its own policy. Accordingly, in its White Paper of 1939, the Government declared that it thought that those who drafted the Mandate in which the Balfour Declaration was embodied did not intend to convert Palestine into a Jewish state against the will of the Arab population of that country.[166] According to MacDonald:

> His Majesty's Government therefore now declare unequivocally that it is not part of their policy that Palestine should become a Jewish State. They would indeed regard it as contrary to their obligations to the Arabs under the Mandate, as well as to the assurances which have been given to the Arab people in the past, that the Arab population of Palestine should be made the subjects of a Jewish state against their will.[167]

The British Government was of the opinion that it would be 'contrary to the whole spirit of the Mandate system that the population of Palestine should remain forever under Mandatory tutelage'.[168] It therefore came to the following conclusion:

> It is proper that the people of the country should as early as possible enjoy the rights of self-Government which are exercised by the people of neighbouring countries. His Majesty's Government are unable at present to foresee the exact constitutional forms which Government in Palestine will eventually take, but their objective is self-government, and they desire to see established ultimately an independent Palestinian State. It should be a State in which the two in Palestine, Arabs and Jews, share authority in Government in such a way that the essential interests of each are secured.[169]

After it became apparent to the US that partition was unenforceable because it could not be secured by the necessary majority in the Security Council (the partition resolution explicitly requested the Security Council to take the necessary measures to secure its implementation by acting under its enforcement powers provided for by Article 39 and 41 of the Charter), partly because Britain would not enforce it, and partly because the Arabs and Jews were preparing for war, it changed its policy.[170] Addressing the Security Council, Warren Austin, the US Ambassador to the UN, announced that his government believed that a temporary trusteeship for Palestine should now be established under the Trusteeship Council of the UN to maintain the peace between the Jews and Arabs of Palestine.[171] It had finally dawned upon the Americans that just as the British had discovered to their detriment a decade earlier, the partition of Palestine was impracticable, most probably illegal, contrary to the League of Nations Covenant, the Mandate and the UN Charter, manifestly unjust to the Arabs, and ultimately unenforceable.

THE DRAFT UN TRUSTEESHIP FOR PALESTINE

On 18 April 1946, the League of Nations unanimously adopted a resolution which recognised that, 'on the termination of the League's existence, its *functions* with respect to the mandated territories will come to an end, but notes that Chapter XI, XII and XIII of the Charter of the United Nations embody principles corresponding to those declared in Article 22 of the Covenant of the League'.[172] The legal basis of this resolution, pending the conclusion of new arrangements with the UN, was the maintenance of the general principles of the mandatory system as it existed at the time of the dissolution of the League, as Hersch Lauterpacht noted in an opinion he prepared for the Jewish Agency for Palestine.[173] In other words, it was only the functions of the League which came to an end. Consequently, this resolution formally put on record the expressed intention of the mandatory powers to effect future arrangements by agreement with the UN. In this respect, the US was perfectly entitled to call upon the UN to establish a temporary trusteeship for Palestine. After all, the provisions of the Charter referred to in the League's resolution, contained principles, which essentially provided for the eventual exercise of self-determination by the peoples of non-self-governing territories and those who were placed under the system of trusteeship.

Article 76 of the UN Charter provides that one of the basic objectives of the trusteeship system, in accordance with the purposes of the UN as laid down in Article 1 of the Charter is 'to promote the political, economic, social, and educational advancement of the inhabitants of trust territories, and their progressive development towards self-Government *or independence* as may be appropriate to the particular circumstances of each territory and its peoples and the freely expressed wishes of the people concerned'.[174]

On 20 April 1948, the US introduced to the UN General Assembly the text of a draft Trusteeship Agreement for Palestine.[175] It was drafted by the US delegate, Philip C. Jessup and had the support of almost all the Latin

American states.[176] As he recalled in his memoirs of his time as the American representative on the UN Security Council:

> Partition clearly could not have been carried out, and the suggestion for a UN trusteeship was the strongest kind of evidence of confidence in the Organization's capacity to deal with the thorny Palestine problem.[177]

The document he drafted specifically referred to Articles 75 and 77 of the Charter in the preamble, providing in Article 2 that: 'The United Nations, acting through the Trusteeship Council, is hereby designated as the Administering Authority for Palestine.'[178] Article 4 provided that the UN was to administer Palestine in such a manner as to achieve the basic objectives of the international trusteeship system laid down in Article 76 of the Charter.[179] Article 5 provided that the UN would assure the territorial integrity of Palestine. Article 13 provided that executive authority would be vested in a Governor-General who would represent the UN in Palestine.[180] In this respect, the Governor was to ensure peace, good order and good government in Palestine.[181] Article 20 provided for a bicameral legislature comprised of a House of Representatives and a Senate; Articles 21–26 provided for elections to the legislature, the functioning thereof, and immunity for its members.[182] Article 29 provided that immigration into Palestine would be permitted 'without distinction between individuals as to religion and or blood, in accordance with the absorptive capacity of Palestine as determined by the Governor-General', subject to the requirements of public order and security and of public morals and public health.[183] As a temporary measure, a mutually agreed number of 'Jewish displaced persons' would be permitted into Palestine 'per month, for a period not to exceed two years'.[184] Article 31 provided that a commission of impartial experts, neither Arab nor Jew, would be called to recommend the criteria upon which a land system appropriate to the needs of Palestine would be based.[185] Most importantly, in the context of self-determination, Article 47 provided that the temporary trusteeship was to be determined after a period of three years after which the UN General Assembly, upon a recommendation of the UN Trusteeship Council, would agree to a plan of government for Palestine, which would be approved by a majority of both the Arab and Jewish communities in Palestine by means of a referendum.[186] It was envisaged that the draft trusteeship agreement would come into force upon the approval by a majority vote of two-thirds of the General Assembly.[187] It is ironic that the draft trusteeship agreement envisaged the creation of an independent and sovereign Palestinian state with strong protections for minorities, exactly what the Arabs states had proposed in Sub-Committee 2 in the UN General Assembly which had been rejected by the European powers.

Unlike partition, however, a draft trusteeship agreement of the kind proposed by the US was consistent with the self-determination of all peoples. Moreover, it was also consistent with expectations of that period which, in the aftermath of the Second World War, placed a high priority on fundamental human rights and freedoms, explicitly provided for by Article 9 of the draft trusteeship.

Accordingly, in the envisaged Palestinian state there was to be amongst other guarantees, the following: (1) the freedom of conscience for all Palestinian citizens, subject only to the requirements of public order, public morals and public health, including freedom of religion and worship, language, education, speech and press, assembly and association, and petition, including petition to the Trusteeship Council; (2) no discrimination of any kind on grounds of race, religion, language or sex; (3) equal protection of the laws; (4) a right not to be arrested, detained, convicted, or punished except according to legal process; and (5) that property within Palestine would not be subject to search or seizure except according to legal process.[188]

However, the draft trusteeship plan was too little, too late. War had already broken out in Palestine with Zionist militias and King Abdullah's Arab Legion effectively implementing their own interpretation of partition by recourse to armed force. As a member of the Jewish Agency, reacting to the US decision to do a U-turn on partition in favour of trusteeship, told the correspondent of *The Times* (of London): 'It does not matter what America says; the Jews in Palestine have already put a sort of partition into force, and we are maintaining it.'[189] In April 1948 a series of massacres perpetrated by the Irgun and Lehi took place in those areas assigned to the Arab state by the UN Partition Plan as well as in Jerusalem and Bethlehem which was supposed to be in the *corpus separatum*, such as the massacre in the village of Deir Yassin just outside Jerusalem. Coincidentally, this was also when 'Plan Dalet', described by some Israeli and Palestinian historians as the 'master plan' for the expulsion of the Palestinian Arabs, was implemented.[190] Consequently, the draft UN Trusteeship Agreement was never put to vote, Palestine disappeared from the map, and the UN faced another refugee crisis.

7
The Arab–Israeli Conflict

'… the Jewish story that the Arabs are the attackers and the Jews the attacked is not tenable'.

Sir Alexander Cadogan, statement to UN Palestine Commission,
First monthly progress report to the Security Council,
UN Doc. A/AC.21/7, 29 January 1948, para. 7 (c)

'If the Arab armies invade the territory of Palestine but without coming into conflict with the Jews, they would not necessarily be doing anything illegal, or contrary to the United Nations Charter.'

Foreign Office Legal Advisers, May,
1948 FO 371/68664 Palestine, Eastern, para. 9 (b)

'Whoever attempts to oppose us – will die.'

Extract from leaflets dropped on Arab towns by the Israeli Air Force

'Expel them (*garesh otam*).'

David Ben-Gurion, Orders to IDF High Command, July 1948

International lawyers have tended to overlook the armed conflict between Palestine's Jewish-settler community, its indigenous Arab population and the wider Arab world that confronted the United Nations in the late 1940s in their various treatises on related aspects of international law.[1] This is even when they address the conflict directly.[2] Instead, the emergence of the state of Israel is treated as a question of fact with little or no regard for the lawfulness of the manner through which that state came into being.[3] The mainstream accounts on self-determination, statehood and the law of armed conflict simply do not deal with it.[4] The International Court of Justice even glossed over it in its historical description of the conflict in its *Wall* advisory opinion.[5] It would seem that some scholars prefer silence, rather than critical engagement with a conflict that still resonates today.[6] This gaping hole in the literature is intriguing, however, since the manner through which Israel achieved its statehood in 1948–49 raises serious and difficult questions for international lawyers. Whether or not one agrees with the conclusions reached by the Foreign Office legal advisers in the passage quoted above, what cannot be doubted is that international law was deemed relevant. Nor can international lawyers plead ignorance, for the atrocities that accompanied that conflict have been exposed by Israeli and Palestinian historians over the last six decades, but particularly since Israel declassified its files on the 1948 war and made them available to the general public in the mid 1980s.

The words 'expulsion' and 'expelled' are used throughout this chapter to refer to two acts: (1) the threat or use of force by the various Zionist militias to coerce the Palestinians to leave their homes; and (2) the policy of the Government of Israel in refusing to allow these people to return to the homes from which they fled. When both of these factors are taken into consideration, it seems apposite to describe the manner in which some 750,000 Palestinian Arabs were forced to flee their homes and Israel's concomitant refusal to let them return, as an act of expulsion.[7] In the words of the German-Jewish political theorist Hannah Arendt:

> ... no matter how their exodus came about ... their flight from Palestine, prepared by Zionist plans for large-scale population transfers during the war and followed by the Israeli refusal to readmit the refugees to their old home, made the old Arab claim against Zionism finally come true: the Jews simply aimed at expelling the Arabs from their homes.[8]

Despite the claims advanced by the Israeli Government that the Palestinian Arabs ran away and were not compelled to flee, the Palestinians have always insisted that they were expelled from their homeland in 1948.[9] Moreover, many Palestinian, Israeli and Western historians have reached the same conclusion.[10] Contemporary eyewitness accounts, official UN documentation and journalists' press reports have chronicled the atrocities, which swept through Palestine in 1948 – some of which will be partly reproduced in the following pages. In addition to this, there are of course the memories of the victims themselves, the Palestinian refugees, which anthropologists have been collecting and publishing as oral-histories.[11]

One project of specific interest is the Nakbah Archive, created by anthropologists, which has, since 2002, recorded over 1,000 hours' worth of video testimony with first generation Palestinian refugees living in Lebanon about the events of 1948.[12] It is envisaged that copies of this archive, which contains a detailed database and search engine, will be held at Oxford University, Birzeit University, Harvard University, and the American University of Cairo, and as part of a Remembrance Museum being established by the Welfare Association in the West Bank.[13] First-hand accounts like these, in addition to the voluminous secondary literature, and the primary sources in archives in Israel, Europe, and North America, provide yet another additional source for historians investigating the events that saw the expulsion of 750,000 Palestinians in 1948.

THE SCHOLARSHIP OF THE NEW HISTORIANS

In the late 1980s, a number of Israeli historians, labelled the 'new historians' or the 'revisionists' achieved notoriety in Israel by publishing several books, initially based on their doctoral research at Oxbridge on the causes of the 1947–48 conflict.[14] These scholars are, principally, Avi Shlaim, Professor of International Relations at Oxford University; Benny Morris, Professor of

History at Ben-Gurion University; Ilan Pappé, Professor of History at the University of Exeter; and the late Simha Flapan who although not a historian, had been in his youth the director of the Arab Affairs Department of Israel's Mapam Party, and who wrote many books on the subject. Tom Segev, an Israeli historian and journalist who writes regularly for the Hebrew daily *Ha'aretz*, and who at the time of writing is a visiting Professor at Berkeley, the University of California, is also occasionally referred to as one of the revisionists.[15]

Collectively, these scholars, who will occasionally be cited in the following pages, dispelled a number of myths about the founding of the state of Israel after consulting archival sources there and elsewhere that had been declassified. As they readily admit, there is nothing new about their version of history that had not been written about before.[16] What was different, however, was the fact that they were able to cite official Israeli Government documents in support of their theories, which as it happened, led them closer to the conclusions reached by veteran Palestinian historians such as Walid Khalidi.[17] Although these scholars do not agree on everything, they soon discovered that the evidence they uncovered simply did not support the myths surrounding the birth of Israel. Instead their research led them to the following conclusions:

1. That Britain did not arm and secretly encourage her Arab allies to invade Israel. Rather, Britain felt that if Palestine had to be partitioned, the Arab area could not stand on its own but should be united with Transjordan.[18]
2. Israel's victory in the 1948 conflict was not achieved in the face of insurmountable odds. It was not a case of 'David against Goliath'.[19]
3. The Arabs did not flee Palestine of their own volition or on the orders of their leaders. Instead, the Arab claim that in 1948 the Zionists seized on the opportunity to displace and dispossess the Arab inhabitants of the country is closer to the truth.[20]
4. The Arabs did not unite as one to attack the fledgling Jewish state. On the contrary, they were bad allies, divided, disloyal and more interested in propping up their own fragile regimes than sending troops to fight in Palestine.[21]
5. At the end of the conflict in 1949, it was not the Arab states who were intransigent, but Israel. Ben-Gurion did not want to conclude a peace treaty with the Arab world that would result in territorial concessions or a return of refugees.[22]

Revisionist history is not unique to Israel. Knowledge of American, British, Irish, Japanese, and other histories, have benefited enormously from those scholars who, with the benefit of hindsight and with access to now declassified official government documentation, have revisited what many took for granted to be 'the truth' and have presented a history more in tune with actual events and facts.[23] In this regard it is noteworthy that since the late 1990s, the revisionists' account of the 1948 war is progressively being approved of by

Israel's Education Ministry and is even taught in some Israeli high schools and used in their history textbooks.[24]

HISTORICAL REVISIONISM AND INTERNATIONAL LAW

History is integral to international law, especially as the discipline operates on precedent, in the form of treaties, custom, general principles and case law.[25] Moreover, when lawyers make a case or assert an argument before a court of law they are beholden to the facts.[26] Bearing in mind that there is, at present, consensus among historians on most of the facts pertaining to the 1948 conflict (although minor disagreements, which are mostly academic, remain), it is astonishing that no international lawyer who has written on the history of the Arab–Israeli conflict has felt it necessary to revisit their scholarship in the light of this new factual material. As international lawyers, what do we do when confronted with this evidence? Simply ignore it because it offends our political sensibilities? Or side with the small but vocal minority who dispute it? Alternatively, do we address the narrative, which brings Israeli, Palestinian and Western scholarship together, one that is also supported by archival evidence? On balance it might be fair to consider the voices of the refugees, as well as the scholarship of Israeli, Palestinian and Western historians supported by documentary evidence in Israel's own archives, as more convincing than, say, people in the Israeli Government, orthodox Israeli historians and others, who rather unconvincingly, maintain the view that Israel's birth amounted to what might be described as an 'immaculate conception'.[27] It is noticeable, for instance, that there are no Palestinian historians supporting this latter view, and few Western scholars. In contrast, many Israeli historians have, after consulting the Israeli archives, reached the conclusion that the Palestinians did not flee Palestine in 1948 of their own volition.

This is not the place to engage with all the intricacies of the debate over 1948 and no attempt will be made to give an exhaustive account of the war, its numerous battles or ceasefire violations, as these have already been written about.[28] Instead, a few salient features of the conflict will be addressed in this chapter with specific attention being devoted to the course of the conflict and some of the atrocities that took place. The purpose of this approach is to challenge the prevailing view in legal scholarship that the Palestinian Arabs and the Arab states were the aggressors of the 1948 war who wanted 'to throw the Jews into the sea'. It will hopefully become apparent in the following pages that this view represents a gross oversimplification and a factually inaccurate characterisation of that conflict. Indeed there is a strong argument to make that the Jewish Agency, the Provisional Government of Israel and its numerous militias sanctioned all kinds of horrific atrocities, and expulsions. Although there were massacres committed by the Arab armies against Jewish civilians, by and large it was Palestine's Arab civilian population who bore the brunt of the conflict, with over 750,000 Palestinian Arabs being forced into exile. The question as to whether or not the Zionists had conspired to expel the Palestinians, which is still disputed by some, will not, however, be addressed in this chapter, and in any event it is only relevant for the purposes of international criminal law.[29] Nevertheless, an attempt is made to show that, whether or not they were intended, expulsions did take place. It will also be argued that these expulsions, and many of the atrocities which accompanied them, were contrary to international law as it existed in 1948.

In this regard it should be noted that for the purposes of state responsibility, as opposed to individual criminal responsibility, the conduct of an insurrectional movement, which becomes the new government of a state, will be considered an act of that state under international law.[30] In other words, there is state practice, and arbitral decisions to suggest that those members of the Jewish Agency, who would form the Provisional Government of Israel in May 1948, could have been held to account for their prior conduct. This probably provides some explanation as to why Israel inserted a reservation when it deposited its notification of accepting the compulsory jurisdiction of the ICJ in 1950. Then, it declared that its acceptance of compulsory jurisdiction was not to apply to 'any dispute between the State of Israel and another State which refuses to establish or maintain normal relations with it'.[31] In 1956, Israel made its reservation more explicit, stipulating that it was not to apply to 'disputes arising out of events occurring between 15 May 1948 and 20 July 1949'.[32] These reservations effectively put an end to any attempt to bring a case before that Court to adjudicate the legal issues surrounding the 1947–49 Arab–Israeli hostilities.[33] In November 1985, Israel revoked its 1956 declaration accepting the compulsory jurisdiction of the ICJ.[34] Although Israel is still *ipso facto* a party to the ICJ as a member of the UN as provided for by Article 93 (1) of the UN Charter, cases can only be adjudicated before that court if Israel consents to it, which is unlikely to happen, or if it concerns the interpretation or application of a bilateral or multilateral treaty that has been ratified by Israel and which specifically provides for a referral to the ICJ in cases of dispute (the so-called 'compromissory clause'), or where there is a special agreement between Israel and another state explicitly providing for jurisdiction at the ICJ.[35]

THE JUS AD BELLUM AND THE JUS IN BELLO

The laws of war are usually divided into the *jus ad bellum* and the *jus in bello*. The former is the law that governs the resort to armed conflict, and the latter is the law that applies to the conduct of hostilities. In this regard, it should be noted that even a war of self-defence that is in compliance with the *jus ad bellum* may nevertheless still breach the *jus in bello*. In other words, in the context of the Arab–Israeli dispute, even if the Haganah (which became the Israeli Army after 15 May 1948) acted defensively in the 1948 war, it could still violate international humanitarian law if it deliberately killed civilians, destroyed buildings, and depopulated villages, without military necessity. In fact, these actions would probably amount to war crimes and crimes against humanity.[36]

War has been prohibited as an instrument of national policy since the Kellogg–Briand Pact of 1928.[37] Prior to this it was restricted by the League of Nations Covenant.[38] The threat or use of armed force is proscribed in Article 2 (4) of the UN Charter of 1945 which provides that: 'All Members shall refrain in their international relations from the threat or use of force against the territorial integrity or political independence of any state, or in any other manner inconsistent with the Purposes of the United Nations.'[39] International humanitarian law further proscribes the conduct of hostilities which are set out most elaborately in the four Geneva Conventions of 1949. However, because the 1948 war occurred before those conventions entered into force, only those provisions which embodied pre-existing customary international law, that is, the *lex lata*, were applicable. Therefore, one must rely on the 1907 Hague Regulations and customary international law in examining allegations of violations of the laws of war in relation to the conflict's impact on the civilian population during the course of the 1948 Arab–Israeli conflict.

QUESTIONING AN ACCEPTED TRUTH

It is almost an article of faith amongst some international lawyers that Israel's conduct during the 1948 conflict was defensive. The staunchest advocate of this view is Alan Dershowitz, the Felix Frankfurter Professor of Law at Harvard Law School, who, in a recent book on the subject, defended his position that Israel was fighting against a 'genocidal war of extermination' in 1948.[40] Other scholars have expressed similar views,[41] although using less inflammatory language. They argue that the Arab states committed an act of aggression (as opposed to genocide) against Israel when they sent their troops into Palestine to defend its inhabitants. According to this view, Israel's conduct was strictly defensive. Stephen Schwebel, an American jurist and former judge of the International Court of Justice, has described the situation thus:

> The facts of the 1948 hostilities between the Arab invaders of Palestine and the nascent state of Israel further demonstrate that Egypt's seizure of the Gaza strip, and Jordan's seizure and subsequent annexation of the West Bank and the old city of Jerusalem, were unlawful. Israel was proclaimed to be an independent state within the boundaries allotted to her by the General Assembly's partition resolution. The Arabs of Palestine and of neighbouring Arab states rejected that resolution. But that rejection was no warrant for the invasion by those Arab states of Palestine, whether of territory allotted to Israel, to the projected, stillborn Arab state, or to the projected, internationalized city of Jerusalem. It was no warrant for attack by the armed forces of neighbouring Arab states upon the Jews of Palestine, whether they resided within or without Israel. But that attack did justify Israeli defensive measures, both within and, as necessary, without the boundaries

> allotted her by the partition plan (as in the new city of Jerusalem). It follows that the Egyptian occupation of Gaza, and the Jordanian annexation of the West Bank and Jerusalem, could not vest in Egypt and Jordan lawful, indefinite control, whether as occupying Power or sovereign: *ex injuria jus non oritur*.[42]

In this article, which was recently republished in an edited collection,[43] Schwebel goes on to argue that according to 'the doctrine of according no weight to conquest' Israel has better title to the territory of what was Palestine than Jordan and Egypt, who were then occupying the West Bank and Gaza respectively, because it acted defensively.[44] There is, however, a serious fallacy inherent in this argument, for if one is to take it to its logical conclusion, it could be argued that if Israel was the aggressor, rather than the Arab states, then the latter could have advanced territorial claims to the territory allotted to the Jewish state in the UN Partition Plan had they captured and occupied it during the 1948 conflict on the basis of 'defensive conquest', the doctrine Schwebel advocates. In any event, since Israel proclaimed to be an independent state *solely* within the boundaries allotted to it by the UN Partition Plan, surely it would be estopped from advancing claims to sovereignty beyond the partition lines in the stillborn Arab state? This is because self-defence does not give a state, assuming that Israel was a state in May 1948, a right to annex territory, a point Schwebel conceded in the same article just quoted regarding his analysis of the 1967 conflict.[45] Besides, the underlying rationale of Schwebel's argument is predicated on the assumption that Israel was acting defensively. But what if it was not? Then, it is submitted, his argument fails at the first hurdle. Moreover, if the resolution containing the UN Partition Plan was not legally binding then what title did the Zionists have to Palestine? The Balfour Declaration and the League of Nations Covenant did not give the Zionists title to Palestine, nor did the Mandate and certainly not Britain's 1939 White Paper. To his credit, Schwebel is one of the few international lawyers to accurately describe the 1948 conflict as an act of conquest, except that his characterisation of Israel's actions in that war as defensive is highly questionable. But Schwebel is not alone in expressing this point of view. Yehuda Z. Blum, who was Israel's Permanent Representative to the United Nations in New York from 1978 to 1984 during the administration of Menachem Begin (the leader of the Irgun), concurred:

> It must, therefore, be concluded that the armed intervention of the various Arab States – including Transjordan – was a violation of international law. Its real aim was of course to crush by military force the newly-established State of Israel which had come into being on the expiry of the British Mandate, in pursuance of General Assembly Resolution 181 (II) of November 29, 1947.[46]

In the light of recent Israeli historical scholarship, Blum may be exonerated for thinking that Transjordan had designs to crush by military force the newly established state of Israel when he wrote this article. But he must have known, even when he wrote these words, that Transjordan's Arab Legion, which was commanded by British officers, did not, with the exception of Jerusalem, advance into the Jewish state as envisaged in the UN Partition Plan.[47] Sir John Bagot Glubb, the British commander in chief of the Arab Legion, actually withdrew his units that were stationed in the West Bank in April 1948 only to send them back across the Jordan River into Palestine after 15 May.[48] In his memoirs, which he published eleven years *before* Blum published his article, he wrote:

> Yet although the British Army insisted on the withdrawal of the Arab Legion, war had already been in progress in Palestine for several weeks. The Jewish forces were already well across the United Nations partition line and were in occupation of considerable areas allotted to the Arabs, even while British troops were in nominal control.[49]

If there were any aggressors in 1948, it was the *Yishuv* (the Jewish-settler community in Palestine) which initiated a large-scale assault on that part of Palestine which had been allotted to the Arabs in the UN Partition Plan six weeks *prior* to its declaration of independence. In the words of Benny Morris: 'During the first half of April [1948], the Yishuv had gone over to the offensive and was engaged in a war of conquest. That war of conquest was prefigured in Plan D.'[50] Moreover, had Transjordan's Arab Legion not come to Palestine's defence on 15 May 1948, Israel could quite easily have gone on to conquer the remainder of it. But for some, all of this would probably be irrelevant because according to international lawyers like Istvan Pogany, the issue was, apparently, clear: '... the Arab intervention in Palestine constituted a *clear* violation of international law. In addition, it amounted to a "threat to the peace, breach of the peace, or act of aggression" within the meaning of Article 39 of the Charter.'[51] And yet the UN Security Council never condemned the Arab intervention as an act of aggression. Moreover, was it really correct to say that the Arab states should simply have remained passive in the face of the atrocities that the Haganah, the Irgun and Lehi were committing against the Palestinian Arabs? Did those states really not have a right of collective self-defence to come to the aid of the stillborn Palestinian state? Alternatively, could the Arab intervention not be described as an early form of 'humanitarian intervention'? Did the Arabs of Palestine not have an inherent right to defend territory that was in their possession from an armed attack in violation of customary international law and the laws of war? In his pamphlet *Jerusalem and the Holy Places*, Professor Elihu Lauterpacht writes:

> ... the physical attack by the Arab forces upon the Jews in Jerusalem, and indeed upon the Jewish state as such, left the Israeli forces with no option but to respond in kind and maintain such hold as they could upon the areas then in Jewish possession, to the point – by way of defensive rationalisation of their positions – of moving in places beyond the lines laid down by the Partition Resolution.[52]

Lauterpacht has a point. If the Haganah needed to enter places beyond the UN Partition Plan for the sole purpose of defending the Jewish population from armed attack, then it could arguably have done so. But then, surely so could the Arabs also defend their own.

But the war did not start on 15 May 1948 as these lawyers allege. It began at the beginning of April 1948, when the Haganah launched a full-scale invasion of Palestine, with a massive armed force, some six weeks *before* the Arab states intervened with their regular armies.[53] The arguments advanced by the scholars quoted above, which have been accepted as gospel truth by many others,[54] are all formulated on the underlying premise that the conflict started on 15 May 1948 so that they can claim that Israel was a 'state' to bring into play Article 2 (4) of the UN Charter which prohibits the threat or use of force against a state. This is rather convenient for it ignores the six months of fighting which preceded the Arab intervention when hundreds of thousands of Arabs, and a smaller number of Jews, were evicted from their homes and displaced by the fighting.[55] Count Folke Bernadotte, who was the UN mediator for Palestine in 1948, before he was assassinated by the Jewish terrorist group Lehi,[56] mentioned numerous reports from what he described as 'reliable sources' of large-scale looting, pillaging and plundering, and of instances of the destruction of villages without apparent military necessity.[57] He reported that by the time Israel declared its independence on 14/15 May, some 350,000 Palestinian Arabs had already fled from the area allotted to the Jewish state in the UN Partition Plan.[58] In other words, almost half of the Arab population of Palestine had fled or been expelled from their homes *before* the Arab states came to their defence on 15 May. Were the Arab states really expected to sit on the sidelines and do nothing?

THE OUTBREAK OF THE HOSTILITIES

Although international lawyers like to categorise conflicts into international and non-international armed conflicts, this paradigm can be difficult to apply in actual practice since there is almost always an international element to an armed conflict. Palestine is a particular case in point since it was supposed to be an international trust as provided by Article 22 of the League of Nations Covenant whose existence as an independent nation had been provisionally recognised. In any event, it was after the UN partition vote, some six months *before* Israel declared its independence in May 1948, that the Arab–Israeli conflict started on 30 November 1947, when fighting broke out between Arabs and Jews, the former protesting against partition.[59] In the following months the fighting would progressively deteriorate with attacks by Jews on Arabs and vice-versa.[60] However, some of the terrorist atrocities undertaken by the Irgun were particularly horrific, especially its assaults on Haifa, Jaffa and Deir Yassin which are described in more detail in the following pages. One explanation as to why the Arab states did not intervene before this date, even when the exodus of the Palestinian Arabs had turned into a torrent, was because they did not want to enter into conflict with Britain, whose armed forces were then still in effective control of Palestine as it remained the mandatory power.[61] In describing the outbreak of local hostilities in December 1947, Sir Alan Cunningham, who was then the British High-Commissioner of Palestine, sent the following cable to London:

> The initial Arab outbreaks were spontaneous and unorganized and were more demonstrations of displeasure at the UN decision [to partition Palestine] than determined attacks on Jews. The weapons initially employed were sticks and stones and had it not been for Jewish resource to firearms, it is not impossible that the excitement would have subsided and little loss of life been caused. This is more probable since there is reliable evidence that the Arab Higher Committee as a whole and the Mufti in particular, although pleased at the strong response to the strike call were not in favour of serious outbreaks.[62]

Moreover, in January 1948, in a statement to the UN Palestine Commission sent to implement the terms of the UN's recommendation to partition Palestine, Sir Alexander Cadogan, Britain's representative to the UN, informed them thus:

> ... in the present circumstances the Jewish story that the Arabs are the attackers and the Jews the attacked is not tenable. The Arabs are determined to show that they will not submit tamely to the United Nations Plan of Partition; while the Jews are trying to consolidate the advantages gained at the General Assembly by a succession of drastic operations designed to intimidate and cure the Arabs of any desire for further conflict. Elements on each side are thus engaged in attacking or in taking reprisals indistinguishable from attacks.[63]

The first stage of fighting, which lasted from December 1947 to May 1948, took place within the borders of the British Mandate of Palestine and could be classified as a civil war, although there were outside forces assisting both sides throughout that period.[64] The Zionists received millions of dollars from Europe and the US and had Second World War veterans in their ranks.[65] Prior to May 1948, the Haganah was able to field 30,000 front-line troops backed up by 32,000 garrison forces, 15,410 settlement police and the 32,000 men of the Home Guard.[66] The Irgun had 5,000 men and Lehi had approximately 1,000 'freedom fighters'.[67] The Palestinian Arabs, on the other hand, had to rely on the *Jaysh al-Jihad al-Muqaddes*, which was their only indigenous defence force, numbering 5,000 men, which had no modern weapons, few sources of finance, and fought with weapons discarded in earlier wars, mostly rifles.[68] The *Jaysh al-Inqadh*, the so-called 'Arab Liberation Army', numbered between 3,000 and 4,000 men, of whom 1,500 were Palestinian Arab.[69] They were described as being poorly trained both militarily and politically, and lacking the formation necessary for mobilising popular resistance. They gave no help to the Palestinian villages they were ostensibly in Palestine to defend and were mockingly dubbed by Palestinians as the *Jaysh al-Rikad* (the 'Run-Away Army').[70] It was only during the second phase of fighting, that there was direct-armed intervention from neighbouring countries. Transjordan, Egypt, Hashemite Iraq, Lebanon and Syria claimed they were coming to the assistance of the Palestinian Arabs, many of whom had fled their homes during the first stage of hostilities, into the borders of those countries.[71] The Syrian Government alleged that Israeli warplanes had dropped bombs on villages near its border, and in Lebanon, and warned British diplomats in Damascus that a further exodus of Palestinians from Safed and Acre into Syria, which were under attack by Zionist militias, would cause them to intervene for humanitarian reasons.[72]

WHEN SELF-DEFENCE BECOMES AGGRESSION

The argument that the Arab states were the aggressors in 1948 rests on the assumption that the state of Israel came into being on 14/15 May, and presumes that they had no other justification for entering Palestine. However, it is arguable that the Arab states were entitled to come to Palestine's rescue in an act of collective self-defence. Moreover, it is simplistic to characterise the action of the Arab states as 'aggressive' and a breach of the UN Charter and that of Israel as 'defensive'.[73] This is because for an act to qualify as aggression it is usually necessary for a state to send its troops across a frontier by launching an invasion of the territory of another state.[74] Yet the Lebanese Army never crossed the border.[75] Moreover, the Syrian Army only made minor inroads into Palestine with a force of two infantry battalions supported by light infantry, and retreated five days later.[76] With the exception of Jerusalem, which was supposed to have been internationalised, Transjordan's Arab Legion and the Iraqi forces that were under Abdullah's command never crossed the UN Partition Plan's boundaries into the proposed Jewish state.[77] Latrun, where most of the fighting took place between the Haganah and Transjordan, had been allotted to the Arab state in the UN Partition Plan.[78] The Jordanians, under the command of Sir John Bagot Glubb, resolutely confined themselves to occupying the West Bank as they had agreed to with the Zionists through their emissary Golda Meyerson.[79] The Zionists, on the other hand, were not so careful. The only army which clashed with the Haganah in territory allocated to the Jewish state by the UN Partition Plan of 1947 was the Egyptian Army with a small contingent of 10,000 troops, who were accustomed to maintaining internal stability in Egypt rather than undertaking offensive military action.[80] It crossed over the partition lines to link up with Transjordan, bypassing the many Jewish settlements on the way, a catastrophic strategic error, which the Israelis fully exploited.[81] The Egyptian Army would be fully routed by the Israelis during the latter stages of the war, with Israel even entering and occupying parts of the Sinai Peninsula triggering the application of the 1936 Anglo-Egyptian Defence Treaty.[82] The Israelis retreated after the UN proposed a ceasefire in January 1949.[83]

The war, therefore, was not a simple case of a monolithic Arab world coming down on the Jews. This becomes clear from looking at the 1949 ceasefire lines between Israel and Egypt, Transjordan, Lebanon and Syria which are highlighted in Map 8. It is quite clear from this map, which is a digital scan from the British Foreign Office archives, that the Zionists did not hesitate to cross the proposed boundaries of the UN Partition Plan, which they had avowedly claimed to have accepted. Indeed, if Transjordan had not intervened when it did the Israelis could have captured the rest of Palestine. In his memoirs, Menachem Begin, the leader of the Irgun, who was not a party to the Jewish Agency's agreement with King Abdullah, (the Irgun was then allied with the Haganah,[84] and partook in combined military operations), confided that at the end of January 1948 they had established plans to conquer (1) Jerusalem, (2) Jaffa, (3) the Lydda-Ramleh plain, and (4) Jenin, Nablus and Tulkarem. They would succeed with all their objectives, except for the fourth.[85] The Zionists and their spokemen, until this very day, never hesitate to mention that they accepted the UN Partition Plan and the Arab states rejected it. But they fail to mention that their forces never adhered to it when they were ordered to conquer the West Bank. In this respect the old adage, that 'actions speak louder than words', rings true.

Typically the UN Security Council did not blame either side for initiating the fighting. Nor did it accept the argument that Israel was acting in self-defence or that the Arabs were the aggressors. Instead, it passed a series of resolutions in which it called for an end to the violence on both sides. In April 1948, the Security Council called upon 'Arab and Jewish armed groups in Palestine to cease acts of violence immediately'.[86] Seventeen days later, it passed a further resolution in which it called on the Jewish Agency and the Arab Higher Committee to 'cease all acts of a military or paramilitary nature, as well as acts of violence, sabotage and terrorism'.[87] On 22 May, the Security Council called upon 'all Governments and authorities, without prejudice to the rights, claims or positions of the parties concerned, to abstain from any hostile military action in Palestine'.[88] Seven days later, the Security Council imposed an arms embargo over the whole of the Middle East, including Palestine.[89] On 15 July, the Security Council determined that the violence in Palestine constituted a threat to the peace within the meaning of Article 39 of the UN Charter, and ordered 'the Governments and authorities concerned, pursuant to Article 40 of the Charter, to desist from further military action and to this end to issue cease-fire orders to their military and para-military forces'.[90]

In this respect, it is arguable that the Arab intervention was an act of collective self-defence aimed at protecting the population of Palestine and preserving its political independence and territorial integrity.[91] After all, the Pact of the League of Arab States of 1945 includes a special annex on Palestine stipulating that Palestine could participate in the work of the Arab League because its existence and independence 'among the nations can ... no more be questioned *de jure* than the independence of any of the other Arab States'.[92] Consequently, upon a request from the Arab Higher Committee for protection, which is what in fact happened, the Arab states would arguably have been justified in coming to Palestine's rescue in self-defence even though Palestine was not technically a state.[93] This is because as members of the UN they all have an inherent right of collective self-defence under Article 51 of the UN Charter. Although Palestine was not a member of the UN in 1948, it would be formalism of an un-evenhanded sort to argue that the Arab states could not rely on their *inherent* right of self-defence to come to the aid of a territory which had been subject to a mandate just as Iraq, Transjordan, Lebanon and Syria had been.[94] When the Republic of South Korea, a non-member of the UN, was attacked by forces from north of the 38th parallel on 24 June 1950, the Security Council referred to it as an 'armed attack' which is usually associated with the right of self-defence recognised by Article 51 of the UN Charter.[95] Presumably the same principle would have applied to Palestine. In any event, the question as to whether or not Palestine and Israel were states in 1948 is probably irrelevant as both the Arab Higher Committee and the Jewish Agency justified their actions before the UN Security Council on the basis of defending the lives and properties of their civilian populations.[96] The Security Council did not seem to think that these claims were inconsistent with the UN Charter.[97] It has even been suggested that the decisions reached by the UN in the Palestine and Korean cases provides support for the view that conflicts between two distinct and relatively permanent territorial units are to be treated as though they are conflicts between established states.[98]

But as the United States Military Tribunal at Nuremberg noted in the *Ministries Trial*, there can be no self-defence against self-defence.[99] So who was acting defensively in 1948, the Arab states or the Zionists? Surely, it was Palestine's indigenous Arab population who were literally fighting for their survival in the 1948 war. They were caught between the Zionists who were hungry for more territory and Transjordan who saw an opportunity to go and get what they thought they had been promised in the Hussein–McMahon correspondence. This time, however, the latter would get Britain's blessing to enter Palestine. When Transjordan's Prime Minister Tawfiq Abu al-Huda met in secret with Foreign Secretary Ernest Bevin in London on 7 February 1948 to get the British Government's approval to occupy that part of Palestine awarded to the Arab state in the UN Partition Plan, Bevin was reported to have replied: 'It seems the obvious thing to do … but do not go and invade the areas allotted to the Jews.'[100]

Nevertheless, what cannot be doubted is that the primary reason why Palestine did not become an 'independent nation' as envisaged by Article 22 of the League of Nations Covenant was because the Haganah, the Irgun and Lehi drove 750,000 Palestinian Arabs from their homes. In this regard it would certainly strike one as odd if a minority community, could commit atrocities against the majority, expel them from their homeland, and claim to be acting in accordance with the law of self-defence. The Zionists were, after all, the first side to launch large-scale military operations with the intention of capturing as much of Palestine as was possible, including the area allotted to the Arab state in the UN Partition Plan, at the beginning of April by implementing Plan Dalet, some six weeks *before* the Arab states intervened in defence of the Palestinian Arabs. Although Plan Dalet (named after the fourth letter in the Hebrew alphabet) was supposed to have been implemented after Israel's Declaration of Independence in May 1948,[101] it was brought forward by almost two months and rigorously implemented:

> Actions [would be launched] against enemy settlements located within or near our defended areas, with the aim of preventing their being used as bases for an active armed force. [These actions will include] the destruction of such villages, the carrying out of searches and, in the event of resistance, the elimination of the armed force *and the expulsion of the [village] population to [territory] outside the borders of the State*, [and in cases where there is no resistance] any army unit will be garrisoned in the village.[102]

It would be difficult to characterise the phrase 'the expulsion of the [village] population to [territory] outside the borders of the State', as an act of self-defence. In this connection it has even been suggested that the Arab states could have entered Palestine to protect it as an act of collective self-defence on the basis that Palestine's Jewish community was being used by foreign interests to commit indirect aggression/subversion against Palestine.[103] A memorandum submitted to the UN by the Arab Higher Committee in June 1948, entitled 'Why the Arab States Entered Palestine: Their Action Justified in Fact and in International Law', defended their entry on precisely this point:

> (a) The Arab armies entered Palestine on the invitation of the native Arabs of Palestine who are 'resisting attempted subjugation by the armed (Jewish) minority and outside (Jewish) pressure.' In the same way the British forces went into Greece at the invitation of the Greek people who were resisting subjugation by the armed Communist minority and outside pressure. Furthermore the Arab States are part of the Arab league, established in order to safeguard the independence and sovereignty of the Arab states. Palestine is an integral part of the Arab world. It was recognised by the Charter of the Arab league as an independent country and was allowed the right of participation in the work of the Council of the League.[104]

Alternatively, it is entirely plausible that those Arab states which bordered Palestine and which were directly affected by the fighting there, i.e. Egypt, Lebanon, Syria and Transjordan, would have been entitled to enter Palestine in an act of *individual* self-defence, especially as the influx of so many refugees into the borders of those countries as a result of direct military action undertaken by these Zionist militias, which was also accompanied by threats, did in fact affect their territorial integrity, and the stability and independence of their governments.[105] Had Transjordan's Arab Legion not entered Palestine when it did, the Irgun, Lehi and quite possibly the Haganah, may have continued their assault eastwards as it is well known that David Ben-Gurion, and Menachem Begin, harboured territorial ambitions there. In this regard, the following extract from Ben-Gurion's diary gives one a sense of his aggressive intentions:

> The weak link in the Arab coalition is Lebanon. Muslim rule is artificial and easy to undermine. A Christian state should be established whose southern border would be the Litani. We shall sign a treaty with it. By breaking the power of the Legion and bombing Amman, we shall also finish off Transjordan and then Syria will fall. If Egypt still dares to fight – we shall bomb Port Said, Alexandria and Cairo.[106] This will be in revenge for what they (the Egyptians, the Aramis and Assyrians) did to our forefathers during Biblical times.[107]

Although it might be arguable that the Zionists had, in principle, a right to create a Jewish state in Palestine in the area allocated to them in the UN Partition Plan, it may seriously be questioned whether they had any right to use *armed force* to create it. Moreover, invoking a plea of 'self-defence' would not give the Haganah a warrant to expel civilians. In fact, it may be questioned whether the Haganah was acting in self-defence at all or whether the term was being abused as a subterfuge for undertaking reprisals. In this regard, the text of Plan Gimmel (Plan C), which preceded Plan Dalet, is illuminating:

> A. The aim of a counterattack is *to strike at each source at the beginning of an Arab outbreak* in order to deter the instigators of the incidents and to prevent the participation and support of the Arab masses. *Forceful and severe blows* will serve to identify and isolate the active elements.
> B. Because of the difficulty in directly engaging the active Arab forces while they are carrying out their activities, the countermeasures we will adopt will mostly take the form of *retaliatory operations. Like all retaliatory operations, they will not always be directed only against the executors of a particular action, but will also be aimed at other active groups or those who provide them with assistance.*
> C. Counterattacks must be appropriate in kind to the operations which led to the retaliation. These attacks must be as immediate as possible, and *must affect large areas*. The reasons for the retaliation must be detailed to the Arabs in full, using all available means of communication: leaflets, announcements, radio broadcasts, etc.
> D. It is preferable that these operations should *strike* the Arab rear in order *to undermine Arab sense of security*.
> E. Counterattacks must be divided into two kinds: warning operations and *strike operations*.[108]

In many respects, Plan Gimmel gave the Haganah greater leeway in expelling civilians than even Plan Dalet. But under international law, self-defence is predicated on the existence of a prior armed attack[109] or where, in the words of the *Caroline* formulation, it can be clearly shown by the state invoking its right of self-defence that there was 'a necessity of self-defence, instant, overwhelming, leaving no choice of means, and no moment for deliberation'.[110] This was clearly not applicable here. Plans Gimmel and Dalet are not the kind of documents one would expect to come across when assessing a plea of self-defence. They were cool and calculating and clearly intended to strike fear into the hearts of Palestine's Arabs. 'Forceful and severe blows', that 'must affect large areas' as a form or retaliation 'in order to undermine Arab sense of security' is hardly consistent with the notion of self-defence which must be necessary, immediate and proportional to the seriousness of the armed attack. Self-defence does not include a right of armed reprisals.

It might not therefore come as a surprise that Palestinian scholars have argued that there was a direct correlation between Plan Gimmel, Plan Dalet and the expulsion of the Palestinians, to the extent that the combined effect of these military operations could be described as a 'master plan' for the conquest of Palestine.[111] Whilst some Israeli scholars, notably Ilan Pappé, accept this argument, others such as Benny Morris argue that although numerous atrocities did occur, including expulsions, the Arab exodus was not premeditated by the Haganah but was an unintended consequence of the war.[112] Rather than engaging fully with this debate, it is perhaps best to simply list the operations, along with their dates and whether or not they succeeded with their objectives, from Walid Khalidi's original 1961 article 'Plan Dalet: The Master Plan for the Conquest of Palestine':

1. *Operation Nachshon*: 1 April –
   To carve out a corridor connecting Tel Aviv to Jerusalem and by so doing to split the main part of the Arab state into two. (Defeated)*
2. *Operation Harèl*: 15 April –
   A continuation of Nachshon but centered specifically on Arab villages near Latrun. (Defeated)*
3. *Operation Miparayim*: 21 April –
   To capture Haifa and rout its Arab population. (Successful)
4. *Operation Chametz*: 27 April –
   To destroy the Arab villages round Jaffa and so cut Jaffa off from physical contact with the rest of Palestine as a preliminary to its capture. (Successful)*
5. *Operation Jevussi*: 27 April –
   To isolate Jerusalem by destroying the ring of surrounding Arab villages and dominating the Ramallah–Jerusalem road to the north, the Jericho–Jerusalem road to the east and the Bethlehem–Jerusalem road to the south. This operation by itself would have caused the whole of Jerusalem to fall and would have made the Arab position west of the Jordan altogether untenable. (Defeated)*
6. *Operation Yiftach*: 28 April –
   To purify eastern Galilee of Arabs. (Successful)
7. *Operation Matateh*: 3 May –
   To destroy Arab villages connecting Tiberias to eastern Galilee. (Successful)

8. *Operation Maccabi*: 7 May –
   To destroy the Arab villages near Latrun and by an outflanking movement to penetrate into Ramallah district north of Jerusalem. (Defeated)*
9. *Operation Gideon*: 11 May –
   To occupy Beisan and drive away the semi-sedentary Bedouin communities in the neighbourhood. (Successful)
10. *Operation Barak*: 12 May –
   To destroy the Arab villages in the neighbourhood of Bureir on the way to the Negev. (Partially successful)
11. *Operation Ben Ami*: 14 May –
   To occupy Acre and purify western Galilee of Arabs. (Successful)*
12. *Operation Pitchfork*: 14 May –
   To occupy the Arab residential quarters in the New City of Jerusalem. (Successful)*
13. *Operation Schfifon*: 14 May –
   To occupy the Old City of Jerusalem. (Defeated)*[113]

Regardless of whether or not one is of the opinion that Plan Dalet amounted to a 'Master Plan', it is noteworthy that the operations marked with single asterisks all took place in those areas that were allotted to the Arab state in the UN Partition Plan.[114] In other words, of the 13 specific full-scale operations under Plan Dalet, eight – operations Nachshon, Harèl, Chametz, Jevussi, Maccabi, Ben Ami, Pitchfork and Schfifon – were *outside* the area which the UN had recommended allotting to the Jewish state.[115] Moreover, these operations all occurred *before* 15 May 1948, when Britain relinquished the Mandate and when the Arab states sent their troops into Palestine at the request of the Arab higher committee to defend its Arab population. In this regard there is at the very least a *prima facie* case to be made that this was a conquest and not a defensive war. It would be difficult to describe the Arab states as aggressors – rather, this adjective is, perhaps, more suited to describe the actions of the Haganah, the Irgun and Lehi.

Moreover, it is generally accepted by most scholars that the attacks on Haifa and Jaffa and the massacre in Deir Yassin, in particular, acted as a precursor to later expulsions, and directly contributed to the Arab exodus. The desperate situation was summed up succinctly in an editorial in *The Times* published in August 1948:

> The stream of Arab men, women, and children fleeing in terror from their little farms, their small businesses, and their humble homes in Zionist-controlled territory was first set in motion by Jewish attacks upon Haifa and Jaffa. It was quickened after the frightful massacre at Deir Yassin, and it swelled into a torrent when the armies of Israel, heartened by victory, went over to the offensive.[116]

The Zionists were able to capture so much territory in so short a period of time as their soldiers were better trained, organised and supplied, and showed more initiative than the Arabs.[117] They were also able to field more battle-trained soldiers, rather than conscripts and volunteers, than the Arabs were able to, and they had shorter lines of communication.[118] Moreover, Egypt, Iraq and Syria were obliged to leave a considerable part of their forces at home for internal security reasons.[119] Furthermore, the Arab League, under British command, refused to engage with the Zionists beyond those areas assigned to the Arabs in the UN Partition Plan. It was only in Jerusalem, which was supposed to be internationalised according to the Partition Plan, where the Arab Legion inadvertently came into conflict with the Zionists.[120] According to Benny Morris: 'By mid-July the IDF [the Israeli Army] was fielding nearly 65,000 troops; by early spring 1949, 115,000. The Arab armies probably had about 40,000 troops in Palestine and Sinai by mid-July, and 55,000 in October, the numbers perhaps rising slightly by the spring of 1949.'[121] Even if one were to accept for argument's sake that the *Yishuv* were acting in self-defence, that they had a right to use armed force to create a Jewish state, and that their decision to send the Haganah across the partition boundaries was not unlawful because the resolution was only a recommendation, the tactics they used – summary executions, bombings, forcing civilians onto trucks to transfer them across the borders, burning villages, rape, pillaging – were contrary to established norms of customary international humanitarian law.[122] Moreover, unlike the Arabs, the Zionists based their claim to statehood on the legitimacy of the UN Partition Plan. Yet they had no intention of ever abiding by its terms. It may therefore be said that the actions of the Zionist militias were aggressive, their tactics unlawful, and their justifications hypocritical.

SOVEREIGNTY IN A VACUUM

Of course, one could also question the intentions of the Arab states in deciding to intervene, particularly Egypt and Transjordan. Were they really acting in self-defence or was their decision to intervene based on considerations of *realpolitik* and self-interest? What of the tacit agreement between King Abdullah and the Zionists to carve up Palestine between themselves? Was this intervention lawful? Were they really acting in the interests of the population of Palestine? Whatever the answer might be, the argument has been advanced that they were not all acting contrary to the UN Charter. This is because Transjordan was not a member of the UN in May 1948. Nor was Israel. And Palestine never became a member. In this connection it has been questioned whether the prohibition on the use of armed force had crystallised as a rule of customary international law binding on non-members in May 1948.[123] As the Foreign Office legal advisers noted in a minute they were instructed to prepare on the legal status of Palestine after termination of the Mandate, which addressed the possibility of an Arab invasion:

> If the Arab armies invade the territory of Palestine but without coming into conflict with the Jews, they would not necessarily be doing anything illegal, or contrary to the United Nations Charter. If they cross the frontier recommended in the United Nations Resolution of November 29th for the Jewish state [the UN Partition Plan], they would ... not *ipso facto* be doing anything illegal though in practice they would no doubt be laying themselves open to public criticism. If they came into conflict with the Jews a situation would no doubt be created of which the Security Council would be asked to take cognizance as a breach of the peace.[124]

The Foreign Office legal advisers were essentially making the point that the Arab states were going into a territory, which, while not belonging to them, did not belong to anyone else.[125] Besides, they did so at the request of the majority of the inhabitants of Palestine, who asked for their assistance.[126] There was nothing inherently unlawful about what they were doing – so the argument advanced by the Foreign Office goes – as there was a legal vacuum caused by the departure of the British, which needed to be filled in order to prevent the chaos engulfing Palestine from spreading further afield.[127]

It should be said that the Foreign Office's suggestion that the Arabs were not doing anything contrary to the UN Charter, which was predicated on the assumption that Palestine became 'a sort of *res nullius*', was rather tenuous.[128] First, Article 2 (6) of the UN Charter provides that the organisation is to ensure that states which are not members of the United Nations act in accordance with its principles so far as may be necessary for the maintenance of international peace and security. Therefore, the Arab states should have refrained from undertaking military action in Palestine unless this was in lawful self-defence, which it arguably was. Second, there is no justification for any argument that Palestine became *res nullius* upon Britain's departure in May 1948 so as to create a legal vacuum. As the Israeli international lawyer Yehuda Z. Blum wrote in the same article referred to earlier:

> ... no mandated territory can be regarded, on the termination of the mandate over it, as a *res nullius* open to acquisition by the first comer. Any other conclusion would lead to the absurd result that a mandated territory would become, upon the termination of the mandate over it, the helpless prey of external forces.[129]

This is a view supported by the vast majority of international lawyers[130] and by the jurisprudence of the principal judicial organ of the United Nations.[131] As described in Chapter 5, upon the relinquishment of the mandate sovereignty was vested in its population.

Nevertheless, as already noted, Yehuda Blum and Stephen Schwebel have advanced the argument that although Palestine was not *res nullius*, Israel has a better claim to sovereignty over the West Bank than either the Palestinians or Jordan so as to justify its retention of that territory today on the basis of 'defensive conquest'.[132] Assuming that such a notion actually exists in international law, these lawyers seem to be arguing that sovereignty over the whole of Palestine was vested in Israel because when the Mandate was terminated in 1948, the Jewish people had a better title to sovereignty over the West Bank and Gaza than Jordan and Egypt.[133] Consequently, when Jordan was in possession of the West Bank and when Egypt was occupying Gaza, they were not entitled to any reversionary rights as legitimate sovereigns and the legal standing of Israel was that of a state in lawful control of territory in respect of which no other state could show a better title.[134]

However, this argument is fallacious on several grounds.[135] First, despite all the evidence to the contrary, it assumes that Israel acted defensively in the 1948 war, which is highly questionable. Second, it presumes that sovereignty did not vest in the population of Palestine upon Britain's relinquishment of the Mandate in May 1948 despite the fact that Article 22 of the League of Nations Covenant stipulated that '[c]ertain communities formerly belonging to the Turkish Empire have reached a stage of development where their existence as independent nations can be provisionally recognized'. The sovereign rights of the Palestinian people had already been recognised at Paris in 1919, subject only to the rendering of administrative advice and assistance by the mandatory power. Whilst sovereignty was probably in abeyance during the mandatory years, once Britain's advice and assistance ceased, that is, once it left the territory subject to the Mandate, sovereignty was vested in the peoples concerned. Third, it is difficult to see how sovereignty could be vested exclusively in the Zionists when they did not have any sovereignty in Palestine prior to, or during, the British Mandate of Palestine. As Lord Curzon noted, the Zionists never had any title to Palestine. The word 'title' appears nowhere in the Balfour Declaration, the Mandate or the Covenant of the League of Nations. As described in Chapters 2 and 5, the Zionists' attempt to include the word 'title' during the drafting of the Mandate failed. Moreover, a special unit set up within the Foreign Office to redraft the Mandate under Lord Curzon's tenure, rejected the claim that the Zionists had *any* claim to Palestine.[136] Instead the Mandate speaks of the 'historical connection of the Jewish people' with Palestine and of 'the grounds for reconstituting their national home in that country'. It did not, as the Zionists desired, provide that Palestine was to be reconstituted as *the* National Home. Moreover, whatever claims the Zionists had to Palestine were always qualified by the safeguard clause in the Balfour Declaration regarding Palestine's indigenous inhabitants and the status of Jews in other countries. And even if one was to argue that the Zionists were given a right to advance claims to sovereignty in those areas allotted to the Jewish state in the UN Partition Plan, this did not give them a right to claim sovereignty over the West Bank and the Gaza Strip which had been consigned to the Arab state in that Plan. Finally, in the *Eritrea v. Yemen* case, the Permanent Court of Arbitration questioned whether the doctrine of reversion was a part of international law.[137] Therefore, even if the Zionists did have title to the whole of Palestine, which is highly debatable, they would be hard pressed to rely on any alleged doctrine of reversion to claim it, as would Egypt and Jordan. And even if either of these states relied on it, title would surely revert to the population of Palestine in May 1948 as a whole.

The better view would be that with the relinquishment of the mandate in 1948, sovereignty was vested in the people of Palestine. It was not up for grabs for whichever state or entity could forcibly take control of Palestine. This would be contrary to the whole raison d'être of the mandates system established in the aftermath of the First World War which was established to give practical effect to the principle that 'the well-being and development' of the peoples subject to the Mandate 'form a sacred trust of civilisation'. In this regard, the Foreign Office legal advisers did concede that with the end of the Mandate, Palestine's theoretical sovereignty 'will probably lie in the people of Palestine'.[138] They conceded this, even though they thought that Palestine, at that particular moment, was not a sovereign state.[139] If this position is correct, then it is arguable that with the lapse of the Mandate, sovereignty was vested in Palestine to be exercised by its peoples – Arabs and Jews – who were left to their own devices to determine their political futures. As the Foreign Office legal advisers conceded: 'If the Jews claim to set up a state in the boundaries of the Jewish areas as defined by the United Nations Resolution of November 29th and the Arabs claim to set up a state covering the whole of Palestine, there would be nothing legally to choose between these claims.'[140] As nationality provides the link between the individual and the state, as described in Chapter 5, it is arguable that sovereignty could only be vested in Palestinian nationals as opposed to foreign immigrants.[141] But even if this view is not accepted, and it is maintained that the people of Palestine included foreign Jewish immigrants who had been given rights of sovereignty there as a result of the UN Partition Plan and the international community's acquiescence in the creation of a Jewish state, this did not give them a right to expel its indigenous Arab population and advance a claim to the whole of the land of Palestine including Jerusalem and the Holy Places.

In any event, the Zionists already had an embryonic government in place in the form of the Jewish Agency, as did the Arab Higher Committee.[142] However, the Zionists had, by the late 1940s, effectively developed a 'state within a state' with British assistance, whereas the Arab Higher Committee was in turmoil, especially after the Haganah's offensive in 1947–48, which saw the exodus of 750,000 Arabs, the destruction of much property, and the collapse of governmental authority.[143] This provides one explanation as to why the Palestine Arabs were in no position to lay the foundations for creating a state in the face of Zionist aggression, when they could not defend themselves, as with the departure of the British Army they were too weak to stand up to the hostile tactics employed by the Haganah, the Irgun and Lehi without outside assistance.[144] They were being driven from their homeland to cleanse it for a Jewish state.

IMPLEMENTING PLAN DALET

As already mentioned, the real war did not begin on 15 May 1948 but earlier in April when Plan Dalet was implemented. One probable explanation for this is that Ben-Gurion wanted to clear the field for the coming battle with the Arab states, and so pre-empted them. However, there is another cogent explanation. In March, the United States turned its back on the UN Partition Plan because it was suspicious of Soviet motives and also because it realised that the Plan was impracticable and could not be enforced in the way it was envisaged. Instead, the US decided to draft a UN Trusteeship Agreement for a Palestinian state in a single geographic unit, which the Zionists would have seen as abandonment by the US of its support for partition and consequently Jewish statehood.[145] This would explain Ben-Gurion's reaction when he first heard of the Americans' volte-face, when he cabled Moshe Shertok saying: 'This is the most terrible day since the beginning of the war.'[146] Evan Wilson, who was working on the Palestine desk at the US Department of State in 1947–48 and therefore privy to the exchanges of correspondence between his government, Great Britain, and the Zionists, deduced the following:

> ... after Austin's [the US Ambassador to the United Nations] Security Council statement on March 1948 had indicated that the United States was rethinking its support for partition, the Zionists must have seen that in order to achieve their Jewish state they would have to redouble their efforts and lead from a position of strength – hence the shift in the direction of ridding Palestine of its Arab inhabitants that was to characterize Zionist policy in the last weeks of the Mandate.[147]

Various press reports from the time also support this contention. For instance, the correspondent for *The Times* reported that in the aftermath of the US announcement in favour of Trusteeship, members of the Jewish Agency threatened to intensify the violence and proclaim a 'Hebrew Republic' on 16 May.[148] Morris argues that the gradual withdrawal of British troops was of help to the *Yishuv* and that by early April, 'the Haganah felt relatively certain that they would not interfere with its planned offensives'.[149] Also, that month, the Haganah had received a major injection of arms from Czechoslovakia, which emboldened them to go on the offensive.[150]

The leadership of the *Yishuv* were clearly aware of the effect that their offensive would have on the composition of the population of Palestine. On 3 December 1947 in a speech in front of senior members of the Mapai Party (Israel's Workers Party), Ben-Gurion outlined how to deal with the realities of the 1947 UN Partition Plan:

> There are 40 per cent non-Jews in the areas allocated to the Jewish state. This composition is not a solid basis for a Jewish state. And we have to face this new reality with all its severity and distinctness. Such a demographic balance questions our ability to maintain Jewish sovereignty ... Only a state with at least 80 per cent Jews is a viable and stable state.[151]

Speaking to the Zionist Actions Committee in April 1948, Ben-Gurion declared:

> We will not be able to win the war if we do not, during the war, populate upper and lower, eastern and western Galilee, the Negev and Jerusalem area ... I believe that war will also bring in its wake a great change in the distribution of the Arab population.[152]

Two months prior to this, he boasted before the Mapai Party Council, that:

> From your entry into Jerusalem, through Lifta, Romema ... there are no Arabs. One hundred percent Jews. Since Jerusalem was destroyed by the Romans, it has not been so Jewish as it is now. In many Arab neighbourhoods in the west one sees not a single Arab. I do not assume that this will change ... What had happened in Jerusalem ... is likely to happen in many parts of the country ... in the six, eight or ten months of the campaign there will certainly be great changes in the composition of the population in the country.[153]

On 1 April 1948, the Haganah implemented Operation Nachshon, the first of many such operations undertaken as part of Plan Dalet, which aimed at carving out and holding a corridor from Tel Aviv on the Mediterranean coast to Jerusalem in the interior of the country.[154] This involved the occupation and destruction of a score of Arab villages and culminated in the battle of Castel on 11 April, which led to the exodus of 10,000–15,000 Palestinian Arabs.[155] Two days earlier, on 9 April, it was thought that more than 200 Arabs, mostly women and children, were murdered in the village of Deir Yassin[156] in a combined operation by the Irgun and Lehi, which the British said was undertaken with the knowledge of the Haganah in a complaint they filed to the UN.[157] According to Benny Morris:

> Whole families were riddled with bullets and grenade fragments and buried when houses were blown up on top of them; men, women, and children were mowed down as they emerged from houses, individuals were taken aside and shot. At the end of the battle, groups of old men, women, and children were trucked through West Jerusalem's streets in a kind of 'victory parade' and then dumped in (Arab) East Jerusalem.[158]

Rape was also a method of warfare used by the Irgun and Lehi at Deir Yassin. The Assistant Inspector General of the Criminal Investigation Division, Richard C. Catling, and a team of British police officers were sent by the British Government to the village of Silwan in Jerusalem, where survivors of the massacre had found refuge. The team reported that they had great difficulty in interviewing the young girls. The following extract is from a dossier signed by Catling and containing reports of the interviews along with corroborating physical evidence obtained through medical examination of the survivors by a doctor and nurse from Government Hospital in Jerusalem:

> On 14th April at 10 A.M., I visited Silwan village accompanied by a doctor and nurse from Government Hospital in Jerusalem and a member of the Arab Women's Union. We visited many houses in this village in which approximately some two to three hundred people from Deir Yassin village are housed. I interviewed many of the women folk in order to glean some information on any atrocities committed in Deir Yassin but the majority of those women are very shy and reluctant to relate their experiences especially in matters concerning sexual assault and they need great coaxing before they will divulge any information. The recording of these statements is hampered also by the hysterical state of the women who often break down many times whilst the statement is being recorded. There is, however, no doubt that many sexual atrocities were committed by the attacking Jews. Many young school girls were raped and later slaughtered. Old women were also molested. One story is current concerning a case in which a young girl was literally torn in two. Many infants were also butchered and killed.[159]

Crimes against *al-'ard* (the honour of the women of the family) tore at the fabric of Palestinian village life, which was based on family obligations and communal duties.[160] Family honour is an integral component of Palestinian culture and would have brought home the necessity, particularly of the men of the family, to protect their women by fleeing, if necessary, to safer grounds. As Rosemary Sayigh, a leading social anthropologist on the subject, noted: 'It was through such methods that a people with a thirty-year tradition of resistance to British occupation and Zionist immigration were terrorized into flight.'[161] On the massacre at Deir Yassin and the role played by the Hanagah, the Irgun and Lehi in executing it, a statement prepared for a Draft Parliamentary Question and Answer that was to take place in the House of Commons submitted to Hector McNeil, the Minister of State, noted:

> It now seems clear that members of Hagana [*sic*] co-operated with the terrorist groups in granting them facilities for mounting their attack on Deir Yassin, and the statement of the Jewish Agency issued on the 12th April expressing horror and disgust at the barbarity of the manner in which this action had been carried out by the terrorists is curiously at variance with the ratification by the Zionist General Council meeting in Tel Aviv on the same day of an agreement for co-operation between Hagana and Irgun Zvai Leumi. Units of Hagana have now taken over occupation of Deir Yassin from the members of the terrorist groups who originally attacked the village.[162]

News of the massacre, which Morris and Pappé claim the Zionists deliberately propagated in order to contribute to the general pandemonium spreading throughout Palestine, caused thousands of people to flee for safety.[163] Similar atrocities occurred throughout Palestine in the following months.[164] An article published in *The Scotsman* on 10 April 1948 quoted one of the perpetrators of the Deir Yassin massacre threatening: 'This is the first step.

We intend to attack, conquer, and hold Arab territory as much as we can. That includes all of Palestine and Transjordan if possible.'[165]

On 13 April, Operation Jephtha was initiated on the same day as a ten-vehicle convoy en route to Hadassah Hospital was attacked by Arabs: 39 Jews, 6 Arabs and 2 British were killed in the seven-hour battle which followed.[166] On 14 April, the day before Operation Harèl was put into effect, there was a massacre at the village of Nasr El Din in the Tiberias District where it was said that many women and children were killed by the Irgun.[167] Two days earlier, the *Manchester Guardian* had described what happened in Tiberias as follows:

> Jewish troops went over to the offensive in the Tiberias area to-night with a heavy attack on an Arab village with automatic weapons and mortars. British Army reports say that large clouds of smoke were seen billowing over the village. Some women and children escaped to safety in the Tiberias police station, but to-night about forty were still in the village.[168]

On 16 April, the Zionists claimed a 'victory' by inflicting 200 casualties in the Nablus–Tulkarem–Jenin triangle.[169] On 17 April, Haganah troops reached Jerusalem. On 18 April, the bodies of eight young Arab men were discovered on Mount Carmel – their hands and legs were amputated.[170] On 19 April the Haganah took Tiberias expelling 4,500 Arabs and occupied Haifa three days later, during Operation Miparayim, where some 30,000–40,000 Arabs were 'held up'. They would be 'evacuated' with the assistance of the British military authorities under the command of General Stockwell, who was subsequently admonished by Bevin.[171] A British observer told the *Manchester Guardian* that the 'pitiful remnants' of the Arab inhabitants in the bazaar area of Haifa had to be ferried across the bay by the British Army to refuge in Acre 'because the Jews have blocked the road round the bay'.[172] This account of the fighting in Haifa and the exodus of its Arab population is also corroborated by the semi-official Zionist paper, *The Palestine Post* (now *The Jerusalem Post*), which reported that 'Haganah forces in a thirty-hour battle ... crushed all resistance, occupied major buildings forcing thousands of Arabs to flee by the only escape route – the sea.'[173] On 28–29 April, during Operation Chametz, the Haganah surrounded Jaffa, which was vividly described in a telegram to the Foreign Office from the last British High Commissioner of Palestine:

> Position in town is now absolutely quiet. Roughly estimate that some 30,000 of the original population of 50,000 Arabs left and more are leaving ... Evacuees are going mainly to Gaza and some by sea to Beirut, others to Ramallah and Nablus. It should be made clear that I.Z.L. [that is, the Irgun] attack with mortars was indiscriminate and designed to create panic amongst civilian inhabitants.[174]

The British authorities in Palestine had been instructed to keep hold of Jerusalem, Jaffa and Haifa until 15 May, when Britain was to relinquish the mandate.[175] The fall of Haifa and Jaffa to the Zionists before that date, infuriated Bevin so much that he insulted the British Army causing a rift with Field-Marshall Montgomery.[176] The Irgun pillaged what they could get their hands on in Jaffa, which was described by Jon Kimche, the editor of the London *Jewish Observer*, who was then in Palestine:

> For the first time in the still undeclared war a Jewish force commenced to loot in wholesale fashion. At first the young Irgunists pillaged only dresses, blouses and ornaments for their girl friends. But this discrimination was soon abandoned. Everything that was movable was carried from Jaffa – furniture, carpets, pictures, crockery and pottery, jewellery and cutlery. The occupied parts of Jaffa were stripped, and yet another traditional military characteristic raised its ugly head. What could not be taken away was smashed. Windows, pianos, fittings and lamps went in an orgy of destruction.[177]

On 5 May, the Haganah attacked Arab villages located on the banks of the Jordan River near Beit El Khouri where they purportedly fired on women and children before disfiguring some of their bodies.[178] On 6 May, they attacked the villages of Elghaweer, Samakh and El-Zaytoun.[179] On 10 May, the Haganah took Safad and three days later they took Jaffa. On 14 May, during Operation Ben Ami, the Haganah captured Acre, encountering little resistance, before declaring independence at midnight on 14/15 May.[180] The Arab Legion halted them in their attempts to occupy Jerusalem's Old City, although they captured the New City during Operation Pitchfork on the same day.[181]

THE EXPULSION OF THE PALESTINIANS

According to an internal assessment by the Israeli Defence Forces Intelligence Service Analysis, between December 1947 and May 1948 approximately 390,000 Palestinian Arabs were displaced from their homes, either through expulsion or fear of expulsion.[182] The assessment stipulated that of the 219 Arab villages in the areas earmarked for the Jewish state, 180 were 'cleansed' of their inhabitants by 1 June 1948 and the inhabitants of a further 70 villages and three towns – Jaffa, Jenin and Acre – were expelled. It is important to note that all three of these towns were supposed to be in the Arab state as envisaged in the UN Partition Plan. This evidently did not prevent the Haganah, the Irgun and Lehi from attacking them. The IDF document outlined what the Israeli military regarded in June 1948 as the primary factors precipitating the exodus, which were listed in order of importance:

1. Direct, hostile Jewish [Haganah/IDF] operations against Arab settlements.
2. The effect of our [Haganah/IDF] hostile operations on nearby [Arab] settlements ... (... especially – the fall of large neighbourhood centres).

3. Operations of the [Jewish] dissidents [the Irgun Z'vai Leumi and Lohamei Herut Yisrael].
4. Orders and decrees by Arab institutions and gangs [irregulars].
5. Jewish whispering operations [psychological warfare], aimed at frightening away Arab inhabitants.
6. Ultimate expulsion orders [by Jewish forces].
7. Fear of Jewish [retaliatory] response [following] major Arab attacks on Jews.
8. The appearance of gangs [irregular Arab forces] and non-local fighters in the vicinity of a village.
9. Fear of Arab invasion and its consequences [mainly near the border].
10. Isolated Arab villages in purely [predominantly] Jewish areas.
11. Various local factors and general fear of the future.[183]

The report gave a detailed breakdown and explanation of the factors causing the exodus, noting, 'without doubt, hostile [Haganah/IDF] operations were the main cause of the over movement of population'.[184] The report concluded by stating that 55 per cent of the total exodus was caused by the Haganah and that the effects of operations undertaken by the Irgun and Lehi contributed to 15 per cent of the exodus.[185] Altogether, the report stated that operations undertaken by the Haganah, the Irgun and Lehi accounted for 70 per cent of the Arab exodus from Palestine.[186]

Even after the Arab armies intervened in May 1948, the expulsions continued. Operation Dani, which was drawn up by the Operation Command of the Israeli Army and by General Yigal Allon, had the objective of capturing Lydda airfield, which was Palestine's international airport (it is now known as Ben-Gurion airport), and the towns of Lydda and Ramle which had also been allocated to the Arab state in the UN Partition Plan.[187] One of the aims of Operation Dani was to induce civilian panic and flight as a means of precipitating military collapse.[188] Various tactics were used to achieve this. For example, on 11 July in a common tactic amounting to a psychological warfare ploy, the Israeli air force showered the Arab towns of Ramle and Lydda with leaflets stating: 'You have no chance of receiving help. We intend to conquer the towns. We have no intention of harming persons or property. [But] whoever attempts to oppose us – will die'.[189] In discussing what to do with the civilians, Morris writes that:

> Ben-Gurion spent the early afternoon at Operation Dani HQ. Also present were IDF OC Operations General Yadin, Deputy Chief of Staff General Zvi Ayalon, Yisrael Galilee ... Allon, and his deputy, Operation Dani OC Operations Yitzhak Rabin ... According to the best account of that meeting, someone, possibly Allon, proposed expelling the inhabitants of the two towns. Ben-Gurion said nothing, and no decision was taken. Then Ben-Gurion, Allon and Rabin left the room. Allon asked: 'What shall we do

> with the Arabs?' Ben Gurion made a dismissive, energetic gesture with his hand and said 'expel them' (*garesh otam*).[190]

When Yitzhak Rabin candidly wrote about this event in his memoirs, a special ministerial committee censored it even though the Israeli military censor had already approved it.[191] Rabin's account, which was subsequently published in *The New York Times* in October 1979 and in the following year in *Ha'olam Hazeh*, was as follows:

> We walked outside, Ben-Gurion accompanying us. Alon repeated his question: 'What is to be done with the population?' BG waved his hand in a gesture which said: Drive them out! Alon and I held a consultation. I agreed that it was essential to drive the inhabitants out ... The population of Lod (Lydda) did not leave willingly. There was no way of avoiding the use of force and warning shots in order to make the inhabitants march the 10–15 miles to the point where they met up with the Legion.[192]

The bulk of the exodus from Ramle and Lydda took place on 13 July, where many had to make their way on foot to the lines controlled by the Arab Legion.[193] There was little doubt that this was an expulsion operation, as most of the signal traffic between operational command and individual Israeli Army units used language that could give them no doubt in this regard (e.g. 'Lydda police fort has been captured. The troops are busy expelling the inhabitants [oskim begeirush hatoshavim]').[194] According to Benny Morris, they were faithfully responding to the following order, signed by Rabin:

1. The inhabitants of Lydda must be expelled quickly without attention to age. They should be directed towards Beit Nabala. Yiftah [Brigade HQ] must determine the method and inform [Operation] Dani HQ and 8th Brigade HQ.
2. Implement immediately.[195]

A similar order, concerning the expulsion of the inhabitants of Ramle, was communicated to Kiryati Brigade headquarters at the same time:

1. In light of the deployment of 42nd Battalion out of Ramle – you must take [over responsibility] for the defence of the town, the transfer of the prisoners [to PoW camps] and the emptying of the town of its inhabitants.
2. You must continue the sorting out of the inhabitants, and send the army-age males to a prisoner of war camp. The old, women and children will be transported by vehicle to al Qubab and will be removed across the lines – [and] from there will continue on foot ...[196]

Prior to the expulsions both towns had populations of roughly 50,000–70,000 people.[197] Although the Arab Legion had a presence in both towns, it withdrew because they could not be defended in the face of a sustained assault by the Haganah.[198] On 11 July, Sir John Bagot Glubb, the British Commander in charge of the Arab Legion ordered his soldiers to retreat from the two towns, an act that was seen as a great betrayal by the Palestinian Arabs which irrevocably sullied Abdullah's reputation amongst the people he had avowedly claimed to be in Palestine to protect.[199] In his diary, Ben-Gurion repeatedly jotted down that he wanted the towns 'destroyed'.[200] He would have his way, as they were to fall to the Haganah. Lt Colonel Moshe Dayan led the initial attack on Lydda. His battalion drove through the town spraying machine-gun fire at anything that moved.[201] One of his troopers described his experiences conquering Lydda in these words:

> [My] jeep made the turn and here at the ... entrance to the house opposite stands an Arab girl, stands and screams with eyes filled with fear and dread. She is all torn and dripping blood – she is certainly wounded. Around her on the ground lie the corpses of her family. Still quivering, death has not yet redeemed them from their pain. Next to her is a bundle of rags – her mother, hand outstretched trying to draw her into the house. And the girl understands nothing ... Did I fire at her?[202]

In his memoirs, the UN mediator Count Folke Bernadotte described what he experienced when he came face to face with these refugees who had fled to Ramallah:

> Before we left Jerusalem, I visited Ramallah, where thousands of refugees from Lydda and Ramleh were assembled. I have made acquaintance of a great many refugee camps; but I have never seen a more ghastly sight than that which met my eyes here, at Ramallah. The car was literally stormed by excited masses shouting with Oriental fervour that they wanted food and wanted to return to their homes. There were plenty of frightening faces in the sea of suffering humanity. I remember not least a group of scabby and helpless old men with tangled beards who thrust their emaciated faces into the car and held out scraps of bread that would certainly have been considered uneatable by ordinary people, but this was their only food. Perhaps there was no danger of this camp becoming a breeding ground for epidemic diseases that would spread all over Palestine. But what would happen at the beginning of October, when the rainy season began and the cold weather set in? It was a thought one preferred not to follow to its conclusion.[203]

On 17 July, the Haganah captured Nazareth and shelled it so severely that it caused an exodus of Arab inhabitants from the city. As the correspondent for the *Manchester Guardian* described it: 'The shelling was reported to have created complete confusion among some twenty-five thousand Arab refugees – mainly Christians – thronging the area. The road leading north-east out of

Nazareth was described as packed with an almost helpless mass of refugees.'[204] Like Jaffa, Lydda and Ramle, Nazareth was supposed to be assigned to the Arab state in the UN Partition Plan. Yet this did not prevent it from being attacked by the Haganah. Israel's conquest of Palestine continued throughout the remainder of 1948 and into 1949. In October 1948, there was a massacre at Safsaf (now Sifsufa), which was described in the following account by the inhabitants of that village:

> As we lined up, a few Jewish soldiers ordered four girls to accompany them to carry water for the soldiers. Instead they took them to our empty houses and raped them. About seventy of our men were blindfolded and shot to death, one after the other, in front of us. The soldiers took their bodies and threw them on the cement covering the village's spring and dumped sand on them.[205]

Later that month there was another massacre, even worse than Safsaf, at the Palestinian Arab village of Dawaymeh, where according to an Israeli soldier, his colleagues

> ... killed some eighty to one hundred Arabs, women and children. The children were killed by smashing their skulls with clubs ... In the village there remained Arab men and women who were put in the houses without food. Then the sappers came to blow up the houses. One officer ordered a sapper to put two old women into the house he was about to blow up. The sapper refused, and said that he will [*sic*] obey only such orders are handed down to him by his direct commander. So the officer ordered his own soldiers to put the old women in and the atrocity was carried out. Another soldier boasted that he raped an Arab woman and then shot her. Another Arab woman with a day-old baby was employed in cleaning jobs in the yard ... she worked for one or two days and then was shot together with her baby ... Cultured and well mannered commanders who are considered good fellows ... have turned into low murderers, and this happened not in the storm of battle, but because of a system of expulsion and annihilation. The less Arabs remain, the better.[206]

When soldiers from mechanised battalion No. 89 of the Israeli Army approached the Sufi mosque of Zaywa in Dawaymeh where the *Darawiesh* were gathered for Friday prayer, they killed some of the faithful. One of the survivors, Khalil Muhammed Mahmoud Salime Hudeib, recalled the way in which the troops approached the mosque:

> The soldiers were laughing and joking loudly as they marched in. The Sheikhs and Darawish began to plead with the soldiers for mercy. One of the soldiers said 'Arabs you have to die so that you go to God.' I heard the shooting and simultaneously the calling of 'There is but One God' by

> the Sheikhs, giving their religious witness as they died. The voice of the Mosque's Imam, Sheikh Muhammed Mutlak Al-Ghawanme, calling with pain 'God' and then I heard a shot and the voice was extinguished. And I heard one of the Daraweish saying 'Oh God, Oh great one' and a soldier shouted 'die because you are great.' After that a frightening silence engulfed the Mosque.[207]

The Arab Refugee Congress of Ramallah subsequently submitted a report to the Technical Committee of the UN Conciliation Commission for Palestine, which specifically addressed the massacre in the village of Dawaymeh in these words:

> Little is known about the brutal massacre of Arab peasants in the village of Dawaymeh on 28/10/48. Dawaymeh is situated a few kilometres West of Hebron. It had a population of six thousand people. Some four thousand Arab refugees had taken refuge in the village prior to the massacre. The reason why so little is known about this massacre which, in many respects, was more brutal than the Deir Yassin massacre, is because the Arab Legion (the Army in control of that area) feared that if the news was allowed to spread, it would have the same effect on the moral of the peasantry that Deir Yassin had, namely to cause another flow of Arab refugees.[208]

Clearly then, there was a link between the massacres and the flow of refugees. In other words, it was the massacres, and the fear they aroused, that led many Palestinians to flee for safety. They did not, as the Zionists claimed, flee so that the Arab states could invade the fledgling Jewish state.[209] 'There is no evidence', Simha Flapan wrote, to support Israel's claims that the Arabs fled in order to open the way for the invading armies.[210] 'In fact', he added, 'the declassified material contradicts the "order" theory, for among these new sources are documents testifying to the considerable efforts of the AHC [Arab Higher Committee] and the Arab states to constrain the flight.'[211] For instance, one letter from the Arab Higher Committee, dated 8 March 1948, implored the Arab governments to cooperate in preventing Palestinians from leaving their country: 'The Arab Higher Committee has resolved that it is in the interests of Palestine that no Palestinian should be permitted to leave the country except under special circumstances, such as for political, commercial or extreme health reasons.'[212] Another scholar raised the obvious, but often overlooked question, as to how the *fellaheen* could have been ordered to flee by the 'invading' Arab armies when the smaller villages did not even have radios.[213] Further support for the position that Arabs did not flee on anyone's orders but through fear for their own safety and well-being appears in a document prepared by the British Foreign Office to correct what they described as 'inaccurate Jewish political propaganda', and which is worth partly reproducing from the declassified Foreign Office files in Kew:

B. – ARAB REFUGEES AND JEWS

The Jews claim that the British and the Arab rulers are responsible for their flight and present plight.

The facts are:-

(a) That very many fled before the Arab invasion of 15th May owing to the brutality and the atrocities of IZL [the Irgun] and Haganah, e.g. at Deir Yassin. This policy of intimidation had since been pursued fairly consistently.
(b) Britain has led voluntary relief and also relief measures through the United Nations.
(c) Jewish settlers have systematically moved into houses and land of Arab refugees.
(d) Jews have obstructed United Nations efforts to obtain return of Arab refugees to their homes.[214]

The events that gripped Palestine in the years 1946–48 are probably best summed up in a speech that Mr Henry Cattan, a member of the Palestine Arab Delegation, gave before the Political Committee of the UN General Assembly, which was held in Paris in November 1948. Although his use of language was both emotional and forceful, it gives one a good impression of the feeling of bitterness that characterised the feelings of most Palestinians displaced by the fighting in 1948. Moreover, he traces the conflict further back in time, not only to the aftermath of partition, when fighting between Arabs and Jews broke out, but to the Jewish terrorist attacks against the British authorities in Palestine which preceded it. Clearly, he saw a link between these events:

> It will be sufficient to recall that in order to force the British authorities out of Palestine, the Zionists embarked upon a campaign of terrorism that began with the assassination of Lord Moyne (British Cabinet Minister), and was followed, to mention only a few of their outrages, by the attempted assassination of the High Commissioner for Palestine and his wife, the blowing-up during office hours of a wing of the King David Hotel (causing the mass murder of some hundred persons), the murder of scores of troops and police, the flogging of British police officers, and finally the hanging of two young Britishers in a forest. That was the way in which the Jews expressed their gratitude to the nation that had promised them a national home in Palestine. I pass over the blowing up of buildings, bridges, roads and railway installations which was, so to speak, a daily occurrence. Eventually, the British were forced out or allowed themselves to be forced out, I do not know, but the policy of terrorism certainly succeeded …
>
> … since the end of November, 1947, when the General Assembly recommended the partition of Palestine, the Jews committed all imaginable and unimaginable terrorist outrages with the object of driving out the Arab population from their homes and their lands. The treacherous blowing-

> up of Arab homes during hours of darkness, burying underneath whole families – men, women and children – was a common occurrence. Here, there and everywhere terrorists struck: the only object was to spread terror and more terror in the hearts of civilian population and force them to move out of their homes. I do not propose to be exhaustive. I shall refer to some incidents only. The Semiramis Hotel was blown up at Jerusalem on the night of the 5th January, 1948, and two entire Arab families and a Spanish diplomatic representative – some twenty innocent residents in all – were thus foully murdered during their sleep and buried under the debris. In Jaffa, the offices of Social Welfare were blown up, causing some hundred Arab casualties. There were mass slaughters of Arab civilians at Tireh, Abassieh, Nasser il Din, Abn Kishk, Ein Zaitoun and other places under circumstances of utmost savagery.[215]

It is noteworthy that the events described by Cattan all occurred *before* 14/15 May 1948, when the *Yishuv* declared their independence, and when the Arabs came to Palestine's defence. In a minute from the British delegation in Paris to the Foreign Office, accompanying the text of Cattan's speech, Lance Thirkell commented: 'The first two thirds of the speech ... give an accurate picture of the methods of terrorism pure and simple by which the Jews have succeeded in driving the Arabs out of the greater part of Palestine. Almost every incident described by Mr CATTAN can be substantiated from our own records.'[216] Thirkell's only cause of complaint was the length of Cattan's speech and the method of its presentation.[217] But he did not dispute the facts.

Even after Israel had signed the armistice agreements with Egypt, Jordan, Lebanon and Syria in the first few months of 1949, it continued to expel Arabs and prevent them from returning to their homes. In his personal recollections of the 1948 war, Mordechai Bar-on, a former member of the Knesset, who served as a company commander in the Giv'ati Brigade, recalled being given orders to prevent a refugee return:

> ... when my company was still deployed near the Gaza Strip, I received information from my superiors that Palestinian refugees were perched on one of those sand dunes, intending to cross the lines and march back into the areas held by the Israeli army. I was ordered to stop them, even with fire if need be. I clearly remember being fully aware of the cruelty involved, but I would not have hesitated to open fire since by then I already understood that the struggle was not only for the establishment of our political sovereignty but also for the land.[218]

Such justifications for acts of expulsion were typical. In September 1949 the Israeli Army destroyed all the houses in the village of Wadi Fukin after the UN Mixed Armistice Commission had decided that the villagers had a right to return there.[219] In 1950, citing security considerations, Israel expelled a further 14,000 residents of al-Majdal (Ashkelon) by trucking them to the nearby border with the Gaza Strip and forcing them to cross.[220] It continued expulsions into

1951, and for several years thereafter forcing out thousands of Palestinian Bedouins from the Negev Desert.[221] Although it has become fashionable to describe what took place in the war of 1948 as an act of 'ethnic cleansing', this is not a term of art in international law – it only came into popular usage during the Balkan wars in the 1990s.[222] However, it does seem to provide an accurate *description* of what transpired in Palestine in the late 1940s.[223]

BROKEN PLEDGES

Evidently, law or morality did not sanction these actions. In addition to being contrary to well-established rules of customary international humanitarian law, they conflicted with the safeguard clause of the Balfour Declaration as it was incorporated into the Mandate, as well as with the Covenant of the League of Nations which had its origins in the Conference of Berlin of 1884–85, Balfour's letter to Lord Curzon, British policy as enunciated in its numerous White Papers, the declared policies of the Allied powers during both World Wars and President's Roosevelt's personal pledge to King Abdul Aziz ibn Saud when they met on the US cruiser, the *Quincy*, as it made its way through the Suez Canal in 1945. On that occasion Roosevelt personally promised Ibn Saud that he would take no action in his capacity as Chief of the Executive Branch of the US Government 'which might prove hostile to the Arab people'.[224] And after Roosevelt passed away, President Harry Truman made a further pledge:

> In supporting the establishment of the Jewish National Home in Palestine the United States had no thought of embarking upon a policy which would be prejudicial to the interests of the indigenous population of Palestine ... We would be firmly opposed to any solution of the Palestine problem which would permit a majority of the population to discriminate against a minority on religious, racial, or other grounds ... I am convinced, furthermore, that the responsible Jewish groups and leaders interested in developing the Jewish National Home in Palestine have no intention of expelling now or at a later date the indigenous inhabitants of that country or of using Palestine as a base for aggression against neighbouring Arab States.[225]

It is clear then, that the United States never supported the expulsion of the Palestinian people from their homeland. On the contrary, the Americans were aghast at what took place. Truman simply could not comprehend how, after what had happened to the Jews in the concentration camps of Europe, the Zionists could even contemplate harming Palestine's indigenous Arab population. He expressed his opinion that:

> No people has suffered more than the Jews during recent years from aggression and intolerance. No people stands more in need of world sympathy and support at the present time. It is therefore inconceivable that responsible Jewish groups or leaders could be contemplating acts

of intolerance and aggression against Arabs in Palestine or elsewhere which would be sure to arouse public opinion and to provoke indignation throughout the world.[226]

THE LAWS OF WAR

Many of the tactics adopted by the Zionists to coerce the Arabs to flee from Palestine – such as summary executions, pillage, torture and the wanton destruction of private and public property, when there was no military necessity – were contrary to established norms of customary international humanitarian law, as they existed in the years preceding the 1947–49 hostilities.[227] In fact, as far back as the seventeenth century, it was already a well-established customary rule of international law that children, old men, women, and anyone who could not carry arms, were not to be made the objects of armed attack.[228] By the nineteenth century this was extended to anyone who did not take an active part in hostilities, which included men of military age, such as doctors and medical personnel, even if they were in the 'enemy's camp'.[229] The life, honour, family rights and religion of the 'peaceful population' were to be protected.[230] These rules subsisted throughout the nineteenth century and found expression in the Hague Regulations of 1899 and 1907 and in the numerous national codes on the laws of war prepared for the armies of numerous states.[231]

There was even doctrinal support in the nineteenth century, although it was contested by some, for a rule of international law that prohibited the deportation of civilians from occupied territory.[232] If this rule was still in dispute at the turn of the twentieth century, it was not by the end of the Second World War, when the International Military Tribunals in Nuremberg and Tokyo had condemned mass deportations as being contrary to the laws of and customs of war.[233] At Nuremberg, the Tribunal specifically cited the 'evacuation' of the inhabitants of the Crimea and its settlement by Germans and the colonisation by Germans of regions in Poland and Russia as being contrary to Article 6 (b) of the Charter of the International Military Tribunal.[234]

The reason why deportations were not explicitly discussed at the Hague Peace Conferences in 1899 and 1907 was because the practice was considered to have been alien to modern warfare, not because deportations were considered to be lawful.[235] In fact, the Commission on the Responsibility of the Authors of War and Enforcement of Penalties at the Paris Peace Conference in 1919 specifically listed deportations as a war crime.[236] In this regard it should be said that in 1946, one year before the outbreak of the Arab–Israeli conflict, the 1907 Hague Regulations were held by the Nuremberg Tribunal to have reflected customary international law since at least 1939.[237] The Tokyo Tribunal also considered the Hague Regulations of 1907 'as good evidence of the customary law of nations, to be considered by the Tribunal along with all other available evidence in determining the customary law to be applied in any given situation'.[238] In this regard it cited the 'Martens Clause' in the preamble to the IV Hague Regulation of 1907:

> Until a more complete code of the laws of war has been issued, the High Contracting Parties deem it expedient to declare that, in cases not included in the Regulations adopted by them, the inhabitants and the belligerents remain under the protection and the rule of the principles of the law of nations, as they result from the usages established among civilized peoples, from the laws of humanity, and the dictates of the public conscience.[239]

Moreover, although the four Geneva Conventions did not enter into force until 21 October 1950, by which time the fighting in mandatory Palestine was already over, many of its provisions, such as the prohibition of deportations, pillage and reprisals, embodied pre-existing law.[240] As the Foreign Office legal advisers noted in another legal opinion they drafted in November 1948, concerning the conduct of the Arab–Israeli conflict:

> *Apart from the laws of war recognised by customary international law*, there are various conventions which in effect are a partial codification of this part of international law including, for instance, the conventions on the treatment of sick and wounded and of prisoners of war. No doubt the provisional State of Israel are [*sic*] not strictly speaking bound by these conventions. Nonetheless they represent a code of civilised conduct to which appeal is frequently made.[241]

As the Foreign Office legal advisers noted, the laws of war recognised by customary international law were applicable during the hostilities in 1948, which prohibited much of the conduct undertaken by the Haganah, the Irgun and Lehi, especially armed attacks against a civilian population. The Arab–Israeli conflict did not, therefore, occur in a normative vacuum. There were legal issues at stake with serious consequences for the parties concerned. In 1949, the United States Military Tribunal at Nuremberg ruled in the *Ministries Trial*[242] – which was a case concerning the participation by members of Germany's Foreign Ministry and other government departments of alleged crimes against peace, war crimes, and crimes against humanity – that although the Hague and Geneva Conventions, the Constitutions and Charter of the League of Nations, and the Kellogg–Briand treaties had given definitive shape to limited fields in international law, they were not exclusive and did not cover the entire field of the law. It then held that:

> The initiation of wars and invasions, with their attendant horror and suffering, has for centuries been universally recognised by all civilised nations as wrong, to be resorted to only as a last resort to remedy wrongs already or imminently to be inflicted. We hold that aggressive wars and invasions have, since time immemorial, been a violation of international law, even though specific sanctions were not provided.[243]

When it came to the treatment of civilians, the Tribunal did not hesitate to conclude that:

> Measures which result in *murder*, *illtreatment*, enslavement *and other inhuman acts* perpetrated on prisoners of war, *deportation*, extermination, enslavement, and persecution on political, racial and religious grounds, *and plunder and spoliation of public and private property*, are acts which shock the conscience of every decent man. These are criminal *per se*.[244]

In the *German High Command Trial*, the same Tribunal ruled on the law relating to hostages and reprisals which concerned the question as to whether, under certain very restrictive conditions and subject to extensive safeguards, hostages could be sentenced to death.[245] The Court ruled that even in this scenario:

> If so inhumane a measure as the killing of innocent persons for offences of others, even when drastically safeguarded and limited, is ever permissible under any theory of International Law, killing without full compliance with all requirements would be murder. If killing is not permissible under any circumstances, then a killing with full compliance with all the mentioned prerequisites still would be murder.[246]

Therefore, those men and women who were captured by the numerous Zionist militias during the course of the 1948 conflict, such as at Deir Yassin, where they were lined up against walls, shot, and thrown down wells, was tantamount to murder, even if they had taken part in hostilities or aided the enemy. In order to try civilians for committing offences against the laws of war, certain strict safeguards had to be met, which were not adhered to during the Arab–Israeli conflict. In the words of the Tribunal, '[k]illings without full compliance with such pre-conditions are merely terror murders'.[247]

The 15 volumes of the *Law Reports of Trials of War Criminals Selected and Prepared by the United Nations War Crimes Commission* are full of cases where soldiers were prosecuted and, in some cases, sentenced to death, for killing civilians.[248] For instance, in the *Trial of Robert Wagner*, the Permanent Military Tribunal at Strasbourg found the accused guilty of orchestrating the mass expulsion and deportation from Alsace of Jews and other French nationals.[249] In the *Trial of Franz Holstein*, the Permanent Military Tribunal at Dijon ruled that the killing of civilians by reprisals, the destruction of inhabited buildings, the ill-treatment of civilians, and pillage were also unlawful:

> That murder, premeditated or not, is punishable as a war crime, has had a long recognition in the laws and customs of war. Its latest expression can be found in the Charter of the International Military Tribunal at Nuremberg (Article 6) and also at that of Tokyo (Article 5). It can also be found in the municipal law of many nations dealing with war crimes, as it emerged during or after the war 1939–45.[250]

The US Military Tribunal at Nuremberg in the *Trial of Edward Milch* specifically condemned deportations.[251] In his concurring opinion, Judge

Phillips ruled: 'If the transfer is carried out without a legal title, as in the case where people are deported from a country occupied by an invader while the occupied enemy still has an army in the field and is still resisting, the deportation is contrary to international law'.[252] He added: '... the final condition under which deportation becomes illegal occurs whenever generally recognized standards of decency and humanity are disregarded'.[253] In his opinion, this flowed 'from the established principle of law that an otherwise permissible act becomes a crime when carried out in a criminal manner'.[254] The judgment then continued:

> Article II (1) (c) of Control Council Law No. 10 specifies certain crimes against humanity. Among those is listed the deportation of any civilian population. The general language of this subsection as applied to deportation indicates that Control Council Law No. 10 has unconditionally contended as a crime against humanity every instance of deportation of civilians.[255]

The US Military Tribunal in the *Krupp Trial* cited the whole of Judge Phillips' concurring opinion with approval.[256] There the Tribunal ruled:

> The law with respect to the deportation from occupied territory is dealt with by Judge Phillips in his convincing opinion in the United States of America v. Milch, decided by Tribunal No. 11. We regard Judge Phillips' statement of the applicable law as sound and accordingly adopt it.[257]

On the question of deportations, the commentary prepared by the United Nations War Crimes Commission to accompany the summaries of these judgments, noted that:

> While in practice cases of alleged deportation and 'slave labour' have usually arisen for treatment together, for deportation to become a war crime or a crime against humanity *it need not have enslavement as its objective*. This conclusion appears to have been accepted by a study of certain French, Australian, Chinese and Yugoslav provisions relating to the trial of war criminals.[258]

In the *Trial of Gauleiter Artur Greiser*, the Supreme National Tribunal of Poland sentenced him to death after finding him guilty of numerous crimes, which also included the deportation of Poles.[259] Although the summary of the judgment reproduced by the War Crimes Commission does not set out the legal basis for its finding that deportations are unlawful, although it implicitly accepted that they were by finding Greiser guilty of the crime, its description of the deportations bear an uncanny similarity to that of the expulsion of the Palestinians at the hands of Zionist troops in 1948:

> On Sunday, 22nd October, 1939, the deportation of Poles from Poznan had already begun. It was carried out with the help of the Field Police and

> the Selbstschutz. The first victims were prosperous Poznan merchants; they were turned out of their homes, the keys of which were handed over to the *Umsiedlungsamt*, and they were loaded into lorries and taken away.
>
> In this way Poznan, of whose 279 thousand inhabitants before the war some 2% were of German nationality, was gradually depopulated. Up to February, 1940, some 70 thousand of the citizens of Polish nationality had already been deported. In their place came Baltic Germans and a large number of officials and army personnel with their families from the Reich. During 1940 some 36,000 Baltic Germans were settled in this manner, taking over houses, and flats, from which Poles had been driven. These homes still contained all the previous occupant's possessions, for the Poles were only allowed to take hand luggage with them.
>
> These deportations, of course, took place throughout the entire Province of Wartheland. Deportations began with the towns. From the country the landowners were the first to be deported, then the Germans began driving away the peasants.
>
> The city of Lodz received particular attention, for of its 700 thousand inhabitants more than 450 thousand were Poles and some 200 thousand Jews. Deportation of Poles began in December, 1939, at a time of severe frost. On 21st February, 1940, the newspaper *Grenzzeitung* announced triumphantly that the centre of Lodz had been entirely cleared of Poles and was reserved exclusively for Germans. In September, 1940, the number of those deported from Lodz was estimated at 150,000. The name of the town has changed to Litzmannstadt, all inscriptions in Polish were removed and an attempt was made to give the town a purely German character.[260]

It would therefore seem that deportations were considered unlawful before, during, and after the Second World War. Although there was no specific legal instrument prior to the adoption of the four Geneva Conventions of 1949, outlawing the practice of deportations and population transfer, the manner in which they were carried out would have breached several provisions of the 1907 Hague Regulations such as Articles 46 and 47 which outlawed pillage and provided that family honour and rights, the lives of persons, and private property, as well as religious convictions and practice, must be respected and that private property must not be confiscated.[261] In fact, Pierre Mounier, the assistant prosecutor for the French Republic, told the International Military Tribunal at Nuremberg on the first day of the proceedings on 20 November 1945 that deportations specifically violated Article 46 of the Hague Regulations. He said that deportations were 'contrary to the international conventions, *in particular to Article 46 of the Hague Regulations, 1907*, the laws and customs of war, the general principles of criminal law as derived from the criminal laws of all civilised nations, the internal penal laws of the countries in which such crimes were committed, and to Article 6 (b) of the Charter'.[262]

It is highly unlikely that a legal tribunal informed of the full facts of the 1948 Arab–Israeli conflict would have ruled that the conduct of the Haganah, the Irgun and Lehi was lawful. In fact, even members of the Provisional Government of Israel accepted that the soldiers under its command were committing war crimes and crimes against humanity. As Aharon Cizling, the Minister of Agriculture in the Israeli Government told his colleagues at a cabinet meeting on 17 November 1948, after being told that Israeli soldiers had been accused of raping civilians before doing away with them:

> I often disagreed when the term Nazi was applied to the British. I wouldn't like to use the term, even though the British committed Nazi crimes. But now Jews too have behaved like Nazis and my entire being has been shaken ... Obviously we have to conceal these actions from the public, and I agree that we should not even reveal that we're investigating them. But they must be investigated.[263]

What is interesting about this statement is not the parallel Cizling draws between the Nazis, the British and the actions of certain Israeli soldiers, or that he wanted to cover up these atrocities, but that he admitted that what he called their 'crimes' were under investigation. Is this not tacit recognition by an Israeli government minister that the laws of war did apply to the hostilities and that those who breached them could be held to account for their conduct? It would seem so. In July 1948, after hundreds of thousands of Palestinian Arabs had fled or been expelled from their homes, the same government minister gave the following order:

> Except in the course of actual fighting, it is forbidden to destroy, burn or demolish Arab towns and villages, or to expel Arab inhabitants from their villages, neighbourhoods and towns, or uproot inhabitants from their homes without express permission of an order from the Minister of Defence, in each and every case. Anyone violating this order will be liable to prosecution.[264]

It may be questioned whether the destruction, burning and demolishing of towns and villages can ever be considered lawful even during the course of armed conflict, where there is no military necessity, even if an order has been given.[265] What is interesting about this particular order, however, is that it affords further evidence that Palestinian Arabs were uprooted from their homes and expelled, that the Government of Israel was aware of this, and that those who partook in these operations were liable to prosecution.

But what was the fate of the 750,000 Palestinian Arabs displaced from their homes by the Zionists? If their expulsion was unlawful, then what does international law have to say about their rights to return, restitution and compensation, and what was the reaction of the Great Powers to their plight at the Lausanne Peace Conference?

8
The Palestinian Refugees

'... every Jew in the world is regarded as having the right to settle in Palestine, which was deserted by his forefathers 2,000 years ago, while at the same time the Palestinian is not recognised as having even the shadow of a right to return to the land which he was forced to quit a mere 20 years ago, or, indeed a bare month ago, as a result of the present conflict. This is certainly a very peculiar line of reasoning.'

Extract from the inaugural address delivered by Mohammed Bedjaoui,* Minister of Justice, 22 July 1967 at the seminar of Arab Jurists on Palestine in Algiers, Algeria, 22–27 July 1967, translated from French by Edward Risk and published in Beirut by the Institute of Palestine Studies, 1968, p. 9

Today, the Palestinian refugees constitute the largest single refugee community anywhere in the world, numbering some 4.4 million persons, outnumbering even Afghan refugees.[1] And yet they are the only known refugee group not to be afforded explicit protection by the UN High Commissioner for Refugees (UNHCR) due to an article inserted into the 1951 UN Refugee Convention which provides that its mandate does not apply to persons receiving protection or assistance from other UN organs.[2] Instead, the problems facing the Palestinian refugees are due to a mishap of history, they being the only group of displaced persons in the world to have a specific UN Agency established to provide for their welfare, the UN Relief and Works Agency for Palestinian Refugees in the Near East (UNRWA), whilst not being afforded the protection provided by the UNHCR. This is because UNRWA's mandate only provides for Palestinian refugee relief, but not their protection, since it was envisaged that they would be allowed to return to their homes one day and/or be resettled in the surrounding Arab countries in line with the recommendations of the UN Conciliation Commission for Palestine (UNCCP) upon the conclusion of peace. Since there has been no peace, the vast majority of Palestinian refugees continue to linger in the camps established after the war in 1948, which these days resemble Brazilian *favelas* or shanty towns rather than tented cities.

One feature unique to the Palestinian refugee problem which, although obvious, is often overlooked, is that their country of origin, Palestine, ceased to exist in 1948. The use of the word 'refugee' is therefore something of an anomaly since this is usually understood to refer to a person fleeing his/her place of origin due to a well-founded fear of being persecuted for reasons of race, religion or nationality and who is unable or unwilling to return to their place of origin through fear of persecution.[3] This definition is, however, not appropriate to describe the predicament of the Palestinian refugees since

* Mohammed Bedjaoui was later appointed a judge at the International Court of Justice.

many of them would like to return to their homes.[4] Instead the Palestinian refugees have been *prevented* from returning to their former homes by the state of Israel which was created, for the most part, in place of Palestine, their properties being confiscated and given to Jewish refugees from occupied Europe. Nevertheless, the term 'refugee' is frequently used as a form of collective identity, and it will be used here in a general sense to refer to those Palestinians displaced in 1948. Since Israel was largely responsible for their flight and consequent plight it becomes necessary to examine in the first place the controversy concerning whether the Palestinians have a 'right of return' which is recognised by international law.

THE RIGHT OF RETURN

The right of peoples to return to their homes is an ancient principle. It is mentioned in the Old Testament in the Book of Ezra where the King of Persia allowed the Jews to return to Jerusalem to rebuild their Temple.[5] It was also mentioned in the Cyrus Cylinder, which some have described as the world's first human rights charter.[6] Not only did Cyrus help the Jews return to their homeland, but he went further and offered them restitution and compensation for the loss of their property which had been pillaged and confiscated by Nebuchadnezzar during the First Temple's destruction.[7] Positive international law, however, does not look kindly on such lofty ecclesiastical ideals, humanitarian gestures or religious edicts, which partly explains why international lawyers have long argued over whether the 750,000 Palestinians displaced from their homes by the fighting in 1948 have a right of return to the homes from which they were forcibly displaced.[8] It might seem odd to the layman, that a right which many would deem natural or intrinsic to human survival – to be able to leave and go from their place of abode without let or hindrance, or to return to their homes of origin after a conflict has drawn to a close – should have been such a cause of controversy in the twentieth century. Even the Magna Carta of 1215, which remains in force in British law, provides in clause 29 that 'no freeman shall be ... exiled ... but by lawful judgement of his peers, or by the law of the land'. In other words, even in medieval Britain there was no arbitrary right to expel people and prevent them from returning to their homes without due process or by the requirements laid down by law.

Typically, Israeli international lawyers have argued that the Palestinian Arabs displaced from their homes in 1948 do not have such a right whilst Palestinian lawyers, supported by some Western scholars, have argued that they do.[9] The arguments advanced can be complex and they will not be repeated here. It is, however, often overlooked that the Zionist claim to Palestine is based on a 'right of return'. That is, it is based on the argument that Palestine belonged to the Jewish people who were displaced by the Romans some 2,000 years ago (although it should be said that even 2,000 years ago Jews did not only live in Palestine, but in Egypt, Iraq and elsewhere). The Palestinian claim, on the other hand, relates to an event, which only happened 60 years ago, after the creation of the UN and after its General Assembly had proclaimed a 'right of return' in its Universal Declaration of Human Rights.[10] Moreover, the UN General Assembly reaffirms this right annually.[11] In fact, and as will be explained in the following pages, that body established a UN commission that was specifically charged with aiding those Palestinians displaced by the fighting with their claims to return, restitution, compensation and resettlement. Whereas the 17,000 Palestinian Jews displaced by the fighting in 1948 were allowed to return to their homes after the cessation of hostilities, the overwhelming majority of Palestinian Arabs have been prevented from doing so.[12] In other words, it is not the concept of a 'right of return' that Israel is opposed to, but of *who* can return to Israel. According to Israel's Law of Return, only Jews can return to Israel.[13]

POPULATION EXCHANGES

Benny Morris, a Professor of History at Ben-Gurion University, who has done much admirable work to uncover the atrocities that took place at the hands of the Haganah, the Irgun and Lehi in 1948 (see previous chapter), has cited the exchange of populations between Greece and Turkey in the 1920s as a justification for Israel's actions during the course of the 1948 conflict.[14] However, the exchange of populations between Greece and Turkey was regulated by way of treaty whereas in Palestine there was no such agreement between Israel and any other Arab state. On the contrary, what took place was a unilateral act on the part of Israel. The Palestinians were expelled; they were not transferred or exchanged with any other Arab state in exchange for their Jewish populations. Moreover, any exchange of populations between Arabs in Palestine and Jews in Palestinian or in other countries in the Middle East would have been impracticable, as the British Government admitted:

> [E]xchange of populations is rendered impracticable by the fact that there are forty times as many Arabs in Jewish areas as there are Jews in Arab areas. If suggestion were to include the possibility of settling of Arabs in other parts of the Arab world there would be a grave danger of Arab governments adopting policy of expulsion of their Jews as well as minorities.[15]

The British Government was clearly warned about the possibility of an adverse reaction by Arab governments to the expulsion of the Palestinians and indeed their political status in many Arab states was prejudiced as a result. The US Government was also warned. The Prime Minister of Iraq, Nuri as-Said, told the US Ambassador in Baghdad that:

> Expulsion of Iraqi Jews to make room for Arab refugees not policy Iraqi Government would normally adopt as Iraq treats its Jews as Iraqi nationals entitled to same rights as Iraqi Arabs. If pressed too hard, however, firebrand Iraqis might take matter into own hands and cause untold misery to thousands [of] innocent persons.[16]

Although there was upheaval and unrest throughout the Arab world in the aftermath of Israel's creation in 1948, many Jews continued to live in the Arab world after its existence became a *fait accompli*, and some still do, although their numbers are small. For instance, in Lebanon, there remained a thriving Jewish community after 1948.[17] Attempts to persuade them to immigrate to Israel failed. In fact their numbers actually increased, to the lament of the Jewish Agency in Jerusalem.[18] It was only when civil war broke out in Lebanon in 1958 and 1975 that many chose to leave to go to Europe, the US and Latin America.[19] In Yemen, in the years 1948–49, Jews were actually airlifted out *en masse* in operations carried out by the Jewish Agency, funded by American Jews through the United Jewish Appeal at a cost of $3.5 million, and which were collectively referred to as 'Operation Magic Carpet'.[20] Again this was a unilateral act on the part of Israel. There was no agreement to an exchange of populations between Israel and Yemen. Few, if any, Palestinian refugees settled in Yemen. Rather, Israel encouraged Arabs to leave Palestine and Jews from Arab countries to come to Israel to settle in the homes and take possession of the properties of the Palestinian Arabs. In Iraq, it has even been alleged that Israeli agents used violence to engineer an exodus of Iraqi Jews from a country in which they had a long and proud history going back 3,500 years.[21] Similarly, in Egypt, Israeli agents were accused of planting bombs at the Alexandria Post Office, in the US Information Service Library in Cairo, and at Cairo train station during Operation Susannah (known as the 'Lavon Affair').[22] When Britain, France and Israel invaded Egypt in 1956, Nasser's government responded by expelling 13,000 French and British citizens, among them many Jews.[23] In addition, 500 Jews not holding British or French citizenship were expelled, some 400 Jewish businesses were sequestered amongst others owned by foreign nationals, and many of these people lost their jobs.[24] This very sad state of affairs brought to an end Egypt's once vibrant and cosmopolitan cities with their ancient Jewish communities, which predated the Islamic era.

From a legal and historical perspective, it would be difficult to argue that an exchange of populations took place in 1948. Legally, there was no agreement between Israel and the Arab states over an exchange of populations.[25] Moreover, an exchange would have been impracticable because in Palestine there were forty times as many Arabs in Jewish areas as there were Jews in Arab areas. Therefore, an 'exchange' as such, did not take place. The Palestinians were expelled in 1948, whereas the 'immigration' of *Mizrahim* (Oriental Jews) into Israel took place later and over a number of years. Furthermore, those Jews who had the financial means chose not to immigrate to Israel but to move to Europe, North and Latin America where they established new communities.[26]

INTERTEMPORAL LAW

In assessing whether the Palestinians displaced by the fighting in 1948 have a right of return one must take into account the rule of intertemporal law as enunciated by Max Huber in his arbitral award in the *Island of Palmas* case, which was briefly mentioned in Chapter 2. There are two features to this rule:

1) a juridical fact must be appreciated in the light of the law contemporary with it, and not of the law in force at the time such dispute in regard to it arises or falls to be settled.
2) ... a distinction must be made between the creation of rights and the existence of rights. The same principle which subjects the act creative of a right to the law in force at the time the right arises, demands that the existence of the right, in other words its continued manifestation, shall follow the conditions required by the evolution of law.[27]

Therefore, if one views the expulsion of the Palestinian Arabs as an act which came to an end in the late 1940s, the question as to whether they have a right to return to their homes must be assessed in the light of international law as it existed then. However, if one views the expulsions in 1948 in the light of Israel's concomitant and persistent refusal to let them return as an act of a *continuing* character, it is arguable that the applicable law is that at the time the dispute arises to be settled. In this regard the International Law Commission's Articles on Responsibility of States for Internationally Wrongful Acts sheds some further light on the link between time and law in Article 14:

1. The breach of an international obligation by an act of a State not having a continuing character occurs at the moment when the act is performed, even if its effects continue.
2. The breach of an international obligation by an act of a State having a continuing character extends over the entire period during which the act continues and remains not in conformity with the international obligation.
3. The breach of an international obligation requiring a State to prevent a given event occurs when the event occurs and extends over the entire period during which the event continues and remains not in conformity with that obligation.[28]

The first question one must answer in any discussion of Article 14 is whether there existed an international obligation in 1948 not to murder, massacre, rape, pillage, plunder, destroy towns and villages, and expel their inhabitants. If an obligation did exist at this time, then the *Yishuv* and its predecessor the Government of the state of Israel, are under an obligation to allow a refugee return. If, however, no such obligation existed one could argue that the rule of intertemporal law is completely irrelevant. To answer this, it is necessary to examine the law relating to expulsions that had been carried out prior to 1948. Now whilst the League of Nations had sanctioned population exchanges, this, as has already been mentioned, is not the same thing as an expulsion, which is a unilateral act carried out during wartime and which involves an element of coercion such as being removed from one's place of habitual residence at gunpoint or fleeing through fear for one's safety and well-being. As already indicated in the previous chapter, from an analysis of the jurisprudence of the numerous Military Tribunals established after the Second World War in France, Germany, Poland, Japan and elsewhere, such atrocities were always considered contrary to customary international law by the 'civilised' world.

Although certain expulsions had been sanctioned by the Great Powers, such as the Sudetenland Germans at Potsdam, the expulsions of Gypsies, Jews, Poles, and others, had been specifically condemned at the Nuremberg Trials as a war crime. The difference between these two sets of events is that the Great Powers sanctioned the former in Article XIII of the Potsdam Protocol, which provided that it be undertaken 'in an orderly and humane manner', whereas the latter were unilateral actions carried out during the course of an armed conflict.[29] Moreover, in December 1946, the UN General Assembly '*affirm[ed]* the principles of international law recognized by the Charter of the Nürnberg Tribunal and the judgment of the Tribunal' and asked the committee on the codification of international law 'to treat as a matter of primary importance plans for the formulation, in the context of a general codification of offences against the peace and security of mankind, or of an International Criminal Code ...'[30] On the same day, the UN General Assembly passed a separate resolution condemning the crime of genocide.[31] It has been argued that the crime of genocide was a rule of customary international law *before* its codification in the Genocide Convention which entered into force on 12 January 1951.[32] In its advisory opinion on *Reservations to the Genocide Convention*, the International Court of Justice noted that it was the intention of the United Nations to condemn and punish genocide as a crime under international law which involved:

> a denial of the right of existence of human groups, a denial which shocks the conscience of mankind and results in great losses to humanity, and which is contrary to moral law and to the spirit and aims of the United Nations (Resolution 96 (1) of the General Assembly, December 11th 1946). The first consequence arising from this conception is that the principles underlying the Convention are principles which are recognized by civilized nations as binding on States, even without any conventional obligation. A second consequence is the universal character both of the condemnation of genocide and of the co-operation required 'in order to liberate mankind from such an odious scourge.' (Preamble to the Convention).[33]

Although the atrocities committed during the course of the conflict in 1948 did not amount to genocide, they certainly amounted to the kind of war crimes condemned at Nuremberg. Many of the rules of humanitarian law are so fundamental to the respect for the human person that they are considered 'elementary considerations of humanity', as the International Court of Justice noted in the *Corfu Channel Case*.[34] This provides a convincing explanation as to why the Hague Regulations of 1907 and the Geneva Conventions of

1949 have been so widely ratified.[35] Moreover, many of their provisions reflected pre-existing customary international law.[36] These provisions were not intended to be exhaustive and cover every imaginable atrocity that might occur in wartime as the Martens Clause in the Hague Regulations, mentioned in the previous chapter, attests.[37] In this regard it would certainly strike one as odd to argue that whilst acts of genocide were prohibited by customary international law since the Nuremberg Trial of 1946, war crimes, which were equally condemned by that Tribunal, were not.[38]

Furthermore, the lack of agreement between Israel and the Arab states concerned meant that the sovereignty and territorial integrity of the Arab states to where the refugees had fled was violated by Israel.[39] This is in contrast to the situation at Potsdam where there was agreement between the three heads of the government of the Soviet Union, the United States and the United Kingdom over the German expulsions from Czechoslovakia and Poland.[40] In contrast, there was no agreement between Israel and the Arab states over the expulsion of the Palestinians. Consequently, their expulsion violated the sovereignty and territorial integrity of Transjordan, Lebanon, Syria and Egypt, the countries to which most had fled. Moreover, Article 107 of the UN Charter specifically provides that nothing in the UN Charter shall invalidate or preclude action, 'in relation to any state which during the Second World War has been an enemy of any signatory to the present Charter, taken or authorised as a result of that war by the Governments having responsibility for such action'.[41] In other words, so long as the German Government was an enemy state it was precluded from invoking any provisions of the UN Charter that may have been violated as a result of the mass population transfer sanctioned at Potsdam by the Allies in 1945. Palestine was a British Mandate during the Second World War and not an enemy state. Potsdam, therefore, cannot be cited as a precedent retroactively justifying the expulsion of the Palestinians as has been argued.[42] Moreover, their expulsion at the hands of the Zionists was arguably contrary to Articles 1 (2), 2 (3), (4), (6), and 73 of the UN Charter, the last providing that UN members which had assumed responsibilities for the administration of territories whose peoples had not yet attained a measure of self-government, which included League of Nations mandates, were to 'recognise the principle that the interests of the inhabitants of these territories are paramount, and accept as a sacred trust the obligation to promote to the utmost, within the system of international peace and security established by the present Charter, the well-being of the inhabitants of these territories'.[43] Article 73 (a) added that, to this end, the colonial power was 'to ensure, with due respect for the culture of the people concerned, their political, economic, social, and educational advancement, their just treatment, and their protection against abuses'. By sitting on the sidelines and not doing more to prevent acts of violence against the Palestinian Arabs at the hands of the Haganah, the Irgun and Lehi, in the months before it relinquished the Mandate in May 1948, it could be argued that Britain breached Article 73 of the UN Charter to which it was bound to by international law. The Palestinian Arab's 'well-being', 'just treatment' and 'protection against abuses' were certainly not advanced by the numerous atrocities inflicted on them as described in the previous chapter. In this regard it is telling that rather than sanction the expulsion of the Palestinian Arabs, the Great Powers acting through the aegis of the UN, called for a comprehensive solution, which involved return, repatriation and resettlement.[44] As an account of the diplomatic negotiations at the Lausanne Conference in 1949 will show, the Great Powers favoured a refugee return to Israel and did not sanction their expulsion. The US Government even threatened to withhold $49 million of unallocated funds from a $100 million Export-Import Bank loan to Israel if it did not comply with the UN General Assembly's request to allow the Palestinian refugees to return to their homes.[45]

If one were to conclude that there was an obligation in 1948 not to harm civilians and expel them *en masse* from their place of habitual residence, the next question which must be considered is whether the act of expulsion was a one-off event which began and ended in 1948 or whether it was an act of a continuing character. It could of course be argued that the expulsions came to an end when the civilians crossed into the borders of the surrounding Arab states. But this would only be so if they were then allowed to return after the end of the hostilities. If, however, they are prevented from returning then the expulsion is effectively continuing. In other words, if X is expelled from state Y and then allowed to return to state Y in year 1000, then the law that applies is the law as it existed then. But if X is expelled from state Y and then prevented from returning to state Y then the law that would be applicable would be that at the time the dispute arises to be settled. This would of course depend on when the dispute was actually settled. According to the commentary to the International Law Commission's articles on state responsibility, international tribunals have interpreted forced or involuntary disappearances and 'creeping' or disguised occupations as continuing wrongful acts.[46] Accordingly, there is a continuing responsibility incumbent on Israel for legislation passed by its Knesset (Parliament) which prohibits a refugee return, confiscates refugee property, or arbitrarily denationalises them by stripping Palestinians of the citizenship they had in Palestine during the mandatory years, if this is still in force, which happens to be the case.[47] In the Progress Report on Palestine which the UN mediator Count Folke Bernadotte presented to the UN General Assembly in September 1948, he specifically concluded:

> The Arab inhabitants of Palestine are not citizens or subjects of Egypt, Iraq, Lebanon, Syria and Transjordan, the States which are at present providing them with a refuge and the basic necessities of life. As residents of Palestine, a former mandated territory for which the international community has a *continuing responsibility* until a final settlement is achieved, these Arab refugees understandably look to the United Nations for effective assistance.[48]

If the UN has a continuing responsibility towards the refugees until a final settlement is achieved, then surely so does that state of Israel which caused their flight. Therefore, if the second interpretation of intertemporal law is adopted in the case of the Palestinian refugees, then one would have to consider the law as it developed from 1948 to the date when the dispute came to be settled which may be in a court of law or in Final Status Negotiations.[49] In this regard it is noteworthy that the drafting of UN General Assembly resolution 194 (III) coincided with the drafting of the Universal Declaration of Human Rights.[50] In fact, the fighting in Palestine interrupted several meetings of the drafting committee.[51] Dr Charles Malik, a Professor of Philosophy from the Lebanon who taught at Harvard as well as at the American University of Beirut, was chairing the meetings at the Palais de Chaillot in Paris. It was the Lebanese representative, Mr Karim Azkoul, who proposed that if a person had the right to leave any country, including his own, he should also be able to return to it.[52] In his opinion the right to leave a country would be strengthened by the assurance of the right to return.[53] This was a sentiment that the delegates from Belgium, Chile, Greece, India, the Philippines and the US concurred with.[54] The delegate from Chile said that the 'freedom of movement was the sacred right of every human being' and the delegate from Greece described the Lebanese amendment as 'logical'.[55] As a result the final draft on the freedom of movement as it would appear in Article 13 included the additional words, 'and to return to his country', which found their way into the Universal Declaration of Human Rights without a dissenting vote.[56]

Article 13

(1) Everyone has the right to freedom of movement and residence within the borders of each state.
(2) Everyone has the right to leave any country, including his own, and to return to his country.

It is significant that since the Universal Declaration of Human Rights was adopted by the UN General Assembly in December 1948, the right of return has been included in all the major human rights treaties such as the International Covenant on Civil and Political Rights[57] and the International Convention on the Elimination of All Forms of Racial Discrimination[58] which have both been ratified by Israel's Knesset.[59] Therefore, if one views Israel's expulsion of the Palestinian Arabs as giving rise to a continuing obligation then international human rights law as it developed in the aftermath of the Second World War would have to be taken into consideration. In other words, the human rights covenants of 1966, which have been ratified by Israel, would come into play, as would customary international law as it developed from 1948 onwards. Scholars who have adopted this approach have reached the conclusion that in such a situation Israel would be obliged to provide for a refugee return as well as offer restitution and compensation.[60]

UN GENERAL ASSEMBLY RESOLUTION 194 (III)

However, for the sake of argument, it will be assumed that it is the restrictive interpretation of intertemporal law that applies. In other words, the law as it existed in 1948. And yet, even according to this restrictive view, there is a body of law and practice *specific* to the Palestine issue that would support their claim to return, restitution and compensation. In contrast to the Sudetenland Germans, whose expulsion was specifically sanctioned by the Great Powers at Potsdam in 1945, in the case of the Palestinians, those same powers, particularly the US and Britain, supported them in their quest to return to their homes. Moreover, in the Progress Report on Palestine, the UN Mediator explicitly *affirmed* that the Palestinian Arabs displaced by the fighting had a right of return. He was also of the opinion that no settlement would be just or complete if recognition was not accorded to the right of the Arab refugees to return to their homes from which they were displaced in 1948:

> ... notwithstanding the views expressed by the Provisional Government of Israel, it was my firm view that the right of the refugees to return to their homes at the earliest practicable date should be *affirmed* ... no settlement can be just and complete if recognition is not accorded to the right of the Arab refugee to return to the home from which he has been dislodged by the hazards and strategy of the armed conflict between Arabs and Jews in Palestine. The majority of these refugees have come from territory which, under the Assembly resolution of 29 November, was to be included in the Jewish State. The exodus of Palestinian Arabs resulted from panic created by fighting in their communities, by rumours concerning real or alleged acts of terrorism, or expulsion. It would be an offence against the principles of elemental justice if these innocent victims of the conflict were denied the right to return to their homes while Jewish immigrants flow into Palestine, and, indeed, at least offer the threat of permanent replacement of the Arab refugees who have been rooted in the land for centuries.[61]

It is worth bearing in mind that before Bernadotte presented his report to the UN General Assembly in September 1948, he had visited the refugee camps in Palestine and had seen for himself the appalling conditions there. The correspondent for the *Observer* newspaper vividly described the situation in August 1948 in the following words:

> I have to-day visited a refugee camp at Ramallah. Lying listlessly on the dusty ground, sheltered from the blazing sun by scraps of canvas and other materials stretched between olive trees, were hundreds of men, women and children whose emaciated faces and filthy, tattered clothing bore evidence of what they have experienced.
>
> A few of the more fortunate had managed to find tattered tents – discarded probably by British troops – but most of them have no more shelter than a strip of canvas to keep off the sun; during the nights, which are still cool and refreshing, they sleep under the stars. A short distance from the camp is a small stream, from which they get little water. Ramallah refugee committee provides a little bread, which, apart from anything the refugees may be able to beg, seemed to be their entire and only sustenance. The children

> were grubbing in the earth trying to find edible roots, but most of these have long since disappeared. Women are giving birth to babies in ditches by the roadside and abandoning their newly born children. There are no possible means of rearing them. Milk or anything remotely approaching baby food is scarcer than rain, which will not fall again until December.[62]

The UN responded to the refugee crisis by adopting the recommendations of Bernadotte in his last Progress Report, which was submitted the day before his assassination. In that report, Bernadotte listed as one of his seven basic premises for resolving the conflict the following principle:

> (e) The right of innocent people, uprooted from their homes by the present terror and ravages of war, to return to their homes, should be affirmed and made effective, with assurance of adequate compensation for the property of those who may choose not to return.[63]

In his specific conclusions he recommended:

> (i) The right of the Arab refugees to return to their homes in Jewish-controlled territory at the earliest possible date should be affirmed by the United Nations, and their repatriation, resettlement and economic and social rehabilitation, and payment of adequate compensation for the property of those choosing not to return, should be supervised and assisted by the United Nations conciliation commission described in paragraph (k) below.
> ...
> (k) In view of the special nature of the Palestine problem and the dangerous complexities of Arab–Jewish relationships, the United Nations should establish a Palestine conciliation commission. This commission, which should be appointed for a limited period, should be responsible to the United Nations and act under its authority ...[64]

In December 1948, the UN General Assembly in resolution 194 (III), heeding Bernadotte's advice, proposed in paragraph 11:

> ... that the refugees wishing to return to their homes and live at peace with their neighbours should be permitted to do so at the earliest practicable date, and that compensation should be paid for the property of those choosing not to return and for loss of or damage to property which, under principles of international law or in equity, should be made good by the Governments or authorities responsible'.
>
> *Instructs* the Conciliation Commission to facilitate the repatriation, resettlement and economic and social rehabilitation of the refugees and the payment of compensation, and to maintain close relations with the Director of the United Nations Relief for Palestine Refugees and, through him, with the appropriate organs and agencies of the United Nations.[65]

Paragraph 2 of UN General Assembly 194 (II) established a three-member UN Conciliation Commission for Palestine (UNCCP), composed of representatives from Turkey, France, and the United States to facilitate the return of the refugees.[66]

As is clear from the final text of paragraph 11 of the General Assembly resolution, changes were made to Bernadotte's original formulation on the floor of the UN General Assembly where the right of return was debated. Palestinian refugees wishing to return to their homes would have to be prepared 'to live at peace with their neighbours', and were to return to their homes 'at the earliest practicable date', rather than at 'the earliest possible date'. In this regard it has been suggested that there were cogent reasons for including these phrases and that the words 'live at peace' were probably drafted in anticipation that some of the refugees were not prepared to live under Israeli sovereignty.[67] These people could therefore remain abroad. However, *a contrario*, no obstacle was to be placed in the way of those refugees who were willing to live at peace with Israel from returning to their homes. As regards the date of implementation, it has been noted that the final draft of the French text of paragraph 11 uses the language '*le plus tôt possible*', as soon as possible, as it did in the original British text, which implies that repatriation should be accomplished as soon as it could be done.[68] In this regard, it has been suggested that the UN General Assembly changed the phraseology to 'at the earliest practicable date' because they contemplated that return would be effectuated by diplomatic means through the UN Conciliation Commission and that the logistics of a return would require a period of time to organise.[69] On the question of compensation, a background paper prepared by the UNCCP concluded that UN General Assembly resolution 194 (III) covered compensation for both returning and non-returning refugees.[70] In other words, it was envisaged that compensation was to be paid both for the property left behind by refugees who do not return to live in their homes as well as to repatriated refugees whose property had been looted or otherwise destroyed without military necessity during the course of the conflict.[71]

In brief, the Commission asked Israel to implement the General Assembly's call for the repatriation of displaced Palestinians.[72] Israel, however, only admitted 8,000 Palestinians on the basis of reuniting divided families, which fell well short of the number of people actually displaced by the fighting, which was estimated to be over 750,000 refugees.[73] Israel did not, however, raise any difficulties in repatriating 17,000 displaced Jews. Thus, Israel's return policy, on the face of things, seemed to be inherently discriminatory: only Jews could return to Israel, but not its indigenous inhabitants who had inhabited that land for centuries. However, at the Lausanne Conference in 1949, Israel did agree, under US pressure, to the repatriation of a limited number of refugees, before subsequently reneging on it. This set of events will be addressed in the following pages.

NATIONALITY AND STATE SUCCESSION

Before turning to the negotiations at Lausanne, a brief mention should be made about the law of nationality upon state succession, and more pertinently, what happened after Israel's creation in 1948 to the nationality of those persons habitually resident in Palestine and who had Palestinian citizenship during the British Mandate.[74] Whilst the law of state succession has not been without controversy, particularly during and after decolonisation, the state practice of the relevant period indicated that persons habitually resident in a territory undergoing succession *ipso facto* acquired the nationality of the successor state.[75] In other words, nationality followed the change of sovereignty so that those persons habitually resident in a territory that became a new state or part of a new state would automatically acquire the nationality of that state. The Treaty of Neuilly (1919), the Rumanian Minorities Treaty (1919), the Treaty of Versailles (1919), the Treaty of St Germain (1919), the Treaty of Trianon (1920), the Treaty of Sèvres (1920), and the Treaty of Lausanne (1923), all support this view, as do the classical authors of international law.[76] In view of this uniformity of practice and the importance of the treaties concerned, it has been suggested that the precedent value of these treaties is considerable.[77] Moreover, an attempt to codify the law of nationality in 1929, for the purposes of international law, concluded that nationality followed the change of sovereignty, unless the persons concerned declined the nationality of the successor state.[78] In other words, it was up to the individuals concerned to decline the nationality of the successor state and not for the successor state to arbitrarily revoke their nationality so as to render them stateless.[79] That nationality followed the change of sovereignty accorded to state practice in the first half of the twentieth century, is further supported by an early decision of the Tel Aviv District Court:

> It seems to me ... that the point of view according to which there are no Israeli nationals, is not compatible with public international law. The prevailing view is that, in the case of transfer of a portion of the territory of a State to another State, every individual and inhabitant of the ceding State becomes automatically a national of the receiving State (see Oppenheim, *International Law*, vol. 1, § 219, and particularly notes 3 and 4 on page 503 of the 7th edition). The same opinion is expressed in Schwarzenberger, *International Law*, 2nd edition, vol. 1, page 166. Lauterpacht also states the same rule in a case of subjugation, *loc cit.*, page 522, particularly footnote 6. If that is the case, is it possible to say that the inhabitants of part of a State which is transformed into an independent State are not *ipso facto* transformed into nationals of that State? So long as no law has been enacted providing otherwise, my view is that every individual who, on the date of the establishment of the State of Israel was resident in the territory which today constitutes the State of Israel, is also a national of Israel.[80]

In other words, the learned judge reached the conclusion that those citizens of the British Mandate of Palestine living in the territory that became the state of Israel in 1948, should have become nationals of Israel, irrespective of their religion or ethnicity. Therefore, the Palestinian Arabs displaced by the fighting in 1948 who had been habitually resident in the towns and cities conquered by the Haganah, the Irgun and Lehi, should have become nationals of Israel after its declaration of statehood and its assertion of Jewish sovereignty over the subjugated areas that comprised their former homes. If this position is correct, then Israel would surely be required to repatriate its own nationals and not only those persons of the Jewish faith as in fact happened? However, instead of doing this, in 1952 Israel enacted a Nationality Law which arbitrarily and retrospectively denationalised all those Palestinian Arabs outside of its borders whose exodus the *Yishuv* had engineered.[81]

Lauterpacht, writing in 1948, noted that the discretion which a state enjoys in matters of nationality 'is subject to general principles of law, to legitimate rights of other states, and to those rights of human personality which international law was increasingly recognizing even before the Charter of the United Nations gave recognition to fundamental human rights and freedoms'.[82] By denationalising the 750,000 Palestinian Arabs who had fled or been expelled from their homes in 1948, Israel undoubtedly infringed upon their human rights. Although the Nationality Law was a domestic law of Israel and therefore could not have extraterritorial application *per se*, its effect was to also denationalise all those persons who fell under Israel's jurisdiction, which included those Palestinian refugees inhabiting East Jerusalem, the West Bank and the Gaza Strip after it was conquered in the June 1967 Six-Day War. Those Palestinians who did not acquire the nationality of a third state such as Jordan have also remained stateless, because there has been, to date, no Palestinian state that could grant them its nationality. And statelessness is a most unpleasant phenomenon because stateless persons have no voting rights, are excluded from many types of professions, are occasionally liable to deportation, and have a difficult time travelling abroad due to the fact that states usually issue passports only to their own nationals. They also have no state to turn to when faced with hardships in foreign countries because this is usually facilitated by means of diplomatic protection, which a state can usually only exercise in respect of its nationals.[83]

THE LAUSANNE CONFERENCE OF 1949

In much of the legal literature, the debate on the right of return and the diplomatic struggle that took place in Lausanne in 1949 between the US, Israel, and the Arab states concerned has been almost completely overlooked. This is lamentable, as those debates provide an interesting insight into the approaches adopted by the Great Powers to resolve the Palestinian refugee question. The Lausanne Conference officially opened on 27 April 1949.[84] A month prior to this, the Archbishop of York told the House of Commons that:

> They [the Palestinian Arab refugees] have been driven out of the land they have occupied for nearly a thousand years and are asking when are they going back to their homes. In many cases their homes have been taken over by the State of Israel and given to Jewish immigrants or have been destroyed or looted. It would be breaking every law of justice if the United Nations accepted the position that these people must be permanently expelled from their homes.[85]

But the UN did not accept the position that the Palestinian Arabs should be permanently expelled from their homes and nor for that matter did the US Government. On 13 April, during the negotiations in Lausanne, Mark F. Ethridge, the US delegate on the UNCCP sent a secret memorandum to the US Secretary of State reporting on his talks with Comay, the second man at Israel's Foreign Office in Sharett's absence (Moshe Sharett was then the Foreign Minister of Israel). In the memorandum Ethridge pointed out to Comay that 'since Israel had once accepted [a] state with 400,000 Arabs in it she should be prepared to take back at least 250,000 refugees and compensate others'.[86] At the time, there were 150,000 Arabs remaining in Israel. Ethridge was making the point that if Israel had really been sincere about accepting the 1947 UN Partition Plan with its population of 400,000 Arabs, then it should not have a problem with repatriating at least 250,000 of those Arabs which had been displaced during the war. However, Comay responded by telling Ethridge that his suggestion was 'completely impossible'.[87] This prompted Ethridge to comment in his memo to US Secretary of State, Dean Acheson:

> Israel does not intend to take back one refugee more than she is forced to take and she does not intend to compensate any directly if she can avoid it. Ben-Gurion and Comay have both argued that refugees are inevitable result of war and no state in modern history has been expected to repatriate them. Both cite Baltic states and Turkey. They contend also that number greatly exaggerated and they can prove it. Israel refuses to accept any responsibility whatever for creation of refugees. I flatly told Ben-Gurion and Comay that while Commission was not tribunal to judge truth of contentions, I could not for moment accept that statement in face of Jaffa, Deir Yassin, Haifa and all reports that come to us from refugee organizations that new refugees are being created every day by repression and terrorism such as now being reported from Haifa. I have repeatedly pointed out political weakness and brutality of their position on refugees but it has made little impression.[88]

As regards the Gaza Strip, Ethridge commented:

> Israel's position as to Gaza Strip is, I believe, that she does not want it with 330,000 Arabs in it, 230,000 of them refugees, particularly since she has back country upon which they have been living. She is probably content at the moment to let it wither.[89]

A month later, on 12 May 1949, the US Government through the UN Conciliation Commission induced Israel to sign a Protocol with the Arab states. An Israeli appeal to the UN to be accepted as a full member was due to be voted upon in the General Assembly on the day before, and its acceptance by the UN depended to a large extent on the American position.[90] It would have been the worst time for Israel to refuse an American demand.[91] With this in mind, Walter Eytan, the Director of Israel's Foreign Ministry, convinced his government to accept the 12 May Protocol, which provided:

> 'The UN PCC anxious achieve quickly possible objectives GA resolution 11, December 1948 re refugees, respect for their rights and preservation of their property, as well as territorial and other questions, has proposed to Israeli delegation and Arab States delegation that working document attached hereto be taken as basis for talks with Commission.
>
> The interested delegations have accepted proposal with understanding that exchanges of views which be carried on by Commission with two parties will bear upon territorial adjustments necessary to above indicated objectives.'[92]

The Protocol included a map of the 1947 UN Partition Plan although it was not labelled 'plan of partition'. The Israeli delegation signed the document with reservations that:

(1) Israeli delegation could not be party to any exchange of views with Syrian delegation until armistice agreement was concluded;
(2) No communication re protocol was made to press and;
(3) Signing in no way prejudiced right of Israeli delegation to express itself freely on matters at issue on which it fully reserved its position.[93]

The position of the Israeli Government was that the Protocol did not bind them to commit to anything other than to talk to the Arab states concerned, although this view did not go uncontested, particular by the US Government.[94] Moreover, it is clear from the Israeli archives that their Foreign Ministry was pushing for the Palestinian Arab refugees to be resettled in the Arab states rather than be returned to Israel.[95] In a letter to Mr de Boisanger, the French chairman of the UNCCP, Walter Eytan wrote:

> There can be no return to the *status quo ante*, as I have been at pains to demonstrate, since the destruction wrought by war and the changes brought about by immigration have decisively and unalterably transformed the whole aspect of the country. The clock cannot be turned back ... If an Arab refugee counts upon living again in the house he abandoned, or plying his trade in the workshop he formerly rented, or tilling the fields in the vicinity of the village he once knew, he is living under an illusion which it seems to me essential to dispel.[96]

On 29 May, Ben-Gurion received a letter from James G. McDonald, the first US Ambassador to Israel, by which the US President informed the Government of Israel that it was 'seriously disturbed by the attitude of Israel with respect to a territorial settlement in Palestine and to the question of Palestine refugees'.[97] The letter continued:

> As a member of the U.N. Palestine Conciliation Commission and as a nation which has consistently striven to give practical effect to the principles of the U.N., the United States Government has recently made a number of representations to the Israeli Government, concerning the repatriation of refugees who fled from conflict in Palestine. These representations were made in conformity with the principles set forth in the resolution of the General Assembly of December 11th, 1948, and urged the acceptance of the principle of substantial repatriation and the immediate beginnings of repatriation on a reasonable scale which would be well within the numbers to be agreed in a final settlement.[98]

The letter reiterated that the Israeli Government 'should entertain no doubt whatever' that the US Government expected it 'to take responsible and positive action concerning the Palestine Refugees'.[99] It then concluded:

> If the Government of Israel continues to reject the basic principles set forth by the resolution of the General Assembly of December 11, 1948 and the friendly advice offered by the United States Government for the sole purpose of facilitating a genuine peace in Palestine, the United States Government will regretfully be forced to the conclusion that a revision of its attitude toward Israel has become unavoidable.[100]

In response to this letter, Foreign Minister Sharett wrote a stern reply, verging on a rebuke, to McDonald, in which Israel disclaimed any responsibility for creating the Palestine refugee problem.[101] He also rejected any idea of territorial compensation for land the Haganah/Israeli Army had acquired beyond the boundaries established by the UN Partition Plan.[102] An elderly Chaim Weizmann, who by 1948 had been elevated to the position of President of Israel, also joined in the fray, writing a personal letter to President Truman in which he claimed that the Palestinian refugees were 'part of an aggressor group'. Despite all the evidence to the contrary, he wrote: 'It was not the birth of Israel which created the Arab refugee problem, as our enemies now proclaim, but the Arab attempt to prevent that birth by armed force. These people are not refugees in the sense in which that term has been sanctified by the martyrdom of millions in Europe'.[103] The US Government did not, however, accept Israel's view of its role in the 1948 conflict. Instead it issued Israel the following aide-mémoire:

> The United States Government regards the solution of the refugee problem as a common responsibility of Israel and the Arab States, which neither side should be permitted to shirk. It is for this reason that it has urged Israel to accept the principle of substantial repatriation and to begin immediate repatriation on a reasonable scale, and has urged the Arab States to accept the principle of substantial resettlement of refugees outside Palestine.[104]

The US Government envisaged a solution to the refugee problem, which involved both repatriation and resettlement as provided for in UN General Assembly resolution 194 (III). This show of strength from the US Government induced the Israelis to discuss figures for a potential refugee return between themselves. In July, Sharett sent a telegram to Aubrey Eban, Israel's UN Ambassador in New York, in which he said that he had been authorised 'to admit total 100,000 on peace', which included 25,000 refugees they claimed had already 'infiltrated' back into Israel.[105] In other words, they envisaged a net refugee return of 75,000 people.[106] However, Dean Acheson, the US Secretary of State did not think the Israeli offer of 100,000 met the provisions of paragraph 11 of UN General Assembly resolution 194 (III).[107] On 13 August, Truman replied to Weizmann:

> With regard to the general question of the Arab refugees, you may recall that the General assembly resolution of December 11 provided that the refugees wishing to return to their homes and live at peace with their neighbours should be permitted to do so at the earliest practicable date, and that compensation should be paid for the property of those choosing not to return. I am, therefore, glad to be reassured by your letter that Israel is ready to cooperate with the United Nations and the Arab states for a solution of the refugee problem; that Israel pledges itself to guarantee the civil rights of all minorities; that Israel accepts the principles of compensation for land abandoned by Arabs; that Israel declares its readiness to unfreeze Arab accounts under certain conditions; that Israel has set up a custodian of absentee property; and that Israel is ready to readmit members of Arab families.[108]

Truman added that he 'would be less than frank' if he did not tell Weizmann that he was 'disappointed' when he read the reply of the Israeli Government written by its Foreign Minister Sharett.[109] He wrote that he thought the views of the Israeli Government 'are in many respects at variance with the General Assembly resolution of December 11' and failed 'to take into account the principles regarding territorial compensation advanced by the United States as indicated in our Aide-Mémoire of June 24'.[110] (See Chapter 9)

On 15 August, the UNCCP sent the Israeli Government a memorandum which they were asked to sign.[111] It provided in part:

> CHAPTER I
>
> Refugees
>
> Is the Delegation of ... prepared to sign a declaration according to which:
> 1. The solution of the refugee problem should be sought in the repatriation of refugees in Israeli-controlled territory and in the re-settlement of those not repatriated, in Arab countries or in the zone of Palestine not under Israeli control?
>
> It is understood that the repatriated refugees will become *ipso facto* citizens of Israel and that no discrimination will be practised against them both with regard to the civil and the political rights which they will exercise and to the obligations imposed upon them by the law of the land.
>
> It is also understood that repatriation in Israel as well as re-settlement in the Arab countries or in the zone of Palestine not under Israeli control, will take place subject to technical and financial aid given to each party by the international community ...[112]

On 31 August, Mr R. Shiloah, the Head of the Israeli Delegation at Lausanne sent a reply to Mr Boisanger, the chairman of the UNCCP, in reply to the memorandum they were asked to sign.[113] It included the following substantive provisions:

> (1) The Delegation of Israel is prepared to sign a declaration along the general lines suggested in Chapter I of the Commission's memorandum, subject to precision on the following specific points:
> (a) The Government of Israel considers that the solution of the refugee problem is to be sought primarily in the resettlement of the refugees in Arab territories, but it is prepared for its part, as already indicated to the Commission, to make its own contribution by agreeing to a measure of resettlement in Israel.
> (b) While the Government of Israel cannot bind itself in advance to the implementation of such a solution as the survey group may propose, it will undertake to facilitate the task of this group and to give full consideration to any proposals the group may put forward.
>
> (2) The Delegation of Israel wishes to offer certain further comments on Chapter I of the Commission's memorandum, in order to make its attitude perfectly clear:
> (a) The Delegation of Israel has taken note of the proviso that 'it is understood that the repatriated refugees will become ipso facto citizens of Israel and that no discrimination will be practised against them both with regard to the civil and political rights which they will exercise and to the obligations imposed upon them by the law of the land'. The Delegation is astonished, however, that there is no

mention of any similar understanding with regard to the refugees to be resettled elsewhere.

(b) The Delegation of Israel desires to stress its understanding that any repatriation in Israel, as indicated by the Commission, would take place subject to financial assistance furnished by the international community and that such assistance would be extended to include the resettlement of Jewish refugees from the Arab-controlled areas of Palestine.

(c) The Delegation of Israel already presented to the Commission a provisional estimate of the number of refugees which the Government of Israel would be ready to accept. It is desired, in this connection, to point out that the Government of Israel's willingness to facilitate the task of the survey group rests within the framework of the contribution which it had declared itself ready to make to the solution of the refugee problem.

(d) The Delegation of Israel desires to take this opportunity of reiterating its earlier statement to the Commission, that the Government of Israel can agree to the repatriation of refugees to Israel only as part of an overall settlement of the refugee problem and of the Palestine conflict.[114]

As already indicated, Israel agreed to a refugee return of approximately 100,000 persons, that is, 75,000 net, as long as their repatriation was funded by the 'international community', by which they presumably meant the US and Europe. However, they made this conditional upon it being part of an overall settlement of the refugee problem and of the Palestine conflict. In September, Boisanger, chairman of the UNCCP, sent a letter to the Israeli Government announcing a recess of the Commission's meetings. Enclosed with this letter was a declaration, which Israel was requested to sign. It provided in part:

1. The solution of the refugee problem should be sought in the repatriation of refugees in Israeli-controlled territory and in the resettlement of those refugees not repatriated in such areas of Palestine as may be under Arab control, or in Arab countries.
2. The Delegations of Syria, Lebanon, Egypt, and the Hashemite Jordan Kingdom, and the Delegation of Israel, consider that their respective countries are not in a position to carry out repatriation and resettlement on a large scale without technical and financial assistance from the international community.
3. The Delegations of Syria, and the Hashemite Jordan Kingdom are in a position to state that their Governments, in conjunction with the recommendations of the Economic Survey Group of the Conciliation Commission and provided that international technical and financial assistance are made available, are able to receive those refugees who may not be repatriated in Israeli-controlled territory or resettled in such areas of Palestine as may be under Arab control. Because of population

pressures and for geographic reasons, it would be difficult for Egypt and Lebanon to receive sizeable numbers of refugees, but the Governments of Egypt and Lebanon are prepared to give careful study to the question in light of the findings of the Economic Survey Group.

4. The refugees who are repatriated in Israeli-controlled territory or resettled in Arab States will become *ipso facto* citizens of Israel or of the Arab States concerned, and no discrimination will be practised against them both with regard to the civil and political rights which they will exercise and to the obligations imposed upon them by the law of the land.[115]

The last paragraph of this declaration on the question of citizenship provides further support for the view that persons habitually resident in a territory undergoing territorial change acquire the nationality of the successor state *ipso facto*. In other words, the very change of sovereignty was supposed to result in persons habitually resident in the territory concerned acquiring the new state's nationality. However, in this particular instance, the Arab states were also expected to grant their nationality to Palestinian refugees who had fled from Israeli-controlled territory to their countries. However, there was a trade off. If Israel did not allow for a substantial repatriation then the Arab states could not be expected to grant the refugees their nationality. Otherwise, it would be to confer a benefit on Israel through its unlawful conduct violating the principle *ex injuria non oritur jus*, which provides that a right should not arise from a wrong.

In reply to Israel's note of 31 August in which it replied to the UNCCP's questionnaire, the Conciliation Commission noted that Israel's insistence that the solution to the refugee problem was chiefly resettlement of the refugees in Arab territories, was 'not in conformity with the terms of paragraph 11 of the General Assembly's resolution of 11 December 1948'.[116] On 27 October, Eban, Israel's UN Ambassador sent a letter to Mr Yalçin, the Turkish member of the UNCCP, in which he wrote:

> The Government of Israel, in the fulfilment of its duty to preserve the security, welfare and, indeed, the very existence of the State, must retain full responsibility for deciding at which point the return of refugees would prejudice the prospect of Arabs and Jews living in peace with each other, and at which point such return would raise insurmountable practical difficulties at any time. It may be added that recent developments in the Middle East have aggravated our fear that any measure of Arab repatriation is liable to prove gravely prejudicial to Israel's security.[117]

Israel seemed to be relenting on its offer to resettle 100,000 Arabs, which the UNCCP thought was unacceptable in any event, as they wanted Israel to readmit 250,000. On 15 November, in his reply to Eban, Yalçin wrote:

> ... in the light of the statement made in your letter that 'recent developments in the Middle East have aggravated our fear that any measure of Arab

> repatriation is liable to prove gravely prejudicial to Israel's security' it is not clear that the Government of Israel is still prepared to accept within its borders a total Arab population of 250,000, in accordance with its offer made to the Commission in Lausanne. The Commission assumes that the terms of this offer remain unchanged.
>
> On the general question of the right of refugees to return, the Commission would again point out that the Israeli position does not conform to the terms of paragraph 11 of the resolution of 11 December 1948 which was passed by the General Assembly after listening to the several interested parties.[118]

Talks between the Arab states and Israel broke down as Israel refused to relent from its position of barring a refugee return.[119] As mentioned already, the US State Department threatened Israel with financial sanctions, but they were forced to back down, due to possible opposition from Congress where continued funding for the Economic Survey Mission was being made dependent on the progress of peace talks at Lausanne.[120] It may, however, be questioned whether Israel's uncompromising position at the Lausanne talks did itself any good as it could have ended the conflict then and there had it been more willing to compromise. The US delegate at Lausanne was certainly upset:

> If there is to be any assessment of blame for stalemate at Lausanne, Israel must accept primary responsibility ... Israel's refusal to abide by the GA assembly resolution, providing those refugees who desire to return to their homes, etc., has been the primary factor in the stalemate. Israel has failed even to stipulate under what conditions refugees wishing to return might return; she has given no definition of what she regards as peaceful co-existence of Arabs and Jews in Israel and she consistently returns to the idea that her security would be endangered; that she cannot bear the economic burden and that she has no responsibility for refugees because of Arab attacks upon her. I have never accepted the latter viewpoint. Aside from her general responsibility for those who have been driven out by terrorism, repression and forcible rejection.[121]

He continued:

> Israel was a state created upon an ethical concept and should rest upon an ethical base. Her attitude toward refugees is morally reprehensible and politically short-sighted. She has no security that does not rest in friendliness with her neighbours. She has no security that does not rest upon the basis of peace in the Middle East. Her position as conqueror demanding more does not make for peace. It makes for more trouble.[122]

In his memoirs, UN mediator Bernadotte recorded his recollections of a meeting he had in August 1948 with Moshe Sharett (in Hebrew, Shertok), the Provisional Government of Israel's Minister of Foreign Affairs, in which he told him that he could not understand why the Zionists were so hostile to the UN and to the Palestinian Arab refugees. His account of the meeting, when he tried to persuade Sharett to ask his government to review its policies, which he dictated to his secretary, Miss Barbro Wessel, and which were published posthumously in Sweden were as follows:

> In the first place [the Provisional Government of Israel] must surely realise that there could be no longer any doubt as to the continued existence of the Jewish state in Palestine. In the second, it must also recognise that what mattered most for the Jews was to increase their good-will in the world at large, and that they ought to set themselves forthwith to counteract the prevailing hatred between Arabs and Jews – whatever happened, the Jews must always reckon to have Arabs for their neighbours. To take one example: the Israeli Government had had a very great opportunity in connection with the Arab refugee question. It had missed that opportunity. It had shown nothing but hardness and obduracy towards those refugees. If instead of that it had shown a magnanimous spirit, if it had declared that the Jewish people, which itself had suffered so much, understood the feelings of the refugees and did not wish to treat them in the same way as it itself had been treated, its prestige in the world at large would have been immeasurably increased.[123]

Alas, Bernadotte's advice was ignored. The refugees were prevented from returning to their homes and the UN Mediator was assassinated by a Lehi hit squad allegedly dispatched on the orders of Yitzhak Shamir,[124] who was elected Israel's Prime Minister in 1983. As is clear from the records of the negotiations in Israel's own archives, some of which have been reproduced in the text above, the Jordanians and the Syrians were prepared to resettle a substantial number of Palestinian refugees in their territories in the interests of peace. However, they also desired a refugee return, especially for those Palestinians who had families remaining in the territories conquered by the Haganah, the Irgun and Lehi in 1948.

9
The Creation of Israel

THE STATE OF ISRAEL ... will foster the development of the country for the benefit of all its inhabitants; it will be based on freedom, justice and peace as envisaged by the prophets of Israel; it will ensure complete equality of social and political rights to all its inhabitants irrespective of religion, race or sex; it will guarantee freedom of religion, conscience, language, education and culture; it will safeguard the Holy Places of all religions; and it will be faithful to the principles of the Charter of the United Nations.

THE STATE OF ISRAEL is prepared to cooperate with the agencies and representatives of the United Nations in implementing the resolution of the General Assembly of the 29th November, 1947, and will take steps to bring about the economic union of the whole of Eretz-Israel.

The Declaration of the Establishment of the State of Israel, 14 May 1948

An eminent international lawyer has described the creation of the first Jewish state to be established in 'the land of Israel' in over two millennia as an act of 'secessionary independence'.[1] This is a novel term to describe what other lawyers might simply call a *fait accompli*, a question of fact that had as much to do with Great Power politics as with international law.[2] However one seeks to describe it, the fact is that Israel emerged as a state from the throes of battle rather than from any legal entitlement bestowed upon it by the UN. As the veteran Israeli international lawyer, Yoram Dinstein wrote: 'Israel became a State when the Jewish nation managed to hold on to a territory in Palestine, ruled by its own independent Government. The scales of statehood were tipped by a sword.'[3] What is missing, however, from all of these descriptions of what transpired in 1948, is the appropriate legal terminology to describe it. It was not the case that Israel merely managed to hold on to territory. Rather, it was that the Haganah, the Irgun and Lehi were trying to capture as much territory as they could. In a word, the birth of Israel in 1948 was quite simply one of the twentieth century's last examples of a successful *conquest*.[4]

RECOGNITION AND STATEHOOD

Although Israel formally proclaimed its 'independence' at midnight on 14/15 May 1948 by making reference to the UN General Assembly resolution of 29 November 1947, which contained the Partition Plan, it did not, at that particular moment, exercise effective control over the territory allocated to it in that Plan. Nor would it adhere to most of the stipulations outlined in that UN Partition Plan despite referring to it in its Declaration of Independence. These were issues that the British Foreign Office legal advisers raised in a minute they had drafted to send to the British delegation at UN Headquarters in New York and in Washington DC on 14 May 1948:

> The decision of November 29th instructed the United Nations Commission to take various steps in Palestine culminating in the establishment of Jewish and Arab states with economic union, e.g. in particular, each state had to draft a constitution and to make a declaration about the Holy Places, minority rights, citizenship, etc. Most of these steps have not been taken and if a Jewish state is proclaimed it will be setting itself up by its own efforts and not through acts of the United Nations Commission.[5]

Five days later, the Foreign Office sent another telegram to its delegation at the UN in New York saying that they would not support Israel's application to become a member:

> The present juridical situation as regards Palestine is obscure and we cannot be sure whether other governments besides that of the Jewish state will emerge. It would be unfair and *legally wrong* in these circumstances to admit the Jewish State to the United Nations at this early stage and thus to give it international recognition, while not taking any similar steps for the rest of Palestine.[6]

In contrast to the position taken by the British Government, the President of the United States, Harry Truman, recognised 'the Provisional Government [of Israel] as the *de facto* authority of the new State of Israel' on 15 May, to the shock and consternation of his own diplomats who were completely unaware of this development.[7] Truman was responding to an address to him from the Provisional Government of Israel's representative in Washington DC, Eliahu Epstein:

> ... I have the honor to notify you that the state of Israel was proclaimed as an independent republic *within frontiers approved by the General Assembly of the United Nations in its Resolution of November 29, 1947*, and that a provisional government has been charged to assume the rights and duties of government for preserving law and order *within the boundaries of Israel*, for defending the state against external aggression, and for discharging the obligations of Israel to the other nations of the world *in accordance with international law*. The Act of Independence will become effective at one minute after six o'clock on the evening of 14 May, Washington time.[8]

By according *de facto* recognition to Israel, which was extended to *de jure* recognition on 31 January 1949,[9] after a government had been democratically elected there, the US Government seemed to be under the impression that Israel's boundaries were commensurate with those of the UN Partition Plan. If so, it is arguable that Israel's entitlement to territorial sovereignty could have only extended to the boundaries delineated in that Plan and that it would be estopped from advancing claims to sovereignty over territories it acquired beyond those boundaries in the 1948 conflict. Two days later, on 17 May 1948, the Soviet Union 'decided to recognize officially the State of Israel and its Provisional Government'.[10] From these statements it was apparent that whereas the US, prior to its granting of *de jure* recognition to Israel in January 1949, merely recognised the fact that Israel had declared its independence in May 1948 and recognised its existence as a fact which it could withdraw if the conditions for recognition failed to materialise, the Soviet Union went one step further and recognised it as a matter of law. In the words of one commentator writing in the *American Journal of International Law*:

> The Soviet Union, acting as a kind of godfather, accorded a diplomatic baptism to the newborn infant and thus assumed by implication a benign interest and responsibility for the child's welfare. President Truman did not imply anything more than the acknowledgement of the child's existence and its *de facto* guardians.[11]

Ernest Gross, the State Department's legal adviser, counselled the White House that any premature recognition of a new state's existence would be wrongful in international law because it would constitute an unwarranted interference in the affairs of the previously existing state (or sovereign).[12] In a legal memorandum he wrote that the policy of the State Department on the recognition of Israel should be based on three factors: (1) *de facto* control of the territory and the administrative machinery of state, including the maintenance of public order; (2) ability and willingness of a Government to discharge its international obligations; and (3) general acquiescence of the people of a country in the Government in power.[13] One prominent international lawyer was even of the opinion that recognition would be unlawful if it was granted *durante bello*, that is, during the course of an armed conflict.[14] It might therefore be fair to conclude that the Soviet Union acted unlawfully in conferring *de jure* recognition on Israel in 1948. Correspondingly, the US acted prematurely in conferring recognition upon Israel because even *de facto* recognition was not warranted when the situation in Palestine was still precarious due to the armed conflict between the Arab states, and the Haganah, the Irgun and Lehi.[15]

In stark contrast to the position adopted by the US and the Soviet Union, Great Britain, which as the mandatory power was then in the process of evacuating its troops from Palestine, considered affording belligerent status to the Jewish Government and the Arab Higher Committee, but then decided against this.[16] Instead, the Foreign Office legal advisers counselled the British Government not to recognise Israel 'for the time being' because, in their opinion, it did not fulfil the 'basic criteria' of an independent state.[17] The French Foreign Minister also disapproved of Truman's premature recognition of the Jewish state.[18] It was evident that Israel could not claim to be an independent state on 14 May because on that date British troops were still occupying Palestine (they did not complete their evacuation until 29 June

1948). Britain also opposed Israel's application to the UN because in its opinion the Jewish state's frontiers were not clearly defined and because it did not exercise effective control over the territories it claimed for itself.

In a letter to Alexander Cadogan, Britain's UN representative, dated 18 August 1948, Aubrey Eban argued that, after the evacuation of British troops, Israel fulfilled the conditions to secure admission to the UN because it satisfied that organisation's admissions criteria provided for in Article 4 (1) of the UN Charter: (a) it was a state; (b) it was a peace-loving state; (c) it was willing to accept the obligations contained in the UN Charter; and (d) it was able and willing to carry out those obligations.[19] Eban claimed that the Provisional Government of Israel exercised effective control in the areas allotted to it in the UN Partition Plan and in those areas of Palestine where its militias had 'repelled attacks launched by the armies of the Arab states'.[20] In support of Israel's application, Eban pointed out that Israel had become 'a signatory to the Geneva Convention' and had 'been invited to send a delegation to the Conference of the International Red Cross'.[21] However, a policy paper prepared by the Foreign Office rejected Eban's contention that Israel was a peace-loving state that was willing and able to accept and carry out the obligations contained in the UN Charter:

> In the case of the Jewish authorities in Palestine it is by no means clear what are the exact boundaries of the area which they at present administer. In any event this area is not identical with that which they claim for permanent inclusion within their State. Originally they maintained their right to establish a State within the frontiers recommended by the General Assembly of the United Nations last November. Statements are now being made, however, which show that the Jewish leaders no longer regard themselves as bound by the General Assembly recommendation, and that they will in due course present claims to additional territory. The limits of these claims have not yet been precisely stated.[22]

The paper also suggested 'the effectiveness of the authority claimed over the Jewish population of Palestine by its present leaders' had not yet been 'sufficiently demonstrated'.[23] This was because 'the right-wing dissident military organization known as Irgun Zvai Leumi' did not accept 'the authority of Mr. Ben Gurion [the leader of the Provisional Government of Israel and its first Prime Minister] and his colleagues'.[24] In this respect, the paper pointed out that five British subjects had been kidnapped by that organisation and that Ben-Gurion's men had only been able to secure their release by making concessions in which two of the five British subjects were put on trial despite the 'illegal action' which led to their kidnapping:

> It thus appears that there is no certainty either about the extent of Jewish territory or about the effectiveness of the control exercised by the authorities in Tel Aviv. In present circumstances, therefore, H.M.G. do not propose to recognize the Jewish State.

> It follows that H.M.G. will not support the application of this State for membership of the United Nations.[25]

In any event, by 1949 when Israel had signed armistice agreements with Egypt, Syria, Jordan and Lebanon,[26] Britain decided that Israel had fulfilled the conditions necessary to support its application to the UN. Upon a recommendation from the Security Council which was opposed by Egypt and from which Britain abstained, it was decided that Israel was a 'peace loving State' that was 'able and willing to carry out the obligations contained in the Charter'.[27] Accordingly, the General Assembly decided to admit Israel to membership in the UN on 11 May 1949 subject to the pledges its ambassador had made to that body regarding the Partition Plan and the return of refugees.[28]

ISRAEL'S OBLIGATIONS AS A UN MEMBER

Israel's membership of the UN was subject to two declarations made by its permanent representative at the General Assembly. The first was that it 'unreservedly accepts the obligations of the United Nations Charter and undertakes to honour them from the day when it becomes a Member of the United Nations'.[29] The second was a statement made by Aubrey Eban, Israel's Ambassador to the UN, to the ad hoc political committee which was issued seven days before it signed the 12 May Protocol with the Arab states (as described in Chapter 8).[30] In a statement before the UN General Assembly, Eban said that he had been authorised by his government to make a statement of principles governing its approach to the negotiations for a peaceful resolution of the conflict. On the question of refugees, this was the position of the Government of Israel:

> 3. The Government of Israel was earnestly anxious to contribute to the solution of that problem although the problem was not of its making. That anxiety proceeded from moral considerations and from Israel's vital interest in stable conditions throughout the Middle East ... A study of the economic, irrigation and other potentialities of the under-populated and under-developed areas of the Arab States revealed greater possibilities for a stable solution by the latter method than by resettlement in Israel. Therefore, the Government of Israel contended that resettlement in neighbouring areas should be considered as the main principle of solution. Israel, however, would be ready to make its own contribution to a solution of the problem. It was not yet ascertainable how many Arabs wished to return under conditions that might be *prescribed by the Assembly or how many Arabs Israel could receive* in the light of existing political and economic considerations. Israel's first objective at Lausanne would be to reach an agreement by direct negotiation on the contribution to be made by each Government toward the settlement of that grave problem. The extent of the contribution of the Israeli Government would depend entirely

on the formal establishment of peace and relations of good neighbourliness between Israel and the Arab States.[31]

Israel's position that the refugee problem was not of its own making was, of course, patent nonsense. Nonetheless, it accepted the principle of repatriation and not only resettlement, although it preferred the latter, subject to (a) those who wished to return; and (b) existing political and economic considerations in Israel. Thus Israel made a solemn declaration to all the members of the UN General Assembly that it accepted the principle of repatriation and not only resettlement upon the formal establishment of peace. There were to be direct negotiations with the governments concerned but the UN General Assembly was responsible for prescribing the number of refugees that might wish to return to their homes in line with resolution 194 (III). As already mentioned in Chapter 8, Israel initially agreed to repatriate 100,000 Palestinian Arabs at the peace talks in Lausanne in 1949 before reneging on that promise.[32]

However, Israel cannot unilaterally interpret its obligations under international law alone. Eban's statement must be read in the light of UN General Assembly resolutions 181 (II) on partition and 194 (III) on refugees, as the General Assembly resolution on Israel's UN membership recalled in its preamble.[33] At Lausanne, the UN mediators and the US Government wanted Israel to repatriate 250,000 refugees because Israel had accepted the UN Partition Plan with its population of over 400,000 Palestinian Arabs.[34] Whilst Israel was opposed to repatriating 250,000 Palestinians it did accept the premise that the refugees had a right of return *to Israel* when Eban said that '[i]t was not yet ascertainable how many Arabs wished to return under conditions that might be prescribed by the Assembly *or how many Arabs Israel could receive* in the light of existing political and economic considerations'.[35] Israel also agreed to compensate the Palestinians. It apparently had no problem with this at all. This is what Eban said:

4. The Government of Israel had already announced its acceptance of obligations to make compensation for abandoned lands. The entire question of compensation as well as the general question of reparations and war damage might well be settled by negotiations at Lausanne.[36]

Of course nothing was settled at Lausanne, but the fact is that Israel had made a declaration to the UN General Assembly committing itself to return, repatriation and compensation in the context of an overall peace settlement. Israel's membership in that organisation is therefore predicated on reaching an agreement on these issues. On the territorial question, this is what is in the UN records:

Mr. Eban then stated the views of his Government on the boundary question, remarking that they did not seem to constitute a major obstacle on the road to a settlement. The fact that an Arab State had not arisen in the part of

> Palestine envisaged by the resolution of 29 November 1947, as well as the circumstances of war and military occupation, *rendered essential a process of peaceful adjustment of the territorial provisions laid down in that resolution.* The General Assembly itself had twice endorsed the need of such a peaceful adjustment and its representatives had even from time to time made proposals for effecting changes in the territorial dispositions of that resolution. The view expounded by the Israeli Government during the first part of the third session was that the adjustment should be made not by arbitrary changes imposed from outside, but through agreements freely negotiated by the Governments concerned.[37]

Eban added that his government interpreted paragraph 5 of UN General Assembly resolution 194 (III) 'as a directive to the Governments concerned to settle their territorial and other differences and claims by a process of negotiation'.[38] Accordingly:

> ... Israel drew encouragement from the success of the armistice negotiations which had led to the establishment of agreed demarcation lines between the military forces of the Governments concerned. Those agreements had been reached through free discussion and reciprocal concession. The United Nations mediating agencies had attempted to lay down no fixed principles but to leave the parties to a process of unfettered negotiation, having in mind the general interest of peace and stability rather than the absolute assertion of unilateral claims. *It was to be presumed that the same process would be followed by the parties in the forthcoming boundary discussion.*[39]

In other words, it was never envisaged that the 1949 ceasefire lines would become Israel's permanent borders. Rather, Israel was required to negotiate over them and was being subjected to pressure to relinquish its control over the territories it captured beyond the 1947 UN Partition Plan's boundaries in the envisaged Arab state. In fact, the US Government and the UN Conciliation Commission for Palestine took a very hard line on the territorial question. The US Government, in particular, was perturbed by Israel's expansionist aims in Palestine. On 29 May 1949, J.G. McDonald, the US Ambassador to Israel, sent a letter to Ben-Gurion from his government, according to which:

> In the interests of a just and equitable solution of these critical questions the United States Government, in the U.N. and as a member of the Palestine Conciliation Commission, has supported the position that *Israel should be expected to offer territorial compensation for any territorial acquisitions which it expects to effect beyond the boundaries set forth in the resolution of the General Assembly of November 29, 1947* [containing the UN Partition Plan]. The Government of Israel has been well aware of this position and of the view of the United States Government that it is based upon elementary principles of fairness and equity.[40]

The letter continued:

> The Government of Israel should entertain no doubt whatever that the United States Government relies upon it to take responsible and positive action concerning Palestine Refugees and that, *far from supporting excessive Israeli claims to further territory within Palestine*, the United States Government believes that it is necessary for Israel to offer *territorial compensation* for territory which it expects to acquire beyond the boundaries of the November 29, 1947 resolution of the General Assembly.[41]

In other words, the US did not support the principle that Israel could benefit from the fruits of aggression. In response, to this letter, the Israeli Government replied as follows:

> The principle of territorial compensation, related to the 1947 award, is one which the Government of Israel cannot accept. That territorial award was based on a series of assumptions which failed to materialize. The hopes of peaceful implementation were dashed by the Arab revolt from within and the Arab invasion from without. The Arab State of Palestine and the Economic Union did not come into being. The Resolution of November 1947 was indeed a source of tremendous encouragement to the Jewish people, and the part played by the United States in promoting its acceptance by the Assembly will never be forgotten. Yet in the decisive struggle which preceded and followed the termination of the British Mandate, the Resolution itself proved of little avail.[42]

Israel's position did not impress the US Government. This was its response:

> The Government of the United States notes that the Government of Israel maintains that it cannot accept the principle of territorial compensation, related to the 1947 partition award, since that award was based on a series of assumptions which failed to materialize. It is observed, however, that the Government of Israel places considerable emphasis upon the continuing validity of the 1947 award where such emphasis supports its own position, for example, in connection with the military occupation by Israel of the southern part of the Negev during a period of truce and in connection with the presence of Syrian troops in a portion of Palestine allotted in 1947 to Israel. In any event, the partition of 1947 is the only authoritative expression of the views of the United Nations with respect to a just territorial division of Palestine between Arabs and Jews. The General Assembly has not indicated in which respects, if any, it believes the territorial basis of that award should be modified in the light of any changes in the assumption on which that partition was based.[43]

In the end the US backed down from this position, as the Israelis were evidently not willing to budge. Ernest Bevin expressed his frustrations when he had a meeting with Dean Acheson at the State Department on 13 September 1949. He said the United Nations appointed commissions which got nowhere and which led to more and more *faits accomplis*, which could not be changed. He said this happened in the matters of Jerusalem, boundaries and Arab territories.[44] On 17 October, a report by the National Security Council on United States Policy Toward Israel and the Arab States, observed:

> b. The present Government of Israel is intensely nationalistic in character, and maintains an internal policy of compromise dictated by the necessity of reconciling the demands of its extremist elements with the more moderate tendencies of the government party. The necessity of maintaining this internal balance makes it difficult for Israel's leaders to meet external demands for compromise with respect to relinquishment of territory and readmission of refugees which are essential to final settlement in Palestine. It also results in further increasing Israel's isolation among the neighbouring Arab states and in reinforcing the charges of intransigence and expansionism which have been levelled against Israel.[45]

On the territorial question, the report concluded that although the US would be prepared to accept a solution freely agreed to by the parties, and to state its views, it should advance a policy which was consistent with that approved by the President:

> If Israel wishes to retain any areas in Palestine allocated to the proposed Arab state under the UN resolution of November 29, 1947 and now occupied by Israeli forces, Israel should, if the Arab states so demand, make territorial compensation elsewhere and/or make other concessions of a non-territorial character as required to reach an equitable agreement which could provide the basis for a lasting peace.[46]

In light of all this, it would seem that the formula for a lasting peace as it was envisaged surrounded three essential issues: the refugees, territory and Jerusalem. As a member of the UN, Israel is obliged to negotiate over these in the interests of a lasting peace. As for the principle of territorial compensation, it should be noted that this was not a new concept but an old principle going back centuries. Compensations of a territorial nature were provided for in all the great peace treaties, including the Treaty of Utrecht (1713), the Congress of Vienna (1815), and the Treaty of Versailles (1919).[47]

CONQUEST OR SECESSION?

It has been noted by one of the leading authorities of international law that the state of Israel was created by the use of force, without the consent of the previous sovereign,[48] without complying with any valid act of disposition of territory, or to a valid and subsisting authorisation.[49] This description, which is undoubtedly correct, seems to be a diplomatic way of describing what transpired in Palestine in 1948 without having to actually engage with the legal consequences of such a conclusion.[50] The missing word for describing precisely this scenario, which should be on every international lawyer's lips, is conquest.[51] Secession, unilateral or otherwise, is not the appropriate mode to describe what happened, because the Zionists were not just a mere minority seeking to break away from the majority to create a Jewish state in a part of Palestine because they were being denied their human rights there, or their right to self-determination, which was clearly not the case. Rather, the Zionists wanted as much of Palestine as they could get, with as few Palestinian Arabs in it as possible, including territories well beyond the UN Partition Plan's boundaries to create their Jewish state. The *Yishuv* accomplished this through war, occupation and annexation after which the Provisional Government of Israel extended its administration and laws there.[52] Israel's title to Palestine is therefore based on conquest and not on 'unilateral secession', 'auto-emancipation', 'defensive conquest', or any other novel term or legal fiction created by international lawyers to describe it.[53] As noted in Chapter 3, there was simply no other way Israel could obtain title over Palestine other than to conquer it, as all the other methods through which it could acquire territorial sovereignty there were not applicable.

It is also difficult to see how Israel could in all seriousness invoke the UN Partition Plan as a basis for its creation when it had no intention of complying with it, as Dean Rusk noted in a meeting he had with Israeli officials on 8 May 1948 six days before Israel issued its Declaration of Independence.[54] This is because the UN Partition Plan explicitly provided that the independent Arab and Jewish states and the special international regime for the City of Jerusalem were to come into existence in Palestine two months after the evacuation of the armed forces of the mandatory power had been completed and not *before* then.[55] Moreover, Israel did not adhere to the territorial limitations of the UN Partition Plan[56] or to the protection of minorities.[57] No Arab state was established and nor was an economic union linking it to the Jewish state or a special regime for Jerusalem established as required by that Plan.[58] The Zionists, despite their protestations, evidently never had any intention of abiding by the UN Partition Plan.

Even if one were to conclude that Israel was created through a process of secessionary independence, this would still be legally problematic. For instance, after considering the opinion of the Committee of Jurists in the Aaland Islands dispute as described in Chapter 5, the Commission of Rapporteurs, which was comprised of politicians as opposed to lawyers, denied the existence of any absolute entitlement to secession by a segment of the population of a state. Although the Rapporteurs did not share the opinion stated by the Commission of Jurists on all points, they did consider that:

> To concede to minorities, either of language or religion, or to any fractions of the population the right of withdrawing from the community to which they belong, because it is their wish or their good pleasure, would be to destroy order and stability within States and to inaugurate anarchy in

> international life; it would be to uphold a theory incompatible with the very idea of the States as a territorial and political unity.[59]

Although Palestine was not a state as such during the Mandate years and although the Zionists did not consider themselves as necessarily belonging to the Palestinian community in 1948, it is submitted that Palestine was as a whole a self-determination unit; a defined territory whose inhabitants had a right to determine their political destiny, through which both Jews and Arabs were destined to live together. Creating a predominantly Jewish state in Palestine only satisfied Jewish self-determination, but the Arabs of Palestine had a right of self-determination too.[60] This is especially as the right of peoples to self-determination is customarily understood to refer to the right of the majority within a generally accepted political unit to exercise power.[61] The fact that the Arabs were willing to create a state with strong protections for minorities was consistent with the self-determination of both peoples, whereas the creation of a Jewish state in place of a Palestinian state was not.

The Rapporteurs also thought that 'the idea of justice and liberty embodied in the formula of self-determination' should be applied 'in a reasonable manner in relations between states and the minorities they include'.[62] They thought that minorities should be able to freely practise their religion and to cultivate language because in their opinion this was 'one of the most noble advances of modern civilization' and were of the opinion that there could be 'no lasting peace apart from justice', which 'constitutes one of the most powerful means of strengthening peace and combating hatred and dissensions both within States and in international relations'.[63] Only in the most exceptional circumstances could a minority separate from the parent state, which might occur when that state 'lacks either the will or power to enact and apply just and effective guarantees'.[64] However, it was apparent that the Zionists had not exhausted alternative remedies for a peaceful resolution of the conflict in 1948, especially as the UN was in the process of creating a Trusteeship, which would have provided such guarantees. In 1945, the drafters of the UN Charter made it clear that the principle of self-determination did not give rise to a right of unilateral secession in any circumstances.[65]

The concept of self-determination in 1948 was, however, not a sufficiently well established principle of law so as to constitute an overriding or peremptory criterion for statehood, meaning that it was a higher norm, which overrode all other considerations. Nevertheless, as argued in Chapter 5, by 1948, the Palestinian Arabs, just like Palestine's Jewish population, had a right of self-determination in Palestine on the basis of the 1947 UN Partition Plan. After all, the continued existence of the 'sacred trust of civilization' inscribed in Article 22 of the League of Nations Covenant did not depend on the continued existence of the League, as the ICJ implicitly accepted in its *Status* opinion and as was evident from Transjordan's independence which occurred *after* the League's demise in 1946.[66] The A-class mandatory system was predicated on the assumption that they would all progressively become independent. Palestine was the only A-class mandate that did not become an 'independent nation' as originally envisaged in 1919. Legally the reason why the Palestinians have the right of self-determination now was that they had it as of 1922 under the Mandate for Palestine.[67] Consequently it could be argued that the Provisional Government of Israel violated the Palestinian people's right of self-determination by sending the Haganah to conquer territories beyond the boundaries delineated in the UN Partition Plan by colluding with Transjordan. In fact, in 1948, there were essentially two conquests: a Zionist one and a Hashemite one.[68] Both parties thwarted the aspirations of the Palestinian Arabs to create an independent state of their own. It would be difficult to describe these acts as lawful even if one was of the opinion that self-determination was not a rule of customary international law in 1948 since it is questionable whether conquest survived the adoption of the UN Charter in 1945.[69] After all, was the *Anschluss* of Austria on 13 March 1938, the annexation on 30 September 1938 of the Sudetenland at the expense of Czechoslovakia, the permission given by the Third Reich to Hungary on 13 March 1938 to seize the Sub-Carpathian Ukraine, the occupation of Prague on 15 March 1939 and the proclamation of the German protectorate over Bohemia and Moravia, as well as the occupation of the territory of Memel on 22 March 1939, not condemned?[70] And what of Japan's earlier invasion of Manchuria on 18 September 1931 which it subsequently annexed on 1 March 1932 by creating the puppet state of Manchukuo. This was not also condemned and not afforded recognition in the light of the Stimson doctrine?[71] Whilst, in the aftermath of the Ethiopian fiasco,[72] League of Nations and state practice, in matters of non-recognition, had been inconsistent, it had nevertheless demonstrated a clear trend in favour of the non-recognition of territorial conquests.[73] If Transjordan was really sincere about entering Palestine on the basis of self-defence, then it should have withdrawn from that territory upon the termination of the war so that the Palestinian Arabs could have set up an independent state. Instead Jordan annexed it in 1950, an act that was only recognised by Britain and Pakistan (and even then, Britain only afforded *de facto* recognition to Jordan's occupation of East Jerusalem and the Holy Places, and likewise to Israel's occupation of West Jerusalem, withholding *de jure* recognition pending a peaceful settlement of the Palestine problem).[74] It was not until 1988 that Jordan withdrew its claims to the West Bank.[75]

Therefore, even if one were to accept, for argument's sake, that the Zionists were given an entitlement to exercise sovereignty over those parts of Palestine allotted to the Jewish state by virtue of the UN Partition Plan, which is debatable, for various reasons,[76] the fact is that the Zionists acquired territory *beyond* those boundaries in the territory envisaged for the Arab state. A paradigm example of this was Israel's annexation through the use of armed force of Umm-Reshresh, now known as the Port of Eilat, which is situated on the Gulf of Aqaba, and which was occupied and annexed after various UN Security Council resolutions had called upon Israel's troops to ceasefire in southern Palestine,[77] and *after* the conclusion of the Egyptian–Israeli General Armistice Agreement signed in Rhodes on 24 February 1949.[78] Another example of an unlawful annexation was a decision by Israel's Knesset (Parliament) on 22 December 1949 to annex West Jerusalem which occurred after the conclusion of the Israel–Jordan General Armistice Agreement of 3 April 1949.[79] There is no way that any of the military actions and repeated annexations undertaken by the Zionists in the territories envisaged for the stillborn Arab state in the UN Partition Plan could have been described as acts of self-defence as it was the Haganah which launched a large-scale invasion of Palestine in April 1948, implementing Plans Gimmel and Dalet, and expelling half of Palestine's civilian population *en masse* prior to the intervention by the Arab states in May 1948. Through these actions the *Yishuv* increased the territory of the Jewish state as proposed in the UN Partition Plan from 14,500 square kilometres to 20,850 square kilometres and by the same act decreased the territory of the proposed Arab state from 11,800 square kilometres to approximately 5,400 square kilometres.[80] And even if, despite all the evidence to the contrary, one reached the conclusion that Israel was acting defensively in 1948, the law of self-defence would not give a defender in the course of its self-defence a right to seize and keep the resources of the attacker.[81] Schwebel's 'defensive conquest' thesis if literally applied could give the Arabs a right to keep hold of any of the territories they captured in Palestine in 1948 on the basis that they were acting in self-defence. It could also give other states a right to seize territories anywhere else in the world and annex them by simply advancing the argument that their intentions were defensive. This would be inimical to the very concept of self-defence which, to be invoked lawfully, must comply with the customary international law principles of necessity and proportionality and which restricts the use of force to the necessary minimum to repel the attacker. More pertinently, the US Military Tribunal at Nuremberg ruled *In Re* List and Others in 1948 that: 'Any purported annexation of territories of a foreign nation, occurring during the time of war and while opposing armies were still in the field', was invalid and ineffective.[82] In 1948, Palestinian partisans such as the *Jaysh al-Jihad al-Muqaddes* and the *Jaysh al-Inqadh* were fighting in the field, as were the opposing armies of the Arab Legion and the Iraqi, Egyptian and Syrian armies after 15 May 1948. Israel proclaimed itself in the boundaries of the UN Partition Plan and therefore its claims to sovereignty in 1948 could not have extended to territories beyond those lines.[83] Consequently, incorporating any territory beyond the 1948 Partition Plan's boundaries into the state of Israel was an act of unlawful annexation. There would seem to be no other way to describe it. If Jordan's actions in occupying and subsequently annexing the West Bank were unlawful, as Israel contended, then *a fortiori* so must Israel's annexation of territory beyond the lines delineated in the UN Partition Plan. The only logical conclusion is that both these acts must have been contrary to international law. If this proposition is correct then the next question to answer is whether a vice in title can be cured by subsequent acquiescence and recognition. The answer to this, quite simply, must be yes.[84] This is because according to the principle of effectivity, as the Canadian Supreme Court noted in the *Reference re Secession of Quebec*, 'an illegal act may eventually acquire legal status if, as a matter of empirical fact, it is recognized on the international plane'.[85] In the words of the Court, 'through a combination of acquiescence and prescription, an illegal act may at some later point be accorded some form of legal status'.[86] But have the Palestinians actually acquiesced and has the full extent of Israel's territorial acquisitions in 1948 been recognised as lawful by the international community?

ACQUIESCENCE, PRESCRIPTION AND RECOGNITION

Even today, states do not recognise the totality of Israel's acquisition of territory in 1948, such as its annexation of West Jerusalem, which is why, for instance, they refuse to locate their embassies there.[87] Whilst, since 2002, the Arab League has offered Israel recognition in exchange for a full withdrawal from the occupied territories, including East Jerusalem, this does not, pending an Israeli withdrawal, a just solution to the Palestinian refugee problem, and the establishment of a sovereign independent Palestinian state in the West Bank and Gaza with its capital in East Jerusalem, amount to acquiescence.[88] Prescription would also be difficult to prove in the face of over 100 years of continuous Palestinian opposition.[89] Israel has shown no signs of taking the Arab League's offer seriously and continues to construct settlements in the occupied territories in violation of Article 49 (6) of the Fourth Geneva Convention.[90] In any assessment of the acquisition of territory through prescription the fact that the territory in question had been acquired through the use of force might have to be taken into consideration especially if it occurred at a time when conquest was considered contrary to international law.[91] As the arbitrator in the *Island of Palmas* case noted, only 'the continuous and *peaceful* display of territorial sovereignty ... is as good as title'.[92] If there are rival claimants who seek to administer the same territory, their interests would have to be taken into account.[93] And were a resolution of the dispute referred to an international tribunal it might have to consider international law on the use of force and the validity of title by conquest.[94]

Having said this, it is clear that both Egypt and Jordan have acquiesced to Israel's existence by concluding peace treaties with it delineating their mutual borders.[95] Egypt's border with Israel was settled at Camp David and subject to arbitration concerning a small area near Taba,[96] whilst Jordan's border with Israel is commensurate with that of the former British Mandate of Palestine.[97] However, both of these treaties explicitly provided that they were concluded without prejudice to the status of any of the territories which came under Israeli military government control in 1967 (East Jerusalem, the West Bank and the Gaza Strip).[98] In 1993, in an exchange of letters with Yitzhak Rabin, Yasser Arafat recognised the state of Israel, whilst the Israeli Government merely recognised the Palestine Liberation Organisation (PLO) as 'the representative of the Palestinian people'.[99] Since Israel has never declared where its eastern boundary extends, what were the territorial boundaries of the state of Israel that Arafat recognised in 1993? Was it the 1949 ceasefire lines or the lines recommended in the 1947 UN Partition Plan? Or have they not yet been delineated and demarcated and are awaiting final agreement to be negotiated by the parties concerned?

When Arafat recognised Israel in 1993, he accepted Security Council resolutions 242 and 338 as a basis for resolving the conflict. One might surmise that the combined effect of recognising Israel and concomitantly accepting resolutions 242 and 338 as a basis for concluding a peace agreement means that the PLO implicitly acknowledged Israel's existence and the scope of its territorial sovereignty within the 1949 ceasefire lines from which those resolutions require an Israeli withdrawal.[100] Consequently, it has been argued that the 1947 UN Partition Plan is inapplicable because it was superseded by Security Council resolution 242.[101] But can a Security Council resolution not based on Chapter VII supersede the territorial formulation contained in the UN Partition Plan? After all, the 1947 UN Partition Plan is the only authoritative document produced by the United Nations to resolve the Palestine problem. All resolution 242 calls for is the withdrawal of Israeli armed forces from territories occupied in the recent conflict, which referred to those territories Israel captured in the 1967 war.[102] In this connection, the preamble to that resolution emphasised 'the inadmissibility of the acquisition of territory by war', which could be understood to mean that any defect in Israel's title to territory over Palestine which was imperfect when resolution 242 was passed by the Security Council in 1967, could not be perfected by it.[103] This would apply to those territories captured by Israel that were envisaged for the Arab state in the UN Partition Plan. It could therefore be argued that even though the Arab states rejected the UN Partition Plan in 1947 (although 'Palestine' subsequently endorsed it in its 1988 Declaration of Independence[104] in Algiers when it embarked on the process towards a two-state solution) it still has a lease of life especially as Israel explicitly invoked it in its Declaration of Independence of 1948 by saying that it was prepared to cooperate with the agencies and representatives of the United Nations in implementing the resolution. On 27 April 1948, this is what Mr Shertok told the UN:

> With regard to the status of Assembly resolutions in international law, it was admitted that any which touched the national sovereignty of the Members of the United Nations were mere recommendations and not binding. However, the Palestine resolution was essentially different for it concerned the future of a territory subject to an international trust. Only the United Nations as a whole was competent to determine the future of the territory, and its decision, therefore, had a binding force.[105]

Resting on good faith and the principle of consistency in state relations, estoppel may involve holding a government to a declaration which in fact does not correspond to its real intention.[106] In the light of Mr Shertok's statement to the UN, the text of Israel's Declaration of Independence, and Mr Epstein's address to President Truman regarding the territorial limits of the Jewish state that his government said would correspond with the borders set out in the UN Partition Plan which formed the basis for the US Government's decision to afford Israel *de facto* recognition, and which many states and the UN subsequently relied upon and accepted in good faith, it could be argued that the state of Israel would be estopped from asserting sovereignty over territories awarded to the Arab state in the UN Partition Plan. Whether the UN Partition Plan was binding or not seems to be beside the point as the underlying premise of a partition of the territory based on an equitable division is still valid and consistent with the 'two-state formula' and the creation 'of an independent, democratic and viable Palestinian state living side by side in peace and security with Israel and its other neighbours' as envisaged in the Performance-Based Roadmap to a Permanent Two-State Solution to the Israeli–Palestinian Conflict[107] which has been endorsed by the EU, Russia, the US and the UN and could be used as a basis for constructive talks between Israelis and Palestinians with a view to resolving the conflict. Moreover, the UN does have dispository powers and a physical presence in Palestine through its various agencies and could support an equitable partition of the Holy Land by suggesting new proposals, conducting surveys, and supporting direct negotiations with the parties most directly concerned. It is submitted that the alternative, which is likely to be a non-viable, fragmented failed state-like entity in the West Bank and Gaza based on the 1949 ceasefire lines and dependent on international aid for its economic viability, is not an appealing prospect for either Israel or the Palestinians. Moreover, the principle of territorial compensation is not out of the question or completely unheard of, especially since the US Government was its greatest champion at the 1949 Lausanne Peace Conference.

Continued Palestinian acquiescence to the state of Israel is also predicated on the assumption that Fatah remains the dominant party in the Palestinian Authority in the foreseeable future. Should the next leader of the Palestinian Authority be from Hamas, then things might be different especially if they refuse to subscribe to the Oslo Accords. Whilst Fatah have accepted the existence of Israel, in principle, the jury is still out as to whether Hamas has done so, or is ever likely to. The answer to the question of Palestinian acquiescence will also depend to a great extent on the success of the negotiations currently taking place behind closed doors as a result of the process launched at Annapolis. Should a Palestinian state eventually be established in treaty relations with Israel then it will depend on what that treaty says. If the treaty recognises Israel's territorial sovereignty within the 1949 ceasefire lines, then the Palestinians will have effectively acquiesced to the 1948 conquest. Israel's original sin will have been cured. One hopes, however, that by this stage, those other bones of contention – Jerusalem, the refugees, water, compensation, security, and the settlements – will have been finally settled. Otherwise, the conflict is likely to fester on for the foreseeable future.

Epilogue

To bolster their case for a Jewish state in Palestine Israeli leaders are accustomed to referring to the Balfour Declaration with admiration. In November 2007, in a speech to commemorate the Declaration's 90th anniversary, Israel's Prime Minister Ehud Olmert said: 'The Balfour Declaration constitutes one of the basic milestones in the establishment of the state of Israel – the right of the Jewish people to a national home.'[1] One wonders whether Olmert and others who proudly proclaim the Balfour Declaration would give it such prominence if they were aware of its true provenance. It certainly strikes one as odd why any Israeli would want to commemorate a declaration named after someone who shared the racial prejudices of Cosima Wagner.[2] But, perhaps, this is the paradox that lies at the heart of Zionism. Edwin Montagu may have lost the debate in the cabinet in 1917, which was so acrimonious that he allegedly wept in front of Balfour and his colleagues, but as history has shown, he was right to point out the dangers inherent in Zionism. For it too contributed to anti-Semitism whilst at the same time providing a pretext for people like Balfour to encourage the Jews to uproot themselves from Europe.

In 1919, Lord Eustace Percy, Balfour's Private Secretary, wrote the following in *The Responsibilities of the League*: 'We might almost dismiss the "national home" as irrelevant were it not for the tremendous forces which the Balfour Declaration has already set in motion – the stirring of all Jewry in Eastern Europe, the growing pressure of whole communities anxious to migrate immediately ...'[3] This statement might initially appear as rather uncontroversial until one realises what Percy thought of the Jews, whom he described as rejecting 'the enlightenment of a new era' and preferring 'the ghetto' which 'has been more a real home to the Jews than forums and parliaments'.[4] For Percy, the victory of the Zionists over the anti-Zionists characterised by the struggle between Montagu and the majority of British Jews against those from Eastern Europe, 'was won by no mere sympathy for the oppressed Jew in other lands; it arose also from a growing conviction that, in the increasing consolidation of the Western nations, it is no longer possible to reckon on complete toleration – that there is a steady tendency to present the alternative between assimilation and exclusion in a more and more inexorable form'.[5] It would seem that British politicians like Percy saw the Jews as a danger to Western civilisation because in addition to their anti-Semitism they thought the Jews were in arms with the Bolsheviks and their Marxist ideology, then sweeping Central and Eastern Europe. They wanted to prevent this from happening in Britain by encouraging the Jews to go to Palestine:

> The horrors of the war just ended turned [the Jew's] eyes more than ever to his traditional home; but it is the conditions of the peace, the nationalism

> of the new Europe, that seems to give the final signal for his exodus. In a world of completely organised territorial sovereignties he has only two possible cities of refuge: he must either pull down the pillars of the whole national state system or he must create a territorial sovereignty of his own. In this perhaps lies the explanation both of Jewish Bolshevism and of Zionism, for at this moment Eastern Jewry seems to hover uncertainly between the two ...[6]

We can only understand this logic if we realise that in 1919 people actually believed in the false philosophy of the *Protocols of the Elders of Zion*, disliked East European Jewish immigrants in Britain who were suspected of dual loyalty and felt slighted when these Jews refused the 'offer' of British assimilation. In Percy's own words:

> Liberalism and nationalism, with a flourish of trumpets, threw open the doors of the ghetto and offered equal citizenship to the Jew. They passed out into the Western world, saw the power and the glory of it, used it and enjoyed it, laid his hand indeed on the nerve centres of its civilisation, guided, directed and exploited it, and then – refused the offer.[7]

But Zionism, like many political ideologies, is a false god.[8] It was foreboding that Palestine's inhabitants would not be willing to have their country turned into a 'Jewish national home' without a struggle. As the two rabbis sent to Palestine in 1897 to investigate its suitability for Jewish colonisation cabled Vienna, 'the bride is beautiful, but she is married to another man'.[9] Lord Curzon, who was the only member of the cabinet who had physically been to Palestine, and Edwin Montagu, the only Jew invited to participate in the cabinet debate, warned their colleagues that Palestine's indigenous inhabitants would not be content to be merely hewers of wood and drawers of water for these Jewish immigrants. It was only because of their efforts that the two safeguard clauses were inserted into the Balfour Declaration providing that nothing should be done which may prejudice the civil and religious rights of existing non-Jewish communities in Palestine, or the rights and political status enjoyed by Jews in any other country.[10]

It is often forgotten that two years before the British Government viewed with favour the establishment of a Jewish national home in Palestine the British High Commissioner in Cairo had already pledged it to Hussein Ibn Ali, the Sherif of Mecca. And regardless of whether or not Britain actually did intend to promise Palestine to the Sherif in 1915, as it has been argued was the case in this book, what this agreement evinces at the *very minimum* is (1) the existence of Arab nationalism; (2) that a prominent Arab leader was prepared to secede from the Ottoman Empire; (3) that he had pledged his allegiance to Britain; (4) that his men fought side by side with British soldiers for the Allied cause, and (5) that the question of self-determination was in principle applicable. In contrast, the British belief in 'the combined power of international Jewry' to foment revolution in Russia and collapse whole dynasties was a fallacy, a mirage, and a fantasy. The Bolshevik revolution had nothing to do with Zionism. But so long as the British Government sincerely believed that it did and that in Zionism there was a solution to the Jewish Question they were bound to offer it their support.

In view of all this, it is perhaps not so surprising that international law was jettisoned by the Great Powers when it clashed with Zionism. 'The four Great Powers are committed to Zionism', Balfour wrote.[11] 'And Zionism, be it right or wrong, good or bad, is rooted in age-long tradition, in present needs, in future hopes, of far profounder import than the desires and prejudices of the 700,000 Arabs who now inhabit that ancient land.'[12] In cruder terms, what Balfour was really saying is that the Great Powers wanted to solve their 'Jewish problem' by discouraging the westward immigration of Jews from the Pale of Settlement into their countries and instead redirect it towards Palestine – precisely as Theodor Herzl had advised the British Government before the Royal Commission on Alien Immigration in 1902 when he presented Zionism as a novel form of 'immigration control', which he repeated to the Colonial Secretary who offered the Jews a tract of land in East Africa. If establishing a Jewish national home in Palestine was not quite lawful or if it was going to cause difficulties with that country's indigenous inhabitants then so be it. As for the principle of self-determination, that was to be set aside. This is what Balfour told a meeting of the English Zionist Federation in 1923:

> ... the critics of this movement shelter themselves behind the phrase – but it is more than a phrase – behind the principle of self-determination, and say that, if you apply that principle logically and honestly, it is to the majority of the existing population of Palestine that the future destinies of Palestine should be committed. My lords, ladies and gentlemen, there is a technical ingenuity in that plea, and on technical grounds I neither can nor desire to provide the answer; but, looking back upon the history of the world, I say that the case of Jewry in all countries is absolutely exceptional, falls outside all the ordinary rules and maxims, cannot be contained in a formula or explained in a sentence. The deep, underlying principle of self-determination really points to a Zionist policy, however little in its strict technical interpretation it may seem to favour it.[13]

In short, the principle of self-determination got in the way of doing the 'right thing'. And the 'right thing' in Balfour's view was to direct the energies of this 'exceptional' and 'highly endowed people', who he was prone to referring to as the 'Hebrew race', to his 'great experiment' in Palestine. This is the gist of what he said in a speech he presented at a dinner given by the Anglo-Palestine Club in his honour to celebrate the tenth anniversary of the Balfour Declaration on 10 November 1927, at the Hotel Cecil:

> I could never have thrown myself with the enthusiasm which I have always felt for this cause into it if it had been merely a question of taking out of the most unhappy conditions a certain number of the Jewish race and re-

> planting them in the land of their forefathers. If it had been merely that, I should have been, I hope, an enthusiast for the cause. But I think it is going to be much more than that. I hope and I believe that the highly endowed people who have done so much for Western civilisation in some of the highest walks of human effort will do even more, if you give them the chance, in the original land of their inspiration, to carry out the work side by side with all the great civilised nations of the world – the chance to work side by side with them for the common advancement of knowledge.
>
> I cannot help thinking that this experiment – I have used this word more than once in my speech, but I use it without remorse – is a great experiment, because nothing like it has ever been tried in the world, and because it is entirely novel.[14]

The novelty of this experiment and the 'absolutely exceptional' nature of the Zionist project were to set a precedent, which has never since been abandoned. The Jewish national home was not to be subject to the laws in the same way as they were applied to other nations. Rather, in Balfour's own words, the experiment fell 'outside all the ordinary rules and maxims'. It was special. It was *sui generis*. This at least provides one plausible explanation as to why self-determination for the Palestinian Arab population was delayed so that the Zionists could create their national home first, why Arab opposition to Zionism was brutally repressed throughout the duration of the British Mandate, why international law was set aside when the UN recommended partitioning Palestine, why the Great Powers turned a blind eye to the atrocities inflicted by the Haganah, the Irgun and Lehi upon Palestine's indigenous Arab population in the 1947–49 conflict, why they did not press the Provisional Government of Israel to readmit the Palestinian Arabs it expelled from their homes, why they ignored the ordinary rules for the recognition of states and overlooked the illegality of conquest under customary international law in 1948, why UN General Assembly and Security Council resolutions on the Palestine question have been routinely ignored for the last six decades and why the International Court of Justice's 2004 advisory opinion on the Wall was confined, in the words of Ra'anan Gissin, a senior adviser to Israeli Prime Minister Ariel Sharon, to 'the garbage-can of history'.[15]

THE ROLE OF INTERNATIONAL LAW

In light of all this, one might deem international law irrelevant. But this was not so. Balfour knew, as did the Zionists, that their experiment needed a sound legal basis. This they accomplished by inserting the Balfour Declaration into the British Mandate of Palestine and by encouraging the other Great Powers to acquiesce in it by getting approval from the Council of the League of Nations at San Remo in 1920. And Britain must have known that the other Great Powers in the League, such as France, Germany, Italy and Russia, countries with long histories of anti-Semitism, were not going to kick up much of a fuss. We must also remember that at that time the population disparities between

Arabs and Jews in Palestine was so vast (the country being in 1918, 93 per cent Arab and 7 per cent Jewish) that many statesmen naively believed that in time both Arabs and Jews would coalesce and be content to live together with one single Palestinian nationality. Moreover, the Zionists justified their project by invoking the colonial language of the period, which they knew would appeal to Britain in particular. It was good for the British Empire, they argued, and for the 'civilising mission'. As Herbert Samuel told a meeting of the Zionist Organisation in a speech he gave in London to celebrate the second anniversary of the Balfour Declaration on 2 November 1919, one year prior to being appointed Palestine's first High Commissioner: '... our ideal will not be fully attained unless Palestine becomes a State in which all its inhabitants are helped to attain a higher standard of civilisation ...'[16] The Zionists claimed the Arabs would materially benefit from the Jewish national home and that it would not affect their rights or prejudice those of Jews from other countries as Montagu feared it would.

However, the Zionists were wrong on all accounts. The creation of Israel in 1948 adversely affected the interests of the Arabs as well as detrimentally affecting the political status of Jews in other countries in Europe, North Africa, and the Middle East. As Montagu had warned Balfour in 1917, '[w]hen the Jews are told that Palestine is their national home, every country will immediately desire to get rid of its Jewish citizens'.[17] And with the notable exception of the United States, a nation of many immigrants, where there was no 'Jewish Question' as such, this is precisely what happened. Throughout the duration of the Mandate (1922–48), many Jews, but especially those from Germany, Poland and Russia, countries abutting the Pale of Settlement, were encouraged to leave and immigrate to Palestine, which was now their 'national home'. And when the Zionists conquered Palestine in 1948, the Arab world retaliated for their expulsion of the Palestinians by forcibly ejecting their own Jewish populations to Palestine. Consequently, the second safeguard clause inserted into the Balfour Declaration, which provided that nothing should be done which might prejudice the political status of Jews in other countries, was violated first by Europe and then by the Arab world. Moreover, it would be extremely difficult to reconcile the atrocities associated with the 1947–49 conflict and the exile of 750,000 Palestinian Arabs with the language inscribed in Article 22 of the League of Nations Covenant which provided that 'the *well-being* and development ... form a sacred trust of civilization'. This is completely inconsistent with the notion that the Palestinian Arabs could be harmed in any way or displaced from their homeland. As the International Court of Justice observed in its advisory opinion on South-West Africa in 1950: 'The Mandate was created, in the interests of the *inhabitants* of the territory, and of *humanity* in general, as an international institution with an international object – a sacred trust of civilization.'[18]

In this connection, the minutes of a meeting of the Permanent Mandates Commission on 17 June 1939, record the statement of policy laid out for Palestine by the Colonial Secretary, which specifically referred to the meaning of the phrase 'well-being' in the sacred trust in paragraph 1 of Article 22 of the League of Nations Covenant:

> ... the well-being to which paragraph 1 of Article 22 of the Covenant referred did not simply mean material and physical well-being, it meant the physical, mental and moral well-being of the people ... The mandate was very much concerned with the moral well-being of all peoples ... [which] meant that these peoples should be regarded as having an equal moral status with any other people in the world, that they had certain fundamental rights as human beings and as a people. They were equal with the other peoples who came under the mandates system in their possession of certain fundamental rights, and the whole purpose of the mandates system was that those fundamental rights should not be interfered with in the stresses of the modern world, and that they should not be injured or destroyed by forces which were materially or physically more powerful than they were.[19]

In other words, any measures, which harmed the physical, mental and moral well-being of the Palestinian people, would be contrary to the 'sacred trust' enunciated in Article 22 of the League of Nations Covenant. In light of this, it would be fair to conclude that the infliction of physical and mental harm upon Palestine's Arab population through the use of violence, force and intimidation in the 1948 conflict was unlawful.

This brings us to the root of the Palestine problem. Was the Zionist project to create a Jewish national home in Palestine lawful? It was certainly novel. On the face of things it seemed lawful. After all, the objective of the Mandate was to establish a Jewish national home in Palestine, which many – though by no means all – understood to be a stepping-stone to statehood. At the turn of the twentieth century, the British would have viewed most Jews, particularly the *Ashkenazim* as 'civilised'. Only a handful of Arabs, particularly those from the upper classes, and the Christians, would have satisfied that description during the Mandate years. Consequently, the British Government would have had no difficultly sympathising with Zionist aspirations rooted in the Bible and Christian-Zionism to colonise the Holy Land and bring it civilisation after it had been 'misgoverned' by the Turks for four centuries. Yet international law did not give the Zionists a blank cheque to colonise Palestine. Leaving aside the question as to whether Palestine had been promised to the Arabs in the Hussein–McMahon correspondence of 1915, the creation of a Jewish national home in Palestine was conditional upon:

1. Article 22 of the League of Nations Covenant, which provided for the principle of self-determination and ultimately independence;
2. The provisions of the Mandate, which provided for Jewish immigration and settlement in Palestine on the condition that the civil and religious rights of Palestine's Arab population were safeguarded which included their political rights;
3. Safeguarding the political status of Jews in other countries;
4. Ensuring equality in law between Arabs and Jews in Palestine.

Arguably, the creation of a Jewish state in two-thirds of mandatory Palestine has infringed most, if not all, of these conditions. First, whilst a Jewish state satisfied the self-determination of Palestine's Jewish population, the manner through which it was established violated the self-determination of Palestine's Arab population because no Arab state was created as envisaged by the 1937 Peel Partition Plan, Churchill's secret Partition Proposal of 1945, the UN Partition Plan of 1947 or the draft UN Trusteeship Agreement of 1948. Secondly, the way in which the state of Israel was created in 1948 through the use of armed force infringed upon the civil and religious rights of Palestine's Arab population who were forcibly displaced from their homeland and permanently exiled. Thirdly, it prejudiced the political status of Jews in other countries, in Central and Eastern Europe especially, as well as in the Middle East and North Africa. Fourthly, many Palestinians in Israel, that is, Israeli Arabs, were discriminated against on a number of accounts, a practice that continues to the present day.[20] Consequently, the manner through which Israel was created in 1948 violated the letter and the spirit of the League of Nations Covenant, the Balfour Declaration, and the British Mandate of Palestine.

In 1937, the Peel Commission, recalling Wilson phraseology in which the President objected to peoples being bartered from sovereignty to sovereignty as if they were mere chattels and pawns in a game, expressed a similar opinion:

> To foster Jewish immigration in the hope that it might ultimately lead to the creation of a Jewish majority and the establishment of a Jewish State with the consent or at least the acquiescence of the Arabs was one thing. It was quite another to contemplate, however remotely, the forcible conversion of Palestine into a Jewish State against the will of the Arabs. For that would clearly violate the spirit and intention of the Mandate System. It would mean that national self-determination had been withheld when the Arabs were a majority in Palestine and only conceded when the Jews were a majority. It would mean that the Arabs had been denied the opportunity of standing by themselves: that they had, in fact, after an interval of conflict, been bartered about from Turkish sovereignty to Jewish sovereignty.[21]

The Zionists were under the impression that they could create their Jewish national home in Palestine, subject to the safeguard clauses, once they formed a majority of the population through waves of Jewish immigration. However, the point is that they *never* formed a majority of the population of Palestine during the mandatory years. In 1948, the Zionists were still a minority. Instead they expelled the Palestinian Arabs from those areas in which they wanted the Jews to form a majority of the population. Although it is arguable that Israel was created through the use of force in pursuance of the Jewish people's right of self-determination assuming that such a right existed in international law at that particular moment in time that allowed them to do this, this went beyond the area delineated by the UN in the Partition Plan of 1947. Moreover, by sending their forces to capture territory beyond the partition lines the Zionists violated the self-determination of the Arab population. Taking this into consideration, one cannot help but conclude that Israel was created through the use of force in the face of persistent Palestinian Arab opposition, after which the Provisional Government of Israel extended its administration, laws and jurisdiction over two-thirds of the territory of Palestine, which it annexed.[22] Under international law this is known as conquest or subjugation.[23]

Although the right of self-determination could in no way have amounted to a peremptory norm of international law in 1948, the UN had spoken authoritatively on the issue. The Great Powers all supported the partition of Palestine in principle, which was a method through which two mutually antagonistic communities inhabiting the same territory could exercise their respective rights to self-determination. So long as Arabs and Jews could not get along and coalesce as a single Palestinian community, united in citizenship and working together in government, then partition had to be considered. As for the Balfour Declaration, this was to disappear. As Britain's Colonial Secretary told the Permanent Mandates Commission at a special session on Palestine in 1937:

> The Balfour Declaration, in itself a compromise document, was not expressed in definitive political terms. It was a gesture, the expression of a hope then existing that the Jews and Arabs would compose their differences and eventually coalesce into a single commonwealth united in Palestinian citizenship. That evolution had not taken place, and was not likely to take place; and it was therefore necessary to go back to fundamentals ... [this] meant that the Balfour Declaration must itself disappear and be replaced, if there was to be peace, progress and good government in Palestine, by a Jewish State in one part of Palestine, an Arab State in the other part, and a special regime for the Holy Places.[24]

Partition sounded nice in principle. After all, India would be partitioned in August 1947, so why not Palestine as well. The problem was that the Great Powers could not agree on how to go about carving up the Holy Land. Their failure to stand by the UN Partition Plan gave the Zionists time to gather their forces and conquer the land.

In 1948, Britain's Foreign Secretary, Ernest Bevin, supported a plan that would have allowed Transjordan to annex the West Bank because of the question of viability.[25] He did not think that a rump Palestinian state in the West Bank could stand-alone. However, today the right of self-determination as a peremptory norm of international law would trump territorial issues. As Judge Dillard wrote in *Western Sahara*, '[i]t is for the people to determine the destiny of the territory and not the territory the destiny of the people'.[26] Even if a Palestinian state would be more viable if it were linked to Jordan so that both the East and the West Bank were united, this could only be accomplished if the Palestinian people expressed a desire to do this. In other words, it could not be accomplished through annexation or through a deal between Israel and Jordan. Moreover, Bevin wanted the Negev to be awarded to the Arab state so as to ensure territorial contiguity between the Sinai, Gaza, the West Bank and Transjordan. It is unlikely that the state of Israel would agree to this today. However, if the Palestinian people and their representatives the Palestine Liberation Organisation were to organise a referendum on the issue, and providing that the Government of Jordan agreed to this, there is no reason why, in principle, both Banks of the Jordan could not form one state. For the time being, however, the international consensus is in favour of an independent, sovereign and viable Palestinian state in the West Bank and Gaza with its capital in Jerusalem. Whether such a state will actually be independent, sovereign or viable is another matter entirely.

THE *SHOAH* AND JEWISH REFUGEES

In the aftermath of the worst European catastrophe in recent history, in which some 6 million Jews, including a million children, were systematically murdered in the most appalling circumstances, the question of what to do with hundreds of thousands of Jewish refugees who survived it confronted the United Nations in one of its first major challenges.[27] And at the heart of the matter was the Palestinian conundrum. The US wanted the refugees to go to Palestine but Britain resisted, saying that it would lead to conflict. A special Anglo-American commission sent to Palestine in 1946 concluded that whilst 100,000 Jews should be allowed into Palestine immediately, it should become a bi-national state where neither Jew nor Arab could dominate the other.[28] Whilst this sounded nice on paper, the Commission provided no political blueprint to achieve this in actual practice. Moreover, the Arabs argued that the problem of displaced Jews was a concern for the whole of humanity and that a comprehensive solution was required. They said that Palestine alone, could not bare the burden. As Sir Mohammed Zafrullah Khan told the UN General Assembly in a debate on the matter with a heavy hint of sarcasm:

> Shall they [the displaced European Jews] be repatriated to their own countries? Australia says no; Canada says no; the United States says no. This was very encouraging from one point of view. Let these people, after their terrible experiences, even if they are willing to go back, not be asked to go back to their own countries ... Shall they be distributed among the Member States according to the capacity of the latter to receive them? Australia, an over-populated small country with congested areas, says no, no, no; Canada, equally congested and over-populated, says no; the United States, a great humanitarian country, a small area, with small resources, says no. That is their contribution to the humanitarian principle. But they state: let them go into Palestine, where there are vast areas, a large economy and no trouble; they can easily be taken in there.[29]

Theodor Herzl must have had a premonition when he wrote the following sentence in his diary: 'The antisemites will become our most loyal friends, the antisemitic nations will become our allies.'[30] This lack of compassion for these Jewish refugees in Australia, Canada and the US, countries which all refused to ease their immigration restrictions, and which are some of Israel's staunchest supporters today, may provide one cogent explanation as to why the Jewish state envisaged in the 1947 UN Partition Plan was much larger than what the British Government was prepared to grant them in 1937 and why it paid no heed to demographics, Palestinian land ownership, their consent to the proposed dismemberment of their homeland, or the wider feelings of peoples throughout the Arab and Islamic world, to the creation of a Jewish state in the heart of the Middle East. And yet when these Jewish refugees were actually asked for their preferences as regards the countries in which they would like to seek asylum and refuge, Palestine was often their last choice. Most Austrian and German Jewish refugees, for instance, preferred to stay in Europe or go to the US. These were the findings contained in a report submitted by Sir Herbert Emerson, the High Commissioner for Refugees to the League of Nations at its final session in Geneva in April 1946:

> The problem of German and Austrian refugees may prove to be more tractable than that of other categories, because they were, and are still, less intent on a single destination – namely, Palestine – than some of the new groups. Many of those who wished to go there were able to satisfy their wishes while certificates were still obtainable. The information available goes to show that, among those belonging to this group and not yet permanently established, there are comparatively few who give Palestine as their first choice. A survey carried out by voluntary organisations in the United Kingdom gave the following results. About 75% wished to stay in the United Kingdom; of the remaining 25% about one-half, namely 12½%, for Palestine. A comprehensive survey carried out by the International Migration Service in Switzerland showed a surprisingly low proportion of German and Austrian refugees who gave Palestine as their first choice, but probably the lack of facilities had something to do with this, since there was a similar low proportion in regard to the United States of America. Of those now in the Western countries of Europe, the majority wish to stay there if they have the opportunity, with the United States as the second priority; of those who wish in any case to leave these countries, the United States is the first priority. The choice of Palestine depends on individual religious and ideological convictions. The majority of those now in Sweden wish to stay there, with the United States as the second priority. Of those in Switzerland, Portugal and Spain, the order of preference is probably: (i) the countries of Western Europe if they were there previously to the war, (ii) the United States, (iii) Palestine.[31]

In other words, even after the genocide of European Jewry, the majority of Jews still did not want to go to Palestine. They wanted to remain in Western Europe in the countries in which they had found refuge, such as

Britain, Switzerland, Portugal and Spain, or alternatively, if this was not an option, they preferred to go to the USA. However, instead of assisting these refugees find comfort in the countries in which they had found refuge, the Zionists sought to capitalise on this atrocity. David Ben-Gurion and the Jewish Agency were more interested in establishing their Jewish state in Palestine and preparing for the coming war with the Arabs in the wake of Britain's departure.[32] And what a departure it was. Instead of fulfilling its Mandate, Britain left the Arabs and Jews to fight it out. The stronger side won. The result was that three-quarters of a million Palestinian Arabs were forcibly displaced from their homes. Once citizens of the British Mandate of Palestine, free to travel without let or hindrance with their Palestinian passports entitled 'British Passport, Palestine', the majority were now refugees, ousted from their homeland, stripped of their former citizenship, ostracised in the countries in which they found refuge, and seen as subversive elements and 'terrorists' in the West.

ZIONISM AND ANTI-SEMITISM

Before the hostilities in 1948, the Arabs had formed a majority of the population of Palestine for hundreds, if not a thousand, years. The creation of a wholly Jewish state was an artificial construct that was alien to the region and which provoked a bitter conflict with a people who historically had no qualms with the Jews. Under the Ottoman *millet* system, each recognised religious community, which included numerous Christian sects, Jews as well as Muslims, could govern their respective affairs with little interference from central government in Istanbul.[33] The *millets*, usually headed by a religious figure, could even pass their own laws and collect their own taxes.[34] For hundreds of years Jews and Arabs had lived in relative harmony in the Middle East and North Africa. Zionism and European colonialism were, however, to change all this. As Mr Ormsby-Gore prophetically warned the Permanent Mandates Commission at an extraordinary session that was singularly devoted to the question of Palestine in Geneva in the summer of 1937:

> I do not exaggerate when I say that the continuance of a policy of repression and nothing else is likely to embroil, not merely Great Britain, but the Jews all over the world, in a conflict with the Mohammedans. It is something of a tragedy that, when in the Middle Ages, on religious grounds, the Christian world took an attitude to the Jews which is not one on which enlightened countries to-day can look back with satisfaction, in those days it was the Mohammedan world peculiarly that befriended the Jews in Spain, in the Near and Middle Easts, with the result that, after the Jews were driven out of Spain, it was in Bagdad [*sic*] and in places of that kind that you had a large settlement of Jewish refugees. To-day those settlements are in danger because of Palestine, and the whole relation between the Jews all over the world and the Moslem all over the world is likely to become a

> serious one, and is likely to deteriorate, unless we can find a solution to the Palestine problem.[35]

Over seventy years later, and Ormsby-Gore's words still hold true. In fact today the conflict in Palestine has became a part and parcel of the larger struggle between political Islam and the West, as is clear from the rhetoric of Osama Bin Laden and Iran's current president Mahmoud Ahmadinejad.[36] Anti-Semitism, once a purely European disease, is now a growing phenomenon in the Arab world and is being fuelled by the conflict between Israelis and Palestinians,[37] although it is not of the pseudo-scientific sort which convulsed Europe a century ago.[38] Unqualified Western support for Israel has not helped matters, especially when that country grossly infringes basic principles of international law such as the non-annexation of territory, engages in population transfers by constructing settlements in the Occupied Palestinian Territories, and uses excessive force against Palestinian civilians, which have, on occasion, led to allegations of war crimes being levelled at Israeli generals and commanders in its army and air force.

In this connection, it will be recalled that one of the major underlying justifications for Zionism is that it would be a panacea for anti-Semitism. All that needed to be done, according to this theory, was to encourage the Jews to extricate themselves from their countries of origin and encourage them to move to Palestine where they would become 'pioneers' of a sovereign Jewish state, 'a light unto the nations'.[39] As a direct consequence, anti-Semitism would disappear. As Herzl wrote in *Der Judenstaat*:

> The departure of the Jews will involve no economic disturbances, no crises, no persecutions; in fact, the countries they abandon will revive to a new period of prosperity. There will be an inner migration of Christian citizens into the positions evacuated by the Jews. The outgoing current will be gradual, without any disturbance, and its initial movement will put an end to Anti-Semitism.[40]

But this was not so. Indeed, today, it would be scandalous to suggest that the exodus of Jews from Europe, North Africa, and the Middle East to Palestine involved 'no crises', 'no persecutions', could be described as 'gradual', and 'without any disturbance'. Whilst relations between Arabs and Jews may not have been absolutely perfect in North Africa and the Middle East, the Jews inhabiting the Arab world were far better off than the Jews of Europe during the first half of the twentieth century.[41] In this regard it ought to be emphasised that historically there was no serious conflict of interest between Arabs and Jews until the British arrived on the scene with their Balfour Declaration in 1917. Before then, Palestine's Jews intermingled with Muslims and Christians with whom they communicated in Arabic and Turkish.[42] It was only with later waves of Jewish immigration caused by European anti-Semitism that conflict ensued. It was British colonialism and Zionism that caused the Arab–Israeli conflict, not any alleged hatred between Arabs and Jews from the biblical era. The callous disregard that European politicians displayed towards the inhabitants of the Orient allowed them to dismember the Middle East into fragmented territories without taking into consideration its ethnic composition. Palestine was essentially a British experiment in demographic engineering and it was this factor above all which has led to the present predicament, something which successive Israeli governments have continued through their settlement policy. And tinkering with national demographics is a very dangerous practice indeed. One has only to think of the Balkans, the Kurds in Iraq, the Chinese in Tibet and numerous other territories where demographic engineering has led to violent confrontation.

In a world as divided as today, it is lamentable that Palestine, the centre for the three monotheistic religions is a place of conflict rather than a place of pilgrimage. It is equally lamentable that neither the League of Nations nor the United Nations has managed to resolve the conflict. And it is a real travesty that Israelis and Palestinians keep killing each other when neither is to blame for starting the conflict. Perhaps if they had a better grasp of their own shared histories in Palestine they would think thrice before resorting to violence. There is little doubt that a culture of intolerance and racism, and the domestic and foreign policies of Great Britain, Germany and Russia at the turn of the twentieth century directly contributed to the origins of the Arab–Israeli conflict and they have, above all, a moral responsibility to do far more than they have done to date to seek a resolution.[43] There are many ways in which the conflict could be resolved if politicians on both sides of the divide were to be more courageous and imaginative. A one-state solution with equal rights for all; a bi-national state; or a two-state solution that really does provide for a contiguous, sovereign and viable Palestinian state next to the state of Israel, would all be better than maintaining the status quo sustained as it is by force and violence. However, if the two-state solution is to be realistic and viable today, it will entail territorial concessions from Israel, as the US and British governments recognised at the Lausanne Peace Conference in 1949, and a special regime for the Holy Places in Bethlehem, Jerusalem and Nazareth. The settlements in the West Bank and those surrounding East Jerusalem will either have to go or the settlers will have to face the prospect of living under Palestinian control as equal citizens in a state which does not discriminate on any grounds. If this entails a re-partitioning of the Holy Land in accordance with the freely expressed wishes of all of its inhabitants then so be it. But any re-partition today will also need to ensure that both states are economically viable and territorially contiguous so far as is practicable and this will undoubtedly entail forging stronger links with Jordan and the other countries of the Middle East. As for the refugees, their interests must be considered paramount, whether this entails their return, repatriation, resettlement and compensation in line with UN General Assembly resolution 194 (III), equity, and international law. Whilst a solution to the conflict may ultimately be political, in the sense that Israelis and Palestinians will have to reach some sort of compromise at some point in time, it is likely to make reference to legal principles.[44] After all, a peace treaty is a legal document. In the end it is unlikely that a lasting peace would subsist unless it is based on equity, justice and principles of international law, which have been sidelined throughout the course of the Arab–Israeli conflict to the detriment of all concerned. In the absence of such conditions any peace agreement is doomed to fail, as evinced by the collapse of the Oslo Peace Process in the 1990s and all the other failed peace endeavours.

Notes

INTRODUCTION

1. This is the standard explanation in most Israeli and Western textbooks on the conflict. See e.g. Alan Dowty, *Israel/Palestine* (Cambridge: Polity Press, 2008), p. 4 ('The core of the Israeli–Palestinian conflict is the claim of two peoples to the same piece of land'). For another example see Kirsten E. Schulze, *The Arab–Israeli Conflict* (London: Longman, 1999), p. 1 ('... the Arab–Israeli conflict emerged with the advent of nationalism in the Middle East and that the conflict, in simplistic terms, is one of competing nationalisms').
2. Israeli politicians are also accustomed to describing the conflict in this way. See e.g. Shlomo Ben-Ami, *Scars of War, Wounds of Peace: The Israeli–Arab Tragedy* (London: Weidenfeld & Nicolson, 2005), p. 1 ('The encounter between Zionism and the Palestinian Arabs started as an experiment in mutual ignorance, an obsessive determination by each to overlook the powerful, genuine national sentiments and the spirit of communal identity that motivated the other'). But this explanation overlooks the fact that Zionism could never have succeeded in Palestine without the assistance of British colonialism and the acquiescence of the other Great Powers.
3. On Irish history from the perspective of international law, see Anthony Carty, *Was Ireland Conquered?* (London: Pluto Press 1996).
4. As will be explained elsewhere in this book there are also Oriental Jews, those from Iberia who settled in the Arab world such as *Sephardim* and the *Mizrahim*, the latter Arab Jews from Iraq, Iran and Syria, who immigrated to Palestine or were expelled after the creation of Israel in 1948, their status in the Arab world being prejudiced as a result of the expansionist aims of Zionism and the expulsion of the Palestinian Arabs from their homeland. See generally, Howard M. Sachar, *A History of Israel: From the Rise of Zionism to Our Time* (Oxford: Basil Blackwell, 1977).
5. See Bernard Lewis, *Semites and Anti-Semites: An Inquiry into Conflict and Prejudice* (London: Phoenix Giant paperbacks, 1997), p. 49 ('Clearly, in Palestine as elsewhere in the Middle East, the modern inhabitants include among their ancestors those who lived in the country in antiquity').
6. See Frank H. Epp, *Whose Land is Palestine? The Middle East Problem in Historical Perspective* (Michigan: Wm. B. Eerdams Publishing Co., 1971), pp. 39–40 (displaying a table listing the peoples or powers in effective control of Palestine from ancient times to the present). See also, Moshe Menuhin, *The Decadence of Judaism in Our Times* (New York: Exposition Press, 1965), p. 18 (describing the Palestinian Arabs as descendants of the Philistines, the Canaanites and other early tribes, the Greeks, Romans, Arabs, Crusaders, Mongols and Turks).
7. See Lewis, *Semites and Anti-Semites*, *supra* note 5, p. 49.
8. See Epp, *Whose Land*, *supra* note 6, p. 14.
9. Ibid.
10. The website of Israel's Ministry of Foreign Affairs contains a section on the history of Israel tracing its roots back to the biblical times and referring to the period in between the dispersal of the Jews during Roman times some 2,000 years ago to the creation of Israel in 1948 as a period of 'foreign domination'. See the historical overview at http://www.mfa.gov.il/mfa/history/history%20of%20israel/ (last retrieved 20 October 2008).
11. See Henry Cattan, *Palestine, the Arabs and Israel: The Search for Justice* (London: Longman Group, 1969), p. 3.

12. See Lewis, *Semites and Anti-Semites*, *supra* note 5 at p. 49 ('The Arab case in Palestine would not be strengthened by showing that the ancient Canaanites were Arabs; it is not weakened showing they were not').
13. However, see e.g. David J. Bercuson who argues that 1948 is the crucial event in *The Secret Army* (New York: Stein & Day, 1984), p. xiii ('The 1948 war is the key event in the history of the Arab–Israeli conflict because Israel was born out of its victory in that war, and the face of the Middle East was unalterably changed by that birth').
14. However, see e.g. Jeremy Bowen who argues that 1967 is the crucial event in *Six Days: How the 1967 War Shaped the Middle East* (London: Simon & Schuster, 2004, paperback), p. 359 ('Arabs and Israelis were fighting over the land long before 1967. But decisive victories change conflicts decisively. The 1967 war made the Arab–Israeli conflict what it is today. The only way to make peace is to unravel what 1967 left behind').
15. On the legal aspects of Jordan's occupation and annexation of the West Bank see Marjorie M. Whiteman, 2 *Digest of International Law* (Washington, DC: Department of State Publication, 1963), pp. 1163–8.
16. See U.O. Umozurike, *International Law and Colonialism in Africa* (Enugu: Nwamife Publishers, 1979), pp. 24–36.
17. See generally Margaret MacMillan, *Peacemakers: The Paris Conference of 1919 and its Attempt to End War* (London: John Murray, 2003, paperback).
18. See Justin McCarthy, *The Population of Palestine: Population History and Statistics of the Late Ottoman Period and the Mandate* (New York: Columbia University Press, 1990), table 2.2, p. 26. The population figures cited for Arabs include Muslims (611,098), Christians (70,429), Druze (7,268) and Shii (162).
19. Ibid., Christians outnumbered Jews in Palestine by 11,701 persons.
20. For a brief explanation of these various agreements see the introductory chapter of Victor Kattan (ed.), *The Palestine Question in International Law* (London: British Institute of International and Comparative Law, 2008).
21. On the Oslo Accords see Geoffrey Watson, *The Oslo Accords: International Law and the Israeli–Palestinian Peace Agreements* (Oxford: Oxford University Press, 2000), (reproducing the agreements in the appendix).
22. See Proposed New Constitution for Palestine, Prepared by the Secretary of State for the Colonies to Parliament by Command of His Majesty, 12 March 1936 (London: HMSO, 1936), Cmd 5119. (The proposals concerned reforming the composition of the Legislative Council, the powers and duties of the Council and the powers and duties of the High Commissioner.)
23. This was despite the fact that this was recommended by Britain's man on the ground, the High Commissioner of Palestine. See 310 *Parliamentary Debates*, Commons, cols 1079–150, and cols 1166–73, 24 March 1936.
24. See The Eternal Thought (1), 'We Support the Intifada', Address by the Eminent Leader of the Islamic Republic of Iran, Ayatollah Khamenei, on the Occasion of the International Conference on Palestinian Intifada, Tehran, 24 April 2001 (London: Centre for Islamic Political Studies, 2001).
25. The attack on the UN headquarters in Baghdad in 2003 is but one example. Attacks on UN personnel have also been reported in Algiers, Lebanon and elsewhere. See 'Recent attacks on the United Nations', *Agence France-Presse*, 11 December 2007.
26. See Jean Allain, *International Law in the Middle East: Closer to Power than Justice* (Aldershot: Ashgate Publishers, 2004).
27. See *The Trials of Major War Criminals, Agreement and Principal Speeches*, Treaty Series No. 27 (1946), Prosecution and Punishment of the Major War Criminals of the European Axis, and the Charter of the International Military Tribunal, London, 8 August 1945; Charter for the International Military Tribunal in the Far East in Joseph Keenan (ed.), *Trial of Japanese War Criminals* (US Department of State, 1946); and *Law Reports of Trials of War Criminals Selected and Prepared by the United Nations War Crimes Commission*, Vols I–XV (London: Published for the United Nations War Crimes Commission by His Majesty's Stationery Office, 1948).

28. A puppet state is a term used to describe nominal sovereigns under effective foreign control. See James Crawford, *The Creation of States in International Law* (Oxford: Oxford University Press, 2006), pp. 78–83, at p. 78. On the practice of apartheid in the occupied territories, see the forthcoming report published by South Africa's Human Sciences and Research Council in Pretoria which is provisionally entitled *Occupation, Colonialism, Apartheid? A Re-Assessment of Israel's Practices in the Occupied Palestinian Territories under International Law*.
29. See Nur Masalha, *Expulsion of the Palestinians: The Concept of 'Transfer' in Zionist Political Thought, 1882–1948* (Washington, DC: Institute for Palestine Studies, 1992).
30. See 445 *Parliamentary Debates*, Commons, 12 December 1947, col. 1396.
31. See Philip C. Jessup, *The Birth of Nations* (New York: Columbia University Press, 1974), p. 289.
32. On human rights violations in the occupied territories see the numerous reports of the UN Special Rapporteur for Human Rights in the Occupied Arab Territories, available on the website of the Office of the High Commissioner for Human Rights in Geneva, Switzerland: http://www.ohchr.org/EN/countries/MENARegion/Pages/PSIndex.aspx (last retrieved 22 January 2008).
33. On Zionism as a 'solution' to a European minority problem see James Parkes, *The Emergence of the Jewish Problem 1878–1939* (London: Oxford University Press, 1946).
34. See Theodor Herzl, *Der Judenstaat* (Leipzig und Wien: M. Breitenstein, 1896).
35. British Museum, Balfour Papers, 49734/154–60, Curzon to Balfour, 20 August 1919, cited in MacMillan, *Peacemakers*, *supra* note 17, p. 435.

1 ANTI-SEMITISM, COLONIALISM AND ZIONISM

1. The word 'Semite' was always understood to refer exclusively to Jews in nineteenth-century anti-Semitic literature. This has not, however, stopped people from making the argument that the Arab–Israeli conflict is not racial because both Arabs and Jews are Semites. See e.g. Quincy Wright, 'The Middle East Crisis', in Isaac Shapiro (ed.), *The Middle East: Prospects for Peace, Background Papers and Proceedings of the Thirteenth Hammarskjöld Forum, Published for the Association of the Bar of the City of New York* (New York: Oceana Publications, 1969), p. 1 ('The recent history of Palestine has been dominated by the conflict between Arabs and Zionists. Both recognise that the conflict is not racial because both claim to be Semites, nor is it religious because Islam has always tolerated Jews and Christians as "people of the book"'). The supposition that the conflict between the Arabs and the Zionists is not racial is not, however, uncontested. This is because the Zionists, particularly in the days of Herzl, considered the Jews to be a separate race from the Arabs, linguistically, culturally and ethnically. By race they likely meant 'nation'. This is why A.J. Balfour, Herbert Asquith, Lloyd George, George Curzon and others referred to the Zionists specifically as a race, the 'Hebrew race', being a common terminology. Most prominent Zionists of that generation also referred to themselves as a race including Theodor Herzl and Nahum Sokolow. This does not, however, mean that Zionism is racism. At the time considering oneself to be of a particular race was not considered derogatory. It was considered to be consistent with the evolution of the species. In the late nineteenth century and at the dawn of the twentieth century this is how most people distinguished themselves from 'the other'. It was a time when ethnography was used in international law textbooks, when Charles Darwin published his *Origin of the Species*, and when Thomas Huxley published his *Man's Place in Nature*.
2. On the mechanics of the Final Solution see Raul Hilberg, *The Destruction of the European Jews* (London: W.H. Allen, 1961).
3. On anti-Semitism in England in the Middle Ages see Léon Poliakov, *The History of Anti-Semitism, Vol. 1, From Roman Times to Court Jews*, trans. from the French by Richard Howard (London: Routledge & Kegan Paul, 1974), pp. 203–9.

4. On the Jewish expulsions from the Iberian Peninsula see Léon Poliakov, *The History of Anti-Semitism, Vol. II, From Mohammed to Marranos*, trans. from the French by Natalie Gerardi (London: Routledge & Kegan Paul, 1974).
5. See Albert M. Hyamson, *Palestine: The Rebirth of an Ancient People* (London: Sidgwick & Jackson Ltd, 1917), p. 103.
6. See Justice Louis D. Brandeis, *The Jewish Problem: How to Solve It* (Cleveland: Joseph Saslaw, 1934), p. 13.
7. Sarah Gordon in her study includes Karl Marx, Friedrich Nietzsche and Arthur Dinter as further examples of German anti-Semites. See Sarah Gordon, *Hitler, Germans and the 'Jewish Question'* (New Jersey: Princeton University Press, 1984), pp. 24–9. In this context, Houston Stewart Chamberlain, a British born naturalised German who married the German composer Wagner's daughter and who wrote a very influential anti-Semitic book that was a best seller in Germany should also be mentioned.
8. See Francis R. Nicosia, *The Third Reich and the Palestine Question* (London: I.B. Tauris, 1985), pp. 20–1. See also, Isaiah Friedman, *Germany, Turkey, and Zionism 1897–1918* (Oxford: Clarendon Press, 1977), chapter I, 'The Birth of Zionism in Germany', pp. 3–19.
9. See Nicosia, *The Third Reich*, p. 20.
10. Ibid., p. 21.
11. Ibid., pp. 21–6.
12. See Bruno Bauer, 'The Jewish Problem (1843)', in Paul Mendes-Flohr and Jehuda Reinharz (eds), *The Jew in the Modern World: A Documentary History* (Oxford: Oxford University Press, 1995), pp. 321–4. Bauer asks at p. 322: 'Can the Jews really possess [human rights] as long as he lives in perpetual segregation from others, as long as he therefore must declare that the others are not really his fellowmen?'
13. See e.g. *Aspects of the Jewish Question by a Quarterly Reviewer with a Map* (London: John Murray, 1902). (The author, who is anonymous in this book, but who was evidently personally acquainted with Dr Herzl, criticised the Zionists for siding with the anti-Semites in trying to remove themselves from Europe and into Palestine, instead of fighting for the civil and political rights in their countries of origin. The book has been attributed in library catalogues to Laurie Magnus.)
14. See Nicosia, *Third Reich*, *supra* note 8, pp. 19–21.
15. This, coming from a man who thought the Jews were a 'state within a state', and who was against granting the Jews civil rights, 'except perhaps, if one night we chop off all their heads and replace them with new ones, in which there would not be one single Jewish idea'. See the English translation by M. Gerber of the passage in Johann Gottlieb Fichte, 'Beitrag zur Berichtung der Urteils des Publicums ueber die Franzoesische Revolution' (1793), quoted in Mendes-Flohr and Reinharz, *The Jew in the Modern World*, *supra* note 12, p. 309.
16. See Nicosia, *Third Reich*, *supra* note 8, p. 19.
17. Ibid.
18. See Raphael Patai (ed.), *The Complete Diaries of Theodor Herzl*, Vol. I (New York: Herzl Press, 1960), p. 182 (quote from 'Address to his family', 15 June 1895).
19. Ibid. (emphasis in original).
20. *Aspects of the Jewish Question*, *supra* note 13, at pp. 18–19.
21. See Lucien Wolf, 'The Zionist Peril', 17 *The Jewish Quarterly Review* (1904), pp. 1–25 at pp. 22–3 ('The characteristic peril of Zionism is that it is the natural and abiding ally of anti-Semitism and its most powerful justification').
22. See Arthur Hertzberg (ed.), *The Zionist Idea: A Historical Analysis and Reader* (New York: Harper & Row, 1959), pp. 226–30 (reproducing a translation of the full text of Herzl's address). The quote appears at p. 226 ('Anti-Semitism – you know it, alas, too well! – is the up-to-date designation of the movement').
23. See Lenni Brenner, *Zionism in the Age of the Dictators* (London: Croom Helm, 1983), p. 15.

24. Adolf Hitler, *Mein Kampf*, with an introduction by D. Cameron Watt, trans. by Ralph Marheim (London: Pimlico, 1992), p. 52 (emphasis added, apart from the word 'Zionists' which is emphasised in the original).
25. Palestine Royal Commission Report, July 1937, Cmd 5479, p. 279.
26. See *A Survey of Palestine*, prepared in December 1945 and January 1946 for the Information of the Anglo-American Committee of Inquiry, Vol. 1 (HMSO, reprinted with permission by the Institute for Palestine Studies, Washington DC, 1991), p. 210 ('... the Jewish population may now include between 50,000 and 60,000 illegal immigrants who have settled in Palestine at any time since 1920 when the first Immigration Ordinance was enacted').
27. An English translation of this law is available online at the University of West England: http://www.ess.uwe.ac.uk/documents/gerblood.htm (last retrieved 20 October 2008). However, this link does not include the law's introductory and accompanying notes.
28. *Die Nuernberger Gesetze*, 5th edition (Berlin, 1939), pp. 13–14, cited and translated in Regina S. Sharif, *Non-Jewish Zionism: Its Roots in Western History* (London: Zed Press, 1983), p. 5.
29. See Jon and David Kimche, *The Secret Roads: The 'Illegal' Migration of a People 1938–1948* (London: Secker & Warburg, 1954), p. 29.
30. Quote from Kimche, ibid., pp. 29–30.
31. See *A Survey of Palestine*, *supra* note 26, pp. 187–203.
32. Ibid.
33. The full texts of the District Court and Supreme Court judgments translated from the Hebrew into English are available in E. Lauterpacht (ed.), 36 *International Law Reports* (London: Butterworths, 1968), pp. 5–276 and pp. 277–344 (reproducing the Supreme Court judgment along with a very useful bibliography). The decision was upheld on appeal to the Israel Supreme Court which concerned the controversy over the jurisdiction of the Israeli courts to try Eichmann retroactively for crimes that he had committed before the state of Israel came into being in May 1948. He was hanged at midnight on 31 May 1962 at Ramla Prison. The jurisdictional aspects of the case provoked quite a debate in the literature. See J.E.S. Fawcett, 'The Eichmann Case', 27 *British Yearbook of International Law* (1962), pp. 181–215; L.C. Green, 'The Eichmann Case', 23 *Modern Law Review* (1960), pp. 507–15; Ian Brownlie, 'Eichmann: A Further Comment', *The Criminal Law Review* (1962), pp. 817–19; and Georg Schwarzenberger, 'The Eichmann Judgment', 15 *Current Legal Problems* (1962), pp. 248–65.
34. See Hannah Arendt, *Eichmann in Jerusalem: A Report on the Banality of Evil* (London: Penguin Books, 1994), pp. 40–1. (Herzl's *Der Judenstaat* was said to have 'converted Eichmann promptly and forever to Zionism'.)
35. Ibid., p. 41.
36. Ibid., p. 56.
37. See Lord Russell of Liverpool, *The Trial of Adolf Eichmann* (London: Pimlico, 2002), pp. 201–11.
38. On Eichmann and the Madagascar Plan see David Cesarani, *Eichmann: His Life and Crimes* (London: William Heinemann, 2004), pp. 84–6.
39. Attorney-General of the Government of Israel v. Adolf Eichmann, Israel, District Court of Jerusalem, 12 December 1961, in 36 *International Law Reports*, *supra* note 33 at pp. 100–1.
40. Ibid., p. 100.
41. Ibid., p. 101.
42. See Hani A. Faris, 'Israel Zangwill's Challenge to Zionism', 4 *Journal of Palestine Studies* (1975), pp. 74–90. Zangwill proposed establishing a Jewish state in Cyrenaica, Angola, Australia, Mesopotamia, Manchuria, Cuba and Canada. He thought that the Zionist project in Palestine was doomed because the Arabs would never accept it. He was consequently condemned by the Zionists.

43. See Robert Weinberg, *Stalin's Forgotten Zion: Birobidzhan and the Making of a Soviet Jewish Homeland: An Illustrated History 1928–1996* (Berkeley: University of California Press, 1998).
44. See Theodor Herzl, *The Jewish State* (1896), trans. from the original German by Sylvie D'Avigdor (New York: Dover Publication Inc., 1988).
45. See Léon Poliakov, *The History of Anti-Semitism, Vol. IV, Suicidal Europe*, trans. from the French by George Klin (Oxford: Oxford University Press, 1985), pp. 195–6 ('The key figure of British policy in the Near East, Sir Mark Sykes, thought and said even more offensive things, indulging in classic caricatures until he became enthused by the Zionist project').
46. Meinertzhagen was the first Chief Political Officer in Palestine. His views of Jews were very strange and on occasion violently anti-Semitic. He objected to people thinking that he was Jewish because of his foreign sounding surname and expressed admiration for Hitler when he first met him. See Colonel R. Meinertzhagen, *Middle East Diary 1917–1956* (London: The Cresset Press, 1959), p. x (preface), pp. 49–50 (anti-Semitism and Zionism) and pp. 149–50 (writing that Hitler struck him 'as being a man of immense strength both physical and mental, possessing a magnetic personality, very sincere and absolutely truthful. This latter characteristic struck me most').
47. See David Fromkin, *A Peace to End all Peace* (London: Andre Deutsche, 1989), p. 294 ('As of 1913, the last date for which there were figures, only about one per cent of the world's Jews had signified their adherence to Zionism').
48. See Bernard Gainer, *The Alien Invasion: The Origins of the Aliens Act of 1905* (London: Heinemann Educational Books, 1972).
49. See Frederick Bradshaw (pro) and Charles Emanuel (con), *Alien Immigration: Should Restrictions Be Imposed?* (London: Ibister & Co., 1904).
50. Ibid., p. 4.
51. See B. Disraeli, M.P., *Tancred*, in *Disraeli's Novels and Tales*, Vol. II (London: Routledge, Warne & Routledge, 1862), pp. 3–364.
52. See Bradshaw, *Alien Immigration, supra* note 49, p. 7.
53. See e.g. Colin Holmes, *Anti-Semitism in British Society, 1876–1939* (London: Edward Arnold, 1979); Gisela C. Lebzelter, *Political Anti-Semitism in England 1918–1939* (London: Macmillan, 1978); and Tony Kushner, *The Persistence of Prejudice: Anti-Semitism in British Society During the Second World War* (Manchester: Manchester University Press, 1989).
54. See *The Jew in London: A Study of Racial Character and Present-Day Conditions Being Two Essays Prepared for the Toynbee Trustees* by C. Russell, BA, and H.S. Lewis, MA with an Introduction by Canon Barnett and a Preface by the Right Hon. James Bryce, MP (London: T. Fisher Unwin, 1900).
55. James Bryce MP, ibid.
56. Canon Barnett, ibid.
57. Ibid., pp. xxix–xxv (from the introduction by Canon Barnett).
58. Ibid.
59. See Patai, *Herzl Diaries, supra* note 18, Vol. I, p. 9.
60. Ibid.
61. On the Dreyfus affair, see Alain Pagès (ed.), *Emile Zola: The Dreyfus Affair* (New Haven: Yale University Press, 1996); on Saratoga, see Brandeis, *The Jewish Problem, supra* note 6; on the Marconi affair, see Frances Lonsdale Donaldson, *The Marconi Scandal* (London: R. Hart-Davis, 1962).
62. See Lloyd P. Gartner, *The Jewish Immigrant in England 1870–1914* (London: Vallentine Mitchell, 2001), p. 280 ('The immigration of Jews to England decisively altered the Jewish community. In the forty years from 1880 it approximately quintupled from its original 60,000 not only by direct addition from the dock-side but from the immigrants' high birth rate').
63. See Report of the Royal Commission on Alien Immigration with Minutes of Evidence and Appendix, Vol. 1, The Report (London: HMSO, 1903), Cd 1741. The Members of the

Royal Commission were Lord James of Hereford, Lord Rothschild, Alfred E. Lyttleton, KC, MP, Sir Kennelm Digby, KCB, Henry Norman, MP, and William Vallance.

64. Ibid., pp. 3–5.
65. Ibid., p. 6, para. 37.
66. Ibid.
67. See James L. Gelvin, *The Israel–Palestine Conflict: One Hundred Years of War* (Cambridge: Cambridge University Press, 2007), p. 43.
68. Ibid.
69. Mr A.J. Balfour, Evening Sitting, Aliens Bill, [Second Reading], 145 *Parliamentary Debates*, Commons, 2 May 1905, col. 795 ('The treatment of the [Jewish] race has been a disgrace to Christendom, a disgrace which tarnishes the fair name of Christianity even at this moment ...').
70. A.J. Balfour, 149 *Parliamentary Debates*, Commons, 10 July 1905, cols 177–9 at col. 178.
71. See the statements made by Mr Samuel, ibid., cols 159–61. See also, the statements made by Sir Charles Dilke, ibid., cols 150–1 ('... this Bill was recommended to the constituencies on anti-Semitic grounds. A considerable portion of the London Press supported it on that ground; and hon. Members had received a great mass of correspondence which showed them the same feeling').
72. See A.J. Balfour, 149 *Parliamentary Debates*, Commons, 10 July 1905, col. 155.
73. See Jason Tomes, *Balfour and Foreign Policy: The International Thought of a Conservative Statesman* (Cambridge: Cambridge University Press, 1997), p. 204.
74. Ibid., p. 201 ('Balfour the anti-Semite liked Cosima Wagner and told Weizmann that he shared many of her anti-Semitic ideas. He complained of a pompous dinner with the Sassoon family, where "the Hebrews were in an actual majority" – "I began to understand the point of view of those who object to alien immigration!"'). See also, Jehuda Reinharz, *Chaim Weizmann: The Making of a Zionist Leader* (Oxford: Oxford University Press, 1985), p. 274 ('... to the tens of thousands of Jews who had in the meantime found asylum on British shores, Balfour's statements in the Commons were not substantially different from those of any anti-Semite in Stepney and Whitchapel, or of a member of the British Brothers League').
75. See Tomes, *Balfour and Foreign Policy*, p. 202 (citing a conversation between Balfour and L. Wolf, 31 January 1917, PRO FO 800/210 ff. 150–2).
76. See Kushner, *Persistence of Prejudice*, *supra* note 53, p. 11 (citing D. Cesarani, 'Anti-Semitism in England After the First World War', in *Immigrants and Minorities*, VI, 1987, p. 22).
77. On religion and Zionism, generally, see Barbara Tuchman, *Bible and Sword: England and Palestine from the Bronze Age to Balfour* (London: Phoenix Paperbacks, 2001).
78. See, generally, Stuart A. Cohen, *English Zionists and British Jews: The Communal Politics of Anglo-Jewry, 1895–1920* (New Jersey: Princeton University Press, 1982).
79. See *Edwin Montagu and the Balfour Declaration*, Arab League Office, 1/11 Hay Hill, London, W1, 1966. (This is a pamphlet reproducing the full texts of Montagu's 1917 three memoranda against Zionism from British Cabinet Records from what was then the Public Records Office.)
80. Ibid., pp. 5–8.
81. See Nahum Sokolow, *History of Zionism 1600–1918* (London: Longmans, Green & Co., 1919), p. xxiii (last paragraph of Balfour's introduction).
82. See Patai, *Herzl Diaries*, *supra* note 18, Vol. 1, p. 171.
83. Ibid.
84. See Tomes, *Balfour and Foreign Policy*, *supra* note 73 and Reinharz, *Chaim Weizmann*, *supra* note 74.
85. See Brian Klug, 'The Other Balfour: Recalling the 1905 Aliens Act', in Stephen W. Massil (ed.), *The Jewish Yearbook* (2005), p. xvi ('[Balfour] ideas about Jews were rooted in the Old Testament brand of Christianity on which he was raised by his Evangelical mother').

86. See Naomi Shepherd, *Ploughing Sand: British Rule in Palestine 1917–1948* (London: John Murray, 1999), p. 6.
87. For a recent and largely sympathetic portrayal of colonialism and British imperialism see Niall Ferguson, *Empire: How Britain Made the Modern World* (London: Penguin Books, 2004).
88. Colonialism was outlawed in 1960 when the UN passed the Declaration on the Granting of Independence to Colonial Countries and Peoples in UN General Assembly resolution 1514 (XV), 14 December 1960. ('The subjection of peoples to alien subjugation, domination and exploitation constitutes a denial of fundamental human rights, is contrary to the Charter of the United Nations and is an impediment to the promotion of world peace and co-operation.')
89. On Zionism and colonialism, generally, see Gershon Shafir, 'Zionism and Colonialism: A Comparative Approach', in Ilan Pappé (ed.), *The Israel/Palestine Question: A Reader* (Abingdon: Routledge, 1999), pp. 78–93.
90. See Thomas Alfred Walker, *A History of the Law of Nations* (Cambridge: Cambridge University Press, 1899), p. 1 ('The term [international law] is by its employers used to denominate certain rules which are asserted to be observed *between states*' – italics in original).
91. The German word *öffentlich-rechtlich* or 'public law' was apparently used instead of the term *völker-rechtlich* or 'public international law', so as to allay Ottoman fears that this was not an expansionist project. See Aharon Cohen, *Israel and the Arab World* (New York: W.H. Allen, 1970), note at p. 39. However, despite the terminology there is little doubt that it was public *international* law and not Swiss constitutional law that aided the Zionist project.
92. See Gelvin, *One Hundred Years of War*, *supra* note 67, p. 54.
93. Ibid.
94. Ibid.
95. Reproduced in Mendes-Flohr and Reinharz, *The Jew in the Modern World*, *supra* note 12, p. 540 (emphasis added).
96. See e.g. Jacob Oettinger, *Jewish Colonization in Palestine: Methods, Plans and Capital* (London: Head Office of the Jewish National Fund, 1919). Even after the establishment of the state of Israel in 1948–49, the word 'colonisation' was still in vogue. See e.g. Yaakov Morris, *Pioneers from the West: A History of Colonization in Israel by Settlers from English-Speaking Countries* (Jerusalem: Youth and Hechalutz Department, World Zionist Organisation, 1953). There are many other examples of such literature.
97. See Gershon Shafir, 'Settler Citizenship in the Jewish Colonization of Palestine', in Caroline Elkins and Susan Pedersen (eds), *Settler Colonialism in the Twentieth Century: Projects, Practices, Legacies* (New York: Routledge, 2005), pp. 41–57 at p. 44.
98. Ibid., p. 44 (noting that Rothschild's first envoy and director of agriculture, Justin Dugourd, who had worked in Algeria and Egypt, recommended developing viticulture in Palestine and that Gerard Ermens gained his experience in Senegal and Egypt and became the Inspector General of Agriculture after 1888).
99. See Ran Aaronsohn, *Rothschild and Early Jewish Colonization in Palestine* (Jerusalem: The Hebrew University Magnes Press, 2000), pp. 35–8 (describing Jewish colonisation in Argentina).
100. Ibid., p. 282.
101. See Simon Schama, *Two Rothschilds and the Land of Israel* (London: William Collins Sons & Co. Ltd, 1978), pp. 142–7.
102. Ibid., p. 144.
103. See Zvi Shilony, *Ideology and Settlement: The Jewish National Fund, 1897–1914* (Jerusalem: The Magnes Press, The Hebrew University, 1998), pp. 53–4. (Naming Dr Selig Soskin, Prof. Warburg, Dr Franz Oppenheimer and Dr Arthur Ruppin as being influenced by the German colonisation of Posen which they sought to emulate in Palestine. Prof. Warburg, for instance, actually founded the Committee for German Colonial Economy and

in 1901 he was appointed a member of the Prussian Colonisation Committee. Moreover, Dr Ruppin was born, raised and educated in the Posen region.)

104. See Shafir, 'Settler Cizenship', *supra* note 97, p. 45.
105. See Gelvin, *One Hundred Years of War*, *supra* note 67, p. 63.
106. See Aaronsohn, *Rothschild and Early Jewish Colonization*, *supra* note 99, at pp. 162–3. Rothschild even inserted clauses into contracts stipulating that employment would be offered to Jewish workers only (p. 96).
107. Shafir, 'Settler Cizenship', *supra* note 97, at p. 45.
108. See Yossi Katz, *The 'Business' of Settlement: Private Entrepreneurship in the Jewish Settlement of Palestine, 1900–1914* (Jerusalem: The Hebrew University Magnes Press, 1994), pp. 252–6 (giving the example of the Tiberias Land and Plantation Company, established by Russian Jewish businessman in 1909 to purchase 5,500 dunams of land in a place called Majdal, which was then Hebraised to Migdal. In 1911–12 when the income from marketing vegetables and grain was lower than expected the management decided to employ some Arabs as regular workers because they were less expensive than Jewish workers. However, this was met with strong opposition from the Jewish workers who approached the heads of the Tiberias Land and Plantation Company directly to secure the abolition of Arab labour in Migdal (p. 269). Following the workers' demand, the number of Arab workers was radically reduced).
109. See Yael Ikan, *The World Zionist Organization: The National Institutions, Structure and Functions* (Jerusalem: The Department of Organisation and Community Relations, The World Zionist Organisation, 1997), p. 44.
110. Ibid.
111. See Nachum T. Gross, 'The Anglo-Palestine Company: The Formative Years, 1903–1914', in Gad G. Gilbar (ed.), *Ottoman Palestine 1800–1914: Studies in Economic and Social History* (Leiden: Brill, 1990), pp. 219–53, at p. 219.
112. Ibid.
113. See Aaronsohn, *Rothschild and Early Jewish Colonization*, *supra* note 99, p. 286. Gelvin, *One Hundred Years of War*, *supra* note 67, p. 62.
114. See Schama, *Two Rothschilds*, *supra* note 101, pp. 192–3.
115. See Walid Khalidi, 'The Jewish-Ottoman Land Company: Herzl's Blueprint for the Colonization of Palestine', 22 *Journal of Palestine Studies* (1993), pp. 30–47.
116. Ibid., p. 31 citing Adolf Böhm, *Die Zionistische Bewegung*, 2nd ed., Vol. 1 (Berlin, 1935), p. 191.
117. Ibid. Khalidi reproduces the full text of the Charter for a Jewish-Ottoman Land Company translated from its original German into English, which is annexed to this article at pp. 44–7. The original document is available at the Herzl Archives in Vienna.
118. A *dunum* is the equivalent of 1,000 square metres.
119. See Khalidi, 'Jewish-Ottoman Land Company', *supra* note 115, pp. 34–7.
120. Ibid., p. 37.
121. See Raphael Patai (ed.), *The Complete Diaries of Theodor Herzl*, Vol. II (New York: Herzl Press, 1960), p. 711.
122. It was also in Britain where on 8 April 1907 the Jewish National Fund was first incorporated as an English company with its registered office in London. See Joseph D. Jacobs, *The Jewish National Fund* (London: The Zionist, Jewish National Fund Commission of the United Kingdom, not dated).
123. See Sharif, *Non-Jewish Zionism*, *supra* note 28, pp. 58–9, citing Palmerston to Ponsonby, Public Records Office MSS, F.O. 78/390, (No. 134), 11 August 1840.
124. Ibid., pp. 50–63.
125. Another plausible explanation is that Britain wanted a protégé in the Middle East to guard its interests and whereas France had the Catholics, and Russia the Greek-Orthodox, Britain had no comparable group to whom, by merit of common religion, it could extend its protection. See Sharif, *Non-Jewish Zionism*, *supra* note 28, pp. 55–6 citing Isaiah Friedman, 'Lord Palmerston and the Protection of Jews in Palestine, 1839–1851', in *Jewish Social Studies*.

126. See Niall Ferguson, *The House of Rothschild: The World's Banker 1849–1998* (London: Penguin Books, 2000), pp. 298–302 (describing the purchase of the shares).
127. The exact amount was £3,976,582:2:6. The Khedive had overestimated the number of shares he had (176,602 as opposed to 177,642 shares).
128. See Ferguson, *House of Rothschild*, *supra* note 126, p. 302. Apparently, the British Government did not have the time or the inclination to ask for such a colossal amount of money from the Bank of England.
129. See Ferguson, ibid., p. 302, cites Disraeli saying that the ownership of the shares gave Britain an additional 'leverage' – a justification to retaliate – in the event of a threat to her communications.
130. See Ferguson, ibid., p. 315 ('There can be no question that the Rothschilds benefited directly from the British occupation of Egypt').
131. See Lord Rothschild, *'You have it Madam', The Purchase, in 1875, of Suez Canal Shares by Disraeli and Baron Lionel de Rothschild* (London: W. & J. Mackay Ltd, 1980), p. 22.
132. See Ferguson, *House of Rothschild*, *supra* note 126, pp. 356–64 (describing how the Rothschilds financed Cecil Rhodes' activities in southern Africa). He writes at p. 361 that the Rothschilds did not 'have any qualms about Rhodes' use of force against the Matebele and other black African tribes who got in his way'.
133. See Ferguson, ibid., p. 360.
134. See Ferguson, ibid., p. 450. Ferguson seems to take it at face value that the Rothschilds were all Zionists. But this was not so as becomes clear from the Montagu memorandum mentioned in chapter 2.
135. For a thorough refutation of the Protocols see Hadassa Ben-Itto, *The Lie that Wouldn't Die: The Protocols of the Elders of Zion* (London: Vallentine Mitchell, 2005). This book, written by a former Israeli judge, painstakingly reproduces the transcripts of numerous court trials that found the Protocols to be forged.
136. See Raphael Patai (ed.), *The Complete Diaries of Theodor Herzl*, Vol. IV (New York: Herzl Press, 1960), pp. 1360–4.
137. Ibid., p. 1360.
138. Ibid., p. 1361.
139. Ibid.
140. Ibid.
141. Ibid.
142. Ibid., p. 1362.
143. Ibid.
144. Entry dated 24 October, on the train, between London and Folestone, ibid., pp. 1364–5 (emphasis added).
145. See Minutes of Evidence taken before the Royal Commission on Alien Immigration, Vol. II (London: HMSO, 1903), Cd. 1742, testimony of Dr Theodore Herzl, pp. 211–21.
146. Ibid., p. 211.
147. Ibid., p. 212 (emphasis added).
148. Ibid., p. 213.
149. Pattai, *Herzl Diaries*, Vol. IV, *supra* note 136, pp. 1446–7 (Herzl described Cromer as 'the most disagreeable Englishman I have ever faced').
150. See Rashid Ismail Khalidi, *British Policy Towards Syria and Palestine 1906–1914* (London: Ithaca Press, 1980), especially chapter 1, pp. 1–56 on the Aqaba incident and chapter 2 on its aftermath.
151. See Patai, *Herzl Diaries*, Vol. IV, *supra* note 136 at p. 1447 (Herzl describes Boutros as 'an old, seedy-looking, obese man, a Copt').
152. Ibid., p. 1428 (describing the Boutros document).
153. Ibid., p. 1501.
154. Ibid., p. 1473.
155. Ibid.
156. Ibid.
157. Ibid.

158. Ibid., p. 1474 (emphasis in original).
159. See Dr Oskar K. Rabinowicz, 'New Light on the East Africa Scheme', in Israel Cohen (ed.), *The Rebirth of Israel: A Memorial Tribute to Paul Goodman* (London: Edward Goldston & Son, 1952), pp. 78–9.
160. For the original draft of the Jewish Colonisation Scheme for East Africa see FO 2/785, Africa (East) Jewish Settlement 1903. Cecil James Barrington Hurst would become the British judge at the Permanent Court of International Justice from 1929 to 1942 and was its President from 1934 to 1936.
161. See Article 7, FO 2/785.
162. See FO 2/785, Africa (East) Jewish Settlement 1903. See also, Rabinowicz, 'New Light on the East Africa Scheme', *supra* note 159, pp. 82–3.
163. FO 2/785, Africa (East) Jewish Settlement 1903.
164. Article 1, FO 2/785, Africa (East) Jewish Settlement 1903.
165. Article 5 (d), ibid.
166. See Article 1 of the Montevideo Convention on the Rights and Duties of States, 26 December 1933, 165 *League of Nations Treaty Series*, p. 19.
167. Hurst was referring to Article 5 (h) of the Draft Agreement of the Jewish Colonisation Scheme for East Africa, *supra* note 160.
168. Article 5 (k), ibid.
169. See Article VI, General Act of the Conference of Berlin Conference, 76 *British and Foreign State Papers* (1885), p. 4 (reproduced in French).
170. See Patai, *Herzl Diaries*, Vol. I, *supra* note 18.
171. Ibid., Book 1, Paris, 12 June 1895, at p. 88.
172. See *The Times*, 28 August 1903 ('... their plan is not limited to emigration. It contemplates an experiment in Jewish self-government; and in that respect I venture to say that it is quite unnecessary, and is even likely to prove mischievous').
173. See the rather astonishing letter with anti-Semitic overtones from W.G. Mombasa to Sir Charles N.E. Elliot of 8 September 1903 in FO 2/785 ('... always as long as Jews are Jews, the incoming aliens will be a barrier to progress in the freedom of *Christian* religion; not to speak of the inevitable attitude against *Christian* preaching, and of the bigoted hostility towards the advocates of the Risen and Ascended *Christ*, the Son of God' – italics in original).
174. See the letter from L.J. Greenberg to the Rt. Hon. Joseph Chamberlain, MP, 13 July 1903, FO 2/785.
175. See Raphael Patai (ed.), *The Complete Diaries of Theodor Herzl*, Vol. III (New York: Herzl Press, 1960), *supra* note 170, Book Eight, 4 January 1900, pp. 1023–4 (on Cyprus), Vol. IV and pp. 1500–1 (on Sinai).
176. Ibid., pp. 1499–1500 (on Mozambique).
177. Ibid., letter to Mr Philippson, 12 July 1903, Vol. IV, pp. 1511–12. Philippson refused to approach the King and advised Herzl that the Congo was not appropriate for a Jewish settlement. For further reading on the Belgian colonisation of the Congo, and Leopold's part in it, see Adam Hochschild, *King Leopold's Ghost: A Story of Greed, Terror, and Heroism in Colonial Africa* (Boston: Mariner Books, 1999).
178. See Patai, *Herzl Diaries*, vol. III, 12 December 1903, pp. 1595–1600.
179. Ibid., p. 1600.
180. See FO 2/785, dated 20 July 1903.
181. Ibid., dated 23 July 1903.
182. See Robert G. Weisbord, *African Zion: The Attempt to Establish a Jewish Colony in the East Africa Protectorate 1903–1905* (Philadelphia: The Jewish Publication Society of America, 1968), pp. 206–19.
183. Ibid., citing the *Report on the Work of a Commission Sent Out by the Zionist Organization to Examine the Territory offered by His Majesty's Government for the Purposes of a Jewish Settlement in British East Africa* (London: Wertheimer, Lea & Co., 1905).

184. This quote is taken from Weisbord, ibid., at note 59 citing *Stenographisches Protokoll der Verhandlungen des VII Zionisten-Kongresses und des Ausserordentlichen Kongresses in Basel* (Berlin: Juedischer Verlag, 1905), p. 69.
185. See Arieh L. Avneri, *The Claim of Dispossession: Jewish Land-Settlement and the Arabs 1878–1948* (New York: Herzl Press, 1982), pp. 111–12.
186. See Yossi Katz, *The Battle for the Land: The History of the Jewish National Fund (KKL) before the Establishment of the State of Israel* (Jerusalem: The Hebrew University Magnes Press, 2005), p. 4 and p. 28.
187. See Gross, 'The Anglo-Palestine Company', *supra* note 111 at p. 224 (quoting from a report written by the British consul in Palestine saying that 'it must be admitted that the company does very little commercial business, it is concerned chiefly with banking transactions and with granting loans to Jews for the purpose of enabling them to buy land').
188. Abraham Granovsky, *Land Policy in Palestine* (New York: Bloch Publishing Company, 1940), p. 5 ('Expressed in figures, all the land purchased by Jews from the foundation of Rishon Lezion until today amounts to no more than 5.8% of the total area of Palestine ...').
189. See *The Jewish National Fund: The Key to the Development of Eretz Yisrael* (The Hague: Head Office of the Jewish National Fund, 1923), p. 2.
190. See ibid., resolution 2, and the preamble to the Covenant between the State of Israel and the Keren Kayemeth Le'Israel, signed on 28 November 1961. This is reproduced in English in Appendix No. 18, Ikan, *World Zionist Organization*, *supra* note 109, p. 131.
191. See Shafir, 'Settler Cizenship', *supra* note 97, p. 49.
192. See *Trial and Error: The Autobiography of Chaim Weizmann* (London: Hamish Hamilton, 1949), pp. 142–5 (describing his first encounter with A.J. Balfour when the latter was contesting the Clayton division of North Manchester in the 1906 General Election where he took the opportunity to explain to Balfour why some Zionists were opposed to the British Government's Uganda offer and why they preferred Palestine).
193. See Norman Rose (ed.), *From Palmerston to Balfour: Collected Essays of Mayir Vereté* (London: Frank Cass, 1992), pp. 14–15, and p. 18. ('The occupation, coupled with support of the Zionist cause, was the neatest, most convenient and becoming way of making France abandon her share in Palestine.')
194. See Tom Segev, *One Palestine, Complete: Jews and Arabs under the British Mandate* (London: Little, Brown & Co., 2000), pp. 42–3.
195. Ibid.

2 PALESTINE AND THE SCRAMBLE FOR THE MIDDLE EAST

1. See Paul C. Helmreich, *From Paris to Sèvres: The Partition of the Ottoman Empire at the Peace Conference of 1919–1920* (Columbus: Ohio State University Press, 1974), pp. 12–14.
2. Ibid., pp. 207–13.
3. Ibid., pp. 20–1.
4. See Raphael Patai (ed.), *The Complete Diaries of Theodor Herzl*, Vol. IV (New York: Herzl Press, 1960), p. 1474.
5. See, generally, Rashid Ismail Khalidi, *British Policy Towards Syria and Palestine 1906–1914* (London: Ithaca Press, 1980).
6. Ibid., chapters I and II.
7. See Proceedings of a Meeting, War Office, 29 October 1919 to discuss reconnaissance for an oil pipeline across the Arabian Desert in Political, Turkey Files, 1919–20, FO 371/4231. The War Office wanted a corridor between Haifa and Baghdad for a railway, oil pipeline and air route. Despite objections from the Foreign Office that the laws of war prohibited prospecting or concessions in occupied enemy territory, the War Office persuaded the Government to press ahead with surveying the area for 'strategic considerations'.

8. This explains why if one looks at a geographic map of Jordan its boundary with Syria and Iraq is in the shape of a funnel directed at Mosul.
9. For further reading on this era of history see e.g. T.E. Lawrence, *The Seven Pillars of Wisdom: A Triumph* (London: Penguin Books, new edition, 2000); George Antonius, *The Arab Awakening: The Story of the Arab National Movement* (London: Hamish Hamilton 1938); C. Ernest Dawn, *From Ottomanism to Arabism: Essays on the Origins of Arab Nationalism* (Urbana: University of Illinois Press, 1973); Elie Kedourie, *In the Anglo-Arab Labyrinth: The McMahon–Husayn Correspondence* (Cambridge: Cambridge University Press 1976); A.L. Tibawi, *Anglo-Arab Relations and the Question of Palestine 1914–1921* (London: Luzac & Co., 1977); and David Fromkin, *A Peace to End All Peace: The Fall of the Ottoman Empire and the Creation of the Modern Middle East*, (London: Andre Deutsche, 1989).
10. See the correspondence between Grey and McMahon on 19 June 1915 and on 23 August 1915. See also, the comments by Mr Chamberlain and the India Office, of 24 August 1915, File No. 118580, as well as the correspondence cited in FO 371/2486. For instance, in a telegram sent on 6 November 1915 to McMahon (File No. 34982), Grey wrote that: 'Our primary and vital object is not to secure a new sphere of British influence, but to get Arabs on our side against Turks.' See also, Elie Kedourie, 'Cairo and Khartoum on the Arab Question, 1915–18', 7 *The Historical Journal* (1964), pp. 280–97.
11. See the various telegrams exchanged between Sir Henry McMahon and Sir Edward Grey, 14 May 1915 and 19 May 1915, as well as the appeal by Sayed Ali el Morghani of Khartoum of 6 May 1915 enclosed in a letter from Sir R. Wingate to Sir E. Gray. Political: Turkey (War) File, 34982, FO 371/2486.
12. See correspondence between Sir Henry McMahon, G.C.M.G., G.C.V.O., K.C.I.E., C.S.I., His Majesty's High Commissioner in Cairo, and the Sherif of Mecca, 5957 *Command Paper* (1939) at pp. 3–18, 27 Great Britain House of Commons, Parliamentary Publications, Sessional Papers 1938–9, Vol. 27.
13. The 20-page memorandum on 'The British commitments to King Hussein', and other such papers form part of the 'Westermann Papers' collected by the late Professor William Linn Westermann, one-time Professor of History at Columbia University and adviser on Turkish affairs to the American Peace Conference delegation. He gave his papers to the Hoover Institution at Stanford University, California, with instructions that they were not to be opened until his death. He died in 1954. See 'Light on Britain's Palestine Promise', *The Times*, 17 April 1964, pp. 15–16. A copy of a similar document is available at the National Archives in Kew, entitled 'Memorandum on British Commitments to King Hussein', Political Intelligence Department, Foreign Office, Special 3, FO 608/92 Peace Conference British Delegation 1919.
14. See 50 *Parliamentary Debates*, Lords, 21 June 1922, col. 1008.
15. Although it is often referred to as the 'Sykes–Picot agreement', it actually consisted of an exchange of letters dated 15–16 May 1916, between Sir Edward Grey, the Foreign Minister, and Paul Cambon, the French Ambassador in London. See 'The Sykes–Picot Agreement, 16 May 1916', in John Norton Moore (ed.), *The Arab–Israeli Conflict, Vol. III: Documents* (New Jersey: Princeton University Press, 1977), at pp. 25–8, reproducing copies of the correspondence from 4 *Documents on British Foreign Policy 1919–1939*, p. 244 at pp. 245–7.
16. See Norton Moore, ibid., pp. 25–6 (emphasis added).
17. See 5 *Foreign Relations of the United States* 1919 (Washington: United States Government Printing Office, 1946), pp. 1–14 at p. 7. The Council of Four: Minutes of Meetings, 20 March to 24 May 1919, Notes of a Conference Held in the Prime Minister's Flat at 23 Rue Nitot, Paris, on Thursday , 20 March 1919 at 3 p.m., Paris Peace Conf. 180.03401/101 IC-163A.
18. It is arguable that the establishment in Palestine of a national *home* for the Jewish people would not be entirely incompatible with the Hussein–McMahon correspondence or the Sykes–Picot agreement if that home was to be established within Palestine subject to

Hussein's acquiescence and so long as Palestine formed a part of the independent Arab state or confederation of Arabs states. In other words, a Jewish refuge or home within Palestine would not be inconsistent with the pledges made to Hussein if he agreed to it and so long as the Zionists were not vested with sovereignty over Palestine.

19. See *The Times*, 'Palestine for the Jews: Official Sympathy', 9 November 1917, p. 7, col. F.
20. For the Rothschilds' association with Zionism and the Balfour Declaration see Niall Ferguson, *The World's Banker: The History of the House of Rothschild* (London: Weidenfeld & Nicolson, 1998), pp. 977–81.
21. A photo-static copy of the original Balfour Declaration is reproduced in Norton Moore, *The Arab–Israeli Conflict*, *supra* note 15 at p. 885 (emphasis added).
22. See generally, Walter Laqueur, *The History of Zionism* (London: I.B. Tauris, 2003), who discusses the reaction of Orthodox Jews to Zionism at pp. 410–11.
23. See Secretary of State to President Wilson in 2 *Foreign Relations of the United States, The Lansing Papers, 1914–1920* (Washington, DC: Government Printing Office, 1940), p. 71.
24. See Protests of Palestinians in America against Zionism, 19 January 1919. Anti-Zionism Society, NYC. They requested PM Lloyd George that no special concessions be granted to Zionists or any religious sect in Palestine (Registry No. 763, No. 162); Petition from 'Patriotic Society of Palestinians', Linares, N.L., Mexico, 18 December 1918. As natives of Palestine they protested against the delivery of their country to the Jews, who, they declared, had always been hostile to them, and pleaded with the members of the Peace Conference for some better solution for the future of Palestine, in Registry No. 1204, No. 204, signed by the president of the Society, Juan M. Buchaar, Pacifico Chahin. See also, letter from pro-Palestine Committee, Chile (Santiago) protesting against establishment of a Jewish state in Palestine (Registry No. 2263, No. 649, 17 December 1918); and 'Comité Pro-Libertad Palestina', Oruro, Bolivia, 28 November 1918. (Registry Number 2625, No. 783). The comité claimed it represented 'more than four thousand Palestinians and Syrian residents in Bolivia'. These documents can be seen in their original form at FO 608/98.
25. Ibid.
26. See Decision submitted to the Peace Conference in Paris by all the Delegates of the Districts of Palestine or Southern Syria, 5 February, 1919, FO 608/98.
27. See 'The Palestine Conference', Jerusalem, (sd.) J.N. Camp, Captain, Intelligence (E), 15 February, 1919, FO 608/98.
28. Ibid.
29. At the steps of the Citadel, just inside Jaffa Gate, General Allenby's Proclamation was read in Arabic, Hebrew, English, French, Italian, Greek and Russian, and posted up on the walls: 'To the inhabitants of Jerusalem the Blessed and the People dwelling in its vicinity. The defeat inflicted on the Turks by the troops under my command has resulted in the occupation of your city by my forces. I therefore here and now proclaim it to be under Martial Law, under which form of administration it will remain so long as military considerations make it necessary.' See 'Palestine under Mandate' by Sir Thomas W. Haycraft, Late Chief Justice in Palestine, talk given at the Central Asian Society on 28 February 1928, CO 733/150/11.
30. However, it has been argued that a conquest of sorts was still considered legitimate even after the First World War. See e.g. Sharon Korman, *The Right of Conquest: The Acquisition of Territory by Force in International Law* (Oxford: Clarendon Press, 1996) p. 143. (The Mandates System served as a kind of surrogate for the right of conquest, whereby the fruits of conquest were still reaped by the victors but according to means more sensitive to the ideological needs of the twentieth century.)
31. For an argument that the mandates system marked a reaction against the policy of acquisition which had hitherto characterised the relations of the Great Powers to backward peoples see Norman Bentwich, *The Mandates System* (London: Longmans, Green & Co., 1930), at p. 5. For a somewhat different argument see Anthony Anghie, 'Colonialism and the Birth of International Institutions: Sovereignty, Economy, and the Mandate System

of the League of Nations', 34 *New York University Journal of International Law and Politics* (2001–02), pp. 513–633 (arguing that the mandates system was an extension of colonialism).

32. See 'Maximalist Coup: Forcible Seizure of Power' and 'Jewish Zionists: British Government Support' in the *Manchester Guardian*, 9 November 1917, both on p. 5.
33. When Lenin came to power, one of the first objectives of his new government was to abolish secret diplomacy, hence the exposure of the secret treaties. See R. St J. MacDonald, 'Soviet International Law and Policy in the Early Years: Is Anything Left?' in Karel Wellens (ed.), *International Law: Theory and Practice, Essays in Honour of Eric Suy* (The Hague: Martinus Nijhoff, 1998), at p. 77–9.
34. The Sykes–Picot agreement was found by Leon Trotsky amongst the secret papers of the Russian Foreign Office. The memorandum was subsequently published in the *Isvestia* on 24 November 1917 and in the *Manchester Guardian* on 19 January 1918. See F. Seymour Cooks, *The Secret Treaties and Understandings* (London: Union of Democratic Control, 1918), p. 44.
35. See Alexei Vassiliev, *Russian Policy in the Middle East: From Messianism to Pragmatism* (Reading: Ithaca, 1993), pp. 8–9 ('The efforts aimed at destroying the old system of international relations included, among other things, a public "denouncing of secret diplomacy" and the publication of secret agreements extracted from the archives of Russia's Diplomatic Department. An important example of the latter was the Sykes–Picot agreement concerning the division of the Asian part of Turkey, concluded between Britain and France on 16 May 1916 in coordination with the Russian government. The Ottoman Government was informed about the Agreement and the text was handed over to Sherif Hussein, leader of the Arab revolt against the Turks in the Hedjaz').
36. At the time Arabs constituted 93 per cent of the population and owned 97.5 per cent of the land. See Janet L. Abu-Lughod, 'The Demographic Transformation of Palestine', in Ibrahim Abu Lughod (ed.), *The Transformation of Palestine: Essays on the Origin and Development of the Arab–Israeli Conflict – with a foreword by Arnold J. Toynbee* (Evanston: Northwestern University Press, 1987, second edition), pp. 139–63.
37. See, generally, Maxime Rodinson, *Israel: A Colonial Settler State?* (London: Pathfinder Press, 2004) (arguing that Israeli is a colonial power like any other).
38. In this sense the movement was at the time perceived by many to be very radical, especially as there were Christians and Muslims inhabiting the Holy Land and not only Jews. It was partly due to this that the right of the Jewish people to self-determination was not considered on a par with the claims of Poles, Czechs or Albanians, especially as the vast majority of Zionists did not even live in Palestine. See Philip Marshall Brown, 'Editorial Comment: Jewish Nationalism', 13 *American Journal of International Law*, (1919), pp. 755–8 at p. 757.
39. See 53 *Parliamentary Debates*, Lords, 27 March 1923, col. 655.
40. See 54 *Parliamentary Debates*, Lords, 27 June 1923, cols 677–8.
41. See 53 *Parliamentary Debates*, *supra* note 39, col. 656.
42. See the telegram from Sir Edward Grey to Sir Henry McMahon on the instructions given to the latter regarding his reply to the Arabs, 20 October 1915, File No. 155203, FO 371/2486.
43. Ibid. (emphasis added).
44. See the telegram from Sir Henry McMahon to Sir Edward Grey, informing the latter about his pledge to Hussein, 26 October 1915, Cairo, File No. 163832, FO 371/2486 (emphasis added).
45. Although in the nineteenth century there were no clear-cut definitions of what exact borders constituted Palestine, it was always understood to refer to *southern* Syria which had been mapped out as a separate administrative unit or a *mutessariflik*, under a governor who ruled from Jerusalem and reported directly to the Imperial government in Istanbul. See Gideon Biger, *An Empire in the Holy Land: Historical Geography of British Administration in Palestine 1917–1929* (Jerusalem: The Hebrew University Magnes Press, 1994), p. 39.

46. As quoted in 50 *Parliamentary Debates*, Lords, 21 June 1922, col. 1005 (emphasis added).
47. As quoted in 145 *Parliamentary Debates*, Commons, 25 July 1921, col. 36 (emphasis added).
48. The Headquarters of the Zionist Organisation was based in Vienna until Herzl's death in 1904. They were then moved successively to Cologne and Berlin. In 1918 they were transferred to London and only in 1935 to Jerusalem.
49. See The Hogarth Message, January 1918, 5974 *Command Paper* (1939), Annex F, pp. 48–9 (emphasis added).
50. See the collection of contributions on this subject in Stig Förster, Wolfgang Justin Mommsen and Ronald Robinson (eds), *Bismarck, Europe and Africa: The Berlin Africa Conference 1884–1885 and the Onset of Partition* (Oxford: Oxford University Press, for the German Historical Institute, London, 1988).
51. As pointed out by Judge Ammoun in his Separate Opinion in the ICJ's advisory opinion on *Western Sahara*, ICJ Reports (1975) at p. 78: 'In short, the concept of *terra nullius*, employed at all periods, to the brink of the twentieth century, to justify conquest and colonization, stands condemned.'
52. At the Berlin Conference territory was acquired in Africa by the colonial powers by means of cession from local leaders. In other words, they agreed to allow the colonial powers to use their territories but not to acquire them. See Malcolm Shaw, *Title to Territory in Africa: International Legal Issues* (Oxford: Clarendon Press, 1986) pp. 33–4. See also, M.F. Lindley, *The Acquisition and Government of Territory in International Law: Being a Treatise on the Law and Practice of Colonial Expansion* (London: Longmans, Green & Co., 1921) pp. 32–40 (who argues that Africa at the time of the Berlin Conference was not considered *terra nullius*).
53. (Emphasis added.) As Judge Ammoun noted in 1971: 'By one of fate's ironies, the declaration of the 1885 Berlin Congress which held the Dark Continent to be *terra nullius* related to regions which had seen the rise and development of flourishing states and empires. One should be mindful of what Africa was before there fell upon it the two greatest plagues in the recorded history of mankind: the slave-trade, which ravaged Africa for centuries on an unprecedented scale; and colonialism, which exploited humanity and natural wealth to a relentless extreme.' It is submitted that whilst Ammoun was undoubtedly correct in highlighting the negative effects of colonialism in Africa, he is incorrect in his assumption that Africa was considered *terra nullius* by the colonial powers. This is because the European Powers of the day implicitly recognised that the land was inhabited and that its peoples had sovereignty by concluding hundreds of treaties with African tribal leaders. See Separate Opinion of Vice-President Ammoun, Advisory Opinions on the Legal Consequences for States of the continued presence of South Africa in Namibia (South-West Africa) notwithstanding Security Council resolution 276 (1970), 21 June 1971, ICJ Reports (1971) pp. 55–88 at p. 86. See also, Article VI, General Act of the Conference of Berlin Conference, 76 *British and Foreign State Papers* (1885), p. 4 which is translated and reproduced in English in R.J. Gavin and J.A. Betley (eds), *The Scramble for Africa: Documents on the Berlin West African Conference and Related Subjects 1884–1885* (Nigeria: Ibadan University Press, 1973), p. 291. The translation of the Berlin Declaration which appears in the *American Journal of International Law*, Supplement, Vol. 3, at p. 12 uses slightly different language to the version quoted: 'All Powers exercising rights of sovereignty or an influence in the Said territories engage themselves to watch over the conservation of the indigenous populations and the amelioration of their moral and material conditions of existence and to strive for the suppression of slavery and especially of the negro slave trade …' America never ratified this treaty.
54. Hence the same language was used in the Treaty of St Germain-en-Laye of 1919 which was signed and ratified by Belgium, France, Italy, Japan, the United Kingdom and the United States of America. Article 11 of that treaty extends the provisions of the 1885 Berlin Act to all the African territories of the powers, who will continue 'to watch over the preservation of the native populations and to supervise the improvement and the

conditions of their moral and material well-being'. This was also essentially the same doctrine (the doctrine of trusteeship) that found its way into Article 22 of the Covenant of the League of Nations and Chapter XII of the UN Charter. See Patrick Thornberry, *Indigenous Peoples and Human Rights* (Manchester: Manchester University Press, 2002), p. 77.

55. See General Act of the Conference of Berlin Conference, *supra* note 53 and FO 2/785, Africa (East) Jewish Settlement 1903, and reference to C.J.B. Hurst in chapter one.
56. For a classical example of international law's racist origins see James Lorimer, *The Institutes of the Law of Nations: A Treatise of the Jural Relations of Separate Political Communities*, Vol. 1 (Edinburgh: William Blackwood & Sons, 1883). (Lorimer used ethnography, reflecting, perhaps, a wider view of his profession, to justify the difference in the way peoples of different civilisations were treated by international law.)
57. See Charles Henry Alexandrowicz, 'The Juridical Expression of the Sacred Trust of Civilisation', 65 *American Journal of International Law* (1971), pp. 149–59 at p. 154.
58. See David Hunter Miller, *The Drafting of the Covenant*, Vol. I (New York: G.P. Putnam's Sons, 1928), p. 102.
59. See Mark Carter Mills, 'The Mandatory System', 17 *American Journal of International Law* (1923), pp. 50–65 at p. 52.
60. For the full text of Wilson's Fourteen Points, 8 January 1918, see Edward Hallet Carr, *International Relations since the Peace Treaties* (London: MacMillan & Co., 1937), Appendix 2, pp. 265–7.
61. Ibid.
62. Ibid.
63. Ibid.
64. See the Report of the American Section of the International Commission on Mandates in Turkey (The King–Crane Commission), 28 August 1919, in 5 *Foreign Relations of the United States* (Washington: United States Government Printing Office, 1946), p. 751 at p. 787 (1947). Excerpts are also reproduced in Norton Moore, *The Arab–Israeli Conflict*, *supra* note 15 at pp. 51–63.
65. See Memorandum Presented to the King–Crane Commission by the General Syrian Congress, 2 July 1919. This is reproduced in Walter Laqueur, *The Israel/Arab Reader: A Documentary History of the Middle East Conflict* (London: Weidenfeld & Nicolson 1969), pp. 31–3 ('We the undersigned members of the General Syrian Congress, meeting in Damascus on Wednesday, July 2nd 1919, made up of representatives of the three Zones, viz., the Southern, Eastern and Western, provided with credentials and authorisations by the inhabitants of the various districts, Moslems, Christians, *and Jews*, have agreed upon the following statement of the desires of the people of the country who have elected us to present them to the American Section of the International Commission').
66. See Laqueur, *The Israel/Arab Reader*, at pp. 32–3.
67. See ibid., at p. 28 and Norton Moore, *The Arab–Israeli Conflict*, *supra* note 15 at p. 56.
68. Lacquer, *The Israel/Arab Reader*, p. 29 and Norton Moore, *The Arab–Israeli Conflict*, p. 56.
69. Lacquer, *The Israel/Arab Reader*, p. 29.
70. Ibid.
71. Ibid., pp. 29–30.
72. See the Island of Palmas Case (or Miangas), United States of America v. the Netherlands, Permanent Court of Arbitration, 4 April 1928, 2 *Reports of International Arbitral Awards* (United Nations Publications, 1949), pp. 831–71.
73. On 29 September 1925, Max Huber was asked by the Netherlands and the US whether he would act as arbitrator. He duly accepted. See ibid., p. 834.
74. Ibid., pp. 838–40 at p. 840.
75. Ibid., p. 857 (emphasis added).
76. Ibid., p. 839.
77. Ibid., p. 870 (emphasis added).

78. Ibid., p. 840.
79. See Isaiah Friedman, *Germany, Turkey, and Zionism 1897–1918* (Oxford: Clarendon Press, 1977), chapter 3 at pp. 32–49.
80. See the Minquiers and Ecrehos Case (France v. United Kingdom), 17 November 1953, ICJ Reports (1953), pp. 4–29.
81. Ibid., p. 14.
82. Ibid.
83. Advancing claims to Palestine based on biblical texts would also be very controversial historically. See e.g. Keith W. Whiteman, *The Invention of Ancient Israel: The Silencing of Palestinian History* (London: Routledge, 1996).
84. See Declaration of Judge Alvarez, Minquiers and Ecrehos case, *supra* note 80, p. 30.
85. Ibid.
86. See Western Sahara (Sahara Occidental), Advisory Opinion, 3 January 1975, ICJ Reports (1975) at p. 12 at p. 43.
87. Although the Balfour Declaration was incorporated into the Treaty of Sèvres in Article 95 the treaty made no mention of the transfer of sovereignty. See Part III Political Clauses, Treaty Series No. 11 (1920) signed at Sèvres, 10 August 1920 (London: HMSO) p. 26. Due to the revolution in Turkey, the Treaty of Sèvres was never ratified. The Treaty of Peace with Turkey signed at Lausanne on 24 July 1923 made no reference to the establishment of the Jewish national home in Palestine. According to Article 16: 'Turkey hereby *renounces* all rights and title whatsoever over or respecting the territories situated outside the frontiers laid down in the present Treaty and the islands other than those over which her sovereignty is recognised by the said Treaty, the future of these territories and islands being settled or to be settled by the parties concerned' (emphasis added). See The Treaty of Peace with Turkey signed at Lausanne, 24 July 1923, *Treaties of Peace 1919–1923*, Vol. II (New York: Carnegie Endowment for International Peace, 1924), pp. 959–1022.
88. See Lighthouses in Crete and Samos, judgment of 8 October, 1937, PCIJ, Series A./B., p. 94 at p. 103.
89. Ibid.
90. The Palestinian jurist Henry Cattan after citing historian George E. Kirk was of the opinion that Palestine, due to its level of cultural development and political maturity could well have been exempted from being assisted by a mandatory power. See Henry Cattan, *Palestine, the Arabs and Israel: The Search for Justice* (London: The Longman Group, 1969), p. 8. The Khalidis, the Husseinis and the Nashashibis, all achieved high office in Palestine under the Ottomans. See Yehoshua Porath, 'The Political Awakening of the Palestinian Arabs and their Leadership towards the end of the Ottoman Period', in Moshe Ma'oz (ed.), *Studies on Palestine during the Ottoman Period* (Jerusalem: The Hebrew University Magnes Press, 1975), pp. 366–7.
91. See Laqueur, *Israel/Arab Reader*, *supra* note 65, at p. 32, para. 3.
92. See Arnold McNair and Hersch Lauterpacht (ed.), *Annual Digest of Public International Law Cases*, (1927–28), p. 47 citing a decision of the *Alta Corte de Justicia de Uruguay*, 7 March 1928, in a case regarding extradition between the British and Uruguayan governments. The Court held that territories under mandate are not colonies or possessions of His Britannic Majesty.
93. See M.F. Lindley, *The Acquisition and Government of Backward Territory in International Law: Being a Treatise on the Law and Practice of Colonial Expansion* (London: Longmans, Green & Co., 1921), p. 257.
94. See Article 22, Covenant of the League of Nations, 1 *League of Nations Official Journal* (1920), p. 9.
95. Ibid.
96. See Permanent Mandates Commission, Minutes of the Fourth Session, Held at Geneva from 24 June to 8 July, 1924, LON Doc. A.13 1924. VI, eleventh meeting, 30 June 1924, p. 87.

97. The draft explicitly referred to 'those territories formerly belonging to Turkey which include Armenia, Kurdistan, Syria, Mesopotamia, Palestine and Arabia ...' See Hunter Miller, *The Drafting of the Covenant*, Vol. II, *supra* note 58 at p. 552.
98. On the attitude of the US towards the League of Nations and its refusal to become a member see Philip C. Jessup, *International Security: The American Rôle in Collective Action for Peace* (Westport: Greenwood Press, 1935, reprinted in 1975), pp. 3–11.
99. See the statement by Lord Balfour to the League of Nations, 16 September 1922, regarding Article 25 of the Mandate for Palestine in *League of Nations Official Journal*, November 1922, pp. 1188–9. See also, the memorandum by Lord Balfour to the Council of the League of Nations revoking specific articles pertaining to the Jewish national home from the Mandate for Transjordan in *League of Nations Official Journal*, November 1922, pp. 1390–1. The territorial delimitation between Palestine and Transjordan was described as follows: 'The Palestine Order-in-Council, 1922, shall not apply to the territory lying East of a line drawn from a point two miles West of Akabah in the Gulf of Akabah up to the centre of Wady Arabah, the Dead Sea and the River Jordan to the junction of the latter with the River Yarmuk, thence up the centre of the River Yarmuk to the Syrian Frontier.' See *Legislation of Palestine, 1918–1925, Including the Orders-In-Council, Ordinances, Public Notices, Proclamations, Regulations etc.*, compiled by Norman Bentwich, Vol. II (Alexandria: Whitehead Morris Ltd, 1926), p. 405. After the Sherif lost control the Hejaz to the Ibn Saud and the Wahhabis on 13 October 1924, he fled to Cyprus and then Transjordan and the Kingdom of Hejaz faded into history and became an integral part of 'Saudi Arabia'. See Joshua Teitelbaum, *The Rise and Fall of the Hashemite Kingdom of Arabia* (London: Hurst & Company, 2001).
100. See Julius Stone, *Israel and Palestine: Assault on the Law of Nations* (Baltimore: Johns Hopkins University Press, 1981), pp. 22–5.
101. To argue, as some have done, that 'Palestine-is-Jordan' on the basis of a few months of British rule over Transjordan in 1921–22, when it lacked any ruler and had the sparsest of populations, is, in the words of two contemporary neoconservative commentators, 'historically wrong, legally superficial, geographically ignorant, and politically procrustean'. See Daniel Pipes and Adam Garfinkle, 'Is Jordan Palestine?', Commentary, October 1988, available via the following link: http://www.danielpipes.org/article/298 (last retrieved 21 October 2008).
102. See *Jawdat Badawi Sha'ban v Commissioner for Migration and Statistics*, Supreme Court of Palestine sitting as a High Court of Justice, 14 December 1945, reported in Vol. 12, *The Law Reports of Palestine* (1945), pp. 551–3, quote at p. 553 (the case concerned the interpretation of Article 15 of the Palestine Citizenship Order in Council 1925).
103. See Lt.-Gen. The Rt. Hon. J.C. Smuts, P.C. *The League of Nations: A Practical Suggestion* (London: Hodder and Stoughton, 1918).
104. See Pitman B. Potter, 'The Origin of the System of Mandates under the League of Nations', 16 *The American Political Science Review* (1922), pp. 563–83 at p. 582.
105. Smuts, *League of Nations, supra* note 103, p. 16.
106. Ibid., pp. 16–17.
107. See *League of Nations Official Journal, supra* note 94, p. 9 (emphasis added).
108. See J.C. Hales, 'The Reform and Extension of the Mandates System', 26 *Transactions of the Grotius Society* (1940), p. 153 at p. 185. See also, Ralph Wilde, *International Territorial Administration: How Trusteeship and the Civilizing Mission Never Went Away* (Oxford: Oxford University Press, 2008), p. 338.
109. The South African argument that the C-class mandates were tantamount to annexation was not accepted. Indeed the issue of that country's administration of South-West Africa would be adjudicated before the International Court of Justice on several occasions. See generally, John Dugard (ed.), *The South West Africa/Namibia Dispute: Documents and Scholarly Writings on the Controversy between South Africa and the United Nations* (Berkeley: University of California Press, 1973).
110. It is noteworthy that the Zionists feared such an interpretation so much so that they solicited a legal opinion by William Finlay KC on the compatibility of Article 22 of the

Covenant with the Mandate for Palestine. In Finlay's opinion there was no conflict based upon a principle of construction between the principles enshrined in Article 22 and the articles in the Mandate conferring special privileges on a minority. He based his reasoning on the terms of Article 95 of the Treaty of Sèvres, which provided for the establishment of a Jewish national home in Palestine. He said that in case of conflict between Article 22 of the Covenant and the Treaty of Sèvres, the latter would prevail. This is, however, a highly questionable conclusion as the Covenant specifically provides in Article 20 that all obligations and understandings that were inconsistent with the Covenant would be abrogated. In any case, the Treaty of Sèvres was never ratified by Turkey and the Treaty of Lausanne made no mention of a Jewish national home. He wrote his opinion on 8 April 1921. See 2 *League of Nations Official Journal* (1921), pp. 443–4.

111. It was also argued that the mandate was illegal. See generally, W.F. Boustany, *The Palestine Mandate: Invalid and Impracticable: A Contribution of Arguments and Documents towards the Solution of the Palestine Problem* (Beirut: The American Press, 1936).
112. In this respect see Quincy Wright, *Mandates under the League of Nations* (Chicago: University of Chicago Press, 1930), p. 119 ('The [Permanent Mandates] Commission has refused to consider numerous petitions from the Arabs of Palestine protesting the inclusion of the Balfour declaration in the mandates ...').
113. See the *League of Nations Official Journal*, *supra* note 94 at p. 10.
114. For a general and succinct overview, see E. Lauterpacht (ed.), *Hersch Lauterpacht, International Law Being the Collected Papers of Hersch Lauterpacht, Vol. 3, The Law of Peace* (Cambridge: Cambridge University Press, 1977), pp. 64–9. See also, R.N. Chowdhuri, *International Mandates and Trusteeship Systems: A Comparative Study* (The Hague: Martinus Nijhoff, 1955), p. 230.
115. See Lauterpacht, *Hersch Lauterpacht* (being of the opinion that sovereignty was vested in the League). In contrast, see the opinion expressed by Quincy Wright, 'Sovereignty of the Mandates', 17 *American Journal of International Law* (1923), pp. 691–703, writing at p. 696 that '[c]ommunities under "A" mandates doubtless approach very close to sovereignty'. See also the Separate Opinion expressed by Judge McNair in International Status of South West Africa, ICJ Reports (1950), p. 146 at p. 150 that the doctrine of sovereignty had no application to the mandates system because it was in abeyance. He wrote: '[I]f and when the inhabitants of the Territory obtain recognition as an independent State, as had already happened in the case of some of the Mandates, sovereignty will revive and vest in the new State.'
116. See Judge Ammoun's Separate Opinion in Legal Consequences for States of the Continued Presence of South Africa in Namibia (South West Africa) notwithstanding Security Council resolution 276 (1970), Advisory Opinion, ICJ Reports (1971), at 69 who cites with approval the French edition of Stoyanovsky thesis, *La théorie générale des mandates internationaux*, (1925), at p. 83 and Paul Pic who both thought that sovereignty resided in the people of A-class mandates, and upheld the notion of virtual sovereignty residing in a people deprived of its exercise by domination or tutelage.
117. See Chowdhuri, *International Mandates and Trusteeship Systems*, *supra* note 114 at p. 236. See also, the chapter on self-determination for elaboration on this point.
118. See D. Campbell Lee, *The Mandate for Mesopotamia and the Principle of Trusteeship in English Law* (London: St Clements Press, 1921). This pamphlet, which is available in the British Library, was comprised of a lecture the author delivered under the Cecil Rhodes Benefaction at University College, London University, Monday 23 May, 1921. (At p. 13, he writes: 'I affirm that it is not the Continental principle of Mandate that has prompted and produced the Mandatory system, but the English idea of Trust. That great doctrine has been, I believe, the real inspiration of Article XXII, and is today its sole dynamic force and saving grace.')
119. As Judge Bustamante opined in his Separate Opinion concerning the preliminary objections in the *South-West Africa* cases: 'In an objective sense the achievement of the purposes of the Mandate is entrusted, *as a fiduciary attribution of responsibility*, to an advanced nation in the capacity of Mandatory' (emphasis added). See *South-West Africa cases*, (Ethiopia v.

Liberia; Liberia v. South Africa), Preliminary Objections, 21 December 1962, ICJ Reports (1962) p. 319.

120. See Lord Herschell in *Bray v. Ford* [1896] *Law Reports, Appeal Cases*, 44 at 51–2; and James L.J in *Parker v. McKenna* [1874] *Law Reports*, 10 Chancery Division, 96. For one of the leading textbooks on the English laws of trusts see A.J. Oakley, *Parker and Mellows: The Modern Law of Trusts* (London: Sweet & Maxwell, 2003).
121. See Millet L.J. in *Bristol and West Building Society v. Mothew* [1998] *Law Reports, Chancery Division*, at 18. This case is also cited in Oakley, *Parker and Mellows*, at p. 331.
122. See International Status of South-West Africa, Advisory Opinion, 11 July 1950, Separate Opinion by Judge McNair, ICJ Reports (1950) p. 128 at p. 148. He opined that: 'Any English lawyer who was instructed to prepare the legal instruments required to give effect to the policy of Article 22 [of the Covenant of the League of Nations] would inevitably be reminded of, and influenced by, the trust of English and American law, though he would soon realize the need of much adaptation for the purposes of the new international institution.'
123. For a brief comment on the concept of trusts and mandates see James Lesley Brierly, 'Trusts and Mandates', 10 *British Yearbook of International Law* (1929), pp. 217–19. On the origins of mandates and trusteeships in international law see Aaron M. Margalith, *The International Mandates* (Baltimore: Johns Hopkins Press, 1930); Duncan Hall, *Mandates, Dependencies and Trusteeship* (Washington, DC: Carnegie Endowment for International Peace, 1948); and Chowdhuri, *International Mandates and Trusteeship Systems*, *supra* note 114 at pp. 16–20.
124. McNair, Separate Opinion, *supra* note 122, p. 149 (emphasis in original).
125. Francisco de Vitoria, *De Indis et De Ivre Belli Relectiones*, edited by Ernest Nys (Washington, DC: Carnegie Institute of Washington, 1917), p. 161. Vitoria's exact words when translated were: 'It might, therefore, be maintained that in their own interests the sovereigns of Spain might undertake the administration of their country, providing them with prefects and governors for their towns, and might even give them new lords, so long as this was clearly for their benefit.'
126. Ibid., p. 161. According to Vitoria: 'Let this, however, as I have already said, be put forward without dogmatism and subject also to the limitation that any such interposition be for the welfare and in the interests of the Indians and not merely for the profit of the Spaniards.'
127. See Hugo Grotius, *Mare Liberum*, translated by R. Magoffin (New York: Oxford University Press, 1916), p. 13 (emphasis added).
128. See Nele Matz, 'Civilization and the Mandate System under the League of Nations as Origin of Trusteeship', 9 *Max Planck Yearbook of United Nations Law* (2005), pp. 47–95, at p. 56.
129. See Norman Bentwich, 'Le Systèm Des Mandats', 29 (IV) *Recueil Des Cours* (1929), pp. 115–86.
130. See Norman Bentwich, *The Mandates System* (London: Longmans, Green & Co., 1930), Editor's Preface by Arnold D. McNair, at p. vi.
131. See Matz, 'Civilization and the Mandate System', *supra* note 128, p. 55.
132. See W.T. Mallison, Jr., 'The Balfour Declaration: An Appraisal in International Law', in Ibrahim Abu Lughod (ed.), *The Transformation of Palestine: Essays on the Origin and Development of the Arab–Israeli Conflict* (Evanston: Northwestern University Press, 1987, second edition), pp. 61–111.
133. On the legal effects of unilateral declarations made by government officials see the Nuclear Tests Case (Australia v. France), 20 December 1974, ICJ Reports (1974), p. 253 at pp. 267–8, paras 43–6.
134. Ibid., para. 51 (where the ICJ analysed a number of statements made by the French Government to the effect that it would cease atmospheric nuclear testing at its Centre d'experimentations du Pacifique in the territory of French Polynesia, after a complaint submitted to the Court by Australia).

135. For the English and French text of the British Mandate of Palestine see Terms of League of Nations Mandates, UN Doc. A/70 (October, 1946) pp. 2–7. See also, Annex 391, 'British Mandate for Palestine', 3 *League of Nations Official Journal* (1922), pp. 1007–12 (emphasis added).
136. See *Jerusalem-Jaffa District Governor and Another Appellant; v. Suleiman Murra and Others Respondents*, Privy Council, 16 February 1926 [1926] A.C. 321, Viscount Cave L.C., Viscount Dunedin, and Lord Parmour. (The case concerned an order to expropriate water from a spring at Urtas village near Soloman's Pools, for use by the Jerusalem Water Supply Commission. The issue was whether full compensation had to be given for the expropriation.)
137. Even if this was Britain's intention, it is highly doubtful whether Article 22 of the Covenant of the League of Nations provided it with a legal basis to do this.
138. See generally, Francis Bennion, *Statutory Interpretation: A Code* (London: Butterworths, 2002), Section 355, p. 993 ('On the presumption that Parliament does nothing in vain, the Court must endeavour to give significance to every word of an enactment. It is presumed that if a word or phrase appears, it was put there for a purpose and must not be disregarded').
139. See Ernst Frankenstein, 'The Meaning of the Term "National Home for the Jewish People"', 1 *The Jewish Yearbook of International Law* (1948), pp. 27–41 at pp. 28–9.
140. See Vienna Convention on the Law of Treaties, 1969, 1155 *United Nations Treaty Series*, p. 331. The Vienna Convention is reproduced in Ian Brownlie (ed.), *Basic Documents in International Law* (Oxford: Oxford University Press, 2002), pp. 270–97.
141. Although Article 4 of the Vienna Convention provides that it only applies to treaties which are concluded after the entry into force of the Convention, Professor D.W. Greig writes in his study on intertemporality that there can be 'little doubt' that the general rules in Article 31 (1) would have been familiar to a lawyer of 1890 (citing Hall). See D.W. Grieg, *Intertemporality and the Law of Treaties* (The British Institute of International and Comparative Law, 2001), pp. 112–18. In the *Iron Rhine Arbitration* between Belgium and the Netherlands (award of 24 May, 2005) and which is available on the website of the Permanent Court of Arbitration at http://www.pca-cpa.org/showpage.asp?pag_id=1155 (last retrieved 22 October 2008). The Arbitral Tribunal, which included three ICJ judges (Judges Higgins, Simma and Tomka) and two Professors (Alfred H.A. Soons and Guy Schrans), held at para. 45 that Articles 31 and 32 of the Vienna Convention reflect pre-existing customary international law, and thus may be (unless there are particular indications to the contrary) applied to treaties concluded before its entry into force in 1980. They reached this conclusion by referring to the ICJ's jurisprudence in the *Kasikili/Sedudu Island* and *Pulau Ligitan/Sipadan* cases, which concerned treaties concluded in the nineteenth century, well before the Mandate was drafted.
142. Minutes of a meeting of the War Cabinet discussing the text of the Balfour Declaration, 31 October 1917, CAB 21/58. Lord Curzon, the only member of the Cabinet to have actually been to Palestine, was more sceptical about the Declaration than some of his colleagues.
143. Ibid. ('It did not necessarily involve the early establishment of an independent Jewish State, which was a matter for gradual development in accordance with the ordinary laws of political evolution.')
144. Interestingly, Nahum Sokolow in his *History of Zionism 1600–1918* (London: Longmans, Green & Co., 1919), pp. xxiv–xxv wrote that the claim that the Zionists were seeking a state was 'wholly fallacious'. See also, Leonard Stein, *The Balfour Declaration* (London: Vallentine, Mitchell, 1961), pp. 523–4 (making the same point).
145. See the preamble to the British Mandate of Palestine, *supra* note 135.
146. See Leonard Stein, *The Balfour Declaration* (Jerusalem: The Magnes Press, 1983), p. 545 and David Gilmour, *Curzon* (London: John Murray, 1994), p. 482.
147. The text is reproduced in *Trial and Error: The Autobiography of Chaim Weizmann* (London: Hamish Hamilton, 1949), p. 256.

148. See e.g. the opinions of two Law Officers on the Royal Niger Company in response to a question asked of them from Lord Salisbury, dated 13 December 1897, in 26 *The British Yearbook of International Law* (1949), pp. 41–4.
149. Ibid., p. 43 ('The Royal Niger Company is not a mere trading Company, but also has power to acquire, retain, and govern territory. It resembles the East India Company ...').
150. See Weizmann, *Trial and Error*, *supra* note 147, p. 260.
151. Ibid.
152. See Stein, *The Balfour Declaration*, *supra* note 146, p. 545 and Gilmour, *Curzon*, *supra* note 146, p. 481 citing PRO CAB 23/4; C memo, 26 Oct 1917 CP 112/266. A copy of Curzon's original memo is reproduced in David Lloyd George, *The Truth About the Peace Treaties*, Vol. II (London: Victor Gollancz, 1938), pp. 1123–32.
153. See Stein, *The Balfour Declaration*, *supra* note 146, p. 545.
154. See ibid., pp. 514–32, Gilmour, *Curzon*, *supra* note 146, p. 481, Lloyd George, *The Truth About the Peace Treaties*, *supra* note 152 at pp. 1133–4.
155. FO 839/12, Eastern Conference, Lausanne, Armenian Question, File 33.
156. Ibid. See e.g. Supplementary Memorandum of the Armenian National Homes presented on behalf of the Armenia American Society, Lausanne, 16 December 1922 which suggested the following location for the Armenian National Home: 'a zone as lying between the northern boundary of Syria as fixed by the League of Nations in giving the mandate to France, and the boundary as drawn in the separate agreement between France and Angora ...'
157. Although it did provide for the protection of non-Muslim minorities in Turkey, see Articles 37–45 of the Treaty of Peace with Turkey signed at Lausanne, 24 July 1923, reproduced in *The Treaties of Peace 1919–1923*, Vol. II (New York: Carnegie Endowment for International Peace, 1924), pp. 970–3.
158. See FO 839/23, Autonomy for Assyrian Christians (claims of Assyro-Chaldeans). This file contains letters and pamphlets outlining the claims of the Assyrian Christians for autonomy in 'a Christian and warrior nation, as a buffer state, separating the Turkish empire from Persia, Kurdistan and Mesopotamia'. (This was outlined in a memorandum from Général Agha Petros Ellow, 23 November 1922, which was handed to a Mr Adams after a meeting in Lausanne on 25 November at the Hotel Central Bellevue.) In 1934, the British Government was seriously contemplating sending a small community of Assyrians to establish a settlement in North Borneo. CO 874/1079 Assyrian Settlement Scheme (1934). See the letter from D.J. Jawline, Governor, North Borneo to the President of the British North Borneo Company, 6 October 1934. The Island of Banguay was particularly recommended as being suitable from both an administrative and agricultural standpoint. Cyprus and Brazil were also other locations considered for Assyrian settlement although they did not work out. A small number of Assyrians were settled at a location in Syria called Khabur. However, it was infested with mosquitoes and many Assyrians fell ill from malaria. Some died. See FO 371/21840, Settlements of the Assyrians of Iraq (1938).
159. See Walid Sharif, 'Soviet Marxism and Zionism', 6 *Journal of Palestine Studies* (1977), pp. 77–97 at pp. 94–5; Robert Weinberg, 'Purge and Politics in the Periphery: Birobidzhan in 1937', 52 *Slavic Review* (1993), pp. 13–27; and Terry Martin, 'The Origins of Soviet Ethnic Cleansing', 70 *The Journal of Modern History* (1998), pp. 813–61, at p. 825.
160. See Robert Weinberg, *Stalin's Forgotten Zion: Birobidzhan and the Making of a Soviet Jewish Homeland: An Illustrated History 1928–1996* (Berkeley: University of California Press, 1998).
161. The *travaux préparatoires*, which include the various drafts agreed upon between the Zionist organisation and the Political Section of the British Peace Delegation, are available at the National Archives. See Peace Conference (British Delegation) Eastern Mission (Turkey) Files 76–91 (1920). CO 733/248/19. The British Government was also being lobbied by 'certain prominent English Jews', who were 'antagonistic to Zionism'. See e.g., 'From the Political Report of the XII Zionist Congress', 1921.
162. Ibid., CO 733/248/19 (emphasis added).

163. See e.g. 'Proposal for Palestine Mandate: On behalf of the Zionist Organisation in Paris transmits a draft scheme for the above, Mr. Frankfurter to Col. Meinertshagen', 20 March, 1919, FO 608/100 (emphasis added).
164. The phrase '*the* national home' appears in Article 2 of the Mandate but it is referring to '*a* national home' as it appears in the preamble and in the original Balfour Declaration.
165. See Doreen Ingrams, *Palestine Papers 1917–1922: Seeds of Conflict* (London: John Murray, 1972), p. 98, citing FO 371/5245.
166. See Frankenstein, '"National Home for the Jewish People"', *supra* note 139 at p. 29.
167. See Earl Curzon to Field-Marshall Viscount Allenby (Cairo) No. 1216 Telegraphic, Foreign Office, 7 November 1919, reproduced in E.L. Woodward and Rohan Butler (eds), *Documents on British Foreign Policy 1919–1939* (London: HMSO, 1952), p. 508.
168. See Ingrams, *Seeds of Conflict*, *supra* note 165, p. 102, citing FO 371/5248.
169. See Proposal for Palestine Mandate (on behalf of the Zionist Organisation in Paris transmits a draft scheme for the above), 20 March 1919, FO 608/100.
170. See Command Paper 1700, Great Britain House of Commons, 23 *Sessional Papers* 1922, pp. 17–21.
171. Ibid.
172. Ibid.
173. See Palestine: Proposed Formation of an Arab Agency, Correspondence with the High Commissioner for Palestine, XXV *Parliamentary Papers* (1923), para. 7. See also, United Nations Special Committee on Palestine, Report to the General Assembly, Official Records of the Second Session of the General Assembly, Supplement No. 11, UN Doc. A/364, 3 September 1947, Vol. 1, Chapter 2 at para. 101.
174. Ibid., p. 10.
175. See Mogannam E. Mogannam, 'Palestine Legislation under the British', 164 *Annals of the American Academy of Political and Social Science* (Nov. 1932), pp. 48–9.
176. Ibid.
177. See Jamaal Bey Husseini, 'The Proposed Palestine Constitution', 164 *Annals of the American Academy of Political and Social Science* (Nov. 1932), p. 24 ('To find themselves in a position to accept legally and execute actually the terms of the Balfour Declaration is a thing the Arabs of Palestine – Moslems and Christians – could not countenance').
178. See Bernard Wasserstein, *Herbert Samuel: A Political Life* (Oxford: Clarendon Press, 1992), p. 208.
179. Ibid., p. 209.
180. Ibid.
181. Ibid., pp. 210–11.
182. See John Bowle, *Viscount Samuel: A Biography* (London: Victor Gollancz Ltd, 1957), pp. 172–7 at pp. 175–6 (Bowle reproduces the full text of Samuel's second memorandum).
183. See Asquith to Venetia Stanley, 13 March 1915 (ii) in Michael and Eleanor Brock (eds), *H.H. Asquith: Letters to Venetia Stanley* (Oxford: Oxford University Press, 1982), pp. 477–8 at p. 477.
184. See Wasserstein, *Herbert Samuel*, *supra* note 178 at pp. 213–19.
185. Ibid., p. 216.
186. Ibid.
187. Ibid.
188. Ibid.
189. Ibid., pp. 218–19.
190. The Zionists also skilfully tried to link support for their cause with British imperialism. Vladimir Jabotinsky proposed the establishment of a Jewish Legion to assist the British war effort by 'liberating' Palestine. See James Renton, *The Zionist Masquerade: The Birth of the Anglo-Zionist Alliance, 1914–1918* (Basingstoke: Palgrave Macmillan, 2007), pp. 59–61.
191. Samuel was the first of seven High Commissioners who would govern Palestine until 1948. See Sahar Huneidi, *A Broken Trust: Herbert Samuel, Zionism and the Palestinians*

with a foreword by Walid Khalidi (London: I.B. Tauris, 2001). See especially chapter 4, 'Herbert Samuel's vision of Zionism' at pp. 79–97.

192. See Norman and Helen Bentwich, *Mandate Memories, 1918–1948* (London: The Hogarth Press, 1965), p. 11 ('I mention first Herbert Samuel because I was nearest to him of the British statesmen who were protagonists for Weizmann and the National Home. He was my wife's uncle, and from the time of my marriage in 1915, we had corresponded about Zionism. And in years to come I had the happy fortune to work under him in Palestine').
193. The article appears in full enclosed in a letter dated 4 July 1918 from the British Embassy in Washington DC to the Foreign Office. See FO 371/3410.
194. Ibid.
195. The statement was also sharply criticised by the graduates and members of the Universities of Oxford, Cambridge, and London. See *Edwin Montagu and the Balfour Declaration* (London: Arab League Office, 1966), p. 15.
196. See e.g. Palestine: Disturbances in May, 1921, Reports of a Commission of Inquiry with Correspondence Relating Thereto, Presented to Parliament by Command of His Majesty, October, 1921 (also known as the Haycraft Commission of Inquiry into Disturbances in Jaffa). See also, Report of the Commission on the Palestine Disturbances of August, 1929, (also known as the Shaw Commission of Inquiry into Disturbances in Jerusalem), 288 *Parliamentary Papers of Interest to the Foreign Office* (1930).
197. See Colonel R. Meinertzhagen, *Middle East Diary 1917–1956* (London: The Cresset Press, 1959), pp. 49–53 at pp. 49–51. This letter is four pages long and so it could not be reproduced in its entirety here. According to Meinertzhagen, Lord Curzon, who the letter must have been passed onto in the Foreign Office, responded to the letter thanking him for a frank expression of his views.
198. See Shane Leslie, *Mark Sykes: His Life and Letters*, with an introduction by the Right Hon. Winston Churchill (London: Cassell & Co. 1923), pp. 283–4.
199. See Elizabeth Monroe, *Britain's Moment in the Middle East, 1914–1971* (London: Chatto & Windus, 1981), p. 43 ('Measured by British interests alone, [the Balfour Declaration] was one of the greatest mistakes in our imperial history').
200. Leslie, *Mark Sykes*, *supra* note 198, p. 270.
201. Ibid.
202. See Renton, *Zionist Masquerade*, *supra* note 190, p. 7 ('It is therefore a central contention of this book that the Zionists were undoubtedly used by the Government. They were not, however, unwitting pawns, duped by the British. It was in fact the Zionists themselves who established the rationale for using Zionism as a propaganda weapon, and consistently showed the Government how and why this should be done').
203. Leslie, *Mark Sykes*, *supra* note 198, p. 271.
204. See Roger Adelson, *Mark Sykes: Portrait of an Amateur* (London: Jonathan Cape, 1975), p. 208.
205. Ibid., p. 226 and Fromkin, *A Peace to End All Peace*, *supra* note 9, p. 198.
206. Adelson, *Mark Sykes*, *supra* note 204, p. 212.
207. Ibid., pp. 242–3.
208. See Leslie, *Mark Sykes*, *supra* note 198, pp. 269–70 (emphasis added).
209. See Report of the Royal Commission on Alien Immigration with Minutes of Evidence and Appendix, Vol. 1, The Report (London: HMSO, 1903), Cd. 1741. See also, the Minutes of Evidence taken before the Royal Commission on Alien Immigration, Vol. II (London: HMSO, 1903), Cd. 1742, testimony of Dr Theodore Herzl, pp. 211–21. And see Raphael Patai (ed.), *The Complete Diaries of Theodor Herzl*, Vol. IV (New York: Herzl Press, 1960), pp. 1360–4.
210. See Nahum Sokolow, *History of Zionism 1600–1918* (London: Longmans, Green & Co., 1919), p. 299 (emphasis added).
211. See Adelson, *Mark Sykes*, *supra* note 204, p. 204 and p. 207. See also, Renton, *Zionist Masquerade*, *supra* note 190, pp. 54–5.

212. See Fromkin, *A Peace to End All Peace*, *supra* note 9, pp. 41–3 (on alleged Jewish freemason network to control Ottoman Empire) and p. 198 (writing that Sykes and Fitzmaurice attended the same public school and shared 'many of the same views and prejudices' about Jews).
213. Ibid., pp. 41–2.
214. Memorandum by Mr Frankfurter of an Interview in Mr Balfour's Apartment, 23 Rue Nitot, Paris, on Tuesday, 24 June, 1919, at 4.45p.m., in E.L. Woodward and Rohan Butler (eds), 4 *Documents on British Foreign Policy* (1919), (London: HMSO, 1952), pp. 1276–8 at p. 1276.
215. See M.W.V. Temperley, *A History of the Peace Conference*, Vol. VI (London: Henry Frowde and Hodder & Stoughton, 1924), pp. 172–3.
216. See Frankenstein, 'The Meaning of the Term "National Home for the Jewish People"', *supra* note 139 , p. 30.
217. Ibid.
218. See *Palestine, A Study of Jewish, Arab and British Policies Published for the ESCO (Ethel S. Cohen) Foundation* (New Haven: Yale University Press 1947), p. 75.
219. See Maxime Rodinson, *Israel: A Colonial Settler State?* (London: Pathfinder Press, 2004) at p. 45 ('It is by no means coincidental that the Balfour Declaration preceded by five days the fateful date of November 7 (October 25 on the Julian calendar) when the Bolsheviks took power. One of the aims of the declaration was to support Kerensky').
220. See Doreen Ingrams (ed.), *Palestine Papers 1917–1922: Seeds of Conflict* (London: John Murray, 1972), p. 8.
221. See Laqueur, *History of Zionism*, *supra* note 22, at p. 177 ('In a conversation with the German ambassador shortly before the Balfour Declaration, Djemal [the Turkish governor of Syria] said he would be willing to concede a national home to the Jews, but for what purpose, since the Arabs would only kill them. The Turks would have greatly preferred not to make any concessions at all, but there was no doubt that if hard-pressed they would opt for the Arabs. This must have been clear to the Germans, who reached the conclusion that the goodwill of the Zionists was not worth a major crisis in their relations with the Turks').
222. See Marian Kent, 'Great Britain and the End of the Ottoman Empire 1900–1923', in Marian Kent (ed.), *The Great Powers and the End of the Ottoman Empire* (London: George Allen, 1984), p. 187.
223. See generally, Jill Hamilton, *Gods, Guns and Israel: Britain, the First World War and the Jews in the Holy City* (Stroud: Sutton Publishing, 2004). (Explaining how the members of the British War Cabinet in 1917 were influenced by the Bible and especially the Old Testament in supporting the creation of a Jewish homeland.)
224. See Renton, *Zionist Masquerade*, *supra* note 190, p. 149.
225. See Robert John, *Behind the Balfour Declaration: The Hidden Origins of Today's Mideast Crisis* (Costa Mesa: The Institute for Historical Review, 1988), p. 70 ('Yale said he had a talk with Weizmann "somewhere in the Mediterranean in 1919", and asked him what might happen if the British did not support a national home for the Jews in Palestine. Weizmann thumped his fist on the table and the teacups jumped, "if they don't", he said, "we'll smash the British Empire as we smashed the Russian Empire."')
226. See e.g. Mark Levene, 'The Balfour Declaration: A Case of Mistaken Identity', 107 *The English Historical Review* (1992), pp. 54–77. (Levene argues that the Balfour Declaration could only have arisen in the context of an overwhelming crisis, such as war, and that widespread anti-Semitism and notions of Jewish power affected the decisions of policymakers in the corridors of Whitehall. As he writes at p. 76: 'In the last analysis ... the Balfour Declaration was the product not of assessment, but of perception: a perception of the world, and of Jews within it, through the narrow, socially and cultural confined prism of Britain's traditional ruling class'.)
227. See Dov S. Zakheim, 'The British Reaction to Zionism: 1895 to the 1990s', 350 *The Round Table* (1999), pp. 321–32.

228. See *Edwin Montagu and The Balfour Declaration* (London: Arab League Office, 1966) reproducing the original memorandum from the Public Records Office, Cab. 24/24, 23 August 1917.
229. Ibid., p. 6.
230. See generally, Daud Abdullah (ed.), *The Israeli Law of Return and its Impact on the Struggle in Palestine* (London: Palestine Return Centre, 2004); Mark J. Altschul, 'Israel's Law of Return and the Debate of Altering, Repealing or Maintaining its Present Language', 5 *University of Illinois Law Review* (2002), pp. 1345–71; Nancy C. Richmond, 'Israel's Law of Return: Analysis of its Evolution and Present Application', 12 *Dickinson Journal of International Law* (1993), pp. 95–133.
231. See *Edwin Montagu and The Balfour Declaration*, *supra* note 228, p. 6.
232. See e.g. *World Conquest through World Government, The Protocols of the Learned Elders of Zion*, trans. from the Russian of Sergyei A. Nilus by Victor Marsden (Britons Publishing Co., 1972).
233. See Gisela C. Lebselter, *Political Anti-Semitism in England 1918–1939* (London: Macmillan 1978), p. 60.
234. See Norman Cohn, *Warrant for Genocide: The Myth of the Jewish World-Conspiracy and the Protocols of the Elders of Zion* (Harmondsworth: Penguin Books, 1970), p. 168 quoting *The Spectator* in its issue of 15 May 1920.
235. See *The Truth about 'The Protocols' A Literary Forgery, from The Times of August 16, 17, and 18, 1921* (London: Printing House Square, 1921).
236. The *Protocols* were a forgery of an earlier book published in France entitled, 'Dialogue in Hell between Machiavelli and Montesquieu; or, the Politics of Machiavelli in the Nineteenth Century', which had nothing to do with the Jews. See John S. Curtiss, *An Appraisal of the Protocols of Zion* (New York: Columbia University Press, 1942), (comparing passages between the two books). See also, Lucien Wolf, *The Myth of the Jewish Menace in World Affairs or the Truth about the Forged Protocols of the Elders of Zion* (New York: Macmillan & Co., 1921).
237. Stephen Eric Bronner, *A Rumour about the Jews: Reflections on Antisemitism and the Protocols of the Learned Elders of Zion* (New York: St Martin's Press, 2000), p. 2 ('International sales of the pamphlet were astronomical during the 1920s and 1930s; Henri Rollin, the French scholar of antisemitism, called the *Protocols* the most widely distributed book in the world other than the Bible, and its distribution was accompanied by a mountain of secondary literature comprising well more than one thousand titles').
238. This quote is reproduced in Curtiss, *An Appraisal*, *supra* note 236, p. 22 citing an American translation entitled *The Protocols and World Revolution* (Boston, 1920), pp. 6–7.
239. *The Jews' Who's Who. Israelite Finance. Its Sinister Influence, Popular Edition* (London: The Judaic Publishing Co., H.H. Beamish, Proprietor, 1921), p. 45 (emphasis in original). Inside the front cover of this book are two cartoons. One is an illustration of Jewish members of the Privy Council along with their names (Edwin Montagu, Herbert Samuel, Lionel Rothschild and Sir Eric Cassel, among others) with the words, 'Jewish control of Finance, Land, Gold, Silver, Diamonds, Base Metals, Petroleum, Electrical, Chemicals, Food, Clothing etc'. The second illustration shows two gentlemen, presumably Jewish, drinking 'vin de Frankfurt' and smoking cigars with the captions 'Britannia rules the waves' and then 'Yeth, but *we* rule Britannia'. There are also selective quotations from Deuteronomy saying that the Jews can lend money but never borrow it so that they can 'rule over many nations'. The book also contains a list of German Jewish surnames which had been Anglicised. For example, Grünwald became Greenwood, Gugenheimer became Gilbert and Schwabacher became Shaw.
240. See *Edwin Montagu and The Balfour Declaration*, *supra* note 228, p. 7.
241. See 'Zionism' by Edwin Montagu, Cab. 24/28, 9 October 1917, ibid., pp. 12–17.
242. See 50 *Parliamentary Debates*, Lords, 21 June 1922, cols 994–1034.
243. See 50 *Parliamentary Debates*, Lords, 21 June 1922, col. 1008.
244. Ibid.

245. See Huneidi, *A Broken Trust*, *supra* note 191, p. 58 citing at endnote 62: United States, Department of State, Records of the Department of State Relating to the Internal Affairs of Turkey, 1910–1029. Telegram, Green to Secretary of State. Record Group. Microcopy No. 353, Roll No. 80, National Archives.
246. See 156 *Parliamentary Debates*, Commons, 4 July 1922, cols 292–342.
247. Ibid., p. 298.
248. Ibid.
249. Ibid., p. 329.
250. Whilst Brandeis was a Zionist, Trotsky was not, and he attacked Zionism as imperialist. Strangely, Churchill even recognised this when he wrote in an article published in the *Illustrated Sunday Herald* on 8 February 1920, that: 'Nothing could be more significant than the fury with which Trotksy has attacked the Zionists generally and Weissmann, [*sic*] in particular.' A copy of this article is republished in Lenni Brenner (ed.), *51 Documents: Zionist Collaboration with the Nazis* (New Jersey: Barricade Books, 2002), pp. 23–8. The statement regarding Trotsky appears at p. 27.
251. Michael Makovsky, *Churchill's Promised Land: Zionism and Statecraft* (New Haven: Yale University Press, 2007), p. 82 ('Consideration of Jewish power played a role in Churchill's premier foreign policy fixation as secretary of state for war and air (1919–1921) and even as colonial secretary (1921–1922): confronting the Bolshevik threat to western civilisation and European stability. In late 1919, he received a copy of the Protocols; it is unclear whether he read it, but he certainly advanced a number of its themes and the anti-Semitic conspirational ideas propagated by other sources. He genuinely considered the Bolsheviks an illegitimate minority consisting mostly of Jews ruling over the majority "real" Russians').
252. See Brenner, *51 Documents*, *supra* note 250 where the full text of the article is reproduced.
253. Ibid., p. 27.
254. Ibid.
255. See Michael J. Cohen, *Churchill and the Jews* (London: Frank Cass, 1985), pp. 55–6.
256. See Cohn, *Warrant for Genocide*, *supra* note 234, pp. 112–13 ('One would normally expect the mysterious rulers to be called Elders of Jewry or Elders of Israel. There must be some reason why they bear the absurd name of Elders of Zion, and there is in fact a very plausible one. As we have seen, the first Zionist Congress at Basel was interpreted by antisemites as a giant stride towards Jewish world-domination. Countless editions of the Protocols have connected that document with the congress; and it does seem likely that this event inspired if not the forgery itself, then at least its title').
257. Makovsky, *Churchill's Promised Land*, *supra* note 251, p. 82.
258. Cohen, *Churchill and the Jews*, *supra* note 255, p. 51. (Churchill then added for good measure: 'Three Jews among only seven Liberal cabinet ministers might I fear give rise to comment.')
259. On Germanic racism, Hitler, and the *Protocols*, see Cohn, *Warrant for Genocide*, *supra* note 234, pp. 187–213.
260. See Hadassa Ben-Itto, *The Lie that Wouldn't Die: The Protocols of the Elders of Zion* (London: Vallentine Mitchell, 2005), pp. 249–55. (Ben-Itto reproduces the testimony of Nahum Sokolow who was questioned at a trial in 1934 in Grahamstown in South Africa about the authenticity of the *Protocols of the Elders of Zion* which the Court condemned as a forgery. During the cross-examination Sokolow was asked whether the *Protocols* was promulgated by Dr Herzl at the first 1897 Zionist Congress at Basel. Sokolow replied: 'There is not one word of truth in the allegation.')
261. Palestine Defence Policy: Military Aspects of Partition. Memorandum by the Minister for the Co-ordination of Defence, 1937–38, CAB 104/5.

3 ARAB OPPOSITION TO POLITICAL ZIONISM

1. See Sir Robert Jennings and Sir Arthur Watts (eds), *Oppenheim's International Law*, Vol. 1, Peace, Parts 2 to 4 (Harlow: Longman Group, 1992), p. 679.
2. Ibid., pp. 706–8.
3. The Feisal–Weizmann agreement which is analysed in the next chapter could not be described as a treaty of cession because it did not provide for a transfer of sovereignty from Palestine to the Zionist movement. Moreover, it was never effectuated and in any event contained a reservation.
4. See, generally, Neville J. Mandel, *The Arabs and Zionism before World War I* (Berkeley: University of California Press, 1976).
5. As Mandel argues, ibid., p. 37 ('There was scarcely a Jewish colony which did not come into conflict at some time with its Arab neighbours, and more often than not a land dispute of one form or another lay behind the graver collisions').
6. Ibid., p. 39.
7. Ibid., p. 40.
8. Ibid., pp. 39–40.
9. Ibid., p. 340.
10. Ibid.
11. See Samih K. Farsoun and Naseer H. Aruri, *Palestine and the Palestinians: A Social and Political History* (Boulder: Westview Press, 2006), p. 52.
12. Ibid.
13. Mandel, *Arabs and Zionism*, *supra* note 4, p. 231.
14. See Baruch Kimmerling and Joel S. Migdal, *The Palestinian People: A History* (Cambridge, MA: Harvard University Press, 2003), p. 6.
15. Ibid.
16. Ibid., p. 8.
17. Ibid.
18. Ibid., p. 11.
19. See A.P. Rogers, *Law on the Battlefield* (Manchester: Manchester University Press, 1996, third edition, 2004, paperback), p. 1, citing R.C. Algase, 'Protection of Civilian Lives in Warfare: A comparison between Islamic law and modern international law concerning the conduct of hostilities', 16 *Revue de Droit Militaire et de Droit de la Guerre (Military Law and Law of War Review)*, 1977, p. 246 ('Islamic law is now being recognized by Western writers in its true context as the oldest legal system containing detailed rules for warfare'). See also, Gerald J. Adler, 'Targets in War: Legal Considerations', in Richard A. Falk (ed.), *The Vietnam War and International Law*, Vol. III (New Jersey: Princeton University Press, 1968–76), pp. 280–326 at p. 288. See further, Percy Bordwell, *The Law of War between Belligerents: A History and Commentary* (Chicago: Callaghan & Co., 1908), ('It [the Qur'an] is the first example we have of a systematic war code'). Finally, see A. Querry, *Droit Musulman. Recueil de Lois Concernant les Musulmans Schyites* (Paris, translated: 1871–72).
20. See Francisco de Vitoria, *De Indis et De Jure Belli Relectiones*, edited by Ernest Nys (Washington, DC: The Carnegie Institution, 1917).
21. See Alberico Gentili, *De Iure Belli Libri Tres* (Oxford: Clarendon Press, 1933).
22. Balthazar Ayala, *De Jure et Officialis Bellicis et Disciplina Militari Libri III*, edited by John Westlake (Washington, DC: Carnegie Institution, 1912).
23. See Hugo Grotius, *De Jure Belli et Pacis Libri Tres*, translated by William Whewell (Cambridge: Cambridge University Press, 1853).
24. Such as Giovanni da Legnano, *Tractatus De Bello, De Represaliis et De Duello*, edited by Thomas Erskine Holland (Washington, DC: The Carnegie Institution, 1917).
25. For summaries of the development of international humanitarian law from ancient times until the present day, see C.F. Amerasinghe, 'History and Sources of the Law of War', 16 *Sri Lanka Journal of International Law* (2004), pp. 263–87; Leon Friedmann, *The Law of War: A Documentary History – Vol. 1 with a foreword by Telford Taylor* (New York:

Random House, 1972), pp. xiii–xxv; and L.C. Green, *The Contemporary Law of Armed Conflict* (Manchester: Manchester University Press, 2000), pp. 20–33.

26. See the Instructions for the Government of Armies of the US in the Field (the 'Leiber Code'), General Orders, 24 April 1863, which is reproduced in Dietrich Schindler and Jiri Toman, *The Laws of Armed Conflicts: A Collection of Conventions, Resolutions and Other Documents* (Leiden: Martinus Nijhoff Publishers, 2004), pp. 3–120.
27. International Convention with respect to the Laws and Customs of War by Land between Austria-Hungary, Belgium, Bulgaria, Denmark, France, Germany, Great Britain, Greece, Italy, Japan, Luxemburg, Mexico, Montenegro, the Netherlands, Portugal, Roumania, Russia, Servia, Siam, Spain, Sweden and Norway, Turkey and the United States, signed at the Hague and its Annex, in Clive Parry (ed.), 187 *The Consolidated Treaty Series* (1898–99), pp. 429–43 (in French).
28. See Sobhi Mahmassani, 'The Principles of International Law in the Light of Islamic Doctrine', 117 (1) *Recueil Des Cours* (Leyden: A.W. Sijthoff, 1967), pp. 201–326, at p. 301.
29. On the concept of jihad in Islamic international law, see e.g. Shaheen Sardar Ali and Javaid Rehman, 'The Concept of Jihad in Islamic International Law', 10 *Journal of Conflict & Security Law* (2005), pp. 321–43. See also, Niaz A. Shah, 'Self-Defence in Islamic Law', 12 *Yearbook of Islamic and Middle Eastern Law* (2005–06), pp. 181–208.
30. See Schindler and Toman, *Laws of Armed Conflicts*, *supra* note 26, at p. vi.
31. See the preface to the Oxford manual, No. 3, Schindler and Toman, *Laws of Armed Conflicts*, *supra* note 26, pp. 29–40.
32. See the preambles to the Hague Conventions of 1899, *supra* note 27.
33. See Lieut.-Col. Norman Bentwich, Chief Judicial Officer, Occupied Territories, Palestine, 'The Legal Administration of Palestine under the British Military Occupation', 1 *British Yearbook of International Law* (1920–21), pp. 139–48 (describing the administration of the occupied territory).
34. This is explained by John J. McTague Jr. 'The British Administration in Palestine 1917–1920', 7 *Journal of Palestine Studies* (1978), p. 57.
35. See Allenby to War Office, 2 March 1918, Foreign Office Papers, FO 371/2070/77141.
36. See the Annex to the Convention, *supra* note 27. For status of ratifications see the website of the International Committee of the Red Cross at the following link: http://www.icrc.org/ihl.nsf/WebSign?ReadForm&id=150&ps=P (last retrieved 2 October 2007).
37. See 1899 Hague Regulations, *supra* note 27.
38. See Edmund Schwenk, 'Legislative Power of the Military Occupant under Article 43, Hague Regulations', 54 *Yale Law Journal* (1945), p. 393, note 1.
39. See *Manual of Military Law*, War Office (St Martin's Lane: HMSO, 1914). Chapter XIV, on the Laws and Usages of War on Land at pp. 234–365 was written by Col. J.E. Edmonds, C.B. and Mr L. Oppenheim, LL. D. The subchapter on the general effects of occupation begins at p. 288.
40. Allenby to War Office, 23 October 1918. FCO 371/3384/358, cited in Bernard Wasserstein, *The British in Palestine: The Mandatory Government and the Arab–Jewish Conflict 1917–1929* (Oxford: Basil Blackwell, 1991), p. 20.
41. *Manual of Military Law*, *supra* note 39, p. 288.
42. Ibid. (emphasis added).
43. For case law on Article 43, see *Commune of Grace-Berleur case*, 1 *Annual Digest* 1919, p. 461 (where the Belgian Court of Cassation held that German modifications to tax laws could not be regarded as a measure for restoring and assuring public order and safety). See further, the decisions in *In re* X 1 *Annual Digest* p. 468, French Court of Appeal 1920 (ruling that certain penal laws as being invalid because they were not among those which could jeopardise the security of the Army). See further, the decisions in *Societe v. Brum de Belie* and *Adriaenssens v. Ministere Public*, both in 1 *Annual Digest*, p. 466 and p. 467 respectively.
44. Ibid.

45. The events are described in some detail by Tom Segev, *One Palestine, Complete: Jews and Arabs under the British Mandate* (New York: Henry Holt, paperback, 1999), pp. 127–144.
46. Figures are provided by Segev, ibid., p. 138 and by the Report of the Court of Inquiry, *infra* note. 49.
47. Segev, *supra* note 45, p. 128.
48. Ibid.
49. See Report of the Court of Inquiry Convened by Order of H.E. the High Commissioners and Commander-in-Chief, dated the 12th day of April, 1920, Political Eastern (Turkey) Files 85, pp. 8154–9913 (1920), FO 371/5121. For the original text of the judgment signed by the members of the courts, (and it should be said in a very poor condition), see the records of the War Office in WO 32/9614.
50. Ibid.
51. Ibid.
52. Ibid., p. 80, para. 69.
53. See Weizmann to Balfour, 30 May 1918, FO 371/3410. See also McTague, 'British Administration in Palestine', *supra* note 34 at p. 63, footnote 23.
54. Ibid.
55. Ibid.
56. McTague, 'British Administration in Palestine', *supra* note 34, p. 65.
57. See the numerous correspondences on the matter in FO 141/686/9.
58. Ibid.
59. See Report of the Court of Inquiry, *supra* note 49.
60. Ibid.
61. Ibid.
62. See Telegram from H. Samuel to Foreign Office, 15 July 1920, File E 8436/85/44 regarding publication of Jerusalem Riot Enquiry report, FO 371/5121.
63. Ibid.
64. Ibid.
65. See Neil Caplan, *Palestine Jewry and the Arab Question, 1917–1925* (London: Frank Cass, 1978) for a description of the violence and its aftermath.
66. An Interim Report on the Civil Administration of Palestine, during the period 1 July 1920 – 30 June 1921, presented to the League of Nations, 30 July 1921.
67. See *Palestine: Disturbances in May, 1921, Reports of the Commission of Inquiry with Correspondence Relating Thereto*, Presented by Command of His Majesty, October, 1921 (London: His Majesty's Stationery Office, 1921).
68. Ibid., p. 3.
69. Ibid., p. 44.
70. Ibid.
71. Ibid., p. 45.
72. Ibid.
73. Ibid., p. 51.
74. Ibid.
75. Ibid., p. 52.
76. Ibid., p. 53.
77. Ibid., p. 54.
78. Ibid.
79. See Report of the Commission on the Palestine Disturbances of August, 1929, *Parliamentary Papers of Interest to the Foreign Office*, 288 (HMSO, 1930), Cmd 3540 at pp. 26–8.
80. On the disagreement see Leonard Stein, 'The Jews in Palestine', 4 *Foreign Affairs* (1925–26), p. 419.
81. Report on the Palestine Disturbances 1929, *supra* note 79, p. 28.
82. These were demolished by the Israelis after they captured the Old City in the 1967 war. Approx. 100 families were given three hours to vacate their homes before they were demolished on the orders of Teddy Kollek, the first Israeli Mayor of Jerusalem. For Kollek's justifications see Teddy and Amos Kollek, *For Jerusalem: A Life* (New York: Random

House, 1978), p. 197. For a critique of his decision see Joost R. Hiltermann, 'Teddy Kollek and the Native Question', 182 *Middle East Report*, May–June 1993, pp. 24–7.

83. See Yehoshua Porath, *The Emergence of the Palestinian-Arab National Movement, 1918–1929* (London: Frank Cass, 1974), pp. 258–9.
84. For Zionist statements about rebuilding the Temple, see CO 733/4.
85. For a detailed description of these events, see Porath, *Emergence of the Palestinian-Arab National Movement*, *supra* note 83, pp. 258–73.
86. For a brief description of the attack in Hebron, see Report of the Commission on the Palestine Disturbances, *supra* note 79 at p. 64. For a more elaborate description see Segev, *One Palestine, Complete*, *supra* note 45 at pp. 314–27.
87. Ibid.
88. See Wasserstein, *The British in Palestine*, *supra* note 40 at p. 237 for the figures and also for a description of events in Hebron.
89. See Report of the Commission on the Palestine Disturbances, *supra* note 79 at pp. 97–132.
90. Ibid., p. 132.
91. Ibid., pp. 133–4.
92. Ibid., p. 129.
93. Ibid., p. 150.
94. Ibid.
95. See Report of the Commission Appointed by His Majesty's Government in the United Kingdom of Great Britain and Northern Ireland, with the Approval of the Council of the League of Nations, to determine the Rights and Claims of Moslems and Jews in Connection with the Western or Wailing Wall at Jerusalem (London: HMSO, December, 1930), p. 34.
96. Ibid.
97. Ibid., pp. 34–5.
98. See General Treaty for the Re-Establishment of Peace between Austria, France, Great Britain, Prussia, Sardinia, Turkey and Russia, signed at Paris, 30 March 1856, reproduced in Clive Parry (ed.), 114 *The Consolidated Treaty Series* (1855–56), pp. 409–20.
99. Ibid.
100. See Article LXII of the Treaty between Austria-Hungary, France, Germany, Great Britain, Italy, Russia and Turkey for the Settlement of Affairs in the East, signed at Berlin, 13 July 1878, reproduced in Clive Parry (ed.) 153 *The Consolidated Treaty Series* (1878), pp. 171–91, at p. 190. ('Les droits acquis à la France sont expressément réservés, et il est bien entendu qu'aucune atteinte ne saurait être portée au *statu quo* dans les Lieux Saints.')
101. Ibid.
102. See Western Wall Report, *supra* note 95, pp. 57–8.
103. Ibid., pp. 58–9.
104. Cmd 3686. See the one-paragraph summary of his report in *A Survey of Palestine*, Prepared in December 1945 and January 1946 for the information of the Anglo-American Committee of Inquiry, Vol. 1 (Printed by the Government Printer, Palestine), p. 27.
105. Ibid.
106. Ibid.
107. Ibid.
108. Cmd 3692. See *A Survey of Palestine*, *supra* note 104.
109. *A Survey of Palestine*, ibid., p. 28.
110. Ibid.
111. See Ritchie Ovendale, *The Origins of the Arab–Israeli Wars* (Harlow: Pearson Longman, 2004), pp. 72–3.
112. For text of the letter, see Walter Laqueur, *The Israel/Arab Reader: A Documentary History of the Middle East Conflict* (London: Weidenfeld & Nicolson, 1969), at pp. 50–6.
113. *A Survey of Palestine*, *supra* note 104, p. 29.
114. Ibid., p. 30.

115. See Porath, *Emergence of the Palestinian-Arab National Movement*, *supra* note 83, pp. 272–3. This event can be seen as the precursor to the creation of the Organisation of the Islamic Conference which was established in 1969 in the aftermath of an arson attack by an Australian citizen of a Christian evangelical sect which set a part of the Al-Aqsa mosque ablaze. For the OIC's provisions on Palestine see the Charter of the Islamic Conference, Adopted by the Third Islamic Conference of Foreign Ministers at Djidda, on 4 March 1972, 914 *United Nations Treaty Series* (1974), p. 103, pp. 104–10 (Arabic text), pp. 111–16 (English text), pp. 117–22 (French text). For a description of its founding, see Michelle Lombardini, 'The International Islamic Court of Justice: Towards an International Islamic Legal System?', 14 *Leiden Journal of International Law* (2001), p. 665.
116. See Porath, *Emergence of the Palestinian-Arab National Movement*, *supra* note 83 at p. 266 (quoting the paper *al-J mi'ah al-'Arabiyyah*).
117. See Philip Mattar, *The Mufti of Jerusalem: Al-Hajj al-Husayni and the Palestinian National Movement* (New York: Columbia University Press, 1988).
118. For statistics see *A Survey of Palestine*, *supra* note 104, p. 30. The total population of Palestine in 1932 was 1,035,154.
119. See Justin McCarthy, *The Population of Palestine: Population History and Statistics of the Late Ottoman Empire and the Mandate* (New York: Columbia University Press, 1990), p. 213, table 2.13.
120. In 1918 it was estimated that there were only 58,728 Jews in Palestine. See McCarthy, ibid., table 2.2., p. 26.
121. See Palestine Royal Commission Report, July 1937, Cmd 5479, pp. 280–2. These predictions were calculated on the basis of 'Verhulst's Logistic'.
122. Ibid., p. 282.
123. Ibid.
124. Ibid., see the note indicated by an asterisk on p. 280.
125. See Dr Paul Weis, 'The Undermining of the Nationality Concept by German Law', which is an extract from the author's unpublished study on 'The Legal Status of German and Austrian Refugees in Great Britain'. This is a Microfilm 454/75, 15 February 1943. It can be viewed in the Wiener Library, 4 Devonshire Street, London W1W 6BH.
126. See e.g. Louise London, *Whitehall and the Jews 1933–1948 British Immigration Policy and the Holocaust* (Cambridge: Cambridge University Press, 2000); and David S. Wyman, *The Abandonment of the Jews: America and the Holocaust 1941–1945* (New York: Pantheon Books, 1985).
127. See 'German Jews Pouring into this Country', by Daily Mail Reporter, *The Daily Mail*, 20 August 1938, p. 11.
128. Ibid. They were John Samuel Brokner, Mendel Fierman and Henrietta Weis.
129. Although there was sympathy for the plight of Germany's Jews amongst the educated elite. See 'Plight of the Jews: Growing Concern, Liberals' Letter to the Prime Minister', *The Times*, 17 November 1938, p. 9 (including messages from President of Cambridge University and the Chancellor of Oxford University as well as an appeal from the Zionist General Council).
130. 'German Jews Pouring into this Country', *supra* note 127 ('In these words, Mr. Herbert Metcalfe, the Old-street magistrate yesterday referred to the number of aliens entering this country through the "back door" – a problem to which *The Daily Mail* has repeatedly pointed').
131. See Jewish Refugees, German Press Comments on Commons Debate: 'Empire's Empty Spaces', *The Scotsman*, 23 November 1938, p. 12.
132. See Martin Kolinsky, *Law, Order and Riots in Mandatory Palestine, 1928–35* (London: St Martin's Press, 1993), pp. 172–7.
133. Ibid., p. 176.
134. Ibid., p. 178.
135. *A Survey of Palestine*, *supra* note 104, pp. 32–3.
136. The armed military wing of HAMAS is called the Izzed Din al-Qassam brigades.
137. *A Survey of Palestine*, *supra* note 104, p. 33.

138. Ibid.
139. See Proposed New Constitution for Palestine, Prepared by the Secretary of State for the Colonies to Parliament by Command of His Majesty, 12 March 1936 (London: HMSO, 1936), Cmd 5119.
140. *A Survey of Palestine*, *supra* note 104, p. 34.
141. Ibid.
142. See 310 *Parliamentary Debates*, Commons, cols 1079–150, and cols 1166–73, 24 March 1936.
143. See W.F. Abboushi, 'The Road to Rebellion: Arab Palestine in the 1930s', 6 *Journal of Palestine Studies* (Spring, 1977), pp. 23–46 at p. 33.
144. See, generally, Ted Swedenburg, *Memories of Revolt: The 1936–1939 Rebellion and the Palestinian National Past* (Fayetteville: University of Arkansas Press, 2003).
145. *A Survey of Palestine*, *supra* note 104, p. 36.
146. Ibid.
147. Ibid., p. 37.
148. See Charles Townsend, 'The Defence of Palestine: Insurrection and Public Security, 1936–1939', 103 *The English Historical Review* (Oct., 1988), p. 919.
149. *A Survey of Palestine*, *supra* note 104, pp. 35–6.
150. See Summary of the Report of the Palestine Royal Commission presented by the Secretary of State for the Colonies to the United Kingdom Parliament by Command of His Britannic Majesty, July 1937, distributed at the request of the United Kingdom Government to the League of Nations, Geneva, 30 November 1937. LoN Doc No. C.495.M.336.1937.VI, Official Communique 9/37.
151. Table of Figures provided in *A Survey of Palestine*, *supra* note 104, p. 38.
152. Palestine Royal Commission Report, July 1937, Cmd 5479, pp. 381–2 at p. 382 ('We think it would accord with Christian sentiment in the world at large if Nazareth and the Sea of Galilee (Lake Tiberias) were also covered by this Mandate').
153. Ibid., p. 381 and p. 386.
154. Ibid., p. 382 ('... the policy of the Balfour Declaration would not apply').
155. Ibid., pp. 382–3.
156. Ibid., p. 386 ('There have been recent precedents for equitable financial arrangements of this kind in those connected with the separation of Sind from Bombay and of Burma from the Indian Empire').
157. Ibid., 'Exchange of Land and Populations' at pp. 389–93 at p. 389 ('If Partition is to be effective in promoting a final settlement it must mean more than drawing a frontier and establishing two States. Sooner or later there should be a transfer of land and, as far as possible, an exchange of population'). See also, Palestine Royal Commission, Minutes of Evidence Heard at Public Sessions (London: HMSO, 1937). For further reading on the concept of population transfer during the inter-war period, see Catriona Janet Drew, 'Population Transfer: The Untold Story of the International Law of Self-Determination, A Thesis Presented for the Degree of Doctor of Philosophy in the Department of Law, London School of Economics and Political Science, University of London, November 2005', PhD thesis submitted to the London School of Economics and Political Science, 2005, particularly chapters 2, 3 and 4.
158. In a statement before the Permanent Mandates Commission the Colonial Secretary said that he was not prepared to commit himself to compulsory population transfer. He said that he did not like the talk about compulsory population transfer because the rights of the native population were inherent. He added that he would hesitate to envisage any obligatory transfer of Arabs from the Jewish state into the Arab state, save where the Government of the latter state agreed. See League of Nations, Permanent Mandates Commission, Minutes of the Thirty-Second (Extraordinary) Session devoted to Palestine, held at Geneva from July 30th to August 18th, 1937, including the Report of the Commission to the Council, Official No. C.330. M.222. 1937. VI, p. 26 (Mr Ormsby-Gore replying to a question from the Chairman) and p. 177 (Mr Ormsby-Gore replying to a question from Mlle. Dannevig).

159. *A Survey of Palestine*, *supra* note 104, p. 41.
160. See Neville Barbour, *Nisi Dominus: A Survey of the Palestine Controversy* (London: George G. Harrap & Co., 1946), p. 184 ('Meanwhile the Twentieth Zionist Congress had met in Zürich. After prolonged discussions a majority of 300 to 158 rejected the Partition Scheme put forward by the Royal Commission ...').
161. See the general discussion at the Permanent Mandates Commission, Minutes of the Thirty-Second (Extraordinary) Session devoted to Palestine, *supra* note 158.
162. On the deportation to the Seychelles and the Mufti's escape see FO 141/678/1.
163. For further reading on the life of Haj Amin al-Husseini, see Mattar, *The Mufti of Jerusalem*, *supra* note 117.
164. See Palestine (Defence) Order in Council, 1937, *Government of Palestine, Ordinances, Regulations, Rules, Orders and Notices, Annual Volume for 1937, Vol. III* (Jerusalem: Government Printing Press, 1937), p. 1138. This is to be read as one with the Emergency Regulations, 1936, *Government of Palestine, Ordinances, Regulations, Rules, Orders and Notices, Annual Volume for 1936, Vol. II* (Jerusalem: Government Printing Press, 1936), p. 354.
165. Ibid., Article 10, Palestine (Defence) Order in Council, 1937 ('Every sentence of death shall direct that the person condemned shall be hanged by the neck until he is dead'). See also, FO 371/21870.
166. See Part II, Article 6, 2, (g), (v), Palestine (Defence) Order in Council, 1937, *Government of Palestine, Ordinances, Regulations, Rules, Orders and Notices, Annual Volume for 1937, Vol. II* (Jerusalem: Government Printing Press, 1937), p. 260, at p. 262 ('for the infliction of fines upon bodies of persons or upon corporations and the forfeiture or destruction of property as punitive measures, whether the actual offenders can or cannot be identified'). See also, CO 733/379/8.
167. See Collective Fines Ordinance, No. 57 of 1936. Palestine Gazette Extraordinary, No. 618, 4 August 1936. See also, *The Laws of Palestine*, Revised Edition, 1933, (London: Waterlow & Sons Ltd, 1934), and FO 371/21870.
168. See Article 19c. Palestine (Defence) Order in Council, 1937, amended 19 January 1938, CO 733/379/8.
169. See the numerous regulations in *Government of Palestine, Ordinances, Regulations, Rules, Orders and Notices, Annual Volume for 1939* (Jerusalem: Government Printing Press, 1939).
170. I am grateful to Anis Qasem for sharing his personal recollections of the torture meted out against his grandfather and uncle. Torture techniques included being moved from one very hot room to a very cold one for days in an attempt to get a suspect to confess to things he may not have known of. Other techniques included lowering suspects into water wells time and again to make them confess for fear of being drowned.
171. See Barbour, *Nisi Dominus*, *supra* note 160 at p. 192.
172. For graphic photographs of the damage to Jaffa via aerial photography, see FO 371/21870. For a description of these events, see WO 191/70.
173. Ibid.
174. See Emergency Regulations (Compensation for Jaffa Demolitions) 1936, *Government of Palestine, Ordinances, Regulations, Rules, Orders and Notices, Annual Volume for 1936, Vol. II* (Jerusalem: Government Printing Press, 1936), p. 1077. (Compensation covered both movable and immovable property. Persons seeking compensation had to submit their claim within one calendar month of the date of the demolitions.)
175. See Townsend, 'Defence of Palestine', *supra* note 148, at p. 933.
176. Ibid.
177. Ibid., p. 934.
178. Ibid., citing Harris to Nicholl, 5 September 1938, PRO AIR 23/765.
179. Aerial Bombarding of Houses, 17 June 1938, E 3598/2/31.
180. Ibid.

181. See Protection of Civilian Populations Against Bombing from the Air in Case of War, Resolution of the League of Nations Assembly, 30 September 1930, League of Nations Official Journal, Special Supplement No. 182, October 1938, pp. 15–16.
182. See Military Lessons of the Arab Rebellion in Palestine, 1936, General Staff, Headquarters, the British Forces, Palestine & Transjordan, February, 1938, p. 7. WO 191/70.
183. See Appendix IV in Walid Khalidi (ed.), *From Haven to Conquest: Readings in Zionism and the Palestine Problem until 1948* (Washington, DC: Institute of Palestine Studies, 1987), pp. 846–9.
184. See e.g. John Bierman and Colin Smith, *Fire in the Night: Wingate of Burma, Ethiopia and Zion* (London: Macmillan, 2000), pp. 88–118; and Trevor Royle, *Orde Wingate: Irregular Soldier* (London: Weidenfeld & Nicolson, 1995), pp. 104–54.
185. See Royle, ibid., p. 150 ('future Israeli commanders such as Moshe Dayan were amongst those members of the Haganah who received their first formal military training from the Special Night Squads'), Bierman and Smith, ibid., p. 138. Dayan described Wingate as having 'unconventional ideas about how to deal with Arab terrorism and sabotage' and noted that unlike many of his colleagues in the British Army, he 'thought well of the Jews'. See Moshe Dayan, *Story of My Life* (London: Weidenfeld & Sons, 1976), p. 28.

4 THE HUSSEIN–McMAHON CORRESPONDENCE

1. See generally, George Antonius, *The Arab Awakening: The Story of the Arab National Movement* (London: Hamish Hamilton, 1938); Isaiah Friedman, 'The McMahon–Hussein Correspondence and the Question of Palestine', 5 *Journal of Contemporary History* (1970), pp. 83–122; Arnold Toynbee, 'The McMahon–Hussein Correspondence: Comments and a Reply', 5 *Journal of Contemporary History* (1970), pp. 185–201; Elie Kedourie, *In the Anglo-Arab Labyrinth: The McMahon–Husayn Correspondence* (Cambridge: Cambridge University Press, 1976); A.L. Tibawi, *Anglo-Arab Relations and the Question of Palestine 1914–1921* (London: Luzac & Co., 1977); David Fromkin, *A Peace to End All Peace: The Fall of the Ottoman Empire and the Creation of the Modern Middle East* (London: Phoenix Press, 2000); and Isaiah Friedman, *Palestine, A Twice-Promised Land? The British, the Arabs and Zionism 1915–1920*, Vol. I (New Brunswick: Transaction Publishers, 2000).
2. See e.g. Friedman, *Journal of Contemporary History*, ibid., p. 122 and *Palestine, A Twice-Promised Land?* ibid., at p. li ('From the point of view of international law, the McMahon–Hussein correspondence had no validity'). See also, Timothy J. Paris, *Britain, the Hashemites and Arab Rule 1920–1925: The Sherifian Solution* (London: Frank Cass, 2003) who argues at p. 31 that the correspondence 'did not embody a treaty or even an agreement; it was a decidedly ambiguous exchange and there was in no sense a "meeting of the minds", a *sine qua non* for any binding agreement'. However, having said this, he goes on to write at p. 32 that '... it cannot be denied that Britain *did* promise to support Arab independence and, in exchange, Husain *did* revolt against the Turks' (his emphasis). Paris' second statement seems to directly contradict what he said about the correspondence being 'ambiguous' because there was 'no meeting of minds'.
3. Several hundred secret treaties are listed in Edward Grosek, *The Secret Treaties of History* (Buffalo, New York: William S. Hein & Co., 2007), including 'the Husayn–McMahon Correspondence', on p. 269 as secret treaty number 781.
4. Samuel B. Crandall, *Treaties: Their Making and Enforcement* (Washington, DC: John Byrne & Co., 1916), p. 58 ('Treaties are frequently (especially in time of war) of such a nature, that it would be extremely improper to publish them, or even commit the secret of their negotiation to any great number of persons').
5. On the Molotov–Ribbentrop Pact to partition Poland see Krystna Marek, *Identity and Continuity of States in Public International Law* (Genève: Librairie Droz, 1968), pp. 417–545. Another example of a treaty regularly cited as 'secret' is the so-called 'Hoare–Laval Pact' between the British and French Foreign Ministers to partition Ethiopia. The outline of an agreed settlement of the Italian–Ethiopian conflict concluded

on 10 December 1935 is reproduced in Stephen Heald (ed.), *Documents on International Affairs 1935*, Vol. II (Oxford: Oxford University Press, 1937), pp. 360–2.

6. See Case Concerning Maritime Delimitation and Territorial Questions between Qatar and Bahrain, Jurisdiction and Admissibility, judgment, ICJ Reports (1994), p. 112 at p. 122, para. 29 (where the ICJ held that an unregistered agreement would be binding between the parties to it even if it was not registered with the UN or with the League of Arab states).
7. For further light on the background to the Hussein–McMahon correspondence see Paris, *Britain, the Hashemites and Arab Rule 1920–1925*, *supra* note 2 at pp. 24–44.
8. In this regard, see e.g. C. Ernest Dawn, *From Ottomanism to Arabism: Essays on the Origins of Arab Nationalism* (Urbana: University of Illinois Press, 1973); T.E. Lawrence, *Revolt in the Desert* (Combined Publishing, New Edition, 1998); and Fred J. Khouri, *The Arab–Israeli Dilemma* (New York: Syracuse University Press, 1985), p. 8.
9. See the letter from the Sherif of Mecca to Sir H. McMahon, 18 February 1916 and the reply from Sir H. McMahon to the Sherif of Mecca, 10 March 1916, reproduced in John Norton Moore (ed.), *The Arab–Israeli Conflict. Vol. III: Documents* (New Jersey: Princeton University Press, 1974), pp. 5–21. (Hussein requested £50,000 in gold for the monthly pay of the troops levied, 20,000 sacks of rice, 15,000 sacks of flour, 3,000 sacks of barley, 150 sacks of coffee, 150 sacks of sugar, 5,000 rifles and the necessary ammunition and 100 boxes of Martini-Henry cartridges and 'the rifles from the factory of St. Etienne in France'. McMahon agreed to these requests: 'I am pleased to be able to inform you that His Majesty's Government have approved of meeting your requests, and that which you asked will be sent with all haste ...')
10. As noted in Malgosia Fitzmaurice and Olufemi Elias, *Contemporary Issues in the Law of Treaties* (Utrecht: Eleven International Publishing, 2005), p. 13.
11. Translation of a letter from Sir H. McMahon, His Majesty's High Commissioner at Cairo, to the Sherif of Mecca, 24 October 1915, Command Paper 5957 (1939), in Norton Moore, *The Arab–Israeli Conflict*, *supra* note 9 (emphasis added).
12. Translation of a letter from the Sherif of Mecca to Sir H. McMahon, His Majesty's High Commissioner at Cairo, 14 July 1915, ibid., pp. 6–7 (emphasis added).
13. Islam's Holy Places include Al-Masjid al-Haram in Mecca, Al-Masjid al-Nabawi in Medina and the compound that houses Al-Masjid Al-Aqsa and the Dome of the Rock in Jerusalem. Although of course it is also conceivable that what was meant by the term 'Holy Places', were the Christian Holy Places, most of which happen to be in Palestine, in any event.
14. Translation of a letter from Sir H. McMahon, His Majesty's High Commissioner at Cairo, to the Sherif of Mecca, 14 December 1915, *supra* note 9, p. 15.
15. Ibid.
16. Translation of a letter from Sir H. McMahon, His Majesty's High Commissioner at Cairo, to the Sherif of Mecca, 25 January 1916, ibid.
17. Translation of a letter from Sir H. McMahon, His Majesty's High Commissioner at Cairo, to the Sherif of Mecca, 10 March 1916, ibid.
18. See the articles in Matthew Craven, Malgosia Fitzmaurice and Maria Vogiatzi (eds), *Time, History and International Law* (Leiden: Martinus Nijhoff Publishers, 2007).
19. Article 18 of the Covenant of the League of Nations provided: 'Every treaty or international engagement entered into hereafter by any Member of the League shall be forthwith registered with the Secretariat and shall as soon as possible be published by it. No such treaty or international engagement shall be binding until so registered.' The Hussein–McMahon correspondence was exchanged in 1915–16, three years before the Covenant entered into force.
20. Qatar and Bahrain, Jurisdiction and Admissibility, *supra* note 6, p. 121, para. 25.
21. See Fitzmaurice and Elias, *Contemporary Issues in the Law of Treaties*, *supra* note 10, p. 24.
22. See J.L. Weinstein, 'Exchange of Notes', 29 *British Yearbook of International Law* (1952), pp. 205–26.

23. See Arnold Duncan McNair, *The Law of Treaties: British Practice and Opinions* (Oxford: Clarendon Press, 1938), pp. 47–58 and related documentation. On agreed minutes constituting an international agreement, see Maritime Delimitation and Territorial Questions between Qatar and Bahrain, *supra* note 6, pp. 120–1 at para. 25 ('The [minutes] enumerate commitments to which the Parties have consented. They thus create rights and obligations in international law for the Parties. They constitute an international agreement').
24. See 4 *Documents on British Foreign Policy 1919–1939*, p. 244, at pp. 245–7.
25. Ibid.
26. See Legal Status of Eastern Greenland, PCIJ, Series A./B., No. 53, 5 April 1933, (1933), p. 22 at pp. 21–75 (where Norway and Denmark disputed ownership of a sector of Greenland, and Norway's foreign minister told Denmark's foreign minister that Norway would 'make no difficulties' for Denmark over Greenland, and Denmark's foreign minister made a note of the remark, the remark as thus recorded was binding on Norway, precluding it from claiming sovereignty).
27. See Case Concerning the Temple of Preah Vihear (Cambodia v. Thailand), Preliminary Objections, judgment of 26 May 1961, ICJ Reports (1961), p. 17 at p. 31 ('Where ... as is generally the case in international law, which places the principal emphasis on the intention of the parties, the law prescribes no particular form, parties are free to choose what form they please provided their intention clearly results from it').
28. See Customs Régime between Germany and Austria, PCIJ, Series A./B. No. 41, Advisory Opinion, 5 September 1931, p. 37 at p. 47.
29. In this regard see Ian Brownlie, *Treaties and Indigenous Peoples: The Robb Lectures, 1991*, edited by F.M. Brookfield (Oxford: Clarendon Press, 1992), pp. 8–9. Brownlie was discussing the Treaty of Waitangi of 6 February 1840, which was concluded between the Chiefs of the Confederation of the subtribes of New Zealand (that is, the leaders of the indigenous Maori people of what became 'New Zealand') and the government of the Queen of England (that is, Queen Victoria). In discussing the capacity of peoples to enter into treaty relationships with states, Brownlie cites Lord McNair, *The Law of Treaties* (Oxford: Clarendon Press, 1961) at pp. 52–4. After citing an ambiguous passage from the *Island of Palmas* case, McNair writes at p. 53: 'Whilst this is believed to be the modern doctrine [that international law does not recognise treaties concluded with tribes and peoples], such agreements have been described as treaties in the past ...'
30. In this respect, see Case Concerning Maritime Delimitation and Territorial Questions Between Qatar and Bahrain, Merits, judgment, 16 March 2001, ICJ Reports (2001), p. 40 at pp. 54–5, paras 38–40. Many of these treaties contained obligations on the Sheikhs not to enter into relations with other foreign powers, hence it would not have been in Britain's interest to argue that they were not binding.
31. Ibid.
32. These treaties are reproduced in J.C. Hurewitz (ed.), *Diplomacy in the Near East: A Documentary Record, Vol. II* (Princeton: D. Van Nostrand Co., 1956), pp. 12–13 and pp. 17–18. See also, Clive Parry (ed.), 221 *The Consolidated Treaty Series* (1915–16), pp. 66–7, for the treaty between Great Britain and the Idrisi.
33. For an example of a treaty concluded between Britain and a 'non-state entity' after the First World War, see the Treaty between Great Britain and Ireland, signed at London, 6 December 1921, 26 *League of Nations Treaty Series* (1924), pp. 9–18. This treaty was concluded *before* the creation of the Irish Free State in the following year on 6 December 1922. The treaty was signed on behalf of the Irish delegation by Arthur Griffith, among others. Griffith was the founder and first leader of Sinn Féin.
34. For a description of the Sherif's authority in the Hejaz during this period of history, see Haifa Alangari, *The Struggle for Power in Arabia: Ibn Saud, Hussein and Great Britain 1914–1924* (Reading: Ithaca Press, 1998), pp. 46–71.
35. See Saleh Muhammad Al-Amr, *The Hijaz under Ottoman Rule 1869–1914: Ottoman Vali, the Sherif of Mecca, and the Growth of British Influence* (a thesis for the degree of Doctor

of Philosophy at the University of Leeds, published by Riyad University Publications, March 1978), p. 111.

36. Ibid., p. 112.
37. See *A Handbook of Arabia*, Vol. 1 (compiled by the Geographical Section of the Naval Intelligence Division, Naval Staff, Admiralty, London, HMSO, 1920), pp. 34–5.
38. Ibid.
39. See *Handbook of Hejaz Prepared by the Arab Bureau, Cairo* (Cairo: Government Press, 1917), p. 50.
40. In fact, the Sublime Porte was desperate for Hussein to endorse the Sultan's declaration of *jihad* when they sided with the Central Powers in the war, something he refused to do, much to their chagrin. One of the reasons underlying Britain's support for the Sherif was precisely because he could prevent the unified Islamic opposition to the Allies sought by the Sultan's call to *jihad.* In this respect, one should bear in mind there was a very large Muslim population in British India. See Gerald de Gaury, *Rulers of Mecca* (London: George G. Harrap & Co., 1951), pp. 268–9.
41. See agreement signed and exchanged at Rafah on 1 October 1906, between the Commissioners of the Turkish Sultanate and the Commissioners of the Egyptian Khediviat, concerning the fixing of a Separating Administrative Line between the Vilayet of Hejaz and Governorate of Jerusalem and the Sinai Peninsula, in Vol. 99, *British and Foreign State Papers* (1905–06), pp. 482–4.
42. De Gaury, *Rulers of Mecca, supra* note 40, p. 270.
43. Ibid., p. 272. (De Gaury gives the date of recognition in January 1917, whereas the Handbook of Hejaz prepared by the Arab Burea in Cairo, Government Press, 1917 gave it as December 1916.)
44. Ibid.
45. Ibid., p. 273.
46. On estoppel generally, see D.W. Bowett, 'Estoppel before International Tribunals and its Relation to Acquiescence', 33 *British Yearbook of International Law* (1957), pp. 176–202.
47. H.W.V. Temperley (ed.), *A History of the Peace Conference of Paris*, Vol. VI (London: Henry Frowde and Hodder & Stoughton, 1924).
48. Ibid., p. 137 ('The Hejaz was already an independent sovereign State. Great Britain was pledged by her undertakings to the Sherif of Mecca to "recognise and support" Arab independence within certain areas which included the greater part of Syria').
49. According to the 'traditional' criteria for statehood a case could be made that after the expulsion of the Turks, his Emirate satisfied the criteria of a state having a permanent population, a defined territory and a government in effective control of the territory, with the capacity to enter into international relations which was recognised by Great Britain and France. See Article 1 of the Montevideo Convention on the Rights and Duties of States, 26 December 1933, 165 *League of Nations Treaty Series*, p. 19.
50. On the legal status of these countries see Hussein al-Baharna, *The Arabian Gulf States: Their Legal and Political Status and their International Problems* (Beirut: Librairie du Liban, 1975).
51. Letter to Mr W.A.F. Erskine, (Rome), H.M. Chargé d'Affaires from the Hon. Mr R. Graham (the Secretary of State) at the Foreign Office, 28 July 1918, attaching a memorandum which is to be communicated to the Italian government. Registry No. 123010/W/44, FO 371/3410.
52. Ibid. (emphasis added).
53. See the Treaty of Peace between the Allied and Associated Powers and Germany, signed at Versailles, 28 June 1919 (in force from 10 January 1920) in 112 *British and Foreign State Papers* (1919), compiled and edited by Edward Parkes, O.B.E., with assistance of John W. Field, M.B.E., and R.C. Thomson, M.B.E. (London: HMSO, 1922), pp. 1–212.
54. Ibid.

55. See Convention relative to the Control of the Trade in Arms and Ammunition – Saint-Germaine-en-Laye, 10 September 1919, 112 *British and Foreign State Papers* (1919), *supra* note 53 at pp. 909–24.
56. See the Convention relative to Air Navigation, Paris, 13 October 1919, 112 *British and Foreign State Papers* (1919), *supra* note 53 at pp. 931–70 (including annexes).
57. See the Treaty of Peace between the British Empire and Allied and Associated Powers and Bulgaria – Neuilly-sur-Seine, 27 November 1919 and the Protocol relative to the Conditions in which certain provisions of the Bulgarian Peace Treaty are to be carried out – Neuilly-sur-Seine, 27 November 1919, 112 *British and Foreign State Papers* (1919), *supra* note 53, at pp. 781–895 and 895–6, respectively.
58. The Treaty of Sèvres was signed on 10 August 1920 and is reproduced in *The Treaties of Peace 1919–1923* (New York: Carnegie Endowment for International Peace, 1924), pp. 789–941.
59. Ibid., p. 817.
60. See Quincy Wright, 'Sovereignty of the Mandates', 17 *American Journal of International Law* (1923), pp. 691–703, at p. 696.
61. See the Case of the S.S. 'Wimbledon', PCIJ, Series A, (judgment of 17 August 1923), p. 25.
62. See C.U. Aitchison, B.C.S., *A Collection of Treaties, Engagements and Sanads Relating to India and Neighbouring Countries, Vol. XI Containing the Treaties, & c., Relating to Aden and the South Western Coast of Arabia, the Arab Principalities in the Persian Gulf, Muscat (Oman), Baluchistan and the North-West Frontier Province* (Delhi: Manager of Publications, 1933).
63. In this regard, see Hasan Kayali, *Arabs and Young Turks: Ottomanism, Arabism, and Islamism in the Ottoman Empire, 1908–1918* (Berkeley: University of California Press, 1997), p. 145 ('In the aftermath of the Tanzimate provincial reorganisation, the Hijaz was designated as a distinct province governed by a governor sent from Istanbul'); and Suraiya Faroqhi, *The Ottoman Empire and the World Around it* (London: I.B. Tauris, 2004), p. 88 ('... at least in the sixteenth and seventeenth centuries, the sherifs did not see themselves as mere dependents of the Ottoman sultan, but attempted to play a role in "international politics"'). See also, *Records of the Hijaz: 1798–1925*, edited by A.L.P. Burdett (London: Archive Editions, 1996) for diplomatic correspondence between London and the British diplomats based in Jeddah.
64. See Case Concerning Right of Passage over Indian Territory (Portugal v. India), Merits, Judgment of 12 April 1960, ICJ Reports (1960), p. 6 at p. 37. The Court concluded that the validity of a treaty concluded in the last quarter of the eighteenth century should not be based upon the basis of practices and procedures which have since developed only gradually. For further reading see Charles Henry Alexandrowicz, 'The Afro-Asian World and the Law of Nations (Historical Aspects)', 123 (I) *Recueil Des Cours* (1968), pp. 206–7.
65. See Dissenting Opinion of Judge Moreno Quintana in Case Concerning Right of Passage over Indian Territory, ibid., p. 91.
66. Ibid.
67. See Pleadings, Oral Arguments, Documents, Western Sahara, Vol. V, Exposé Oral De M. Dupuy, p. 209 ('En premier lieu, les traités de paix, de commerce et d'amitié conclus par le Maroc aux XVIIIe et XIXe siècles constituent une reconnaissance implicite de la souveraineté chérifienne au Sahara occidental').
68. The relevant passage from McMahon's letter is: 'With the above modification, and without prejudice of our existing treaties with Arab chiefs, we accept those limits.'
69. See Nuclear Tests Case (New Zealand v. France), judgment, ICJ Reports (1974), p. 457 at p. 472, para. 46 ('It is well recognized that declarations made by way of unilateral acts, concerning legal or factual considerations, may have the effect of creating legal obligations. Declarations of this kind may be, and often are, very specific').

70. See the telegram from Sir Henry McMahon to Sir Edward Grey, informing the latter about his pledge to Hussein, 26 October 1915, Cairo, File No. 163832, FO 371/2486 (emphasis added).
71. See the letter published by McMahon in *The Times* on 23 July 1937 after he came under pressure for Britain's Zionist lobby. The letter is reproduced in Norton Moore, *The Arab–Israeli Conflict*, *supra* note 9, p. 23.
72. Qatar v. Bahrain case, Preliminary Objections, *supra* note 6 at pp. 121–2, para. 27.
73. *Report of a Committee Set Up to Consider Certain Correspondence between Sir Henry McMahon and the Sharif of Mecca in 1915 and 1916*, Presented by the Secretary of State for the Colonies to Parliament by Command of His Majesty, 16 March 1939, XIV Parliamentary Papers (1938–39), Cmd 5974 (London: HMSO, 1934).
74. See Statement by Sir Michael McDonnell on certain legal points arising out of the Lord Chancellor's statement at the second meeting of the committee on 24 February, (Annex C), ibid. p. 34.
75. Ibid.
76. For the facts see Ellery C. Stowell, *Intervention in International Law* (Washington, DC: John Byrne & Co., 1921) at pp. 63–6.
77. See the Protocol for the Pacification of Syria signed in Paris on 3 August 1860 and subsequently embodied in a convention signed in Paris on 5 September 1860. The official French texts and the English translations of those agreements may be found in 68 *Parliamentary Papers* (1861), pp. 1–7. For further documentation on this episode, see Louis B. Sohn and Thomas Buergenthal, *International Protection of Human Rights* (New York: The Bobbs-Merrill Company, Inc., 1973), pp. 143–78.
78. For a critique of the thesis that France's intervention in Syria was purely on humanitarian grounds see Istvan Pogany, 'Humanitarian Intervention in International Law: The French Intervention in Syria Re-Examined', 35 *International and Comparative Law Quarterly* (1986), pp. 182–90.
79. See the Convention between Great Britain and France for the settlement of certain points connected with the mandates for Syria and the Lebanon, Palestine and Mesopotamia – Paris, 23 December 1920 (signed by Hardinge of Penshurst and G. Leygues), 113 *British and Foreign State Papers* (1920), pp. 355–60.
80. See Statement by Sir Michael McDonnell, *supra* note 74, p. 38, citing Lord Blackburn, *River Wear Commissioners v. Adamson* (1877) 2 A.C. p. 763 and Wightman J. in *Lewis v. Nicholson* (1852) 18 Q.B. 512.
81. This is why the letter published by McMahon in *The Times* on 23 July 1937, some 22 years after he had written to the Sherif, is really beside the point. It is clearly evident from what he wrote to Lord Grey after he had corresponded with the Sherif that he only intended to exclude 'Mersina, Alexandretta and those districts *on the northern coast of Syria*, which cannot be said to be purely Arab, and where I understand that French interests have been recognised'. See the telegram from Sir Henry McMahon to Sir Edward Grey, informing the latter about his pledge to Hussein, 26 October 1915, Cairo, File No. 163832, FO 371/2486.
82. See Lassa Oppenheim, *International Law: A Treatise, Vol. I, Peace* (London: Longmans, Green & Co., 1912), p. 542 ('... there exists a customary rule of international law that treaties are binding'); Charles G. Fenwick, *International Law* (New York: Appleton-Century-Crofts, 1948), p. 430 ('The oldest and doubtless the most fundamental rule of international law is that of the sanctity of treaties'); and Hersch Lauterpacht (ed.), *International Law: A Treatise by L. Oppenheim* (London: Longmans, Green & Co., 1955), p. 900 ('... the determination of the extent of the obligation of a State, although lying within the competence of the interested State, must take place in accordance with the legal duty to act in good faith'). See also, Boleslaw A. Boczek, *International Law: A Dictionary* (Lanham, MD: Scarecrow Press, 2005), p. 334 ('It gives expression to the principle of the sanctity of treaties which underlies the entire system of the law of treaties and is believed to be the very foundation of the legal relations among nations, as in particular produced by Hans Kelsen's pure theory of law').

83. See the telegram from Sir Henry McMahon to Sir Edward Grey, informing the latter about his pledge to Hussein, 26 October 1915, Cairo, File No. 163832, FO 371/2486 and reproduced in Chapter 2.
84. MFQ 1/357.
85. See e.g. the conclusions of the arbitrator, Gerald Fitzmaurice, in the *Beagle Channel Arbitration*, 18 February 1977, in E. Lauterpacht (ed.), 52 *International Law Reports*, para. 142 at p. 85 ('Clearly, a map emanating from Party X showing certain territory as belonging to Party Y is of far greater evidential value in support of Y's claim to that territory than a map emanating from Y itself, showing the same thing').
86. Ibid., p. 86 ('maps appearing contemporaneously with the territorial settlement or within a relatively short period after it will, other things being equal, have greater probative value than those produced later when the mists of time have obscured the landscape and the original participants have left it').
87. Memorandum on British Commitments to King Hussein, Political Intelligence Department, Foreign Office, Special 3, FO 608/92, Peace Conference, British Delegation 1919.
88. See Susan Silsby, 'George Antonius: The Formative Years', 15 *Journal of Palestine Studies* (1986), pp. 81–98.
89. See 'Juridical Basis of the Arab Claim to Palestine' (attaches a memorandum discussing the main points on which the Arab legal claim is based, to which answers may be required), 21 December 1938, Political Eastern, Palestine and Transjordan (1939), FO 371/23219.
90. Letter to H.F. Downie, Esq. OBE, Colonial Office, 19 January 1939, (E6/6/31), FO 371/23219.
91. 5 *Foreign Relations of the United States* 1919 (Washington: United States Government Printing Office, 1946), pp. 1–14. The Council of Four: Minutes of Meetings, 20 March to 24 May 1919, Notes of a Conference Held in the Prime Minister's Flat at 23 Rue Nitot, Paris, on Thursday, 20 March 1919 at 3 p.m., Paris Peace Conf. 180.03401/101 IC-163A.
92. Ibid., p. 7.
93. Ibid.
94. Ibid.
95. Ibid. (emphasis added, 'Treaty' is capitalised in the original).
96. Ibid.
97. Ibid.
98. Ibid.
99. Ibid., pp. 807–12. Notes of a Meeting Held at Mr Lloyd George's Residence, 23 Rue Nitot, Paris, on Thursday, 22 May 1919 at 11 a.m. (discussing the oil pipeline project and saying that treaty obligations should be respected). See also, the statement by Clemenceau in Paul Matoux, *The Deliberations of the Council of Four (24 March – 28 June 1919), Notes of the Official Interpreter, Vol. II, From the Delivery of the Peace Terms to the German Delegation to the Signing of the Treaty of Versailles*, trans. by Arthur S. Link (New Jersey: Princeton University Press, 1992), p. 163. The partition of Greater Syria was dictated by Imperial strategic considerations. The War Office wanted a corridor between Haifa and Baghdad for a railway, oil pipeline and air route. Despite objections from the Foreign Office that the laws of war prohibited prospecting or concessions in occupied enemy territory, the War Office persuaded the Government to press ahead with surveying the area for 'strategic considerations'. See Proceedings of a Meeting, War Office, 29 October 1919 to discuss reconnaissance for an oil pipeline across the Arabian Desert in Political, Turkey Files, 1919–20, FO 371/4231.
100. Friedman, *Palestine, A Twice-Promised Land? supra* note 1 at p. 59. Friedman also argues that the Palestinian Arabs did not deserve to benefit from Britain's agreement with the Sherif in the Hussein–McMahon correspondence because they fought for the Turks. This, however, seems to be beside the point. This is because Britain's correspondence was with the Sherif of Mecca and not with any other Arab leader. During the First World War, the Palestinian Arabs were under Turkish sovereignty and so it is hardly surprising that many of them were obliged to fight against Britain by being conscripted into the Turkish army.

In fact, many Palestinians, but especially Christians and Jews, fled the country precisely to avoid conscription. For criticisms of Friedman's thesis see Charles D. Smith, 'The Invention of a Tradition: The Question of Arab Acceptance of the Zionist Right to Palestine during World War I', 22 *Journal of Palestine Studies* (1993), pp. 48–61.

101. See Khouri, *Arab–Israeli Dilemma*, *supra* note 8 at p. 8 ('While the Arabs did not play a large role in the overall war picture, their revolt was of great military value because it diverted a considerable number of Turkish reinforcements and supplies to the Hejaz, protected the right flank of the British armies as they advanced through Palestine, removed any danger of the establishment of a German submarine base on the Red Sea, and prevented the proclamation of jihad by the Sultan from having any serious consequences in Allied-controlled areas').

102. See translation of a letter from Sir H. McMahon, His Majesty's High Commissioner at Cairo, to the Sherif of Mecca, 14 December 1915, *supra* note 9, p. 15 ('It is on the *success* of these efforts and on the more active measures which the Arabs may hereafter take in support of our cause, when the time for action comes, that the permanence and strength of our agreement must depend' – emphasis added).

103. See Enclosure No. 334, Mr Lloyd George to M. Clemenceau, 18 October 1919, in E.L. Woodward and Rohan Butler (eds), *Documents on British Foreign Policy 1919–1939* (London: HMSO, 1952), p. 483.

104. It is interesting to note that Loder, who worked for the Political Intelligence Department in Egypt during the war and who was present at the Versailles Conference, and who had clearly been privy to the negotiations between McMahon and the Sherif in 1915 (indeed, he reproduced the relevant passage from the correspondence in his book that was published in 1923, even though the correspondence had been kept secret) thought that it was binding. See J. De V. Loder, *The Truth About Mesopotamia, Palestine & Syria* (London: George Allen & Unwin Ltd, 1923), pp. 19–23 at p. 19 ('In July 1916 a correspondence began, and continued until the beginning of the following year, between Hussein and the British High Commissioner in Egypt, representing His Majesty's Government, in the course of which the condition of Arab intervention on behalf of the Allies were discussed. Great importance is to be attached to these documents, since they contain those engagements *binding* the British and Arab Governments which were to prove such a fertile source of trouble in the sequel' emphasis added).

105. See the views of Loder, ibid. See also the views of Arnold Toynbee who worked for the Foreign Office's Political Intelligence Department in 1918 in Toynbee, 'McMahon–Hussein Correspondence', *supra* note 1. See also, Arnold Toynbee and Louis Eaks, 'Arnold Toynbee on the Arab–Israeli Conflict', 2 *Journal of Palestine Studies* (Spring, 1973), pp. 3–13.

106. Moreover, undertakings made in private meetings can be binding. See e.g. the 'Ihlen Declaration' in the Status of Eastern Greenland, *supra* note 26 and the Nuclear Tests Case, *supra* note 69. An agreement can still be binding even if it is not registered. See Case Concerning Maritime Delimitation and Territorial Questions between Qatar and Bahrain, Jurisdiction and Admissibility, *supra* note 6, p. 122, para. 29.

107. See the Aegean Sea Continental Shelf Case, (Greece v. Turkey) Jurisdiction of the Court, judgment of 19 December 1978, ICJ Reports (1978), p. 3, at p. 39 at para. 96. See also, the Nuclear Tests Case, *supra* note 69 at p. 473, para. 48 ('Whether a statement is made orally or in writing makes no essential difference, for such statements made in particular circumstances may create commitments in international law, which does not require that they should be couched in written form').

108. See Selected Reference Documents on Israel's Foreign Ministry Website at http://www.mfa.gov.il/mfa/peace%20process/reference%20documents/ (last retrieved 22 October). The Feisal–Weizmann agreement is listed after the Balfour Declaration.

109. The French Army would boot Feisal out of Damascus after the Syrian National Congress had crowned him King of Greater Syria in 1920. He would settle in Iraq where the British made him King in 1921 after holding a referendum which showed that 96 per cent of the population wanted an Arab monarchy rather than direct British rule, although Britain remained in control as the mandatory power until 1932, when Iraq became nominally

independent. Antonius was given exclusive access to Feisal's diaries in the spring of 1933, shortly before Feisal's death of a heart attack, when he visited Baghdad.

110. For French hostility towards Feisal and for further reading on French policy towards the region see Jan Karl Tanenbaum, *France and the Arab Middle East 1914–1920* (Philadelphia: The American Philosophical Society, 1978).

111. See Article IV, Feisal–Weizmann Agreement in Norton Moore, *The Arab-Israeli Conflict*, *supra* note 9, at pp. 39–41. The agreement also provided that 'The Mohammedan Holy Places shall be under Mohammedan control' (Article VI) and that any dispute between the Arabs and the Zionists were to be referred to the British Government for arbitration (Article IX).

112. See George Antonius, *The Arab Awakening: The Story of the Arab National Movement* (London: Hamish Hamilton, 1938), pp. 285–6.

113. Moreover, as the Assistant Political officer in Jerusalem, Mr J.N. Camp noted: '... Dr. Weizmann's agreement with Emir Feisal is not worth the paper it is written on or the energy wasted in conversation to make it ... if it becomes sufficiently known among the Arabs, it will be somewhat in the nature of a noose about Feisal's neck, for he will be regarded as a traitor'. See Colonel French (Cairo) to Earl Curzon (received 6 September), No. C.P.O. 31/110, 26 August 1919 in E.L. Woodward and Rohan Butler (eds), *Documents on British Foreign Policy 1919–1939* (London: HMSO, 1952), p. 364.

114. This is especially as Feisal did not speak good English and was reliant on a British agent, Colonel T.E. Lawrence, in his negotiations with Feisal.

115. Ibid. The Feisal-Weizmann agreement is reproduced in Appendix F, pp. 437–9. The reservation is at the bottom of p. 439, translated in English by Antonius. It is noteworthy that the reservation is not reproduced in the Feisal–Weizmann agreement which is reprinted in Norton Moore's *Arab–Israeli Conflict*, *supra* note 9, as this was copied from a book by David Hunter Miller which does not include it. A copy of the original Feisal–Weizmann agreement is, however, available in the National Archives at FO 608/98/9. The agreement is dated 3 January 1919. A British translation of Feisal's reservation by Col. T.E. Lawrence is as follows: 'If the Arabs are established as I have asked in my manifesto of January 4th addressed to the British Secretary of State for Foreign Affairs, I will carry out what is written in this Agreement. If changes are made, I cannot be answerable for failing to carry out this agreement.' This is also reproduced in Arabic and in English in Issa Al-Sifri, *Arab Palestine: Between the Mandate and Zionism* (Jaffa: New Palestine Library Press, 1937), p. 18.

116. Ibid., note by A. Toynbee written on 17 January 1918, FO 608/98/9 ('Colonel Lawrence tells me that in the first draft of the present document, Dr. Weizmann used the phrases 'Jewish State', 'Jewish Government' and that the Emir Feisal altered these to 'Palestine', 'Palestinian Government').

117. Ibid.

118. See Constitution of New Arab State by Emir Feisal, 1 January 1919, FO 608/80/5.

119. See the statement by Dr Weizmann in Official Records of the UN General Assembly, Supplement No. 11, United Nations Special Committee on Palestine, Report of the General Assembly, Vol. III, Annex A: Oral Evidence Presented at Public Meeting, Lake Success, New York, UN Doc. A/364/Add.2 PV.21, 8 July 1947.

120. See Majid Khadduri, 'The Arab League as a Regional Arrangement', 40 *American Journal of International Law* (1946), pp. 756–77, at p. 759 ('Thus failing to achieve unity and independence the Arab nationalists naturally contended that European imperialism had deliberately followed a policy of divide et impera since it was easier to dominate the Middle East by creating small and helplessly weak states than to allow a vast area of Western Asia to unite, and hence to become difficult to control').

121. See 'The Emir Faisal on Palestine and the Jews: Interview for the Jewish Chronicle with His Highness the Emir Faisal', *The Jewish Chronicle*, 3 October 1919, pp. 14–15 at p. 14.

122. Ibid. p. 14.

123. See Robert Lansing, *The Big Four and Others of the Peace Conference* (London: Hutchinson & Co., 1922), p. 168.

124. See Memorandum on British Commitments to King Hussein, *supra* note 87.
125. See letter to Clemenceau, 18 October 1919 in Woodward and Butler, *Documents on British Foreign Policy*, *supra* note 113, pp. 486–487 (emphasis added).
126. Within the Foreign Office there was a dispute over the meaning of the Hussein–McMahon correspondence. For instance, there is reference to a document prepared by Arnold J. Toynbee when he worked at the Foreign Office on the Middle East during the First World War. He accused Britain of betraying the Arabs after concluding the Hussein–McMahon correspondence because of what he termed 'Jewish pressure'. He claimed that he drafted a document to the effect that Palestine was included in McMahon's pledge to the Sherif and that this was subsequently considered by the Eastern Committee of the Cabinet, which did not question his interpretation of the correspondence. Lacy Baggallay, who was put in charge of investigating Toynbee's accusations, wrote that 'it would be difficult to establish that the changes in outlook of His Majesty's Government, which does undoubtedly seem to have taken place between 1918 and 1922, was due to Jewish pressure. I doubt whether the change was conscious ... What probably happened was that after 1918 the Zionist interpretation of the Balfour Declaration was accepted by His Majesty's Government and ordered to be put into effect by persons who had forgotten or never known about the pledges to the Arabs. Later, when the irreconcilable elements in the situation began to make themselves felt, arguments were sought to show that the pledges did not exclude what was being done for the Zionists.' This is all recorded in a number of letters and memoranda. See, for instances, British Commitments in the Middle East, 1914–18, and Ms Baggallay's minute, 18 April 1940, FO 371/24569.

5 THE QUESTION OF SELF-DETERMINATION

1. Eustace Percy, *The Responsibilities of the League* (London: Hodder & Stoughton, 1919), p. 150.
2. For a collection of essays on self-determination see Robert McCorquodale (ed.), *Self-Determination in International Law* (Aldershot: Ashgate, 2000). See further, U.O. Umozurike, *Self-Determination in International Law* (Hamden: Archon Books, 1972); A. Rigo Sureda, *The Evolution of the Right of Self-Determination: A Study of United Nations Practice* (Leiden: A.W. Sijthoff, 1973); Michla Pomerance, *Self-Determination in Law and Practice: The New Doctrine of the United Nations* (The Hague: Martinus Nijhoff, 1982); Hurst Hannum, *Autonomy, Sovereignty, and Self-Determination: The Accommodation of Conflicting Rights* (Philadelphia: University of Pennsylvania Press, 1992); Antonio Cassese, *Self-Determination of Peoples: A Legal Reappraisal* (Cambridge: Cambridge University Press, paperback, 1995); and David Raič, *Statehood and the Law of Self-Determination* (The Hague: Kluwer Law International, 2002).
3. See 'The Right of Nations to Self-Determination' which was written by Lenin between February and May 1914, being first published in the journal *Prosveschcheniye* before being republished in *V.I. Lenin: Collected Works*, Vol. 20, December 1913 – August 1914 (Moscow: Progress Publishers and in London by Lawrence & Wishart, 1977), pp. 395–454 at p. 397. Lenin was critiquing Rosa Luxemburg's stance against nations having a right of self-determination. She thought that Poland would have been better off as an autonomous region with Russia. In the end, Lenin won the argument: Poland became an independent state in 1919, although Luxemburg never witnessed this as she was assassinated by Germany's Freikorps after she was accused of being involved in a socialist uprising in Berlin. In his article Lenin concluded by saying on p. 451: 'No one can seriously question the London resolution of 1896 [of the International Congress declaring that it stands for the full right of all nations to self-determination], or the fact that self-determination implies only the right to secede, or that the formation of independent national states is the tendency in all bourgeois-democratic revolutions.'
4. See Erez Manela, *The Wilsonian Moment: Self-Determination and the International Origins of Anticolonial Nationalism* (Oxford: Oxford University Press, 2007), p. 37.

5. See Arno J. Mayer, *Wilson vs. Lenin: Political Origins of the New Diplomacy 1917–1918* (New York: The World Publishing Co., Meridian Books, 1963), p. 298. See also, Alfred Cobban, *National Self-Determination* (London: Oxford University Press, 1944), p. 12. For the text of the Brest-Litovsk Treaty see Jane Degras (ed.), *Soviet Documents on Foreign Policy, Vol. 1, 1917–1924* (London: Oxford University Press, 1951), pp. 50–5. Article 3 of that treaty provides that Germany and Austria-Hungary agree 'to determine the future status' of the territories from which Russia had withdrawn its troops 'in agreement with their population'.
6. See Article 17 of the Constitution (Basic Law) of the Union of Soviet Socialist Republics, confirmed by the Eighth Congress of Soviets of the USSR, 5 December 1936, as amended to 1 October 1968 ('The right shall be preserved for each Union Republic freely to secede from the USSR'). See also, Article 15 of the Constitution (Basic Law) of the Russian Soviet Federated Socialist Republic, adopted by the Fifth All-Russian Congress of Soviets on 19 July, 1918, as confirmed by the Seventeenth All-Russian Congress of Soviets, 21 January 1937, as amended 1 October, 1968 ('The Russian Soviet Federated Socialist Republic reserves for itself the right to secede from the Union of Soviet Socialist Republics'). These are reproduced in English in Harold J. Berman and John B. Quigley, Jr. (trans. and eds), *Basic Laws on the Structure of the Soviet State* (Cambridge: Harvard University Press, 1969), p. 3 at p. 7 and p. 30 at p. 32. A right to secession also appeared in the constitution of Burma, that of the former Socialist Federal Republic of Yugoslavia, and in the 1968 Constitution of Czechoslovakia. It currently appears in the constitution of Ethiopia. See David Raič, *Statehood and the Law of Self-Determination*, *supra* note 1, pp. 313–14.
7. For instance it was explicitly mentioned in Lenin's Decree on Peace of 26 October 1917 and put into actual practice in Ukraine (17 December 1917), Finland (31 December 1917), Turkish Armenia (11 January 1918), and Estonia, Latvia and Lithuania (7 December 1918). See Bill Bowring, 'The Return of Politics to Self-Determination: From Lenin to Lavrov; from the Baltic States and Georgia, to Abkhazia and Transdniestra', unpublished manuscript presented to the Conference on New Approaches to Self-Determination at the School of Oriental and African Studies on Thursday 12 June 2008 (on file with author) citing Igor P. Blishchenko, *Antisovyetism I Mezhdunarodnoye Pravo* [Antisovietism and International Law], (Moscow: 1968).
8. See Derek Heater, *National Self-Determination: Woodrow Wilson and His Legacy* (London: Macmillan, 1994), pp. 36–7.
9. Ibid., p. 36.
10. Ibid.
11. Ibid., p. 37.
12. See Lenin, 'The Right of Nations to Self-Determination', *supra* note 3. Bill Bowring, 'The Return of Politics to Self-Determination', *supra* note 7, points out that the Soviet Union was the greatest champion of self-determination and was responsible for getting it enshrined in the UN Charter in 1945, in the Declaration on the Granting of Independence to Colonial Countries and Peoples in 1960 and was instrumental in getting it included in common Article 1 to the two human rights conventions of 1966.
13. For instance, in a debate at the UN in 1965, forty years after the end of the First World War, Britain even quoted Wilson in support of the claims of the Falkland islanders to self-determination over Argentina's claims to sovereignty there based on historic title, even though at the time only 2,000 settlers lived on the islands. See the statement by Mr Brown at the proceedings of the Fourth Committee of the UN General Assembly, Twentieth Session, 16 November 1965, para. 91. See further, Raphael Perl (ed.), *The Falkland Islands Dispute in International Law and Politics: A Documentary Sourcebook* (New York: Oceana Publications, 1983). See also, Thomas M. Franck and Paul Hoffman, 'The Right of Self-Determination in Very Small Places', 8 *New York University Journal of Law and Politics* (1975–76), pp. 379–84. Britain would advance similar arguments in support of its claims to Gibraltar. See e.g. Franck and Hoffman, ibid., pp. 371–9.
14. See Erez Manela, *The Wilsonian Moment: Self-Determination and the International Origins of Anticolonial Nationalism* (Oxford: Oxford University Press, 2007), pp. 59–60

(describing the multitude of different ethnic groups and nationalities that would come to petition Wilson at Paris).

15. Ibid., p. 25.
16. Ibid.
17. Robert Lansing, *The Peace Negotiations: A Personal Narrative* (London: Constable & Co., 1921), p. 87.
18. See Robert Lansing, *The Big Four and Others of the Peace Conference* (London: Hutchinson & Co., 1922), p. 168.
19. See James Brown Scott (ed.), *President Wilson's Foreign Policy: Messages, Addresses, Papers* (New York: Oxford University Press, 1918), pp. 364–73 at p. 368.
20. Ibid., p. 371.
21. See Heater, *National Self-Determination*, *supra* note 8, p. 53 ('...Wilson travelled to Paris armed with two firm objectives, of which the honouring of the principle of self-determination was one ... The other was, of course, the creation of a League of Nations').
22. This was subject only to the rendering of administrative advice and assistance by a Mandatory until such time as they are able to stand alone. See Article 22, Covenant of the League of Nations, 1 *League of Nations Official Journal* (1920), p. 9.
23. See Document No. 47756/2117/M.E. 44/1919, National Archives. This is cited in a confidential memorandum on the 'Arab choice of His Majesty's Government as mandatory power for Palestine' (emphasis added).
24. Iraq became independent in 1933, Lebanon in 1943, Syria in 1944 and Transjordan in 1946. In 1948–49, Palestine would be unilaterally partitioned between Israel and Transjordan.
25. See Palestine: General Statement by the Principal Accredited Representative, the Right Hon. W. Ormsby-Gore, Permanent Mandates Commission, Minutes of the Thirty-Second (Extraordinary) Session devoted to Palestine, held at Geneva from 30 July to 18 August, 1937, including the Report of the Commission to the Council, Official No. C.3330. M.222. 1937 VI., p. 17.
26. Palestine: Statement of Policy, Presented by the Secretary of State for the Colonies to Parliament by Command of His Majesty, (1 May 1939), Cmd. 6019.
27. See Balfour's memorandum to the British Foreign Secretary, Curzon, 11 August 1919, Foreign Office No. 371/4183 (1919). This is reproduced in E.L. Woodward and Rohan Butler (eds), *Documents on British Foreign Policy 1919–1939* (London: HMSO, 1952), p. 345.
28. Ibid.
29. As to their different views on Palestine see David Gilmour, 'The Unregarded Prophet: Lord Curzon and the Palestine Question', 25 *Journal of Palestine Studies* (1996), pp. 60–8. It has been said that Balfour actually complained to his colleagues lamenting the fact that they had made Palestine an A-class Mandate because he said this meant 'self-determination'. See 'Arnold Toynbee on the Arab–Israeli Conflict', 2 *Journal of Palestine Studies* (1973), pp. 3–13 at p. 3 (where in an interview Toynbee recollects seeing a note to this effect).
30. See Doreen Ingrams (ed.), *Palestine Papers 1917–1922: Seeds of Conflict* (London: John Murray, 1972), pp. 96–7.
31. Curzon was also referring to Robert Vansittart who was liaising with the Zionists, Ingrams, ibid., p. 98 (he was very upset that Vansittart had put the phrase 'historical connection' in the preamble to the Mandate).
32. Ibid., pp. 94–104.
33. Ibid., pp. 98–9 (emphasis in original).
34. Ibid., p. 97 ('As to the Palestine mandate, Berthelot said that Millerand had nearly jumped out of his skin when he had shown it him. Berthelot added that, frankly, he himself was both surprised and alarmed by it. They both think it much too judaised and judaising – full of red flags indeed').
35. Ibid., p. 102.
36. Ibid., pp. 102–3 (emphasis added).

37. See Ernst Frankenstein, 'The Meaning of the Term "National Home for the Jewish People"', 1 *The Jewish Yearbook of International Law* (1948), pp. 27–41 at p. 29.
38. As quoted in 50 *Parliamentary Debates*, Lords, 21 June 1922, col. 1005 (emphasis added).
39. See H.W.V. Temperley, *A History of the Peace Conference of Paris*, Vol. VI (London: Henry Frowde and Hodder & Stoughton, 1924), p. 141 ('The promise that the native populations should exercise the right of self-determination regarding the form of National Government under which they should live was thought conclusive. Indeed, it convinced the people that they were to have a free choice in wider questions than, perhaps, the Declaration ever intended ...').
40. See the Nuclear Tests Case (Australia v. France), 20 December 1974, ICJ Reports (1974), p. 253 at pp. 267–8, paras 43–6.
41. See Memorandum by Balfour in Woodward and Butler, *Documents on British Foreign Policy 1919–1939*, *supra* note 27, pp. 343–4.
42. See Paul J.I.M. De Waart, *Dynamics of Self-Determination in Palestine: Protection of Peoples as a Human Right* (Leiden: E.J. Brill, 1994), p. 112 ('The intention of both the Mandatory Power and the Council of the League of Nations to create an independent state for Jews *and* Arabs in Palestine is the red thread in an otherwise zigzag policy on the part of both bodies, resulting from undertakings given at various times to various parties' – emphasis in original).
43. 'The Welfare and Development of the Natives in Mandated Territories', Report by M. Yanaghita, Annex 6, in Annexes to the Minutes of the Third Session of the Permanent Mandates Commission, held at Geneva from 20 July – 10 August 1923, pp. 279–86, at p. 280.
44. See Indians in Kenya. Memorandum presented to Parliament by Command of His Majesty, 23 July, 1923, Cmd. 1922 (London: HMSO), General Statement of Policy, p. 10. The memorandum added that: 'Obviously the interests of the other communities, European, Indian or Arab, must *severally* be safeguarded' (emphasis added).
45. Delimitation provides the definition of the separating line between the authority of the neighbouring states through a verbal description of the location of the boundary, sometimes accompanied by maps and sketches. Demarcation is a technical decision limited to the transformation of the verbal, graphical and digital definitions to the terrain surface which is usually accomplished by marking it on the ground. See Ron Adler, 'Geographical Information in Delimitation, Demarcation and Management of International Land Boundaries', 3 (4) *Boundary and Territory Briefing* (International Boundaries Research Unit, 2001), p. 10.
46. See Yehoshua Porath, 'The Political Awakening of the Palestinian Arabs and their Leadership towards the end of the Ottoman Period', in Moshe Ma'oz (ed.), *Studies on Palestine during the Ottoman Period* (Jerusalem: The Hebrew University Magnes Press, 1975), pp. 351–81.
47. Ibid., p. 360.
48. Ibid., pp. 358–9.
49. Ibid., p. 357.
50. Ibid., p. 359.
51. Ibid., p. 360.
52. Palestinian historians, as well as some Israeli sociologists, trace the roots of a modern collective Palestinian identity to Egypt's occupation of Palestine from 1831 to 1840 as described in Chapter 3. See Samih K. Farsoun and Naseer H. Aruri, *Palestine and the Palestinians: A Social and Political History* (Boulder: Westview Press, 2006), pp. 27–8 ('From then on [after the nationwide revolt against Egyptian rule], but especially after the end of the Crimean War in 1856, varied processes and factors progressively gave the area of Palestine social, economic, administrative, and political coherence, which culminated in the twentieth-century (mandate) Palestine').
53. See A. Rigo Sureda, *The Evolution of the Right of Self-Determination: A Study of United Nations Practice* (Leiden: A.W. Sijthoff, 1973), pp. 126–7.

54. Ibid.
55. See Command Paper 1700, Great Britain House of Commons, 23 *Sessional Papers* 1922, pp. 17–21.
56. See Annex 391, 'British Mandate for Palestine', 3 *League of Nations Official Journal* (1922), pp. 1007–12.
57. Writing in the 1920s, Jacob Stoyanovsky argued in his thesis on the theory and practice of international mandates which was supervised by Arnold McNair, that the mandate system had been applied to Palestine 'chiefly, on account of the fact that the people whose connection with Palestine had been recognised is still outside its boundaries'. In Stoyanovsky's opinion, Britain had assumed an obligation not only towards the actual population of Palestine but also to the virtual population of Palestine (that is, to Jews living in other countries). See Jacob Stoyanovsky, *The Mandate for Palestine: A Contribution to the Theory and Practice of International Mandates* (London: Longmans, Green & Co., 1928), pp. 41–2.
58. See John Strawson, 'Mandate Ways: Self-Determination in Palestine and the "Existing Non-Jewish Communities"', in Sanford R. Silverburg (ed.), *Palestine and International Law* (Jefferson: McFarland & Co., 2002), pp. 251–70.
59. See David Lloyd George, *The Truth About the Peace Treaties*, Vol. II (London: Victor Gollancz, 1938), p. 1151 quoting a Foreign Office memorandum (emphasis added). No date is given but it is probably circa 1918–20.
60. See Norman Bentwich, *The Mandates System* (London: Longman, Green & Co., 1930), pp. 27–8.
61. See Permanent Mandates Commission, Minutes of the Fourth Session, Held at Geneva from 24 June to 8 July, 1924, LON Doc. A.13 1924. VI at p. 88.
62. See Palestine: Proposed Formation of an Arab Agency, Correspondence with the High Commissioner for Palestine, XXV *Parliamentary Papers* (1923), para. 7.
63. Ibid. It is telling that the right of self-determination enshrined in common Article 1 to the International Covenant on Civil and Political Rights and the International Covenant on Economic, Social and Cultural Rights provides that: 'All peoples have the right of self-determination. By virtue of that right they freely determine their political status and freely pursue their *economic, social and cultural development*.' See vol. 993, United Nations Treaty Series, p. 3 (ICCPR) and vol. 999, United Nations Treaty Series p. 171 (ICESCR).
64. See eighth meeting, 28 October 1924, in Permanent Mandates Commission, Minutes of the Fifth Session (extraordinary) held at Geneva from 23 October – 6 November, 1924, p. 56.
65. See the comments by Sir Herbert Samuel in reply to M. Van Rees, ibid., p. 66.
66. Although these proposals were rejected by Parliament. See 310 *Parliamentary Debates*, Commons, cols 1079–150, and cols 1166–73, 24 March 1936.
67. See The Hogarth Message, January 1918, 5974 *Command Paper* (1939), Annex F, pp. 48–9 (emphasis added). This is reproduced in John Norton Moore (ed.), *The Arab–Israeli Conflict, Vol. III: Documents* (New Jersey: Princeton University Press, 1977), pp. 33–4.
68. See the document reproduced in Lloyd George, *The Truth About the Peace Treaties*, *supra* note 59, p. 1174.
69. For the argument that it does not include political rights see Frankenstein, '"National Home for the Jewish People"', *supra* note 37 and Julius Stone, *Israel and Palestine: Assault on the Law of Nations* (Baltimore: Johns Hopkins University Press, 1981), p. 9. Both jurists seem to predicate their argument on the fact that the word 'political rights' is not explicitly used as regards the non-Jewish population without considering whether civil rights would cover this.
70. Lloyd George, *The Truth About the Peace Treaties*, *supra* note 59 at p. 1174.
71. Ibid.
72. Ibid.
73. Ibid.

74. Permanent Mandates Commission, Minutes of the Thirty-Sixth Session, held at Geneva from 8 June to 29 June, 1939, including the Report of the Commission to the Council, Official No. C.170.M.100.1939. VI., p. 121.
75. The 'Top Secret' seven-page memorandum is entitled 'Palestine: Reference to the United Nations', dated 13 January 1947. File no. C.P. (47) 28. According to the Foreign Office Lists for 1947–48, William Eric Beckett, Gerald Gray Fitzmaurice, Richard Samuel Berrington Best, James Edmund Fawcett and Francis Aime Vallat were legal advisers at the Foreign Office in London and in Britain's Washington Embassy. See Godfrey E.P. Hertslet (ed.), *Foreign Office List and Diplomatic and Consular Yearbook* (London: Harrison & Sons Ltd, 1947), p. 11.
76. Ibid.
77. Palestine defence policy: military aspects of partition. Memorandum by the Minister for Co-ordination of Defence, 1937–38. CAB 104/5.
78. The Aaland (or Åland) Islands are located between Finland and Sweden where the Baltic Sea meets the Gulf of Bothnia. In 1809 Sweden had ceded the islands along with Finland to Russia. When Finland became independent of Russia in 1917 (it joined the League in 1920) the islanders asked Finland to return the islands to Sweden. However, Finland opposed this and the dispute was referred to the Council of the League of Nations, which ruled in favour of Finland. For literature on this dispute see Lauri Hannikainen and Frank Horn (eds), *Autonomy and Demilitarisation in International Law: The Åland Islands in a Changing Europe* (The Hague: Kluwer Law International, 1997).
79. The Aaland Islands Question. Report of the Committee of Jurists, *League of Nations, Official Journal*, Special Supplement No. 3, October, 1920, pp. 3–10 at p. 6. In fact, one author writing in 1922 was of the opinion 'that the adoption of the principle of a Jewish national home runs directly counter to the doctrine of the *right* of each people to self-determination' (emphasis added). See Berriedale Keith, 'Mandates', 4 *Journal of Comparative Legislation and International Law* (1922), p. 78.
80. Ibid.
81. Ibid., p. 10.
82. See International Status of South-West Africa, Advisory Opinion of 11 July 1950, Separate Opinion by Sir Arnold McNair, ICJ Reports (1950), pp. 146–63 at p. 150. See also, Judge Ammoun in his Separate Opinion in Legal Consequences for States of the Continued Presence of South Africa in Namibia (South West Africa) notwithstanding Security Council Resolution 276 (1970), Advisory Opinion, ICJ Reports (1971), at 69, para. 2 who cites with approval the French edition of Stoyanovsky thesis, *La théorie générale des mandates internationaux* (1925), at p. 83.
83. See the Treaty of Peace with Turkey signed at Lausanne, 24 July, 1923. *Treaties of Peace 1919–1923*, Vol. II (New York: Carnegie Endowment for International Peace, New York, 1924), pp. 959–1022.
84. In this regard, see the pamphlet by D. Campbell Lee, *The Mandate for Mesopotamia and the Principle of Trusteeship in English Law* (London: St Clements Press, 1921), who makes the same argument. ('I do not see how the League of Nations can possess sovereignty in its present state of development, but it is highly probable that from the view-point of international law the proper conclusion is that the Allied Powers, by creating the Mandatory system, have placed the sovereignty of all Mandated areas in *suspense* during the operation of the respective Mandates. The important and practical consideration is that the Mandatory must possess legal dominion. This is conferred on him by his selection as a Mandatory and by the approval of his Mandate by the Council of the League. So long as he fulfils an unrevoked Mandate, he has legal dominion within the compass of his powers. He has no rights of sovereignty beyond this limit. Full sovereignty will come in due time to the territory, but only when its people assume the dignity of an independent state' – emphasis added).
85. This provided that the territories concerned had 'ceased to be under the sovereignty of the States which formerly governed them'. It does not, however, say where that sovereignty

resides. The only logical answer to this, one may deduce, is that it must have resided in the peoples of the territories concerned.

86. See Antonio Cassese, *Self-Determination of Peoples: A Legal Reappraisal* (Cambridge: Cambridge University Press, 1995), p. 324.
87. In the case *Mabo v. Queensland* (No. 2), the High Court of Australia considered the theory of *terra nullius* 'false in fact and unacceptable in our society'. See Mabo v. Queensland (No. 2) [1992] HCA 23; (1992) 175 CLR (3 June 1992), para. 39.
88. Western Sahara, Advisory Opinion, ICJ Reports 1975, p. 12, at p. 39, para. 80.
89. Thirteenth Meeting, St James's Palace, London, 24 July 1922, 3 *League of Nations Official Journal* (1922), p. 823.
90. See Justin McCarthy, *The Population of Palestine: Population History and Statistics of the Late Ottoman Period and the Mandate* (New York: Columbia University Press, 1990), table 2.2., p. 26. The population figures cited in 1918 included Muslims (611,098), Christians (70,429), Jews (58,278), Druze (7,268) and Shii (162).
91. See the statements made by Herbert Samuel at the eighth meeting of the Permanent Mandates Commission, Minutes of the Fifth session (extraordinary), in Geneva on 28 October 1924 at pp. 59–94 (describing the number of Palestinians employed in the civil service, the political system in Palestine, the Turkish land law, the judicial system in Palestine, labour organisation, school system, the system of public health, the Turkish system of taxation etc.).
92. See The Mavrommatis Jerusalem Concessions, judgment, Series A, No. 5, Permanent Court of International Justice, 26 March 1925, p. 6.
93. On effective occupation see, generally, Ian Browlie, *Principles of Public International Law* (Oxford: Oxford University Press, 1998), pp. 136–42. On the application of Turkish law to Palestine before the British conquest see Robert Eisenman, 'The Young Turk Legislation, 1913–17 and its Application in Palestine/Israel', in David Kushner (ed.), *Palestine in the Late Ottoman Period: Political, Social and Economic Transformation* (Leiden: Brill, 1986), pp. 59–73.
94. See Edward Said, *The Question of Palestine* (London: Routledge & Kegan Paul, 1980), p. 9.
95. See Judge McNair, Separate Opinion, International Status of South West Africa, ICJ Reports (1950), p. 146 at p. 150.
96. See *Palestine: Correspondence with the Palestine Arab Delegation and the Zionist Organization*, Presented to Parliament by Command of His Majesty, June, 1922. XXIII *Parliamentary Papers* (HMSO, 1922), pp. 243–73: 'It is the object of providing *the people of Palestine* with a constitutional channel for the expression of their opinions and wishes that the draft constitution has been framed' (emphasis added).
97. Ibid. (emphasis added).
98. Lecture by David Ben-Gurion in Berlin, 1931 (emphasis added). This quote is reproduced in Eric Rouleau, 'The Palestinian Question', 53 *Foreign Affairs* (1975) at p. 266 citing Cahiers Bernard Lazare (Paris), December 1972 – January 1973 issue.
99. In 1931, *L'Institut de Droit International* met at Emmanuel College, University of Cambridge, from 28 July to 4 August to consider various aspects of international law. M. Henri Rolin was rapporteur and the resolution was adopted on 31 July. According to the relevant text of the Institute's resolution: 'The powers conferred upon the mandatory are in the *exclusive interest of the population subject to Mandate* ... 6. The communities under Mandate *are subjects of international law*. They have a patrimony distinct from that of the mandatory State; they possess a national status, and they may acquire rights or be held to their obligations. 7. The functions of the mandatory State end by renunciation or revocation of the Mandate ... by the recognition of *the independence of the community* which has been under Mandate ... 8. The rights and duties of the communities under Mandate *are not affected by the expiration of the Mandate* or the change of the mandatory' (emphasis added). The English text is reproduced in James Brown Scott, 'Two Institutes of International Law', 26 *American Journal of International Law* (1932), pp. 91–2. The original French text of the resolution is available on the *L'Institut de Droit International*'s

website at the following link: http://www.idi-iil.org/idiF/resolutionsF/1931_camb_01_fr.pdf (last retrieved 22 October 2008).

100. See the Ottoman Law of Nationality, 19 January 1869 in R.W. Flournoy Jr. and M.O. Hudson (eds), *A Collection of Nationality Laws of Various Countries as Contained in Constitutions, Statutes and Treaties* (New York: Oxford University Press, 1929), pp. 568–9. The preamble to the Palestine Citizenship Order provided that 'it is desirable to regulate the grant and acquisition of Palestinians *citizenship*' (emphasis added). See the Palestinian Citizenship Order, *Official Gazette*, 16 September 1925, pp. 459–66. The citizenship order and its amendments can be accessed in Robert Harry Drayton, 8 *The Laws of Palestine* (London: Waterlow & Sons, 1934), pp. 2640–52.

101. See 4 *League of Nations Official Journal* (1923), p. 604. The League adopted this resolution after considering a report by the Permanent Mandates Commission on the national status of inhabitants of territories under B- and C-class mandates.

102. Bentwich was of the opinion '[t]hat English nationality does not apply to the inhabitants of protectorates and mandated territories [as] stated in Dicey's *Conflict of Laws*, on the ground that these countries are not included in His Majesty's Dominions, and the population do not owe allegiance to His Majesty'. See Norman Bentwich, 'Nationality in Mandated Territories Detached from Turkey', 7 *British Yearbook of International Law* (1926), pp. 97–109 at p. 101.

103. In a decision by the English High Court in *R. v. Ketter* [1940] 1 K.B. 787 it was held that a Palestinian national in Great Britain was not a British subject. A native of Palestine born at a time when that territory was under Turkish sovereignty, but holding a passport marked 'British passport – Palestine', had not become a British subject by virtue of Article 30 of the Treaty of Peace with Turkey, nor under the terms of the Mandate of 24 July 1922, since Palestine was not transferred to and was not annexed by Great Britain by either the Treaty or the Mandate. The position that Palestinians were not British subjects was further confirmed by decisions in the High Court in Palestine (*A.G. v. Goralschwili et al. Annual Digest*, 1925–26, Case No. 33) and the Egyptian Mixed Court (*Saikaly v. Saikaly*, *Annual Digest*, 1925–26, Case No. 34).

104. See Paul Weis, *Nationality and Statelessness in International Law* (Alphen and Rijn: Sijthoff and Noordhoff, 1979), p. 22.

105. See First Report on succession of States in respect of rights and duties resulting from sources other than treaties, by Mr Mohammed Bedjaoui, Special Rapporteur, UN Doc. A/CN.4/204, 5 April 1968, reprinted in Vol. II, *Yearbook of the International Law Commission* (1968), pp. 94–117, at p. 103 (saying that a mandate was regarded in theory and practice as a state).

106. According to British statistics published in 1937, 68 per cent of the Civil Service was staffed by Arabs and only 16 per cent by Jews. See Palestine Royal Commission Report, Presented by the Secretary of State for the Colonies to Parliament by Command of His Majesty, (London: HMSO, 1937), Cmd 5479, p. 318. On the judiciary, see League of Nations, Permanent Mandates Commission, Minutes of the Thirty-Second (Extraordinary) Session, p. 117 ('Mr. Hall could not give separate figures in regard to senior and junior staff; but, taking the service as a whole, there were in the Judicial Department 265 Arabs, 65 Jews, and 22 others'). And Palestine was at this time, manifestly *Arab*, in its language and culture, and Arabic was the language most commonly used to record a Court file, even in criminal trials when the presiding judge was British and the advocates addressed the Court in English. See Norman Bentwich, *England in Palestine* (London: Kegan Paul, Trench, Trubner & Co., 1932), p. 288.

107. It was described as such by S.D. Myres, Jr. in 'Constitutional Aspects of the Mandate for Palestine', 164 *Annals of the American Academy of Political and Social Science* (Nov. 1932), p. 3.

108. Ibid., pp. 3–4.

109. See League of Nations, Permanent Mandates Commission, Minutes of the Thirty-Second (Extraordinary) Session devoted to Palestine, held at Geneva from July 30th to August

18th, 1937, including the Report of the Commission to the Council, Official No. C.330.M.222 1937. VI, pp. 86–7 (emphasis in orginal).

110. See Article 30, Treaty of Lausanne, reprinted in *The Treaties of Peace 1919–1923*, Vol. II (New York: Carnegie Endowment for International Peace, New York, 1924), at p. 969 (emphasis added).

111. The Mixed Court at Mansura had jurisdiction over the Governorates of Damietta, El Arish, the Suez Canal, the *Moudiriehs* of Charkieh, Dakelia, and the Eastern Frontier territories. The official languages of the Mixed Courts were French, Arabic and Italian. Each Court consisted of five judges and these were of various nationality over the years, including Egyptian, Italian, American, Russian, British, Austrian, German, Belgian, Danish, Spanish, Greek, Dutch, Norwegian and Swedish. See Mark Hoyle, *Mixed Court of Egypt* (London: Graham & Trotman, 1991), p. 12 and pp. 22–3.

112. *Antoine Bey Sabbagh v. Mohamed Pacha Ahmed and Others*, Mixed Court of Mansura, Egypt, 15 November, 1927, reported in Arnold D. McNair and H. Lauterpacht (eds), 4 *Annual Digest of Public International Law Cases* (1927–28), pp. 48–9.

113. League of Nations, Permanent Mandates Commission, Minutes of the Thirty-Second (Extraordinary) Session devoted to Palestine, *supra* note 109, statement dated 5 August 1937, Mr Ormsby-Gore, p. 87.

114. Some support for this latter proposition can be gleaned from a Foreign Office minute prepared by their legal advisers, on the legal status of Palestine after the termination of the Mandate: '... when the Mandate comes to an end, and pending the emergence of one or more states in Palestine to which international recognition can be accorded, Palestine will be a sort of res nullius. Its theoretical sovereignty will probably lie *in the people of Palestine* but it will be latent and there will certainly be no international entity recognised as a sovereign state or states in comprising Palestine.' The legal advisers added that if the Zionists set up a state in the boundaries accorded to the Jewish state by the UN Partition Plan, and the Arabs did likewise, 'there would be nothing legally to choose between these two claims'. In other words, it was really up to the Arabs and the Jews to establish their own states which would be recognised in time according to the 'ordinary standards of international law'. See legal status of Palestine after termination of the Mandate, from Sir O. Sargent, F.O. Minute, 14 May 1948, to UK delegation in New York, and Washington (prepared by FO Legal Advisers). FO 371/68664 Palestine, Eastern, 1948, para. 7 (emphasis added, the words underlined appear in the original). The application of the doctrine of *terra nullius* to inhabited territories is largely discredited today and would have no application to Palestine. See Western Sahara, *supra* note 88.

115. Michael Akehurst, 'The Arab–Israeli Conflict and International Law', 5 *New Zealand Universities Law Review* (1973), p. 234.

116. As Weiler notes: '... sovereignty may rest in the inhabitants of the territory in question ... when the Mandate came to an end, the Mandatory power relinquished its role as supervisor; but the problem of determining in whom sovereignty vests still remains. In other words, we can ask the following question: At the moment that the British left, but one moment before the West Bank was invaded by Jordan: In whom did sovereignty over the West Bank vest? There can, as we noted, be no vacuum in title. The answer must be that it vested, at least in potential, in the *indigenous population* for whom the Mandate was established' (emphasis added). See Joseph H.H. Weiler, 'Israel, the Territories and International Law: When Doves are Hawks', in Alfred E. Kellerman (ed.), *Israel Among the Nations: International and Comparative Law Perspectives on Israel's 50th Anniversary* (Leiden: Brill, 1999), pp. 381–91 at p. 386.

117. Article 22, Covenant of the League of Nations, 1 *League of Nations Official Journal* (1920), p. 9. See James Crawford, 'Israel (1948–1949) and Palestine (1998–1999): Two Studies in the Creation of States', in Guy S. Goodwin-Gill and Stefan Talmon (eds), *The Reality of International Law: Essays in Honour of Ian Brownlie* (Oxford: Clarendon Press, 1999), pp. 95–124, citing A. Calogeropoulos Stratis, *Le Droit des Peuples à Disposer d'Eux-Mêmes* (Brussels, 1973), footnote 47, p. 104. See also James Crawford, *The Creation of States in International Law* (Oxford: Oxford University Press, 2006), pp. 428–9.

118. See South-West Africa cases, (Ethiopia v. Liberia; Liberia v. South Africa), Preliminary Objections, 21 December 1962, ICJ Reports (1962), at p. 329 ('The essential principles of the Mandates system consist chiefly in the recognition of certain *rights of the peoples* of the underdeveloped territories; the establishment of a regime of tutelage for each of such peoples to be exercised by an advanced nation as a "Mandatory" "on behalf of the League of Nations"; and the recognition of "a sacred trust of civilisation" laid upon the League as an organised international community and upon its Member States. This system is dedicated to the avowed object of promoting the well-being and development *of the peoples concerned* and is fortified by setting up safeguards for the protection of *their rights*' – emphasis added).
119. Bentwich, *The Mandates System*, *supra* note 60, p. 5.
120. South-West Africa cases, *supra* note 118 at pp. 330–1 ('The Mandate, in fact and in law, is an international agreement having the character of a treaty or convention ... It is an instrument having the character of a treaty or convention and embodying international engagements for the Mandatory as defined by the Council and accepted by the Mandatory').
121. See e.g. Julius Stone, *Israel and Palestine: Assault on the Law of Nations* (Baltimore: Johns Hopkins University Press, 1981). In this book Stone attacks the authors of two UN reports on Palestine on resolutions and self-determination. He argues that the Palestinians were not entitled to self-determination until the 1970s, that they did not constitute a 'people' until the emergence of the PLO, and that Jordan is really Palestine.
122. See Heater, *National Self-Determination*, *supra* note 8 at p. 179 ('With regard to Iraq, Syria and Lebanon, there was no real disagreement that the mandatories would hand over the countries after a relatively short period of time; and this was even the case with Palestine, despite the difficulties of reconciling Arab and Jewish claims').
123. Article 28 of the British Mandate provided: '*In the event of the termination of the mandate hereby conferred upon the Mandatory*, the Council of the League of Nations shall make such arrangements as may be deemed necessary for safeguarding in perpetuity, under guarantee of the League, the rights secured by Articles 13 and 14, and shall use its influence for securing, under the guarantee of the League, that the Government of Palestine will fully honour the financial obligations legitimately incurred by the Administration of Palestine during the period of the mandate, including the rights of public servants to pensions or gratuities' (emphasis added).
124. See David Hunter Miller, *The Drafting of the Covenant, Vol. Two* (London: G.P. Putnam's Sons, 1928), p. 103 (emphasis added).
125. Miller, ibid., Document 14, Wilson's Fourth Draft or Third Paris Draft, 2 February 1919, p. 153 (emphasis added).
126. See Article 64 of the Vienna Convention on the Law of Treaties, 23 May, 1969, 1155 United Nations Treaty Series, p. 331.
127. See East Timor (Portugal v. Australia), judgment, ICJ Reports (1995), p. 90 at p. 102, para. 29.
128. Legal Consequences of the Construction of a Wall in the Occupied Palestinian Territory, Advisory Opinion, ICJ Reports (2004), p. 136 at p. 199, at paras 155–6.
129. See Legal Consequences for States of the Continued Presence of South Africa in Namibia (South-West Africa) Notwithstanding Security Council Resolution 276 (1970), Advisory Opinion, 26 January 1971, ICJ Reports (1971), p. 31, para. 53. This passage is cited with approval in the Wall advisory opinion, ibid., p. 172, para. 88.
130. See M.C. Bassiouni, '"Self-Determination" and the Palestinians', 65 *Proceedings of the American Society of International Law* (1971), pp. 31–40, at p. 36.
131. Henry Cattan, 'Recollections on the United Nations Resolution to Partition Palestine', 4 *Palestine Yearbook of International Law* (1987–88), pp. 260–4 at p. 263. The number of Jewish immigrants that entered Palestine from 1920 until 1945 was about half a million persons. Notwithstanding the facilitation by the Government of Palestine of the acquisition of Palestinian citizenship by Jewish immigrants during the Mandate only 132,616 of them had acquired citizenship by the year 1945. See immigration and naturalisation figures in

Statistical Abstract of the Government of Palestine, (1944–45), pp. 36 and 46, and *A Survey of Palestine*, also published by the Government of Palestine, Vol. 1, p. 208.

132. See Nottebohm Case (second phase), judgment of 6 April, 1955: ICJ Reports (1955), at p. 22.
133. Ibid., pp. 22–3.
134. The *Nottebohm* case concerned a factual scenario which occurred before and after the Second World War. For subsequent endorsement of the rule see Iran–United States, Case No. A/18, 6 April 1984 in S.R. Pirrie, J.S. Arnold and E. Lauterpacht (eds), *Iran–United States Claims Tribunal Reports, 1984–1* (Cambridge: Grotius Publications, 1985), p. 263 ('While *Nottebohm* itself did not involve a claim against a State of which Nottebohm was a national, it demonstrated the acceptance and approval by the International Court of Justice of the search for the real and effective nationality based on the facts of the case, instead of an approach relying on more formalistic criteria. The effects of the *Nottebohm* decision have radiated throughout the international law of nationality').
135. For the text of the convention see 24 *American Journal of International Law*, Supplement, (1930), pp. 192–200. On its application to Palestine see Mufaz Qafish, 'The International Law Foundations of Palestinian Nationality, A Legal Examination of Palestinian Nationality under British Rule', in Thèse présentée à l'Université de Genève pour l'obtention du grade de Docteur en relations internationales (droit international) at pp. 232–9. This has been recently been published in Mutaz M. Qafisheh, *The International Law Foundations of Palestinian Nationality: A Legal Examination of Nationality in Palestine under Britain's Rule* (Leiden: Martinus Nijhoff Publishers, 2008), pp. 179–84.
136. See the Nationality Convention, ibid., p. 193, Article 5: 'Within a third State, a person having more than one nationality shall be treated as if he had only one. Without prejudice to the application of its law in matters of personal status and of any conventions in force, a third State shall, of the nationalities which any such person possesses, recognise exclusively in its territory either the nationality of the country in which he is *habitually and principally resident, or the nationality of the country with which in the circumstances he appears to be in fact most closely connected*' (emphasis added).
137. Qafish, *supra* note 135, at pp. 239–40 (thesis) and pp. 184–5 (book).
138. See the Palestinian Citizenship Order, *Official Gazette*, 16 September 1925, pp. 459–66. The citizenship order and its amendments can also be examined in Robert Harry Drayton, 8 *The Laws of Palestine* (London: Waterlow & Sons, 1934), pp. 2640–52.
139. See Part III, Article 7, *Official Gazette*, ibid., p. 462.
140. The oath of allegiance was as follows: 'I, A.B., Swear by Almighty God that I will be Faithful and Loyal to the Government of Palestine.', ibid., p. 466.
141. See the form of application for naturalisation as a Palestinian citizen, ibid., pp. 470–1.
142. See Cattan, 'Recollections', *supra* note 131.
143. On the demographics, see Janet L. Abu-Lughod, 'The Demographic Transformation of Palestine', in Ibrahim Abu Lughod, *The Transformation of Palestine: Essays on the Origin and Development of the Arab–Israeli Conflict – with a foreword by Arnold J. Toynbee* (Evanston: Northwestern University Press, 1987, second edition), pp. 139–63.
144. See Rosalyn Higgins, *Problems and Process: International Law and How We Use It* (Oxford: Clarendon Press, 1994), pp. 111–12 at p. 111 ('There is a general assumption that self-determination is to do with independence. It is also widely assumed that the UN Charter provides for self-determination in such terms. In fact, there is no such provision in the UN Charter').
145. The original draft of Article 80 used the following language: '... nothing in the Charter should be construed in and of itself to alter in any manner the *rights* of any State or any peoples in any territory, *or the terms of any mandate*'. See *Documents of the United Nations Conference on International Organisation*, San Francisco, 1945, Vol. 10, p. 477 (emphasis added). The text of the US representative was adopted by a majority vote of 29 to 5 and became that which is enshrined, with minor modifications, in Article 80.
146. See Sally V. Mallison and W. Thomas Mallison Jr, 'The Juridical Bases for Palestinian Self-Determination', 1 *Palestine Yearbook of International Law* (1984), pp. 36–65 at

p. 39. See also, W. Thomas Mallison and Sally V. Mallison, *The Palestine Problem in International Law and World Order* (Harlow: Longman Group, 1986), p. 193.

147. See Higgins, *Problems and Process*, *supra* note 144 at p. 112 ('self-determination is *not* provided for by the text of the UN Charter – at least not in the sense that it is generally used'). The essential tenet of Higgins' analysis is that this was a right of states, and not peoples.
148. This was further supplemented by Article 55, which viewed that the respect for the principle of equal rights and self-determination of peoples would be promoted through 'universal respect for, and observance of, human rights and fundamental freedoms for all without distinction as to race, sex, language or religion'. See Article 55, UN Charter, XV *Documents of the United Nations Conference on International Organisation*, *supra* note 145, p. 335.
149. International Status of South-West Africa, Advisory Opinion, 11 July 1950, ICJ Reports (1950), p. 133 (expressing the opinion that the obligations contained in Article 22 of the League of Nations Covenant did not depend on the existence of the League of Nations. In the words of the Court: 'Their *raison d'être* and original object remain').
150. Ibid., p. 134.
151. Ibid., p. 137.
152. Ibid., pp. 137–8.
153. See UN General Assembly resolution 24 (1), 12 February 1946 (transferring to the UN supervision of League treaties).
154. The latter, which is now called Namibia, only became an independent state on 21 March 1990 after decades of struggle by the South-West Africa People's Organisation (SWAPO) against the white-minority Government of South Africa which refused to give up its administration and domination of the former German colony (its Mandate was 'terminated' in 1966 by the UN General Assembly). For further reading on the legal history see Michla Pomerance, 'The ICJ and South West Africa (Namibia): A Retrospective Legal/Political Assessment', 12 *Leiden Journal of International Law* (1999), pp. 426–39.
155. See General Assembly resolution 2145 (XXI), 27 October 1966.
156. See John Dugard, 'The Revocation of the Mandate for South West Africa', 62 *American Journal of International Law* (1968), p. 85. As an analogy to South-West Africa, it could be argued that as the UN General Assembly is obliged to secure self-determination for the Palestinian people it should declare that Israel's prolonged occupation of East Jerusalem, the West Bank and the Gaza Strip for more than four decades is contrary to international law and should be terminated forthwith. After all, it is primarily because Israel is in the occupied territories as the Occupying Power, supporting a settler society, that the Palestinians are unable to exercise their right to self-determination and independence. If Israel was not in the occupied territories, there would be no obstacle to prevent the Palestinians from establishing an independent and sovereign Palestinian state there in line with UN Security Council resolutions 242 and 338 as enshrined in the Arab Peace Plan. See Letter Dated 24 April 2002 from the Chargé d'Affaires a.i. of the Permanent Mission of Lebanon to the United Nations Addressed to the Secretary-General, Annex II, UN Doc. S/2002/932, A/56/1026, 15 August 2002 (relaying to the UN the resolutions of the Arab Peace Initiative at the Summit-level Council of the League of Arab States in Beirut).

6 THE PARTITION OF PALESTINE

1. See T.G. Fraser, *Partition in Ireland, India and Palestine: Theory and Practice* (London: Macmillan, 1984). On the partition of British India specifically, see Mian Muhammad Sadullah, *The Partition of the Punjab 1947: A Compilation of Official Documents*, Vols 1–4 (Lahore: National Documentation Centre, 1983) and Nicholas Mansergh (ed.), *Transfer of Power, 1942–7: Constitutional Relations between Britain and India*, Vols 1–12 (London: HMSO, 1970–83).

2. See Brendan O'Malley and Ian Craig, *The Cyprus Conspiracy: America, Espionage and the Turkish Invasion* (London: I.B. Tauris, 2001).
3. See Jongsoo Lee, *The Partition of Korea after World War II: A Global History* (New York: Palgrave Macmillan, 2006).
4. See Tony Sharp, *The Wartime Alliance and the Zonal Division of Germany* (Oxford: Clarendon Press, 1975).
5. These cases are dealt with in A. Rigo Sureda, *The Evolution of the Right of Self-Determination: A Study of United Nations Practice* (Leiden: A.W. Sijthoff, 1973).
6. See International Assistance to Refugees: Report Submitted by Sir Herbert Emerson, G.C.I.E., K.C.S.I., C.B.E., High Commissioner for Refugees, Annex 20, 11 March 1946, (presented at Geneva session in April 1946), in League of Nations, Official Journal, Special Supplement No. 194, Records of the Twentieth (Conclusion) and Twenty-First Ordinary Sessions of the Assembly, Text of the Debates at the Plenary Meetings and Minutes of the First and Second Committees, Final Assembly, Geneva, 1946, pp. 228–35 at p. 233.
7. See paras 1 and 6 of UN General Assembly resolution 106 (S-1), 15 May 1947.
8. See *Yearbook of the United Nations* (1947–48), p. 227.
9. See Official Records of the Second Session of the General Assembly, Supplement No. 11, United Nations Special Committee on Palestine, Report to the General Assembly, Vol. 1, Lake Success, New York 1947, UN Doc. A/364, 3 September 1947, Chapter II at para. 176.
10. See Ilan Pappé, *A History of Modern Palestine: One Land, Two Peoples* (Cambridge: Cambridge University Press, 2004), p. 124.
11. Ibid.
12. The numerous statements in support of partition at the UN General Assembly as recorded in UN Doc. A/PV. 125, 26 November 1947, attest to the link between partition and the self-determination of peoples. See, for example, the statement by the delegate from Poland, Mr Lange: 'We therefore have to establish two States, an Arab State and a Jewish State, to provide for the national aspirations of the two communities which live in Palestine.' See also the statement by the Uruguayan delegate Mr Rodriguez Fabregal: 'Those of us who are voting for partition are not voting against either of these two peoples, against either of these two sectors of social reality in Palestine. We are voting for both of them, for their progress, their civil development, their advancement within the community of nations, so that they may not only never come into conflict, but may combine a multitude of productive undertakings, thus ensuring that economic unity for which the plan under discussion definitely provides.' See further, the statement by the Soviet delegate, Mr Gromyko: 'The decision to partition Palestine ... is in keeping with the principle of the national self-determination of peoples.'
13. UNSCOP report, *supra* note 9, para. 162.
14. Ibid., para. 164.
15. Ibid., chapter V, Recommendations, para. 3.
16. Ibid., para. 4.
17. Ibid., para. 5.
18. Ibid., para. 6.
19. See *UN Yearbook*, *supra* note 8, p. 227.
20. Nabil Elaraby, 'Some Legal Implications of the 1947 Partition Resolution and the 1949 Armistice Agreements', 33 *Law and Contemporary Problems* (1968), pp. 97–109 at p. 101.
21. See *UN Yearbook*, *supra* note 8, p. 235.
22. Ibid.
23. Ibid.
24. Ibid., p. 237.
25. Ibid., p. 240.
26. Ibid.
27. See General Assembly, 126th Plenary Meeting, held in the General Assembly Hall at Flushing Meadow, New York, UN Doc. A/PV.126, 28 November 1947.

28. Ibid.
29. Ibid.
30. Ibid. As Khan said: 'Now we are told: you must accept either partition or nothing. But is that so? Is that the only choice? How much genuine support has the scheme of partition received? In the *Ad Hoc* Committee, it received the support of twenty-five delegations. Some of these twenty-five delegations said they supported the partition plan with a heavy heart; others said they supported it with reluctance. Why? Because there is nothing else. This shows that the General Assembly as a whole is, at least, not happy to commit itself to this so-called solution.'
31. See UN Doc. A/PV.128, 29 November 1949.
32. See *UN Yearbook*, *supra* note 8, pp. 240–1.
33. Ibid., p. 241. The full-text of the resolution is provided in the annex.
34. Ibid.
35. Ibid.
36. Ibid.
37. Ibid.
38. Article 96 (1) of the UN Charter provides: 'The General Assembly or the Security Council may request the International Court of Justice to give an advisory opinion on any legal question.' Article 65 (1) of the Statute of the ICJ provides: 'The Court may give an advisory opinion on any legal question at the request of whatever body may be authorized by or in accordance with the Charter of the United Nations to make such a request.'
39. Ad Hoc Committee on the Palestinian Question, Summary Record of the Thirty-Second Meeting, Lake Success, New York, Monday, 24 November 1947, at 830pm. UN Doc. A/AC.14/SR.32, 25 November 1947.
40. See *UN Yearbook*, *supra* note 8, p. 241.
41. The vote was as follows: *In favour*: Afghanistan, Argentina, Brazil, Colombia, Cuba, Egypt, El Salvador, Greece, Haiti, Iran, Iraq, Lebanon, Liberia, Pakistan, Saudi Arabia, Syria, Turkey, Yemen. *Against*: Australia, Belgium, Byelorussian Soviet Socialist Republic, Canada, Chile, Costa Rica, Czechoslovakia, Denmark, Dominican Republic, France, Guatemala, Iceland, Luxembourg, New Zealand, Norway, Panama, Peru, Poland, Sweden, Ukrainian Soviet Socialist Republic, Union of South Africa, Union of Soviet Socialist Republics, United States of America, Uruguay, Venezuela. *Abstentions*: Bolivia, China, Ecuador, Ethiopia, Honduras, India, Mexico, Netherlands, Nicaragua, United Kingdom, Yugoslavia.
42. The vote was as follows: *In favour*: Afghanistan, Argentina, Brazil, Colombia, Cuba, Egypt, El Salvador, France, Greece, Haiti, India, Iran, Iraq, Lebanon, Liberia, Pakistan, Saudi Arabia, Syria, Turkey, Yemen. *Against*: Australia, Byelorussian Soviet Socialist Republic, Canada, Chile, Costa Rica, Denmark, Dominican Republic, Guatemala, Iceland, New Zealand, Norway, Panama, Peru, Poland, Sweden, Ukrainian Soviet Socialist Republic, Union of South Africa, Union of Soviet Socialist Republics, United States of America, Uruguay, Venezuela. *Abstentions*: Belgium, Bolivia, China, Czechoslovakia, Ecuador, Ethiopia, Honduras, Luxembourg, Mexico, Netherlands, Nicaragua, United Kingdom, Yugoslavia.
43. See Edvard Hambro, 'The Authority of the Advisory Opinions of the International Court of Justice', 3 *International and Comparative Law Quarterly* (1954), pp. 2–22 at p. 15.
44. Ad Hoc Committee, Summary Record, 24 November 1947, *supra* note 39.
45. Ibid.
46. See Nationality Decrees Issues in Tunis and Morocco, Advisory Opinion, PCIJ, Series B, No. 4, 7 February 1923, pp. 6–32.
47. Pitman B. Potter, Editorial Comment, 'The Palestine Problem before the United Nations', 42 *American Journal of International Law* (1948), pp. 859–61 at p. 860.
48. Ibid., p. 859.
49. Ibid., p. 860.
50. Ibid.
51. See UN General Assembly resolution 171 (III), 14 November 1947.

52. Ibid. (emphasis added).
53. UN General Assembly resolution 181 (II) (A+B), 29 November 1947. The vote was as follows. *In favour*: Australia, Belgium, Bolivia, Brazil, Byelorussian Soviet Socialist Republic, Canada, Costa Rica, Czechoslovakia, Denmark, Dominican Republic, Ecuador, France, Guatemala, Haiti, Iceland, Liberia, Luxembourg, Netherlands, New Zealand, Nicaragua, Norway, Panama, Paraguay, Peru, Philippines, Poland, Sweden, Ukrainian Soviet Socialist Republic, Union of South Africa, Union of Soviet Socialist Republics, United States of America, Uruguay, Venezuela. *Against*: Afghanistan, Cuba, Egypt, Greece, India, Iran, Iraq, Lebanon, Pakistan, Saudi Arabia, Syria, Turkey, Yemen. *Abstentions*: Argentina, Chile, China, Colombia, El Salvador, Ethiopia, Honduras, Mexico, United Kingdom, Yugoslavia. See UN Doc. A/PV.128.
54. The figure provided for by the UNSCOP was 407,000. See UN Doc. A/364, 3 September 1947. However, for a more accurate figure see the population statistics in UN Doc. A/AC.14/SR.32, 25 November 1947.
55. See Official Records of the Second Session of the General Assembly, Ad Hoc Committee on the Palestinian Question, 25 September – 25 November 1947, UN Doc. A/AC. 14/32 and Add. 1, 11 November 1947 at paras 61–6, at 64 ('It will thus be seen that the proposed Jewish State will contain a total population of 1,008,800, consisting of 509,780 Arabs and 499,020 Jews. In other words, at the outset, the Arabs will have a majority in the proposed Jewish State').
56. Khan claimed it was 60 per cent. See the speech by Khan in UN Doc. A/PV.126, 28 November 1947.
57. See speech by Khan, ibid.
58. Ibid.
59. Ibid. For exact figures see Ad Hoc Committee on the Palestinian Question, Report of Sub-Committee 2, UN Doc. A/AC.14/32, 11 November 1947, para. 65.
60. See Bevin Memorandum, 18 September, 1947, CP (47) 259, Cab 129/21.
61. See inward telegram from General Sir A. Cunningham, 19 January 1948, describing Partition Plan as 'manifestly unfair to the Arabs', FO 371/68613, Eastern, Palestine.
62. See Walter Laqueur, *The Israel/Arab Reader: A Documentary History of the Middle East Conflict* (London: Weidenfeld & Nicolson, 1969), p. 108.
63. See Declaration Adopted by the Extraordinary Zionist Conference, Biltmore Hotel, New York City, 11 May 1942 (calling for Palestine to be established as a Jewish commonwealth), reproduced in John Norton Moore (ed.), *The Arab–Israeli Conflict, Vol. III: Documents* (New Jersey: Princeton University Press, 1977) at pp. 230–2.
64. See Menachem Begin, *The Revolt* (London: W.H. Allen, 1979), pp. 334–5.
65. This frustrated the Foreign Office. See the numerous telegrams in FO 371/68664 Palestine East 1948. The following extract appeared in one telegram from the Foreign Office to New York, sent on 19 May 1948: '...for totally improper reasons Transjordan, which has for a considerable time enjoyed the qualifications necessary for admission to the United Nations, has failed to secure this'.
66. See Palestine: An attempt to forecast the possible result of reference to the United Nations, Foreign Office, 16 January 1947, FO 371/61858.
67. On the impact of the Zionist lobby on the partition vote, see Michael J. Cohen, *Palestine and the Great Powers 1945–1948* (New Jersey: Princeton University Press, 1982), pp. 292–300. In his memoir Truman admitted that he had never been subject to so much pressure and propaganda in all his life over the question of partitioning Palestine from Zionist lobby groups in the US. See Harry S. Truman, *Years of Trial and Hope 1946–1953* (Bungay: Hodder & Stoughton, 1956), pp. 168–9 ('I do not think I ever had as much pressure and propaganda aimed at the White House as I had in this instance'). On the Zionist lobby, more generally, see e.g. Edward Tivnan, *Jewish Political Power and American Foreign Policy* (New York: Simon & Schuster, 1987); James F. Petras, *The Power of Israel in the United States* (Atlanta: Clarity Press, 2006); and John J. Mearsheimer and Stephen M. Walt, *The Israel Lobby and US Foreign Policy* (New York: Farrar, Straus & Giroux, 2007).

68. See the statement of Mr Romulo (Philippines), UN Doc. A/PV.124, 26 November 1947.
69. A.H. Batlavi (ed.), *The Forgotten Years: Memoirs of Sir Muhammad Zafrullah Khan* (Lahore: Vanguard Books, 1991), p. 180.
70. See Palestine: An attempt to forecast the possible result of reference to the United Nations, *supra* note 66.
71. See, for instance, Hersch Lauterpacht's opinion for the Jewish Agency where he was asked to rebut the charges which the Agency thought may have been brought by the Arab states before the ICJ in arguing that a resolution calling for a partition of Palestine would only be a recommendation and not a legally binding decision. See E. Lauterpacht, Q.C., *International Law: Being the Collected Papers of Hersch Lauterpacht*, Vol. III, The Law of Peace (Cambridge: Cambridge University Press, 1977), pp. 508–13. For the other view, see Hans Kelsen, *The Law of the United Nations: A Critical Analysis of its Fundamental Problems* (London: Stevens & Sons, 1950), pp. 195–7, footnote 7, who thought that the resolution was not binding. Professor Hans Kelsen taught Lauterpacht law at Vienna University. See 10 *International and Comparative Law Quarterly* (1961), pp. 2–3.
72. See Ian Brownlie, *Principles of Public International Law* (Oxford: Oxford University Press, 2003) pp. 163–4 ('It is doubtful if the United Nations has a "capacity to convey title", in part because the Organization cannot assume the role of territorial sovereign: in spite of the principle of implied powers the Organization is not a state and the General Assembly only has a power of recommendation. Thus the resolution of 1947 containing a partition plan for Palestine was probably *ultra vires*, and, if it was not, was not binding on member states in any case').
73. It could be argued that the UN General Assembly has this power by virtue of Article 11 (2) of the UN Charter. See, for example, the debates over the creation of Eritrea which was based on Article 11 (2) when they were considering separating it from Ethiopia in 1947–48. Although UN General Assembly resolution 390 A, 2 December 1950 decided to keep the country together the debate suggests that the assembly must have had an implied power of partition.
74. See Reparation for Injuries suffered in the Service of the United Nations, Advisory Opinion, 11 April 1949, ICJ Reports (1949), p. 12. On implied powers, generally, see F.A. Vallat, 'The Competence of the United Nations General Assembly', 97 (II) *Recueil Des Cours* (1959), pp. 203–92.
75. See e.g. Articles 11 (2) and 14 of the UN Charter.
76. See the International Status of South-West Africa, Advisory Opinion, 11 July, 1950, ICJ Reports (1950), p. 128 at p. 144 (the *dispositif*).
77. Ibid., Oral Arguments, Documents, II (1950), pp. 134–5 and p. 137 (written statement of the USA), pp. 213–14, p. 236 (statement by Mr Kerno of the United Nations), p. 246 (statement by M. Ingles of the Philippines); and ICJ pleadings, *South-West Africa*, (1966), Vol. II, pp. 68–70 (counter-memorial of South Africa); Vol. VII, pp. 294–7 (argument of Mr Gross); Vol. VIII, pp. 161–6 (argument of Mr Moore); pp. 493–500 (argument of Mr De Villiers); Vol. IX, pp. 175–87 (reply of Mr Gross), and pp. 436–43 (rejoinder of Mr De Villiers).
78. As it will be recalled, the preamble to the Charter reaffirms 'faith in fundamental human rights, in the dignity and worth of the human person, in the equal rights of men and women and of nations large and small'.
79. See International Status of South-West Africa, *supra* note 76.
80. UN Security Council resolution 652, 17 April 1990.
81. See A. Rigo Sureda, *Evolution of the Right of Self-Determination*, *supra* note 5, p. 48.
82. See Andrew W. Cordier and Wilder Foote (eds), *Public Papers of the Secretaries-General of the United Nations*, Vol. 1, *Trygve Lie, 1946–1953* (New York: Columbia University Press, 1969), pp. 106–15. At p. 107 Lie is quoted from his memoir *In the Cause of Peace* as writing at p. 167: 'The United Nations does not have the power to impose a political settlement, whether it be unification or partition, except in special circumstances. Such circumstances exist when all the parties in control of a territory hand it over to the United Nations to determine its fate. In the case of Korea all the parties did not do that. In the

case of Palestine, on the other hand, the United Kingdom was the sole Mandatory Power, and it handed over the whole territory to the United Nations for disposition. Clearly, I felt, the Organization in these circumstances had full constitutional power not only to maintain order inside the territory but, even more, to resist any attempt from outside to overthrow its decision.'

83. See Declaration of the Establishment of the State of Israel, 14 May, 1948, 1 *Laws of the State of Israel* (1948), pp. 3–5 ('On the 29th November, 1947, the United Nations General Assembly passed a resolution calling for the establishment of a Jewish State in Eretz-Israel; the General Assembly required the inhabitants of Eretz-Israel to take such steps as were necessary on their part for the implementation of that resolution. This recognition by the United Nations of the right of the Jewish people to establish their State is irrevocable').
84. See Attorney-General of Israel v. El-Turani, Israel, District Court of Haifa, 21 August 1951, Hersch Lauterpacht (ed.), *International Law Reports*, Vol. 18, 1951 (London: Butterworth & Co., 1957), p. 167 ('From the point of view of international law, the demilitarized zone is included within the Partition Resolution, which is a document having validity under international law').
85. See Jorge Castañeda, *Legal Effects of United Nations Resolutions*, translated by Alba Amoia (New York: Columbia University Press, 1969), p. 73 and pp. 132–3.
86. See Clyde Eagleton, 'Palestine and the Constitutional Law of the UN', 42 *American Journal of International Law* (1948), pp. 397–9 at p. 397 ('It is clear to any student of the Charter that a resolution of the General Assembly, such as that for the partition of Palestine, is no more than a recommendation, and that it can have no legally binding effect upon any state whatsoever').
87. See the statement of Warren Austin at 271st meeting of the Security Council, UN Doc. S/PV.271, 19 March 1948. See also, UN Press Release PAL/145, 12 March 1948. Even if the Security Council had voted to enforce the Partition Plan by acting under Chapter VII of the Charter and invoking its enforcement provisions provided by Articles 25 and 39, it would still be subject to the terms of the Charter as Article 25 provides that: 'The Members of the United Nations agree to accept and carry out the decisions of the Security Council *in accordance with the present Charter*.' In his Dissenting Opinion in the ICJ's 1971 Namibia advisory opinion, Judge Sir Gerald Fitzmaurice of the United Kingdom was of the opinion that the Security Council, even when acting under Chapter VII, has no power to abrogate or alter territorial rights. See Dissenting Opinion of Judge Sir Gerald Fitzmaurice, Legal Consequences for States of the Continued Presence of South Africa in Namibia (South-West Africa) Notwithstanding Security Council Resolution 276 (1970), Advisory Opinion, 26 January 1971, ICJ Reports (1971), p. 294 at para. 115.
88. See the statement by Ernest Bevin, 445 *Parliamentary Debates*, Commons, 12 December 1947, col. 1396 ('I am not going, and His Majesty's Government are not going, to oppose the United Nations decision. The decision has been taken. As someone said we have tried our best. We have no intention of opposing that decision, but we cannot ourselves undertake, either individually or collectively, in association with others, to impose that decision by force').
89. UN General Assembly resolution 181 (II) (A+B), 29 November 1947.
90. See Philip C. Jessup, *The Birth of Nations* (New York: Columbia University Press, 1974), p. 264.
91. See United Nations Palestine Commission Relations between the United Nations Commission and the Security Council (Working Paper Prepared by the Secretariat). UN Doc. A/AC.21/13, 9 February 1948.
92. Ibid., p. 13, para. 4.
93. See UN Doc. 1/286, 3 April 1947.
94. Although there is some doctrinal debate as to whether this might also apply to decisions made under Chapter VI of the Charter. See Rosalyn Higgins, 'The Advisory Opinion on Namibia: which UN resolutions are binding under Article 25 of the Charter?' 21 *International & Comparative Law Quarterly* (1972), pp. 270–86, at pp. 281–2. In referring to UN resolutions on the Namibia question, Higgins writes: 'The binding or

non-binding nature of those resolutions turns not upon whether they are to be regarded as "Chapter VI" or "Chapter VII" resolutions ... but upon whether the parties intended them to be "decisions" or "recommendations".'

95. See e.g. Michael Virally, 'The Sources of International Law', in Max Sørensen (ed.), *Manual of Public International Law* (London: Macmillan, 1968), pp. 160–2.
96. See generally, ibid. at p. 162.
97. On the possibility of undue influence, see the comments of Pitman B. Potter, 'The Palestine Problem before the United Nations', *supra* note 47 at p. 861 ('The United States came close to exercising undue influence to get the partition plan adopted ...'). For a vivid description of the types of pressure which UN delegates faced from the Zionist lobby during the partition vote, see the memoirs of the Philippine UN delegate, Carlos P. Romulo with Beth Day Romulo, *Forty Years: A Third World Soldier at the UN* (New York: Greenwood Press, 1980), pp. 65–8. The Philippines was not the only country to be lobbied and harassed. Haiti and several other countries were also coerced to change their votes. See *The Palestine Question: Seminar of Arab Jurists on Palestine, Algiers, 22–27 July, 1967*, translated from French by Edward Rizk (Beirut: The Institute for Palestine Studies, 1968), p. 77. For instance, Harvey S. Firestone, Jr, of the Firestone Tire & Rubber Company, which had a concession in Liberia, brought pressure on the president of that country, William Tubman to vote in favour of partition (which they did). See Robert J. Donovan, *Conflict and Crisis: The Presidency of Harry S. Truman 1945–1948* (New York: W.W. Norton & Company, 1977), p. 330. And Cuba, Greece, Haiti, the Philippines and Liberia were specifically mentioned on a list that was to be lobbied by the Zionists. See Donovan, pp. 329–31. Certain delegates from Latin America were even offered $75,000 to vote in favour of partition. Donovan, p. 331 (quoting a record of a conversation between Guilermo Belt and a US official on the bribing of Latin American officials). The Zionists went so far as to offer assistance to the Cuban Ambassador to get elected president of his country if he would vote in favour of partition (he turned down this offer). See Richard Stevens, *American Zionism and US Foreign Policy, 1942–1947* (New York: Pageant Press, 1962), pp. 176–85. All this prompted the US Secretary of Defense, James Forrestal to make the following note in his diary: 'I thought the methods that had been used by people outside of the Executive Branch of government to bring coercion and duress on other nations in the General Assembly bordered closely on scandal.' See Walter Millis (ed.), *The Forrestal Diaries: The Inner History of the Cold War* (London: Cassell & Co., 1952), p. 346. Yet it was not just the Zionists who were doing the lobbying. According to Sumner Welles, the former Under-Secretary of State, American officials were also exerting pressure on recalcitrant states to vote for partition. See Sumner Welles, *We Need Not Fail* (Cambridge, MA: The Riverside Press, 1948), p. 63 ('By direct order of the White House every form of pressure, direct and indirect, was brought to bear by American officials upon the countries outside the Moslem world that were known to be either uncertain or opposed to partition. Representatives or intermediaries were employed by the White House to make sure that the necessary majority would at length be secured').
98. UN Palestine Commission, Statement of 6 February 1948 communicated to the Secretary-General by Mr Isa Nakleh, Representative of the Arab Higher Committee, UN Doc. A/AC.21/10, 16 February 1948), para. 2.
99. Ibid., para. 6.
100. See 5 *Foreign Relations of the United States* 1947 (Washington: United States Government Printing Office, 1971), p. 1157.
101. As argued by Elihu Lauterpacht in *Jerusalem and the Holy Places* (London: The Anglo-Israel Association, 1968), p. 18.
102. See Michael Akehurst, 'The Arab–Israeli Conflict and International Law', 5 *New Zealand Universities Law Review* (1973), p. 236.
103. Ibid., p. 235, citing Article 37 (2) of the Vienna Convention on the Law of Treaties 1969.
104. On the question of equity in boundary disputes generally, see e.g. Masahiro Miyoshi, *Considerations of Equity in the Settlement of Boundary Disputes* (Dordrecht: Martinus

Nijhoff, 1993). Interestingly, this book which was based upon a University of London PhD thesis was supervised by Sir Francis Aime Vallat, who was one of the Foreign Office legal advisers during the partition of Palestine.

105. See Official Records of the Second Session of the General Assembly, Ad Hoc Committee on the Palestinian Question, *supra* note 39 at paras 67 and 68. See also Appendix VI.
106. Ibid., para. 67, table showing percentage of ownership per sub-district.
107. See UNSCOP Report, *supra* note 9 ('The proposed Jewish State leaves considerable room for further development and land settlement').
108. See Report of the Anglo-American Committee of Enquiry regarding the problems of European Jewry and Palestine, Miscellaneous No. 8 (1946), Lausanne, 20 April, 1946 (London: HMSO, 1946, Cmd. 6808).
109. The Committee's Recommendation No. 2 was that 100,000 certificates be authorised for the admission into Palestine of Jews who had been victims of Nazi persecution. However, in Recommendation No. 1, the Committee concluded that 'Palestine alone cannot meet the emigration needs of the Jewish victims of Nazi and Fascist persecution. The whole world shares responsibility for them and indeed for the resettlement of all "Displaced Persons".' In Recommendation No. 3 they advised that Palestine 'shall be neither a Jewish state nor an Arab state'. See Anglo-American Committee of Enquiry, ibid., pp. 1–4.
110. See 5 *Foreign Relations of the United States 1947* (Washington: United States Government Printing Office, 1971), p. 1271 and footnote 2.
111. Ibid. See also, Evan M. Wilson, *Decision on Palestine: How the U.S. Came to Recognize Israel* (Stanford: Stanford University, Hoover Institution Press, 1979), p. 124.
112. See War Cabinet, Palestine, Memorandum by the Secretary of State for Foreign Affairs for the Personal Use of the Prime Minister, 10 April 1945, PREM 4/52/1, Palestine: Post-War (Partition) 1945.
113. See UN Doc. A/648 16 September 1948 (resume of negotiations).
114. See the statement of Amir Arslan in UN Doc. A/PV.125, 26 November 1947.
115. See Armenia–Turkey Boundary Case of 1920, Hackworth (ed.), 1 *Digest of International Law*, p. 715.
116. Ibid.
117. See Article XII of the Treaty between Great Britain and Ireland, signed at London, 6 December 1921, 26 *League of Nations Treaty Series* (1924).
118. See Geoffrey J. Hand (ed.), *Report of the Irish Boundary Commission* (Shannon: Irish University Press, 1969), p. 30. Although the findings of this commission were suppressed it still evinces a 'judicial mindset' when partitioning a particular territory. The commission was conscious of the fact that they had not only to delineate the border in line with the wishes of the inhabitants but that the economic viability of Northern Ireland had to be taken into consideration as well. For a critique of the Irish Boundary Commission's findings from an international lawyer, see Anthony Carty, *Was Ireland Conquered? International Law and the Irish Question* (London: Pluto Press, 1996), pp. 135–66.
119. Ibid., pp. 30–1.
120. See Question of Jaworzina, (Polish–Czechoslovakian Frontier), Advisory Opinion, Series B, No. 8, 6 December 1923, pp. 6–57 at p. 57.
121. See Acts and Documents Relating to Judgments and Advisory Opinions Given by the Court, Series C, No. 4, (November 13th – December 6th 1923), Documents Relating to Advisory Opinion No. 8 (Jaworzina), p. 131 (referring to the Resolution of the Conference of Ambassadors on July 28th, 1920).
122. See Chapter XXII. A Plan of Partition, 3. The Frontier, the Palestine Royal Commission, Summary of Report (with extracts), (London: HMSO, 1957).
123. See Sadullah, *Partition of the Punjab 1947*, Vol. 1, *supra* note 1, pp. 80–1.
124. If there existed a customary rule of international law, prior to the adoption of the Partition Plan, that the wishes of the population should be taken into consideration when delimiting the boundary, then it is arguable that it was illegal as a violation of a prior customary rule.

125. See Armenia–Turkey Boundary Case, *supra* note 115 ('The conflicting territorial desires of Armenians, Turks, Kurds and Greeks along the boundaries assigned to my arbitral decision could not always be harmonized. In such cases it was my belief that considerations of a healthy economic life for the future state of Armenia should be decisive').
126. See Ad Hoc Committee on the Palestinian Question, 25 September – 25 November 1947, *supra* note 39 at paras 80–3.
127. See War Cabinet, Palestine, Memorandum, 10 April 1945, PREM 4/52/1, *supra* note 112. See also the note to the Prime Minister by Sir Edward Griggs, the Minister Resident in the Middle East, who was also opposed to partitioning Palestine. W.P. (45) 214, 4 April 1945.
128. The Atlantic Charter of 14 August 1941 is reproduced in 35, *Supplement to the American Journal of International Law: Official Documents* (1941), pp. 191–2.
129. In the General Assembly the argument was advanced that the problem of Palestine could not be dealt with under Article 14 of the UN Charter because what was being proposed was not the peaceful adjustment of a situation but the imposition by force of a settlement contrary to the wishes of the people concerned. If the General Assembly adopted the plan for partition, it would have to use force to carry it out. See *Repertory of Practice of United Nations Organs* (New York: United Nations, 1955), p. 471. According to Cohen's book, *Palestine and the Great Powers*, *supra* note 67 at pp. 340–1, Maj. Gen. Alfred Greunther, head of the Joint Chiefs, estimated in a meeting with President Harry Truman that the implementation of partition by force would require a minimum of 80,000 and a maximum of 160,000 American troops.
130. 'I am, therefore, instructed to repeat explicitly that the United Kingdom Government cannot allow its troops and administration to be used in order to enforce decisions which are not accepted by both parties in Palestine.' Sir Alexander Cadogan (United Kingdom), UN Doc. A/PV.124, 26 November 1947.
131. See Cohen, *Palestine and the Great Powers*, *supra* note 67 at pp. 346–7.
132. See Rann of Kutch Arbitration (India and Pakistan), The Indo-Pakistan Western Boundary Case, constituted pursuant to the Agreement of 30 June, 1965, Award, 19 February 1968, 7 *International Legal Materials* (1968), pp. 633–705.
133. Ibid., p. 692.
134. On 21 September 1999, the Islamic Republic of Pakistan filed in the Registry of the Court an Application instituting proceedings against the Republic of India in respect of a dispute relating to the destruction, on 10 August 1999, of a Pakistani aircraft. Pakistan asked the ICJ to adjudge and declare that India's action in shooting down the Pakistani aircraft constituted breaches of various obligations under the UN Charter, customary international law and a number of other treaties. The ICJ by a majority vote of 14 to 2 found that it had no jurisdiction to entertain the application filed by Pakistan. See Case Concerning the Aerial Incident of 10 August 1999 (Pakistan v. India), judgment of 21 June 2000, ICJ Reports (1999), pp. 8–35.
135. See Arbitral Tribunal for Dispute over Inter-Entity Boundary in Brčko Area, The Republika Srpska v. The Federation of Bosnia and Herzegovina, Award, 14 February 1997, 36 *International Legal Materials* (1997), pp. 399–437, at p. 421. In the Final Award the tribunal established a new institution under a new multi-ethnic democratic government known as 'The Brčko District of Bosnia and Herzegovina' under the exclusive sovereignty of Bosnia and Herzegovina. See The Federation of Bosnia and Herzegovina v. The Republika Srpska, Arbitration for the Brčko Area, Final Award, 5 March 1999, 38 *International Legal Materials* (1999), pp. 536–50. For commentary, see Christoph Schreuer, 'The Brčko Award of 14 February 1997', 11 *Leiden Journal of International Law* (1998), pp. 71–80 and the commentary by the same author on the Final Award in 38 *International Legal Materials* (1999), pp. 534–5.
136. See Mutaz Qafisheh, 'The International Law Foundations of Palestinian Nationality, A Legal Examination of Palestinian Nationality under British Rule', thesis, Université de Genève, 2007, p. 261.
137. Ibid., p. 261 (citing figures from the *Survey of Palestine*).

138. See statement by Mr Dihigo in UN Doc. A/PV. 126, 26 November 1947.
139. Ibid.
140. Piños Island – the Island of Pines – was renamed in 1978 as *Isla de la Juventud* – the Island of Youth.
141. See statement by Mr Dihigo, *supra* note 138.
142. Ibid.
143. See UN Doc. A/PV.124, 26 November 1947.
144. See the statement by Amir Arslan (Syria), in UN Doc. A/PV.125, 26 November 1947.
145. Statement by Amir Arslan, ibid.
146. See Oles M. Smolansky, 'The Soviet Role in the Emergence of Israel', in Wm. Roger Louis and Robert N. Stookey (eds), *The End of the Palestine Mandate* (London: I.B. Tauris, 1986), pp. 61–78 at p. 65. (The Soviet Union encouraged Jews in the concentration camps of Eastern Europe to move to those areas under the western zones of occupation in Germany and Austria. 'The Soviet Government did so in full awareness of the fact that most emigrants were determined to proceed to Palestine and to do what they could to ensure the establishment of a Jewish state.') See also, Yaacov Ro'i, *Soviet Decision Making in Practice: The USSR and Israel 1947–1954* (New Brunswick: Transaction Books, 1980), p. 28 ('The new Polish regime seems to have agreed to this Jewish emigration in the wake of the active anti-Semitism which, despite government legislation, overtook Poland immediately after the war'). See further, Arnold Krammer, *The Forgotten Friendship Israel and the Soviet Bloc, 1947–53* (Urbana: University of Illinois Press, 1974), p. 51 ('Large numbers of Jewish refugees had returned to rebuild their former lives in Poland, Hungary, or Czechoslovakia, but in the face of continued hostility from the local populace, now preferred to go to Palestine. The governments of these countries realized that the traditional communist solution of the Jewish problem was not applicable, and that the enforcement of strict measures to assimilate them would only serve to bring upon the governments themselves the odium of anti-Semitism').
147. See Annex 391a, 'French Mandate for Syria and the Lebanon', 3 *League of Nations Official Journal* (1922), pp. 1013–17 at p. 1013.
148. See the Partition Plan, in General Assembly resolution 181, *supra* note 53 at Chapter 4, D 1, and 3.
149. See Ad Hoc Committee on the Palestinian Question, 25 September – 25 November 1947, *supra* note 39 at paras 78–9.
150. See the statement by Viscount Cecil of Chelwood (United Kingdom) during the last session of the Assembly of the League of Nations, *Official Journal*, Special Supplement No. 194, Records of the Twentieth (Conclusion) and Twenty-first Ordinary Sessions of the Assembly, Text of the Debates at the Plenary Meetings and Minutes of the First and Second Commissions, p. 29 ('... Until the three African Territories have actually been placed under trusteeship and until fresh arrangements have been reached in regard to Palestine – whatever those arrangements may be – it is the intention of His Majesty's Government in the United Kingdom *to continue to administer these Territories in accordance with the general principles of the existing Mandates*' – emphasis added).
151. International Status of South-West Africa, Advisory Opinion, ICJ Reports (1950), *supra* note 76 at p. 157.
152. See paragraph 4 of the unanimous resolution adopted by the League of Nations in its final session on 18 April 1946, in 1 *United Nations Yearbook* (1946–47), pp. 745–75.
153. See Question of Palestine, letter from the United Kingdom delegation (Alexander Cadogan) to the UN (Dr Victor Chi Tsai Hoo), UN Doc. 1/286, 3 April 1947.
154. See UN Palestine Commission: Communication received from the UK delegation concerning the date of the termination of the Mandate (received from Mr Fletcher-Cooke), Restricted, UN Doc. UK/142, 12 May 1948.

My dear Bunche,

Would you be so good enough to inform the Commission that the following communiqué will be released in Jerusalem at 1.50pm (Palestine time) on the 12th May:-

'Legally the Mandate terminates immediately after midnight on the night of the 14th/15th May. In consequence, His Excellency the High Commissioner will leave Jerusalem for Haifa on 14th May and will sail from Haifa in H.M.S. "Luryalus" at midnight. The withdrawal of troops from Jerusalem and parts of Palestine will also commence on 14th May.'

155. This provides: 'The trusteeship system shall apply to such territories in the following categories as may be placed thereunder by means of trusteeship agreements: (a) territories now held under mandates ...'
156. It is interesting to note that although the legal advisers at the Foreign Office did not think that Britain was under any legal obligation to bring any new policy for Palestine to the UN for approval, they thought that it would have been unwise to have done this on political grounds. They advised that: 'The experience which the South African Government are now going through seems to demonstrate conclusively that it would be politically most unwise for H.M.G. to seek to continue British administration on any other terms than trusteeship.' They added that as an alternative, Britain could allow for Palestine to become an independent state as the Arabs wished or be partitioned as the Zionists desired. They thought it significant that 'the Soviet delegate, in the course of the current debate on South West Africa, has put forward the view that trusteeship or independence are the only two courses envisaged by the Charter for mandated territories'. See Reference of the Palestine Question to the United Nations, 4 December, 1946, memorandum addressed to Sir Orme Sargeant, K.C.M.G., CB of the Colonial Office.
157. Emphasis added.
158. See Documents of the *United Nations Conference on International Organization*, San Francisco, 1945, Vol. 10, p. 477. (The text of the US representative was adopted by a majority vote of 29 to 5 and became that which is enshrined, with minor modifications, in Article 80.)
159. On the termination of the Mandate, see UN Doc. UK/142, 12 May 1948, *supra* note 154.
160. Inward Telegram, From Palestine (O.A.G.) to S. of S., Colonies, 8 September 1947. No. 1691 Top Secret and Personal.
161. See Henry Cattan, 'Recollections on the United Nations Resolution to Partition Palestine', 4 *Palestine Yearbook of International Law* (1987–88), p. 263.
162. It was rejected by the Twentieth Zionist Congress, which met in Zurich in August 1937, see Neville Barbour, *Nisi Dominus: A Survey of the Palestine Controversy* (London: George G. Harrap & Co., 1946), p. 184.
163. See Sir John Woodhead, 'The Report of the Palestine Partition Commission', 18 *International Affairs* (1939), pp. 171–93.
164. See Report of the Palestine Royal Commission presented by the Secretary of State for the Colonies to the United Kingdom Parliament by Command of His Brittanic Majesty (July 1937), League of Nations Doc. C. 495.M.336.1937.VI (30 November 1937); and see War Cabinet, Palestine, Memorandum, 10 April 1945, PREM 4/52/1. For an analysis of these various partition proposals see Roza I.M. El-Eini, *Mandated Landscape: British Imperial Rule in Palestine, 1929–1948* (London: Routledge, 2006), especially pp. 314–68.
165. Palestine: Statement by His Majesty's Government in the United Kingdom, Presented by the Secretary of State for the Colonies to Parliament by Command of His Majesty, 11 November, 1938, Cmd 5893.
166. Palestine: Statement of Policy, Presented by the Secretary of State for the Colonies to Parliament by Command of His Majesty, (1 May 1939), Cmd 6019.
167. Ibid.
168. Ibid.
169. Ibid.
170. See the statement made by the US representative at the UN Warren Austin at UN Doc. S/PV.271, 19 March 1948: 'From what has been said in the Security Council and in consultations among the several members of the Security Council, it is clear that the Security Council is not prepared to go ahead with efforts to implement this plan in the

existing situation. We had a vote on that subject, and only five votes could be secured for that purpose.'

171. Ibid.
172. 1 *United Nations Yearbook* (1946–47), pp. 745–75 (emphasis added). The resolution also recalls the role of the League in assisting Iraq progress from an 'A-class' Mandate to complete independence, and 'welcomes the termination of the mandated status of Syria, Lebanon and Trans-Jordan, which have, since the last session of the Assembly, become independent members of the world community'. Paragraph 4 of that resolution: 'TAKES NOTE of the expressed intentions of the Members of the League now administering territories under Mandate to continue to administer them for the well-being and development of the peoples concerned in accordance with the obligations contained in the respective mandates, *until other arrangements have been agreed between the United Nations and the respective mandatory powers*' (emphasis added). At that time only the mandates of Palestine, Namibia and Nauru were still in force and had not yet been terminated. Nauru would be placed under UN Trusteeship.
173. See Hersch Lauterpacht, 'The United Nations General Assembly-Voting and Competence in the Palestine Question', in E. Lauterpacht (ed.) *Inter-national Law Being the Collected Papers of Hersch Lauterpacht, Vol. 3: The Law of Peace* (Cambridge: Cambridge University Press 1977), pp. 509–10.
174. Emphasis added. For a discussion of the Philippines' struggle against the colonial powers to include the words 'or independence' in the UN Charter's provisions on trusteeship, see the memoirs of Carlos Romulo who described it as one of his proudest achievements in *Forty Years*, *supra* note 97 at pp. 37–45.
175. The Draft Trusteeship Agreement, UN Doc. A/C.1/277, 20 April 1948. For the political debate surrounding the trusteeship decision see Michael J. Cohen, *Palestine and the Great Powers 1945–1948*, *supra* note 67, at pp 345–90.
176. See Jessup, *Birth of Nations*, *supra* note 90, pp. 268–72. (He recalls the views of the Latin American states over dinner with Austin at the Waldorf. With the exception of Jorge García-Granados of Guatemala, all were in favour of trusteeship.) On Zionist efforts to influence the Latin American vote, see Edward B. Glick, 'Zionist and Israel Efforts to Influence Latin America: A Case Study in Diplomatic Persuasion', 9 *The Western Political Quarterly* (1956), pp. 329–43. On the views of García-Granados, see *The Birth of Israel: The Drama as I saw It* (New York: Alfred A. Knopf, 1949).
177. Jessup, *Birth of Nations*, ibid., p. 269.
178. See Draft Trusteeship Agreement in UN Doc. A/C.1/277, 20 April 1948, *supra* note 175.
179. This provides, *inter alia*, that one of the basic objectives of the trusteeship system is 'to promote the political, economic, social, and educational advancement of *the inhabitants of the trust territories*, and their progressive development towards self-Government or *independence* as may be appropriate *to the particular circumstances of each territory and its peoples* and *the freely expressed wishes of the peoples concerned*, and as may be provided by the terms of each trusteeship agreement' (emphasis added).
180. See Article 5, Draft Trusteeship Agreement, *supra* note 175.
181. Ibid., Article 13, Draft Trusteeship Agreement.
182. Ibid., Articles 20–26, Draft Trusteeship Agreement.
183. Ibid., Article 29, Draft Trusteeship Agreement.
184. Ibid.
185. Ibid., Article 31, Draft Trusteeship Agreement.
186. Ibid., Article 47, Draft Trusteeship Agreement.
187. Ibid., Article 45, Draft Trusteeship Agreement.
188. Ibid., Article 9, Draft Trusteeship Agreement.
189. 'Plan to Drop Partition of Palestine', *The Times*, 20 March 1948, p. 4, col. A.
190. See generally, Ilan Pappé, *The Ethnic Cleansing of Palestine* (Oxford: Oneworld Publications, 2006); Walid Khalidi, 'Plan Dalet: Master Plan for the Conquest of Palestine', 18 *Journal of Palestine Studies* (1988), pp. 4–33; and literature cited in the next chapter.

7 THE ARAB–ISRAELI CONFLICT

1. See e.g. D.W. Bowett, *Self-Defence in International Law* (Manchester: Manchester University Press, 1958) (who refers to the conflict several times but does not go into details); Ian Brownlie, *International Law and the Use of Force by States* (Oxford: Clarendon Press, 1963), p. 390 (mentioning the 1949 armistice without referring to the hostilities which preceded it); Lord McNair and A.D. Watts, *The Legal Effects of War* (Cambridge: Cambridge University Press, 1966) (not mentioning it at all); Malcolm N. Shaw, *International Law* (Cambridge: Cambridge University Press, 1997), pp. 140–1 (hinting at the 1948 conflict when making the point that a state need not have defined borders to constitute a state, obviously referring to Israel in 1948, though without mentioning this, and then saying that despite the 1988 Declaration of Independence Palestine is not a state because the PLO does not control territory); David Raič, *Statehood and the Law of Self-Determination* (The Hague: Kluwer Law International, 2002), only mentioning Palestine fleetingly in two footnotes on p. 210, note 169 (on the UN Partition Plan) and at p. 412, note 37 (pointing out that Palestine is not a state); and Christine Gray, *International Law and the Use of Force* (Oxford: Oxford University Press, 2002), p. 112 ('Israel had been involved in cross-border actions against irregular forces operating from neighbouring states since 1948 ...'). Gray does not, however, mention what happened in 1948 or refer to the 1948–49 conflict even though it involved cross-border actions and invocations of self-defence.
2. Antonio Cassese's account of the conflict in his book *Self-Determination of Peoples: A Legal Reappraisal*, which won him a Certificate of Merit for Creative Scholarship from the American Society of International Law, is typical:

   > ... when Britain withdrew from the region and Zionist leaders (led by David Ben Gourion [*sic*]) declared the birth of the State of Israel on 15 May 1948, Egypt, Syria, Lebanon, and Jordan invaded.
   >
   > At the end of the war, Transjordan had absorbed the West Bank of the river Jordan, thus forming the Hashamite [*sic*] Kingdom of Jordan; Egypt was in possession of the Gaza Strip; the State of Israel included approximately 3 per cent more of Palestine than had been allotted to the Jewish State by the UN and 750,000 Palestinians were living in exile.

   This tells us nothing about the conflict or even how 750,000 Palestinians ended up 'living in exile'. See Antonio Cassese, *Self-Determination of Peoples: A Legal Reappraisal* (Cambridge: Cambridge University Press, 1995), p. 234. One scholar writing in a very prominent international law journal even had the audacity to overlook the Haganah's offensive in April 1948 when a number of ghastly atrocities and expulsions occurred, by claiming that it was voluntary – as though 350,000 Palestinians just decided to leave the country they had been living in for hundreds of years willingly. See Kurt René Radley, 'The Palestinian Refugees: The Right to Return in International Law', 72 *American Journal of International Law* (1978), p. 589 ('An unusual feature of this stage of the conflict [referring to April 1948 when Plan Dalet was implemented] was the complete and apparently voluntary evacuation by the Arabs of their towns and villages').
3. See e.g. D.P. O'Connell, *State Succession in Municipal Law and International Law, Vol. II, International Relations* (Cambridge: Cambridge University Press, 1967), p. 155 ('Israel came into existence, by its own act, on 14 May 1948. The British mandate was terminated on the following day'). One noteworthy exception is Geoffrey R. Watson who briefly mentions the 1948 conflict and Plan Dalet in his historical chapter in *The Oslo Accords: International Law and the Israeli–Palestinian Agreements* (Oxford: Oxford University Press, 2000) at pp. 24–5.
4. See e.g. Sharon Korman, *The Right of Conquest: The Acquisition of Territory by Force in International Law and Practice* (Oxford: Clarendon Press, 1996), p. 251 ('... the problem of the future of Palestine was settled by armed force, in the first of the Arab–Israeli wars, starting on 15 May 1948, the date on which Britain unilaterally relinquished its Mandate

in Palestine'). Note, that there is no mention of the war crimes, expulsions or the exodus of 750,000 Palestinian Arabs or to the fact that the conflict was already well underway *before* 15 May 1948. See also, Thomas M. Franck, *Recourse to Force: State Action Against Threats and Armed Attacks* (Cambridge: Cambridge University Press, 2002). In his analysis of state practice, Franck glosses over 1948 and straight to the 1956 Israel–Egypt conflict. See also, Yoram Dinstein, *War, Aggression and Self-Defence* (Cambridge: Cambridge University Press, 2005), p. 7 ('Thus, Israel's War of Independence started on 30 November 1947 as a civil war between the Arab and Jewish populations of the British Mandate in Palestine. But on 15 May 1948, upon the declaration of Israel's independence and its invasion by the armies of five sovereign Arab countries, the war became inter-State in character'). It is interesting that Dinstein stresses that the Arab states were sovereign. Does this mean that Israel was not? Moreover, how can the struggle between the Arab and Jewish *populations* of Palestine be commensurate with his description of the conflict as interstate in character? Notice too, how Israel only becomes a state when the Arab armies 'invaded' it. But what of the expulsions, the atrocities and the exodus of 350,000 Arabs *before* 15 May 1948? And what of their uprooting and destruction of their villages, the looting of their properties, the denial of their return?

5. See Legal Consequences of the Construction of a Wall in the Occupied Palestinian Territory, Advisory Opinion, ICJ Reports (2004), p. 136, at pp. 165–6, at paras 71–2 ('... on 14 May 1948, Israel proclaimed its independence on the strength of the General Assembly resolution; armed conflict then broke out between Israel and a number of Arab States and the Plan of Partition was not implemented').
6. It may also be the case that scholars fear the consequences for their reputations as academics by writing on the Arab–Israeli conflict. For example, James Crawford, the current Whewell Professor of Public International Law at Cambridge University was advised to omit his analysis of the creation of the state of Israel which he addressed in his doctoral thesis at Oxford University when he came to publish it in his book *The Creation of States in International Law* (Oxford: Clarendon Press, 1979). See James Crawford, 'Israel (1948–1949) and Palestine (1998–1999): Two Studies in the Creation of States', in Guy Goodwin-Gill and Stefan Talmon (eds), *The Reality of International Law: Essays in Honour of Ian Brownlie* (Oxford: Clarendon Press, 1999), p. 96. To his credit his second edition *The Creation of States in International Law* (Oxford: Oxford University Press, 2006), pp. 421–48 devotes 13 pages to the creation of Israel and 14 pages to attempts to create Palestine. Another scholar, John Borneman, a Professor of Anthropology at Princeton University, faced political objections to a workshop he organised at Princeton University on the case against Ariel Sharon in Belgium. See John Borneman (ed.), *The Case of Ariel Sharon and the Fate of Universal Jurisdiction* (New Jersey: Princeton University Press, 2004), pp. 7–8 (describing how several Princeton faculty members after agreeing to participate in his workshop, all of a sudden withdrew, after influential alumni threatened to withdraw funds). The author of this book was also subject to unwarranted political pressure when he published *The Palestine Question in International Law* (London: British Institute of International and Comparative Law, 2008). Three members of the Board of Governors of the British Institute of International and Comparative Law (a solicitor, a judge and a QC) complained to the Institute's director and threatened to resign over the book even though it was an edited collection of previously published peer-reviewed articles from international law journals. Incredibly, not one of them had read the book prior to their complaint and when one of the lawyers demanded copy approval he was rebuffed by the Institute's publisher. However, they successfully persuaded the Institute to withdraw two invitations that had already been sent to a famous Israeli historian and a well regarded Palestinian historian because they did not agree with their views of the conflict. They said that they wanted someone from the Israeli Government to be given a platform to speak at the book launch. This did not happen but the book was recalled from the printing press and examined page by page by an authority on international law who, in the event, approved it for publication. However, a disclaimer was inserted in the book, the first time this has happened in any Institute publication in its 50 year history. It

is noteworthy that not one of the complainants were authorities in public international law and nor did they have any specialist knowledge of the Arab–Israeli conflict. Nevertheless they felt it necessary to identify their religion on the telephone to the director as if this were relevant. The QC in question even had the gall to call up one of the Israeli contributors (who he did not know, but he obtained his telephone number from an employee at the Institute) to ask why he had agreed to have his article republished in the edited collection and the solicitor even hinted at withdrawing funds to the Institute from a trust fund based in Jerusalem over lunch with the Director and the Development Director. A 'complaint' regarding the book was then sent to an Israeli NGO called 'Israel Academia Monitor' which specifically highlighted the article that was republished in the book by three Israeli international lawyers on their website as an example of 'extremist views'. For a book which argues that academic freedom has never existed for scholars who write on the question of Palestine see Matthew Abraham, *Out of Bounds: Academic Freedom and the Question of Palestine* (London: Pluto Books, forthcoming 2009).

7. The figure 750,000 is used as this is the most commonly figure cited for Palestinian Arab displacement in 1948 in the prevailing literature. Statistics for refugee figures have been as high as 935,573 according to UNRWA registrations, and as low as 530,000 (Israeli figure). However, in internal correspondence, Walter Eytan apparently noted the UNRWA registration figures saying they were 'immaculate' and that the real figure was close to 800,000. The British Foreign Office estimated the total number of refugees to be 810,000 in February 1949 and then issued a revised estimate of 600,000. The UNCCP Technical Office gave a figure of 760,000. The US Government estimated a total refugee population of 875,000 as of 1953. For further information see *Survey of Palestinian Refugees and Internally Displaced Persons 2002* (Bethlehem: Badil Resource Center, 2003), p. 25, note to table 1.1.
8. See Hannah Arendt, *The Jew as Pariah: Jewish Identity and Politics in the Modern Age* edited by Ron H. Feldman (New York: Grove Press, 1978), pp. 215–16 (quote taken from an article called 'Peace of Armistice in the Near East' which was originally published in 1950).
9. For early propaganda pamphlets produced by Israel's Information Office in New York see M. Comay, *The Future of the Arab Refugees* (1954) and G. Meir, *Arab Refugee Problem Toward a Solution* (1961), (both disclaiming Israel of any responsibility for creating the Arab refugee problem).
10. See the numerous articles and books cited in the following pages by Khalidi, Pappé, Morris, Shlaim, Segev, Finkelstein, Gilmour, Sayigh, Flapan, Cattan, Palumbo, Said, Hitchens, etc.
11. See e.g. Mia Grandahl, *In Hope and Despair: Life in the Palestinian Refugee Camps* (Cairo: The American University Press, 2003), which is a photographic study. See also, Nur Masalha (ed.), *Catastrophe Remembered: Palestine, Israel and the Internal Refugees – Essays in Memory of Edward Said* (London: Zed Books, 2005); Muna Hamzeh, *Refugees in Our Own Land: Chronicles from a Palestinian Refugee Camp in Bethlehem* (London: Pluto Press, 2001); Staughton Lynd, Alice Lynd and Sam Bahour, *Homeland: Oral Histories of Palestine and Palestinians* (Northampton: Interlink Books, 1998); Jamil I. Toubbeh, *Day of the Long Night: A Palestinian Refugee Remembers the Nakbah* (Jefferson: McFarland & Co. 1998); and Walid Khalidi, *Before their Diaspora: A Photographic History of the Palestinians, 1876–1948* (Washington, DC: Institute for Palestine Studies, 1984).
12. The word *Nakbah* means 'catastrophe' in Arabic, and refers to the displacement, dispersal and dispossession of the Palestinian Arabs during the 1948 war.
13. See the project's website at http://www.nakba-archive.org (last retrieved 23 October 2008).
14. See Avi Shlaim, 'The Debate about 1948', 27 *International Journal of Middle East Studies* (1995), pp. 287–304.
15. See Tom Segev, *1949: The First Israelis* (New York: The Free Press, 1986) and *One Palestine, Complete: Jews and Arabs under the British Mandate* (New York: Henry Holt, paperback, 1999).

16. Shlaim, 'The Debate about 1948', *supra* note 14, p. 289 ('The first thing to note about the new histiography is that much of it is not new').
17. Walid Khalidi is an eminent Oxford educated Palestinian historian who has written extensively on the Palestinian exodus. He is the General Secretary and co-founder of the Institute of Palestine Studies. He taught history at the University of Oxford, Princeton University, the American University of Beirut and Harvard University.
18. Britain encouraged Transjordan to invade Palestine but only on the strict condition that they did not invade the area allocated to the Jewish state in the UN Partition Plan. In other words, Britain did not attempt to abort the birth of the Jewish state in 1948. On the contrary, it thwarted the creation of the Arab state that was envisaged in the UN Partition Plan by agreeing to its annexation by Transjordan. See generally Ilan Pappé, *Britain and the Arab–Israeli Conflict, 1948–1951* (London: Macmillan Press, in association with St Antony's College, Oxford, 1988).
19. Rather the Haganah, which would become the Israeli Army after the founding of the Jewish state, fielded more troops than the Arabs, drew on a large reserve of Western-trained officers, had an effective and centralised system of command and control, and shorter lines of communication that enabled it to operate with greater speed and efficiency. The Arabs, on the other hand, were divided and relied on conscripts and volunteers who were less disciplined and numerically inferior. See Simha Flapan, *The Birth of Israel: Myths and Realities* (New York: Random House, 1988), especially 'Myth Six'. See also, Ilan Pappé, *The Making of the Arab–Israeli Conflict 1947–1951* (London: I.B. Tauris, 2001), pp. 108–13.
20. Disagreement still remains, however, over the question as to whether the Zionists intended to expel Palestine's Arab population or whether this was an unintended consequence of the war. Benny Morris argues that it is the latter, whereas his critics say that the evidence of the atrocities he has uncovered in his research does not support his conclusion. See Benny Morris, *The Birth of the Palestinian Refugee Problem, 1947–1949* (Cambridge: Cambridge University Press, 1987). For a criticism of this account see Norman G. Finkelstein, *Image and Reality of the Israel–Palestine Conflict* (London: Verso Books, 2003), pp. 51–87. His critics also argue that the concept of 'transfer' had been prevalent in Zionist political thought in the decades prior to the 1948 conflict, something which Morris readily admits, however he disagrees with their contention that this led them to act with malice aforethought when they allegedly conspired to expel Palestine's Arab population in 1948. See Nur Masalha, *Expulsion of the Palestinians: The Concept of 'Transfer' in Zionist Political Thought, 1882–1948* (Washington, DC: Institute for Palestine Studies, 1992). See also, Walid Khalidi, 'Plan Dalet: Master Plan for the Conquest of Palestine', 18 *Journal of Palestine Studies* (1988), pp. 4–33 and by the same author, *Why Did the Palestinians Leave? An Examination of the Zionist Version of the Exodus of 1948* (London: Arab Information Centre, 1963). See further, 'The Debate on the 1948 Exodus', 21 *Journal of Palestine Studies* (1991), pp. 66–114 (with contributions from Norman Finkelstein, Benny Morris and Nur Masalha).
21. Moreover, King Abdullah of Transjordan had entered into a covert alliance with the Zionists to partition Palestine between them in the event of conflict. In the words of Avi Shlaim, the Zionists and the Hashemites had entered into an alternative partition plan which was 'consciously and deliberately intended to frustrate the will of the international community, as expressed through the United Nations General Assembly, in favour of creating an independent Arab state in part of Palestine'. See Shlaim, 'The Debate about 1948', *supra* note 14, p. 298.
22. In contrast, the Arab world bent over backwards to make peace with Israel – as Shlaim notes, the files of Israel's Foreign Ministry are 'burst at the seams with evidence of Arab peace feelers and Arab readiness to negotiate with Israel from September 1948 onward'. See Shlaim, 'The Debate about 1948', *supra* note 14, pp. 300–1. For instance, during the armistice negotiations between Israel and Syria, the latter offered to resettle 300,000 Palestinian refugees (100,000 were already in Syria, but they were offering to resettle an additional 200,000 from the other Arab countries) if Israel agreed to redraw the border

to allow it access to half of the Sea of Galilee. See Avi Shlaim, *The Iron Wall: Israel and the Arab World* (London: Penguin Books, 2000), p. 46. See also, Ilan Pappé, *The Making*, *supra* note 19 at pp. 226–228; and Tom Segev, *1949*, *supra* note 15, pp. 14–17. Ben-Gurion's response was to reject this offer 'out of hand'. Quote from Shlaim, ibid., p. 300. When Syria dropped its demand on the Galilee, whilst maintaining its offer to settle 300,000 refugees, Ben-Gurion ignored the advice of his ministers and refused to meet with the Syrians.

23. See e.g. Stephen Howe, 'The Politics of Historical "Revisionism": Comparing Ireland and Israel/Palestine', *Past and Present* (2000), pp. 227–53.
24. Although it has not been without controversy. See Ethan Bronner, 'Israel's History Textbooks Replace Myths with Facts', *New York Times*, 14 August 1999. See also, Elie Podeh, *The Arab–Israeli Conflict in Israeli History Textbooks, 1948–2000* (Westport: Greenwood Press, 2002), pp. 58–61 and especially pp. 105–10, p. 110 ('... first- and second-generation textbooks reflected the Israeli position on the refugee question ... This one-sided narrative, however, is replaced in third-generation textbooks by a multicausal explanation that includes Israel's partial role in the creation of the refugee problem ...').
25. See, generally, the collection of essays in Matthew Craven, Malgosia Fitzmaurice and Maria Vogiatzi (eds), *Time, History and International Law* (The Hague: Martinus Nijhoff Publishers, 2006).
26. See Rosalyn Higgins, 'Time and Law: International Perspectives on an Old Problem', 46 *International and Comparative Law Quarterly* (1997), pp. 501–20 (examining some aspects of the rule of inter-temporal law).
27. To coin a phrase from Shlaim in 'The Debate about 1948', *supra* note 14 at p. 292 and p. 297.
28. See e.g. David Tal, *The War in Palestine 1948: Strategy and Diplomacy* (New York: Routledge, 2004).
29. See Monique Chemillier-Gendreau, 'Israel's Violent Attacks on Palestinian Arabs in 1948–49: Qualifying Crimes in Light of International Law and Consequences', 12 *Palestine Yearbook of International Law* (2002–03), pp. 117–44. The standard of proof in any criminal law proceedings would be 'beyond reasonable doubt', whereas it seems that the International Court of Justice would be satisfied with the 'balance of probabilities test', the test of 'reasonableness' or 'persuasiveness'. See Brendan Plant and Anna Riddell, *Evidence in the International Court of Justice* (London: British Institute of International and Comparative Law, forthcoming 2009).
30. See James Crawford, *The International Law Commission's Articles on State Responsibility: Introduction, Texts and Commentaries* (Cambridge: Cambridge University Press, 2002), pp. 116–20, citing arbitral decisions in Mexico and Venezuela from the early twentieth century.
31. See 5 *International Court of Justice Yearbook* (1950–51), p. 193. The declaration was signed by M. Sharett on 4 September 1950.
32. See 8 *International Court of Justice Yearbook* (1956–57), pp. 214–15 (declaration signed by Golda Meir).
33. It would also be difficult, though perhaps not impossible, to bring a case concerning Britain's responsibility as the mandatory power, for allowing the refugee crisis to escalate whilst it was still in effective control of Palestine in 1948. See Iain Scobbie, 'The Responsibility of Great Britain in Respect of the Creation of the Palestine Refugee Question', 10 *Yearbook of Islamic and Middle Eastern Law* (2003–04), pp. 39–58.
34. Israel followed the US in withdrawing its consent to the compulsory jurisdiction of the ICJ in the aftermath of the *Nicaragua* judgment. The notification of termination of the declaration of 17 October 1956 received from the Government of Israel on 21 November 1985 reads as follows: 'On behalf of the Government of Israel, I have the honour to inform you that the Government of Israel has decided to terminate, with effect as of today, its declaration of 17 October 1956 as amended, concerning the acceptance of the compulsory jurisdiction of the International Court of Justice.' This statement was signed by Benjamin

Netanyahu. See 'Declarations Recognizing Jurisdiction', 38–40 *International Court of Justice Yearbook* (1983–86), p. 79, at pp. 79–80.

35. See Articles 92–96 of the UN Charter and Article 36 of the Statute of the International Court of Justice which is annexed to the UN Charter of which it forms an integral part. For further reading on jurisdictional issues see Shabtai Rosenne, *The Law and Practice of the International Court 1920–2005*, Vol. II, *Jurisdiction* (Leiden: Martinus Nijhoff Publishers, 2006), pp. 645–9 (the compromissory clause) and pp. 701–802 (compulsory jurisdiction).
36. See Law Reports of Trials of War Criminals Selected and Prepared by the United Nations War Crimes Commission, Vol. XV (London: HMSO, 1949), p. 113 and p. 134.
37. See General Treaty for the Renunciation of War as an Instrument of National Policy (Pact of Paris), 94 *League of Nations Treaty Series* (1928), p. 57.
38. See Articles 10–12 of the Covenant of the League of Nations, 1 *League of Nations Official Journal* (1920), pp. 5–6.
39. See Article 2 (4) of the UN Charter, XV *United Nations Conference on International Organisation*, p. 335.
40. See Alan Dershowitz, *The Case for Israel* (New Jersey: John Wiley & Sons, 2003), p. 74.
41. See e.g. Louis Rene Beres, 'A Rejoinder', 9 *Temple International & Comparative Law Review* (1995), pp. 445–9 at p. 449 (responding to an article by John Quigley criticising Israel's destruction of Iraq's nuclear reactor in the course of which Beres quotes a statement from a dubious source allegedly by Azzam Pasha threatening Israel with genocidal extermination). According to a report published in the *Manchester Guardian* in May 1948, Azzam Pasha was quoted as saying: 'The Zionists were seeking to create a purely Jewish State, but the Arabs were fighting for a Palestinian State in which the Jews would have full and equal citizenship, every facility to develop their Jewish life, and every encouragement to play a full part in the building up of a united Palestine.' This is hardly consistent with threatening Israel with genocidal extermination. See 'Arab Policy: Fighting to Prevent a Zionist State', *Manchester Guardian*, 20 May 1948, p. 5 (reproducing the quote as to what motivated the Arabs to fight in 1948).
42. See Stephen M. Schwebel, 'What Weight to Conquest?' 64 *American Journal of International Law* (1970), pp. 344–7 at p. 346. For criticisms of the Schwebel argument, see Sir Robert Jennings and Sir Arthur Watts (eds), *Oppenheim's International Law*, Vol. 1, Parts 2 to 4 (Harlow: Longman Group, 1992), p. 704 note 8.
43. Although Schwebel's article was published in 1970 it was given a new lease of life when Malcolm Shaw included it in a collection of articles on title to territory. This is despite the fact that since the mid 1980s, Israel has published a plethora of documents from its own archives disproving the David vs. Goliath thesis and the myth that Israel's conquest of Palestine in 1948 was defensive. See Malcolm N. Shaw (ed.), *Title to Territory* (Aldershot: Ashgate, 2005), pp. 393–6. The article also appears in Schwebel's collected writings on international law, provocatively entitled *Justice in International Law* (Cambridge: Grotius Publications, Cambridge University Press, 1994), pp. 521–5.
44. Schwebel, 'What Weight to Conquest?' *supra* note 42, p. 346.
45. Schwebel, ibid., p. 344 ('... on appreciation of the fact that Israel's action in 1967 was defensive, and on the theory that, since the danger in response to which defensive action was taken remains, occupation – though not annexation – is justified, pending a peace settlement'). The forcible acquisition of territory in 'self-defence' would be prohibited by Article 2 (4) of the UN Charter and would go well beyond the confines of self-defence as proscribed in Article 51 of the UN Charter and the principle of proportionality which was already established in customary international law long before the adoption of the UN Charter in 1945. Self-defence is restricted to the preservation of the *status quo ante*. It can never be used to justify conquest for this would be inimical to the very concept of self-defence. See Robert Yewdall Jennings, *The Acquisition of Territory in International Law* (Manchester: Manchester University Press, 1963), pp. 55–6 at p. 55 ('It would be

a curious law of self-defence that permitted the defender in the course of his defence to seize and keep the resources and territory of the attacker').

46. See Yehuda Z. Blum, 'The Missing Reversioner: Reflections on the Status of Judea and Samaria', 3 *Israel Law Review* (1968), pp. 279–301 at p. 287. He expressed the same opinion in Yehuda Z. Blum, *Secure Boundaries and Middle East Peace: In the Light of International Law and Practice* (Jerusalem: Institute for Legislative Research and Comparative Law, 1971), pp. 87–91. In a speech before the UN General Assembly on 2 December 1980, Blum said that the claims of the Palestinians to establish a state in the West Bank and Gaza were unfounded. He said that the Palestinians had already achieved self-determination in their own state, namely Jordan. See General Assembly Official Records, XXXVth session, Plenary Meetings, 77th meeting, 1318, paras 108–13.
47. See Benny Morris, *The Road to Jerusalem: Glubb Pasha, Palestine and the Jews* (London: I.B. Tauris, 2002), p. 147 ('... Abdullah in practice cleaved to his original intention of occupying some of the Arab areas, not attacking the Jewish areas, and avoiding battle with the Haganah').
48. See Sir John Bagot Glubb, *A Soldier with the Arabs* (London: Hodder & Stoughton, 1957), p. 89 ('The greater part of the military units of the Arab Legion were already in Palestine before the British mandate came to an end, having remained there at the end of the Second World War. The British government, however, decided that they must all leave before the end of the mandate, and the greater part of the three mechanized regiments crossed the Jordan and camped near Zerqa before the end of April').
49. Ibid.
50. See Benny Morris, *1948: A History of the First Arab–Israeli War* (New Haven: Yale University Press, 2008), pp. 118–19.
51. See Istvan S. Pogany, *The Security Council and the Arab–Israeli Conflict* (Aldershot: Gower Publishing Co., 1984), p. 41 (emphasis added).
52. See Elihu Lauterpacht, *Jerusalem and the Holy Places* (London: The Anglo-Israeli Association, 1968), p. 22. In 1971, Eileen Denza, the Foreign Office Legal Adviser, was asked to give her opinion on Lauterpacht's pamphlet on Jerusalem. In a four-page minute, she took issue with several of the arguments advanced by Lauterpacht. On the 1948 conflict, she wrote, 'I do not think that the analysis which makes Israel an entirely innocent self-defender in 1948 and the other Arab States aggressors is entirely correct and I do not think that a distinction in any event can be drawn between Israel's title and Jordan's on the basis of their conduct in 1948.' See Foreign Office Minute on Jerusalem and the Holy Place by Eileen Denza, 11 October 1971, FCO 17/1605.
53. See Ilan Pappé, *The Ethnic Cleansing of Palestine* (Oxford: Oneworld Publications, 2006), pp. 86–126.
54. See Julius Stone, *Israel and Palestine: Assault on the Law of Nations* (Baltimore: Johns Hopkins University Press, 1981), p. 46; J.R. Gainsborough, *The Arab–Israeli Conflict: A Politico-Legal Analysis* (Aldershot: Gower, 1986), pp. 44–5; and Allan Gerson, *Israel, the West Bank and International Law* (London: Frank Cass, 1978), pp. 49–51 (all characterising Israel's actions as defensive and that of the Arabs as aggressive).
55. During the first phase of the conflict over 50 per cent of Palestine's Arab population and 3 per cent of its Jewish population were displaced. See Salman Abu-Sitta, *From Refugees to Citizens at Home* (London: Palestine Land Society and Palestine Return Centre, 2001), p. 7.
56. On Bernadotte's assassination see the Report Regarding the Assassination of the UN Mediator, UN Doc. S/1018, 28 September 1948. The Reparation case at the ICJ (1949) came about as a direct result of his assassination.
57. See the Progress Report of the UN Mediator, GAOR, 3rd session, supp. 11, UN Doc. A/648, 16 September 1948, at Chapter V entitled 'Refugees' para. 7.
58. Ibid., Part Three: Assistance to Refugees, I. Nature of the Problem, balance.1 ('As a result of the conflict in Palestine, almost the whole of the Arab population fled or was expelled from the area under Jewish occupation. This included the large Arab populations of Jaffa, Haifa, Acre, Ramleh and Lydda. Of a population of somewhat more than 400,000

Arabs prior to the outbreak of hostilities, the number presently estimated as remaining in Jewish-controlled territory is approximately 50,000').

59. See Edgar O'Ballance, *The Arab–Israeli War 1948* (London: Faber & Faber, 1956), p. 31 ('The Israel–Arab War can properly be said to have begun on 29 November 1947, when the General Assembly of the United Nations passed their resolution on the partitioning of Palestine'). See also, Benny Morris, *The Birth of the Palestinian Refugee Problem Revisited* (Cambridge: Cambridge University Press, 2004), p. 65 and note 1, p. 139 and Pappé, *Ethnic Cleansing*, *supra* note 53, p. 40.
60. For a detailed list of the fighting which engulfed Palestine between December 1947 and May 1948 see Chronology of Events in Palestine, 1 December 1947 – 15 May 1948, 2 *The Middle East Journal* (1948), pp. 215–21 and 329–32 which is reproduced in Appendix VI in Henry Cattan, *Palestine, the Arabs and Israel: The Search for Justice* (London: The Longman Group, 1969), pp. 214–15.
61. See the report of a discussion between British Embassy officials in Damascus and the Syrian Minister of Interior. 'The last things the Syrian government wanted, and he repeated this three times, was to get into conflict with ourselves', but that due to the Zionist aggression they felt they had no choice, especially as Safad and Acre were threatened and that 'Jewish aircraft had dropped bombs on Syrian and Lebanese villages'. See Situation, Outrages, Haifa, Incident, CO 537/3860, cipher, diplomatic (secret) distribution, from Damascus to Foreign Office, 3 May 1948, Mr Broadmead.
62. See Michael Palumbo, *The Palestinian Catastrophe: The 1948 Expulsion of a People from their Homeland* (London: Quartet Books, 1987), pp. 35–6 citing MEC: Cunningham Papers, box 2, file 3.
63. See UN Palestine Commission, First Monthly Progress Report to the Security Council, UN Doc. A/AC.21/7, 29 January 1948, para. 7 (c).
64. Both the Jewish Agency and the Arab Higher Committee received assistance in the form of volunteers, weapons, and money. See O'Ballance, *Arab–Israeli War 1948*, *supra* note 59, at pp. 39–41 (describing the infiltration of Arab irregulars into Palestine from neighbouring countries). See also, David J. Bercuson, *The Secret Army* (New York: Stein & Day, 1984), pp. 50–79 (describing how the Jewish Agency and the World Zionist Organisation brought in volunteers to fight the Arabs in Palestine, and how they received millions of dollars in arms, medical supplies, food and clothing, as well as Second World World veterans).
65. See Bercuson, *The Secret Army*, ibid.
66. See David Gilmour, *Dispossessed: The Ordeal of the Palestinians* (London: Sphere paperbacks, 1982), p. 63.
67. Ibid.
68. See Rosemary Sayigh, *The Palestinians: From Peasants to Revolutionaries* (London: Zed Books, 2007), pp. 79–83.
69. Ibid., p. 79.
70. Ibid., p. 80.
71. For the various justifications for the Arab intervention, see UN Doc. S/748, 17 May, cablegram from King Abdullah of Transjordan to the Secretary-General of the UN and Press Release PAL/167, 16 May 1948; cablegram from the Egyptian Government to the UN Secretary-General UN Doc. S/743, 15 May 1948 and cablegram from the Secretary-General of the Arab League to the UN Secretary-General UN Doc. S/745, 15 May 1948. See also Res. 85, The Policy of the Arab States Towards the Question of Palestine, translated and reproduced in Muhammad Khalil (ed.), *The Arab States and the Arab League: A Documentary Record, Vol. II International Affairs* (Beirut: Khayats, 1962), p. 166.
72. See the report of a discussion between British Embassy officials in Damascus and the Syrian Minister of Interior, *supra* note 61.
73. See A.L.W. Munkman in her review of *Jerusalem and the Holy Places* by Elihu Lauterpacht in 43 *British Yearbook of International Law* (1968–69), pp. 306–10 at p. 308 ('It is not easy to characterize the action of the Arab States as a clear breach of Article 2 (4) – even accepting for the sake of argument that this embodied at that date a customary rule applicable to non-members of the UN – in the factual context in Palestine at that date').

74. Although the definition of an 'aggressor' in international law has proved controversial, it has always been understood to refer to the use of force by a state (invasion, bombardment, attack, etc.) of the territory of another state. See, for instance, Article 1 of the Soviet Draft Declaration on the Definition of the Aggressor, 1933; Article 2 of the Convention for the Definition of Aggression signed in London on 3 July 1933; Article 4 of the Treaty of Non-Aggression between Afghanistan, Iraq and Turkey, signed in Tehran on 8 July 1937; and Articles 1, 2 and 3 of the UN Definition of Aggression annexed to UN General Assembly resolution 3314 (XXIX), 14 December 1974. On the history and formulation of a definition of aggression, see Ahmed M. Rifaat, *International Aggression – A Study of the Legal Concept: Its Development and Definition in International Law* (Stockholm: Almqvist & Wiskell International, 1979).
75. See Benny Morris, *Righteous Victims: A History of the Zionist–Arab Conflict, 1881–1999* (London: John Murray, 1999), p. 233 (writing that two Lebanese battalions, 'supported by armoured cars and two batteries of 75mm artillery, were deployed in southern Lebanon for the planned invasion, but they apparently never crossed the border'). See also, Matthew Hughes, 'Collusion across the Litani? Lebanon and the 1948 War', in Eugene L. Rogan and Avi Shlaim (eds), *The War for Palestine: Rewriting the History of 1948* (Cambridge: Cambridge University Press, 2007, second edition), pp. 204–27 (writing that Lebanon's involvement in the 1948 war could only be described as symbolic).
76. See Morris, *Righteous Victims*, ibid., pp. 232–3 (describing the entry of the Syrian Army).
77. See the map of the Arab invasion in Morris, *Road to Jerusalem*, *supra* note 47, p. 146.
78. See Glubb, *A Soldier*, *supra* note 48 at pp. 166–72 (describing the fighting in Latrun).
79. See Avi Shlaim, *Collusion Across the Jordan: King Abdullah, the Zionist Movement, and the Partition of Palestine* (Oxford: Clarendon Press, 1988), pp. 110–21.
80. See Fawaz A Gergez, 'Egypt and the 1948 War: Internal Conflict and Regional Ambition', in Eugene L. Rogan and Avi Shlaim (eds), *The War for Palestine: Rewriting the History of 1948* (Cambridge: Cambridge University Press, 2001), pp. 151–77 at pp. 156–7.
81. See Gergez, ibid., pp. 159–60.
82. Ibid., p. 168.
83. See Tal, *War in Palestine 1948*, *supra* note 28, pp. 444–61 (providing a description of the fighting in Sinai, the frenzied diplomatic activity this aroused, the Anglo-Egyptian Treaty and the eventual Israeli withdrawal).
84. Begin outlines the terms of a secret agreement between Haganah and his movement the Irgun Zvai Leumi in his memoirs. See Menachem Begin, *The Revolt* (London: WH Allen, 1979) at pp. 345–6.
85. See Begin, *The Revolt*, ibid., at p. 348.
86. UN Security Council resolution 73, UN Doc. S/714, 1 April 1948.
87. UN Security Council resolution 46, UN Doc. S/723, 17 April 1948.
88. UN Security Council resolution 49, UN Doc. S/773, 22 May 1948.
89. UN Security Council resolution 50, UN Doc. S/801, 29 May 1948.
90. UN Security Council resolution 54, UN Doc. S/902, 15 July 1948.
91. See Special Appendix Relating to Palestine (conferring upon it a special status in the Arab league) and Art. 6 Pact of the League of Arab States on collective self-defence, signed at Cairo, on 22 March 1945. Filed and recorded at the request of Egypt on 29 August 1950, 70 *United Nations Treaty Series* (1950), pp. 238–47 (in Arabic), and pp. 248–62 (in English and French). The Arabic text is the official text.
92. Ibid.
93. Article 6, ibid. On Palestine's request and the Arab justifications see *supra* note 71, and for the requirements of collective self-defence see Military and Paramilitary Activities in and against Nicaragua (Nicaragua v. United States of America), Merits, judgment, ICJ Reports (1986), p. 14 at p. 105, para. 199.
94. Article 17 of the British Mandate of Palestine provided for the defence of Palestine albeit subject to the supervision of the mandatory.

95. See UN Security Council resolutions 82, 25 June 1950; 83, 27 June 1950; 84, 7 July 1950; and 85, 31 July 1950. Article 51 UN Charter provides: 'Nothing in the present Charter shall impair the inherent right of individual or collective self-defence if an armed attack occurs against a Member of the United Nations, until the Security Council has taken measures necessary to maintain international peace and security. Measures taken by Members in the exercise of this right of self-defence shall be immediately reported to the Security Council and shall not in any way affect the authority and responsibility of the Security Council under the present Charter to take at any time such action as it deems necessary in order to maintain or restore international peace and security.'
96. See Bowett, *Self-Defence*, *supra* note 1, p. 100.
97. Ibid.
98. See Myres S. McDougal and Florentino P. Feliciano, *The International Law of War: Transnational Coercion and World Public Order* (New Haven: New Haven Press, 1994), p. 221.
99. See *In re* Weizsaecker and Others (Ministries Trial), United States Military Tribunal at Nuremberg, 14 April 1949, in H. Lauterpacht (ed.), 16 *Annual Digest and Reports of Public International Law Cases 1949* (London: Butterworth & Co., 1955), p. 347 ('there can be no self-defence against self-defence').
100. See Lieutenant-General Sir John Bagot Glubb, *A Soldier with the Arabs* (London: Hodder & Stoughton, 1957), pp. 63–6.
101. See Meron Benvenisti, *Sacred Landscape: The Buried History of the Holy Land since 1948* (Berkeley: University of California Press, 2000), p. 109.
102. This is reproduced in Benvenisti, ibid., p. 108 (parenthesis in original, emphasis added).
103. See Michael Akehurst, 'The Arab–Israeli Conflict and International Law', 5 *New Zealand Universities Law Review* (1973) at p. 237.
104. See Why the Arab States Entered Palestine: Their Action Justified in Fact and in International Law. Memorandum to the United Nations Delegations submitted by The Arab Higher Committee Delegation for Palestine, 4512 Empire State Building, New York, N.Y., June, 1948, pp. 7–8, at p. 8, in Memoranda on Palestine, FO 371/68577 at p. 7.
105. See for instance the threats made by Ben-Gurion in his diary and by the Irgun against Transjordan which was reported in *The Scotsman*, 10 April 1948, p. 15. Moreover, the President of Syria, Shukri al-Quwwatli was subsequently overthrown in a coup and Egypt's Premier Nuqrashi was assassinated by a member of the Muslim Brotherhood for their failures in defending Palestine.
106. See Avi Shlaim, 'Israel and the Arab Coalition in 1948', in Rogan and Shlaim, *The War for Palestine*, *supra* note 80 at pp. 79–104 at pp. 93–4 citing Ben-Gurion, Yoman Hamilhama, vol. II, pp. 453–4. The rest of the quote ('This will be in revenge for what they (the Egyptians, the Aramis and Assyrians) did to our forefathers during Biblical times') appears in Pappé's book, *supra* note 53, p. 144.
107. See Pappé, *Ethnic Cleansing*, *supra* note 53 at p. 144 citing Ben-Gurion's *Diary*, 18 July 1948 (Ben-Gurion Archives).
108. See text of Plan Gimmel (Plan C), May 1946: Section on Countermeasures, translated from *Sefer Toldot Hahaganah* [History of the Haganah], Vol. 3, edited by Yehuda Slutsky (Tel Aviv: Zionist Library, 1972), Appendix 39, pp. 1939–43, and reproduced in 18 *Journal of Palestine Studies* (1988), Appendix A, p. 20.
109. See Article 51 UN Charter in Vol. XII, *Documents of the United Nations Conference on International Organization* San Francisco, 1945 (New York: United Nations Information Organizations, 1945), p. 680.
110. See the Letter from Daniel Webster, US Secretary of State, to Henry Fox, British Minister in Washington, DC, 24 April, 1841, in 29 *British and Foreign State Papers* (1840–41), p. 1129 at p. 1138.
111. See Khalidi, 'Plan Dalet: Master Plan', *supra* note 20.
112. According to Pappé 'the Consultancy', which included David Ben-Gurion, Ezra Danin, Yehoshua Palmon, Eliyahu Sasson, Yohanan Ratner, Fritz Eisenshtater, Yossef Weitz, Yaacov Tahon, Yaacov Dori, Israeli Galili, Yigael Yadin, Zvi Leschiner, Yitzhak Sadeh

and Yigal Allon, met several times from December 1947 to March 1948 in Ben-Gurion's house and in the Red House, formerly located on Yarkon Street in north Tel Aviv, to mastermind the expulsion. See Pappé, *Ethnic Cleansing*, *supra* note 53, pp. 37–85. This is disputed by Morris. See Morris, *1948: A History*, *supra* note 50 at pp. 120–1.

113. See Khalidi, 'Plan Dalet: Master Plan', *supra* note 20 at pp. 17–18.
114. The full text of Plan Dalet is reproduced in English in 18 *Journal of Palestine Studies* (1988), pp. 34–7.
115. Khalidi, 'Plan Dalet: Master Plan', *supra* note 20 at p. 18.
116. See *The Times*, Editorial, 9 August 1948, p. 5, col. c.
117. See Major R.D. Wilson, *Cordon and Search: With the 6th Airborne Division in Palestine* (Aldershot: Gale & Polden, 1949), p. 166 (saying that the Zionists showed more initiative than the Arabs in their attacks, and by executing them under cover of darkness they rarely had to contend with the [British] Army), pp. 173–4 (describing how the Zionists would dress like British soldiers when they attacked the Arabs causing all sorts of confusion), and p. 175 (Zionists had good intelligence).
118. See Glubb, *A Solider with the Arabs*, *supra* note 48, pp. 92–5.
119. Ibid., p. 95. Iraq and Syria were experiencing unrest in their Kurdish provinces in 1947–48.
120. See Ilan Pappé, *Britain and the Arab–Israeli Conflict*, supra note 18, pp. 30–3 (providing a brief description of the battle for Jerusalem).
121. See Morris, *Righteous Victims*, *supra* note 75, p. 217.
122. See e.g. Benny Morris, *The Birth*, *supra* note 20, at p. 230 ('In his briefing of 11 November to the Political Committee of Mapam, Galilee detailed some of the atrocities committed in the October fighting. He spoke of "52 men [in Safsaf] tied with a rope and dropped into a well and shot. 10 were killed. Women pleaded for mercy. [There were] 3 cases of rape ... A girl aged 14 was raped. Another 4 were killed"'). There were many other cases like this, some of which are cited later in this chapter.
123. See A.L.W. Munkman, review of *Jerusalem and the Holy Places*, *supra* note 73 at p. 308.
124. See legal status of Palestine after termination of the Mandate, from Sir O. Sargent, Foreign Office Minute, 14 May 1948, to UK delegation in New York, and Washington (prepared by FO Legal Advisers), FO 371/68664 Palestine, Eastern, 1948, para. 9 (b). According to the *Foreign Office List and Diplomatic and Consular Yearbook* for 1947), p. 11, William Eric Beckett, Gerald Gray Fitzmaurice, Richard Samuel Berrington Best, James Edmund Fawcett and Francis Aime Vallat were legal advisers at the Foreign Office in London and in Britain's Washington embassy. The extract just quoted was drafted for the most part by Fitzmaurice, with Beckett's input.
125. See the exchange of views in a FO Minute from Mr Wright about the British attitude towards recognising Palestine, in FO 371/68665, Palestine, Eastern, 1948, where there is some discussion of whether the British Government should afford belligerent status to the Jewish Government and the Arab Higher Committee.
126. See legal status of Palestine after termination of the Mandate, *supra* note 124.
127. The situation in Palestine was in the opinion of the legal advisers, 'a sort of *res nullius*'. See ibid., para. 7. What the Foreign Office lawyers seemed to be suggesting with the addition of the words 'sort of' before '*res nullius*' was that there was a legal vacuum in Palestine caused by the departure of the British. See FO 371/68665, Palestine, Eastern, 1948. However, the concept of *terra nullius* does not apply to territories with politically active and organised populations, as the ICJ would conclude in its 1974 *Western Sahara* advisory opinion. See Western Sahara, Advisory Opinion, 16 October, ICJ Reports (1975), p. 12 at p. 39 at para. 80 ('Whatever differences of opinion there may have been among jurists, the State practice of the relevant period indicates that territories inhabited by tribes or peoples having social and political organization were not regarded as *terra nullius*'). In 1971, Eileen Denza, the Foreign Office Legal Adviser, expressed her opinion after studying various opinions on the subject in the Legal Advisers' files dating back to 1949, in these words: 'I do not think that there was a legal vacuum (such as exists in Taiwan)

at the end of the Mandate. I think that all the powers of sovereignty under the Mandate became temporarily vested in the General Assembly. But the analysis of where sovereignty lay is to some extent an unprofitable exercise. The main point is that Resolutions of the General Assembly acting in effect as the successor to the powers under the Mandate of both the League of Nations and the Mandatory Power have a special force. It is probably true that the Resolutions did not in themselves cede territory, but they had a legal force beyond the moral and persuasive force which is all that General Assembly Resolutions have in the ordinary case.' See Foreign Office Minute on Jerusalem and the Holy Place by Eileen Denza, 11 October 1971, FCO 17/1605.

128. Ibid.
129. See Blum, 'The Missing Reversioner', *supra* note 46, p. 283.
130. See James Crawford, *The Creation of States in International Law* (Oxford: Oxford University Press, 2006), pp. 432–3 and the authorities cited therein at note 232.
131. See *Western Sahara*, *supra* note 127 at p. 39 at para. 80.
132. See Stephen M. Schwebel, 'What Weight to Conquest', *supra* note 42, pp. 344–7. For criticisms of the Schwebel thesis, see Jennings and Watts, *Oppenheim's International Law*, *supra* note 42 at p. 704, note 8.
133. See Schwebel, ibid., p. 346 ('Where the prior holder of territory had seized that territory unlawfully, the state which subsequently takes that territory in the lawful exercise of self-defense has, against that prior holder, better title'). See also, Blum, 'The Missing Reversioner', *supra* note 46 at p. 294, note 60 and Eugene V. Rostow, '"Palestinian Self-Determination": Possible Futures for the Unallocated Territories of the Palestine Mandate', 5 *Yale Studies in World Public Order* (1978–79), pp. 147–72 (who thought the Balfour Declaration and the Mandate were still in force allowing Israel to colonise the whole of Palestine until the present day). It should be said that these claims were advanced, in part, so as to argue that Geneva Convention IV was not applicable to the occupied territories. This view has never been accepted outside of Israel. See Declaration of the Conference of the High Contracting Parties to the Fourth Geneva Convention and Statement of the ICRC, Dec. 5, 2001: http://www.icrc.org/web/eng/siteeng0.nsf/html/5FLDPJ (last retrieved 23 October 2008).
134. See Blum, 'The Missing Reversioner', *supra* note 46, p. 294.
135. See Antonio Cassese, 'Legal Considerations on the International Status of Jerusalem', 3 *Palestine Yearbook of International Law* (1986), pp. 13–39 at pp. 23–5; and Richard A. Falk and Burns H. Weston, 'The Relevance of International Law to Palestinian Rights in the West Bank and Gaza: In Defence of the Intifada', 32 *Harvard International Law Journal* (1991), pp. 129–57 at pp. 138–44 (both criticising the sovereignty vacuum theory).
136. See Doreen Ingrams (ed.), *Palestine Papers 1917–1922: Seeds of Conflict* (London: John Murray, 1972), pp. 98–9 ('It was agreed that they had no *claim*, whatever might be done for them on sentimental grounds; further, that all that was necessary was to make room for Zionists in Palestine, not that they should turn "it", that is the whole country, into their home ...').
137. See Eritrea v. Yemen, Award of the Arbitral Tribunal in the First Stage of the Proceedings (Territorial Sovereignty and the Scope of the Dispute), 3 October 1996, para. 125 ('It has not been established in these proceedings to the satisfaction of the Tribunal that the doctrine of reversion is part of international law'). This decision is available on the Court's website at the following link: http://www.pca-cpa.org/upload/files/EY%20Phase%20I.PDF (last retrieved 21 October 2008).
138. See legal status of Palestine after termination of the Mandate, from Sir O. Sargent, FO Minute, 14 May 1948, to UK delegation in New York, and Washington (prepared by FO Legal Advisers), FO 371/68664 Palestine, Eastern, 1948, para. 7.
139. Ibid. ('Its theoretical sovereignty will probably lie in the people of Palestine but it will be latent and there will certainly be no international entity recognised as a sovereign state or state in or comprising Palestine').
140. Ibid., para. 9 (a).

141. See Henry Cattan, 'Recollections on the United Nations Resolution to Partition Palestine', 4 *Palestine Yearbook of International Law* (1987–88), pp. 260–4.
142. See the Arab Higher Committee's responses to a letter submitted from the President of the UN Security Council, which asked, among other things, whether they were exercising political authority in Palestine. They claimed they were. See UN Doc. A/775, 24 May 1948.
143. The situation was summed up by a contemporary Palestinian historian in the following words: 'Arab Palestine was crumbling, and the implications of the absence of a single Palestinian national authority that could have raised and organized forces to defend it were now acutely clear: as individual cities, towns, and villages, most often defended by their own inhabitants with scarce help from outside, fell to the well-organized, centralized forces of a state that had not yet been declared.' See Rashid Khalidi, *The Iron Cage: The Story of the Palestinian Struggle for Statehood* (Boston: Beacon Press, 2006), p. 134.
144. Although the Arab Higher Committee claimed otherwise, see *supra* note 142.
145. See Benny Morris, *Righteous Victims*, *supra* note 75 at pp. 204–5 (making the link between the US support for Trusteeship and Haganah's offensive in late March 1948).
146. See Morris, *1948: A History*, *supra* note 50 at p. 115.
147. See Evan M. Wilson, *Decision on Palestine: How the US Came to Recognise Israel* (Stanford: Hoover Institution Press, Stanford University, 1979), p. 140 citing John H. Davis, *The Evasive Peace: A Study of the Zionist–Arab Problem* (London: John Murray, 1968), p. 58 and Erskine Childers, 'The Other Exodus', *The Spectator* (London), 12 May 1961.
148. See 'Dangers in Palestine: Effects of US Decision', *The Times*, 22 March 1948, p. 4, col. D and 'Jewish Agency Threat: A Hebrew Republic', *The Times*, 23 March 1948, p. 3, col. D. See also, note of a meeting in Lake Success, 20 April 1948 in The War of 1948, UN Assembly, FO 115/4376 (Mr Creech-Jones noting that 'there seemed to be little doubt that the Jews would proclaim a Hebrew state on 16 May').
149. Morris, *Righteous Victims*, *supra* note 75, p. 205.
150. Ibid. ('... at the beginning of April, the first major injection of arms reached the Haganah, from Czechoslovakia – some 4,700 rifles, 240 machine guns, and 5 million rounds of ammunition').
151. See Pappé, *Ethnic Cleansing*, *supra* note 53, p. 48. The quote is taken from a speech reproduced in a book authored by Ben-Gurion called *In the Battle* (Tel Aviv: Am Oved, 1949), pp. 255–72 which is published in Hebrew. The passage was translated by Pappé.
152. Ben-Gurion, *Behilahem Yisrael* [As Israel Fought], (Tel Aviv: Mapai Press, 1952), pp. 86–7, cited in Masalha, *Expulsion of the Palestinians*, *supra* note 20, p. 181.
153. Ben-Gurion, *War Diary*, Vol. 1, entry dated 7 February 1948, pp. 210–11, cited in Masalha, ibid., pp. 180–1.
154. See Pappé, *Ethnic Cleansing*, *supra* note 53 at pp. 86–126. See also, Khalidi, 'Plan Dalet: Master Plan', *supra* note 20, pp. 4–33; and Khalidi, *Why Did the Palestinians Leave?*, *supra* note 20, p. 11. There were several other military operations which composed Plan Dalet such as Yiftach, Jaffa, Harel, Jebusi, Maccabi and Pitchfork. For a semi-official Israeli account of these various military operations see Lt. Colonel Netanel Lorch, *The Edge of the Sword: Israel's War of Independence, 1947–1949* (New York: G.P. Putnam's Sons, 1961), pp. 87–137.
155. See Khalidi, 'Plan Dalet: Master Plan', ibid. and Chronology of Events in Palestine, *Middle East Journal*, *supra* note 60.
156. See the eye-witness account of the massacre by the Chief delegate of the International Committee of the Red Cross who visited the scene, Jacques de Reynier, in Jacques de Reynier, *A Jérusalem un Drapeau flottait sur la ligne de Feu* (Neuchatel, Switzerland: Editions de la Bacconière, 1950), pp. 69–77, 213. It is now thought that the number killed in that massacre is less, at some 100–150 people.
157. See Michael Palumbo, *The Palestinian Catastrophe*, *supra* note 62 at pp. 47–57, at p. 55 citing UN Archives (New York) 13/3/1/0 ('On 20 April, the British government informed

the United Nations Palestine Commission that the assault in Deir Yassin had been launched by the Irgun and the Stern Gang "with the knowledge of the Haganah"').

158. Morris, *Righteous Victims*, *supra* note 75 at p. 208 (footnotes omitted).
159. See Dominique Lapierre and Larry Collins, *O Jerusalem!* (London: Weidenfeld & Nicolson, 1972), p. 276, note with asterisk.
160. See Samih K. Farsoun and Naseer H. Aruri, *Palestine and the Palestinians: A Social and Political History* (Boulder: Westview Press, 2006), pp. 113–14.
161. See Sayigh, *The Palestinians*, *supra* note 68 at p. 77.
162. Situation in Palestine: Terrorist Activity and Fighting between Jews and Arabs. Palestine Outrages, Deir Yassin Massacre, 15 April 1948, FO 371/68504.
163. Pappé, *Ethnic Cleansing*, *supra* note 53, pp. 90–1 and Morris, *Righteous Victims*, *supra* note 75 at pp. 208–9.
164. For a very comprehensive list of Zionist attacks on Arabs from January to September 1948 with reference to documents in the British National Archives, see Issa Nakhleh, *Encyclopaedia of the Palestine Problem*, Vol. I (New York: Intercontinental Books, 1991), pp. 162–230.
165. See Eric Downton, '200 Killed by Jews in Village Fight: 100 Victims were Women and Children: Irgun-Stern Group Thrust in Palestine', *The Scotsman*, 10 April 1948, p. 15.
166. All these facts are recounted in the Chronology of Events in Palestine, *Middle East Journal*, *supra* note 60 at pp. 215–21 and 329–32.
167. See *Jewish Atrocities in the Holy Land: Memorandum to the United Nations Delegations submitted by the Arab Higher Committee Delegation for Palestine*, 4512 Empire State Building, New York, N.Y., 20 July 1948, p. 4. This is reproduced in Memoranda on Palestine, FO 371/68577. It was accompanied by a minute written by Lance Rinkell, a Foreign Office official. He wrote: 'The document on Jewish atrocities was circulated as UN document S. 925, although probably exaggerated, makes very unpleasant reading. Undoubtedly, from what we know of Jewish extremist organizations, contains a great deal of truth.'
168. See 'Women Escape from Burning Village', *Manchester Guardian*, 12 April 1948, p. 5.
169. See 'Jews Claim a Victory: Arab Guns Captured', *Manchester Guardian*, 16 April 1948, p. 5.
170. See *Jewish Atrocities in the Holy Land*, *supra* note 167, p. 10.
171. See Pappé, *Ethnic Cleansing*, *supra* note 53, at pp. 92–6 and Morris, *The Birth*, *supra* note 20, at pp. 186–211.
172. See 'Jews Gain Control of Haifa', *Manchester Guardian*, 22 April 1948, p. 5.
173. See Gilmour, *Dispossessed*, *supra* note 66 at p. 67 citing *Palestine Post*, 23 April 1948.
174. See Situation, Outrages, Jaffa Incident, CO 537/3861, Inward Telegram from Gen. Sir A. Cunningham, 2 May 1948, to S of S + repeated to Washington. Most immediate. No. 1232. Secret.
175. See *The Memoirs of Field-Marshall The Viscount Montgomery of Alamein, K.G.* (Glasgow: William Collins Sons & Co., Fontana paperback, 1960), p. 480 ('The three main areas which we decided to hold until 15th May were Jerusalem, Jaffa and Haifa').
176. Ibid., pp. 480–2.
177. See Jon Kimche, 'Deir Yassin and Jaffa', in Walid Khalidi, *From Haven to Conquest: Readings in Zionism and the Palestine Problem until 1948* (Beirut: Institute for Palestine Studies, 1971), pp. 775–8 at p. 778.
178. See *Jewish Atrocities in the Holy Land*, *supra* note 167, p. 4.
179. Ibid.
180. See Chronology of Events in Palestine, *Middle East Journal*, *supra* note 60.
181. See Khalidi, 'Plan Dalet: Master Plan', *supra* note 20, p. 18.
182. This document was found in the private papers of Aharon Cohen, Director of Mapam in the Hashomer Hatza'ir Archive in Israel. It is officially entitled: 'The Emigration of the Arabs of Palestine in the period 1/12/1947 – 1/6/1948 (t'nu'at ha'hagira shel arvi' yei eretz yisrael ba't' kufa 1/12/1947 – 1/6/1948) and is reproduced and analysed by Benny Morris in 'The Causes and Character of the Arab Exodus from Palestine: The Israel Defence Forces

Intelligence Service Analysis of June 1948', in Benny Morris, *1948 and After: Israel and the Palestinians* (Oxford: Clarendon Press, 1990), pp. 69–88 at p. 72.

183. Ibid., p. 74, (the inserted words in brackets are by Morris).
184. Ibid.
185. Ibid., p. 75.
186. Ibid., p. 76. As Christopher Hitchens has noted: 'However apprehensive the authors of the report may have been on this score, their own evidence shows that fully 72 per cent of the Palestinian refugees in this crucial period were expelled by Israeli military force. This admission by the IDF deserves, perhaps, more publicity than it has yet received.' Hitchens wrote this in 1988. Yet it is just as poignant today. See Christopher Hitchens, 'Broadcasts', in Edward W. Said and Christopher Hitchens (eds), *Blaming the Victims: Spurious Scholarship and the Palestinian Question* (New York: Verso, 1988), pp. 73–83 at p. 74.
187. See Benny Morris, 'Operation Dani and the Palestinian Exodus from Lydda and Ramle in 1948', 40 *The Middle East Journal* (Winter 1986), pp. 82–109. See also Pappé, *Ethnic Cleansing*, *supra* note 53 at pp. 166–70.
188. See Morris, ibid., p. 86.
189. Ibid., p. 87.
190. Ibid., p. 91 citing Michael Bar-Zohar, *Ben-Gurion* (Tel Aviv: Am Oved, 1977), Vol. II, p. 775. Bar-Zohar cites an interview with Yitzhak Rabin as his source.
191. See Peretz Kidron, 'Truth Whereby Nations Live', in Said and Hitchens, *Blaming the Victims*, *supra* note 186 at pp. 90–3. Kidron was Rabin's ghost writer who had exclusive access to his original notes to write his memoirs. He was also hired as the ghost writer for another war veteran who also partook in the same operation. Both stories were corroborated by the events, dates, and descriptions, which were almost identical.
192. Ibid., p. 92.
193. Morris cites a broadcast from Ramallah Radio, whose text was transmitted to the Foreign Office in London by the British Consul-General in Jerusalem, Sir Hugh Dow: 'Everywhere children and tiny babies and worn-out women and old men, have come in, wave after wave, into this town. Seventy thousand people into a township of ten thousand ... The lucky ones with camels and crowded trucks, the unlucky ones, bleeding, and a women crying out for news of her only child that escaped. People have brought away nothing but blankets. They have seen terrible and unforgettable things in their streets ... Every roadside, the shade of every tree, every corner of every house and hotel is crowded with makeshift families ... The smell is beginning to be bad in so many places ... There won't be a drop of water left in Ramallah in three days.' Morris, 'Operation Dani', *supra* note 187 at pp. 99–100, citing FO 371/68578, Sir H. Dow (Jerusalem) to H. Beeley (London), 29 July 1948.
194. Ibid., p. 96, citing KMA-PA 141–516, Dani HQ to General Staff/Operations, 13 July 1948.
195. Cited from Morris, *The Birth Revisited*, *supra* note 59, p. 429 (parenthesis in original).
196. Morris, ibid. (parenthesis in original).
197. Ibid., p. 425.
198. See Eugene L. Rogan, 'Jordan and 1948: The Persistence of an Official History', in Rogan and Shlaim, *The War for Palestine*, *supra* note 80, pp. 104–24 at pp. 113–14.
199. See Glubb, *A Soldier*, *supra* note 48 at pp. 163–4 (explaining how villagers threw stones at the Arab Legion calling them traitors who were 'worse than the Jews').
200. Morris, *The Birth Revisited*, *supra* note 59 at p. 429 citing Ben-Gurion's diary.
201. Ibid.
202. Ibid., p. 426 citing a book published in Hebrew by Allon Kadish, Avraham Sela and Arnon Golan, *The Conquest of Lydda, July 1948* (Tel Aviv: Haganah Archives, Ministry of Defence Press, 2000), pp. 143–4.
203. See *To Jerusalem: Folke Bernadotte*, trans. from the Swedish by Joan Bulman (London: Hodder & Stoughton, 1951), p. 200.

204. See 'Jews Capture Nazareth: Population Flees', *Manchester Guardian*, 17 July 1948, p. 5.
205. See Nafez Nazzal, *The Palestinian Exodus from Galilee 1948* (Beirut: Institute of Palestine Studies, 1978), at p. 95 citing in note 123, Muhammad Talib Hammad, Muhammed Khalid al-Salih, and Umm Shahadah al-Salih, interviewed at 'Ain al-Hilwah camp, Sidon, Lebanon, March 23 and 24, 1973, who recalled the names of 25 of the 70 men who were blindfolded and shot to death.
206. See Gilmour, *Dispossessed*, *supra* note 66 at p. 68 citing letters of 8 November 1948 from Eyal Kafkafi, 'A Ghetto Attitude in the Jewish State', *Davar*, 6 September 1979.
207. See Saleh Abdel Jawad, 'Zionist Massacres: The Creation of the Palestinian Refugee Problem in the 1948 War', in Eyal Benvenisti, Chaim Gans and Sari Hanafi (eds), *Israel and the Palestinian Refugees* (Heidelberg: Springer, in association with Max-Planck-Institut für ausländisches öffentliches Recht und Völkerrecht, 2007), pp. 59–127 at pp. 90–1, citing M.A.S. Hudeib, *Al-Dawayimah Village*, 1985; A. 'Atharbeh, *Al-Dawayimah*, Birzeit Research Center, The Palestinian Destroyed Villages, 21 April 1997, 215–16; 'Olive Season Massacres: This is how they killed the people in al-Dawayima Mosque during the Friday prayer', *Sawtt al-Haq wa-al Huriya*, 21 October 1994, p. 9.
208. United Nations Conciliation Commission for Palestine Technical Committee. Report Submitted by the Arab Refugee Congress of Ramallah. The Dawaymeh Massacre. UN Doc. Restricted. Com.Tech. /W.3 14 June 1949.
209. See Erskine Childers, 'The Other Exodus', *The Spectator* (London), 12 May 1961. This is reprinted in Walter Laqueur (ed.), *The Israel/Arab Reader: A Documentary History of the Middle East Conflict* (London: Weidenfeld & Nicolson, 1968), pp. 143–51 at p. 146 ('There was not a single order, or appeal, or suggestion about the evacuation from Palestine from any Arab radio station, inside or outside Palestine, in 1948. There is repeated monitored record of Arab appeals, even flat orders, to the civilians of Palestine to stay put'). See further, 'The Spectator Correspondence', reprinted in 18 *Journal of Palestine Studies* (1988), pp. 51–70 (with contributions from Hedley V. Cooke, Jon Kimche, Erskine B. Childers, Walid Khalidi, Edward Atiyah and David Cairns about the controversy over whether or not the Arabs ordered Palestine's Arabs to flee or to stay put during the conflict in 1948). See also, Khalidi, 'Plan Dalet: Master Plan', *supra* note 20 at p. 6 (examining the files of the BBC Cyprus listening post and the CIA-sponsored Foreign Broadcast Information Service which covered local radios and newspapers).
210. See Simha Flapan, 'The Palestinian Exodus of 1948', 16 *Journal of Palestine Studies* (1987), pp. 3–26 at p. 5.
211. Ibid., p. 5. On the alleged broadcasts see also Hitchens 'Broadcasts' in Said and Hitchens (eds), *Blaming the Victims*, *supra* note 186 at pp. 75–83, concluding that: 'Even though nobody has ever testified to having heard them, and even though no record of their transmission has ever been found, we shall hear of these orders and broadcasts again and again.'
212. See Gilmour, *Dispossessed*, *supra* note 66 at p. 67.
213. See Sayigh, *From Peasants to Revolutionaries*, *supra* note 68, p. 64.
214. See Request for a statement of answers correcting inaccurate Jewish political propaganda (for Mr Mayhew), FO Minutes from Mr Reddaway, 19 January 1949, FO 371/75367.
215. See text of speech delivered by Mr Henry Cattan, Member of the Palestine Arab Delegation, before the Political Committee on Nov 22nd. FO 371/68599, pp. 6–7. This is also reproduced in the UN archives as Two Hundred and Seventh Meeting, Held at the Palais de Chaillot, Paris, on Monday, 22 November 1948, at 3 pm, UN Doc. A/648, pp. 697–704.
216. Ibid. The last part of his speech was a critique of the partition of Palestine.
217. Ibid. ('Unfortunately, the method of their presentation, the length of his speech, and the feelings of bitterness and near hysteria lying behind it will have detracted from whatever small effect it might ever have had on that singularly unimpressionable audience the United Nations General Assembly').

218. See Mordechai Bar-on, 'Remembering 1948: Personal Recollections, Collective Memory, and the Search for What Really Happened', in Benny Morris (ed.), *Making Israel* (Ann Arbor: The University of Michigan Press, 2007), pp. 29–46 at p. 43.
219. See 'Israelis Destroy Arab Village: UN Decision Flouted', *Manchester Guardian*, 16 September 1949, p. 7.
220. See John B. Quigley, 'Displaced Palestinians and a Right of Return', 39 *Harvard International Law Journal* (1998), pp. 171–229, at p. 184 and sources cited therein.
221. Ibid.
222. See, generally, Pappé, *Ethnic Cleansing*, *supra* note 53.
223. As a former deputy mayor of Jerusalem conceded, the expulsions which took place in 1948 came 'dangerously close to fitting the definition of "ethnic cleansing"'. See Benvenisti, *Sacred Landscape*, *supra* note 101 at p. 145.
224. See the letter from President Roosevelt to King of Saudi Arabia, 5 April 1945, in 8 *Foreign Relations of the United States* 1945 (Washington, DC: United States Government Printing Office, 1969), p. 698.
225. See the letter from President Truman to the King of Saudi Arabia, 24 January 1947, in 5 *Foreign Relations of the United States* 1947 (Washington, DC: US Government Printing Office, 1971), pp. 1011–14 at pp. 1012–13.
226. Ibid., p. 1013.
227. See Hersch Lauterpacht (ed.), *International Law: A Treatise by L. Oppenheim, Vol. II, Disputes, War and Neutrality* (London: Longmans, 1944), p. 277 ('... in the eighteenth century it became a universally recognized customary rule of the Law of Nations that private enemy individuals shall not be killed or attacked'), and at p. 320 ('... in the nineteenth century it became a universally recognised rule of international law that all useless and wanton destruction of enemy property, be it public or private, was absolutely prohibited ...').
228. See G.F. Von Martens, *A Compendium of the Law of Nations*, trans. William Cobbett (London: Cobbett & Morgan, 1802), pp. 289–90.
229. See William Oke Manning, *Commentaries on the Law of Nations*, revised by Sheldon Amos (Cambridge: Macmillan, 1895), pp. 204–5.
230. See *The Collected Papers of John Westlake on Public International Law*, ed. L. Oppenheim (Cambridge: Cambridge University Press, 1914), p. 251.
231. See e.g. *The War Office: Manual of Military Law, 1929*, reprinted December 1939, (London: His Majesty's Stationery Office, 1943), p. 330 and Appendix 22, p. 414 (relations between the British Military Forces and the Civil Population in enemy country in time of war). This is also reproduced in the Australian edition of the *Manual of Military Law 1941* (Canberra: Commonwealth Government Printer, 1941), p. 275 and p. 356. See also, Department of the Army, *US Field Manual, The Law of Land Warfare, 1956*, p. 106.
232. See Von Martens, *Compendium of the Law of Nations*, *supra* note 228, pp. 293–4, footnote ('It has been, and is yet, a dispute, whether the modern law of nations permits the removal of the subjects of conquered countries or provinces. Their sovereign never fails to complain of it' citing Moser, *Versuch*, v.9, p. 1. p. 299).
233. See The Trial of German Major War Criminals: Proceedings of the International Military Tribunal sitting at Nuremberg, Germany, especially Part 22, judgment, 22nd August, 1946 to 31st August, 1946, 30th September, 1946 and 1st October, 1946 (London: published under the authority of H.M. Attorney-General by His Majesty's Stationery Office, 1950); and The Tokyo Major War Crimes Trial: The Judgment, Separate Opinions, Proceedings in Chambers, Appeals and Reviews of the International Military Tribunal for the Far East, Annotated, Compiled and Edited by R. John Pritchard, A Collection in 124 Volumes (New York: The Edwin Mellon Press, 1998). The Charters of the Tribunals both listed deportations as being a crime against humanity.
234. Ibid., Trial of German Major War Criminals, Part 22, judgment, pp. 456–7.
235. See John H.E. Fried, 'Transfer of Civilian Manpower from Occupied Territory', 40 *American Journal of International Law* (1946), pp. 307–9 ('Deportations of civilians

from such territories had been so alien to modern warfare that it was not even discussed at the Hague Conferences').

236. This reflected the opinion of the majority. See *Carnegie Endowment for International Peace, Division of International Law, Pamphlet No. 32, Violation of the Laws and Customs of War, Reports of Majority and Dissenting Reports of American and Japanese Members of the Commission of Responsibilities, Conference of Paris, 1919* (Oxford: Clarendon Press, 1919), p. 18. The Commission's composition included, amongst others, Robert Lansing, James Brown Scott, Gordon Hewart, Ernest Pollock, W.F. Massey, André Tardieu, F. Larnaude, Mr Rolin-Jaequemyns, and N. Politis. A. de Lapradelle also assisted the commission. In the Annex, they list at p. 35 examples of mass deportations in France, Greece, Italy, Roumania and Serbia.
237. See The Trial of German Major War Criminals, *supra* note 233 at p. 467. The judgment is also reproduced in 41 *American Journal of International Law* (1947) at pp. 248–9 ('by 1939 these rules laid down in the Convention were recognized by all civilized nations, and were regarded as being declaratory of the laws and customs of war ...'). See also, the Cessation of vessels and tugs for navigation on the Danube case, 1 *Reports of International Arbitral Awards* (1921) at p. 104.
238. See The Tokyo Major War Crimes Trial: The Judgment, Vol. 101, *supra* note 233 at p. 48, 491 (this is the page number from the original court transcript).
239. See the preamble to Convention (IV) respecting the Laws and Customs of War on Land and its annex: Regulations concerning the Laws and Customs of War on Land. The Hague, 18 October 1907, reproduced in Clive Parry (ed.), 205 *The Consolidated Treaty Series* (1907), pp. 277–98.
240. See e.g. the comments regarding Article 49 (1) of Geneva Convention IV by Jean S. Pictet, *Commentary: IV Geneva Convention Relative to the Protection of Civilian Persons in Time of War* (Geneva: International Committee of the Red Cross, 1958) at p. 279 ('The Hague Regulations do not refer to the question of deportations; this was probably because the practice of deporting persons was regarded at the beginning of this century as falling into abeyance. The events of the last few years have, however, made it necessary to make more detailed provisions on this point which may be regarded today as having been embodied in international law'). On the prohibition of pillage and reprisals see Pictet, ibid., pp. 226–7.
241. See Palestine and British Treaties with Egypt, Iraq and Transjordan: Request for Legal Advice, 9–15 November 1948, FO 371/68597 (emphasis added).
242. See *In re* Weizsaecker and Others (Ministries Trial), United States Military Tribunal at Nuremberg, 14 April 1949, in H. Lauterpacht (ed.), 16 *Annual Digest and Reports of Public International Law Cases 1949* (London: Butterworth & Co., 1955), pp. 344–62.
243. Ibid., p. 346.
244. Ibid., p. 351 (emphasis added).
245. See *In re* Von Leeb and Others (German High Command Trial), United States Military Tribunal at Nuremberg, Germany, 28 October 1948, in H. Lauterpacht (ed.), 15 *Annual Digest and Reports of Public International Law Cases 1948* (London: Butterworth & Co., 1953), pp. 376–98.
246. Ibid., p. 393.
247. Ibid.
248. See *Law Reports of Trials of War Criminals Selected and Prepared by the United Nations War Crimes Commission*, Vols I–XV (London: Published for the United Nations War Crimes Commission by His Majesty's Stationery Office, 1948).
249. Trial of Robert Wagner, 23 April – 3 May 1946, ibid., Vol. III, pp. 23–55.
250. Trial of Franz Holstein, 3 February 1947, ibid., Vol. VIII, pp. 22–33 at p. 27.
251. Trial of Edward Milch, 20 December 1946 – 17 April 1947, ibid., Vol. VI, pp. 27–66.
252. Ibid., p. 45.
253. Ibid., p. 46.
254. Ibid.
255. Ibid.

256. The Krupp Trial, 17 November 1947 – 30 June 1948, ibid., Vol. X, pp. 69–181.
257. Ibid., p. 144.
258. Ibid., Vol. XV, p. 119, emphasis added.
259. The Trial of Gauleiter Artur Greiser, 21 June – 7 July, 1946, ibid., Vol. XIII, pp. 70–117.
260. Ibid., p. 86.
261. See Articles 46 and 47 of the Convention (IV) respecting the Laws and Customs of War on Land and its annex: Regulations concerning the Laws and Customs of War on Land. The Hague, 18 October 1907, reproduced in Clive Parry (ed.), 205 *The Consolidated Treaty Series* (1907), pp. 277–98.
262. See 2 *Trial of the Major War Criminals before the International Military Tribunal*, Nuremberg, 14 November – 1 October 1946, (published at Nuremberg, Germany, 1947), p. 49 (emphasis added).
263. Quote reproduced from Tom Segev, *The First Israelis* (New York: The Free Press, 1986), p. 26, note at the bottom of the page citing Aharon Cizling, Minister of Agriculture, Minutes of Cabinet Meeting, 17 November 1948, Kibbutz Meuhad Archive, Section 9, Container 9, File 3.
264. Ibid., pp. 27–8, citing Order of Tsvi Ayalon, 6 July 1948, Kibbutz Meuhad Archive (A. Cizling), Section 9, Container 9, File 1.
265. Aharon Cohen, the director during the war of the Mapam Party, was of the opinion that 'the evacuation/clearing out of Arab villages is not always done out of military necessity'. See Memorandum entitled 'Our Arab Policy during the War', in Giv'at Haviva, Hashomer Hatza'ir Archives, 10.10.95 (4), dated 10 May 1948 and addressed to Mapam's Political Committee. This document is cited in Masalha, *Expulsion of the Palestinians*, *supra* note 20 at p. 181.

8 THE PALESTINIAN REFUGEES

1. This includes Palestinians displaced in 1967. See *UNHCR Statistical Yearbook 2006: Trends in Displacement, Protection and Solutions* (Geneva: UNHCR, 2007), p. 29 ('Afghanistan continued to be the leading country of origin of refugees, excluding the 4.4. million Palestinians who fall under the mandate of UNRWA').
2. Article 1 (d) of the 1951 UN Refugee Convention provides that:

   This Convention shall not apply to persons who are at present receiving from organs or agencies of the United Nations other than the United Nations High Commissioner for Refugee protection or assistance.

   When such protection or assistance has ceased for any reason; without the position of such persons being definitely settled in accordance with the relevant resolutions adopted by the General Assembly of the United Nations, these persons shall *ipso facto* be entitled to the benefits of this Convention.

   It has been argued that the drafters of the 1951 Convention intended the word 'protection' in Article 1 (d) to be a reference to the UN Conciliation Commission on Palestine (UNCCP) and therefore the language 'protection or assistance' in that article refers both to the UNCCP as providing protection and UNRWA as providing assistance. Since the UNCCP is now defunct, an argument could be advanced that the UNHCR should take over responsibility for Palestinian refugee protection for those who would fall within the scope of its mandate. See Susan M. Akram and Terry Rempel, 'Recommendations for Durable Solutions for Palestinian Refugees: A Challenge to the Oslo Framework', 11 *Palestine Yearbook of International Law* (2000–01), pp. 1–71.
3. See Article 1 (a) 2 of the 1951 UN Refugee Convention. Note that the definition's temporal stipulation which provided that it only applied to European refugees prior to 1951, was relaxed by a Protocol concluded in 1967 which has been widely acceded to.

4. The use of the word 'refugee' also does not refer to those Palestinians who settled abroad but who are prevented from returning to the land of their birth. This would apply, for instance, to those Palestinians who resided in countries which do not maintain diplomatic relations with Israel. For instance my grandfather always wanted to return to Palestine before his death in 1980 but was unable to do so because his country of residence, Sudan, does not have diplomatic relations with Israel. When my grandparents first moved to the Sudan it was a British colony, so there were no problems affecting their freedom of movement. It was only after 1967, when Bethlehem was occupied by the Israeli Army that they could not go back to see their family. When my grandmother became a British national she was able to visit Israel in 1996, during the peace process, but then only as a tourist. Many other Palestinians face similar problems.
5. See the Book of Ezra 1: The Return from Exile which speaks of the Decree of Cyrus in chapter 1; the census of the inhabitants who were to return in chapter 2; and the restoration of the Altar and the rebuilding of the Temple in chapter 3, in *The New American Bible*, Translated from the Original Languages with Critical Use of All the Ancient Sources by members of the Catholic Biblical Association of America (New York: Thomas Nelson, 1970), pp. 408–10. According to Cecil Roth, who was a leading scholar of Jewish history and editor-in-chief of *Encyclopaedia Judaica*, the returning exiles numbered 400,000. See Cecil Roth, *A History of the Jews: From the Earliest Times Through the Six Day War* (New York: Shocken Books, 1970), p. 58.
6. See Hirad Abtahi, 'Reflections on the Ambiguous Universality of Human Rights: Cyrus the Great's Proclamation as a Challenge to the Athenian Democracy's Perceived Monopoly on Human Rights', in Hirad Abtahi and Gideon Boas (eds), *The Dynamics of International Criminal Justice: Essays in Honour of Sir Richard May* (Leiden: Martinus Nijhoff Publishers, 2006), pp. 1–38, writing at p. 16, 'after his capture of Babylon, Cyrus liberated the displaced populations. Not only did he permit them to return to their homelands, he encouraged them to do so, sometimes even financing this return, as in the Jewish Diaspora's case.'
7. Ibid., pp. 25–6.
8. See the collection of essays in Eyal Benvenisti, Chaim Gans and Sari Hanafi (eds), *Israel and the Palestine Refugees* (Heidelberg: Springer, in association with Max-Planck-Institut für ausländisches öffentliches Recht und Völkerrecht, 2007).
9. John Quigley assesses most of these arguments in his comprehensive article 'Displaced Palestinians and a Right of Return', 39 *Harvard International Law Journal* (1998), pp. 171–229. For differing viewpoints on the right of return see the articles by Yaffa Zilbershats (arguing against a right of return in international law) and Gail J. Boling (arguing in its favour) in Benvenisti, Gans and Hanafi, *Israel and the Palestine Refugees*, *supra* note 8 at pp. 191–251. See also, Gail J. Boling, *The 1948 Palestinian Refugee and the Individual Right of Return: An International Law Analysis* (Bethlehem: Badil Resource Centre, 2001), and the authorities cited therein. This document is available online at http://www.badil.org/Publications/Legal_Papers/RoR48.pdf (last retrieved 24 October 2008). See further, Kathleen Lawand, 'The Right to Return of Palestinians in International Law', 8 *International Journal of Refugee Law* (1996), pp. 532–68.
10. The Universal Declaration of Human Rights was adopted and proclaimed by the UN General Assembly in resolution 217 A (III) on 10 December 1948, the day before that same body passed UN General Assembly resolution 194 (III) affirming a Palestinian right of return.
11. See e.g. UN General Assembly resolution 62/102, 10 January 2008 which notes 'with regret that repatriation or compensation of the refugees, as provided for in paragraph 11 of General Assembly resolution 194 (III), has not yet been effected, and that, therefore, the situation of the Palestine refugees continues to be a matter of grave concern and the Palestine refugees continue to require assistance to meet basic health, education and living needs'. See also, UN General Assembly resolution 62/103, 10 January 2008 which 'reaffirms the right of all persons displaced as a result of the June 1967 and subsequent

hostilities to return to their homes or former places of residence in the territories occupied by Israel since 1967'.

12. A very small number of Arabs were allowed to return under family reunification schemes. For statistics on Jewish refugee displacement during the 1948 war see Final Report of the UN Economic Survey Mission for the Middle East (January 1950) and United Nations Conciliation Commission for Palestine Final Report of the Economic Survey Mission for the Middle East, Part 1. The Final Report and Appendices (Lake Success, New York: United Nations), UN Doc. A/AC.25/6, 28 December 1949, p. 18.
13. See the Law of Return 5710–1950; Law of Return (Amendment 5714–1954); and Law of Return (Amendment No. 2) 5730–1970. These laws can be read in English in *The Laws of the State of Israel* (usually referred to by its acronym, LSI). As Gouldman notes: 'There can thus be no doubt that it is easier for a Jew than a non-Jew to acquire Israel nationality, and the Nationality Law is therefore open to the charge that it discriminates, on ethnic grounds, in favour of Jews.' See M.D. Gouldman, *Israel Nationality Law* (Jerusalem: The Hebrew University of Jerusalem, 1970), p. 67.
14. See Benny Morris, 'In '48, Israel did what it had to do', *LA Times*, 26 January 2004.
15. See Telegram from British Delegate, Middle East Office (Cairo) to Foreign Office, 28 July 1948, Palestine Arab Refugees, 1948, FO 371/68576.
16. See The Ambassador in Iraq (Crocker) to the Secretary of State, Baghdad, 10 May 1949, 6 *Foreign Relations of the United States: The Near East, South Asia and Africa* (Washington: US Government Printing Office, 1977), p. 995.
17. See Kirsten E. Schulze, *The Jews of Lebanon: Between Coexistence and Conflict* (second edition, Sussex Academic Press, forthcoming 2009). The author very kindly agreed to share her manuscript with me prior to publication.
18. Ibid., (writing that 'the Lebanese Jewish community increased rather than decreased after 1948 – so much so that it caused many laments in the Jewish Agency in Jerusalem which had been trying to motivate Lebanese Jews to move to Israel to no avail').
19. Ibid. ('the Jewish community in Lebanon grew after 1948 and it was not until the 1967 Arab–Israel war and the Lebanese civil war of 1975 that the community started to migrate and emigrate').
20. See Tudor Parfitt, *The Road to Redemption: The Jews of Yemen 1900–1950* (Leiden: E.J. Brill, 1996) at p. 283. Parfitt writes at p. 284 that the reason for their departure was down to economic reasons, famine, disease, growing political persecution and increased public hostility (due to Zionism), the state of anarchy after the assassination of Imam Yahya, a desire to be reunited with family members who had already emigrated to Palestine during the mandatory years, incitement and encouragement to leave from agents and emissaries of the Jewish Agency which played on religious sensibilities, promises that their passage would be paid by Israel and a sense that the land of Israel 'would be a veritable Eldorado'. See further, Reuben Aroni, *Jewish Emigration from the Yemen 1951–98: Carpet Without Magic* (Richmond: Curzon Press, 2001) who writes at pp. 133–4 that many Yemeni Jews initially regretted the move to Israel.
21. See Abbas Shiblak, *Iraqi Jews: A History of Mass Exodus* (London: Saqi Books, 2005), pp. 151–65.
22. See Joel Beinin, *The Dispersion of Egyptian Jewry: Culture, Politics, and the Formation of a Modern Diaspora* (Berkeley: University of California Press, 1998), p. 19.
23. Ibid., p. 87.
24. Ibid.
25. See Jan Abu Shakrah, 'Deconstructing the Link: Palestinian Refugees and Jewish Immigrants from Arab Countries', in Naseer Aruri (ed.), *Palestinian Refugees: The Right of Return* (London: Pluto Press, 2001), pp. 208–16 at p. 214.
26. See Beinin, *Dispersion of Egyptian Jewry*, *supra* note 22 at p. 21 ('Only a small minority of Jews were active Zionists, even after 1948 ... Most Jews who left Egypt after 1948, especially those with enough resources to have a choice, did not go to Israel').
27. See Island of Palmas (or Miangas) Arbitral Award, 4 April 1928, 22 *American Journal of International Law* (1928), p. 883.

28. See James Crawford, *The International Law Commission's Articles on State Responsibility: Introduction, Texts and Commentaries* (Cambridge: Cambridge University Press, 2002), p. 135.
29. On Potsdam and the Sudetenland Germans, see Alfred M. de Zayas, *Nemesis at Potsdam: The Anglo-Americans and the Expulsion of the Germans* (London: Routledge and Kegan Paul, 1979), pp. 85–9.
30. See UN General Assembly resolution 95 (1), 11 December 1946.
31. See UN General Assembly resolution 96 (1), 11 December 1946.
32. See Rosalyn Higgins, *Problems and Process: International Law and How We Use It* (Oxford: Clarendon Press, 1994), p. 29 ('The prohibition against genocide clearly pre-existed the Convention as a prohibition of customary international law').
33. Reservations to the Convention on Genocide, Advisory Opinion, ICJ Reports (1951), p. 15 at p. 23.
34. Corfu Channel case, judgment of 9 April 1949, ICJ Reports (1949), p. 4 at p. 22.
35. Legality of the Threat or Use of Nuclear Weapons, Advisory Opinion, ICJ Reports (1996), p. 226, at p. 257, para. 79.
36. As early as 1921, the International Committee of the Red Cross had prepared a preliminary draft Convention, the main provisions of which prohibited the deportation of the inhabitants of occupied countries and the execution of hostages and guaranteed the rights of civilians to exchange correspondence and receive relief. Civilians in enemy territory were to be allowed to return to their home country unless there were reasons of state security to prevent this; internees were to enjoy the same conditions as prisoners of war. However, the Committee's efforts did not meet with success because as the commentary to the Fourth Geneva Convention noted: 'In the state of general optimism which reigned at that time, various people of standing in official circles considered the moment a particularly inappropriate one to propose that Governments should draw up regulations governing the status of civilians in wartime; an initiative of that sort would, they felt, be regarded in international circles as almost equivalent to betraying the cause of peace.' In Tokyo, in 1934, a draft treaty was adopted by the International Red Cross Conference which was to have been submitted to a Diplomatic Conference convened by the Swiss Government. The Committee then arranged to hold the conference at the beginning of 1940 to formalise the text of the treaty, but by then war had broken out. In this connection it is noteworthy that Article 49 of Geneva Convention IV which prohibits mass forcible transfers and deportations was derived from the Tokyo Draft. See Jean S. Pictet (ed.), *Commentary to the Geneva Conventions of 12 August 1949, IV Geneva Convention Relative to the Protection of Civilian Persons in Time of War* (Geneva: International Committee of the Red Cross, 1958), pp. 4–5 and p. 278.
37. It will be recalled that the Martens Clause in the preamble to the IV Hague Regulation of 1907 provided that: 'Until a more complete code of the laws of war has been issued, the High Contracting Parties deem it expedient to declare that, in cases not included in the Regulations adopted by them, the inhabitants and the belligerents remain under the protection and the rule of the principles of the law of nations, as they result from the usages established among civilized peoples, from the laws of humanity, and the dictates of the public conscience.' See also, Part 1, Article 1 (2) of Protocol Additional to the Geneva Conventions of 12 August 1949, and relating to the Protection of Victims of International Armed Conflicts, (Protocol 1), 8 June 1977, which provides: 'In cases not covered by this Protocol or by other international agreements, civilians and combatants remain under the protection and authority of the principles of international law derived from established custom, from the principles of humanity and from dictates of public conscience.'
38. According to Article 6 (b) of the Nuremberg Statute, war crimes consist of 'violations of the laws or customs of war. Such violations shall include, but not be limited to, murder, ill-treatment or deportation to slave labour or for any other purpose of civilian population of or in occupied territory, murder or ill-treatment of prisoners of war or persons on the seas, killing of hostages, plunder of public or private property, wanton destruction of cities, towns or villages, or devastation not justified by military necessity.'

39. In the inter-war years in the context of debates on the effect of denationalisation decrees in Russia, Italy and Germany, it had been argued that the expulsion of a state's nationals or ex-nationals coupled with the refusal to receive them back violated international law. See John Fischer Williams, 'Denationalization', 8 *British Yearbook of International Law* (1927), p. 45 at p. 61 ('a state cannot sever the tie of nationality in such a way as to release itself from the international duty, owed to other states, of receiving back a person denationalized who has acquired no other nationality, should he be expelled as an alien by the state where he happens to be'); Hersch Lauterpacht, *The Function of Law in the International Community* (Oxford: Clarendon Press, 1933), p. 301 (describing it as an abuse of rights); and Paul Abdel, 'Denationalization', 5 *Modern Law Review* (1942), p. 57 at p. 64 (examining the various arguments).
40. See, however, Jochen Abr. Frowein, 'Potsdam Agreements on Germany (1945)', in Rudolf Bernhardt (ed.), *Encyclopedia of Public International Law*, Vol. 3 (Amsterdam: Elsevier, 1997), pp. 1087–92 at p. 1091 ('It is clear, however, that many of the measures agreed upon concerning the international status of Germany, the "administration" of German territory in contrast to occupation, and the transfer of German populations went far beyond what was recognised as legal in 1945 under the rules of belligerent occupation').
41. The so-called 'enemy state clauses' in Article 53 (in part) and Article 107 of the UN Charter have been described as 'anachronistic and obsolete' whose deletion 'is long overdue'. See Michael Wood, 'United States Charter, Enemy State Clauses', *Max Planck Encyclopedia of Public International Law*, available online at http://www.mpepil.com (last retrieved 24 October 2008).
42. See Eliyahu Tal, *Refugees Forever? Issues in the Palestinian–Israeli Conflict*, *The Jerusalem Post* (special supplement) with a foreword by the Chairman of the Board, David Radler. See especially the chapter entitled 'The Penalty of Aggression', where the author cites the Sudetenland 'precedent' to argue that there is no Palestinian right of return because unlike the Germans, the Palestinians 'refuse to accept the universal code that aggressors must pay for their acts'. This pamphlet is available online on the website of *The Jerusalem Post* at http://info.jpost.com/C003/Supplements/Refugees/ (last retrieved 24 October 2008).
43. See Bruno Simma (ed.), *The Charter of the United Nations: A Commentary*, Vol. II (Oxford: Oxford University Press, 2002), pp. 1089–90 (noting that mandate territories are included within the scope of Article 73).
44. See UN General Assembly resolution 194 (III), 11 December 1948.
45. See Donald Neff, 'US Policy and the Palestinian Refugees', 18 *Journal of Palestine Studies* (1988), pp. 96–111 at p. 107, citing Memorandum by William J. McWilliams, Assistant to the Director of the Executive Secretariat, 26 August 1949, 6 *Foreign Relations of the United States* (1949), p. 1332, p. 1389 and p. 1455. He also cites George McGhee, *Envoy to the Middle East: Adventures in Diplomacy* (New York: Harper & Row Publishers, 1983).
46. See Crawford, *The International Law Commission's Articles on State Responsibility*, *supra* note 28, p. 136.
47. See Gail J. Boling, 'Absentee's Property Laws and Israel's Confiscation of Palestinian Property: A Violation of UN General Assembly Resolution 194 and International Law', 11 *Palestine Yearbook of International Law* (2000–01), pp. 73–130; and Sabri Jiryis, 'Settler's Law: Seizure of Palestinian Lands', 2 *Palestine Yearbook of International Law* (2005), pp. 17–36.
48. See Progress Report of the United Nations Mediator on Palestine submitted to the Secretary-General for Transmission to the Members of the United Nations, UN Doc. A/648, 16 September 1948, Part III, Assistance to Refugees, VI, Conclusions, 1, (d) (emphasis added).
49. See Gail J. Boling, 'The Question of "Timing" in Evaluating Israel's Duty under International Law to Repatriate the 1948 Palestinian Refugees', in Benvenisti, Gans and Hanafi, *Israel and the Palestine Refugees*, *supra* note 8 at p. 250 ('... if Israel's actions in 1948 violated at least one viable, existing customary norm of international law in 1948, that is sufficient basis to start the clock running on a continuing violation. The violation

of one valid existing norm will serve to *ground* the claim of illegality. However, since the violation is a continuing and ongoing one, as newly emerging norms crystallise and as treaty obligations are undertaken by the state concerned, such "subsequent" norms and treaty obligations will serve to buttress and strengthen the claim of illegality over time' – emphasis in original).

50. Official Records of the Third Session of the General Assembly, Part 1, Social, Humanitarian and Cultural Questions, Third Committee, Summary Records of Meetings, 21 September – 8 December 1948.
51. Ibid., pp. 194, 206, 277, 289, 473 and 485.
52. Ibid., p. 316. Article 11, Lebanese proposal (A/C.3/260).
53. Ibid. ('If that right were recognized, the right to leave a country, already sanctioned in article 11, would be strengthened by the assurance of the right to return').
54. Ibid., pp. 316–25.
55. Mr Santa Cruz (Chile), p. 316 and Mr Contoumas (Greece), p. 319.
56. Ibid., p. 325 (A/C.3/260). The amendment was adopted by 33 votes to none, with 8 abstentions.
57. Article 12, 999 *United Nations Treaty Series*, p. 171.
58. Article 5 (d) (ii), 660 *United Nations Treaty Series*, p. 195.
59. The website of the Office for the High Commissioner for Human Rights in Geneva contains a list of those states which have ratified these treaties, which includes reservations, at http://www.ohchr.org/EN/Pages/WelcomePage.aspx (last retrieved 24 October 2008).
60. See Boling, *The 1948 Palestinian* Refugee, *supra* note 9, and also by Boling, 'Question of "Timing"', *supra* note 49; and Victor Kattan, 'The Nationality of Denationalized Palestinians', 74 *Nordic Journal of International Law* (2005), pp. 67–102.
61. See Progress Report of the United Nations Mediator on Palestine submitted to the Secretary-General for Transmission to the Members of the United Nations, UN Doc. A/648, 16 September 1948, V. Refugees, at paras 5–6 (emphasis added).
62. See 'Desperate Plight of Arab Refugees', *Observer*, 8 August 1948, p. 5.
63. Seven Basic Premises, para. 3 (e), UN Mediator Report, *supra* note 61.
64. Specific Conclusions, para. 4 (i) and (k), UN Mediator Report.
65. UN Doc. A/Res/194 (III), 11 December 1948.
66. Ibid., para. 2.
67. See Quigley, 'Displaced Palestinians', *supra* note 9, p. 187.
68. Ibid., p. 188.
69. See W. Thomas Mallison and Sally V. Mallison, *The Palestine Problem in International Law and World Order* (Harlow: Longman, 1986), pp. 179–80.
70. See Michael R. Fischbach, *Records of Dispossession: Palestinian Refugee Property and the Arab–Israeli Conflict* (New York: Columbia University Press, 2003), pp. 84–5.
71. Ibid., citing UNSA DAG 13–3, UNCCP. Subgroup: Principal Secretary. Series: Records Relating to Compensation / Box 18/1948–51 / Background Information Relating to Compensation; Document: W/36, 'Returning Refugees and the Question of Compensation', 7 February, 1950.
72. See the Ambassador in France (Bruce) to the Secretary of State, 12 June 1949, 6 *Foreign Relations of the United States* (1949), p. 1124 (asking for Israeli concessions on refugees).
73. See Don Peretz, *Israel and the Palestine Arabs* (Washington, DC: The Middle East Institute, 1958), pp. 50–5, citing statement by Ambassador Michael Comay before the UN Special Political Committee, 19 February 1957.
74. See, generally, Kattan, 'Nationality of Denationalized Palestinians', *supra* note 60, pp. 67–102.
75. On state succession and the controversies concerning decolonisation see Matthew Craven, *The Decolonization of International Law: State Succession and the Law of Treaties* (Oxford: Oxford University Press, 2007).
76. See Articles 39 (Serb-Croat-Slovene nationality), 44 (Greek nationality), 51 and 52 (Bulgarian nationality) of the Neuilly Treaty; Articles 36 (Belgian nationality), 84 (Czecho-

slovakian nationality), 91 (Polish nationality), 105 (nationality of the Free City of Danzig) and 112 (Danish nationality) of the Versailles Treaty; Articles 64–65 (Austrian nationality), 70–71 (Italian nationality) of the St Germain Treaty; Article 57 (Hungarian nationality) of the Trianon Treaty; Articles 102 (Egyptian nationality), 117 (Cypriot/British nationality), 123 (general), 129 (Palestinian nationality) of the Sèvres Treaty; and Article 30 of the Lausanne Treaty. See both volumes of the *Treaties of Peace 1919–1923* (New York: Carnegie Endowment for International Peace, 1924) which contains all the texts of these treaties as well as maps. For authorities which support the view that nationality follows the change of sovereignty and for the text of the relevant provisions of the Rumanian Minorities Treaty see Kattan, 'Nationality of Denationalized Palestinians', *supra* note 60, p. 91.

77. See Ian Brownlie, *Principles of Public International Law* (Oxford: Oxford University Press, 1998), p. 657.
78. See Article 18 of the Draft Convention on Nationality prepared in anticipation of the First Conference on the Codification of International Law, The Hague, 1930, Research in International Law, Harvard Law School, 1929, in 29 *American Journal of International Law Special Supplement* (1929), p. 15.
79. As the commentary to the draft articles noted, this provision was drafted to avoid statelessness. Moreover, it was believed to express a rule of international law which was generally recognised. According to the commentary, 'international law assumes that the successor state confers its nationality upon the nationals of the predecessor state residing in the annexed territory at the time of the annexation'. See Ibid., p. 61.
80. See *A.B v. M.B.* 6 April 1951 reported in 17 *International Law Reports* (1950), p. 111.
81. See Nationality Law 5712 – 1952. Published in Sefer Ha-Chukkim No. 95, 8 April 1952, p. 146, *Laws of the State of Israel*, Vol. XI, p. 50. In May 2003, the Knesset enacted the Nationality and Entry into Israel Law which suspends, subject to limited and subjective exceptions especially in cases of marriages between an Israeli Arab citizen and an Arab resident of the occupied territories. The law directly discriminates between Arab residents of the occupied territories and its Jewish residents (settlers) as it only applies to Arabs; Jews are specifically excluded from its application.
82. See Hersch Lauterpacht, 'The Nationality of Denationalized Persons', 1 *Jewish Yearbook of International Law* (1948), p. 164 at p. 172.
83. Although the PLO has many consulates abroad which try to assist Palestinians with their difficulties in their host countries they do not have the same rights in international law as normal diplomatic missions. Nor do Palestinian diplomats have diplomatic immunity because they are not representatives of a state.
84. See Ilan Pappé, *The Making of the Arab–Israeli Conflict 1947–1951* (London: I.B. Tauris, 2001), p. 206 and discussion therein.
85. See 'Palestine Refugees' Plight. Appeal by Archbishop of York: "Special Responsibility" of UN', *Manchester Guardian*, 30 March 1949, p. 6.
86. See Mr Mark F. Ethridge to the Secretary of State, 13 April 1949, 6 *Foreign Relations of the United States 1949, The Near East, South Asia and Africa* (Washington, DC: US Government Printing Office, 1977), p. 913.
87. Ibid.
88. Ibid., p. 914.
89. Ibid., p. 915.
90. See Pappé, *Making of the Arab–Israeli Conflict*, *supra* note 84 at p. 208. See also, UN General Assembly resolution 273 (III), 11 May 1949.
91. Ibid., citing David P. Forsythe, *UN Peacemaking: The Conciliation Commission for Palestine* (Baltimore, 1972), p. 27.
92. See Mark F. Ethridge to the Secretary of State, enclosing the full text of the Protocol, 12 May 1949, in 6 *Foreign Relations*, *supra* note 86 at p. 998.
93. Ibid., p. 999.

94. See W. Eytan to M. Sharett (New York), 14 May 1949 in Yemima Rosenthal, 4 *Documents on the Foreign Policy of Israel, May–December 1949*, Israel State Archives (Jerusalem: The Government Printer, 1986), p. 51.
95. See E. Elath to M. Sharett, 19 May 1949, ibid., p. 55 ('we consider resettlement main solution and shall consider repatriation only part peace settlement').
96. See W. Eytan to C. de Boisanger (Lausanne), 25 May 1949, ibid., p. 63.
97. See J.G. McDonald to D. Ben-Gurion, 29 May 1949, ibid., pp. 75–6.
98. Ibid., p. 76.
99. Ibid., p. 77.
100. Ibid.
101. M. Sharett to J.G. McDonald (Tel Aviv), 8 June 1949, ibid., pp. 107–11 at p. 109 ('refugees are ... members of an aggressor-group defeated in a war of its own making').
102. Ibid., pp. 108–9.
103. President Weizmann to President Truman (Washington), 24 June 1949, ibid., pp. 168–72 at pp. 170–1.
104. Aide-mémoire by the Government of the United States, 24 June 1949, ibid., p. 174.
105. M. Sharett to A. Eban (New York), 6 July 1949, ibid., p. 207. See also, 6 *Foreign Relations of the United States 1949*, *supra* note 86, pp. 1261–4 (Israeli Ambassador communicating Israel's offer to the US Government of allowing 100,000 refugees to return to Israel).
106. Ibid.
107. The Secretary of State to the US Delegation at Lausanne, Top Secret, 11 August 1949, 6 *Foreign Relations of the United States 1949*, *supra* note 86, p. 1297 ('On balance, the US does not consider present Israeli offer to repatriate 100,000 Arab refugees satisfactory from standpoint of basis for ultimate solution of the refugee problem').
108. President Truman to President Weizmann (Rehovoth), 13 August 1949, Rosenthal, *Documents on the Foreign Policy of Israel*, *supra* note 94, p. 331.
109. Ibid., p. 332.
110. Ibid.
111. Memorandum Handed to the Delegations of the Arab States and to the Delegation of Israel in Lausanne on 15 August 1949, ibid., pp. 340–2.
112. Ibid., p. 341.
113. R. Shiloah to C. de Boisanger (Lausanne), 31 August 1949, ibid., p. 417.
114. Ibid., p. 418.
115. Appendix II, Draft Declaration, ibid., p. 434.
116. Note by the Conciliation Commission to the Israeli Delegation in Lausanne, 12 September 1949, ibid., p. 456.
117. A. Eban to H. Yalçin (New York), 27 October 1949, ibid., pp. 578–9.
118. H. Yalçin to A. Eban (New York), 15 November 1949, ibid., p. 628.
119. See 'Arab Refugee Plan: Opposition in Israeli Parliament', *The Times*, 3 August 1949, p. 3 (reporting that the Israeli Government's decision to discuss at Lausanne the repatriation of a limited number of Arab refugees was angrily received by the opposition in the Knesset).
120. See Memorandum of Conversation, by the Deputy Assistant Secretary of State for Near Eastern and African Affairs (Hare), Top Secret, Washington, 25 August 1949, subject: status of PCC Activities and Export-Import Bank Loan in 6 *Foreign Relations of the United States 1949*, *supra* note 86, pp. 1328–31 (the State Department tried to delay the bank from giving the Israeli Government a loan, allegedly for 'political reasons', provoking a strong reaction from Israel's Ambassador in Washington). See also, Memorandum by the Assistant Secretary of State for Congressional Relations (Gross) to the Assistant Secretary of State for Near Eastern and African Affairs (McGhee), 26 August 1949, p. 1333 (citing problems in Congress of trying to use economic means to handle the Palestine problem, possible congressional opposition from Senators Connally and Vandenberg who were anxious that money was being spent wisely in the Middle East).
121. The Ambassador in France (Bruce) to the Secretary of State, Top Secret, Paris, 12 June 1949, 1 pm, 2413, from Ethridge, USDel at Lausanne commenting separately on Israel note in 6 *Foreign Relations of the United States 1949*, *supra* note 86, p. 1124.

122. Ibid., p. 1125.
123. See *To Jerusalem: Folke Bernadotte*, trans. from the Swedish by Joan Bulman (London: Hodder & Stoughton, 1951), p. 209.
124. See John Quigley, *The Case for Palestine: An International Law Perspective* (Durham: Duke University Press, 2005), p. 85 ('On September 17 three members of LEHI assassinated Bernadotte in Jerusalem, apparently because of his concern for the rights of the Arabs. LEHI leader Itzhak Shamir, according to several of the assassins, authorized the assassination'). Quigley cites as his source a report in the *New York Times*, 12 September 1988, p. A3. See also, Donald Neff, 'Jewish Terrorists Assassinate U.N. Peacekeeper Count Folke Bernadotte', *Washington Report on Middle East Affairs* (September 1995), pp. 83–4, at p. 83 ('The assassins were members of Lehi (Lohamei Herut Israel – Fighters for the Freedom of Israel), better known as the Stern Gang. Its three leaders had decided a week earlier to have Bernadotte killed because they believed he was partial to the Arabs. One of those leaders was Yitzhak Shamir, who in 1983 would become prime minister of Israel'). Neff cites as his sources Marton, *A Death in Jerusalem*, p. 208, Kurzman, *Genesis* 1948, pp. 555 and p. 563, and Avishai Margalit, 'The Violent Life of Yitzhak Shamir', *New York Review of Books*, 14 May 1992. See further, Donald Macintyre, 'Israel's Forgotten Hero: The Assassination of Count Bernadotte – and the Death of Peace', *The Independent*, 18 September 2008, available online at: http://www.independent.co.uk/news/world/middle-east/israels-forgotten-hero-the-assassination-of-count-bernadotte--and-the-death-of-peace-934094.html (last retrieved 8 February 2009). Macintyre writes that the assassination 'was perpetrated by the most extreme of the Jewish nationalist underground groups, Lehi, more commonly known to the British as the Stern Gang, ordered by a three-man leadership which included the future Israeli prime minister Yitzhak Shamir'.

9 THE CREATION OF ISRAEL

1. See James Crawford, *The Creation of States in International Law* (Oxford: Clarendon Press, 2006), p. 433 ('Israel must be considered to have met that standard [of secessionary independence] by 24 February 1949, when the Egyptian–Israel Armistice Agreement was signed').
2. See Letter dated 18 February 1972 from Mr Mohammed Bedjaoui to the Chairman of the International Law Commission on the topic of Succession of States in respect of matters other than treaties, UN Doc. A/CN.4/255, 8 March 1972, p. 11, para. 27 ('The actual creation of Israel on 15 May 1948 is the result of a fait accompli born of violence and defiance of the international community of nations. The Zionists occupied 6,500 square kilometres which the General Assembly had reserved in resolution 181 (II) for the Arab State of Palestine and part of which had already been annexed through Israeli violence even before the war culminating in the proclamation of 15 May 1948').
3. See Yoram Dinstein, 'The United Nations and the Arab–Israeli Conflict', 15 *Encyclopedia Judaica* (1971), p. 1543, reprinted in John Norton Moore (ed.), *The Arab–Israeli Conflict, Vol. II: Readings* (New Jersey: Princeton University Press, 1974), pp. 482–3.
4. Notwithstanding India's conquests of Hyderabad in 1948 and Goa, Damao and Diu in 1961. India justified its intervention in Hyderabad on the basis that the Nizam was violating the standstill agreement and terrorising its Hindu population. See Taraknath Das, 'The Status of Hyderabad During and After British Rule in India', 43 *American Journal of International Law* (1949), pp. 57–72 (arguing that India's actions there were lawful) and Clyde Eagleton, 'The Case of Hyderabad Before the Security Council', 44 *American Journal of International Law* (1950), pp. 277–302 (arguing that India's actions were contrary to international law). India's conquest of Goa was justified, among other things, on the basis that it was 'eliminating colonialism' from the Indian subcontinent. See Quincy Wright, 'The Goa Incident', 56 *American Journal of International Law* (1962), pp. 617–32. It would be difficult to see how the Zionist movement could justify its conquest of Palestine on the basis that it was eliminating colonialism. Nor is there any parallel to

Hyderabad where the Muslim Nizam ruled over a population that was over 80 per cent Hindu. Moreover, Nehru and the Indian Independence Movement were ardent supporters of the Palestinian Arab national cause, something often overlooked in India today.

5. See Legal Status of Palestine after termination of the Mandate, from Sir O. Sargent, FO Minute to New York/Washington, 14 May 1948, FO 371/68664, Palestine, Eastern.
6. Emphasis added. The Telegram added: 'The provocation thus given to the Arab States would be doubly felt owing to the fact that, for totally improper reasons Transjordan, which has for a considerable time enjoyed the qualifications necessary for admission to the United Nations, has failed to secure this.' See Application for membership of the United Nations by the Republic of Israel, Telegram from Foreign Office to New York, 19 May 1948, FO 371/68664, Palestine, Eastern, 1948.
7. See Majorie M. Whiteman (ed.), 2 *Digest of International Law* (Washington, DC: Department of State Publication, 1963), pp. 167–9 at p. 168. On the reaction of US diplomats see Philip C. Jessup, *The Birth of Nations* (New York: Columbia University Press, 1974), p. 289.
8. See Whiteman, ibid., pp. 167–8 (emphasis added).
9. Ibid., p. 169.
10. See Philip Marshall Brown, 'The Recognition of Israel', 42 *American Journal of International Law* (1948), p. 620.
11. Ibid., p. 622.
12. See John Snetsinger, *Truman, the Jewish Vote and the Creation of Israel* (Stanford: Hoover Institution Press, 1974), p. 109.
13. See Memorandum of Legal Opinions on Recognition of the Palestine State, prepared by Ernest A. Gross, State Department legal adviser, 13 May 1948. Gross's opinions were attached to a memorandum from C.H. Humelsine, Office of the Secretary of State, 14 May 1948, Clifford Papers. This is cited in Snetsinger, ibid. at p. 109, endnote 24.
14. See Hersch Lauterpacht, *Recognition in International Law* (Cambridge: Cambridge University Press, 1947), pp. 7–8 ('Recognition is unlawful if granted *durante bello*, when the outcome of the struggle is altogether uncertain').
15. See Crawford, *Creation of States*, *supra* note 1, p. 433 ('United States recognition was correspondingly premature'). See also, Patrick Maitland, 'Recognising Israel: Conundrum for International Lawyers', *The Scotsman*, 22 May 1948, p. 7 (reflecting the difficulty international lawyers faced with Israel's declaration of independence and whether or not it should be granted recognition by Britain since the US and the Soviet Union had already extended recognition).
16. See FO Minute, Mr Wright, British Attitude towards Recognition of Palestine, FO 371/68665. This contains a minute by W.E. Beckett on the issue of belligerent status.
17. See 'Recognition of the Jewish State', Eastern, Palestine (1948), FO 371/68670.
18. See United States recognition of new Jewish state, telegram from Sir O. Harvey, Paris, 17 May 1948 to Foreign Office, FO 371/68664, Palestine, Eastern, 1948 ('M. Bidault in conversation with His Majesty's Minister during the reception yesterday, referred disapprovingly to President Truman's action in recognising the new Jewish State. He said that he had not been in agreement with the French vote at the U.N. in favour of partition and had wished France to abstain but that he had been absent from Paris at the time').
19. See Letter to the Right Hon. Sir Alexander Cadogan, 18 August 1948 from Aubrey S. Eban, Representative of the Provisional Government of Israel, File 6090, FO 371/68670, Eastern, Palestine (1948).
20. Ibid.
21. Ibid.
22. See 'Recognition of the Jewish State', *supra* note 17.
23. Ibid.
24. Ibid.
25. Ibid.
26. See the Egyptian–Israel armistice agreement (UN Doc. S/1264/Corr.1, 23 February 1949); the Israel–Jordan armistice agreement (UN Doc. S/1302/Rev.1, 3 April 1949);

the Israel–Lebanon armistice agreement (UN Doc. S/1296, 23 March 1949); and the Israeli–Syrian general armistice agreement (UN Doc. S/1353, 20 July 1949).

27. See UN Security Council resolution 69 (1949), 4 March 1949.
28. See UN General Assembly resolution 273 (III), 11 May 1949. The vote was 37 in favour, 12 against and 9 abstentions. The vote was as follows: *In favour*: Union of Soviet Socialist Republics, United States of America, Uruguay, Venezuela, Yugoslavia, Argentina, Australia, Bolivia, Byelorussian Soviet Socialist Republic, Canada, Chile, China, Colombia, Costa Rica, Cuba, Czechoslovakia, Dominican Republic, Ecuador, France, Guatemala, Haiti, Honduras, Iceland, Liberia, Luxembourg, Mexico, Netherlands, New Zealand, Nicaragua, Norway, Panama, Paraguay, Peru, Philippines, Poland, Ukrainian Soviet Socialist Republic, Union of South Africa. *Against*: Yemen, Afghanistan, Burma, Egypt, Ethiopia, India, Iran, Iraq, Lebanon, Pakistan, Saudi Arabia, Syria. *Abstentions*: United Kingdom, Belgium, Brazil, Denmark, El Salvador, Greece, Siam, Sweden, Turkey.
29. Ibid., citing UN Doc. S/1093.
30. Ibid.
31. See statement by Aubrey Eban, UN Doc. A/AC.24/SR.45, 5 May 1949 (emphasis added).
32. See M. Sharett to A. Eban, Tel Aviv, 6 July 1949, in Yemima Rosenthal (ed.), *Documents on the Foreign Policy of Israel*, Vol. 4, May–December 1949. Israel State Archives (Jerusalem: The Government Printer, 1986), p. 207.
33. See the preamble to UN General Assembly resolution 273 (III), 11 May 1949 ('*Recalling* its resolutions of 29 November 1947 and 11 December 1948 and taking note of the declarations and explanations made by the representative of the Government of Israel before the *ad hoc* Political Committee in respect of the implementation of the said resolutions').
34. See Mr Mark F. Ethridge to the Secretary of State, 13 April 1949, 6 *Foreign Relations of the United States 1949, The Near East, South Asia and Africa* (Washington, DC: US Government Printing Office, 1977), p. 913.
35. Statement by Aubrey Eban, UN Doc. A/AC.24/SR.45, 5 May 1949 (emphasis added).
36. Statement by Eban, ibid.
37. Ibid. (emphasis added).
38. Ibid.
39. Ibid. (emphasis added).
40. See J.G. McDonald to D. Ben-Gurion, Tel Aviv, 29 May 1949, in Rosenthal, *Documents*, *supra* note 32 at pp. 75–7 at p. 76 (emphasis added). See also, 6 *Foreign Relations of the United States 1949*, *supra* note 34, p. 1073
41. McDonald to Ben-Gurion, ibid., p. 77 (emphasis added).
42. See M. Sharett to J.G. McDonald, Tel Aviv, 8 June 1949, in Rosenthal, *Documents*, *supra* note 32, p. 109.
43. See Aide-Mémoire, 24 June 1949, ibid., p. 174.
44. See 6 *Foreign Relations of the United States* (1949), *supra* note 34 at p. 1377.
45. See Report by the National Security Council on United States Policy Toward Israel and the Arab States, Top Secret, Washington, 17 October, 1949, 6 *Foreign Relations of the United States 1949*, *supra* note 34, p. 1433.
46. Ibid., p. 1438.
47. See The Treaty of Utrecht, 31 March 1713, in George Chalmers, *A Collection of Treaties between Great Britain and other Powers* (London: 1790), p. 340; The Congress of Vienna, 9 June 1815, in Edward Hertslet (ed.), *The Map of Europe by Treaty: Political and Territorial Changes Since the General Peace of 1814*, Vol. 1 (London: Butterworths, 1875), pp. 208–77; the Treaty of Peace between the Allied and Associated Powers and Germany, signed at Versailles, 28 June 1919, in 112 *British and Foreign State Papers*, (1919) (London: HMSO, 1922), pp. 1–212. The principle of territorial compensation was also provided for in the Partition Treaties of 1608 and 1700. See the French King's Treaty made with the King of England, relating to the Settlement of the Succession of Spain on the Electoral Prince of Bavaria, on Condition that Naples, Sicily, Guipulcoa,

& be granted to the Dauphin (which is commonly called, The First Treaty of Partition) concluded August 19, 1698; and the Treaty between the most Christian King, the King of Great Britain, and the States General of the United Provinces, for Settling the Succession of the Crown of Spain, in case his Catholic Majesty die without issues, commonly called the Second Treaty of Partition. These treaties are reprinted in *A General Collection of Treatys, Declarations of War, Manifestos, and Publik Papers, Relating to Peace and War, in Four Volumes*, Vol. I, Second Edition, London, 1732, p. 386 (the First Partition Treaty) and p. 407 (the Second Partition Treaty). This collection can be accessed electronically at the British Library on their database Eighteenth Century Collections Online. Compensations of a territorial nature sometimes referred to as 'indemnities' were also provided in the treaties which created Belgium. See The Treaty for Settling the Barrier, in the Netherlands, between the most Serene and most Potent Prince Charles VI, Emperor of Germany, and the most Serene and Potent Prince George, by the Grace of God, King of Great Britain, France and Ireland, Defender of the Faith, and the High and Mighty Lords the States General of the United Netherlands, concluded at Antwerp on the 15 November, 1715, in Chalmers, *A Collection of Treaties between Great Britain and other Powers*, ibid., p. 209; the Treaty between Great Britain, Austria, France, Prussia, and Russia, and Belgium, relative to the Separation of Belgium from Holland, signed at London, 15 November, 1831, in Hertslet, *The Map of Europe by Treaty*, ibid., p. 858; and the Treaty between Great Britain, Austria, France, Prussia, and Russia, on the one part, and The Netherlands, on the other, signed at London, 19 April, 1839, in Hertslet, *The Map of Europe by Treaty*, ibid., p. 979.

48. As Turkey never assented to the incorporation of the Balfour Declaration into the Treaty of Lausanne, nor for that matter did it agree to the secession of Kurdistan which was explicitly provided for by Article 64 of the Treaty of Sèvres.
49. As noted by Crawford in *Creation of States*, *supra* note 1 at p. 432.
50. See Crawford, ibid., p. 433 ('Secession would thus appear to be the appropriate mode, and the question then becomes at what time Israel qualified as a seceding State in accordance with the criteria for secessionary independence …').
51. On the notion of conquest and subjugation in international law see Sir Robert Jennings and Sir Arthur Watts (eds), *Oppenheim's International Law*, Vol. 1, Parts 2 to 4 (Singapore: Pearson Education, 2005, ninth edition), pp. 698–705.
52. The Provisional Government of Israel extended its administration, laws and jurisdiction over two-thirds of the territory of Palestine, which it then annexed. See the various laws passed by the Provisional Council of State and the Knesset by which Israel extended its administration, laws and jurisdiction over two-thirds of the territory of mandatory Palestine in *Laws of the State of Israel*, Vols 1–7 (1948–53).
53. For the 'unilateral secession' thesis, see Crawford, *Creation of States*, *supra* note 1. For the 'auto-emancipation thesis' see Frank L.M. Van de Craen, 'The Territorial Title of the State of Israel to "Palestine": An Appraisal in International Law', 14 *Revue Belge de Droit International* (1978–79), pp. 500–38 at p. 502 ('The birth of Israel can the [*sic*] best be described by using the legal construction of "auto-emancipation"'). On the notion of 'defence conquest', see Stephen M. Schwebel, 'What Weight to Conquest', 64 *American Journal of International Law* (1970), pp. 344–7. For criticisms of the Schwebel argument, see Sir Robert Jennings and Sir Arthur Watts (eds), *Oppenheim's International Law*, Vol. 1, Parts 2 to 4 (Harlow: Longman Group, 1992), p. 704 note 8.
54. See Meeting: M. Shetok, E. Epstein – G. Marshall, R. Lovett, D. Rusk, Washington, 8 May 1948, CZA Z 6/4/15 (secret) in Gedalia Yogev (ed.), *Political and Diplomatic Documents, December 1947 – May 1948, State of Israel, Israel State Archives and World Zionist Organization, Central Zionist Archives* (New Brunswick: Transaction Books, 1979), pp. 757–69 at pp. 767–8 ('Mr. Rusk expressed his view that if the Provisional Government of Israel set up a Jewish state on 14/15 May it would not be in accordance with the partition plan. He said that the resolution contemplated the setting up of a Provisional Government by the United Nations Commission and the coming into existence of the state in connection with the Economic Union').
55. See General Assembly resolution 181 (II) (A+B), 29 November 1947, Part I, A, 3.

56. Ibid., Part II.
57. Ibid., Part I, Chapter C. II.
58. Ibid., Part 1, D (economic union), Part II, A (Arab state) and Part III (City of Jerusalem).
59. The Aaland Islands Question, Report Submitted to the Council of the League of Nations by the Commission of Rapporteurs, Geneva, 16 April 1921, League of Nations, Official Journal VII (1921), p. 28.
60. See Crawford, *Creation of States*, *supra* note 1 at p. 435 ('The Balfour Declaration had been accepted as incorporated in the Mandate, and the Jewish people accordingly had a right of self-determination in respect of post-1922 Palestine as a whole. But so too did the Palestinian people').
61. See Rosalyn Higgins, *The Development of International Law through the Political Organs of the United Nations* (London: Oxford University Press, 1963), p. 104 ('Self-determination refers to the right of the majority within a generally accepted political unit to the exercise of power').
62. The Aaland Islands Question, *supra* note 59, p. 28.
63. Ibid.
64. Ibid.
65. See VI *The United Nations Conference on International Organization*, UN Doc. 343, p. 296 (1945). Although the position regarding secession might be different today, especially as regards peoples suffering from racial discrimination and massive human rights violations. See Michael P. Scharf, 'Earned Sovereignty: Juridical Underpinnings', 31 *Denver Journal of International Law and Policy* (2003), pp. 373–85.
66. See International Status of South-West Africa, Advisory Opinion, 11 July 1950, ICJ Reports (1950), p. 133 (expressing the opinion that the obligations contained in Article 22 of the League of Nations Covenant did not depend on the existence of the League of Nations. In the words of the Court: 'Their *raison d'être* and original object remain').
67. See James Crawford, 'The Right of Self-Determination in International Law: Its Development and Future', in Philip Alston (ed.), *People's Rights* (Oxford: Oxford University Press, 2001), p. 14.
68. Jordan incorporated East Jerusalem and the West Bank into its Kingdom in 1950 after overrunning the territory in the 1948 war and subsequently occupying it and annexing it. It did this in collusion with the Provisional Government of Israel. See generally, Avi Shlaim, *Collusion Across the Jordan: King Abdullah, the Zionist Movement, and the Partition of Palestine* (Oxford: Clarendon Press, 1988). The United Kingdom granted *de jure* recognition to the union, but most states withheld *de jure* recognition (although they may have granted *de facto* recognition). In particular, the other Arab states denounced the union as a betrayal of the Palestinian cause and as a breach of a resolution passed by the Arab League prohibiting the annexation of any part of Palestine. See The Policy of the Arab States Towards the Question of Palestine, Resolution 320-Sess.12 – Sched.6, Apr. 13, 1950, in Muhammad Khalil (ed.), *The Arab States and the Arab League: A Documentary Record*, Vol. 2 (Beirut: Khayats, 1962), p. 166. Eventually a compromise was reached; Jordan declared that the annexation of the West Bank was without prejudice to the final settlement of the Palestine issue, which the other Arab states accepted. See Michael Akehurst, 'The Place of the Palestinians in an Arab–Israeli Peace Settlement', 70 *Round Table* (1980), p. 443 (discussing Resolution 242, which outlined the terms of the settlement).
69. See Ian Brownlie, *International Law and the Use of Force by States* (Oxford: Clarendon Press, 1963), p. 217 ('Latin-American practice and Article 10 of the Covenant provided cogent evidence that the right of conquest no longer existed. Even in the state practice before 1914 war merely for conquest had in some wise [*sic*] been disapproved. The practice on non-recognition in the period after 1932 confirm the view that conquest could no longer give title to territory').
70. See the Joint Four-Nation Declaration (US, UK, Soviet Union and China) on Austria at the Moscow Conference in October 1943 ('The Governments of the United Kingdom,

the Soviet Union and the United States of America are agreed that Austria, the first free country to fall a victim to Hitlerite aggression, shall be liberated from German domination. They regard the annexation imposed on Austria by Germany on March 15, 1938, as null and void. They consider themselves as in no way bound by any charges effected in Austria since that date'). The text of this declaration is available on the website of the Avalon Project at the Yale Law School Lillian Goldman Law Library: http://avalon.law.yale.edu/wwii/moscow.asp (last retrieved 9 February 2009). As Langer notes, the use of the term 'null and void' is a clear statement of law and the act in question is by definition legally invalid from its inception. See Robert Langer, *Seizure of Territory: The Stimson Doctrine and Related Principles in Legal Theory and Diplomatic Practice* (New Jersey: Princeton University Press, 1947), p. 182. The International Military Tribunal at Nuremberg described the German protectorate over Bohemia and Moravia as 'a flagrant breach of the Munich Agreement'. See International Military Tribunal (Nuremberg), Judgment and Sentences, 1 October, 1946, 41 *American Journal of International Law* (1947), pp. 172–333 at p. 198. The German occupation of the Czechoslovak Republic assumed under the guise of German 'protection' as the Protectorate of Bohemia and Moravia was refused recognition by France, the US and the USSR. President Roosevelt wrote a letter to Dr Beneš in which he wrote that his government had 'not recognized the legal status' of the German occupation of Bohemia and Moravia. See Langer, *Seizure of Territory*, ibid., p. 233. A letter dispatched to the German Ambassador in Moscow contained the following sentence: 'the Soviet Government cannot recognise the inclusion of the Czech provinces and also, in one form or another, of Slovakia in the German Empire to be legitimate and in conformity with the generally accepted rules on international law and justice or the principle of self-determination of nations'. See Langer, *Seizure of Territory*, ibid., p. 222. In contrast, the response of the British Government was equivocal, and the Chamberlain Government was castigated in the House of Commons. In a Parliamentary Debate Mr Alexander, citing the Stimson doctrine, expressed the opinion, which was shared by many, that 'there has grown up in the last few years in international law a clear recognition of a principle ... that ... there must be a definite act taken by way of resolving not to recognise'. In conclusion he said 'if the British Government were to grant recognition to Germany over the annexation of Czechoslovakia at this time, such an action would be inconsistent with the Covenant of the League of Nations'. See Langer, *Seizure of Territory*, ibid., p. 228. For a sophisticated legal analysis of the *Anschluss*, the dismemberment of the Czechoslovak Republic, Italy's invasion of Albania, the Soviet Union's annexation of the Baltic Republics, and the partition of Poland by Germany and the USSR in 1939 see Krystyna Marek, *Identity and Continuity of States in Public International Law* (Genève: Librairie Droz, 1968), pp. 283–545 (arguing that all these invasions, territorial dismemberments, and annexations were contrary to international law).

71. On 7 January 1932, during the Manchuria conflict, US Secretary of State Stimson addressed to China and Japan a note in which it declared, *inter alia*, that the American Government would not recognise any situations, treaties or agreements, including those which related to the sovereignty, the independence or the territorial and administrative integrity of the Republic of China, which had been brought about by means contrary to the League of Nations Covenant or the Kellogg–Briand Pact. The Stimson doctrine found expression in a resolution adopted by the League of Nations Assembly on 11 March 1932. It acquired legal strength for American states after its inclusion in Article 2 of the 1933 Treaty of Non-Aggression and Conciliation of Rio de Janeiro and in Article 17 of the 1948 Bogotá Pact. For further reading on the Stimson Doctrine, see Arnold D. McNair, 'The Stimson Doctrine of Non-Recognition: A Note on its Legal Aspects', 14 *British Yearbook of International Law* (1933), pp. 65–74.
72. On the Italian invasion and annexation of Ethiopia and the League of Nations response see Langer, *Seizure of Territory*, *supra* note 70, pp. 132–54.
73. See John Dugard, *Recognition and the United Nations* (Cambridge: Grotius Publications, 1987), pp. 39–40 ('State practice and League action during the inter-war years were not sufficiently uniform to warrant the conclusion that the principle of non-recognition of

territorial conquests had become a customary rule. However, it would be wrong to dismiss the precedents of this period as isolated incidents in support of non-recognition or as evidence of an American regional rule only. State and League practice, albeit inconsistent, demonstrated a clear trend in favour of the non-recognition of territorial conquests and, if necessary, of the non-recognition of an aspirant State produced by conquest').

74. See the statement made by the Minister of State of the United Kingdom in the House of Commons, 27 April 1950, reproduced in Ruth Lapidoth and Moshe Hirsch (eds), *The Jerusalem Question and Its Resolution: Selected Documents* (Dordrecht: Martinus Nijhoff Publishers, in cooperation with the Jerusalem Institute for Israel Studies, 1994), pp. 147–8 at p. 148. See further, 'Jordan Authority in Jerusalem' (Foreign Office minute by Mr Lawrence), 23 May 1955, FO 371/115663, and the minute from the FCO legal adviser Ms Eileen Denza on the publication of Elihu Lauterpacht's Jerusalem and the Holy Places, 13 October 1971, FCO 17/1605. On Jerusalem Denza wrote: 'I would disagree entirely with Mr. Lauterpacht's account of the status of East Jerusalem prior to 1967. In my view Jordan's position in East Jerusalem was entirely parallel with Israel's in West Jerusalem. The Armistice Agreement did not say that the parties to it could not assert sovereign rights in regard to Jerusalem. It merely provided that the terms of the Agreement itself would not prejudice the terms of an ultimate settlement of the Palestine question. So far as it operated to prevent the establishment of title by prescription it operated against Israel as much as Jordan. Page 47 seems to me to be nonsense ... The British approach does not depend on believing that Israel has annexed Jerusalem. HMG are perfectly well aware that Israel has in virtually all respects of which we are aware treated East Jerusalem as her own territory, but has stopped shortly of the juridical step of annexation. Mr. Lauterpacht flatters himself on page 52 when he says that he has met the British point on its merits. All he has done is to allege falsely that it is based on an incorrect assumption. Mr. Lauterpacht ignores the customary international law, of which he must be perfectly well aware, which lays down in details the duties of an occupying power in the administration of occupied territory. It is not possible to circumvent these rules by describing Israel's action as reunification or integration rather than annexation.'

75. See Jordan: Statement Concerning Disengagement from the West Bank and Palestinian Self-Determination, Address by His Majesty King Hussein to the Nation, 31 July 1988, 27 *International Legal Materials* (1988), pp. 1637–45.

76. See Henry Cattan, *Palestine and International Law* (London: Longman Group, 1973), pp. 74–7 at p. 75 (quoting R.Y. Jennings in arguing that a General Assembly resolution *per se* cannot constitute a source of title or affect any change in sovereignty).

77. See e.g. UN Security Council resolutions 61, UN Doc. S/1070, 4 November 1948; 62, UN Doc. S/1080, 16 November 1948; and 66, UN Doc. S/1169, 29 December 1948.

78. See cablegram dated 22 March 1949 from the Acting Mediator (Ralph Bunche) to the Secretary-General transmitting a supplementary report on the situation in the southern Negev, UN Doc. S/1295, 12 March 1949.

79. See the resolution adopted by the UN Trusteeship Council at the eighth meeting on Tuesday 20 December 1949, concerning the removal to Jerusalem of certain ministries and central departments of the Government of Israel, UN Doc. T/RES/427, 21 December 1949; and the exchange of correspondence between the President of the Trusteeship Council and the Government of Israel and the statement by Ben-Gurion before the Knesset in Question of an International Regime for the Jerusalem Area and Protection of the Holy Places, UN Doc. T/431, 5 January 1950. Note that Article II (1) of the Israel–Jordan Armistice Agreement provides '[t]he principle that no military or political advantage should be gained under the truce ordered by the Security Council is recognised'. See Israel–Jordan armistice agreement, UN Doc. S/1302/Rev.1, 3 April 1949.

80. See Henry Cattan, *Palestine, the Arabs and Israel* (London: Longman Group, 1969), p. 37 citing statistics from Israel Government, *Government Year-Book*, English edition, 5712 (1951/1952), p. 315.

81. See Robert Yewdall Jennings, *The Acquisition of Territory in International Law* (Manchester: Manchester University Press, 1963), pp. 55–6. See also, the exchange of notes

between Derek Bowett and G. Hart, 'International Law Relating to Occupied Territory: A Rejoinder', 87 *Law Quarterly Review* (1971), pp. 473–5.

82. See H. Lauterpacht (ed.), 15 *Annual Digest and Reports of Public International Law Cases 1948* (London: Butterworth & Co., 1953), pp. 632–56 at p. 655. On the rule that belligerent occupation, by itself, cannot produce a transfer of title over territory to the occupying state, see the Arbitral Award in *Affaire de la Dette Publique Ottoman*, 18 April 1925, 1 *Reports of International Arbitral Awards*, p. 529, at p. 555.
83. See Rudolf Bernhardt (ed.), *Encyclopaedia of Public International Law*, Vol. 3 (Amsterdam: Elsevier, 1997), p. 864 ('since May 1948 the state of Israel has seized, partly annexed and partly occupied the "State" territory of Palestine as it was conceived of in terms of the UN partition plan').
84. On acquiescence generally, see Kaiyan Homi Kaikobad, 'Some Observations on the Doctrine of Continuity and Finality of Boundaries', 54 *The British Yearbook of International Law* (1983), pp. 119–41 at pp. 121–6 (analysing various cases on the acquiescence and recognition of boundaries).
85. Reference re Secession of Quebec, [1998] 2 S.C.R. 217, para. 146.
86. Ibid.
87. For this reason most embassies are located in Tel Aviv as opposed to Jerusalem. On the status of Jerusalem in international law see Antonio Cassese, 'Legal Considerations on the International Status of Jerusalem', 3 *Palestine Yearbook of International Law* (1986), pp. 13–39, reprinted in Victor Kattan (ed.), *The Palestine Question in International Law* (London: British Institute of International and Comparative Law, 2008), pp. 295–321.
88. See 'The Beirut Declaration' of the Council of the League of Arab States at the Summit Level, at its 14th Ordinary Session (28 March 2002), reprinted in 12 *The Palestine Yearbook of International Law* (2002/03), pp. 425–6.
89. As Johnson notes, acquiescence may be implied in cases where interested and affected states have failed within a reasonable time to refer the matter to the appropriate international organisation. See D.H.N. Johnson, 'Acquisitive Prescription in International Law', 27 *British Yearbook of International Law* (1950), pp. 332–54 at p. 353. This would not, however, apply to Palestine which has been continuously on the agenda of the UN General Assembly even prior to the creation of Israel in 1948–49, whereby states for over 60 years have lodged thousands of diplomatic protests and complaints relating to various aspects of the Palestine problem. This would seem to suggest a general conviction by a significant number of states that the present condition of things in Israel–Palestine is not in conformity with the international legal order. In the ninth edition of Oppenheim's *International Law*, prescription is defined 'as the acquisition of sovereignty over a territory through continuous and undisturbed exercise of sovereignty over it during such a period as is necessary to create under the influence of historical development the general conviction that the present condition of things is in conformity with international order'. See Sir Robert Jennings and Sir Arthur Watts (eds), *Oppenheim's International Law* (Singapore: Pearson, 2005, ninth edition), p. 706.
90. See Geneva Convention Relative to the Protection of Civilian Persons in Time of War, 12 August 1949, 75 *United Nations Treaty Series*, p. 287. On the applicability of the fourth Geneva Convention of 1949 to the occupied Palestinian territories see Legal Consequences of the Construction of a Wall in the Occupied Palestinian Territory, Advisory Opinion, ICJ Reports (2004), p. 136 at p. 177, para. 101.
91. Acquisitive prescription is a controversial doctrine of international law. Whilst traditionally it has legitimised situations originally established through a violation of international law – such as territories obtained through conquest – it may be questioned whether this remains the case today, especially when many writers consider that the prohibition of the use of force has *jus cogens* status. It ought to be remembered that many of the classical authors of international law who wrote about prescription did so in an era when conquest could legitimately convey title. Moreover, one of the principal justifications adduced for the existence of the doctrine was for the need to preserve international order and stability. See Ian Brownlie, *Principles of Public International Law* (Oxford: Oxford University Press,

2008), pp. 146–51 at p. 146. But what if the state pleading prescription is through its own actions (annexation, aggression, conquest, prolonged military occupation) causing instability in international relations? Then, as Cassese notes, 'the principle of *effectiveness* is overridden by that of legality'. See Cassese, 'Legal Considerations on the International Status of Jerusalem', *supra* note 87, p. 37 (PYIL) and p. 319 (Kattan book). Of primordial importance is the question of self-determination which of course did not exist as law in the nineteenth century. However, it is submitted that in any contemporary analysis of prescription such as in the case of the territories Israel acquired in 1948 and in 1967 the right of self-determination would have to be taken into special consideration. As the authors of the ninth edition of *Oppenheim's International Law*, *supra* note 89, p. 716, argue, in determining the acquisition of territorial title a variety of factors would have to be taken into consideration. These include, *inter alia*, effective occupation and administration, acquiescence and/or protest, the relative strength or weakness of any rival claim, the effect of inter-temporal law (examined in Chapter 8 of this book), the principle of stability in territorial title and boundaries, geographical and historical factors, the attitudes of other states, the requirements of self-determination, 'and also indeed', in the words of Jennings and Watts, 'the possibly unlawful origin of the original taking of possession, and that subjugation is no longer *per se* a recognisable title'.

92. See Island of Palmas Case, Award, The Hague, 4 April, 1928, 2 *Reports of International Arbitral Awards* (1949), p. 831 at p. 839.
93. See A.L.W. Munkman, 'Adjudication and Adjustment – International Judicial Decision and the Settlement of Territorial and Boundary Disputes', 46 *The British Yearbook of International Law* (1972–73), pp. 1–116 at p. 106.
94. Ibid., p. 106 ('where territory has been acquired by force, then international law on the use of force and the validity of title by "conquest" would require consideration also').
95. See Treaty of Peace between the Arab Republic of Egypt and the State of Israel, 26 March 1979, reproduced in 18 *International Legal Materials* (1979), p. 362; and Treaty of Peace between the State of Israel and the Hashemite Kingdom of Jordan, 26 October 1994, reproduced in 34 *International Legal Materials* (1995), pp. 46–66.
96. See Award in the Boundary Dispute concerning the Taba Area, 29 September 1988, in 27 *International Legal Materials* (1988), pp. 1421–538.
97. See Israel–Egypt Treaty, *supra* note 95, Articles 1 (2) and 2 and Israel–Jordan Treaty, *supra* note 95, Article 3.
98. Ibid.
99. See Israel–PLO Recognition: Exchange of Letters between Arafat, Holst and Rabin, 9 September 1993, reproduced in M. Cherif Bassiouni (ed), *Documents on the Arab–Israeli Conflict: The Palestinians and the Israeli–Palestinian Peace Process*, Vol. 2 (New York: Transnational Publishers, 2005), pp. 888–9.
100. See Geoffrey Watson, *The Oslo Accords: International Law and the Israeli–Palestinian Peace Agreements* (Oxford: Oxford University Press, 2000), p. 24 ('... Security Council Resolution 242 ... implicitly superseded the territorial formula in the Partition Resolution, since it called only for an Israeli withdrawal from territories occupied in the 1967 War, not withdrawal to the borders envisaged by the Partition Resolution').
101. Ibid.
102. See UN Security Council resolution 242, UN Doc. S/RES/242, 22 November 1967.
103. See John McHugo, 'Resolution 242: A Legal Reappraisal of the Right-Wing Israeli Interpretation of the Withdrawal Phase with Reference to the Conflict between Israel and the Palestinians', 51 *International and Comparative Law Quarterly* (2002), pp. 851–81 at p. 878.
104. On 15 November 1988, the Palestine National Council (the legislative branch of the Palestine Liberation Organisation) issued a Declaration of Independence. See Letter dated 18 November 1988 from the Permanent Representative of Jordan to the United Nations addressed to the Secretary-General in UN Doc. A/43/827-S/20278, 18 November 1988. This was the second time that such a Declaration had been issued, the first being declared in Gaza by the Mufti Haj Amin al-Husseini in September 1948. See Avi Shlaim, 'The

Rise and Fall of the All-Palestine Government in Gaza', 20 *Journal of Palestine Studies* (1990), pp. 37–53. Neither the Mufti's nor Arafat's declarations resulted in the creation of a Palestinian state even though by 1990, 114 states had recognised 'Palestine', whereas only 93 states maintained diplomatic relations with Israel. It must be stressed that it was the Palestinians, not Israel or the United States, which first called for a solution based on the establishment of two states. Fourteen years before President George W. Bush called for the establishment of a Palestinian state in a speech he gave in the Rose Garden in 2002, Yasser Arafat in a specially convened meeting of the UN General Assembly in Geneva in 1988 had called for the establishment of such a state on the basis of UN Security Council resolutions 242 and 338. In his speech Arafat also called for an end to Israeli settlement activity and a full withdrawal to the 1949 ceasefire lines. At the time the United States and Israel were opposed to Yasser Arafat's PLO, which is why he had to give his speech in Geneva as the US Government would not give him a visa to travel to New York. And it would take well over a decade of settlement construction and land expropriations under the guise of a 'peace process' before a US president would recognise the need for an independent and sovereign Palestinian state.

105. See UN Doc. A/C 1/SR. 127 at p. 7, 27 April 1948.
106. See Brownlie, *Principles of Public International Law*, *supra* note 91, p. 153.
107. See 'A performance-based roadmap to a permanent two-state solution to the Israeli–Palestinian conflict' annexed to a letter dated 7 May 2003 from the Secretary-General addressed to the President of the Security Council, UN Doc. S/2003/529, 7 May 2003.

EPILOGUE

1. See Israeli Cabinet Communique, 4 November 2007, available at http://www.mfa.gov.il/MFA/Government/Communiques/2007/Cabinet%20Communique%204-Nov-2007 (last retrieved 25 October 2008).
2. See Jason Tomes, *Balfour and Foreign Policy: The International Thought of a Conservative Statesman* (Cambridge: Cambridge University Press, 1997), p. 201 (Balfour admitting that he shared Cosima Wagner's racial theories – she was Richard Wagner's wife). See also, Meyer W. Weisgal (ed.), *The Letters and Papers of Chaim Weizmann*, Vol. VII, Series A, August 1914 – November 1917 (Jerusalem: Israel Universities Press, 1975), p. 81 and pp. 114–15 (describing a meeting with Balfour when he said he shared Cosima Wagner's views of the Jews and that they controlled everything in Germany, and that the Jews must either assimilate or go to Palestine). It should be added that Cosima Wagner's daughter, Eva, married Houston Stewart Chamberlain, who was a notorious anti-Semite and who was said to have influenced Alfred Rosenberg, the Nazi ideologue. Chamberlain, a British-born naturalised German, was also friendly with Adolf Hitler who he met several times before his death in 1927. See William L. Shirer, *The Rise and Fall of the Third Reich* (London: The Folio Society, 2005), pp. 111–20 at p. 113 ('It is probably no exaggeration to say, as I have heard more than one follower of Hitler say, that Chamberlain was the spiritual founder of the Third Reich. This singular Englishman, who came to see in the Germans the master race, the hope of the future, worshipped Richard Wagner, one of whose daughters he eventually married; he venerated first Wilhelm II and finally Hitler and was the mentor of both'). H.S. Chamberlain was the author of *Foundations of the Nineteenth Century* (*Grundlagen Des Neunzehnten Jahrhunderts*) which became a bestseller in Germany. The book contains a chapter on the Jews with all the Nazi stereotypes. The book was said to be especially popular with the German aristocracy, the Kaiser and the Nazis who exalted it.
3. See Eustace Percy, *The Responsibilities of the League* (London: Hodder & Stoughton, 1919), p. 154.
4. Ibid., p. 152.
5. Ibid.

6. Ibid., p. 153.
7. Ibid., p. 151.
8. See e.g. Nathan Weinstock, *Zionism: False Messiah* (London: Pluto Press, 1989).
9. See Avi Shlaim, *The Iron Wall: Israel and the Arab World* (London: Penguin paperback, 2000), p. 3.
10. See David Gilmour, *Curzon* (London: John Murray, 1994), p. 482 ('The final version of the letter deferred to the anxieties of both Curzon and Montagu ...').
11. See Balfour's memorandum to the British Foreign Secretary, Curzon, 11 August 1919, Foreign Office No. 371/4183 (1919). This is reproduced in E.L. Woodward and Rohan Butler (eds), *Documents on British Foreign Policy 1919–1939* (London: HMSO, 1952), p. 345.
12. Ibid.
13. See Israel Cohen (ed.), *Speeches on Zionism by the Right Hon. The Earl of Balfour* (London: Arrowsmith, 1928), pp. 25–6. Balfour was delivering a speech at a public demonstration held by the English Zionist Federation under the chairmanship of Lord Rothschild at the Royal Albert Hall for the purpose of celebrating the conferment of the Mandate for Palestine upon Great Britain and the incorporation of the Balfour Declaration into the Treaty of Peace with Turkey although the latter treaty was never ratified by Turkey, and would be expunged from the final draft of the Treaty that was finally concluded at Lausanne in 1923.
14. Ibid., pp. 120–1.
15. See Legal Consequences of the Construction of a Wall in the Occupied Palestinian Territory, Advisory Opinion, ICJ Reports (2004), p. 136. This is also reproduced in 43 *International Legal Materials* (2004), pp. 1009–56. For commentaries see the articles cited in Victor Kattan, 'The Legality of the West Bank Wall: Israel's High Court of Justice v. the International Court of Justice', 40 *Vanderbilt Journal of Transnational Law* (2007), p. 1426, note 2. On Ra'anan Gissin's comments see Aluf Benn, Shlomo Shamir and Yuval Yoaz, 'Israeli Firmly Rejects ICJ Fence Ruling', *Ha'aretz*, 10 July 2004 ('"I believe that after all the rancor dies, this resolution will find its place in the garbage-can of history. The court has made an unjust ruling denying Israel its right of self-defense" said Ra'anan Gissin, a senior adviser to Prime Minister Ariel Sharon').
16. See Rt. Hon. Herbert Samuel, *Zionism: Its Ideals and Practical Hopes* (London: The Zionist Organisation, 1919), p. 3.
17. See *Edwin Montagu and The Balfour Declaration* (London: Arab League Office, 1966), p. 6.
18. See International Status of South-West Africa, Advisory Opinion: ICJ Reports (1950), p. 128 at p. 132 (emphasis added). This passage is cited with approval in the *Wall* advisory opinion, *supra* note 15, at p. 165, para. 70.
19. See the minutes of the statement by the Right Honourable Malcolm MacDonald, 17 June, in Permanent Mandates Commission, Minutes of the Thirty-Sixth Session, held at Geneva from 8 June to 29 June, 1939, including the Report of the Commission to the Council, Official No. C. 170.M. 100. 1939, VI., p. 125.
20. See, generally, Sabri Jiryis, *The Arabs in Israel 1948–1966*, trans. by Meric Dobson (Beirut: Institute for Palestine Studies, 1969).
21. See Walter Laqueur, *The Israel/Arab Reader: A Documentary History of the Middle East Conflict* (London: Weidenfeld & Nicolson, 1969), p. 57.
22. See the various laws passed by the Provisional Council of State and the Knesset in *Laws of the State of Israel*, Vols 1–7 (1948–53). For instance, Law No. 12 of 5708–1948 at p. 25, Vol. 1, L.S.I., entitled 'Abandoned Areas Ordinance' provides in Article 1 (a) that an '"Abandoned Area" means any area or place *conquered* by or surrendered to armed forces or deserted by all or part of its inhabitants, and which has been declared to be an abandoned area' (emphasis added). See also, 'Area of Jurisdiction and Powers Ordinance', No. 29 of 5708–1948, 1 L.S.I., p. 64 which applies retroactively from 15 May 1948. Article 1 of the statute provides that: 'Any law applying to the whole of the State of Israel shall be deemed to apply to the whole of the area including both the area of the State of Israel

and any part of Palestine which the Minister of Defence has defined by proclamation as being held by the Defence Army of Israel.'

23. See Sir Robert Jennings and Sir Arthur Watts (eds), *Oppenheim's International Law*, Vol. 1, Parts 2 to 4 (Singapore: Pearson Education, 2005, ninth edition), p. 699 ('Conquest was a mode of acquisition only if the conqueror, after having firmly established the conquest, and the state of war coming to an end, then formally annexed the territory').
24. See League of Nations, Permanent Mandates Commission, Minutes of the Thirty-Second (Extraordinary) Session devoted to Palestine, held at Geneva from July 30th to August 18th, 1937, including the Report of the Commission to the Council, Official No. C.330. M.222. 1937. VI, pp. 178–9 (Mr Ormsby-Gore replying to a question from the Chairman).
25. See Wm. Roger Louis, 'British Imperialism and the End of the Palestine Mandate', in Wm. Roger Louis and Robert W. Stookey (eds), *The End of the Palestine Mandate* (London: I.B. Tauris, 1986), p. 24.
26. See Separate Opinion of Judge Dillard, Western Sahara, Advisory Opinion, ICJ Reports (1975), p. 122.
27. See generally, Raul Hilberg, *The Destruction of the European Jews* (London: W.H. Allen, 1961) (describing the Nazi machinery of destruction and the roles played by the perpetrators of the *Shoah*); Martin Gilbert, *The Holocaust: A History of the Jews of Europe during the Second World War* (New York: Henry Holt & Co., 1985) and of course the writings of Primo Levi.
28. See Report of the Anglo-American Committee of Enquiry regarding the problems of European Jewry and Palestine, Miscellaneous No. 8 (1946), Lausanne, 20 April 1946 (London: HMSO, Cmd 6808).
29. Sir Mohammed Zafrullah Khan, representative of Pakistan, UN General Assembly debate on the majority and minority proposals regarding partition. UN Doc. A/PV.126, 28 November 1947.
30. Quoted in Tom Segev, *One Palestine, Complete: Jews and Arabs under the British Mandate* (London: Little, Brown & Co., 2000), p. 47, footnote, citing Theodor Herzl, Diary (in Hebrew) (Tel Aviv: Neumann, 1930), Vol. 1, p. 12.
31. See International Assistance to Refugees: Report Submitted by Sir Herbert Emerson, G.C.I.E., K.C.S.I., C.B.E., High Commissioner for Refugees, Annex 20, 11 March 1946, (presented at Geneva session in April 1946), in League of Nations Official Journal, Special Supplement No. 194, Records of the Twentieth (Conclusion) and Twenty-First Ordinary Sessions of the Assembly, Text of the Debates at the Plenary Meetings and Minutes of the First and Second Committees, Final Assembly, Geneva, 1946, pp. 228–35 at p. 233.
32. See Tom Segev, *The Seventh Million: The Israelis and the Holocaust* (New York: Farrar, Straus & Giroux, 1993), pp. 82–3 ('... the leaders of the state-to-be believed it was not their job to save the Jews of Europe. The Jewish Agency's business, David Ben-Gurion said at the height of the Holocaust, was to build the Land of Israel').
33. See Abdulaziz Achedina, *The Islamic Roots of Democratic Pluralism* (Oxford: Oxford University Press, 2001), pp. 96–7.
34. See Benjamin Braude and Bernard Lewis (eds), *Christians and Jews in the Ottoman Empire: The Functioning of a Plural Society*, Vols I and II (New York: Holmes & Meirer Publishers, 1982) (both volumes include various articles by different authors on the millet system in the Arab world during Ottoman rule).
35. See Permanent Mandates Commission, Minutes of the Thirty-Second (Extraordinary) Session devoted to Palestine, held at Geneva from 30 July to 18 August 1937, at p. 17.
36. On 23 February 1998, *Al Quds al-Arabi*, an Arabic newspaper published in London, printed in full the text of a 'Declaration of the World Islamic Front for Jihad against the Jews and the Crusaders', faxed to them under the signature of Us ma bin L din. The declaration refers to the 'petty state' of the Jews, their occupation of Jerusalem and their killing of Muslims in it. See Bernard Lewis, *A Middle East Mosaic: Fragments of Life, Letters and History* (New York: Random House, 2000), pp. 319–20.
37. The Community Security Trust, a British-based body which monitors anti-Jewish racism, has reported a sharp increase in anti-Semitic incidents as a result of Israel's Christmas

assault on Gaza in 2008-09 and during the war in Lebanon in July 2006. See Mark Townsend, 'Rise in antisemitic attacks "the worst recorded in Britain in decades"', *Observer*, 8 February 2009, available online at: http://www.guardian.co.uk/world/2009/feb/08/police-patrols-antisemitism-jewish-community (last retrieved 10 February 2009).

38. See Bernard Lewis, 'The Arab World Discovers Anti-Semitism', in Sander L. Gilman and Steven T. Katz (eds), *Anti-Semitism in Times of Crisis* (New York: New York University Press, 1991), pp. 343–52.
39. Isaiah 42:6.
40. See Theodor Herzl, *The Jewish State* (1896), trans. from the original German by Sylvie D'Avigdor (New York: Dover Publication Inc., 1988), p. 83.
41. See 'Hostages', *Manchester Guardian*, 10 December 1947, p. 4 ('... on the whole the Arabs have a good record in their treatment of the Jews – a far better record, be it said, than that of Europe. If it is not quite true, as is sometimes claimed, that there was no anti-Jewish feeling among the Arab people before the founding of the Jewish National Home in Palestine, it is fair to say that over many centuries Jews and Arabs lived together in peace. The conflict over Palestine naturally changed this').
42. In 1841 the bulk of Palestinian Sephardim spoke a language known as Ladino which was a dialect of antique Spanish, heavily laced with Turkish and Arabic words. See Arnold Blumberg, *Zion before Zionism 1838–1880* (New York: Syracuse University Press, 1985), p. 27.
43. In this regard see the foreword by Arnold Toynbee in Robert John and Sami Hadawi, *The Palestine Diary*, Vol. 1, 1914–45 (New York: New World Press, 1970), p. xiv (arguing that Britain bears primary responsibility for starting the conflict).
44. For an article on how international law can be used to facilitate negotiations between Israelis and Palestinians, see Omar Dajani, 'Shadow or Shade? The Roles of International Law in Palestinian–Israeli Peace Talks', 32 *Yale Journal of International Law* (2007), pp. 61–124.

Select Bibliography

There are hundreds of books and thousands of articles published in international law journals related to the Arab–Israeli conflict listed on the Peace Palace catalogue in The Hague, which holds the largest collection of international legal material in the world. It would not be possible to list more than a selection of books here. Generally, only those books which have actually been referred to or cited within these pages are referred to in this bibliography although the list is not exhaustive. The following list focuses on the Palestine question in the mandate years and international law more generally, although reference is also made to later periods. In addition, reference is also made to case law, international treaties, and Foreign, Colonial and War Office documentation, although specific League of Nations and United Nations documents were too numerous to list here. For further references, please see the endnotes of this book where full citations have been reproduced to aid the researcher locate specific documents.

BOOKS

Aaronson, R. (2000) *Rothschild and Early Jewish Colonization in Palestine*. Jerusalem: The Hebrew University Magnes Press.

Adelson, R. (1975) *Mark Sykes: Portrait of an Amateur*. London: Jonathan Cape.

Ahroni, R. (2001) *Jewish Emigration from Yemen, 1951–98: Carpet Without Magic*. Richmond: Curzon.

Alangari, H. (1998) *The Struggle for Power in Arabia: Ibn Saud, Hussein and Great Britain 1914–1924*. Reading: Ithaca Press.

al-Baharna, H. (1975) *The Arabian Gulf States: Their Legal and Political Status and their International Problems*. Beirut: Librairie du Liban.

Allain, J. (2004) *International Law in the Middle East: Closer to Power than Justice*. Aldershot: Ashgate Publishers.

Antonius, G. (1938) *The Arab Awakening: The Story of the Arab National Movement*. London: Hamish Hamilton.

Arendt, H. (1994) *Eichmann in Jerusalem: A Report on the Banality of Evil*. London: Penguin Books.

Avigdor, S. (1988) *Theodor Herzl: The Jewish State*. New York: Dover Publication Inc.

Avneri, A.L. (1982) *The Claim of Dispossession: Jewish Land-Settlement and the Arabs 1878–1948*. New York: Herzl Press.

Ayala, B. (1912) *De Jure et Officialis Bellicis et Disciplina Militari Libri III*, edited by John Westlake. Washington, DC: Carnegie Institution.

Barbour, N. (1946) *Nisi Dominus: A Survey of the Palestine Controversy*. London: George G. Harrap & Co.

Bar-Joseph, U. (1987) *The Best of Enemies: Israel and Transjordan in the War of 1948*. London: Frank Cass.

Bar-Zohar, M. (1977) *Ben-Gurion*. Tel Aviv: Am Oved.

Bassiouni, M.C. (2005) *Documents on the Arab–Israeli Conflict: Emergence of Conflict in Palestine, the Arab–Israeli Wars and the Peace Process*. New York: Transnational.

Begin, M. (1979) *The Revolt*. London: W.H. Allen.

Beinin, J. (1998) *The Dispersion of Egyptian Jewry: Culture, Politics, and the Formation of a Modern Diaspora*. Berkeley: University of California Press.

Ben-Ami, S. (2005) *Scars of War, Wounds of Peace: The Israeli–Arab Tragedy*. London: Weidenfeld & Nicolson.

Ben-Itto, H. (2005) *The Lie that Wouldn't Die: The Protocols of the Elders of Zion*. London: Vallentine Mitchell.

Bennion, F. (2002) *Statutory Interpretation: A Code*. London: Butterworths.
Bentwich, N. (1930) *The Mandates System*. London: Longmans, Green & Co.
Bentwich, N. (1932) *England in Palestine*. London: Kegan Paul, Trench, Trubner & Co.
Bentwich, N. and. H. (1965) *Mandate Memories, 1918–1948*. London: The Hogarth Press.
Benvenisti, M. (2000) *Sacred Landscape: The Buried History of the Holy Land since 1948*. Berkeley: University of California Press.
Benvenisti, E., Gans, C. and Hanafi, S. (2007) *Israel and the Palestine Refugees*. Heidelberg: Springer, in association with Max-Planck-Institut für ausländisches öffentliches Recht und Völkerrecht.
Bercuson, D.J. (1984) *The Secret Army*. New York: Stein & Day.
Bermant, C. (1971) *The Cousinhood: The Anglo-Jewish Gentry*. London: Eyre & Spottiswoode.
Bernadotte, F. (1951) *To Jerusalem*. London: Hodder & Stoughton.
Blumberg, A. (1985) *Zion before Zionism 1838–1880*. New York: Syracuse University Press.
Bordwell, P. (1908) *The Law of War between Belligerents: A History and Commentary*. Chicago: Callaghan & Co.
Bowen, S. (1997) *Human Rights, Self-Determination and Political Change in the Occupied Palestinian Territories*. The Hague: Martinus Nijhoff Publishers.
Bowen, J. (2004) *Six Days: How the 1967 War Shaped the Middle East*. London: Simon & Schuster.
Bowett, D.W. (1958) *Self-Defence in International Law*. Manchester: Manchester University Press.
Bowle, J. (1957) *Viscount Samuel: A Biography*. London: Victor Gollancz.
Bradshaw, F. and Emanuel, C. (1904) *Alien Immigration: Should Restrictions Be Imposed?* London: Ibister & Co.
Brandeis, L. (1934) *The Jewish Problem: How to Solve It*. Cleveland: Joseph Saslaw.
Braude, B. and Lewis, B. (1982) *Christians and Jews in the Ottoman Empire: The Functioning of a Plural Society*. New York: Holmes & Meirer Publishers.
Brenner, L. (1983) *Zionism in the Age of the Dictators*. London: Croom Helm.
Brenner, L. (2002) *51 Documents: Zionist Collaboration with the Nazis*. New Jersey: Barricade Books.
Bronner, S.E. (2000) *A Rumour about the Jews: Reflections on Antisemitism and the Protocols of the Learned Elders of Zion*. New York: St Martin's Press.
Brownlie, I. (1992) *Treaties and Indigenous Peoples: The Robb Lectures, 1991*. Oxford: Clarendon Press.
Brownlie, I. (2008) *Principles of Public International Law*. Oxford: Oxford University Press.
Buergenthal, T. and Sohn, L.B. (1973) *International Protection of Human Rights*. New York: The Bobbs-Merrill Company.
Caplan, N. (1978) *Palestine Jewry and the Arab Question, 1917–1925*. London.
Carr, E.H. (1937) *International Relations since the Peace Treaties*. London: Macmillan & Co.
Carty, A. (1996) *Was Ireland Conquered? International Law and the Irish Question*. London: Pluto Press.
Cassese, A. (1995) *Self-Determination of Peoples: A Legal Reappraisal*. Cambridge: Cambridge University Press.
Castañeda, J. (1969) *Legal Effects of United Nations Resolutions*. New York: Columbia University Press.
Cattan, H. (1969) *Palestine, The Arabs and Israel: The Search for Justice*. London: The Longman Group.
Cattan, H. (1973) *Palestine and International Law: Legal Aspects of the Arab–Israeli Conflict*. London: Longmans.
Cattan, H. (2000) *The Palestine Question*. New edition. London: Saqi Books.
Cesarani, D. (2004) *Eichmann: His Life and Times*. London: William Heinemann.
Chowdhuri, R.N. (1955) *International Mandates and Trusteeship Systems: A Comparative Study*. The Hague: Martinus Nijhoff.
Cohen, A. (1970) *Israel and the Arab World*. New York: W.H. Allen.

Cohen, I. (1928) *Speeches on Zionism by the Right Hon. The Earl of Balfour*. London: Arrowsmith.

Cohen, I. (1952) *The Rebirth of Israel: A Memorial Tribute to Paul Goodman*. London: Edward Goldston & Son.

Cohen, M.J. (1982) *Palestine and the Great Powers 1945–1948*. New Jersey: Princeton University Press.

Cohen, M.J. (1985) *Churchill and the Jews*. London: Frank Cass.

Cohen, S.A. (1982) *English Zionists and British Jews: The Communal Politics of Anglo-Jewry, 1895–1920*. New Jersey: Princeton University Press.

Cohn, N. (1970) *Warrant for Genocide: The Myth of the Jewish World-Conspiracy and the Protocols of the Elders of Zion*. Harmondsworth: Penguin Books.

Cooks, F.S. (1918) *The Secret Treaties and Understandings*. London: Union of Democratic Control.

Cordier, A.W. and Foote, W. (1969) *Public Papers of the Secretaries-General of the United Nations, Trygve Lie, 1946–1953*. New York: Columbia University Press.

Crandall, S.B. (1916) *Treaties: Their Making and Enforcement*. Washington, DC: John Byrne & Co.

Crawford, J. (2006) *The Creation of States in International Law*. Oxford: Oxford University Press.

Curtiss, J.S. (1942) *An Appraisal of the Protocols of Zion*. New York: Columbia University Press.

Dawn, C.E. (1973) *From Ottomanism to Arabism: Essays on the Origins of Arab Nationalism*. Urbana: University of Illinois Press.

Dayan, M. (1976) *Story of My Life*. London: Weidenfeld & Sons.

Disraeli, B. (1862) *Tancred*. London: Routledge, Warne & Routledge.

Donaldson, F.L. (1962) *The Marconi Scandal*. London: R. Hart-Davis.

Donovan, R.J. (1977) *Conflict and Crisis: The Presidency of Harry S. Truman 1945–1948*. New York: W.W. Norton & Company.

Dowty, A. (2008) *Israel/Palestine*. Cambridge: Polity Press.

Dugard, J. (1987) *Recognition and the United Nations*. Cambridge: Grotius Publications.

El-Eini, R. (2006) *Mandated Landscape: British Imperial Rule in Palestine, 1929–1948*. London: Routledge.

Epp, F.H. (1971) *Whose Land is Palestine? The Middle East Problem in Historical Perspective*. Michigan: Wm. B. Eerdams Publishing Co.

Faroqhi, S. (2004) *The Ottoman Empire and the World Around it*. London: I.B. Tauris.

Farsoun, S.K. and Aruri, N.H. (2006) *Palestine and the Palestinians: A Social and Political History*. Boulder: Westview Press.

Feldman, R.H. (1978) *Hannah Arendt, The Jews as Pariah: Jewish Identity and Politics in the Modern Age*. New York: Grove Press.

Fenwick, C.G. (1948) *International Law*. New York: Appleton-Century-Crofts.

Ferguson, N. (1998) *The World's Banker: The History of the House of Rothschild*. London: Weidenfeld & Nicolson.

Ferguson, N. (2004) *Empire: How Britain Made the Modern World*. London: Penguin Books.

Fischbach, M.R. (2003) *Records of Dispossession: Palestinian Refugee Property and the Arab–Israeli Conflict*. New York: Columbia University Press.

Flohr, P.M. and Reinharz, J. (1995) *The Jew in the Modern World: A Documentary History*. Oxford: Oxford University Press.

Forsyth, D.P. (1972) *United Nations Peacemaking: The Conciliation Commission for Palestine*. Baltimore: The Johns Hopkins University Press.

Fraser, T.G. (1984) *Partition in Ireland, India and Palestine: Theory and Practice*. London: Macmillan.

Friedmann, I. (1977) *Germany, Turkey, and Zionism 1897–1918*. Oxford: Clarendon Press.

Friedmann, I. (2000), *Palestine: A Twice-Promised Land? The British, the Arabs and Zionism 1915–1920*, Vol. I. New Brunswick: Transaction Publishers.

Friedmann, L. (1972) *The Law of War: A Documentary History – Volume 1 with a foreword by Telford Taylor*. New York: Random House.
Fromkin, D. (2000) *A Peace to End All Peace: The Fall of the Ottoman Empire and the Creation of the Modern Middle East*. London: Phoenix Press.
Gainer, B. (1972) *The Alien Invasion: The Origins of the Aliens Act of 1905*. London: Heinemann Educational Books.
Gainsborough, J.R. (1986) *The Arab–Israeli Conflict: A Politico-Legal Analysis*. Aldershot: Gower.
García-Granados. (1949) *The Birth of Israel: The Drama as I saw It*. New York: Alfred A. Knopf.
Gartner, L.P. (2001) *The Jewish Immigrant in England 1870–1914*. London: Vallentine Mitchell.
Gat, M. (1997) *The Jewish Exodus from Iraq 1948–1951*. London: Cass.
Gaury, G. de, (1951) *Rulers of Mecca*. London: George G. Harrap & Co.
Gelvin, J.L. (2007) *The Israel–Palestine Conflict: One Hundred Years of War*. Cambridge: Cambridge University Press.
Gentili, A. (1933) *De Iure Belli Libri Tres*. Oxford: Clarendon Press.
George, D.L. (1938) *The Truth About the Peace Treaties*. London: Victor Gollancz.
Gerson, A. (1978) *Israel, the West Bank and International Law*. London: Frank Cass.
Gilman, S.L. and Katz, S.T. (1991) *Anti-Semitism in Times of Crises*. New York: New York University Press.
Gilmour, D. (1982) *Dispossessed: The Ordeal of the Palestinians*. London: Sphere paperbacks.
Gilmour, D. (1994) *Curzon*. London: John Murray.
Glubb, J.B. (1957) *A Soldier with the Arabs*. London: Hodder & Stoughton.
Gordon, S. (1984) *Hitler, Germans and the 'Jewish Question'*. New Jersey: Princeton University Press.
Granovsky, A. (1940) *Land Policy in Palestine*. New York: Bloch Publishing Company.
Green, L.C. (2000) *The Contemporary Law of Armed Conflict*. Manchester: Manchester University Press.
Grieg, D.W. (2001) *Intertemporality and the Law of Treaties*. London: British Institute of International and Comparative Law.
Grotius, H. (1853) *De Jure Belli et Pacis Libri Tres, translated by William Whewell*. Cambridge: Cambridge University Press.
Grotius, H. (1916) *Mare Liberum*. New York: Oxford University Press.
Hall, D. (1948) *Mandates, Dependencies and Trusteeship*. Washington, DC: Carnegie Endowment for International Peace.
Hamilton, J. (2004) *Gods, Guns and Israel: Britain, the First World War and the Jews in the Holy City*. Stroud: Sutton Publishing.
Heater, D. (1994) *National Self-Determination: Woodrow Wilson and His Legacy*. London: Macmillan.
Heller, J. (1995) *The Stern Gang: Ideology, Politics and Terror, 1940–1949*. London: Frank Cass.
Helmreich, P.C. (1974) *From Paris to Sèvres: The Partition of the Ottoman Empire at the Peace Conference of 1919–1920*. Columbus: Ohio State University Press.
Hertzberg, A. (1959) *The Zionist Idea: A Historical Analysis and Reader*. New York: Harper & Row.
Herzl, T. (1896) *Der Judenstaat*. Leipzig und Wien: M. Breitenstein.
Higgins, R. (1994) *Problems and Process: International Law and How We Use It*. Oxford: Clarendon Press.
Hilberg, R. (1961) *The Destruction of the European Jews*. London: W.H. Allen.
Hitler, A. (1992) *Mein Kampf*, with an introduction by D. Cameron Watt, Trans. by Ralph Marheim. London: Pimlico.
Hochschild, A. (1999) *King Leopold's Ghost: A Story of Greed, Terror, and Heroism in Colonial Africa*. Boston: Mariner Books.
Holmes, C. (1979) *Anti-Semitism in British Society, 1876–1939*. London: Edward Arnold.

Huneidi, S. (2001) *A Broken Trust: Herbert Samuel, Zionism and the Palestinians*. London: I.B. Tauris.

Hyamson, A.M. (1917) *Palestine: The Rebirth of an Ancient People*. London: Sidgwick & Jackson Ltd.

Hyamson, A.M. (1950) *Palestine under the Mandate*. London: Methuen & Co. Ltd.

Ikan, Y. (1997) *The World Zionist Organization: The National Institutions, Structure and Functions*. Jerusalem: The Department of Organisation and Community Relations, The World Zionist Organisation.

Jacobs, J.D. (Not dated) *The Jewish National Fund*. London: The Zionist, Jewish National Fund Commission of the United Kingdom.

Jessup, P.C. (1935) *International Security: The American Rôle in Collective Action for Peace*. Westport: Greenwood Press.

Jessup, P.C. (1974) *The Birth of Nations*. New York: Columbia University Press.

Jiryis, S. (1969) *The Arabs in Israel 1948–1966*. Beirut: Institute for Palestine Studies.

John, R. and Hadawi, S. (1970) *The Palestine Diary, 1914–1945*. New York: New World Press.

John, R. (1988) *Behind the Balfour Declaration: The Hidden Origin of Today's Mideast Crisis*. Costa Mesa: The Institute for Historical Review.

Kattan, V. (2008) *The Palestine Question in International Law*. London: British Institute of International and Comparative Law.

Katz, Y. (1994) *The 'Business' of Settlement: Private Entrepreneurship in the Jewish Settlement of Palestine, 1900–1914*. Jerusalem: The Hebrew University Magnes Press.

Katz, Y. (2005) *The Battle for the Land: The History of the Jewish National Fund (KKL) before the Establishment of the State of Israel*. Jerusalem: The Hebrew University Magnes Press.

Kayali, H. (1997) *Arabs and Young Turks: Ottomanism, Arabism, and Islamism in the Ottoman Empire, 1908–1918*. Berkeley: University of California Press.

Kedourie, E. (1976) *In the Anglo-Arab Labyrinth: The McMahon–Husayn Correspondence*. Cambridge: Cambridge University Press.

Kelsen, H. (1950) *The Law of the United Nations: A Critical Analysis of its Fundamental Problems*. London: Stevens & Sons.

Khalidi, R. (1980) *British Policy Towards Syria and Palestine 1906–1914*. London: Ithaca Press.

Khalidi, R. (2007) *The Iron Cage: The Story of the Palestinian Struggle for Statehood*. Oxford: Oneworld Publications.

Khalidi, W. (1963) *Why did the Palestinians Leave? An Examination of the Zionist Version of the Exodus of 1948*. London: Arab Information Centre.

Khalidi, W. (1984) *Before their Diaspora: A Photographic History of the Palestinians 1876–1948*. Washington, DC: Institute for Palestine Studies.

Khalidi, W. (1987) *From Haven to Conquest: Readings in Zionism and the Palestine Problem Until 1948*. Washington, DC: Institute for Palestine Studies.

Khalidi, W. (1993) *All the Remains: The Palestinian Villages Occupied and Depopulated by Israel in 1948*. Washington, DC: Institute of Palestine Studies.

Khouri, F.J. (1985) *The Arab–Israeli Dilemma*. New York: Syracuse University Press.

Kimche, J. and Kimche, D. (1954) *The Secret Roads: The 'Illegal' Migration of a People 1938–1948*. London: Secker & Warburg.

Kolinsky, M. (1993) *Law, Order and Riots in Mandatory Palestine, 1928–35*. London: St Martin's Press.

Korman, S. (1996) *The Right of Conquest: The Acquisition of Territory by Force in International Law*. Oxford: Clarendon Press.

Kramer, A. (1974) *The Forgotten Friendship: Israel and the Soviet Bloc, 1947–53*. Urbana: University of Ilinois Press.

Kushner, D. (1986) *Palestine in the Late Ottoman Period: Political, Social and Economic Transformation*. Leiden: Brill.

Kushner, T. (1989) *The Persistence of Prejudice: Anti-Semitism in British Society During the Second World War*. Manchester: Manchester University Press.

Lansing, R. (1921) *The Peace Negotiations: A Personal Narrative*. London: Constable & Co.
Lansing, R. (1922) *The Big Four and Others of the Peace Conference*. London: Hutchinson & Co.
Laqueur, W. (1969) *The Israel/Arab Reader: A Documentary History of the Middle East Conflict*. London: Weidenfeld & Nicolson.
Laqueur, W. (2003) *The History of Zionism*. London: I.B. Tauris.
Lauterpacht, E. (1968) *Jerusalem and the Holy Places*. London: The Anglo-Israel Association.
Lauterpacht, E. (1977) *International Law: Being the Collected Papers of Hersch Lauterpacht*. Cambridge: Cambridge University Press.
Lawrence, T.E. (2000) *The Seven Pillars of Wisdom: A Triumph*. New edition. London: Penguin Books.
Lebzelter, G.C. (1978) *Political Anti-Semitism in England 1918–1939*. London: Macmillan.
Lee, D.C. (1921) *The Mandate for Mesopotamia and the Principle of Trusteeship in English Law*. London: St Clements Press.
Lehn, W. (1988) *The Jewish National Fund*. New York: Kegan Paul International.
Legnano, G. da, (1917) *Tractatus De Bello, De Represaliis et De Duello, edited by Thomas Erskine Holland*. Washington, DC: The Carnegie Institution.
Lenin, V.I. (1977) *Collected Works, Vol. 20, December 1913 – August 1914* Moscow: Progress Publishers and in London by Lawrence & Wishart.
Leslie, S. (1923) *Mark Sykes: His Life and Letters*. London: Cassell & Co.
Lewis, B. (1997) *Semites and Anti-Semites: An Inquiry into Conflict and Prejudice*. London: Phoenix Giant paperbacks.
Lewis, B. (2000) *A Middle East Mosaic: Fragments of Life, Letters and History*. New York: Random House.
Lindley, M.F. (1921) *The Acquisition and Government of Territory in International Law: Being a Treatise on the Law and Practice of Colonial Expansion*. London: Longmans, Green & Co.
Liverpool, L.R. (2002) *The Trial of Adolf Eichmann*. London: Pimlico.
Loder, J.D.V. (1923) *The Truth About Mesopotamia, Palestine & Syria*. London: George Allen & Unwin Ltd.
London, L. (2000) *Whitehall and the Jews 1933–1948: British Immigration Policy and the Holocaust*. Cambridge: Cambridge University Press.
Lorch, N. (1961) *The Edge of the Sword: Israel's War of Independence, 1947–1949*. New York: G.P. Putnam's Sons.
Lorimer, J. (1883) *The Institutes of the Law of Nations: A Treatise of the Jural Relations of Separate Political Communities*. Edinburgh: William Blackwood & Sons.
Louis W.R. and Stookey, R.N. (1986) *The End of the Palestine Mandate*. London: I.B. Tauris.
MacMillan, M. (2003) *Peacemakers: The Paris Conference of 1919 and its Attempt to End War*. London: John Murray.
Makovsky, M. (2007) *Churchill's Promised Land: Zionism and Statecraft*. New Haven: Yale University Press.
Magnus, L. (1902) *Aspects of the Jewish Question by a Quarterly Reviewer with a Map*. London: John Murray.
Malcom, J.A. (Not dated) *Origins of the Balfour Declaration: Dr. Weizmann's Contribution*.
Mandel, N.J. (1976) *The Arabs and Zionism before World War I*. Berkeley: University of California Press.
Manning, W.O. (1895) *Commentaries on the Law of Nations, revised by Sheldon Amos*. Cambridge: Macmillan.
Marek, K. (1968) *Identity and Continuity of States in Public International Law*. Genève: Librairie Droz.
Margalith, A.M. (1930) *The International Mandates*. Baltimore: Johns Hopkins Press.
Martens, G.F.V. (1802) *A Compendium of the Law of Nations, trans. William Cobbett*. London: Cobbett & Morgan.
Mattar, P. (1988) *The Mufti of Jerusalem: Al-Hajj al-Husayni and the Palestinian National Movement*. New York: Columbia University Press.

Mayer, A.J. (1963) *Wilson vs. Lenin: Political Origins of the New Diplomacy*. New York: The World Publishing Co.

McCarthy, J. (1990) *The Population of Palestine: Population History and Statistics of the Late Ottoman Empire and the Mandate*. New York: Columbia University Press.

McDougal, M.S. and Feliciano, F.P. (1994) *The International Law of War: Transnational Coercion and World Public Order*. New Haven: New Haven Press.

McNair, A. (1961) *The Law of Treaties*. Oxford: Clarendon Press.

Mearsheimer, J.J. and Walt, S.M. (2007) *The Israel Lobby and US Foreign Policy*. New York: Farrar, Straus & Giroux.

Meinertzhagen, R. (1959) *Middle East Diary 1917–1956*. London: The Cresset Press.

Menuhin, M. (1965) *The Decadence of Judaism in Our Times*. New York: Exposition Press.

Migdal, J.S. and Kimmerling, B. (2003) *The Palestinian People: A History*. Massachusetts: Harvard University Press.

Miller, D.H. (1928) *The Drafting of the Covenant*. New York: G.P. Putnam's Sons.

Miyoshi, M. (1993) *Considerations of Equity in the Settlement of Boundary Disputes*. Dordrecht: Martinus Nijhoff.

Monroe, E. (1981) *Britain's Moment in the Middle East, 1914–1971*. London: Chatto & Windus.

Morris, B. (1987) *The Birth of the Palestinian Refugee Problem 1947–49*. Cambridge: Cambridge University Press.

Morris, B. (1990) *1948 and After: Israel and the Palestinians*. Oxford: Clarendon Press.

Morris, B. (1999) *Righteous Victims: A History of the Zionist–Arab Conflict, 1881–1999*. London: John Murray.

Morris, B. (2002) *The Road to Jerusalem: Glubb Pasha, Palestine and the Jews*. London: I.B. Tauris.

Morris, B. (2004) *The Birth of the Palestinian Refugee Problem Revisited*. Cambridge: Cambridge University Press.

Morris, B. (2008) *1948 A History of the First Arab–Israeli War*. New Haven: Yale University Press.

Morris, Y. (1953) *Pioneers from the West: A History of Colonization in Israel by Settlers from English-Speaking Countries*. Jerusalem: Youth and Hechalutz Department, World Zionist Organisation.

Nakhleh, I. (1991) *Encyclopaedia of the Palestine Problem*. New York: Intercontinental Books.

Nicolson, H. (1969) *Diplomacy*. Oxford: Oxford University Press.

Nicosia, F. (1985) *The Third Reich and the Palestine Question*. London: I.B. Tauris.

Masalha, N. (1992) *Expulsion of the Palestinians: The Concept of 'Transfer' in Zionist Political Thought, 1882–1948*. Washington, DC: Institute for Palestine Studies.

Nilus, S.A. (1972) *World Conquest through World Government, The Protocols of the Learned Elders of Zion*, trans. from the Russian by Victor Marsden, Britons Publishing Co.

Oettinger, J. (1919) *Jewish Colonization in Palestine: Methods, Plans and Capital*. London: Head Office of the Jewish National Fund.

Oppenheim, L. and Edmonds, J.E. (1914) *Manual of Military Law*. London: War Office, St Martin's Lane: HMSO.

Oppenheim, L. (1912) *International Law: A Treatise*. London: Longmans, Green & Co.

Ovendale, R. (2004) *The Origins of the Arab–Israeli Wars*. Harlow: Pearson Longman.

Palumbo, M. (1987) *The Palestinian Catastrophe: The 1948 Expulsion of a People from their Homeland*. London: Quartet Books.

Pappé, I. (1988) *Britain and the Arab–Israeli Conflict, 1948–1951*. London: Macmillan Press.

Pappé, I. (2004) *A History of Modern Palestine: One Land, Two Peoples*. Cambridge: Cambridge University Press.

Pappé, I. (2006) *The Ethnic Cleansing of Palestine*. Oxford: Oneworld Publications.

Parfit, T. (1996) *The Road to Redemption: The Jews of Yemen 1900–1950*. Leiden: E.J. Brill.

Parris, T.J. (2003) *Britain, the Hashemites and Arab Rule 1920–1925: The Sherifian Solution*. London: Frank Cass.

Percy, E. (1919) *The Responsibilities of the League*. London: Hodder & Stoughton.

Peretz, D. (1958) *Israel and the Palestine Arabs*. Washington, DC: The Middle East Institute.

Pictet, J.S. (1958) *Commentary to the Geneva Conventions 1949*. Geneva: International Committee of the Red Cross.

Playfair, E. (1992) *International Law and the Administration of Occupied Territories*. Oxford: Oxford University Press.

Poliakov, L. (1974) *The History of Anti-Semitism, Volume 1, From Roman Times to Court Jews*. London: Routledge & Kegan Paul.

Poliakov, L. (1974) *The History of Anti-Semitism, Volume II, From Mohammed to Marranos*. London: Routledge & Kegan Paul.

Poliakov, L. (1985) *The History of Anti-Semitism, Volume IV, Suicidal Europe*. Oxford: Oxford University Press.

Porath, Y. (1974) *The Emergence of the Palestinian-Arab National Movement, 1918–1929*. London: Frank Cass.

Quigley, J.B. (1990) *Palestine and Israel: A Challenge to Justice*. Durham: Duke University Press.

Quigley, John. (2005) *The Case for Palestine: An International Law Perspective*. Durham: Duke University Press.

Reinharz, J. (1985) *Chaim Weizmann: The Making of a Zionist Leader*. Oxford: Oxford University Press.

Renton, J. (2007) *The Zionist Masquerade: The Birth of the Anglo-Zionist Alliance, 1914–1918*. Basingstoke: Palgrave Macmillan.

Reynier, J. de, (1950) *A Jérusalem un Drapeau flottait sur la ligne de Feu*. Neuchatel: Editions de la Bacconière.

Rigo Sureda, A. (1973) *The Evolution of the Right to Self-Determination: A Study of United Nations Practice*. Leiden: A.W. Sijthoff.

Rizk, E. (1968) *The Palestine Question: Seminar of Arab Jurists on Palestine, Algiers, 22–27 July, 1967*. Beirut: The Institute for Palestine Studies.

Rodinson, M. (2004) *Israel: A Colonial Settler State?*. London: Pathfinder Press.

Rogers, A.P. (1996) *Law on the Battlefield*. Third edition, 2004, paperback. Manchester: Manchester University Press.

Ro'i, Y. (1980) *Soviet Decision Making in Practice: The USSR and Israel 1947–1954*. New Brunswick: Transaction Books.

Romulo, C.B. (1980) *Forty Years: A Third World Soldier at the UN*. New York: Greenwood Press.

Rothschild, L. (1980) *'You have it Madam,' The Purchase, in 1875, of Suez Canal Shares by Disraeli and Baron Lionel de Rothschild*. London: W. & J. Mackay Ltd.

Royle, T. (1995) *Orde Wingate: Irregular Soldier*. London: Weidenfeld & Nicolson.

Rose, N. (1992) *From Palmerston to Balfour: Collected Essays of Mayir Vereté*. London: Frank Cass.

Russell, C. and Lewis, H.S. (1900) *The Jew in London. A Study of Racial Character and Present-Day Conditions Being Two Essays Prepared for the Toynbee Trustees* with an Introduction by Canon Barnett and the Right Hon. James Bryce, M.P. London: T. Fisher Unwin.

Sachar, H.M. (1977) *A History of Israel: From the Rise of Zionism to our Time*. Oxford: Basil Blackwell.

Said, E. (1980) *The Question of Palestine*. London: Routledge & Kegan Paul.

Sanders, R. (1983) *The High Walls of Jerusalem: A History of the Balfour Declaration and the Birth of the British Mandate of Palestine*. New York: Holt, Rinehart & Winston.

Sayigh, R. (2007) *The Palestinians: From Peasants to Revolutionaries*. London: Zed Books.

Schama, S. (1978) *Two Rothschilds and the Land of Israel*. London: William Collins Sons & Co. Ltd.

Schechtman, J.B. (1966) *The United States and the Jewish State Movement. The Crucial Decade: 1939–1949*. New York: Herzl Press.

Schölch, A. (1993) *Palestine in Transformation 1856–1882: Studies in Social, Economic and Political Development*. Washington, DC: Institute for Palestine Studies.

Schulze, K. (1999) *The Arab–Israeli Conflict*. London: Longman.

Schulze, K. (2001) *The Jews of Lebanon: Between Coexistence and Conflict*. Brighton: Sussex Academic Press.

Segev, T. (1986) *1949: The First Israelis*. New York: The Free Press.

Segev, T. (1993) *The Seventh Million: The Israelis and the Holocaust*. New York: Farrar, Straus & Giroux.

Segev, T. (1999) *One Palestine, Complete: Jews and Arabs under the British Mandate*. New York: Henry Holt, paperback.

Shafir, G. (1989) *Land, Labour and the Origins of the Israeli–Palestinian Conflict 1882–1914*. Cambridge: Cambridge University Press.

Sharif, R. (1984) *Non-Jewish Zionism: Its Roots in Western History*. London: Zed Press.

Shamir, R. (2000) *The Colonies of Law: Colonialism, Zionism and Law in Early Mandate Palestine*. Cambridge: Cambridge University Press.

Shapiro, I. (1969) *The Middle East: Prospects for Peace*. New York: Oceana Publications.

Shaw, M. (1986) *Title to Territory in Africa: International Legal Issues*. Oxford: Clarendon Press.

Shiblack, A. (1986) *The Lure of Zion: The Case of Iraqi Jews*. London: Al Saqi.

Shilony, Z. (1998) *Ideology and Settlement: The Jewish National Fund, 1897–1914*. Jerusalem: The Magnes Press, The Hebrew University.

Shirer, W. (2005) *The Rise and Fall of the Third Reich*. London: The Folio Society.

Shepherd, N. (1999) *Ploughing Sand: British Rule in Palestine 1917–1948*. London: John Murray.

Shlaim, A. (1988) *The Politics of Partition: King Abdullah, the Zionists and Palestine 1921–1951*. Oxford: Clarendon Press.

Shlaim, A. (2000) *The Iron Wall: Israel and the Arab World*. London: Penguin Books.

Smith, C. and Bierman, J. (2000) *Fire in the Night: Wingate of Burma, Ethiopia and Zion*. London: Macmillan.

Smuts, J.C. (1918) *The League of Nations: A Practical Suggestion*. London: Hodder & Stoughton.

Snetsinger, J. (1974) *Truman, the Jewish Vote and the Creation of Israel*. Stanford: Hoover Institution Press.

Sokolow, N. (1919) *The History of Zionism 1600–1918*. London: Longmans Green & Co.

Sørensen, M. (1968) *Manual of Public International Law*. London: Macmillan.

Stein, L. (1983) *The Balfour Declaration*. Jerusalem: The Magnes Press.

Stevens, R. (1962) *American Zionism and US Foreign Policy, 1942–1947*. New York: Pageant Press.

Stone, J. (1981) *Israel and Palestine: Assault on the Law of Nations*. Baltimore: Johns Hopkins University Press.

Stowell, E.C. (1921) *Intervention in International Law*. Washington, DC: John Byrne & Co.

Stoyanovsky, J. (1928) *The Mandate for Palestine: A Contribution to the Theory and Practice of International Mandates*. London: Longmans, Green & Co.

Takkenberg, L. (1998) *The Status of Palestinian Refugees in International Law*. Oxford: Oxford University Press.

Tal, D. (2004) *The War in Palestine 1948: Strategy and Diplomacy*. New York: Routledge.

Tanenbaum, J.K. (1978) *France and the Arab Middle East 1914–1920*. Philadelphia: The American Philosophical Society.

Teitelbaum, J. (2001) *The Rise and Fall of the Hashemite Kingdom of Arabia*. London: Hurst & Company.

Temperley, H.W.V. (1924) *A History of the Peace Conference*. London: Henry Froude and Hodder & Stoughton.

Thornberry, P. (2002) *Indigenous Peoples and Human Rights*. Manchester: Manchester University Press.

Tibawi, A.L. (1977) *Anglo-Arab Relations and the Question of Palestine 1914–1921*. London: Luzac & Co.

Tivnan, E. (1987) *Jewish Political Power and American Foreign Policy*. New York: Simon & Schuster.

Toman, J. and Schindler, D. (2004) *The Laws of Armed Conflicts: A Collection of Conventions, Resolutions and Other Documents*. Leiden: Martinus Nijhoff Publishers.

Tomes, J. (1997) *Balfour and Foreign Policy: The International Thought of a Conservative Statesman*. Cambridge: Cambridge University Press.

Truman, H.S. (1956) *Years of Trial and Hope 1946–1953*. Bungay: Hodder & Stoughton.

Tuchman, B. (2001) *Bible and Sword: England and Palestine from the Bronze Age to Balfour*. London: Phoenix Paperbacks.

Umozurike, U.O. (1979) *International Law and Colonialism in Africa*. Enugu: Nwamife Publishers.

Vassiliev, A. (1993) *Russian Policy in the Middle East: From Messianism to Pragmatism*. Reading: Ithaca.

Victoria, F.D. (1917) *De Indis Et De Ivre Belli Relectiones*. Washington, DC: Carnegie Institute of Washington.

Walker, T.A. (1899) *A History of the Law of Nations*. Cambridge: Cambridge University Press.

Waart, P.J.I.M. de (1994) *Dynamics of Self-Determination in Palestine: Protection of Peoples as a Human Right*. Leiden: E.J. Brill.

Wasserstein, B. (1991) *The British in Palestine: The Mandatory Government and the Arab–Jewish Conflict 1917–1929*. Oxford: Basil Blackwell.

Wasserstein, B. (1992) *Herbert Samuel: A Political Life*. Oxford: Clarendon Press.

Watson, G. (2000) *The Oslo Accord: International Law and the Israeli–Palestinian Peace Agreements*. Oxford: Oxford University Press.

Weis, P. (1979) *Nationality and Statelessness in International Law*. Alphen and Rijn: Sijthoff & Noordhoff.

Weisbord, R.G. (1968) *African Zion: The Attempt to Establish a Jewish Colony in the East Africa Protectorate 1903–1905*. Philadelphia: The Jewish Publication Society of America.

Weinberg, R. (1998) *Stalin's Forgotten Zion: Birobidzhan and the Making of a Soviet Jewish Homeland: An Illustrated History 1928–1966*. Berkeley: University of California Press.

Weinstock, N. (1989) *Zionism: False Messiah*. London: Pluto Books.

Weisgal, M.W. (1975) *The Letters and Papers of Chaim Weizmann*. Jerusalem: Israel Universities Press.

Weizmann, C. (1949) *Trial and Error: The Autobiography of Chaim Weizmann*. London: Hamish Hamilton.

Welles, S. (1948) *We Need Not Fail*. Cambridge, MA: The Riverside Press.

Wheatcroft, G. (1996) *The Controversy of Zion: How Zionism Tried to Resolve the Jewish Question*. London: Sinclair-Stevenson.

Whiteman, K.W. (1996) *The Invention of Ancient Israel: The Silencing of Palestinian History*. London: Routledge.

Wilson, E.M. (1979) *Decision on Palestine: How the U.S. Came to Recognize Israel*. Stanford: Stanford University, Hoover Institution Press.

Wilson, M.C. (1987) *King Abdullah, Britain and the Making of Jordan*. Cambridge: Cambridge University Press.

Wilson, R.D. (1949) *Cordon and Search: With the 6th Airborne Division in Palestine*. Aldershot: Gale & Polden.

Wolf, L. (1921) *The Myth of the Jewish Menace in World Affairs or the Truth about the Forged Protocols of the Elders of Zion*. New York: Macmillan & Co.

Wright, Q. (1930) *Mandates under the League of Nations*. Chicago: University of Chicago Press.

Wyman, D.S. (1985) *The Abandonment of the Jews: America and the Holocaust 1941–1945*. New York: Pantheon Books.

BOOK SECTIONS

Crawford, J. (1999) 'Israel (1948–1949) and Palestine (1998–1999): Two Studies in the Creation of States', in *The Reality of International Law: Essays in Honour of Ian Brownlie*, edited by G.S. Goodwin Gill and S. Talmon. Oxford: Clarendon Press.

Gross, N.T. (1990) 'The Anglo-Palestine Company: The Formative Years, 1903–1914', in *Ottoman Palestine 1800–1914: Studies in Economic and Social History*, edited by G.G. Gilbar. Leiden: Brill.

Lauterpacht, H. (1977) 'The United Nations General Assembly-Voting and Competence in the Palestine Question', in *International Law Being the Collected Papers of Hersch Lauterpacht, Volume 3: The Law of Peace*, edited by E. Lauterpacht. Cambridge: Cambridge University Press.

Louis, W.R. (1986) 'British Imperialism and the End of the Palestine Mandate', in *The End of the Palestine Mandate*, edited by W.R. Louis and R.N. Stookey. London: I.B. Tauris 1986.

Porath, Y. (1975) 'The Political Awakening of the Palestinian Arabs and their Leadership towards the end of the Ottoman Period', in *Studies on Palestine during the Ottoman Period*, edited by M. Ma'oz. Jerusalem: The Hebrew University Magnes Press.

Rabinowicz, O.K. (1952) 'New Light on the East Africa Scheme', in *The Rebirth of Israel: A Memorial Tribute to Paul Goodman*, edited by I. Cohen. London: Edward Goldston & Son.

Shafir, G. (2005) 'Settler Citizenship in the Jewish Colonization of Palestine', in *Settler Colonialism in the Twentieth Century: Projects, Practices, Legacies*, edited by C. Elkins and S. Pedersen. New York: Routledge.

Smolansky, O.M. (1986) 'The Soviet Role in the Emergence of Israel', in *The End of the Palestine Mandate*, edited by W.R. Louis and R.N. Stookey. London: I.B. Tauris.

Weiler, J.H.H. (1999) 'Israel, the Territories and International Law: When Doves are Hawks', in *Israel Among the Nations: International and Comparative Law Perspective on Israel's 50th Anniversary*, edited by A.E. Kellerman. Leiden: Brill.

Wright, Q. (1969) 'The Middle East Crisis', in *The Middle East: Propsects for Peace, Background Papers and Proceedings of the Thirteenth Hammarskjöld Forum, Published for the Association of the Bar of the City of New York*, edited by Isaac Shapiro. New York: Oceana Publications.

EDITED BOOKS

Aitchison, C.U. (1933) *A Collection of Treaties, Engagements and Sanads Relating to India and Neighbouring Countries*. Delhi: Manager of Publications.

Batlavi, A.H. (1991) *The Forgotten Years: Memoirs of Sir Muhammad Zafrullah Khan*. Lahore: Vanguard Books.

Betley, J.A. and Gavin, R.J. (1973) *The Scramble for Africa: Documents on the Berlin West African Conference and Related Subjects 1884–1885*. Nigeria: Ibadan University Press.

Burdett, A.L.P. (1996) *Records of the Hijaz: 1798–1925*. London: Archive Editions.

Foote, A.C.W. (1969) *Public Papers of the Secretaries-General of the United Nations, Vol. 1, Trygve Lie, 1946–1953*. New York: Columbia University Press.

Förster, S., Mommsen, W. and Robinson, R. (1988) *Bismarck, Europe and Africa: The Berlin Africa Conference 1884–1885 and the Onset of Partition*. Oxford: Oxford University Press, for the German Historical Institute, London.

Hand, G.J. (1969) *Report of the Irish Boundary Commission*. Shannon: Irish University Press.

Hurewitz, J.C. (1956) *Diplomacy in the Near East: A Documentary Record*. Princeton: D. Van Nostrand Co.

Ingrams, D. (1972) *Palestine Papers 1917–1922: Seeds of Conflict*. London: John Murray.

Kattan, V. (2008) *The Palestine Question in International Law*. London: British Institute of International and Comparative Law.

Keenan, J. (1946) *Trial of Japanese War Criminals*. Washington, DC: US Department of State.

Kent, M. (1984) *Great Britain and the End of the Ottoman Empire 1900–1923. The Great Powers and the End of the Ottoman Empire*. London: George Allen.

Khalidi, W. (1987) *From Haven to Conquest: Readings in Zionism and the Palestine Problem until 1948*. Washington, DC: Institute of Palestine Studies.

Khalil, M. (1962) *The Arab States and the Arab League: A Documentary Record*. Beirut: Khayats.

Lauterpacht, H. (1955) *International Law: A Treatise by L. Oppenheim*. London: Longmans, Green & Co.

Link, A.S. (1992) *Paul Matoux, The Deliberations of the Council of Four (24 March – 28 June 1919), Notes of the Official Interpreter, Vol. II, From the Delivery of the Peace Terms to the German Delegation to the Signing of the Treaty of Versailles*. New Haven: Princeton University Press.

Lughod, I.A. (1987) *The Transformation of Palestine: Essays on the Origin and Development of the Arab–Israeli Conflict – with a foreword by Arnold J. Toynbee*. Evanston: Northwestern University Press.

Millis, W. (1952) *The Forrestal Diaries: The Inner History of the Cold War*. London: Cassell & Co.

Moore, J.N. (1977) *The Arab–Israeli Conflict*, Vols I–III. New Jersey: Princeton University Press.

Oppenheim, L. (1914) *The Collected Papers of John Westlake on Public International Law*. Cambridge: Cambridge University Press.

Pappé, I. (1999) *The Israel/Palestine Question: A Reader*. Abingdon: Routledge, 1999.

Patai, R. (1960) *The Complete Diaries of Theodor Herzl*. New York: Herzl Press.

Pritchard, R.J. (1998) *The Tokyo Major War Crimes Trial*. New York: The Edwin Mellon Press.

Rogan, E. and Shlaim, A. (2007) *The War for Palestine: Rewriting the History of 1948*. Cambridge: Cambridge University Press.

Flournoy, R. and Hudson, M.O. (1929) *A Collection of Nationality Laws of Various Countries as Contained in Constitutions, Statutes and Treaties*. New York: Oxford University Press.

Sadullah, M.M. (1983) *The Partition of the Punjab 1947: A Compilation of Official Documents*. Lahore: National Documentation Centre.

Silverburg, S.R. (2002) *Palestine and International Law*. Jefferson: McFarland & Co.

Temperley, H.W.V. (1924) *A History of the Peace Conference of Paris*. London: Henry Frowde and Hodder & Stoughton.

Wellens, K. (1998) *International Law: Theory and Practice, Essays in Honour of Eric Suy*. The Hague: Martinus Nijhoff.

Yogev, G. (1979) *Political and Diplomatic Documents, December 1947 – May 1948, State of Israel, Israel State Archives and World Zionist Organization, Central Zionist Archives*. New Brunswick: Transaction Books.

JOURNAL ARTICLES

Abboushi, W.F. (1977) 'The Road to Rebellion: Arab Palestine in the 1930s', *Journal of Palestine Studies* 6: 23–46.

Akehurst, M. (1973) 'The Arab–Israeli Conflict and International Law', *New Zealand Universities Law Review* 5: 231–49.

Alexandrowicz, C.H. (1968) 'The Afro-Asian World and the Law of Nations (Historical Aspects)', *Recueil Des Cours* 123 (I): 117–214.

Alexandrowicz, C.H. (1971) 'The Juridical Expression of the Sacred Trust of Civilisation', *American Journal of International Law* 65: 149–59.

Algase, R.C. (1977) 'Protection of Civilian Lives in Warfare: A Comparison between Islamic Law and Modern International Law Concerning the Conduct of Hostilities', *Revue de Droit Militaire et de Droit de la Guerre* 16.

Amerasinghe, C.F. (2004) 'History and Sources of the Law of War', *Sri Lanka Journal of International Law* 16: 263–87.

Anghie, A. (2001–02) 'Colonialism and the Birth of International Institutions: Sovereignty, Economy, and the Mandate System of the League of Nations', *New York University Journal of International Law and Politics* 34: 513–633.

Bentwich, N. (1920–21) 'The Legal Administration of Palestine under the British Military Occupation', *British Yearbook of International Law* 1: 139–48.

Bentwich, N. (1926) 'Nationality in Mandated Territories Detached from Turkey', *British Yearbook of International Law* 7: 97–109.

Bentwich, N. (1929) 'Le Systèm Des Mandats', *Recueil Des Cours* 29 (IV): 115–86.

Brierly, J.L. (1929) 'Trusts and Mandates', *British Yearbook of International Law* 10: 217–19.

Brown, P.M. (1919) 'Editorial Comment: Jewish Nationalism', *American Journal of International Law* 13: 755–8.

Brown, P.M. (1948) 'The Recognition of Israel', *American Journal of International Law* 42: 620–7.

Cattan, H. (1987–88) 'Recollections on the United Nations Resolution to Partition Palestine', *Palestine Yearbook of International Law* 4: 260–4.

Dajani, O. (2007) 'Shadow or Shade? The Roles of International Law in Palestinian–Israeli Peace Talks', *Yale Journal of International Law* 32: 61–124.

Dugard, J. (1968) 'The Revocation of the Mandate for South West Africa', *American Journal of International Law* 62: 78–97.

Eagleton, C. (1948) 'Palestine and the Constitutional Law of the UN', *American Journal of International Law* 42: 397–9.

Elaraby, N. (1968) 'Some Legal Implications of the 1947 Partition Resolution and the 1949 Armistice Agreements', *Law and Contemporary Problems* 33: 97–109.

Faris, H.A. (1975) 'Israel Zangwill's Challenge to Zionism', *Journal of Palestine Studies* 4: 74–90.

Fried, J.H.E. (1946) 'Transfer of Civilian Manpower from Occupied Territory', *American Journal of International Law* 40: 303–31.

Gilmour, D. (1996) 'The Unregarded Prophet: Lord Curzon and the Palestine Question', *Journal of Palestine Studies* 25: 60–8.

Glick, E.B. (1956) 'Zionist and Israel Efforts to Influence Latin America: A Case Study in Diplomatic Persuasion', *The Western Political Quarterly* 9: 329–43.

Gowlland-Debbas, V. (1990) 'Collective Responses to the Unilateral Declaration of Independence of Southern Rhodesia and Palestine: An Application of the Legitimizing Function of the United Nations', *British Yearbook of International Law* 61: 135–53.

Hambro, E. (1954) 'The Authority of the Advisory Opinions of the International Court of Justice', *International and Comparative Law Quarterly* 3: 2–22.

Husseini, J.B. (1932) 'The Proposed Palestine Constitution', *Annals of the American Academy of Political and Social Science* 164.

Kattan, V. (2005) 'The Nationality of Denationalized Palestinians', *Nordic Journal of International Law* 74: 67–102.

Keith, B. (1922) 'Mandates', *Journal of Comparative Legislation and International Law* 4: 71–83.

Khalidi, W. (1988) 'Plan Dalet: Master Plan for the Conquest of Palestine', *Journal of Palestine Studies* 18: 4–33.

Khalidi, W. (1994) 'The Jewish-Ottoman Land Company: Herzl's Blueprint for the Colonization of Palestine', *Journal of Palestine Studies* 22: 30–47.

Levene, M. (1992) 'The Balfour Declaration: A Case of Mistaken Identity', *The English Historical Review* 107: 54–77.

Lynk, M. (2003) 'The Right to Restitution and Compensation in International Law and the Displaced Palestinians', *Refuge* 21: 96–113.

Mahmassani, S. (1967) 'The Principles of International Law in the Light of Islamic Doctrine', *Recueil Des Cours* 117 (I): 201–326.

Mallison, S. and Mallison, Jr. W. Thomas (1984) 'The Juridical Bases for Palestinian Self-Determination', *Palestine Yearbook of International Law* 1: 36–65.
Matz, N. (2005) 'Civilization and the Mandate System under the League of Nations as Origin of Trusteeship', *Max Planck Yearbook of United Nations Law* 9: 47–95.
McTague, J.J. (1978) 'The British Administration in Palestine 1917–1920', *Journal of Palestine Studies* 7: 55–76.
Mills, M.C. (1923) 'The Mandatory System', *American Journal of International Law* 17: 50–65.
Mogannam, M.E. (1932) 'Palestine Legislation under the British', *Annals of the American Academy of Political and Social Science* 164.
Morris, B. (1986) 'Operation Dani and the Palestinian Exodus from Lydda and Ramle in 1948', *The Middle East Journal* 40: 82–109.
Pogany, I. (1986) 'Humanitarian Intervention in International Law: The French Intervention in Syria Re-Examined', *International and Comparative Law Quarterly* 35: 182–90.
Pomerance, M. (1999) 'The ICJ and South West Africa (Namibia): A Retrospective Legal/Political Assessment', *Leiden Journal of International Law* 12: 426–39.
Potter, P.B. (1922) 'The Origin of the System of Mandates under the League of Nations', *The American Political Science Review* 16: 563–83.
Potter, P.B. (1948) 'The Palestine Problem before the United Nations', *American Journal of International Law* 42: 859–61.
Quigley, J. (1998) 'Displaced Palestinians and a Right of Return', *Harvard International Law Journal* 39: 171–229.
Rehman, J. and Ali, S.S. (2005) 'The Concept of Jihad in Islamic International Law', *Journal of Conflict & Security Law* 10: 321–43.
Scobbie, I. (2003–04) 'The Responsibility of Great Britain in Respect of the Creation of the Palestine Refugee Question', *Yearbook of Islamic and Middle Eastern Law* 10: 39–58.
Shah, N.A. (2005–06) 'Self-Defence in Islamic Law', *Yearbook of Islamic and Middle Eastern Law* 12: 181–208.
Silsby, S. (1986) 'George Antonius: The Formative Years', *Journal of Palestine Studies* 15: 81–98.
Townsend, C. (1988) 'The Defence of Palestine: Insurrection and Public Security, 1936–1939', *The English Historical Review* 103: 917–49.
Vallat, F.A. (1959) 'The Competence of the United Nations General Assembly', *Recueil Des Cours* 97 (II): 203–92.
Wolf, L. (1904) 'The Zionist Peril', *The Jewish Quarterly Review* 17: 1–25.
Woodhead, J. (1939) 'The Report of the Palestine Partition Commission', *International Affairs* 18: 171–93.
Zakheim, D.S. (1999) 'The British Reaction to Zionism: 1895 to the 1990s', *The Round Table* 350.

THESES

Al-Amr, S.M. (1978) 'The Hijaz under Ottoman Rule 1869–1914: Ottoman Vali, the Sherif of Mecca, and the Growth of British Influence'. University of Leeds.
Drew, C.J. (2005) 'Population Transfer: The Untold Story of the International Law of Self-Determination', A Thesis Presented for the Degree of Doctor of Philosophy in the Department of Law. London: LSE.
Qafisheh, M. (2007) 'The International Law Foundations of Palestinian Nationality, A Legal Examination of Palestinian Nationality under British Rule', Thèse présentée à l'Université de Genève pour l'obtention du grade de Docteur en relations internationales (droit international).

NEWSPAPERS

The Jewish Chronicle
The Manchester Guardian

The Guardian
The Observer
The Times
The Scotsman
The New York Times

LEGAL RESOURCES

Bernhardt, R. (ed.) *Encyclopedia of Public International Law* (1997)
Max Planck Encyclopedia of Public International Law, http://www.mpepil.com

PUBLISHED ARCHIVES

Parliamentary Papers, Commons
Parliamentary Papers, Lords
Parry's Consolidated Treaty Series
A Handbook of Arabia
Handbook of Hejaz
Records of the Hijaz 1798–1925
British Foreign and State Papers
Foreign Relations of the United States
Documents on the Foreign Policy of Israel
Documents on British Foreign Policy
Minutes of the Permanent Mandates Commission
League of Nations Official Journal
United Nations Conference on International Organisation
Official Records of the General Assembly

LAW REPORTS

Reports of the Permanent Court of International Justice, Series A–C
Annual Digest and Reports of Public International Law Cases
Digest of International Law (Hackworth, Whiteman & Moore)
Reports of International Arbitral Awards
Law Reports of Trials of War Criminals Selected and Prepared by the United Nations War Crimes Commission
The Trials of Major War Criminals, Agreement and Principal Speeches, Treaty Series No. 27 (1946), Prosecution and Punishment of the Major War Criminals of the European Axis, and the Charter of the International Military Tribunal, London, 8 August 1945
Charter for the International Military Tribunal in the Far East in Joseph Keenan (ed.), Trial of Japanese War Criminals, US Department of State, 1946
International Law Reports
ICJ Reports
Palestine Gazette
Drayton's Laws of Palestine
The Law Reports of Palestine
Government of Palestine, Ordinances, Regulations, Rules, Orders and Notices, (Annual Volume)
Laws of the State of Israel
Yearbook of the International Court of Justice
Yearbook of the International Law Commission
International Legal Materials

NATIONAL ARCHIVE DOCUMENTATION

Colonial, Foreign and War Office Files

Africa (East) Jewish Settlement, FO 2/785, (1903).

Exchange of telegrams between Sir Henry McMahon and Sir Edward Grey, 14 May 1915 and 19 May, Political: Turkey (War) File, 34982, FO 371/2486, (1915).

Telegram from Sir Edward Grey to Sir Henry McMahon on the instructions given to the latter regarding his reply to the Arabs, 20 October, File No. 155203, FO 371/2486, (1915).

Telegram from Sir Henry McMahon to Sir Edward Grey, informing the latter about his pledge to Hussein, 26 October, File No. 163832, FO 371/2486, (1915).

Allenby to War Office on the applicability of the laws of war to Palestine, 2 March, FO 371/2070/77141 and FO 371/3384/358, (1918).

Weizmann to Balfour, complaining about the applicability of the laws of war to Palestine, 30 May, FO 371/3410, (1918).

Attempts by Zionists to buy up German owned land in Haifa, FO 141/686/9, (1918).

Letter to Mr W.A.F. Erskine, (Rome), H.M. Chargé d'Affaires from the Hon. Mr R. Graham (the Secretary of State) at the Foreign Office, 28 July, attaching a memorandum which is to be communicated to the Italian Government on the delivery of heavy weaponry to the Sherif of Mecca, Registry No. 123010/W/44, FO 371/3410, (1918).

An article on Norman Bentwich published in the American Jewish Chronicle, enclosed in a letter dated 4 July from the British Embassy in Washington DC to the Foreign Office, FO 371/3410, (1918).

Memorandum on British Commitments to King Hussein, Political Intelligence Department, Foreign Office, Special 3, FO 608/92 Peace Conference British Delegation (1919).

Protests of Palestinians in America, Bolivia, Chile and Mexico against Zionism, FO 608/98, (1919).

Report of an Intelligence Office on the Palestine Conference, FO 608/98, (1919).

Proposal for Palestine Mandate: On behalf of the Zionist Organisation in Paris, Mr Frankfurter to Col. Meinertshagen, 20 March, FO 608/100, (1919).

Proceedings of a Meeting, War Office, 29 October to discuss reconnaissance for an oil pipeline across the Arabian Desert in Political, Turkey Files, FO 371/4231, (1919).

Feisal–Weizmann Agreement, 3 January, FO 608/98/9, (1919).

Constitution of New Arab State by Emir Feisal, 1 January, FO 608/80/5, (1919).

Peace Conference (British Delegation) Eastern Mission (Turkey) Files 76–91, CO 733/248/19, (1920).

Report of the Court of Inquiry Convened by Order of H.E. the High Commissioners and Commander-in-Chief, dated the 12th day of April, Political Eastern (Turkey) Files 85, pp. 8154–9913 (1920), FO 371/5121 & WO 32/9614, (1920).

Telegram from H. Samuel to Foreign Office, 15 July, File. E 8436/85/44 regarding publication of Jerusalem Riot Enquiry report, FO 371/5121, (1920).

Eastern Conference, Lausanne, Armenian Question, File 33, FO 839/12, (1922).

Autonomy for Assyrian Christians (claims of Assyro-Chaldeans), FO 839/23, (1922).

'Palestine under Mandate' by Sir Thomas W. Haycraft, Late Chief Justice in Palestine, talk given at the Central Asian Society on 28 February, CO 733/150/11, (1928).

Collective Fines Ordinance, No. 57, FO 371/21870, (1936).

On the deportation to the Seychelles of six leading Arab politicians and the Mufti's escape, FO 141/678/1, (1937).

Palestine (Defence) Orders-in-Council, FO 371/21870 & CO 733/379/8, (1937).

Palestine (Defence) Order in Council, 1937, amended 19 January, CO 733/379/8, (1938).

Photographs of damage to Jaffa via aerial photography, FO 371/21870. For a description of events, see WO 191/70, (1938).

'Juridical Basis of the Arab Claim to Palestine' (attaches a memorandum discussing the main points on which the Arab legal claim is based, to which answers may be required), 21 December 1938, Political Eastern, Palestine and Transjordan, FO 371/23219, (1939).

British Commitments in the Middle East, 1914–1918, 18 April, FO 371/24569, (1940).

War Cabinet, Palestine, Memorandum by the Secretary of State for Foreign Affairs for the Personal Use of the Prime Minister, 10 April, PREM 4/52/1, Palestine: Post-War (Partition), (1945).

Palestine: An attempt to forecast the possible result of reference to the United Nations regarding partition, Foreign Office, 16 January, FO 371/61858, (1947).

Military Lessons of the Arab Rebellion in Palestine, 1936, General Staff, Headquarters, the British Forces, Palestine & Transjordan, February, WO 191/70, (1948).

Legal status of Palestine after termination of the Mandate, from Sir O. Sargent, FO Minute, 14 May, to UK delegation in New York, and Washington (prepared by FO Legal Advisers), Palestine, Eastern, FO 371/68664, (1948).

Inward telegram from General Sir A. Cunningham, 19 January, describing partition plan as 'manifestly unfair to the Arabs', Eastern, Palestine, FO 371/68613, (1948).

Numerous telegrams from the Foreign Office over their frustration regarding Transjordan's failure to become a member of the United Nations, Palestine, East, FO 371/68664 (1948).

Situation, Outrages, Jaffa Incident, Inward Telegram from Gen. Sir A. Cunningham, 2 May, to S of S + repeated to Washington. Most immediate. No. 1232. Secret, CO 537/3861, (1948).

Recognition of the Jewish State, Eastern, Palestine, FO 371/68670, (1948).

Letter to the Right Hon. Sir Alexander Cadogan, 18 August, from Aubrey S. Eban, Representative of the Provisional Government of Israel, File 6090, Eastern, Palestine, FO 371/68670, (1948).

Minute from the FCO legal adviser Ms Eileen Denza on the publication of Elihu Lauterpacht's Jerusalem and the Holy Places, 13 October, FCO 17/1605, (1971).

INTERNATIONAL AGREEMENTS

'Protocol for the Pacification of Syria signed in Paris on 3 August', in (1860): 68 Parliamentary Papers (1861), p. 1.

'General Act of the Conference of Berlin Conference', in (1885): 76 British and Foreign State Papers, p. 4.

'International Convention with respect to the Laws and Customs of War, signed at the Hague and its Annex', in (1899): The Consolidated Treaty Series (1898–99), p. 429.

'Agreement signed and exchanged at Rafah on October 1, between the Commissioners of the Turkish Sultanate and the Commissioners of the Egyptian Khediviat, concerning the fixing of a Separating Administrative Line between the Vilayet of Hejaz and Governorate of Jerusalem and the Sinai Peninsula', in (1906): 99, British and Foreign State Papers, (1905–06), p. 482.

'Convention (IV) respecting the Laws and Customs of War on Land and its annex: Regulations concerning the Laws and Customs of War on Land. The Hague, 18 October', in (1907): 205 The Consolidated Treaty Series (1907), p. 277.

'Treaty between Great Britain and Ibn Saud, 26 December', in (1915): J.C. Hurewitz (ed.) *Diplomacy in the Near East: A Documentary Record*, Vol. II (Princeton: D. Van Nostrand Co., 1956), p. 12.

'Treaty between Great Britiain and the Idrisi Sayyid of Sabya', in (1915): 221, The Consolidated Treaty Series (1915–16), p. 66.

'Correspondence between Sir Henry McMahon, G.C.M.G., G.C.V.O., K.C.I.E., C.S.I., His Majesty's High Commissioner in Cairo, and the Sherif of Mecca', in (1915–16): 5957 Command Paper (1939), 27 Great Britain House of Commons, Parliamentary Publications, Sessional Papers 1938–39, Vol. 27, p. 3.

'Convention relative to Air Navigation, Paris, 13 October', in (1919): 112 British and Foreign State Papers, p. 931.

'Convention relative to the Control of the Trade in Arms and Ammunition – Saint-Germaine-en-Laye, 10 September', in (1919): 112 British and Foreign State Papers, p. 909.

'Protocol relative to the Conditions in which certain provisions of the Bulgarian Peace Treaty are to be carried out – Neuilly-sur-Seine, 27 November', in (1919): 112 British and Foreign State Papers, p. 895.

'Treaty of Peace between the British Empire and Allied and Associated Powers and Bulgaria – Neuilly-sur-Seine, 27 November', in (1919): 112 British and Foreign State Papers, p. 781.
'Treaty of Peace between the Allied and Associated Powers and Germany, signed at Versailles, 28 June 1', in (1919): 112 British and Foreign State Papers, p. 1.
'Convention between Great Britain and France for the settlement of certain points connected with the Mandates for Syria and the Lebanon, Palestine and Mesopotamia – Paris, 23 December', in (1920): 113 British and Foreign State Papers (1920), p. 355.
'Covenant of the League of Nations', in (1920): 1 League of Nations Official Journal, p. 3.
'The Treaty of Peace with Turkey signed at Sèvres', in (1920): August 10, Treaty Series No. 11, HMSO, p. 26.
'Treaty between Great Britain and Ireland, signed at London, 6 December', in (1921): 26 League of Nations Treaty Series, (1924), p. 9.
Annex 391, 'British Mandate for Palestine', in (1922): 3 League of Nations Official Journal, p. 1007.
'Treaty of Peace with Turkey signed at Lausanne, 24 July', in (1923): Treaties of Peace 1919–1923, Vol. II (New York: Carnegie Endowment for International Peace, New York, 1924), p. 959.
'Montevideo Convention on the Rights and Duties of States, 26 December', in (1933): 165 League of Nations Treaty Series, p. 19.
'Charter of the United Nations, signed in San Francisco, 26 June 1945, entered into force on 24 October 1945', in (1945): XV United Nations Conference on International Organisation, p. 335.
'Pact of the League of Arab States on collective self-defence, signed at Cairo, on 22 March', in (1945): 70 United Nations Treaty Series (1950), p. 238.
'Egyptian–Israel Armistice Agreement, 23 February', in (1949): UN Doc. S/1264/Corr.1.
'Israeli–Syrian Armistice Agreement, 20 July', in (1949): UN Doc. S/1353.
'Israel–Jordan Armistice Agreement, 3 April', in (1949): UN Doc. S/1302/Rev.1.
'Israel–Lebanon Armistice Agreement, 23 March 1949', in (1949): UN Doc. S/1296.

SELECTED CASES

The Aaland Islands Question, Report of the Committee of Jurists, League of Nations, Official Journal, 3, October 1920.
Armenia–Turkey Boundary Case Arbitral Award, Digest of International Law 1920.
Cessation of vessels and tugs for navigation on the Danube Arbitral Award, Reports of International Arbitral Awards 1921.
Nationality Decrees Issues in Tunis and Morocco, Advisory Opinion, Permanent Court of International Justice, PCIJ, 6, 7 February 1923.
Question of Jaworzina, (Polish–Czechoslovakian Frontier), Advisory Opinion, Permanent Court of International Justice, PCIJ, 6, 6 December 1923.
Mavrommatis Palestine Concessions case, Permanent Court of International Justice, PCIJ, 6, 30 August 1924.
Mavrommatis Palestine Concessions case, Permanent Court of International Justice, PCIJ, 4, 26 March 1925.
A.G. v. Goralschwili et al. Case No. 33, High Court of Palestine, Annual Digest 1925–26.
Saikaly v. Saikaly, Case No. 34, Egyptian Mixed Court, Annual Digest 1925–26.
Jerusalem-Jaffa District Governor and another Appellant; v. Suleiman Murra and Others Respondents, Privy Council, A.C., 321, 1926.
Island of Palmas Case, Permanent Court of Arbitration, Reports of International Arbitral Awards, 831, 4 April 1928.
Customs Régime between Germany and Austria, Permanent Court of International Justice, PCIJ, 37, 5 September 1931.
Legal Status of Eastern Greenland, Permanent Court of International Justice, PCIJ, 22, 5 April 1933.
Lighthouses in Crete and Samos, Permanent Court of International Justice, 4, 1937.

R. v. Ketter High Court of England, K.B, 787, 1940.

The Trial of German Major War Criminals: Proceedings of the International Military Tribunal sitting at Nuremberg, Germany, Judgment, International Military Tribunal, Nuremberg, 22–31 August 1946.

International Military Tribunal for the Far East, Judgment, International Military Tribunal for the Far East, Tokyo, R. John Pritchard, The Tokyo Major War Crimes Trial: A Collection in 124 Volumes (New York: The Edwin Mellon Press, 1998), 1948.

International Status of South-West Africa, Advisory Opinion, International Court of Justice, ICJ Reports, 128, 11 July 1950.

A.B. v. M.B, Tel Aviv District Court, International Law Reports, 110, 1950.

Attorney-General of Israel v. El-Turani, District Court of Haifa, International Law Reports, 21 August 1951.

Minquiers and Ecrehos Case (France v. United Kingdom), Merits, International Court of Justice, ICJ Reports, 4, 17 November 1953.

Case Concerning Right of Passage over Indian Territory (Portugal v. India), Merits, International Court of Justice, ICJ Reports, 6, 12 April 1960.

Case Concerning the Temple of Preah Vihear, (Cambodia v. Thailand), Preliminary Objections, Judgment of 26 May 1961, International Court of Justice, ICJ Reports, 17, 26 May 1961.

Attorney-General of the Government of Israel v. Adolf Eichmann, District Court of Jerusalem, judgment, 36 International Law Reports, 12 December 1961.

Attorney-General of the Government of Israel v. Adolf Eichmann, Israel Supreme Court (sitting as a Court of Criminal Appeal), judgment, 36 International Law Reports, 29 May 1962.

South-West Africa cases, (Ethiopia v. Liberia; Liberia v. South Africa), Preliminary Objections, International Court of Justice, ICJ Reports, 319, 1962.

Rann of Kutch Arbitration (India and Pakistan), Abitral Award constituted pursuant to the Agreement of 30 June, 1965, International Legal Materials 633, 1965.

Legal Consequences for States of the continued presence of South Africa in Namibia (South-West Africa) notwithstanding Security Council Resolution 276 (1970), Advisory Opinion, International Court of Justice, ICJ Reports, 55, 21 June 1971.

Nuclear Tests Case (Australia v. France), Merits, International Court of Justice, ICJ Reports, 253, 20 December 1974.

Western Sahara (Sahara Occidental), Advisory Opinion, International Court of Justice, ICJ Reports, 12, 3 January 1975.

Beagle Channel Arbitration, Court of Arbitration, London, pursuant to an arbitration agreement between Chile and Argentina signed in 1902, International Law Reports, 1977.

Aegean Sea Continental Shelf Case, (Greece v. Turkey) Jurisdiction of the Court, judgment, International Court of Justice, ICJ Reports, 3, 19 December 1978.

Boundary Dispute Concerning the Taba Area, Egypt–Israeli Arbitration Tribunal, International Legal Materials 1421, 29 September 1988.

Mabo v. Queensland (No. 2) [1992] HCA 23; (1992) 175 CLR (3 June 1992).

Case Concerning Maritime Delimitation and Territorial Questions between Qatar and Bahrain, Jurisdiction and Admissibility, judgment, ICJ Reports, 1 July 1994, p. 112.

East Timor (Portugal v. Australia), judgment, International Court of Justice, ICJ Reports, 90, 30 June 1995.

Legality of the Use by a State of Nuclear Weapons in Armed Conflict, Advisory Opinion, International Court of Justice, ICJ Reports, 66, 8 July 1996.

Arbitral Tribunal for Dispute over Inter-Entity Boundary in Brčko Area, The Republika Srpska v. The Federation of Bosnia and Herzegovina, Arbitral Award, International Legal Materials 399, 14 February 1997.

Reference re Secession of Quebec, [1998] 2 S.C.R. 217

Case concerning Kasikili/Sedudu Island, (Botswana v. Namibia), Merits, International Court of Justice, ICJ Reports, 1045, 13 December 1999.

The Federation of Bosnia and Herzegovina v. The Republika Srpska, Arbitration for the Brčko Area, Final Award, Arbitral Award, International Legal Materials 536, 5 March 1999.

Case Concerning Maritime Delimitation and Territorial Questions Between Qatar and Bahrain, Merits, International Court of Justice, ICJ Reports, 40, 16 March 2001.
Legal Consequences of the Construction of a Wall in the Occupied Palestinian Territory, Advisory Opinion, International Court of Justice, ICJ Reports, 139, 9 July 2004.

UN DOCUMENTATION

The UN documents cited in this book are too numerous to reproduce here. Scholars can access a plethora of information either at dedicated UN Documentation Centres, or specifically on the Palestine question, at the United Nations Information System on Palestine (UNISPAL) which is accessible online at: http://domino.un.org/unispal.nsf

List of Individuals

King Abdullah (1882–1951)	Second eldest son of Hussein Ibn Ali and Emir of Transjordan. Abdullah was assassinated while visiting the Al-Aqsa Mosque in Jerusalem in 1951. His grandson Hussein bin Talal was at his side during the assassination. Hussein was enthroned King of Jordan in 1952.
Hussein Ibn Ali (1854–1931)	The Sherif of Mecca from 1908 until 1917. King of Hejaz from 1917 to 1924. In 1924, the year he proclaimed himself Caliph, he was defeated in battle by Abdul Aziz al Saud and fled to Transjordan.
Edmund Allenby (1861–1936)	Commander-in-Chief of the Egyptian Expeditionary Force. The main bridge that connects Jericho in the West Bank to Jordan is named by Israelis after him.
George Antonius (1891–1941)	A Christian Greek Orthodox Arab civil servant in Palestine. He authored the *Arab Awakening* which became the classic text for students of Arab nationalism.
Yasser Arafat (1929–2004)	Founded Fatah, the Palestinian National Liberation Movement, in the 1950s along with other Palestinians in the Diaspora. From 1969 until his death on 11 November 2004, Arafat was the Chairman of the Palestine Liberation Organisation. In addition, in 1996, he became President of the Palestinian National Authority. In 1988, he issued on behalf of 'Palestine' a Declaration of Independence in Algiers. In the 1990s Arafat signed several treaties with Israel known collectively as the 'Oslo Accords,' named after the city where the secret negotiations with Israel took place.
Arthur James Balfour (1848–1930)	British Prime Minister from 1902 to 1905 when the Alien's Act was passed. He was appointed Foreign Secretary in Lloyd George's cabinet in 1916, a position he held until 1919. He was one of the main supporters of the movement to establish a national home for the Jews in East Africa in 1902. He told Cosima Wagner, the wife of the famous composer, that he shared many of her anti-semitic views of the Jews. The November 1917 'Balfour Declaration' is named after him.
Menachem Begin (1913–1992)	Leader of the Irgun. Prime Minister of Israel from 1977 to 1983 and the first leader of the Likud to win an election. As Prime Minister he signed a Peace Treaty with Egypt in 1979. He also authorised the Israeli invasion of Lebanon in 1982.
David Ben-Gurion (1886–1973)	Chairman of the Executive Committee of the Jewish Agency. He would become the first Prime Minister of Israel.
Norman Bentwich (1883–1971)	First Attorney-General of Palestine, legal scholar and author. He was a life-long Zionist, the son of Herbert Bentwich. During the First World War he served in the Camel Transport Corps of the British Army in Egypt. In 1918, he became a senior judicial officer in the British military administration in Palestine. In 1929, whilst serving as Attorney-General he was lightly wounded in an assassination

attempt. He was replaced when his open support for Zionism became an embarrassment to the British Government. In 1932, he became a Professor of International Relations at the Hebrew University of Jerusalem. He was the author of several scholarly articles and books on international law and the mandate system.

Folke Bernadotte (1895–1948)

He was the Count of Wisborg and a Swedish diplomat who made his name negotiating the release of 15,000 prisoners from German concentration camps, over half of them Jews. In 1947, he was unanimously chosen to be the UN mediator in Palestine. In his last progress report to the UN he called for a return of the refugees displaced by the conflict and suggested that the Negev be assigned to the Arab state as envisaged in the UN Partition Plan. He was assassinated by Lehi.

Louis D. Brandeis (1856–1941)

Brandeis was the first Jew to be appointed a Justice of the US Supreme Court in 1916 by President Woodrow Wilson. He was also very prominent in the American Zionist movement and saw in Zionism a solution to the Jewish Question.

Henry Cattan (1906–1992)

Palestinian jurist and a British barrister educated at the universities of London and Paris. He represented the Arab Higher Committee before the UN General Assembly in 1947–48 and testified before the Anglo-American Commission of Inquiry. He wrote several books on the Palestine question in international law as well as on the law of oil concessions in the Middle East and North Africa.

Joseph Chamberlain (1836–1914)

The father of future British Prime Minister Neville Chamberlain, Joseph was one of the most important British politicians of his era. He was the Colonial Secretary from 1895 to 1903 and was seen as a key British expansionist and imperialist. It was Chamberlain who first suggested to Theodor Herzl that he consider establishing a Jewish national home in East Africa, the same year in which he gave a speech at Limehouse in London's East End where he spoke out against the dangers of alien immigration.

Winston Churchill (1874–1965)

Among other positions, he was appointed Secretary of State for the Colonies in 1921, and played a pivotal role in formulating Britain's policy towards Palestine. In 1920, Churchill wrote an article in the *Illustrated Sunday Herald* in which he argued that Zionism was the Jewish answer to international communism. He was Prime Minister during the Second World War leading Britain and the Allies to victory.

George Curzon (1859–1925)

British conservative statesman who served as Viceroy of India from 1899 to 1905 and British Foreign Secretary from 1919 to 1924. It was Curzon who inserted the safeguard clause in the Balfour Declaration which provided that 'nothing shall be done which may prejudice the civil and religious rights of existing non-Jewish communities in Palestine'. He also fought with Balfour over the wording of the Palestine Mandate.

Moshe Dayan (1915–1981)

He was an Israeli military leader and politician who was the Chief of Staff of the Israeli Army during the Suez war in 1956. He was the Minister of Defence during the 1967 Six Day War.

Benjamin Disraeli (1804–1881)

A baptised Jew, Disraeli was elected British Prime Minister twice and founded the modern Conservative Party. He was also the author of many novels including *Sybil*, *Vivian Grey* and *Tancred*.

Aubrey Eban (1915–2002)	Israel's first Ambassador to the UN and Israel's Foreign Minister during the June 1967 Six Day War.
Mark F. Ethridge (1896–1981)	US Representative on the UN Conciliation Commission for Palestine at the Lausanne Peace Conference in 1949.
Walter Eytan (1910–2001)	The first Director-General of Israel's Foreign Ministry which he helped to establish in 1948.
Prince Feisal (1883–1933)	Third son of Hussein Ibn Ali. Led Arab revolt against the Turks in 1917 and lobbied for the Arab cause at the 1919 Paris Peace Conference. He was appointed the King of Iraq from 1921 to 1933 by the British where he reigned after the French forced him out of Syria in 1920.
Lloyd George (1863–1945)	Solicitor with the firm Lloyd George, Roberts & Co when he was asked to draft a Jewish colonisation scheme for East Africa in 1903. He was British Prime Minister from 1916 to 1922 and a keen Zionist.
John Bagot Glubb (1897–1986)	Often referred to as 'Glubb Pasha', he was a British soldier who assumed command of Transjordan's Arab Legion in 1938, a position he held until 1956, when he was dismissed for being a 'British stooge' after tempers flared up in the Middle East after the Anglo-French-Israeli invasion of Suez.
Hugo Grotius (1583–1645)	A seventeenth-century Dutch jurist who entered the University of Leiden when he was just eleven years old. He is seen by many European lawyers as one of the founding fathers of international law.
Loy W. Henderson (1892–1986)	US Foreign Services Officer and Diplomat. He served in the US Department of State, where he was director of the Office of Near Eastern and African Affairs, as well as being appointed US Minister in Iraq, the US Ambassador to India and to Iran.
Theodor Herzl (1860–1904)	Austro-Hungarian Jewish journalist who founded political Zionism as a panacea for anti-Semitism. Authored *Der Judenstaat* ('The Jewish State') and was the first president of the Zionist Organisation. He appeared before the Royal Commission on Alien Immigration in 1902 when he presented his vision of a Jewish state as a way of solving Britain's 'immigration problem'. He also met with Joseph Chamberlain who urged him to consider establishing a Jewish state in East Africa.
Cecil Hurst (1870–1963)	Legal adviser at the British Foreign Office. He would later become a judge at the International Court of Justice.
Amin al-Husseini (1895–1974)	Grand Mufti of Jerusalem from 1922 to 1937 when he was deported to the Seychelles for supporting the Arab Revolt.
Philip C. Jessup (1897–1986)	Professor of International Law at Columbia University, and US delegate on the UN Security Council in 1948 when the Provisional Government of Israel declared its independence. He and his colleagues were shocked when Truman recognised the Jewish state in May 1948 without being informed. Jessup had been the primary author of the draft UN Trusteeship Agreement for Palestine. He was appointed a judge at the International Court of Justice in 1961. An International Law Moot Court Competition is named after him.

Mohammed Zafrullah Khan (1893–1985)
British educated Pakistani jurist who studied law at King's College, London. He was Pakistan's first Foreign Minister. Prior to this he represented British India before the League of Nations. He represented the Muslim League before the Radcliffe Boundary Commission on India's partition. A skilful orator, Khan was asked to take on the Arab cause at the request of Britain before the UN General Assembly in 1947 arguing against the UN Partition Plan for Palestine. He became President of the International Court of Justice in 1970.

Robert Lansing (1864–1928)
Legal adviser to the US Department of State at the outbreak of the First World War and a prominent international lawyer. He served as US Secretary of State under President Woodrow Wilson from 1915 to 1920 and was a member of the US delegation to the Paris Peace Conference.

Hersch Lauterpacht (1897–1960)
Whewell Professor of International Law at Cambridge University, he was elected a judge of the International Court of Justice in 1954. He gave legal advice to the Jewish Agency in 1947 on the UN Partition Plan.

Thomas Edward Lawrence (1888–1935)
A British soldier who fought with Arab troops under the command of Prince Feisal against the Ottoman Empire. He developed a close relationship with Feisal and was part of the Arab delegation to the Paris Peace Conference in 1919. He was popularly known as 'Lawrence of Arabia' and was immortalised in a feature movie named after him. He authored *The Seven Pillars of Wisdom*, an account of his experiences as a British soldier fighting in the Arab Revolt against the Ottoman Turks.

Vladimir Ilyich Lenin (1870–1924)
Russian politician who led the October Revolution. He was the first head of the Russian Soviet Socialist Republic and subsequently the Soviet Union. As Head of State, Lenin played an important role in developing the concept of self-determination through granting immediate independence to Ukraine, Finland, Estonia, Latvia, Lithuania and Turkish Armenia.

Malcolm MacDonald (1901–1981)
British politician and diplomat and the son of Prime Minister Ramsay MacDonald. As Colonial Secretary in the late 1930s he was responsible for formulating British policy towards Palestine.

Charles Malik (1906–1987)
Harvard educated Lebanese philosopher and UN diplomat. He served as a Rapporteur for the Commission on Human Rights in 1947 and 1948, when he became President of the Economic and Social Council. He was instrumental in drafting the Universal Declaration of Human Rights in 1948. He succeeded Eleanor Roosevelt as Chair of the UN Human Rights Commission. In 1958 he presided over the thirteenth session of the UN General Assembly. He was appointed to the Lebanese Cabinet several times and founded the Philosophy Department at the American University of Beirut.

Henry McMahon (1862–1949)
British diplomat and Indian Army Officer who served as High Commissioner in Egypt from 1915 to 1917. He is best known for authoring two contentious partition treaties. The first concerning Palestine and the Middle East, and the second between Britain and Tibet concerning the disputed border between India and China.

Arnold McNair (1885–1975) — A British legal scholar, McNair was the Whewell Professor of International Law at Cambridge University from 1935 to 1937. He was elected a judge of the International Court of Justice in 1946 and became the first President of the European Court of Human Rights from 1959 to 1965.

Richard Meinertzhagen (1878–1967) — A British soldier, Meinertzhagen served as Allenby's Chief Political Officer in Palestine. He attended the Paris Peace Conference in 1919 and was involved with the drafting of the Palestine Mandate. In his diary, he expressed admiration for Adolf Hitler. His views on Jews and Zionism can be summed up in an extract from his personal diary. In a letter to Lord Allenby he wrote: 'My inclination towards Jews in general is governed by an anti-Semitic instinct which is invariably modified by personal contact. My views on Zionism are those of an ardent Zionist.'

Edwin Montagu (1879–1924) — Member of the British War Cabinet in 1916 and Secretary of State for India from 1917 to 1922. He was opposed to political Zionism and to the Balfour Declaration which he considered anti-Semitic. It was he who inserted the second safeguard clause in the Balfour Declaration which provided that nothing shall be done which may prejudice 'the rights and political status enjoyed by Jews in any other country'.

Lassa F.L. Oppenheim (1858–1919) — German educated jurist known for his legal positivist school of thought who became in 1908 the Whewell Professor of International Law at Cambridge University. He is the author of the pioneering text on the subject, *International Law: A Treatise*. This has become the standard text in international law and the ninth edition was edited by the late Sir Robert Jennings and the late Sir Arthur Watts and is named after Oppenheim.

William Ormsby-Gore (1885–1964) — British conservative politician who served as Under-Secretary of State for the Colonies from 1922 to 1929. He was the British representative to the Permanent Mandates Commission from 1921 to 1922 and Colonial Secretary from 1936 to 1938. Many of the colonial documents on Palestine from 1919 through the Mandate in the National Archives bear his signature.

Lord Eustace Percy (1887–1958) — He was the youngest son of the seventh Duke of Northumberland who entered the Civil Service after passing a competitive examination in 1909. In 1911 he passed an examination in International Law. He was transferred to the Foreign Office three years later. According to *The Foreign Office List and Diplomatic and Consular Year Book for 1920*, Percy '[a]ccompanied Mr. Balfour, Secretary of State for Foreign Affairs, on a Special Mission to the United States, May and June, 1917'. According to the same *Year Book*, he also '[a]cted as Private Secretary to Mr. Balfour as one of the British Plenipotentiaries to the Peace Conference at Paris, May 1 to July 6, 1919'. In his memoirs, Percy recalled that he arranged 'the breakfast meeting between Balfour and my friend Justice Brandeis, where I suspect (for I was not present) the formula of the "national home" was first adumbrated'. See Eustace Percy, *Some Memories* (London: Eyre & Spottiswoode, 1958), p. 59. In 1921 Percy was elected a Conservative MP for Hastings. He retained his seat there until 1937. In 1929 he was appointed Privy Councillor and from 1935–36 he served as Minister without Portfolio. He authored several books on international politics including *The Responsibilities of the League* (1919), *Maritime Trade in War: Lecture on the Freedom of the Seas* (1930), and *The Heresy of Democracy: A Study in the History of Government* (1954).

Yitzhak Rabin (1922–1995)
Chief Operations Officer of the Palmach, which was the regular fighting force of the Haganah. He subsequently became Prime Minister of Israel. He was assassinated in 1995 by Yigal Amir, a right-wing Jewish extremist who opposed the Oslo Accords.

Carlos P. Romulo (1899–1985)
A Filipino diplomat, politician, soldier, journalist and author. He represented the Philippines at the UN Conference on International Organisation and included among his many achievements, getting the words 'or independence' included in the draft of Article 76 (b) of the UN Charter on Trusteeships. He was the Philippines' UN Ambassador in 1947 during the vote in favour of partition which his Government initially opposed, although it was forced to change its stance due to pressure from the US Government.

Franklin D. Roosevelt (1882–1945)
President of the United States, elected to four terms in office. He concluded the Atlantic Charter with Churchill in 1941 and made a promise to King Abdul Aziz ibn Saud when referring to the situation in Palestine that he would do nothing in his capacity as Chief of the Executive Branch of the US Government 'which might prove hostile to the Arab people'.

Edmond B. James de Rothschild (1845–1934)
A French Baron, banker and philanthropist from the international Rothschild financial dynasty. He financed many of the first agricultural colonies and settlements in Palestine, although he was not, at first, a Zionist and initially opposed Herzl's attempts to cajole him into the movement.

Lionel Walter Rothschild (1868–1937)
A British Lord, banker and zoologist from the international Rothschild financial dynasty. He was a Member of Parliament for Aylesbury from 1899 to 1910 and worked to formulate the Balfour Declaration which was addressed to him. He was the first British Jew to be made a Peer of England and was a member of the Royal Commission on Alien Immigration of 1902–03 which led to Parliament passing the Alien's Act of 1905 restricting Jewish immigration into Britain. Theodor Herzl was said to have greatly impressed Rothschild when he appeared before the Royal Commission on Alien Immigration in 1902.

Herbert Samuel (1870–1963)
The first practising Jew to be appointed to a British cabinet, who put forward the idea of establishing a British protectorate over Palestine in 1915. He was the Home Secretary in 1916 during the troubles with Britain's Russian Jews who refused to enlist in the British Army and his ideas were to influence the drafting of the Balfour Declaration in November of the following year. He was appointed the first High Commissioner of Palestine in 1920, a position he retained for five years.

Yitzhak Shamir (1915–)
The Prime Minister of Israel from 1983 to 1984 and from 1986 to 1992. In his youth he joined the Irgun before breaking away with Avraham Stern to create Lohamei Herut Israel, known as Lehi or the 'Stern Gang'. He is alleged to have authorised the assassination of Count Folke Bernadotte, the UN mediator for Palestine.

Moshe Sharett (1894–1965)	The first Foreign Minister of Israel. He became Prime Minister of Israel when Ben-Gurion retired in 1954.
Nahum Sokolow (1859–1936)	A Zionist leader, author, Hebrew journalist and translator. He was appointed Secretary-General of the Zionist Organisation in 1906. Among other publications, he is the author of *The History of Zionism* (1919). Sokolow participated in meetings with various British politicians including Sir Mark Sykes during the First World War and lobbied for the Balfour Declaration.
Mark Sykes (1879–1919)	An eccentric English traveller, who was brought up a strict Roman Catholic from a very wealthy aristocratic British family, Sykes was a Conservative Party politician and adviser on Middle East affairs. Before the First World War he had a particular interest in Turkey and travelled extensively in the Middle East. He is most often remembered for his role in the Sykes–Picot agreement which partitioned the Middle East into British and French spheres of influence. In his final years Sykes was instrumental in persuading the British Government to back the Zionist cause. He fell victim to the Spanish flu epidemic in 1919, and died in a hotel in Paris where he was attending the Peace negotiations.
Arnold J. Toynbee (1889–1975)	Worked for the Political Intelligence Department of the British Foreign Office during the First World War and was a member of the British delegation to the Paris Peace Conference in 1919. Toynbee was Director of Studies at the Royal Institute of International Affairs (Chatham House) between 1925 and 1955 and was an honorary fellow of Balliol College, at Oxford University where he began his teaching career. A historian, Toynbee wrote several influential books on world history and civilisation. He always maintained that Palestine had been included in the area assigned to the Sherif of Mecca in the Hussein–McMahon correspondence of 1915. He held Britain, and in particular A.J. Balfour, whom he described as 'a wicked man', as responsible for causing the Arab–Israeli conflict.
Harry S. Truman (1884–1972)	Succeeded Roosevelt on his deathbed to become President of the United States. He supported the UN Partition Plan in 1947, partly due to the fact that it was an election year in 1948. In his memoirs, he wrote that he had never been subject to so much pressure and propaganda in all his life over the question of partitioning Palestine from Zionist lobby groups in the US.
Francisco de Vitoria (1492–1546)	Sixteenth-century Spanish renaissance Roman Catholic theologian and scholar, noted for his contributions to the theory of just war and international law. He was a Professor at the University of Salamanca and some of his writings were influenced by Spain's conquest and colonisation of the Americas. Among other publications, he authored *De Indis at De Jure Belli*.
Chaim Weizmann (1874–1952)	A Russian scientist and Professor of Chemistry at the University of Manchester. He became a British subject in 1910 and was President of the English Zionist Federation. He would subsequently become the President of the Zionist Organisation and the Jewish Agency. Weizmann was involved with the negotiations which led to the Balfour Declaration and he signed an agreement with Prince Feisal in 1919 in order to try to reach an understanding over Palestine. He was appointed the first President of the state of Israel in 1948, a position he retained until his death.

Woodrow Wilson (1856–1924)
The 28th President of the US, from 1913 to 1921. Wilson was President of Princeton University from 1902 to 1910. He famously articulated his Fourteen Points to both Houses of Congress in January 1918, and was instrumental in creating the League of Nations mandates system at the Paris Peace Conference in 1919 which was based on the principle of self-determination.

Orde Wingate (1903–1944)
A British soldier who was raised a militant Christian Zionist. He established the Special Night Squads in Palestine, which were armed groups, formed of British and Haganah volunteers. Soldiers like Moshe Dayan claimed they learnt much from him.

Lucien Wolf (1857–1930)
A British journalist, foreign affairs expert, and historian of Jewish decent. Wolf was the first president of the Jewish Historical Society of England. For 20 years he served on the Conjoint Committee of the Board of Deputies of British Jews and the Anglo-Jewish Association. He was opposed to political Zionism and lobbied against the Balfour Declaration in 1917. He authored several books including *The Myth of the Jewish Menace in World Affairs* (1920). Wolf attended the Paris Peace Conference (1919) as part of the Anglo-Jewish delegation, where he was instrumental in drafting the minority treaties.

Israel Zangwill (1864–1926)
A British-born writer of many novels and plays. He was also politically active with the Zionist movement and was a confidant of Herzl in the early days. However, later in life, he broke away from the Zionist Organisation and established the Jewish Territorial Organisation which he led. It sought to establish a Jewish national home somewhere other than Palestine. One of the reasons Zangwill sought to establish a Jewish home in a territory other than Palestine was because he did not think that Palestine's Arab inhabitants would ever acquiesce peacefully to Jewish sovereignty.

Glossary

aliyah — The word *aliyah* originates from a Hebrew word which means 'to ascend'. The Zionists believed that Jewish settlers coming from Europe would 'ascend' from their diaspora condition and be 'reborn' in Palestine. The term is regularly used to refer to the waves of Jewish immigration into Palestine.

Arab Higher Committee — This was the central political organ of the Arab community in Palestine. It was established in 1936.

Arab League — Officially known as the League of Arab States, it is a regional organisation based in Cairo comprised of 22 Arab states in North Africa and the Middle East, which includes Palestine. It was created in 1945.

Ashkenazim — These are Jews who are said to have descended from the communities of the Rhineland in France and Germany. However, it is a general term which is also used to describe Jews from Eastern Europe, particularly Poland, Lithuania, Bohemia, Moravia and the Ukraine where the Pale of Settlement existed.

belligerent occupation — This takes place when a hostile army takes control and authority over territory, triggering the application of international humanitarian law, or the laws of war.

cession — This is the transfer of sovereignty over state territory by agreement, normally a treaty, from one state to another.

conquest — This term is also used interchangeably with the word subjugation. It refers to the acquisition of title to territory through the use of armed force and annexation. It is unlawful in contemporary international law.

customary international law — One of the primary sources of international law, customary international law is composed of two components: the practice of states and *opinio juris sive necessitatis*. It arises from a general and consistent practice of a significant number of states over a period of time followed out of a sense of legal obligation. In the words of the International Court of Justice: 'Not only must the acts concerned amount to a settled practice, but they must also be such, or be carried out in such a way, as to be evidence of a belief that this practice is rendered obligatory by the existence of a rule of law requiring it.'

estoppel — In international law estoppel (also known as 'preclusion') prevents or 'estopps' a party from successfully adopting different subsequent statements on the same issue without regard for truth or accuracy. The party invoking estoppel must have been induced to undertake legally relevant action or abstain from it by relying in good faith upon clear and unambiguous representations by the other state. Subsequent deviation from the original representation must cause damage to the relying state, or result in advantages for the representing state. As Judge Percy Spender explained in his dissenting opinion in the *Temple of Preah Vihear* case (1962) at pp. 143–4: '[T]he principle operates to prevent a State contesting before the Court a situation contrary to a clear and unequivocal representation previously made by it to another State, either expressly or impliedly, on which representation the other State was, in the circumstances, entitled to rely and in fact did rely, and as a result that other State has been prejudiced or the State making it has secured some benefit or advantage for itself'.

fellaheen — These are the peasants, farmers and agricultural labourers who are thought to be descended from the ancient Egyptians who mixed with various occupying peoples, including Arabs, Persians, Greeks and Turks.

Geneva Conventions of 1949 — These are four separate conventions that opened for ratification in 1949. They are comprised of the Convention for the Amelioration of the Wounded and Sick in Armed Forces in the Field; for those Wounded, Sick and Shipwrecked at Sea; for the Treatment of Prisoners of War; and for the Protection of Civilian Persons in Time of War. The Fourth Geneva Civilians Convention is the most commonly cited.

Haganah — This was a Jewish paramilitary organisation which became the Israeli Army (the 'Israel Defence Force') after the creation of Israel. It was the main armed tool used by the Zionists to create their state in 1948, after it had agreed to coordinate the fighting with the Irgun and Lehi.

Hague Regulations of 1899 and 1907 — These are international treaties negotiated at the First and Second Peace Conferences at The Hague in 1899 and 1907. The most important provisions regulating the conduct of warfare affecting a civilian population are those contained in the Annex on the Law and Customs of War on Land.

International Court of Justice — This is the principal judicial organ of the United Nations based in the Peace Palace in The Hague. It was established in 1945 by the UN Charter and it can only settle disputes between states and international organisations that consent to its jurisdiction. However, it can also issue advisory opinions to UN organs and its specialised agencies which, although not formally binding, reflect the Court's authoritative view on important issues of international law. The ICJ is composed of 15 judges of various nationalities elected to nine-year terms.

international humanitarian law — This is a general term to describe the laws of war and specifically the application of those conventions that become applicable during warfare such as the Hague Regulations of 1907 and the Geneva Conventions of 1949.

Irgun — The Irgun Zvai Leumi, sometimes referred to by its Hebrew acronyms as Etzel, was a militant offshoot of the Haganah. It was widely referred to as a terrorist organisation in its day and was the political predecessor of the Herut Party, which merged with the Likud Party in 1988. The Irgun was responsible for the bombing of the King David Hotel in Jerusalem in July 1946, among many other violent acts, including the Deir Yassin massacre.

Jewish Agency — Served as the pre-state Jewish government before the establishment of Israel. It is mentioned in Article 4 of the British Mandate of

Palestine and was charged with facilitating Jewish immigration into Palestine, land purchase and planning the general policies of the Zionist leadership.

jus ad bellum This refers to the rules governing the resort to armed conflict which are set out in Chapter VII of the UN Charter.

jus in bello This refers to the rules governing the actual conduct of armed conflict which are set out in numerous conventions the most important ones in the case of occupied territories being the 1907 Hague Regulations and the Fourth Geneva Convention and the 1977 Additional Protocols.

League of Nations An international organisation created at the Paris Peace Conference in 1919 to coordinate international affairs between its members. It was based in Geneva at the Palais des Nations. It was dissolved in 1946.

League of Nations Council This was the executive body of the League of Nations.

League of Nations Mandates These applied to the colonies formerly belonging to Imperial Germany and the Ottoman Empire. Article 22 of the League of Nations Covenant provided the constituent document for their administration. They were classified into A-, B- and C-class mandates, depending on their stage of development.

Lehi This is the Hebrew acronym for Lohamei Herut Israel or 'the freedom fighters of Israel'. In the West, Lehi was known as 'the Stern Gang', named after its founder Avraham Stern, and was responsible for carrying out numerous acts of terrorism and assassinations, including that of the UN mediator in Palestine, Count Folke Bernadotte in 1948 and Lord Moyne, Britain's Resident Minister of State in Cairo in 1944.

Mizrahim These are Jews descended from communities in the Middle East, North Africa, Central Asia and the Caucasus.

Nakbah This is an Arabic word meaning catastrophe. It is used by Palestinians to refer to the expulsion and dispossession of 750,000 Palestinian Arabs from their homes in 1948.

occupation Not to be confused with belligerent occupation, occupation is a mode of acquisition by a state of title to a territory which at the time in question is not under the sovereignty of any other state. In other words, it can only take place when the territory subject to occupation is *terra nullius* (territory belonging to no other sovereign).

pacta sunt servanda In Latin this means that 'agreements must be kept'. It is a basic principle of international law. Article 26 of the Vienna Convention on the Law of Treaties of 1969 provides that: 'Every treaty in force is binding upon the parties to it and must be performed by them in good faith.'

Palestine Liberation Organisation This is the National Liberation Movement of the Palestinian People, which has since 1974 been recognised by the Arab League as being 'the sole legitimate representative of the Palestinian people'. It has UN Observer Status and consulates in over 100 states. In the 1990s Israel and the PLO concluded several treaties providing for the creation of a Palestinian National Authority in the West Bank and Gaza Strip.

Palestinian National Authority An administrative organ established by Israel and the PLO to govern parts of the West Bank and the Gaza Strip.

peremptory norm Also called *jus cogens* or *ius cogens*, which is Latin for 'compelling law'. This refers to a rule of international law which is deemed to be so fundamental to the international community that no derogation is permitted.

Permanent Court of Arbitration Established at the Hague Peace Conference in 1899, the PCA is an intergovernmental organ based in the Peace Palace in The Hague, providing a variety of dispute resolution services for states.

Permanent Court of International Justice This was the international court of the League of Nations established in 1922 and situated in the Peace Palace in The Hague. It was replaced in 1946 by the International Court of Justice.

Permanent Mandates Commission This was a League of Nations commission, based in Geneva, which was responsible for overseeing the administration of the Mandates. Each Mandatory was required to submit annual reports to it.

Prescription This is a concept which refers to the acquisition by a state of sovereignty over a territory which at one time was under the sovereignty of another state, through uninterrupted and uncontested peaceful exercise of state authority which has persisted for an undefined period of time, sufficiently long to legitimise the status of the territory in the eyes of other states as based on a valid title acquired under international law by the possessor state.

public international law This is the law that applies between states and international organisations.

recognition When a new state comes into existence, other states are confronted with the problem of deciding whether or not to recognise the new state. Recognition therefore means the willingness to deal with the new state as a member of the international community. The distinction between *de jure* and *de facto* recognition is that the former is the fullest kind of recognition whilst the latter is a lesser degree of recognition. *De facto* recognition takes place when the new authority of the state, although independent and wielding effective power in the territory under its control, has not acquired sufficient stability.

secession The creation of a new independent entity through the separation of part of the territory and population of an existing state, without the consent of the latter.

self-defence This is one of the exceptions to the prohibition on the use of force contained in the UN Charter. Article 51 of the UN Charter provides: 'Nothing in the present Charter shall impair the inherent right of individual or collective self-defence if an armed attack occurs against a Member of the United Nations, until the Security Council has taken measures necessary to maintain international peace and security.' Anglo-American international lawyers often cite the *Caroline* incident in support of a rule of self-defence in customary international law. According to the *Caroline* formulation it must be clearly shown by the state invoking its inherent right of self-defence that there was 'a necessity of self-defence, instant, overwhelming, leaving no choice of means, and no moment for deliberation'.

self-determination This generally refers to the right of peoples to determine their own political destiny without outside interference. Under the colonial system it was applied to all A-class League of Nations mandates. In addition it also has a human rights component. Common article 1 to the 1966 Human Rights Covenants defines it thus: 'All peoples have the right of self-determination. By virtue of that right they freely determine their political status and freely pursue their economic, social and cultural development.'

Sephardim These are Jews who originated from the Iberian Peninsula. They were expelled from Spain in 1492 and from Portugal in 1497.

Shoah A Hebrew word signifying catastrophe, calamity, disaster and destruction. It is the term used in Israel by many to refer to the Holocaust.

sovereignty This is a concept which is tantamount to independence, that is, the right to exercise in a territory the functions of a state to the exclusion of any other state, and with no other authority over the state than that of international law.

state practice This is quite literally the practice of states, that is, what states do. Evidence of state practice is usually found in government press releases, declarations, statements, and other papers on foreign ministry websites, as well as through the explanations they give for voting in various UN bodies and other international organisations.

succession The replacement of one state by another in the responsibility for the international relations of territory.

terra nullius Also known as *res nullius*, this refers to territory under no sovereignty. During the early years of international law opinion was divided as to whether this system of law applied to indigenous peoples. Naturalists argued that all peoples of the world enjoyed certain inalienable rights, whilst positivists denied such rights to indigenous peoples and claimed that international law applied to Christian, civilised nations only. During the nineteenth century, the positivist view prevailed, with the result that indigenous, non-European peoples in loosely organised societies were viewed as having no sovereign rights under international law. As a result their territory was viewed as *terra nullius*, a designation which gave legal backing to colonial expansion and the conquest of that territory.

treaty This is an international agreement concluded between states or between states and international organisations. They come under various names, such as protocol, covenant, convention, exchange of letters, notes, and memoranda, among other descriptions. Most treaties are registered with the UN, with the exception of secret treaties. There is no requirement that a treaty be published for it to be considered binding between states.

United Nations This is the premier international organisation created by the UN Charter in 1945 to replace the League of Nations. Its headquarters are based in New York City. Many of its specialised agencies are based in Geneva as well as in Vienna, Paris and The Hague. The UN is divided into five main administrative bodies: The Secretariat, the Security Council, the General Assembly, the Economic and Social Council, and the International Court of Justice.

UN Charter This is the founding constituent document of the United Nations. It was signed at the United Nations Conference on International Organisation in San Francisco in 1945. Article 103 of the Charter provides: 'In the event of a conflict between the obligations of the Members of the United Nations under the present Charter and their obligations under any other international agreement, their obligations under the present Charter shall prevail.'

UN Conciliation Commission for Palestine This was a commission established by the UN General Assembly to implement the requirements set out in resolution 194 (III) which included coming up with a detailed proposal for Jerusalem and facilitating the repatriation, resettlement and economic, social and rehabilitation of the Palestinian refugees and the payment of compensation. It was comprised of delegates from France, Turkey and the US who attempted, but ultimately failed, to bridge the gaps between Israel and the Arab states concerned at the 1949 Lausanne Peace Conference.

UN General Assembly This is the only UN organ in which all member states have equal representation. Its powers are to oversee the budget of the organisation, to appoint the non-permanent members to the Security Council, to receive reports from other agencies of the UN and to make recommendations in the form of General Assembly resolutions. Voting in the General Assembly on important questions such as recommendations on peace and security; election of members to organs; admission, suspension, expulsion of members, and budgetary matters is by a two-thirds majority of those present and voting. Other questions are decided by a majority vote. Each member state has one vote. Observers cannot vote. Although most UN General Assembly resolutions are not legally binding they may constitute evidence of customary international law. The UN General Assembly is in session annually at its base in New York City from September to December.

UN Security Council This is the organ of the UN charged with maintaining peace and security. It may establish peacekeeping operations, implement international sanctions, and authorise military action. Unlike the UN General Assembly, the Security Council functions continuously throughout the year and its resolutions if passed under Chapter VII of the Charter are binding.

UN Special Committee on Palestine UNSCOP was established in May 1947 in response to Great Britain's decision to terminate the mandate over Palestine and hand responsibility over it to the UN. It was asked to come up with a solution to the Palestine problem. The majority on the Committee favoured the partition of Palestine into two states with an economic union, and the minority produced a report that favoured a unitary state.

UN Trust Territories These were the successors to the remaining League of Nations mandates (B- and C-class mandates) which came into being when that body was dissolved in 1946. Palestine and South-West Africa (Namibia) were the only two mandates that were not converted into UN Trusteeships in 1946. Namibia became an independent state in 1990 after South Africa withdrew from the territory after decades of struggle with SWAPO.

Universal Declaration of Human Rights This was a declaration adopted and proclaimed by the UN General Assembly on 10 December 1948. Although it was not technically legally binding, many of its provisions reflect customary international law today.

Yishuv A Hebrew word which refers to the body of Jewish settlers in Palestine before the establishment of the state of Israel.

World Zionist Organisation The Zionist Organisation was established at the First Zionist Congress in Basel in 1897. It served as an umbrella organisation for the Zionist movement, to assist it with creating a Jewish state in Palestine. It was renamed the World Zionist Organisation in 1960.

Index

Compiled by Sue Carlton

Page numbers in **bold** refer to the glossary